INQUIRIES INTO EASTERN CHRISTIAN WORSHIP

EASTERN CHRISTIAN STUDIES

A Series of the Institute of Eastern Christian Studies
Nijmegen, the Netherlands

edited by

Wil van den Bercken
Adelbert Davids
Herman Teule
Peter Van Deun
Joseph Verheyden

Volume 12

EASTERN CHRISTIAN STUDIES 12

INQUIRIES INTO
EASTERN CHRISTIAN WORSHIP

Selected Papers of the Second International Congress
of the Society of Oriental Liturgy
Rome, 17-21 September 2008

Edited by
Bert Groen, Steven Hawkes-Teeples
and Stefanos Alexopoulos

PEETERS
LEUVEN – PARIS – WALPOLE, MA
2012

A catalogue record for this book is available from the Library of Congress.

© 2012 Uitgeverij Peeters, Bondgenotenlaan 153, B-3000 Leuven (Belgium)

D/2012/0602/8
ISBN 978-90-429-2492-5

PREFACE

The Society of Oriental Liturgy, or Societas Orientalium Liturgiarum (SOL), was founded in 2006, at the initiative of the prominent scholar of Byzantine liturgical studies, Robert F. Taft. The Society, though respectful of all churches and religious traditions, is academic without religious affiliation. It is dedicated to the scholarly study of Eastern Christian liturgies, fostering such study in all its aspects (origins in early liturgy, history, current practice, theology, spirituality), including related disciplines (hymnography and musicology, architecture, archaeology, iconography, ...), and using various methodologies (from philology, textual analysis, historiography, philosophy, practical or pastoral theology, the social sciences, ritual studies, gender studies, ...).

The first congress of the new Society was held in the Collegium Orientale at Eichstätt, Germany, from 23 to 28 July 2006. Its acts were published in the *Bollettino della Badia Greca di Grottaferrata*, third series, vol. 4 (2007), pp. 5-287 and vol. 5 (2008), pp. 5-325. The second congress took place in the Casa La Salle in Rome, from 17 to 21 September 2008. In this volume, selected papers of that congress are published. While writing this foreword, the third congress has just come to an end. It took place from 26 to 30 May 2010 in the Theological Academy of the Holy Metropolis of Demetrias, Volos, Greece. We plan to edit the proceedings of this conference in this same series of 'Eastern Christian Studies'.

In editing and preparing the manuscript for publication the editors could rely on the help and assistance of several native speakers. We would like to thank in particular André Lossky, Saskia Löser, Georges Ruyssen, Massimo Pampaloni, Carmelo Giuffrida, Daniel Galadza, Marco Bais, and Rafał Zarzeczny. We also wish to thank the library of the Pontifical Oriental Institute in Rome and the Institute for Liturgy, Christian Art and Hymnology of the University of Graz for their institutional and material support. Finally, we thank the editors of the 'Eastern Christian Studies' for their willingness to accept the manuscript in the series.

Several noted scholars in the field of the study of Eastern Christian worship have left us in the past years. Respectfully we mention the names of three of them: Miguel Arranz, Ioannis Foundoulis, and Gregory Woolfenden. 'Everlasting Memory'!

The Editors

CONTENTS

LIST OF CONTRIBUTORS

1. **Stefanos Alexopoulos** is assistant professor of liturgy at the Ecclesiastical Academy of Athens, Greece.
2. **Susan Ashbrook Harvey** is Willard Prescott and Annie McClelland Smith Professor, and Chair, Department of Religious Studies, Brown University, Providence, Rhode Island, USA.
3. **Margot Fassler** holds the Keough-Hesburgh Chair of music history and liturgy, is a fellow of the Medieval Institute, and co-director of the Master of Sacred Music Program, University of Notre Dame, Indiana, USA.
4. **Emmanuel Fritsch** is a research fellow at the French Centre of Ethiopian Studies (CFEE) in Addis Ababa, Ethiopia.
5. **Stig Simeon R. Frøyshov** is professor of liturgical studies at the Faculty of Theology, University of Oslo, Norway.
6. **Nina Glibetić** is a graduate student at the Pontifical Oriental Institute in Rome, Italy.
7. **Bert Groen** is professor of liturgical studies and sacramental theology and holds the UNESCO-Chair of intercultural and interreligious dialogue in South-Eastern Europe at the University of Graz, Austria.
8. **Steven Hawkes-Teeples** is adjunct professor of Byzantine liturgical studies at the Pontifical Oriental Institute, Rome, Italy.
9. **Sebastià Janeras** is visiting professor of Oriental liturgy and church history at the Catalonian Faculty of Theology, Barcelona, Spain.
10. **Peter Jeffery** holds the Michael P. Grace Chair of medieval studies, is concurrent professor of theology, and co-director of the Master of Sacred Music Program, University of Notre Dame, Indiana, USA.
11. **Maxwell E. Johnson** is professor of liturgical studies at the University of Notre Dame, Indiana, USA.
12. **Panayotis Kalaïtzidis** is a research fellow of Byzantine liturgical studies and teaches religion in secondary education in Thessalonica, Greece.
13. **Vassa Larin** is a university assistant at the Institute of Liturgical Studies of the University of Vienna, Austria.
14. **Hlib Lonchyna** is bishop and Apostolic Administrator of the Ukrainian Greek-Catholic Exarchate of Great Britain.

15. **André Lossky** is professor of liturgical studies at the Saint Sergius Institute of Orthodox Theology, Paris, France.

16. **Šimon Marinčák** is researcher at the Research Institute affiliated with the Faculty of Theology, University of Trnava, and chorus master at the State Opera House in Košice, Slovakia.

17. **Marcel Mojzeš** teaches liturgical theology and spirituality at the Greek-Catholic Faculty of Theology at the University of Prešov, Slovakia.

18. **Mark M. Morozowich** is associate dean of seminary and ministerial studies, and assistant professor of liturgy in the School of Theology and Religious Studies at the Catholic University of America, Washington, D.C., USA.

19. **Chrysostom Nassis** is lecturer in liturgical sources and teleturgics at the Department of Pastoral and Social Theology at the University of Thessalonica, Greece.

20. **Michael Petrowycz** is dean of the Department of Theology, Ukrainian Catholic University, Lviv, Ukraine.

21. **Gerard Rouwhorst** is professor of liturgical studies at the Faculty of Catholic Theology of the University of Tilburg, the Netherlands.

22. **Nino Sakvarelidze** is research associate and lecturer at the Institute of Biblical Studies and Historical Theology of the University of Innsbruck, Austria.

23. **Robert F. Taft** is professor emeritus of Oriental liturgical studies at the Pontifical Oriental Institute, Rome, Italy.

24. **Gabriele Winkler** is professor emerita of liturgical studies at the University of Tübingen, Germany.

25. **Gregory (Graham) Woolfenden** († 2008) was professor of liturgical studies at St Sophia Seminary, South Bound Brook, New Jersey, and a visiting professor at Yale Institute of Sacred Music, New Haven, USA.

26. **Michael Zheltov** is professor of liturgical studies at the Post-Graduate and Doctoral School of the Russian Orthodox Church and at the Moscow Spiritual Academy, Moscow, Russia.

TRADITION AND NATURAL DISASTER
THE ROLE OF LITURGICAL SCHOLARSHIP

Mark M. MOROZOWICH

1. Introduction

Liturgical scholarship often seems removed from the actual liturgical life of the Christian community. Popular pundits have quipped that liturgical studies are in fact the disaster of our time; however, I contend that liturgical studies provide a vibrant source of renewal for the church. Liturgical scholarship reflects upon the worship experience of the Christian community in order to challenge and engage it more completely in realizing the corporate worship of God. This challenge calls us to treat tradition in its fullest sense and see how it continues in the present liturgical expression. In order to investigate this reality, I propose an examination of tradition, natural disaster, and liturgical scholarship. This curious choice provokes quizzical reactions, yet Byzantine liturgical history provides an illustrative example of the interaction of tradition and natural disaster. This study focuses on the origin of the commemoration of natural disasters in the Byzantine liturgical calendar in order to clarify the relationship between tradition and liturgy. If one examines the shock and destruction of natural disasters one readily sees the opportunities for liturgical prayer as the faithful try to cope with the various calamities. Today, many churches in the United States have not dealt well with the effects of terrorism and the September 11 events. It seems that the status quo dictates liturgical practice despite an at times incongruous link between real life and the communal prayer life of a church. Hopefully, these reflections will stimulate thought on the future direction of liturgical scholarly endeavors.

[1] S. Kelleher, *Passion and Resurrection: The Greek Catholic Church in Soviet Ukraine 1939-1989* (Lviv, 1993); I. Smolitsch, *Geschichte der Russischen Kirche 1700–1917*, Vol. 1, Studien zur Geschichte Osteuropas 9 (Leiden, 1964); Vol. 2, Forschungen zur osteuropäischen Geschichte 45 (Berlin, 1991); N. M. Zernov, *The Russian Religious Renaissance of the Twentieth Century* (London, 1963); *Eastern Christianity and Politics in the Twentieth Century*, ed. Pedro Ramet (Durham, NC, 1988); *Religion under Siege, Vol. II: Protestant, Orthodox and Muslim Communities in Occupied Europe (1939-1950)*, eds. Lieve Gevers and Jan Bank (Leuven, 2007).

Eastern Christian liturgical scholarship continues to flourish and the second international conference of the Society of Oriental Liturgy clearly demonstrates the health of our discipline with over forty participants. A brief look at the recent history of Eastern Christian Churches easily demonstrates that the twentieth century marked a tumultuous time with numerous wars and conflicts that affected every Eastern Christian faith community. These debilitating social, economic, and political situations have curtailed, hampered, and, at times, seemingly destroyed these faith communities — the enormous suffering that spawned worldwide immigration has destabilized many traditional strongholds of Eastern Christian Churches.[1] However, in the midst of these challenges, a new springtime of liturgical scholarship appeared and continues to grow in the East.[2] The numerous great Byzantine liturgists of the twentieth century, with a few continuing into our own century, bear witness to the great health of our endeavor: Among the most notable figures we find Dmitrievsky, Baumstark, Engberding, Schmemann, Mateos, Arranz, Janeras, Taft, and Winkler. Their litany of achievements includes various subjects of liturgical study; among them are the Eucharist, the Liturgy of the Hours, the Mysteries, and the liturgical year, as well as historical studies of various liturgical manuscripts. The passion for this type of historical liturgical study continues to inspire new scholars as they join the procession of scholars seeking the truth and most importantly seeking to understand the tradition of the various liturgical families. Various recent academic conferences demonstrate the vitality of this scholarly field: the Baumstark Conference, the yearly St Serge Conferences in Paris,[3] the first conference of the Society of Oriental Liturgy held in Eichstätt, Germany,[4] the Fifth International Theological Conference of the Russian Orthodox Church in Moscow from 13-16 November 2007 entirely devoted to liturgical matters, entitled, 'Teaching on the Sacraments of the Church',[5] and

---

[2] For an example of the effects of this increased scholarship see: Mark M. Morozowich, 'Liturgical Changes in Russia and The Christian East? A Case Study: The Mysteries (Sacraments) of Initiation with the Eucharistic Liturgy', *Worship* 83 (2009) 30-47.

[3] A particularly interesting example can be seen in *Les mouvements liturgiques: Corrélations entre pratiques et recherches, Conférences Saint-Serge, Le Semaine d'études liturgiques, Paris, 23-26 Juin 2003*, eds. Carlo Braga and Alessandro Pistoia, Bibliotheca "Ephemerides Liturgicae". Subsidia 129 (Rome, 2004).

[4] The acts have been published. See *Bolletino della Badia Greca di Grottaferrata* 3rd series, 4 (2007) and 3rd series, 5 (2008).

[5] For more information, view these websites: http://theolcom.ru/ru/text.php?SECTION_ID=38, http://theolcom.ru/ru/text.php?SECTION_ID=48, http://www.patriarchia.ru/db/text/209130.html, and for the full English version of the talks see http://theolcom.ru/ru/full_text.php?TEXT_ID=343.

the present 2008 Society of Oriental Liturgy Conference in Rome. These witnesses demonstrate only a few of the important large scale Eastern Christian liturgical scholarly endeavors.

2. What is Liturgical Tradition?

These diverse liturgical studies demonstrate the seriousness that various scholars treat the liturgical tradition of the church. They primarily study this tradition by utilizing methods of historical critical research. However, some scholars look askance at this methodology. This questioning of liturgical history has been the focus of recent presentations at the annual meetings of the North American Academy of Liturgy. John Baldovin's response to the 2007 *Berakah* Award entitled, 'The Usefulness of Liturgical History', presents a sweeping overview of the various ways that liturgical history provides an important and necessary aspect of liturgical study.[6] A year later, Paul Bradshaw reflects on the current state of affairs in liturgical studies in his response to the 2008 *Berakah* Award entitled, 'Is Liturgical History a Thing of the Past'.[7] Bradshaw observes that many have disregarded historical liturgical study and he presents arguments for why liturgical historical study remains centrally important today. Bradshaw develops this position by looking at the interrelationship between the liturgical historical study and tradition. This important relationship provides an insight into the suppositions and claims that people have made regarding these two terms. His explanation illuminates some problems experienced in the historical study of liturgical texts:

'In other words, liturgical scholars from all ecclesiastical bodies were interested not merely in history but in tradition, and in the legitimacy that tradition gave to present practices and those who preformed them. This inevitably affected what they chose to study and the sort of conclusions that they reached. Quite unconsciously, they were selective in what they noticed and how they interpreted the evidence. They focused on similarities and tended to explain away inconvenient differences in historical practices. They chose to treat some elements and strands in the traditions as normative and others as deviations, often without being aware that they were making a choice at all.'[8]

[6] John Baldovin, 'The Usefulness of Liturgical History,' *Proceedings of the North American Academy of Liturgy* (2007) 18-32.
[7] Paul Bradshaw, 'Is Liturgical History a Thing of the Past', *Proceedings of the North American Academy of Liturgy* (2008) 22-33.
[8] *Ibid.*, pp. 22-33.

His reflection on the role of historical study leads us to examine our methodological approach to study. Indeed, the historian must admit biases and aim for a more objective historical study. Bradshaw's utilization of the term 'tradition' describes how the concept of tradition can preclude the investigator from conducting unbiased research. Bradshaw's attention to liturgical history and methodology advanced our science in many demonstrable ways. The findings and challenges in his *Search for the Origins of Christian Worship* hold scholars to new standards of accuracy and excellence.[9] Bradshaw's treatment of tradition in his 2008 response to the *Berakah* Award focuses attention upon the way that research was influenced to select certain types of evidence in order to justify current practice or as he states what has won the day that becomes known as tradition. This meaning of liturgical tradition provokes inquiry into what exactly we understand when we say 'liturgical tradition'. Bradshaw utilizes this term to describe the role that our own present liturgical practices have in limiting our historical critical investigations. I posit that liturgical tradition is more than just what we do today or what the church has been doing for the past few hundred years or the last millennium.

This investigation commences by developing a concept of hermeneutics applied to liturgical study. The very supposition of an unbiased researcher that can be completely free from the influence of all current practices and presuppositions provokes a myriad of questions and issues. The fundamental hermeneutical work of Gadamer, *Wahrheit und Methode* (in English: *Truth and Method*), challenges the concept of a researcher's ability to be totally and completely objective.[10] Gadamer's critique demands introspection on the part of the researcher coupled with an ability to state limits and predispositions. Certainly, the student of the past must eliminate prejudice but Gadamer's critique provokes further reflection and insight into this dynamic relationship between liturgical history and tradition by allowing the researcher to fully acknowledge his or her aims. This does not give license to an abstract historical approach, but it does allow for the historian to develop adequate hypotheses that help to render understandable the development of communal liturgical prayer.

The variant understandings of the beleaguered word 'tradition' continue to be bantered in various debates and discussions with tenuous

---

[9] Paul Bradshaw, *The Search for the Origins of Christian Worship: Sources and Methods for the Study of Early Liturgy*, 2nd ed. (New York, 2002).

[10] Hans Georg Gadamer, *Truth and Method,* 2nd rev. ed. (New York, 1989).

definitions barely revealing the reality it entails. A deeper analysis of tradition provides a useful reflection for practitioners of liturgical history. Some liturgical historians create a golden age in the patristic era of liturgy and define that as the normative tradition to be followed — they seek to return to a bygone era. This idealist appraisal remains under scrutiny among various critics and is nothing more than fantasy. In fact, recent liturgical historical studies like Robert Taft's, *Through their Own Eyes: Liturgy as the Byzantines Saw It*, demonstrates real life accounts of liturgical experiences that contradict the idealized situation of liturgy in the so-called golden age: It questions our understanding of the liturgical practices of that time as well as our own sense of what their liturgical practice was.[11] This certainly qualifies and limits our ability to comprehensively present a definitive understanding of the past. Others have been so beleaguered with trying to find the *ipsissima verba liturgica* based on the *ipsissima verba Christi* or some other ancient strain of evidence in order to uncover the *real* liturgical practice of the church with its roots somewhere in the actual liturgical actions of the apostles in order to demonstrate the real history of the Christian community before it might have been tainted by later developments. It seems that this discussion is based upon a nascent desire to establish a real tradition that is historically accurate to the time of Jesus. The scant evidence from the ante-Nicene period yields very little certainty and, at times, an almost nihilistic notion is conveyed regarding tradition which limits explanations for the liturgical practices that eventually prevail and became normative in various early Christian churches. The lack of historical certainty regarding the earlier practices that became the tradition in no way diminishes the value of the tradition and efforts to explain it.

This illusive concept of liturgical tradition directs our attention to methodology and the definition of key terms as well as thought constructs. Robert Taft's development of this complex concept of tradition in his reflections on liturgical history illuminates this issue:

> 'From what I have said already, it should be obvious that the study of liturgy is not just history. But of course it has an historical dimension because like everything else on the face of the earth, liturgy has a history. And this history is studied not in order to recover the past (which is impossible), much less to recreate it (which would be fatuous), but simply in order to render intelligible the present which can be fully understood only as part of

---

[11] Robert F Taft, *Through Their Own Eyes: Liturgy as the Byzantines Saw It* (Berkeley, CA, 2006).

a larger whole. In other words, liturgy is part of tradition, and tradition is not past, but the present insofar as it is in continuity with the past. Historical research helps us uncover and see the tradition in its totality, thus counteracting the common temptation to mistake the proximate part for the whole.'[12]

This emphasis on the present clarifies the reality that liturgical historical research aims to render intelligible our current practices. This certainly demands a treatment of the complex and at times miniscule fragments of history that taken together explain the mosaic of our liturgical tradition. The search for the whole compels the liturgical historian to grapple with many competing concepts and preconceived notions in order to liberate our historical understanding from the tyranny of the present. In addition to the historical evidence, the researcher looks to patterns and developments. Perhaps Taft's understanding of tradition can be clarified by this more succinct definition:

> 'Liturgical history, therefore, does not deal with the past, but with tradition, which is a *genetic vision of the present,* a present conditioned by its understanding of its own roots. And the purpose of this history is not to recover the past (which is impossible), much less to imitate it (which would be fatuous), but to *understand liturgy* which, because it has a history, can only be understood in motion, just as the only way to understand a top is to spin it.'[13]

Liturgical tradition encompasses a complex variety of ideas, facts, concepts, and thoughts, in short the reality of the worshipping church. This nuanced understanding evokes a comprehensive continuity with what has come before us. Perhaps Taft's biological analogy of a *genetic vision of the present* provides the best workable short hand definition of tradition. As we think about the genetic code, we realize that it includes so much information that can describe details of our ancestors as well as help to indicate our strengths, talents, and even our weaknesses. This metaphor evokes a strong sense of continuity with a determinative pattern while being entirely focused upon the dynamic human person allowing for the uniqueness of the current reality of the individual. So liturgical tradition involves the worship of our ancestors, but it also deals with the dynamics of our worship today. It includes our historical roots and the reality of everything that makes up our world. Our intellectual framework, experiences, cultural filters, and general

---

[12] Robert F Taft, *Beyond East and West: Problems in Liturgical Understanding,* 2nd rev. ed. (Rome, 2001), p. 236.

[13] *Ibid.,* pp. 191-192.

horizon of life all come together in our liturgical life. So if we are to understand liturgy properly, we must enter into a profound historical study in order to see this worship experience as an alive experience, which as Taft reminds us is best studied in motion. This motion includes the various aspects of our life as we interact with the historical liturgical realities that we have inherited and that we assimilate into our worship experience today. The worshippers perform these tasks as part and parcel of their ability to enter into worship, whether or not they have explicitly identified these tasks. Also, this motion includes the formation that the church provides to the believers; in ancient times, it was known as mystagogical teaching proceeded by catechesis.[14] So the church actively assimilates people into its own *Symbolgestalt* as Schulz describes the world view of symbols that comprise any liturgy and in particular the Byzantine liturgy in order to facilitate the worship experience.[15] In the liturgy, the church actively conveys its own self-understanding in order to engage the believer. All of this is part of the motion of the living tradition of the church as it continues the worship patterns that it has inherited and brings them alive to successive generations. But our study is not simply about this dynamic in the present, but how this dynamic has functioned through the centuries and whether or not a genetic understanding of tradition has been operative.

Lawrence Hoffman, a Jewish liturgical historian, reflects upon tradition in much the same manner as Robert Taft. His reflections in his article, 'What Is a Liturgical Tradition?'[16] probe the various usages of the word tradition. He attempts to provide a clear understanding of liturgical tradition in its dynamic reality. An examination of his succinct definition helps to amplify this discussion:

> 'Liturgy is the public act of *tradition*, the symbolic marker by which tradition is owned. Or, put another way: *Tradition* is a public property of the past, which we inherit by means of the equally public and symbolic proclamation of *traditio*, which is our liturgy.'[17]

---

[14] Enrico Mazza, *Mystagogy: A Theology of Liturgy in the Patristic Age* (New York, 1989); Craig Alan Satterlee, *Ambrose of Milan's Method of Mystagogical Preaching* (Collegeville, MN, 2002).

[15] Hans-Joachim Schulz, *Die byzantinische Liturgie: Glaubenszeugnis und Symbolgestalt*, 3rd rev. ed. (Trier, 2000) or the English translation: Hans-Joachim Schulz, *The Byzantine Liturgy: Symbolic Structure and Faith Expression*, trans. Matthew J. O'Connell (New York, 1986).

[16] Lawrence Hoffman, 'What Is a Liturgical Tradition?', in *The Changing Face of Jewish and Christian Worship in North America*, eds. Paul F. Bradshaw and Lawrence A. Hoffman, Two Liturgical Traditions 2 (Notre Dame, IN,1991), pp. 3-25.

[17] *Ibid.*, p. 10.

This definition clarifies the concept that tradition is not something static or old, but rather it is alive. Later in the same article Hoffman proposes an artistic metaphor: 'Liturgical tradition is thus closer to being a painting than an argument; its content is denoted as present rather than connoted as true.'[18] This apt metaphor provides yet another understanding of Taft's notion of tradition as a *genetic* vision of the present. Both notions convey the importance of the participant in the task of understanding liturgical tradition. In order to properly understand liturgy, attention to this dynamic yields a more complete picture of the reality celebrated. One cannot capture the past or even completely describe this present experience, but attention to this dynamic reality assists the researcher in producing a more accurate conceptualization of the event.

Clearly, the liturgical historical task is not simply *academic* in the pejorative sense. Rather, our responsibility to the tradition and the history of the liturgy enables the church to live more completely today. Our ability to explain liturgical history and to bring tradition into focus as part and parcel of the *genetic vision* of the present is our unique privilege and responsibility. This important task cannot be accomplished on an individual basis. In fact, the impact of liturgical scholarly labors may not be immediate, but they will bear fruit collectively. An examination of how liturgical scholarship has affected the way that contemporary Christians worship demonstrates this cumulative impact. One can point to the liturgical renewal spurred by the Second Vatican Council or to the liturgical renewals of individual Eastern churches, even if some were tentative.[19]

---

[18] *Ibid.*, p. 14.

[19] For a good overview, see M. Mojzeš, *Il movimento liturgico nelle chiese bizantine: Analisi di alcune tendenze di riforma nel XX₤ secolo*, Bibliotheca "Ephemerides Liturgicae". Subsidia 132 (Rome, 2005); Pavlos Koumarianos, 'Liturgical "Rebirth" in the Church of Greece Today: A Doubtful Effort of Liturgical Reform', *Bollettino della Badia Greca di Grottaferrata* 3rd series, 4 (2007) 119-144; Н. Балашов, *На пути к литургическому возрождению: Дискуссии Православной Российской Церкви начала XX века. Поместный Собор 1917–1918гг. и предсоборный период* Серия: Церковные реформы (Moscow, 2000), pp. 444-476; А.Г. Кравецкий, 'Священный Собор Православной Российской Церкви: Из материалов Отдела о богослужении, проповедничестве и храме', *Богословские труды* 34 (1998) 200-388. For a contemporary example of liturgical change see Mark Morozowich, 'Liturgical Changes in Russia' (see n. 2), pp. 30-47.

3. Earthquake Commemorations in the Byzantine Liturgy

This genetic understanding of tradition challenges many of our insights and presuppositions. In order to develop a deeper comprehension of liturgical tradition, the Byzantine liturgy's commemoration of earthquakes in Constantinople provides an interesting case study. What does it mean for us to study tradition and see the genetic view of the present in the liturgical commemoration of earthquakes, especially earthquakes that occurred in a distant city in a different time? The examination begins with history, both the broader generic history and the more focused liturgical history detailing when the commemorations of earthquakes began and how they were celebrated. Many general historical studies on these seismological events exist. Twentieth-century Byzantine historians labored to develop an accurate and complete list of the dating of the numerous Constantinopolitan earthquakes. Glanville Downey identified fifty-eight earthquakes that occurred from 342 to 1454.[20] The ancient perception of the cause of earthquakes originated from Aristotle and Seneca. Croke provides a good summary of the ancient world's general geological concepts accompanied by a pre-Christian theological interpretation:

> 'These subterranean winds entered the earth both through openings in the earth's crust and, more frequently, by way of an undersea passage which meant that the regions most prone to earthquakes were those nearest the sea. Hence, Poseidon (Neptune) the god of the sea was also the God of earthquakes — the Homeric 'Earthshaker' ('Εννοσίγαιος). Although rationally explained, this shaking of the earth was interpreted as a divine signal, usually a punishment for misdemeanor. Apollinas of Tyana, for example, reminded the feuding Antiochenes that the earthquake they had experienced was a divine admonition and Libanius offered the Antiochenes the same advice two centuries later. In the fourth and as late as the sixth century A.D., earthquakes were still interpreted in the traditional way though both Ammianus Marcellinus and Agathias expressed dissatisfaction with the Aristotelian explanation.'[21]

This world view provides the backdrop for understanding the mentality of the inhabitants of this new imperial city. The divine manipulates the movements of the underground winds causing calamities because of

---

[20] Glanville Downey, 'Earthquakes at Constantinople and Vicinity, AD 342-1454', *Speculum* 30 (1955) 596-600.
[21] Brian Croke, 'Two Early Byzantine Earthquakes and their Liturgical Commemoration', *Byzantion* 51 (1981), p. 122.

some sort of divine dissatisfaction or judgment of the moral behavior of the inhabitants. This concept of punishment for the misconduct of the inhabitants continues to shape thought even in the late-antique Christian era. The scientifically advanced people of the twenty-first century find these explanations difficult and facile. Already in the sixth century, these geological explanations were being questioned as they searched for more adequate descriptions of these natural events, but the interpretation of divine punishment loomed large in their imaginations and various patristic fathers as well as emperors who often capitalized on this understanding. About the year AD 396 the emperor Arcadius is reported in Orosius', *History* III, 3:1-3 as leading the people in prayer following an earthquake.[22] The emperor and the people were seeking out divine favor in order to have calm so that they might proceed with their lives. This rudimentary liturgy or simply communal prayer sets the pattern for future commemorations.

A sense of divine punishment and dissatisfaction with the general state of human affairs can be witnessed in various homilies. Chrysostom's remarks, in *Homily 41 of Acts* preached around 401 A.D. in Constantinople, provide an important insight into the interpretation given to earthquakes. Chrysostom preaches on the earthquake of 400 A.D.:

> 'But see, I pray you, after such signs had been wrought, what evils within a short space ensue. Such is human nature: it soon forgets. Or, do ye not remember what has been the case among ourselves? Did not God last year shake our whole city? Did not all run to baptism? Did not whoremongers and effeminate and corrupt persons leave their dwellings, and the places where they spent their time, and change and become religious? But three days passed, and they returned again to their own proper wickedness. And whence is this? From the excessive laziness.'[23]

---

[22] '**3:1** Anno ab Vrbe condita CCCLXXVI saeuissimo terrae motu Achaia uniuersa concussa est et duae tunc ciuitates, id est Ebora et Helice, abruptis locorum hiatibus deuoratae. **2** At ego nunc e contrario poteram similia in diebus nostris apud Constantinopolim, aeque modo principem gentium, praedicta et facta sed non perfecta narrare, cum post terribilem denuntiationem conscientiamque mali sui praesciam subter commota funditus terra tremeret; desuper fusa caelitus flamma penderet donec orationibus Arcadii principis et populi Christiani praesentem perditionem Deus exoratus auerteret, **3** probans se solum esse et conseruatorem humilium et punitorem malorum. Sed haec ut commemorata sint magis quam explicita uerecundiae concesserim ut et qui scit recolat et qui nescit inquirat.' See Orosius, *Histoires: contre les païens,* texte établi et traduit par Marie-Pierre Arnaud-Lindet (Paris, 1990), pp. 143-144.

[23] PG 60:291 (CPG 4426) (http://www.newadvent.org/fathers/210141.htm). For a developed discussion of the date of this earthquake to 400 A.D., see Alan Cameron, 'Earthquake 400', *Chiron* 17 (1987) 344-351.

Chrysostom interprets the calamities in light of the wickedness of the people. He thus continues the theme established from the pre-Christian era. This was not a passing theme; it also appears in Chrysostom's *Homily 7 of Acts*:

> 'If you remember how it was when God shook our city with an earthquake, how subdued all men were. (Infra, Hom. xli. §2.) Such was the case then with those converts. No knavery, no villany then: such is the effect of fear, of affliction! No talk of mine and thine then. Hence gladness waited at their table; no one seemed to eat of his own, or of another's; — I grant this may seem a riddle. Neither did they consider their brethren's property foreign to themselves; it was the property of a Master; nor again deemed they anything their own, all was the brethren's.'[24]

So the homilist marshals the contemporary world view with its theological understanding of divine admonition in order to call the faithful to reform their lives and to live more closely according to the Christian ideals. This appeal for divine intervention continues in the year 407 when Arcadius sought out the prayers of the holy Nilus of Ancyra on the occasion of another earthquake. Nilus (*Letters II, 265*) objected to Arcadius' appeal on the grounds that John Chrysostom had been exiled.[25]

This pattern of seeking divine assistance and intervention occurs again a few years later during the earthquake of September 25, 437. Theophanes the Confessor relates the event by saying that the entire populace gathered in the open with the bishop in order to pray.[26] This famous account is recast in a letter from Pope Felix III (483-492) about how Proclus, the bishop of Constantinople, led the people out of the city to pray and a young boy miraculously was lifted up and heard the Trisagion hymn.[27] Of course, the historicity of this account provokes skepticism

---

[24] PG 60:66 (CPG 4426) (http://www.newadvent.org/fathers/210107.htm)

[25] PG 79:336. See also Croke, 'Two Early Byzantine Earthquakes' (see n. 21), p. 124 and Alan Cameron, 'The Authenticity of the letter of Nilus of Ancyra', *Greek, Roman and Byzantine Studies* 17 (1976), p. 187.

[26] *The Chronicle of Theophanes Confessor: Byzantine and Near Eastern History AD 284-813*, trans. Cyril Mango and Roger Scott with the assistance of Geoffrey Greatrex (Oxford, 1997), pp. 144-145.

[27] Felix, *Epistola III Ad Petrum Fullonem*, PL 58 909-910. See also Croke, 'Two Early Byzantine Earthquakes' (see n. 21), p. 127. For a more complete development of the Trisagion Hymn see: Sebastià Janeras, 'Le Trisagion: Une formule brève en liturgie comparée', in *Comparative Liturgy Fifty Years after Anton Baumstark (1872-1948), Rome, 25-29 September 1998*, eds. R. F. Taft and G. Winkler, Orientalia Christiana Analecta 265 (Rome, 2001), pp. 495-562; Gabriele Winkler, *Das Sanctus: Über den Ursprung und die Anfänge des Sanctus und sein Fortwirken*, Orientalia Christiana Analecta 267 (Rome, 2002), pp. 196-197.

regarding the actual content of the revelation, but the reality of the earth-quake and the reality of the people praying together remain as a given. For our purposes, the story underlines the fact that the bishop led his flock in prayer in order to seek divine mercy and consolation for his faithful. This communal prayer and the felt desire for divine intercession provide the impetus for the creation of yearly liturgical commemorations and even processions on certain fixed days commemorating various earthquakes. In fact this widespread acceptance of the necessity of inter-cession is even witnessed in the work of Romanos the Melodist who composes an entire Kontakion around 537 A.D. on the earthquakes invoking God and beseeching God's mercy for the sinful people.[28] This pattern of liturgical prayer became normalized focusing upon the role of the community in public prayer and the all important aspect of God's presence and mercy. Even in the eighth century, the pattern of pairing natural disasters with prayer continues. Theophanes the Confessor describes the great earthquake of October 26, 740:

> 'Many churches and monasteries collapsed and many people died. There also fell down the statue of Constantine the Great that stood above the gate of Atalos as well as that of Atalos himself, the statue of Arkadios that stood on the column of Xerolophos, and the statue of Theodosios the Great above the Golden Gate; furthermore, the land walls of the City, many towns and villages in Thrace, Nicomedia in Bithynia, Prainetos, and Nicaeam where only one church was spared. In some places the sea withdrew from its proper boundaries. The quakes continued for twelve months.'[29]

Theophanes continues by attributing these evils to the impious Leo, so once again earthquakes, as well as other calamities, are seen as punishment for misdeeds.[30]

This study could continue to recount various antidotes and historical tidbits, but the question of their liturgical commemoration is at hand. These liturgical processions and special yearly liturgies, clearly recorded in the calendars of the church and in the liturgical books, demonstrate the wide variety celebrated. *Holy Cross 40*, the tenth-century Synaxarion of the Great Church, presents eight dates for processions and liturgical

---

[28] Romanos le Mélode, 'LIV. Hymne sur le tremblement de terre et l'incendie', in *Hymnes*, tome 5, introduction, texte critique, traduction et notes par José Grosdidier de Matons, Sources Chrétiennes 283 (Paris, 1981), pp. 455-499. See also Gilbert Dagron, 'Quand la terre tremble...', in *Travaux et Mémoires*, Centre de recherche d'histoire et civilisation byzantines 8 (Paris, 1981), p. 92.

[29] *Chronicle of Theophanes Confessor* (see n. 26), p. 572.

[30] *Ibid.*, p. 573.

commemorations of various earthquakes. They are January 9, January 26, March 17, August 16, October 7, October 26, December 14 and the Monday after Pentecost.[31] Delehaye in the Synaxarium of Constantinople includes commemorations on thirteen other dates.[32] So these processional liturgies and their approach to intercession possess a strong hold on the Byzantine liturgical life. Of course, several of the dates for various earthquakes become conflated and their historicity remains in doubt, but the reality of their commemoration and the entrance into the liturgical calendars of various diverse earthquakes remains an important interpretive guide for understanding this tradition of the Constantinopolitan church. These various liturgical commemorations demonstrate the continued need to seek divine mercy in the communal liturgical prayer. The calendar also marked other natural disasters:[33] for example, an eclipse on August 8,[34] comets on October 21,[35] and even fires on September 1.[36] In addition, the Constantinopolitan liturgical tradition included various commemorations of other events and even of victories over foreign invaders. A broad analysis of these commemorations indicates that the Constantinopolitan church responded to the needs of the faithful in a liturgical manner in order to focus prayer for God's intervention on behalf of the people and they willingly added various commemorations to their liturgical calendars. Perhaps the mentality of the Constantinopolitan people aided this type of celebration. Croke provides a comprehensive insight into the Constantinopolitan worldview:

[31] *Le Typicon de la Grande Église: Ms. Sainte-Croix 40, Xe siècle,* vol. I, *Le cycle des douze mois,* ed. J. Mateos, Orientalia Christiana Analecta 165 (Rome, 1962): January 9 (pp. 192-193); January 26 (pp. 212-213); March 17 (pp. 248-251); August 16 (pp. 372-375); October 7 (pp. 63-65); October 26 (pp. 78-81); December 14 (pp. 130-133). *Le Typicon de la Grande Église: Ms. Sainte-Croix 40, Xe siècle,* vol. II, *Le cycle des fêtes mobiles,* ed. J. Mateos, Orientalia Christiana Analecta 166 (Rome, 1963), pp. 140-141.

[32] For additional dates, see Hippolyte Delehaye, *Synaxarium ecclesiae Constantinopolitanae e codice Sirmondiano nunc Berolinensi* (Brussels, 1902): September 25 (pp. 79-80); November 15 (p. 227); December 1 (p. 292); January 11 (p. 385); January 25 (p. 422); March 2 (p. 501); May 22 (p. 701); June 21 (p. 762); July 7 (p. 805); July 8 (p. 806); July 22 (p. 835); August 2 (p. 862); August 12 (p. 865).

[33] For a listing of various events commemorated, see Jakov Kulić, *Ricerca sulle commemorazioni giornaliere bizantine nei menei* (Rome, 1992).

[34] *Le Typicon de la Grande Église,* vol. I (see n. 31), pp. 364-365; Delehaye, *Synaxarium* (see n. 32), p. 878.

[35] *Synaxarium ecclesiae Constantinopolitanae* 154.24 26.

[36] *Le Typicon de la Grande Église,* vol. I (see n. 31), pp. 2-3. Not to mention the numerous fires recorded in A.M. Schneider, 'Brände in Konstantinopel', *Byzantinische Zeitschrift* 41 (1941) 382-403. See also V. Grumel, *La Chronologie,* Traité d'études byzantines 1 (Paris, 1958), pp. 476-481.

'While earthquakes in Graeco-Roman antiquity were no less frequent than in Byzantine times we do get the impression from our literary sources that quakes became more regular from the fourth century onwards: at least they occupy a more prominent position in the extant records. This quantitative increase in the recording of earthquakes is to be explained ultimately by the Christianization of the Roman world, that is to say although quakes were experienced and recorded in antiquity and sometimes interpreted as a manifestation of divine wrath, the God of the Christians assumed a more dominant and consistent role as the *Earthshaker*. Interest in the physical causes of earthquakes declined and they came to be ascribed to the will of God, pure and simple.'[37]

This popular reaction and the pervasiveness of the Aristotelian view provide an interesting historical glimpse into the thought development and popular reaction to natural disasters, which create a backdrop to the liturgical commemorations of these earthquakes. Certainly, the Byzantines grappled with scientific issues: Croke and also Dagron's comprehensive overview of the Byzantine scientific world is helpful in this respect.[38] From the ecclesiastical sphere, this commemoration of earthquakes and other natural disasters intimately combines with an understanding of the divine will and becomes an occasion of prayer and asking mercy from God. Certainly, it remains heavily influenced by the faulty geology and, at times, a theology that poses real questions. For example, some of the theology that André Lossky illustrates in his study of earthquakes speaks of the role of God as placing people in distress in order to illicit repentance.[39] The theology evident in these prayers might seem a bit askew in light of a more developed geology that understands the movements of the earth as a normal part of the geological make up of the planet rather than the result of the whim of a deity, not to mention a deeper theological understanding of God and his relationship to the natural world order. Does it then follow that liturgical tradition must continue to present this outdated world view in order to be faithful to the Constantinopolitan tradition? My simple answer is no. Tradition as a genetic view of the present entails an appreciation of what has come before while providing an adequate celebration of the current liturgical reality.

---

[37] Croke, 'Two Early Byzantine Earthquakes' (see n. 21), p. 145.

[38] Dagron, 'Quand la terre tremble...' (see n. 28), pp. 87-103.

[39] André Lossky, 'Commémoration liturgique des séismes et confession de la toute-puissance divine', in *Liturgie et Cosmos: Conférences Saint Serge, Le semaine d'études liturgiques,* eds. A. Triacca and A. Pistoria (Rome, 1998), pp. 131-151.

This broad overview provides some important insights into the activity of the Constantinopolitan ecclesial world: they intimately involved themselves in the struggles and major calamities that their people faced. The Constantinopolitan liturgical practice provokes much thought and a critique of how our contemporary liturgical life responds to the needs, struggles, and calamities of our time.

4. The Nexus of Tradition and Natural Disaster Commemorations

So what exactly is this Constantinopolitan *tradition*? What is this particular tradition of commemorating the earthquakes and what it can mean for today's communities? If we take seriously the concept of tradition as a genetic understanding of the present, then we need to delve a bit deeper. Certainly the historical study that I have sketched before us today provokes a real sense of the richness of the heritage and of the response of the ecclesial officials by creating various liturgical commemorations. Reflecting again on the words of Taft: '...history is essential to the formation of a *moving point of view*, a sense of relativity, of seeing the present as always in dynamic tension between past and future, and not as a static *given*.'[40] What is this sense of relativity? What is this dynamic tension which sees the present in terms of the past and future? I contend that our example of the earthquakes demonstrates an ecclesial community alive with the creation of prayers and commemorations that assisted people in facing their struggles. They continued to commemorate events from centuries before, but they never hesitated to introduce new commemorations, new moments in the liturgical year for the faithful to gather in prayer and petition for the mercy of God and for divine grace in response to natural disaster. This responsiveness and creativity conveys the Byzantine tradition in a genetic manner, as an alive and dynamic reality of an encounter of people with their God. This type of thinking outside of the box, or realizing that this Constantinopolitan tradition is not simply about the past, but about today, is crucial in our own work and more importantly for the life of the various ecclesial communities that we serve. Simply put, a genetic vision of the present describes a principle of being attentive to the particular reality of the faithful: this tradition elicits a response, in order to

---

[40] Taft, *Beyond East and West* (see n. 12), p. 236.

be truly traditional. The true tradition of the Byzantine liturgical life today must not simply recall calamities or natural disaster events of bygone eras, but the dynamic of responding to the ever changing contemporary situation of the believers by incorporating liturgical commemorations of contemporary events. I assert that this dynamic understanding of the principle of tradition demonstrates the application of Taft's assertion that tradition is a *genetic vision of the present,* a present conditioned by its understanding of its own roots.'[41]

This approach to tradition does not necessitate a wholesale acceptance of the time-bound world view or the questionable theology and concomitant geology of old that do not fit our present understandings as that would be anachronistic. Such an exercise would try to recreate the past, which is indeed totally impossible. What does this task entail? An examination of several contemporary tragedies demonstrates that the reaction of people today to disasters provides some indications for action. Perhaps one of the most shocking experiences to the American psyche was the terrorist attacks of September 11, 2001. Civil authorities continue to commemorate this event and even call for a moment of silence as a way of inexplicitly invoking God. Some churches offer special commemorations that are very well attended. In fact, some religious officials — bishops included — continue to be amazed by the number of faithful who willingly enter churches in order to ask for divine assistance on September 11. This phenomenon even occurs as attendance on Sundays and other holydays wanes. A look at the response to other natural disasters demonstrates similar yearnings. Even though in 2008, Hurricane Ike's impact on Texas paled in comparison to the catastrophic damage of Hurricane Katrina in 2005, the residents suffer and need compassion as they create meaning out of their loss. We can recall the recent floods in Ukraine, the wild fires in Greece, or the catastrophic loss of the 2004 Indian Ocean tsunami: each of these events cast their mark upon the people who experienced them and they need assistance to find meaning. Twenty-first century human beings might not articulate a hurricane or an earthquake as punishment from God, but they still face fear, hardship, and they need help in making sense of calamity, and in many ways it provides a moment to reflect on the course of their life: in short, people continue to question and often times they look to God and even to ecclesial communities for assistance in bringing peace to their lives.

---

[41] *Ibid.*, pp. 191-192.

Some might respond by stating that the Byzantine tradition offers prayers for these events by remembering what happened in Constantinople and, by application, they can assist people by inviting them to prayer and providing understanding and guidance in their time of need. However, as we have seen, the dynamic liturgical tradition of Constantinople didn't simply remain focused upon commemorations of past events, but was intent on marking new events with new liturgical commemorations for specific events. The tradition of the Constantinopolitan liturgy is one of creativity in offering new liturgical opportunities. This wonderful tradition remains an inspiration even today.

5. Conclusion

My contention remains that we as liturgical historical scholars need to continue to articulate our understanding of tradition and that guided by this concept of tradition as a genetic understanding of the present we can more fruitfully engage our modern Eastern faith communities in a vibrant and alive expression of that tradition. This engagement with tradition in no way indicates that we as the academy are directing liturgical reforms, or that by this study, somehow, I am mandating the creation of new commemorations for specific natural disasters. I hope that this discussion has stimulated the beginning of a deeper reflection of what tradition is and that it has challenged us to take another look at what a genetic vision of the present can and should be. This study might best serve to remind us of the important role that each of us plays by researching and studying the rich liturgical history of our various Eastern liturgical families and that we are able to convey that liturgical tradition as an alive genetic vision of the present. As scholars, we must choose our projects wisely so that we might continue to elucidate *the genetic vision of the present*.

'THE MYSTICAL CHORUS OF THE TRUTH ITSELF'
LITURGY AND MYSTERY IN CLEMENT OF ALEXANDRIA

Peter JEFFERY

Over the last half-century,[1] both liturgical scholarship and liturgical renewal have profited much from the rediscovery of mystagogy, the liturgical theology of the great Latin and Greek church fathers.[2] Though the history of this kind of theology has been traced from at least the works of Origen to the Pseudo-Dionysian corpus[3] and beyond,[4] it is most often identified with prominent bishops of the late fourth and early fifth centuries: Cyril of Jerusalem, John Chrysostom, and Theodore of Mopsuestia in the East, Ambrose and Augustine in the West. From each of these men we have one or more series of mystagogical sermons (completely or incompletely preserved) that were addressed to the neophytes, adult converts who had received the sacraments of Christian initiation at the great vigil service that began on Holy Saturday and ended early Easter morning. The purpose of these mystagogical sermons was to

---

[1] In this article I have used the following abbreviations: ACW = Ancient Christian Writers; *ANF* = *Ante-Nicene Fathers*; *ANRW* = *Aufstieg und Niedergang der römischen Welt;* CCSL= Corpus Christianorum: Series Latina; FaCh = Fathers of the Church; FC = Fontes Christiani; *CPG* = *Clavis Patrum Graecorum*, ed. M. Geerard, 6 vols. (Turnhout, 1974-87); LCC = Library of Christian Classics; LCL = Loeb Classical Library; LQF = Liturgiewissenschaftliche Quellen und Forschungen; *PG* = *Patrologia Graeca*, ed. J.-P. Migne; SC = Sources Chrétiennes

[2] See *Mystagogie: Pensée liturgique d'aujourd'hui et liturgie ancienne, Conférences Saint-Serge, XXXIXe Semaine d'Études Liturgiques, Paris, 30 juin – 3 juillet 1992*, eds. A. M. Triacca and A. Pistoia, Bibliotheca "Ephemerides Liturgicae". Subsidia 70 (Rome, 1993).

[3] Alexander Golitzin, *Et Introibo ad Altare Dei: The Mystagogy of Dionysius Areopagita, with Special Reference to Its Predecessors in the Eastern Christian Tradition*, Analekta Vlatadōn 59 (Thessalonica, 1994); Sarah Klitenic Wear, *Dionysius the Areopagite and the Neoplatonist Tradition: Despoiling the Hellenes* (Aldershot, 2007), pp. 85-115.

[4] René Bornert, *Les Commentaires byzantins de la divine liturgie du VIIe au XVe siècle*, Archives de l'Orient Chrétien 9 (Paris, 1966); Karl Christian Felmy, *Die Deutung der göttlichen Liturgie in der russischen Theologie: Wege und Wandlungen russischer Liturgie-Auslegung*, Arbeiten zur Kirchengeschichte 54 (Berlin, 1984); Louis Bouyer, *The Christian Mystery: From Pagan Myth to Christian Mysticism*, transl. Illtyd Trethowan (Edinburgh, 1990; Petersham, Mass., 1995); *Denys l' Aréopagite et sa postérité en orient et en occident: Actes du Colloque International Paris, 21-24 septembre 1994*, ed. Ysabel de Andia (Paris, 1997).

explain the meaning and symbolism of the liturgical rituals that had accompanied these sacraments — baptism, anointing or confirmation, and first Eucharist — even though, for the most part, the sermons were delivered on the weekdays following Easter, after the sacraments of initiation had already been celebrated. Thus we would do well, following the example particularly of Cyril's and Ambrose's works, to distinguish mystagogy from catechesis, the more preliminary kind of instruction given to the catechumens, who were not yet ready for baptism.[5] The two differ not only in function but in content, since catechesis dealt with more basic ethical and doctrinal formation than mystagogy. Where mystagogy described and explained the sacramental rites in great detail,[6] catechesis focused first on the exegesis of Old Testament stories to illustrate Christian moral principles, then on the points of the creed, which the catechumens were required to memorize.[7]

Another feature specific to mystagogy is its employment of a special vocabulary, which recalls (and seems derived from) the non-Christian cults of ancient times that we now lump together glibly as 'mystery religions'[8] — though this vocabulary was also used by Plato and other philosophers to describe the attainment of philosophical knowledge.[9] The

---

[5] The stages of progress are outlined in Edward Yarnold, *The Awe-Inspiring Rites of Initiation: The Origins of the R[ite of] C[hristian] I[nitiation of] A[dults]*, 2nd ed. (Collegeville, MN, 1994), pp. 1-54, and William Harmless, *Augustine and the Catechumenate* (Collegeville, MN, 1995). The Antiochene writers, Theodore of Mopsuestia and John Chrysostom, actually began the mystagogical sermons prior to baptism on Easter, but finished the series during Easter week with their sermons on the eucharist.

[6] Alexis James Doval, *Cyril of Jerusalem, Mystagogue: The Authorship of the 'Mystagogic Catecheses,'* Patristic Monograph Series 17 (Washington, DC, 2001), pp. 55-56; Craig Alan Satterlee, *Ambrose of Milan's Method of Mystagogical Preaching* (Collegeville, MN, 2002).

[7] Marcia L. Colish, *Ambrose's Patriarchs: Ethics for the Common Man* (South Bend, IN, 2005), pp. 13-29; Alexis Doval, 'The Date of Cyril of Jerusalem's Catecheses', *Journal of Theological Studies* 48 (1997) 129-132.

[8] Recent discussions include: Tennyson Jacob Wellman, 'Ancient *Mystēria* and Modern Mystery Cults', *Religion and Theology* 12 (2006) 308-348; Fritz Graf, 'Initiation: A Concept with a Troubled History', in *Initiation in Ancient Greek Rituals and Narratives: New Critical Perspectives*, eds. David B. Dodd and Christopher A. Faraone (London, 2003), pp. 3-24.

[9] For the cultic ritual vocabulary see: Walter Burkert, 'Initiation', in *Thesaurus Cultus et Rituum Antiquorum*, 2 (Los Angeles, 2004), pp. 91-124; George E. Mylonas, *Eleusis and the Eleusinian Mysteries* (Princeton, 1961), pp. 224-285, 287-316, and the glossary 317-320; *The Ancient Mysteries, A Sourcebook: Sacred Texts of the Mystery Religions of the Ancient Mediterranean World*, ed. Marvin W. Meyer (San Francisco, 1987), pp. 3-13. For the philosophical vocabulary see F. E. Peters, *Greek Philosophical Terms: A Historical Lexicon* (New York, 1967). A good selection of ancient artworks depicting the mystery rites is: Ministero per I Beni e le Attività Culturali, Soprintendenza Archeologica di Roma, *Il Rito segreto: Misteri in Grecia e a Roma*, ed. Angelo Bottini (Milan, 2005).

very word *mystagōgos* ('mystagogue') originally referred to one who sponsored the initiate (*mystēs*) and led him to the secret ceremony.[10] Once imported into Christian usage, this language of the mysteries brought with it a number of features that we find problematic today: an attitude of fear and awe,[11] a ritual secrecy reserved for the initiated few (sometimes called *disciplina arcani*), and the implication that Christian ceremonies are to some degree analogous to those of other religions.[12] Why Christian theologians saw fit to adopt such language, and what they really meant by it, has been controversial for centuries.

Obviously the Christian use of mystery terminology represents some sort of accommodation to ancient Greco-Latin culture, and this has encouraged some modern scholars to conclude that it is essentially a product of the Constantinian era. 'It was natural, therefore, that [Constantine] should seek to represent Christianity as the greatest of the mystery-religions', Edward Yarnold supposed.[13] But was it simply a matter of 'representation', or did some Christians assume that Christianity actually was or should be a mystery religion? Confident 'that the rites themselves were hardly influenced', since mystery language only affected 'the explanation given of them', Yarnold nevertheless wondered, 'Was Christianity enriched or distorted by this new emphasis?'[14] On the other hand, the mysterious secrecy could have had the opposite intention of keeping Christianity strictly separate from rival religions. That is the opinion of Casimir Kucharek:

> 'It is in the fourth and fifth centuries, when the masses were flocking into the Church, that the *disciplina arcani* reached its highest point, not out of fear of being betrayed to persecutors, since the persecutions had ended in A.D. 313, but in order to safeguard what was most holy in Christianity from the unworthy and the unprepared who would otherwise have flocked in with the sincere believers. This was excellent psychology even by today's standards.'[15]

[10] Mylonas, *Eleusis* (see n. 9), pp. 237, 244, 319; Doval, *Cyril* (see n. 6), pp. 55-56.

[11] George E. Saint-Laurent, 'The Sacraments as "Fear-Provoking" and "Awe-Inspiring" Rites in the Greek Fathers: Passage from Anxiety and Guilt to Freedom', in *Anxiety, Guilt and Freedom: Religious Studies Perspectives (Essays in Honor of Donald Gard)*, eds. Benjamin J. Hubbard and Bradley E. Starr (Lanham, MD, 1990), pp. 47-71.

[12] See Peder Borgen, '"Yes", "No", "How Far?": The Participation of Jews and Christians in Pagan Cults', in *Paul in his Hellenistic Context*, ed. T. Engberg-Pedersen (Edinburgh, 1994), pp. 30-59; repr. P. Borgen, *Early Christianity and Hellenistic Judaism* (Edinburgh, 1996), pp. 15-43.

[13] Edward Yarnold, 'Baptism and the Pagan Mysteries in the Fourth Century', *The Heythrop Journal* 13 (1972) 247-267, quote from p. 267.

[14] Yarnold, *Awe-Inspiring* (see n. 5), p. 66.

[15] Casimir A. Kucharek, *The Sacramental Mysteries: A Byzantine Approach* (Allendale, NJ and Combermere, Ont., 1976), p. 57.

For Enrico Mazza, on the other hand, mystagogy was less about secrecy than about biblical typology, a type of exegesis that finds in the Old Testament detailed foreshadowings of the New.[16] Each of the authors Mazza examined had his own way of employing typology in his liturgical explanations, but their shared mystagogical vocabulary was a casual, un-self-conscious use of the available cultural idiom.

> 'It is difficult to say why this literary and liturgical phenomenon should have appeared precisely at the end of the fourth century... The rise of the phenomenon at this point in history should not, however, surprise us when we consider that this was a period of major innovations in liturgical practice.... The Fathers were men of their times and shared the culture and philosophical horizons of their age.... Theirs was a general kind of Platonism, unorganized and unsystematic, that allowed them only to derive from the works of the great master what was useful for their theological and pastoral needs.'[17]

For Josef Knupp, on the contrary, the utilization of mystery language in fourth-century sacramental preaching was more deliberate, descended from an earlier Christian usage, exemplified by Clement of Alexandria, in which Christian doctrine was imparted as 'true philosophy'. This was done despite the fact that the rituals of the mystery cults and those of the early church bore only a superficial resemblance.[18]

Was Christian mystagogy, then, fundamentally syncretistic and cultic, or exegetical and typological, or Hellenistic and philosophical? Were the analogies to non-Christian rites limited to theological explanation, or did they actually contribute to shaping the liturgical celebration itself? 'Literally thousands of monographs, dissertations and articles have been addressed to the question ...', wrote Jonathan Z. Smith, a teacher of comparative religion, in an indispensable essay. 'The comparison of early Christianities and the religions of Late Antiquity, especially the so-called 'mystery cults' goes back hundreds of years, extending from early modern to post-modern times.[19] And as Smith shows, most of the

---

[16] See also Wenrich Slenczka, *Heilsgeschichte und Liturgie: Studien zum Verhältnis von Heilsgeschichte und Heilsteilhabe anhand liturgischer und katechetischer Quellen des dritten und vierten Jahrhunderts*, Arbeiten zur Kirchengeschichte 78 (Berlin, 2000).

[17] Enrico Mazza, *Mystagogy: A Theology of Liturgy in the Patristic Age*, transl. Matthew J. O'Connell (New York, 1989), pp. x, 172.

[18] Josef Knupp, *Das Mystagogieverständnis des Johannes Chrysostomos*, Benediktbeurer Studien 4 (Munich, 1995), pp. 5-20.

[19] Jonathan Z. Smith, *Drudgery Divine: On the Comparison of Early Christianities and the Religions of Late Antiquity*, Chicago Studies in the History of Judaism (Chicago, 1990), p. vii.

authors who contributed to this vast literature were seeking to advance deeply-held apologetic agendas. For seventeenth-century Protestants like Isaac Casaubon and John Daillé (who coined the expression *disciplina arcani*), mystery vocabulary and the practice of secrecy 'can be traced to an "accommodation", whether apologetic or paedagogic, to "pagan" converts', a 'direct transmission' of 'doctrinal formulations' 'from the "gentile background" to the early Christian texts'.[20] Over the centuries this interpretation was regularly used by Protestants to delegitimize Catholicism as a degraded, paganized form of Christianity, while Roman Catholics and Tractarians argued that sacramental theology, though implicit in the thought of the New Testament and early Christian authors, was hidden behind 'the discipline of the secret' in order to evade pagan ridicule and persecution.[21] Eighteenth-century Deists expanded the Protestant argument to discredit all of Christianity, to say that 'Platonists and Plotinists' had corrupted the 'pure principles' of Jesus, the 'simple evangelists', and the 'unlettered apostles' by 'the fabrication of the Christian Trinity'[22] and other absurd doctrines. Though Protestantism was not exempt from this indictment, Roman Catholic rituals in particular were seen as nothing but the 'verbal Translations of the old Originals of Heathenism'.[23] By the nineteenth century, such arguments were being used to present Christianity itself as merely one particular cultural expression (and hardly the most attractive one) of allegedly universal religious impulses honoring the sun, the seasons, and other natural phenomena.[24]

In the twentieth century, meanwhile, new attention was given to a fact already noticed in the sixteenth, that the Septuagint and other late antique Jewish writings in Greek also utilize the word *mystērion* and related terms.[25] By arguing that these Jewish usages were unconnected to the pagan mystery religions, writers with Christian loyalties were enabled to allege that mystery terminology demonstrates the pure Semitic pedigree of early Christianity and its independence from paganism, without

---

[20] Smith, *Drudgery* (see n. 19), p. 59.

[21] *The Westminster Dictionary of Christian Spirituality*, ed. Gordon S. Wakefield (Philadelphia, 1983), pp. 116-117; Anscar J. Chupungco, *Liturgical Inculturation: Sacramentals, Religiosity, and Catechesis* (Collegeville, MN, 1992), pp. 142-143; Royal W. Rhodes, *The Lion and the Cross: Early Christianity in Victorian Novels* (Columbus, 1995), pp. 26, 159-160, 202.

[22] Smith, *Drudgery* (see n. 19), pp. 7-26, quotes from pp. 7, 9.

[23] *Ibid.*, pp. 23-26, quote from p. 25.

[24] *Ibid.*, pp. 29-33, 89-111, 128-129.

[25] Johan Lust, Erik Eynikel and Katrin Hauspie, *Greek-English Lexicon of the Septuagint*, rev. ed. (Stuttgart, 2003), p. 411.

prejudice to Christianity's superiority over all ancient and modern forms of Judaism.[26]

My thesis in the present article is this: the glossary of Christian mystagogy is actually a coalescence of several pre-Christian vocabularies that were originally distinct, and had different origins. The merged lexicon was not a product of the Constantinian age, but can be observed taking shape in the second-century writings of Clement of Alexandria, whose worship practices, ironically, were rather different from the fourth-century liturgies of Chrysostom, Ambrose, and the rest. For the fathers of the fourth and fifth centuries, mystery vocabulary was already a traditional dialect of Christian theology, not a direct borrowing from or imitation of the mystery religions. Thus it is in second-century sources that we should look for answers to our questions about relationships between early Christianities and their non-Christian competitors.

The Language of Mystery

The features of mystagogical language and vocabulary as used by Christians are well illustrated in the homilies of John Chrysostom, who seems to have used this kind of terminology more frequently than other fourth-century Greek fathers.[27]

> 'Now let me speak to you of the mysteries themselves, and of the contract which will be made between yourselves and the Master. In worldly affairs, whenever someone wishes to entrust his business to anyone, a written contract must be completed between the trustee and his client. The same thing holds true now, when the Master is going to entrust to you not mortal things which are subject to destruction and death, but spiritual things which belong to eternity. Wherefore, this contract is also called faith, since it possesses nothing visible but all things which can be seen by the eyes of the spirit. There must be an agreement between the contracting parties. However, it is not on paper nor written in ink; it is in God and written by the Spirit....
> See here again the external attitude of captivity. The priests bring you in. First they bid you to pray on bent knees, with your hands outstretched to heaven, and to remind yourselves by your posture from what evil you are delivered and to what good you will dedicate yourselves. Then the priest

---

[26] Smith, *Drudgery* (see n. 19), pp. 62-84.

[27] Some statistics in Philippe de Roten, 'Le vocabulaire mystagogique de Saint Jean Chrysostome', in *Mystagogie*, eds. Triacca and Pistoia (see n. 2), pp. 115-135, especially pp. 117-118.

comes to you one by one, asks for your contract and confession, and prepares you to utter those awesome and frightening words: "I renounce thee, Satan".[28]'

Here, when Chrysostom proposes to speak of 'the mysteries themselves', the word 'mysteries' seems close in meaning to what we would call 'liturgy', the specific ceremonies that make up the rite of sacramental initiation: 'The priests bring you in. First they bid you to pray on bent knees', and so on. They are fittingly called 'mysteries' because they express 'spiritual things which belong to eternity', things which only 'can be seen by the eyes of the spirit'. This quotation also demonstrates a willingness to make favorable comparisons with non-Christian rituals, though in this case the details of contract ratification belong, not to the mystery cults, but to the realm of 'worldly affairs'.

In another sermon, the word 'mystery' is apparently equivalent to 'sacrament', and 'the mystery of initiation', celebrated within the Easter liturgy, is likened to a different civil ceremony — the triumphal victory spectacles put on by 'the kings of foreign nations' upon conquering their enemies, even though 'their kind of honor is rife with dishonor'.

> 'I was seeking to tell you why our fathers passed by all the other seasons of the year and ordained that your souls be initiated during this season, and I said that observance of the time was not a simple or random thing. For it is always the same grace and it is not hindered by the season, for the grace is from God. But the observance of the proper season does have some connection with the mystery of initiation. Why did our fathers ordain this feast at this time? Our King has now conquered in the war against the barbarians. And all the demons are barbarians, and more savage than barbarians. Now He has destroyed sin, now He has put down death and has subjected the devil, He has taken His captives.
>
> And so it is that on this day we celebrate the memory of those victories, and on this account our fathers ordained that the King's gifts be distributed at this time, for this is the custom of conquerors. The kings of foreign nations do this and count the days of the triumphal celebration deserving of many honors. But their kind of honor is rife with dishonor. For what kind of honor is there in spectacles and in what is said and done there? Are these spectacles not filled in every way with shame and loud laughter?
>
> But the honor of this season is worthy of the munificence of Him who gives this honor. Therefore, our fathers ordained the celebration of this

---

[28] John Chrysostom, [untitled baptismal sermon (*CPG* 4466)] series 3, homily 2:17-18; *SC* 50bis: 143-144 (Wenger), *FC* 6/2: 346-349 (Kaczynski); transl. *ACW* 31: 49-50 (Harkins). Another translation in Yarnold, *Awe-Inspiring* (see n. 5), p. 158. On the editions, numberings, and datings of Chrysostom's mystagogical sermons, see Knupp, *Mystagogieverständnis* (see n. 18), pp. 55-65.

season first in order to remind you of the Master by the season of His victory, and then that there might be, in the triumphal celebration, some who
are wearing shining robes and who are about to receive a reward from the
King ....'[29]

In another sermon the 'mysteries' (plural) refer to one specific sacrament: the eucharist, as distinct from baptism. In the very next paragraph,
however, the same word (singular) refers to an exegetical mystery:
something in the Bible that requires explanation to reveal its deeper
meaning.

'St. John says that, when Christ was dead but still on the cross, the soldier
came and pierced his side with a lance, and straightway there came out
water and blood. The one was a symbol of baptism, and the other of the
mysteries. Therefore he did not say, "There came out blood and water",
but first water came forth and then blood, since first comes baptism and
then the mysteries. It was the soldier, then, who opened Christ's side and
dug through the rampart of the holy temple, but I am the one who has
found the treasure and gotten the wealth. So it was with the lamb. The Jews
sacrificed the victim, but I reaped the reward of salvation which came from
their sacrifice.
"There came out from His side water and blood". Beloved, do not pass this
mystery by without a thought. For I have still another mystical explanation
to give. I said that there was a symbol of baptism and the mysteries in that
blood and water. It is from both of these that the Church is sprung "through
the bath of regeneration and renewal by the Holy Spirit", through baptism
and the mysteries. But the symbols of baptism and the mysteries come
from the side of Christ. It is from His side, therefore, that Christ formed
His church, just as He formed Eve from the side of Adam.'[30]

The fact that the same word (mystery) can be used for both a sacramental action and a profound scriptural passage may be difficult for
modern Western Christians to appreciate, given our post-Reformation
outlook that assumes a sharp distinction between Word and Sacrament.
But the language of early Christian mystagogy did not clearly distinguish the two.

---

[29] Chrysostom, [untitled baptismal sermon (*CPG* 4461=Papadopoulos-Kerameus 2)]
series 2, homily 2: 3; *SC* 366: 174-177 (Piédagnel), *FC* 6/1: 200-203; transl. *ACW* 31:
150.
[30] Chrysostom, [untitled baptismal sermon (*CPG* 4467=Papadopoulos-Kerameus 4)]
series 2, homily 4:16-17; *SC* 50bis: 160-161 (Wenger), *FC* 6/1: 272-275; transl.
ACW 31: 61-62.

Word or Sacrament

For early Christian theologians, being able to understand the scriptures and being enrolled in the Christian community were two aspects of the same spiritual state. One can see this in a papyrus text that shows Origen settling an exegetical dispute between parties of orthodox and heretical bishops. Arriving at the disputed biblical passage, Origen says, 'we have come upon a mystical word (*logon mystikon*)'. Later he will also describe the wheels of Ezekiel's vision as 'unspeakable mysteries' (*aporrhēta mystēria*).[31] In the presence of such mysteries, Origen says,

> ' … I am both anxious to speak, and anxious not to speak. Because of those who are worthy I am willing to speak, so that I may not be accused of withholding the word from those who are able to hear [it]. Because of those who are not worthy I hesitate to speak, on account of the [biblical sayings] that were strung together before: that I will never toss holy things to dogs or cast pearls before swine [Matthew 7:6]. It was the task of Jesus alone to know how to separate those among his hearers who were outside from those who were inside, so that he would speak in parables to those outside, and he would solve the parables for those entering his house. The [difference between being] outside and entering the house is a mystical thing. "For what have I to do with judging those outside?" [1 Corinthians 5:12]. Everyone who sins is outside. That is why he had to speak in parables to those [who were] outside, so that somehow, leaving the outside, they might be enabled to become inside. Coming into the house is a mystical thing (*mystikon*). The one who enters into the house of Jesus is his legitimate disciple. He enters because he understands ecclesiastical things, because he lives ecclesiastically. The [difference between the] inside and the outside is a spiritual thing (*pneumatikon*).'[32]

The background for this is Matthew 13, wherein Jesus went out of a house, told the parable of the sower to a great crowd, and was asked by the disciples, 'Why do you speak to them in parables?' He replied, 'To you it has been given to know the mysteries of the kingdom of heaven, but to them it has not been given' (13:10-11), then he proceeded to explain the parable. After telling a few more parables, Jesus returned to the house (13:36) and, once again at the disciples' request, explained the parable of the good seed and the weeds (13:36-43). After a few more

---

[31] Origène, *Entretien avec Héracleide*, ed. Jean Scherer, SC, 67, rev. ed. (Paris, 2002), pp. 86-87, 108-109 [*CPG* 1481].

[32] Origène, *Entretien*, ed. Scherer (see n. 31), pp. 86-87. For additional commentary see *Entretien d'Origène avec Héraclide et les évêques ses collègues sur le père, le fils, et l'âme*, ed. Jean Scherer, Publications de la Société Fouad I de Papyrologie, 9 (Cairo, 1949), pp. 152-155.

parables he asked, 'Have you understood all this?' and continued, 'Therefore every scribe who has been trained for the kingdom of heaven is like the master of a household who brings out of his treasure what is new and what is old' (13:51-52). The hidden meaning of the scriptures, in short, is available to those who have entered the house where Jesus is, the same house where those who have received authority to teach these mysteries reside. Those who remain outside hear only parables they do not understand. 'Coming into the house is a mystical thing' that requires one to both 'understand ecclesiastical things' and 'live ecclesiastically', or according to the church's principles.

Those who have entered the house of the church, of course, will have done so through the church's initiation process. Though the Origen text quoted above gives no details about the rituals involved, Origen himself explicitly stated that the words and gestures of the church's liturgy ('ecclesiastical observances') veiled hidden truths that required exegesis, in the same way that the priestly rituals commanded by Moses were types of the Christ to come.[33] The unicity of word, teaching, and sacrament as the locus of encounter with the living Christ is, of course, already taught in the New Testament itself. For Luke, it is in the breaking of the bread that the disciples recognize the Lord who opens the scriptures (Luke 24:30-35).

The identity between admission to the Christian community and admission to the inner meaning of its holy writings can be felt more jarringly in Rufinus's Latin translation of Origen's *De Principiis*: There the hidden meanings of scripture are frankly called 'sacraments', since Rufinus used the word *sacramenta* where the lost Greek original must have said *mystēria*. For one of Origen's basic principles (*principia*) was

> 'that the Scriptures were composed by the Spirit of God, and have a meaning — not only that [meaning] which is evident in the plain [text], but also a certain other [meaning], which is hidden (*latentem*) from most people. For these things that are described are the shapes (*formae*) of certain mysteries (*sacramentorum*) and the images of divine things'.[34]

---

[33] Origen, *In Num. Hom.* 5.1.4, ed. W. A. Baehrens, GCS 30 (Berlin, 1921), pp. 26-27; SC, 415 (Paris, 1996), pp. 122-125. See also F. Ledegang, *Mysterium Ecclesiae: Images of the Church and Its Members in Origen*, Bibliotheca Ephemeridum Theologicarum Lovaniensium 156 (Leuven, 2001), pp. 310-354.

[34] Origen, *De Principiis*, transl. Rufinus, eds. Crouzel and Simonetti, Pref. 8. *SC* 252: 84-87; *PG* 11:119.

Of course the Latin word *sacramentum*, which originally referred to a Roman soldier's oath of allegiance,[35] was hardly a close translation of the Greek word μυστήριον (*mystērion*), which had originally denoted the closing of the eyes or the lips associated with ritual secrecy.[36] Ancient bilingual glossaries typically render μυστήριον into Latin by such locutions as 'arcanum initiamentum' (a secret initiation), and *sacramentum* into Greek as ὅρκος στρατιωτικός (a soldier's oath) or something similar.[37] It has been argued that Tertullian deliberately used the word *sacramentum* to avoid the pagan associations implied by the Greek loanword *mysterium*.[38] Yet both terms could denote a solemn ritual of entrance into a community, be it a mystery cult or a Roman legion. Hence the word *sacramentum* first occurs in a Christian context in the famous letter of Pliny the Younger, who describes some sort of initiation rite that has obvious parallels with a soldier's oath of allegiance:

> 'But they asserted that this was the height of their fault or error: that they were accustomed to come together on a specific day before dawn, and to say among themselves a spell to Christ, as if to a god, and to bind themselves with an oath (*sacramento*) — not to something wicked, but that they not commit thefts nor robberies nor adulteries, nor betray a trust, nor withhold a deposit of [money that had been] called for.'[39]

In the Latin world, therefore, *sacramentum* became the most common term for the sanctifying celebrations of the Church,[40] while *mysterium* was often used to mean a theological truth or scriptural passage that required explanation. For example, the *Liber Regularum*, an influential exegetical handbook by Tyconius the Donatist, explains that 'there are certain mystical rules (*regulae mysticae*) which preserve the hidden places (*recessus*) of the entire law, and make the treasures of truth invisible to some people'.[41] Such usage can be found in a much-quoted passage from

---

[35] Sara Elise Phang, *Roman Military Service: Ideologies of Discipline in the Late Republic and Early Principate* (Cambridge, 2008), pp. 117-120.

[36] Hjalmar Frisk, *Griechisches etymologisches Wörterbuch*, 2 (Heidelberg, 1970), pp. 279-281 at 'μύω.'

[37] D. Gáspár, 'Quelques remarques concernant le mot "sacramentum" et le serment militaire', *Acta Archaeologica Academiae Scientiarum Hungaricae* 28 (1976) 197-203, on p. 199.

[38] Dimitri Michaélidès, *Sacramentum chez Tertullien* (Paris, 1970), p. 334.

[39] Pliny the Younger, *Ep. Tra.* 10.96(97).7, eds. M. Schuster and R. Hanslik, 3rd ed. (Stuttgart, [1958] 1992), p. 356.

[40] William A. Van Roo, *The Christian Sacrament*, Analecta Gregoriana 262; Series Facultatis Theologiae sectio A, 34 (Rome, 1992), pp. 27-44, 69-97.

[41] 'Sunt enim quaedam regulae mysticae quae universae legis recessus obtinent et veritatis thesauros aliquibus invisibiles faciunt.' See *The Book of Rules of Tyconius newly*

the sermons of Pope Leo the Great, which nonetheless makes clear that Christ is truly present in both the sacramental actions and the proclaimed word.

> 'The sacrament of our salvation, which the creator of the universe valued at the price of his own blood, has been fulfilled through the economy of humility, O dearest ones, from the dawn of his bodily arrival [at the Incarnation] up to the departure of his Passion. And though he also radiated many signs of divinity [while] in the form of a servant, yet his activity at that time properly pertained to demonstrating the truth that he had taken on a human nature ... Therefore, dearest ones, so that we would be able to have the capacity for this blessedness, after he had fulfilled all things which conformed to the evangelical preaching and the mysteries of the New Testament, our Lord Jesus Christ brought his bodily presence to an end. He was lifted up to heaven in the sight of his disciples on the fortieth day after his resurrection, to remain at the right hand of the Father, until the times that have been divinely fixed for multiplying the children of the Church will be completed, and he will come to judge the living and the dead in the same flesh in which he ascended. Therefore what was once conspicuously visible about our Redeemer has passed into the sacraments. And so that faith may be firmer and more excellent, the hearts of believers, illuminated by celestial rays, follow the authority of doctrine, which has become the successor to vision.'[42]

What Jesus did during his earthly life was accomplish 'the sacrament of our salvation', which however consisted in many individual acts or 'mysteries of the New Testament' or covenant that is preached in the gospels. These mysteries, which his contemporaries saw with their own eyes, have 'passed into the sacraments' of the Church, wherein they are also experienced by following 'the authority of doctrine, which has become the successor to vision'. What the disciples saw, that is, we now receive in the Church's teaching. Hence scripture, sacrament, and ecclesiastical teaching are for us what direct acquaintance with the Messiah was for the first Christians (cf. 2 Peter 1:16-21). Leo's well-known text has therefore become a locus classicus in the modern recovery of the liturgical theology of the early church. The 'proclamation of Christ's death by the *word* cannot be dissociated from the liturgical *action* itself ... The word is not simply an interpretation of what takes place in the

---

edited from the mss., ed. F. C. Burkitt, Texts and Studies 3/1 (Cambridge, 1894), p. cxxiii. See also Tyconius, *The Book of Rules*, transl. William S. Babcock, Society of Biblical Literature. Texts and Translations 31; Early Christian Literature Series 7 (Atlanta, GA, 1989), pp. 2-3.

[42] Leo, *Tractatus LXXIV* 1-2, ed. Antoine Chavasse, in *CCSL* 138A: 455-457.

action. It forms a single liturgical whole with it'.[43] However, the fact that Leo can describe the whole economy of redemption as 'the sacrament of our salvation' shows that he did not recognize an absolute distinction between scriptural mysterium and liturgical sacramentum.[44] Indeed this distinction never became absolute in the West, where the word 'mystery' retained a special connection with the sacrament of the eucharist, which eventually developed into the Roman Catholic theology of the Church as Mystical Body.[45]

In Greek Christianity, on the other hand, which never adopted the Latin word *sacramentum*, the word *mystērion* tended to retain the broader semantic field that covered word, teaching and ritual action. Thus for Gregory of Nazianzen the eucharistic mystery (i.e., the sacrament) was 'the antitype of the great mysteries' (i.e. the redemptive acts of Christ).[46] Pseudo-Dionysius had to employ the term *teletē* (τελετή) for the kind of ritual action we would call a 'sacrament'. This word, which implies a process of 'perfecting', was the term for an initiation ceremony in the non-Christian mystery cults. The use of *teletē* by Pseudo-Dionysius allowed *mystērion* to retain its traditional broader field of semantic reference, including 'ineffable conceptions, ... the incarnation in particular', as well as 'certain sacred ceremonies', and the eucharistic elements themselves.[47] In the Dionysian sacramental system there were three mysteries, which align asymmetrically with three stages of Christian initiation, presided over by the three orders of clergy: (1) first the deacons prepare candidates for the illumination or divine birth of baptism, which (2) is actually perfected by the priests, followed by (3) the synaxis (Eucharist) and the mystery of the ointment,

---

[43] E. Schillebeeckx, *Revelation and Theology*, transl. N. D. Smith (New York, 1967), p. 53. See also Paul Janowiak, *The Holy Preaching: The Sacramentality of the Word in the Liturgical Assembly* (Collegeville, 2000).

[44] Marie-Bernard De Soos, *Le mystère liturgique d'après saint Léon le Grand*, LQF 34 (Münster, 1958), pp. 79-94, 136-138, 143-149.

[45] The story is classically recounted in Henri de Lubac, *Corpus Mysticum: The Eucharist and the Church in the Middle Ages*, transl. Gemma Simmonds et al. (South Bend, IN, 2007).

[46] Jaroslav Pelikan, *Christianity and Classical Culture: The Metamorphosis of Natural Theology in the Christian Encounter with Hellenism* (New Haven, CT, 1993), pp. 297-298.

[47] Pseudo-Dionysius, *Hier. Eccl.* 1.1 (372A), 4.III.12 (485A). See the comments in Pseudo-Dionysius, *The Complete Works*, transl. Colm Luibheid and Paul Rorem, The Classics of Western Spirituality (New York and Mahwah, 1987), pp. 195 n. 3, 232 n. 138; Paul Rorem, *Biblical and Liturgical Symbols within the Pseudo-Dionysian Synthesis*, Studies and Texts 71 (Toronto, 1984), pp. 39-46, 49-54.

'for it is the ordinance of God that only the sacramental powers of the God-possessed hierarchs can accomplish the sanctification of the clerical orders, the consecration of the ointment, and the rite of consecrating the holy altar'. Even at the first stage of preparing for baptism, however, it is 'the singing and reading of the scriptures' that 'incubate the uninitiated toward life-giving sonship'.[48] The sequence of Dionysian mysteries seems to parallel the initiation process assumed by the anonymous author of the Epistle to the Hebrews: 'Those who have once been enlightened [i.e., baptized?], and have tasted the heavenly gift [Eucharist?], and have shared in the Holy Spirit [anointing?]', are also enabled to 'have tasted the goodness of the word of God and the powers of the age to come' (Hebrews 6:4-5).

But if the fathers of the church were in continuity with the New Testament, the historical pathway from Luke, 2 Peter and Hebrews to Pseudo-Dionysius has not yet been traced fully. In fact it passes directly through the writings of Clement of Alexandria, who can be seen merging several different vocabularies that were originally discrete, having originated in different historical contexts.

Apocalyptic-Incarnational Vocabulary

The most direct line between Clement and the New Testament can be seen in the transition from apocalyptic to incarnational vocabulary. In the following passages, the word 'mystery' is used in the same way as in Jewish apocalyptic literature, where Greek 'mystērion' translates the Persian loanword 'rāz'.[49]

> 'To you has been given the secret (*mystērion*) of the kingdom of God, but for those outside everything is in parables (Mark 4:11[50]; plural 'secrets/mysteries' in Matthew 13:11 and Luke 8:10).'

---

[48] Pseudo-Dionysius, *Hier. Eccl.* 5.I.5 (505C), 4.III.3 (477A), transl. Luibheid and Rorem, in *The Complete Works* (see n. 47), pp. 237, 227.

[49] F. Mojtabāi, 'The Iranian Background of the Judeo-Christian Concept of Rāz / Mystērion,' in *Mihr – O – dād – O Bahār: Memorial Volume of Dr. Mehrdād Bahār*, ed. Ameer Kavous Balazadeh (Teheran, 1377 [=A.D. 1998]), pp. 343-372; Guy G. Stroumsa, *Hidden Wisdom: Esoteric Traditions and the Roots of Christian Mysticism*, 2nd ed. (Leiden, 2005); Adela Yarbro Collins, *Mark: A Commentary*, Hermeneia (Minneapolis, 2007), pp. 247-250, 404; Baby Varghese, *West Syrian Liturgical Theology* (Aldershot, 2004), pp. 35-42.

[50] Joel Marcus, *The Mystery of the Kingdom of God*, Society of Biblical Literature Dissertation Series 90 (Atlanta, 1986), pp. 45-47. See also R. T. France, *The Gospel of*

'But we speak the wisdom of God hidden in a mystery, which God decreed before the ages for our glorification' (1 Corinthians 2:7).

The mystery here is God's hidden knowledge, especially the divine plan of salvation history to be revealed in the last times. For Christians, of course, this was identical with the gospel:

> 'the proclamation of Jesus Christ, according to the revelation of the mystery that was kept secret for long ages but is now disclosed, and through the prophetic writings is made known to all the Gentiles according to the command of the eternal God' (Romans 16:25-26).[51]

Like its synonyms 'Logos' and 'Wisdom', however, the word 'mystery' in the apocalyptic sense, 'God's plan to sum up all things in Christ',[52] was increasingly identified with the person of Christ himself, incarnate in history. Thus in the post-Pauline epistles, Christians are urged 'to be encouraged and united in love, so that they may have all the riches of assured understanding and the knowledge of God's mystery, that is, Christ himself, in whom are hidden all the treasures of wisdom and knowledge' (Colossians 2:2-3, cf. Ephesians 1:9, 3:1-12).

Clement of Alexandria wrote in the same way, in a gloss on 1 Timothy 3:16 ('The mystery of our religion is great...'):

> 'O mystery! The angels saw Christ while he was with us, [not] having seen Him before — not like men.'[53]

For Clement, the teaching of true doctrine within the Church was a 'mystic marvel', because it proceeded directly from the Incarnation of Christ.

> 'O mystic marvel! The Lord has sunk down, but man rose up; and he who was driven from Paradise gains a greater prize, heaven, on becoming obedient. Wherefore it seems to me, that since the Word Himself came to us from Heaven, we ought no longer to go to human teaching, to Athens and

---

Mark: A Commentary on the Greek Text (Grand Rapids, MI, 2002), pp. 196-199; Suzanne Watts Henderson, *Christology and Discipleship in the Gospel of Mark*, Society for New Testament Studies Monograph Series (Cambridge, 2006), pp. 101-126.

[51] 'The "Mystery" of Romans 11:25-26 Once More', in Seyoon Kim, *Paul and the New Perspective: Second Thoughts on the Origin of Paul's Gospel* (Grand Rapids, 2002), pp. 239-258; Markus N. A. Bockmuehl, *Revelation and Mystery in Ancient Judaism and Pauline Christianity*, Wissenschaftliche Untersuchungen zum Neuen Testament, 2. Reihe 36 (Tübingen, 1990), pp. 226-227.

[52] Peter T. O'Brien, *The Letter to the Ephesians* (Grand Rapids, 1999), pp. 108-115.

[53] *Hypotyp.* Frag. 16, on 1 Tim 3:16, 'seen by angels,' ed. Otto Stählin, *GCS* 17 [= Clemens Alexandrinus 3], p. 200, on which see the editorial edition of '[not].' Translation modified from *ANF* 2: 579 (Wilson).

the rest of Greece ... If our teacher is He who has filled the universe with holy powers, creation, salvation, beneficence, lawgiving, prophecy, teaching, this teacher now instructs us in all things, and the whole world has by this time become an Athens and a Greece through the Word ... we, who have become disciples of God, have entered into the really true wisdom which leaders of philosophy only hinted at, but which the disciples of the Christ have both comprehended and proclaimed abroad.'[54]

Indeed, the scripture is the 'Lord's voice'; his very incarnation (parousia) is an exegesis of the Old Testament.[55] However, the Eucharist is also a mystic marvel, and for the same reason.

'Now that the loving and kind Father has rained down the Word, it is he himself who has become the spiritual nourishment of the chaste. O mystic marvel! The Father of all is one, the Word who belongs to all is one, the Holy Spirit is one and the same for all. And one alone, too, is the virgin Mother. I like to call her the Church. ... Calling her children about her, she nourishes them with milk that is holy: the infant Word. ... "Eat my flesh", he says, "and drink my blood" (John 6:55). He is himself the nourishment that he gives. He delivers up his own flesh and pours out his own blood. There is nothing lacking his children, that they may grow. O paradoxical mystery! He bids us put off the former mortality of the flesh and, with it, the former nourishment, and receive instead this other new life of Christ.'[56]

In this case the mystery is the ingestion of Christ as food — what we would call the sacrament. As H. G. Marsh recognized already in 1936, Clement is referring to 'something more than mere verbal exegesis' of scriptural texts regarding the Eucharist.[57] For Clement, as for Origen, 'the sacramental celebrations are considered the *locus* in which the spiritual sense of Scripture (moral, allegorical, anagogical) becomes explicit and effective'.[58]

---

[54] Clement, *Protr.* 111,3, translation modified from LCL 238-239 (Butterworth).

[55] *Strom.* 7.95.4, 4.134.4.

[56] Clement, *Paed.* 1.41.3-1.43.1, translation modified from FaCh 23:40 (Wood).

[57] H. G. Marsh, 'The Use of Μυστήριον in the Writings of Clement of Alexandria with Special Reference to his Sacramental Doctrine', *Journal of Theological Studies* 37 (1936) 64-80, on pp. 68, 74-76. Cf. *Paed.* 1.46.3 and 2.29.1.

[58] Eliseo Ruffini and Enzo Lodi, *'Mysterion' e 'Sacramentum': La Sacramentalità negli scritti dei padri e nei testi liturgici primitivi* (Bologna, 1987), pp. 83-102, quote from p. 98.

Cultic-Philosophical Vocabulary

Another eucharistic passage, however, shows that Clement was heir to a different vocabulary of mystery, this one going back to Plato. I am referring to the use of terminology from the Greek mystery religions — not in its original sense, but in its derivative use to describe stages of philosophical realization. This passage describes the growth from catechesis to full sacramental participation in the eucharistic sacrifice using terminology from the Eleusinian mysteries.

> 'If, then, 'milk' is said by the apostle to belong to babes (*nēpiōn*), and 'meat' to be the food of the full-grown/perfected (*teleiōn*), milk will be understood to be catechesis — the first food, as it were, of the soul. Meat is the mystical vision (*epoptikē theōria*), for this is the flesh and the blood of the Word, that is, the comprehension of the divine power and essence. "Taste and see that sweet is the Lord", it is said (Ps 33:9 LXX). For so he imparts of himself to those who partake of such food in a more spiritual manner (*pneumatikōteron*), when now the soul nourishes itself, according to the truth-loving Plato (*Ep.* 7; 341 CD). The meat and drink of the divine Word is the knowledge (*gnōsis*) of the divine essence, wherefore also Plato says, in the second book of the *Republic* (378 A), "It is those that sacrifice not a sow, but some great and difficult sacrifice", who ought to inquire respecting God. And the apostle writes, "Christ our passover was sacrificed for us" (1 Cor 5:7) — a sacrifice hard to procure: in truth the Son of God consecrated for us.'[59]

The word *teleiōn*, which here primarily means 'full-grown', could also mean 'perfected' in the language of the mystery cults. Most importantly, the mystical vision (*epoptikē theōria*) was the climactic experience undergone by the initiate in the Great Mysteries of Eleusis, after he had already passed through the more preliminary Little Mysteries.[60] Clement's willingness to quote Plato in the same breath with the Psalms and St Paul offers one of the keys to his use of such cultic language: Just as Plato was willing to use the terminology of the mystery cults allegorically, to describe a disciple's progress toward the profound knowledge

---

[59] Clement, *Strom.* 5.66.2-5, translation modified from *ANF* 2: 460 (Wilson).

[60] For the terminology see: Mylonas, *Eleusis* (see n. 9), pp. 238-239, 274-249; Michael B. Cosmopoulos, *Greek Mysteries: The Archaeology and Ritual of Ancient Greek Secret Cults* (London, 2003), pp. 50-78, 197 and elsewhere; Noel D. Robertson, 'The Two Processions to Eleusis and the Program of the Mysteries', *American Journal of Philology* 119 (1998) 547-575; Peter Jeffery, *The Secret Gospel of Mark Unveiled: Imagined Rituals of Sex, Death, and Madness in a Biblical Forgery* (New Haven, 2007), pp. 193-194.

(*gnōsis*) of philosophy, so Clement was willing to use it to describe progress toward the true Christian gnosis, which Clement carefully distinguished from the false gnosis of Gnosticism. Thus Clement could approvingly quote a prayer to Zeus in the course of comparing the advanced Christian life to the career of an athlete (cf. 1 Cor 9:25).

> 'For to the gnostic [Christian] every kind of good comes as an accessory,[61] seeing that his chief end is in each case knowledge and action in accordance with knowledge. ... I like that story which is told among the Greeks of a famous athlete of former days, who had trained himself for feats of manhood by a long course of discipline. Having gone up to the Olympian games he turned to the image of Pisaean Zeus and uttered these words: "If I, O Zeus, have now done all that was fitting on my part in preparation for the contest, do thou make haste to bestow the victory I deserve". For just so does the gnostic, when he has thoroughly and conscientiously performed his part with a view to learning and discipline and with a view to doing good and pleasing God, find the whole world contributing to perfect his salvation.'[62]

Clement's use of the word 'gnostic' to describe his ideal Christian emphasizes the importance, for Clement's community, of obtaining advanced exegetical and philosophical instruction, beyond the pre-baptismal catechesis given to all Christians. If the *epopteia* or mystical vision of the Great Mysteries of Eleusis could represent the gnostic Christian's experience of receiving the Eucharist — the highest level of Christian initiation — so the same epoptic vision could also stand as a metaphor for the heights of knowledge to be achieved by the gnostic who mastered Clement's philosophical curriculum.

> 'Do you see how the Greeks deify the gnostic life (though not knowing how to become acquainted with it)? And what knowledge it is, they know not even in a dream. If, then, it is agreed among us that knowledge is the food of reason, truly "blessed are they", according to the Scripture, "who hunger and thirst after truth: for they shall be filled" with everlasting food. In the most wonderful harmony with these words, Euripides, the philosopher of the drama, is found in the following words, — making allusion, I know not how, at once to the Father and the Son:
>
> "To thee, the Lord of all, I bring
> Cakes and libations too, O Zeus,
> Or Hades would'st thou choose be called;

---

[61] A Stoic sentiment: Cicero, *De Finibus* 3.30-34.
[62] Clement, *Strom.* 7.48, transl. Hort and Mayor, rev. in *Alexandrian Christianity*, eds. John Ernest Leonard Oulton and Henry Chadwick, LCC 2 (Philadelphia, 1954), pp. 123-124.

Do thou accept my offering of all fruits,
Rare, full, poured forth".

For a whole burnt-offering and rare sacrifice for us is Christ. And that unwittingly he mentions the Saviour, he will make plain, as he adds:

"For thou who, 'midst the heavenly gods,
Jove's sceptre sway'st, dost also share
The rule of those on earth".

Then he says expressly: -

"Send light to human souls that fain would know
Whence conflicts spring, and what the root of ills,
And of the blessed gods to whom due rites
Of sacrifice we needs must pay, that so
We may from troubles find repose".

It is not without reason, then, that in the mysteries that obtain among the Greeks, lustrations (*katharsia*) hold the first place; as also the laver (*loutron*) among the Barbarians [i.e., the Jews]. After these are the Lesser Mysteries, which have some foundation of instruction and of preliminary preparation for what is to come after; and the Great Mysteries, in which nothing remains to be learned of the universe, but only to contemplate (*epopteuein*) and comprehend nature and things. ...

If, then, abstracting all that belongs to bodies and things called incorporeal, we cast ourselves into the greatness of Christ, and thence advance into immensity by holiness, we may reach somehow to the conception of the Almighty, knowing not what He is, but what He is not. And form and motion, or standing, or a throne, or place, or right hand or left, are not at all to be conceived as belonging to the Father of the universe, although it is so written. But what each of these means will be shown in its proper place. The First Cause is not then in space, but above both space, and time, and name, and conception.

Wherefore also Moses says, "Show Thyself to me" (Exodus 33:18) — intimating most clearly that God is not capable of being taught by man, or expressed in speech, but to be known only by His own power. For inquiry was obscure and dim; but the grace of knowledge is from Him by the Son.'[63]

For these advanced students of Christian knowledge, the washings of baptism were just the beginning. This was not the only place where Clement described his philosophical curriculum as a passage through lesser to great mysteries and finally to the mystic *epopteia*,[64] and it shows that, for all Clement's use of mystery vocabulary, his extant writings are

---

[63] *Strom.* 5.70.1-71.5, slightly adapted from ANF 461.
[64] See *Strom.* 4.3.1-4 and 1.176.1-2.

not mystagogy in the classic sense. They were not intended, that is, for the newly baptized, but for very advanced students of Christian learning. At the same time, Clement was extremely critical of the actual mystery cults, devoting many pages of the *Protreptikos* to disparaging their sexual and violent content. For Clement, the ancient Greek mysteries were 'sacred initiations that are really profanities, and solemn rites that are without sanctity'.[65] He even proposed to derive the Greek word μυστήριον etymologically from μύσος ('defilement') (*Protr.* 2.13.1, 2.34.3-5). Clement's mystery vocabulary was a philosophical usage, not an attempt to find common ground with non-Christian cults, even for apologetic purposes.

Typological Vocabulary

Alongside the vocabularies derived from Jewish apocalyptic and from Plato, the third vocabulary was derived from Philo, specifically his allegorical reinterpretation of Old Testament and Jewish ceremonies. Philo, of course, had inherited a Middle Platonist school tradition in which the ritual terminology of the pagan mystery cults was applied metaphorically to the acquisition of philosophical knowledge and growth in ethical maturity, as in Plato's *Symposium* and *Phaedrus*. But Philo reapplied this cultic-philosophical language to the allegorical exegesis of the Bible; from him Clement (and probably also Clement's readers) learned to do the same.[66]

> 'For so it is said, "And he shall put off the linen robe (στολήν), which he had put on when he entered into the holy place; and shall lay it aside there, and wash his body in water in the holy place, and put on his robe" (Lev. 16:23-24). But in one way, as I think, the Lord puts off and puts on by descending into the region of sense; and in another, he who through Him has believed puts off and puts on, as the apostle intimated, the consecrated robe' (1 Cor 15:53 and 2 Cor 5:2-4).[67]

[65] *Protr.* 2.22.3; transl. LCL 92:45 (Butterworth).

[66] Christoph Riedweg, *Mysterienterminologie bei Platon, Philon und Klemens von Alexandrien*, Untersuchungen zur antiken Literatur und Geschichte 26 (Berlin, 1987); Gary Lease, 'Jewish Mystery Cults Since Goodenough,' in *Aufstieg und Niedergang der römischen Welt: Geschichte und Kultur Roms im Spiegel der neueren Forschung* 20/2, eds. Wolfgang Haase and Hildegard Temporini (Berlin, 1987), pp. 858-880.

[67] Clement, *Strom.* 5.40.2-3, transl. modified from *ANF* 2: 454.

One cannot be certain from this that the baptism ritual of Clement's church actually called for the putting off and on of a ceremonial robe. The important thing is that the robe that signifies the adoption of Christian faith, even if it is only metaphorical, is mentioned in the context of Temple typology, by being connected to the linen garments of the High Priest. Here Clement is obviously indebted to Philo, but in the generation after Clement, Origen would state more explicitly that the specific ceremonies of the Christian liturgy were linked typologically to the rituals of the Old Testament, and that this linkage constituted a secret mystery.

'Now therefore let us go back to that tabernacle of the Church of the living God, and let us see how each of these things ought to be observed in the Church of God by the priests of Christ. But if anyone is a priest to whom the sacred vessels — that is the secrets of the wisdom of the mysteries — are committed, let him learn from them, and observe how it is necessary to keep these things within the veil of conscience, and not to proffer them readily to the public.'[68]

'No doubt Moses understood what a true circumcision is. He understood what a true Passover is, he knew what true New Moons and Sabbaths were. And while he understood all these things in spirit, yet he veiled them in words through the species of corporeal things and shadowy outlines. And while he knew that the true Passover to be immolated would be Christ, he commands a corporeal lamb to be immolated on Passover. And while he knew a feast day ought to be done with the unleavened bread of sincerity and truth, yet he prescribed that the feast day be done with unleavened bread made of flour. Also of this kind, therefore, were the Holies of Holies, which, when Moses handed down to be carried with the other [things], that is with things and works to be fulfilled, yet he handed them down covered and veiled by the common speech of words. However the forearms that carried what these deeds signified, we often show forth in many places of Scripture. But also in the ecclesiastical observances are some things of this kind, which indeed it is necessary for everyone to do, yet the reason for them is not evident to everyone. For example: that we bend the knees while praying, and that, out of all the regions of heaven, we pour out prayer while turned only toward the eastern part, are things not easily ascertained by anyone through clear reasoning. But also, who could easily explain the reason for the Eucharist to be perceived or explained in the rite by which it is carried out, or [the reason] for those words and gestures and orders which are carried out in baptism, and for the questions and answers?...[69]

---

[68] Origen, *Hom. Num.* 4.3.1. *SC* 415:108-109. *PG* 12:600-601.
[69] Origen, *Hom. Num.* 5.1.3. *SC* 415:122-123. *PG* 12:603.

The justification for such typology is a tradition going back as far as Clement of Rome (*1 Clem.* 40-41), in which the worship of Christians is a visible, earthly image of the eternal cult celebrated in the idealized heavenly temple.[70] 'The Church of this world is the image of the heavenly Church', as Clement of Alexandria put it.[71] Beneath that is the older biblical view of Christ and the Church manifesting the presence of God in the world, as the Temple had formerly done.[72] But alongside the metaphor of the heavenly Temple, Clement made use of another image, which in some respects sums up the biblical, Platonic, and Philonic heritages in Clement's language of mystery: this is the image of the heavenly chorus.

The Church as Heavenly Chorus

In the most famous passages where Clement invokes the mystery religions, he seems willing to describe Christian rites as the same sort of thing as pagan mysteries, only superior.

> 'Come, O frenzy-stricken one, ... I will show you the Word and the mysteries of the Word, described according to your own image. ... This is the mountain beloved of God, not a subject for tragedies, ... but one devoted to the dramas of truth ...Therein revel (*bakcheuousi*) no Maenads, sisters of "thundersmitten" Semele, who are initiated into the loathsome distribution of raw flesh, but the daughters of God, the beautiful lambs (*amnades*), who enact the solemn orgies of the word, assembling a sober company. The chorus is the righteous, the song is the hymn of the king of all. The maidens play the harp [or sing psalms (*psallousin*)], angels glorify, prophets speak, a sound of music is raised ...'[73]

> 'O truly sacred mysteries! O pure light! In the blaze of torches I have a vision of heaven and of God. I become holy by initiation. The Lord reveals the mysteries; He marks the worshipper with His seal, gives light to guide his way, and commends him, when he has believed, to the Father's care, where he is guarded for ages to come. These are the Bacchic revels of my mysteries! If you will, be initiated yourself also,

---

[70] E. g., *Strom.* 5.40.2-3, 6.107.2. Ledegang, *Mysterium Ecclesiae* (see n. 33), pp. 310-354.

[71] Clement of Alexandria, *Strom.* 4.66.1, as quoted in Henri De Lubac, *The Splendor of the Church*, transl. Michael Mason (San Francisco, 1999), p. 83 n. 156.

[72] Yves M.-J. Congar, *Le Mystère du Temple, ou l'Économie de la présence de Dieu à sa créature de la Genèse à l'Apocalypse* (Paris, 1958).

[73] Clement, *Protr.* 12.119.1-2, transl. modified from *LCL* 255.

and you shall dance with angels around the unbegotten and imperishable and only true God, the Word of God joining with us in our hymn of praise. ... I will anoint you with the ointment of faith, whereby you cast away corruption, and I will display the naked figure of righteousness, whereby you ascend to God.'[74]

The use of Bacchic terminology, indebted to Euripides's *Bacchantes*, has precedent in Philo's description of the singing and dancing of the Therapeutai: 'carried away as if in the Bacchic rites by the undiluted wine of the God-beloved.'[75] A similar thought may underlie Ephesians 5:18-19, 'Do not get drunk with wine, ... but be filled with the Spirit, addressing one another in psalms and hymns and spiritual songs ...'. Thus Clement invited his pagan readers to join in the chorus: 'If you will, be initiated (*muou*) yourself also, and you shall dance (*choreuseis*) with angels around the unbegotten and imperishable and only true God, the Word of God joining with us in our hymn of praise'. However, because Bacchus was identified with Dionysius, the patronal deity of ancient Greek theater, there is also an implied analogy to the chorus of classical Greek drama. The ancient Greek chorus both sang and danced; it performed both choral music and choreography. Since these were highly developed arts that required considerable training, the chorus was also an educational institution. Because of its ritual and educational functions, we should not think of the ancient chorus as a mere company of professional entertainers, like the chorus of a modern Broadway show. Choruses often consisted of young men or young women, and the leader was their teacher.[76] The dual ritual/educational function is also characteristic of Plato's divine choruses,[77] and contributes to the description of the seven Maccabean brothers who 'grouped about their mother as though a chorus', who bravely 'constituted a holy chorus of religion' as

---

[74] Clement, *Protr.* 120.1-2, transl. modified from *LCL* 256-257. The passage's clear literary dependence on Euripides, *Bacchantes*, raises the question of how much Clement's knowledge of the pagan cults was based on firsthand experience, how much on the study of literary texts.

[75] Philo, *De Vita Contemplativa* 11.85. See Peter Jeffery, 'Philo's Impact on Christian Psalmody', in *Psalms in Community: Jewish and Christian Textual, Liturgical, and Artistic Traditions*, eds. Harold W. Attridge and Margot Elsbeth Fassler, Society of Biblical Literature. Symposium Series 25 (Atlanta, GA, 2003), pp. 147-188, quote from p. 173.

[76] Claude Calame, *Choruses of Young Women in Ancient Greece: Their Morphology, Religious Role, and Social Functions*, new and rev. ed., transl. Derek Collins and Janice Orion (Lanham, MD, 2001).

[77] Riedweg, *Mysterienterminologie* (see n. 66), p. 157; Jeffery, *The Secret Gospel of Mark Unveiled* (see n. 60), pp. 193-194.

they went to their martyrdom, 'encircled the sevenfold fear of tortures' and were 'gathered together into the chorus of the fathers' (4 Maccabees 8:4, 13:8, 14:8, 18:23). For a Christian Platonist like Clement, then, it was natural to describe 'the Lord's church', which taught in his name, as 'that spiritual and holy chorus'.

> '"And meats are for the belly and the belly for meats, but the Lord shall destroy them" (1 Cor 6:13), that is, all who so reason and live as if they were born for eating, instead of eating to live as a subordinate aim, but devoting themselves to knowledge as their principal aim. And perhaps he means that these are, as it were, the fleshy parts of the Holy Body, the Lord's Church being figuratively described as a body (Eph 1:23), i.e., that spiritual and holy chorus, of whom those who are only called by the Name and do not live accordingly constitute the flesh. But this spiritual body, i.e., the holy Church, is not for fornication ...'[78]

In fact the Church is 'the mystical chorus of the truth itself', from which the true gnostic —Clement's ideal Christian — receives knowledge of divine things.

> 'At any rate he who has received a clear conception of the things concerning God from the mystical chorus of the truth itself, makes use of the word of exhortation, exhibiting the greatness of virtue according to its worth, ... being united as intimately as possible with things intellectual and spiritual in the way of knowledge along with an inspired exaltation of prayer. ... He presents a soul altogether unyielding and impregnable whether to the assaults of pleasure or of pain. If reason calls him to it, he is an unswerving judge, in no respect indulging his passions, but keeping inflexibly to the path in which it is the nature of justice to walk, being fully persuaded that all things are admirably ordered, and that, for the souls which have made the choice of virtue, progress is always in the direction of what is better, until they arrive at the Good itself, being brought close to the great High Priest (Heb 4:14), in the vestibule[79] so to speak, of the Father. This is the faithful gnostic who is fully persuaded that all things are ordered for the best.'[80]

Like a Greek philosopher, the gnostic Christian is rational, 'in no respect indulging his passions', walking the path of justice, choosing virtue, arriving at Good itself. Both the High Priest of the Epistle to the Hebrews and an allegorical Platonic temple are invoked to describe this progress. It is from 'the mystical chorus of the truth itself' that the gnostic Christian learns these things, so that the heavenly chorus serves

---

[78] Clement, *Strom.* 7.87.3, transl. LCC 2: 149.
[79] Or portico (*prothýrois*); Plato, *Phileb.* 64C.
[80] Clement, *Strom.* 7.45, transl. LCC 2: 121-22.

as the central image in Clement's most informative passage about the worship practices in his own elite community.

> 'Wherefore also he who holds intercourse with God must have his soul undefiled and absolutely pure, having raised himself to a state of perfect goodness if possible, but at any rate both making progress toward knowledge and longing for it, and being entirely withdrawn from the works of wickedness. Moreover it is fitting that he should offer all his prayers in a good spirit and in concert with good men, for it is a dangerous thing to countenance the errors of others. The gnostic will therefore share the prayers of ordinary believers in those cases in which it is right for him to share their activity also. But all his life is a holy festival. For instance, his sacrifices consist of prayers and praises and the reading of the Scriptures before dining, and psalms and hymns during dinner and before going to bed, aye and of prayers again during the night. By these things he unites himself with the heavenly chorus, being enlisted in it for ever-mindful contemplation, in consequence of his uninterrupted thought of heaven while on earth. Again, is he not acquainted with that other sacrifice which consists in the free gift both of instruction and of money among those who are in need? Certainly he is.'[81]

Thus the true gnostic Christian, who is 'making progress toward knowledge', can share the prayers of ordinary believers, provided they are 'good men'. But his proper worship, since 'all his life is a holy festival', consists of spiritual 'sacrifices' that include prayers and praises, 'the reading of the scriptures before dining', 'psalms and hymns during dinner', and again 'before going to bed', with further prayers during the night.

Though it is often said, following Eusebius, that Clement was the head of a catechetical school, his extant works seem to assume a different situation: more like the quasi-monastic Therapeutai sect described in Philo's *On the Contemplative Life*, whether or not those idealized Jewish monastics actually existed.[82] The main ritual was an evening banquet (which Clement calls 'agape;' *Paed.* 2.5-8). It was preceded by Bible reading, then accompanied by psalms and hymns during the dinner itself. Clement's dinner companions were a select group of Christians who saw themselves as advanced students of the Bible. They had already experienced a three-year catechumenate[83] of elementary instruction by bishops

---

[81] Clement, *Strom.* 7.49.4, transl. modified from LCC 2: 124.

[82] Joan E. Taylor, *Jewish Women Philosophers of First-Century Alexandria: Philo's 'Therapeutae' Reconsidered* (Oxford, 2003), pp. 7-12.

[83] *Strom.* 2.96.2. See Paul E. Bradshaw, *The Search for the Origins of Christian Worship: Sources and Methods for the Study of Early Liturgy*, 2nd ed. (New York, 2002), p. 104. For an attempt to reconstruct the three-year catechumenate of Origen's time, see

or presbyters,[84] and the three-day baptismal celebration which perhaps
anticipated the three-day Epiphany period of the later Egyptian church,
commemorating Jesus's baptism in the Jordan.[85] These things were only
the beginning of their journey. They were now embarked on a mission
to learn the true philosophy and appreciate the deep meanings of scripture which were hidden from ordinary believers. Since they were 'know-
ers' (gnostics), their worship, like their scripture study, was above and
beyond the catechesis and mystagogy that every Christian had experienced. That is why, even if Clement was a presbyter himself, 'the church
as institution is not prominent in his works'.[86]

Among themselves, however, Clement and his fellow gnostics spoke
a rich mystical language, combining vocabularies of disparate origins in
fruitful cross-fertilization. Their glossary looked back to the apocalyptic
mystery of the incarnate Christ. It echoed Plato's adaptation of ritual
language from the mystery cults to express the profundity of the new
philosophy. It followed Philo in applying Platonizing ritual language to
the rituals of the Old Testament, and then linked this usage typologically
to the worship of Christians, whose spiritual sacrifices looked forward to
the heavenly Temple just as the Platonist philosopher turns from the
shadow to the reality. At their gatherings they merged biblical, Platonic,
and Philonic imagery in speaking of the church as a heavenly chorus —
an obvious thing to do since their worship combined singing with bible
study, prayer, and gratitude for the sacraments they had received. Though
their worship was doubtless different in many respects from the great
cathedral liturgies of the fourth and fifth centuries, they knew that Christ
was present in everything they did. 'By these things [the gnostic] unites
himself with the heavenly chorus, being enlisted in it for ever-mindful
contemplation, in consequence of his uninterrupted thought of heaven

---

P. Nautin, *Origène: sa vie et son oeuvre* (Paris, 1977), pp. 389-409; P. Nautin and
P. Husson, *Origène: Homélies sur Jérémie*, SC 232 (Paris, 1976), pp. 1, 100-112.

[84] *Quis dives* 42.3-4. 'Clement is a pioneer in using the word [catechesis] to mean
specifically "instruction of those preparing for baptism,"' according to Annewies van den
Hoek, 'The "Catechetical" School of Early Christian Alexandria and Its Philonic Heritage', *Harvard Theological Review* 90 (1997) 59-87, quote from p. 69.

[85] Clement, *Strom.* 5.73.2 for the three days. Jeffery, *The Secret Gospel of Mark
Unveiled* (see n. 60), pp. 69, 78-80.

[86] Annewies van den Hoek, 'How Alexandrian was Clement of Alexandria? Reflections on Clement and his Alexandrian Background,' *The Heythrop Journal* 31 (1990)
179-194, quote from p. 181. For a brief sketch of what little is known of Clement's life,
see Carl P. Cosaert, *The Text of the Gospels in Clement of Alexandria*, Society of Biblical
Literature: The New Testament in the Greek Fathers 9 (Atlanta, GA, 2008), pp. 3-11.

while on earth.' It is no wonder, then, that Clement began his great *Exhortation to the Greeks* with stories that illustrate the failings of pagan music, and then introduced Christ: 'an all-harmonious instrument of God, melodious and holy, the wisdom that is above this world, the heavenly Word, … the Lord, and the New Song'.[87]

---

[87] *Protr.* 1.5.6-1.6.1, transl. LCL 15.

PERFORMANCE AS EXEGESIS
WOMEN'S LITURGICAL CHOIRS IN SYRIAC TRADITION

Susan ASHBROOK HARVEY

1. Syriac Women's Choirs: A Forgotten History[1]

Among the most notable aspects of Syriac liturgical tradition is the striking prominence of women's choirs.[2] These choirs first appear in historical sources in the fourth century, in the hymnography of St Ephrem the Syrian (died 373), where choirs of consecrated virgins are sometimes mentioned and even addressed directly as they lead the congregation in song.[3] Fittingly, sixth-century sources attribute the establishment of Syriac women's choirs to St Ephrem himself, claiming that he founded them in Edessa for the purpose of singing *madrashe*, doctrinal hymns, to counteract the seductive singing of heretics (specifically, the hymns of Bardaisan).[4] An energetic champion of Nicene Orthodoxy, Ephrem did in fact write his hymns in the context of heated polemics,

---

[1] I have employed the following abbreviations: CSCO = Corpus Scriptorum Christianorum Orientalium; Scr. Syr. = Scriptores Syrii; *PO = Patrologia Orientalis*. For the hymns of Ephrem: HNat = Hymns on the Nativity; HPasch = Hymns on Easter; HVirg = Hymns on Virginity (full references to critical editions and translations are in the notes).

[2] See S.A. Harvey, 'Revisiting the Daughters of the Covenant: Women's Choirs and Sacred Song in Ancient Syriac Christianity', *Hugoye: Journal of Syriac Studies* 8.2 (July 2005) [http://syrcom.cua.edu/Hugoye/Vol8No2/HV8N2Harvey.html]; eadem, 'Spoken Words, Voiced Silence: Biblical Women in Syriac Tradition', *Journal of Early Christian Studies* 9 (2001) 105-131.

[3] See, for example, Ephrem, HNat 4: 62b-63, 22: N23. Edited with German translation by Edmund Beck, *Des heiligen Ephraem des Syrers Hymnen de Nativitate (Epiphania)*, CSCO 186-187 / Scr. Syr. 82-83 (Leuven, 1959); English trans. Kathleen McVey, *Ephrem the Syrian: Hymns* (New York, 1989), pp. 63-217. Whether or not Ephrem refers to these choirs in HNat 7: 9-13 and 8: 21-2 is not entirely clear. Compare the similarly ambiguous references in the Anonymous hymns on Mary, 4.1 and 6.1 in Sebastian Brock, *Bride of Light: Hymns on Mary from the Syriac Churches* (Kottayam, Kerala, 1994), pp. 38, 42.

[4] Joseph P. Amar, 'A Metrical Homily on Holy Mar Ephrem by Mar Jacob of Serug', *PO*, 47 (Turnhout 1995), pp. 5-76; idem, *The Syriac 'Vita' Tradition of Ephrem the Syrian* (Ann Arbor, MI, 1988); Kathleen McVey, 'Ephrem the Kitharode and Proponent of Women: Jacob of Serug's Portrait of a Fourth-Century Churchman for the Sixth Century Viewer and its Significance for the Twenty-First Century Ecumenist', in *Orthodox and Wesleyan Ecclesiology*, ed. S.T. Kimbrough (Crestwood, NY, 2007), pp. 229-253.

both in Nisibis and in Edessa, as the church struggled to gain stability and doctrinal unity in the post-Constantinian era.[5]

From the fifth through the ninth centuries, Syriac women's choirs are attested, discussed, and promulgated in Syriac ecclesiastical legislation, hagiography, historiography, hymns and homilies produced in both Roman and Persian territories, and under Islam. They are often (but not always) identified as constituted by Daughters of the Covenant (*Bnat Qyama*), a consecrated office dating perhaps from the late third century and lasting perhaps until the tenth. Members of the Covenant both male and female (*Bnai* and *Bnat Qyama*), took vows of celibacy and simplicity, and worked in the service of their local bishop. Their role of civic ministry was not replicated by the diaconate nor eclipsed by the rise of monasticism. Sons of the Covenant sometimes went on to enter ranks of the clergy. Daughters of the Covenant may have been similar to those women known as *canonicae* or *subintroductae* elsewhere in the fourth century: consecrated virgins in the service of the church.[6]

By the early fifth century, the West Syriac Rabbula canons explicitly designate a liturgical ministry for the Daughters of the Covenant, requiring them to participate in the daily services of the church, to chant the Psalms and to sing the *madrashe*, the doctrinal hymns.[7] This

---

[5] See most recently Christine Shepardson, *Anti-Judaism and Christian Orthodoxy: Ephrem's Hymns in Fourth-Century Syria* (Washington, DC, 2008); and further, Sidney H. Griffith, 'The Marks of the "True Church" according to Ephraem's *Hymns Against Heresies*', in *After Bardaisan: Studies in Continuity and Change in Syriac Christianity in Honour of Professor Han J.W. Drijvers*, eds. G.J. Reinink and A.C. Klugkist (Leuven, 1999), pp. 125-140; idem, 'Setting Right the Church of Syria: Saint Ephraem's *Hymns Against Heresies*', in *The Limits of Ancient Christianity: Essays on Late Antique Thought and Culture in Honor of R.A. Markus*, eds. William Klingshirn and Mark Vessey (Ann Arbor, MI, 1999), pp. 97-114.

[6] Harvey, 'Revisiting the Daughters of the Covenant' (see n. 2); G. Nedungatt, 'The Covenanters of the Early Syriac-Speaking Church', *Orientalia Christiana Periodica* 39 (1973) 191-215, 419-444; Simon Jargy, 'Les "fils et filles du pacte" dans la literature monastique syriaque', *Orientalia Christiana Periodica* 17 (1951) 304-320; J.-M. Fiey, 'Cénobitisme feminin ancien dans les églises syriennes orientale et occidentale', *L'Orient Syrien* 10 (1965) 281-306; Robert Murray, 'Circumcision of the Heart and the Origins of the *Qyama*', in *After Bardaisan*, eds. Reinink and Klugkist (see n. 5), pp. 201-211; Sidney H. Griffith, '"Singles" in God's Service: Thoughts on the *Ihidaye* from the Works of Aphrahat and Ephraem the Syrian', *The Harp* 4 (1991) 145-159; idem, 'Monks, "Singles", and the "Sons of the Covenant": Reflections on Syriac Ascetic Terminology,' in *Eulogema: Studies in Honor of Robert Taft*, eds. Ephrem Carr et al., Studia Anselmiana 110 / Analecta Liturgica 17 (Rome, 1993), pp. 141-160; Naomi Koltun-Fromm, 'Yokes of the Holy Ones: The Embodiment of a Christian Vocation', *Harvard Theological Review* 94 (2001) 205-218.

[7] Canons 20, 27, in 'The Rules of Rabbula for the Clergy and the Qeiama', ed. and trans. Arthur Vööbus, *Syriac and Arabic Documents Regarding Legislation Relative to*

is the practice ascribed to Ephrem's own intentions in the anonymous sixth-century Syriac *vita Ephraemi*, which presents the founding of the choirs accordingly:

> '[Blessed Ephrem] established and arranged the Daughters of the Covenant in opposition to the diversions and popular movements of the deceivers [the Bardaisanites]. He taught them metrical hymns (*madrashe*) and songs (*sblatha*) and antiphons ('*onitha*)... Every day the Daughters of the Covenant gathered in the churches on feasts of the Lord and on Sundays and for the celebration of the martyrs.'[8]

Jacob of Serug (died 521) encouraged Christians to listen closely to the '*madrashe* sung by chaste women with voices of praise, which wisdom of the highest has given to the congregations,' sung in the Divine Liturgy between the Psalm verses and the lectionary readings.[9] Similarly, fifth-century East Syriac canons in Persia mandate that every village and town church must have 'an order (*taxis*) of the sisters', 'educated in doctrine and instruction', 'instructed in the scripture-lesson, and particularly in the service of the Psalms'.[10] A number of sources identify or prescribe that a deaconess must serve as the choir director.[11] The East Syriac Synod of Mar George I in 676, Canon 9, identifies the most important work of these women as the chanting of the Psalms at the offices of the church, as well as the singing of hymns in funeral processions (but not at the cemetery), at the memorial services for the dead, and at vigil services.[12]

Syrian Asceticism, Papers of the Estonian School of Theology in Exile 11 (Stockholm, 1960), pp. 34-50.

[8] Amar, *Syriac Vita*, p. 298, Syriac on pp. 158-159 (see n. 4). Cp. Amar, *Syriac Vita*, p. 157 (trans. p. 296): '[Ephrem] prepared himself a choir to do battle...against the heresies of which we have spoken before, by means of the Daughters of the Covenant who assembled regularly in church. He initiated instruction for them and taught them doctrinal hymns (*madrashe*). Evening and morning they would gather in church before the service and on the feast of the martyrs, and they were singing them at the lamentations of the dead.'

[9] Hugh Connolly, 'A Homily of Mâr Jacob of Serûgh on the Reception of the Holy Mysteries', *Downside Review* 27 (1908) 278-287, on p. 281.

[10] 'Maruta Canons', 26.1-3, 41.1, 26.4, 41.3; ed. and trans. in Arthur Vööbus, *The Canons Ascribed to Maruta of Maipherqat and Related Sources*, CSCO 439-440 / Scr. Syr. 191-192 (Leuven, 1982).

[11] For example, 'Maruta Canons', 41.3 (see n. 10). For a West Syrian example, see *Canons of Iohannon bar Qursos*, 27, ed. and trans. A. Vööbus, *The Synodicon in the West Syrian Tradition*, CSCO 367-368 / Scr. Syr. 161-162 (Leuven, 1975).

[12] The text is edited and translated in J.B. Chabot, *Synodicon Orientale ou Recueil de Synodes Nestoriens* (Paris, 1902), pp. 221-222 (Syr.), p. 486 (Fr.).

We may be sure of the importance of these choirs. When strange natural phenomena in 499/500 AD compelled the bishop of Edessa to summon the population for a special liturgy of supplication in the city streets, his calling of the choirs of the *Bnai* and *Bnat Qyama* was specially noted.[13] In the sixth century, a wandering solitary monk named Simeon stumbled upon an unchurched people isolated deep in the mountains along the Roman/Persian border. As he set about converting them, one of his first tasks was the tonsuring of twelve girls and eighteen boys to be the *Bnat* and *Bnai Qyama* for the tribe. These he schooled for some years together, then separately, in scriptures and psalmody, so that 'thereafter loud choirs were to be heard at the service'. The boys grew up to become readers (and thus entered the ranks of clergy); the girls continued as Daughters of the Covenant, devoted to their instruction of the people.[14]

The duties of the women's choirs are the subject of some discussion in an East Syriac liturgical commentary probably of the ninth century (Ps.-George of Arbela).[15] Concrete evidence may vanish at that point, although the Pontifical of the West Syrian Patriarch Michael the Great (12th century) and a few more recent West Syriac manuscripts refer to, and in at least two cases contain, a consecration service for the office of deaconess, also identified as 'singer'.[16] Whether or not this service was still in use when any of these manuscripts were copied is unknown but seems unlikely. Yet even a millennium's silence can be deceptive. In the late twentieth century and now in the twenty-first, an energetic revival and renewal of these choirs is well underway in local churches of the

---

[13] *The Chronicle of Pseudo-Joshua the Stylite*, trans. Frank R. Trombley and John W. Watt (Liverpool, 2000), at ch. 36, pp. 34-36. See also chs. 43, 100.

[14] John of Ephesus, *Lives of the Eastern Saints*, 16; ed. and trans. E.W. Brooks, *PO* 17 (Paris 1923), on pp. 229-47.

[15] Pseudo-George of Arbela, as cited by Juan Mateos, *Lelya-Sapra: Essai d'interpretation des matines chaldeennes* (Rome, 1959), p. 408.

[16] The service from Mingana Syriac ms 166 was translated by Sebastian Brock in idem, 'Deaconesses in the Syriac Tradition', in *Women in Prism and Focus: Her Profile in Major World Religions and in Christian Traditions*, ed. Prasanna Vazheeparampil (Rome, 1996), pp. 204-217, on pp. 213-217. Another is contained in the Syriac Orthodox Pontifical compiled and edited by Metropolitan Yuhanon Dolabani of Mardin in 1947, which His Eminence Mor Polycarpus I (Aydin) graciously allowed me to see at the Mor Ephrem Monastery, Glane, the Netherlands in September 2007. I am grateful to both His Eminence Mor Polycarpus and to Dr. Brock for discussing this service with me. Fr. Ephrem Carr has also pointed out to me that at least two recensions of Michael the Syrian's Pontifical do not contain such a service, although they mention it, stating that it was no longer in use (the Paris and Vatican recensions).

Middle East, Europe, Scandinavia, and North America for both Syriac Orthodox and Church of the East communities.[17]

In some respects, Syriac women's choirs performed tasks shared by women in the larger Christian community. The chanting of Psalms in private prayer, monastic offices, or in the Liturgy, for example, as well as singing hymns in liturgical processions and at vigils for feast days, for martyrs or saints, or for important funerals, were all activities in which ancient Christian women took part across the Mediterranean world.[18] From the fourth century, this singing often included choral as well as congregational singing. Yet modern historians seem to follow the position of Johannes Quasten in presuming that women were generally forbidden to participate in liturgical singing.[19] To be fair, several Greek and Latin church fathers admonish women to keep silence in church, following the New Testament injunctions to that effect (1 Cor 14: 34-5, 1 Tim 1: 11-12, 1 Pet 3: 1). These patristic passages are not without ambivalence, however, and are surely prescriptive rather than descriptive. Eusebius of Caesarea cites women's choirs as a primary reason for Paul of Samosata's expulsion from Antioch in 268, but the problem was certainly not the women so much as their hymns, sung in honor of Paul himself rather than Christ.[20] Cyril of Jerusalem exhorts that women should keep absolutely silent in church; but he is speaking about catechumens preparing for baptism.[21] It is not clear that the passage precludes singing by the baptized (although scholars have assumed it does). Isidore of Pelusium (died ca. 435) urged that women be forbidden to sing in church, on the grounds that people 'misuse the sweetness

[17] Ms. Sarah Bakker is presently pursuing a doctoral dissertation at the University of California at Santa Cruz on religious identity among Syriac-speaking diaspora Christians, which includes study of the renewed commitment to these women's choirs.

[18] Religious rituals provided the primary (and even the sole) socially permissible location for women's public presence, participation, and speech in ancient Mediterranean societies. There has been excellent work on the Greek pre-Christian traditions for women's choirs and religious singing by Eva Stehle, *Performance and Gender in Ancient Greece* (Princeton, NJ, 1997); Barbara Goff, *Citizen Bacchae: Women's Ritual Practice in Ancient Greece* (Berkeley, CA, 2004); and C. Calame, *Choruses of Young Women in Ancient Greece: Their Morphology, Religious Role, and Social Function*, trans. Derek Collins and Janice Orion (Lanham, MD, 1997).

[19] Johannes Quasten, 'The Liturgical Singing of Women in Christian Antiquity', *Catholic Historical Review* 27 (1941) 149-165; idem, *Music and Worship in Pagan and Christian Antiquity*, trans. Boniface Ramsey (Washington, 1983), pp. 75-86.

[20] Eusebius, *HE* 7. 30.10 = no. 212 in James McKinnon, *Music in Early Christian Literature* (Cambridge, 1987) p. 99 (hereafter = McKinnon, *Music*).

[21] Cyril of Jerusalem, *Procat.* 14 = no. 154, McKinnon, *Music*, pp. 75-76.

of melody to arouse passion', an opinion shared by Jerome.[22] But that was precisely the problem for such men: the women were singing, too well it seemed.

By contrast, Ambrose of Milan mentioned women's singing positively, directly taking issue with the Pauline admonition that women must keep silent in church (1 Cor 14: 34); he advocated the singing of Psalms as beneficial for all people.[23] Victricius of Rouen praised the choir of virgins in his own community.[24]

Indeed, the textual evidence provides a more complicated picture than Quasten allowed. Certainly women's choirs accompanied the rise of monasticism in the fourth century, as women's monastic communities took primary responsibility for their own liturgical practices. The letters of Basil of Caesarea and Gregory of Nyssa's *Life of Macrina*, for example, describe such choirs and their psalmody as prominent in the daily discipline of Cappadocian convents.[25] Here, however, the women's singing seems to have been devoted specifically to the Psalms. As such, the practice was part of the ascetic discipline of the monastic life. When Gregory describes the funeral for Macrina, he explains that he ordered the women's psalmody to control their otherwise excessive grief over the loss of their beloved founder and leader.[26] Such choirs of nuns are mentioned periodically in late antique texts describing liturgies. They were also visibly and audibly evident in the processions that went from city to shrine at the celebration of saints or martyrs' feasts.[27] When the

---

[22] Isidore of Pelusium, *Ep.* 1.90 = no. 121, McKinnon, *Music*, p. 61; Jerome, *dial. c. pel.* 1.25 = no. 334, McKinnon, *Music*, p. 145. Elsewhere, Jerome speaks with warm enthusiasm for women's monastic singing, and psalmody in their private chambers: e.g., *Ep.* 54 = no. 320, McKinnon, *Music*, p. 141 and *Ep.* 107.12 = no. 326, McKinnon, *Music*, pp. 142-143.

[23] E.g., Ambrose, *Explan. Ps.* 1.9 = no. 276, McKinnon, *Music*, pp. 126-127; idem, *de vir. ad Marcelliam* 1.10.60, 3.4.19 = nos. 300-301, McKinnon, *Music*, p. 133.

[24] Victricius of Rouen, *In Praise of Saints*, sec. 5. Celebrating the arrival of relics sent by Ambrose from Milan ca. 396, he writes, 'You, too, holy and inviolate virgins, chant, chant [cf. Ps. 47.6] and in your choirs dance on the paths that lead to heaven.' Is the reference to women's choirs chanting the Psalms, or other hymns? Is the call to dance metaphorical or literal? I cite the translation from Gillian Clark, 'Victricius of Rouen Praising the Saints', *Journal of Early Christian Studies* 7 (1999) 365-399, on p. 382.

[25] Basil, *Ep.* 2.12, 207.3 = nos. 138-9, McKinnon, *Music*, pp. 68-69; Gregory of Nyssa, *Life of Macrina*, 3, 33 = nos. 151-2, McKinnon, *Music*, pp. 73-74. See also the anonymous *de virg.*, 20 = no. 153, McKinnon, *Music*, p. 74. There is much more in the *Life of Macrina* than McKinnon includes. See, e.g., pp. 171, 178, 182-183, 186-187 in the translation by Virginia Callahan, *Saint Gregory of Nyssa: Ascetical Works*, Fathers of the Church 58 (Washington, DC, 1967).

[26] Gregory of Nyssa, *Life of Macrina*, pp. 182-183, 186-187 (see n. 25).

[27] E.g., John Chrysostom, *After the Remains of Martyrs*, in Wendy Mayer and Pauline Allen, *John Chrysostom* (New York, 2000), pp. 85-92, on pp. 90-91; idem, *On St. Phocas,*

Emperor Julian came through Antioch around the year 362, a choir of strident nuns harassed and taunted him with their loud singing of Psalm-verses chosen to mock his rule.[28] According to Egeria, during the late fourth century choirs of male and female ascetics sang antiphonally at daily pre-dawn services in Jerusalem.[29] In later Byzantine tradition, women identified as Myrrophoroi sang in the Easter services in Jerusalem and Constantinople.[30] In twelfth-century Thessalonica, choirs of nuns and 'righteous laywomen' sang in the cathedral for the festival of St Demetrius.[31]

Amidst all this female song, Syriac women's choirs nonetheless followed a distinctive practice. From our earliest attestation, these choirs are notable for their work singing a specific type of Syriac hymn, the *madrasha*. *Madrashe* (plural) were hymns of varied meters, isosyllabic, usually in stanzas (often arranged with acrostics), and generally with a short, repeated refrain.[32] The chanter might sing the stanzas and the choir the refrain; or the choir might sing the stanzas and the congregation the refrain, in different patterns of liturgical exchange. There were

2, in Wendy Mayer with Bronwen Neil, *Saint John Chrysostom: The Cult of Saints* (Crestwood, NY, 2006), pp. 75-87, on p. 78. Jerome, *Ep.* 107. 12, Ep. 108 = nos. 326-7, McKinnon, *Music*, 142-143. See also Gerontius, *Life of Melania the Younger*, 42, 46, 47, trans. Elizabeth A. Clark (New York, 1984) pp. 56, 59-60.

[28] Theodoret of Cyrrhus, *HE* 3.19.1-4 = no. 225, McKinnon, *Music*, pp. 104-105.

[29] Egeria, *Diary of a Pilgrimage*, 24; trans. George E. Gingras, Ancient Christian Writers 38 (New York, 1970), pp. 89-93.

[30] Sources for the Myrrophores are distressingly rare. See Allie Ernst, 'Martha from the Margins: An Examination of Early Christian Traditions about Martha', Ph.D. thesis (University of Queensland 2006), pp. 194, 218-225; Valerie Karras, 'The Liturgical Functions of Consecrated Women in the Byzantine Church', *Theological Studies* 66 (2005) 96-116; eadem, 'Female Deacons in the Byzantine Church', *Church History* 73 (2004) 272-316; eadem, 'The Liturgical Participation of Women in the Byzantine Church', Ph.D. dissertation (Catholic University of America 2002), pp. 153-162.

[31] Pseudo-Lucian, *Timarion*, 55, 59, as cited in Alexander Lingas, 'Sunday Matins in the Byzantine Cathedral Rite: Music and Liturgy', Ph.D. dissertation (University of British Columbia, 1996), pp. 188-190. I am grateful to Dr. Lingas for this reference, and for helpful conversation on the whole question of women's liturgical singing in Byzantium. Important for the larger context of women's presence and roles in Byzantine liturgy is Robert Taft, 'Women at Church in Byzantium: Where, When, and Why?', *Dumbarton Oaks Papers* 52 (1998) 27-87. For women's liturgical singing in later Byzantine hagiographic and monastic texts, see Alice-Mary Talbot, 'The Devotional Life of Laywomen', in *A People's History of Christianity, Vol. 3: Byzantine Christianity*, ed. Derek Krueger (Minneapolis, MN, 2006), pp. 201-220; eadem, 'Blue-Stocking Nuns: Intellectual Life in the Convents of Late Byzantium', in her *Women and Religious Life in Byzantium* (Aldershot, Hampshire, 2001), ch. XVIII (= *Okeanos: Essays presented to Ihor Sevcenko on his Sixtieth Birthday by his Colleagues and Students*, eds. Cyril Mango and Omeljan Pritsak, Harvard Ukrainian Studies, 7 [Cambridge, MA, 1983], pp. 604-618).

[32] See especially Kathleen McVey, 'Were the Earliest *Madrase* Songs or Recitations?', in *After Bardaisan*, eds. Reinink and Klugkist, pp. 185-199 (see n. 5).

different types of *madrashe*, but as their name suggests (from the root *d-r-sh*, to practice, train, or instruct) all were designated as doctrinal — i.e., as devoted to presentation of the primary ecclesiastical teachings of the church. The anonymous *vita Ephraemi* makes the significance of this content explicit in its description of the hymns it claims that Ephrem composed for the Daughters of the Covenant to sing:

> '[Blessed Ephrem] took arrangements of songs (*qale*) and melodies (*qinyatha*) and added true doctrine to them.... He put in the metrical hymns (*madrashe*) words with subtle connotation and spiritual understanding concerning the birth and baptism and fasting and the entire plan of Christ: the passion and resurrection and ascension, and concerning the martyrs.'[33]

We might note that this list of topics is highly reminiscent of the one in the *Didascalia Apostolorum*, ch. 15 — except that there the list indicates that these are precisely the topics on which women should *not* teach![34]

Madrashe took various forms, with an array of performative arrangements by choirs, congregation, chanters and clergy, in different patterns of vocal interaction. In late antiquity, the period with our most abundant evidence for Syriac women's choirs, *madrashe* addressed major feasts of the church as well as biblical instruction through the re-telling of biblical stories. A favorite form was the *soghitha*, the dialogue hymn, sung antiphonally by male and female choirs.[35] These hymns often presented

---

[33] Amar, *Syriac Vita*, pp. 296, 298. On the doctrinal significance of *madrashe*, see the discussion and references in Sidney H. Griffith, *'Faith Adoring Mystery': Reading the Bible with St. Ephraem the Syrian* (Milwaukee, WI, 1997), pp. 9-13.

[34] 'But let [the widow] send those who desire to be instructed to the leader. And to those who ask them let them (namely the widows) give answer only about the destruction of idols and about this that there is only one God. It is not right for the widows to teach nor for a layman. About punishment and about the rest, and about the kingdom of the name of Christ, and about His dispensation, neither a widow nor a layman ought to speak. Indeed, when they speak without the knowledge of doctrine, they bring blasphemy against the word... Indeed, when the gentiles, those who are being instructed, hear the word of God spoken not firmly, as it ought to be, unto edification of life everlasting — and especially because it is spoken to them by a woman — about how our Lord clothed Himself in the body, and about the passion of Christ, they will deride and mock, instead of praising the word of doctrine. ... Therefore, it is not required nor necessary that women should be teachers, and especially about the name of Christ and about the redemption of His passion. Indeed, you have not been appointed to this, O women, and especially widows, that you should teach, but that you should pray and entreat the Lord.' Syriac *Didascalia Apostolorum*, Ch. 15; ed. and trans. A. Vööbus, *The Didascalia Apostolorum in Syriac*, Vol. 1, CSCO 401-402 / Scr. Syr. 175-176, and Vol. 2, CSCO 407-408 / Scr. Syr. 179-180 (Leuven, 1979). Here I cite the translation by Vööbus, CSCO 408 / Scr. Syr. 180, pp. 144-145.

[35] See esp. Sebastian P. Brock, 'Dramatic Dialogue Poems,' in *IV Symposium Syriacum*, eds. H. J. W. Drijvers, R. Lavenant, C. Molenberg, and G. J. Reinink, Orientalia

a biblical story through an imagined dialogue between two characters, such as Sarah and Abraham, or Mary and the Archangel Gabriel or Joseph, or the Sinful Woman and Satan. In these cases, the women's choir sang the biblical woman's voice.[36] The dialogue always revolved around a conflict or disagreement that required resolution; the alternating male and female choirs added an element of performative drama, as the competing figures argued their respective positions. Perhaps again distinctive to Syriac tradition is the almost invariable casting of the biblical woman as the hero in these exchanges, while the male figure argues in feeble opposition against the power of faith. (Comedy as well as drama played a role in these dialogues!)[37] A good number of such hymns are preserved in both West and East Syriac traditions.[38]

All our sources, both East and West Syriac, stress that the women's choirs sang these hymns in the civic churches. In other words, Syriac women's choirs performed a primary teaching function for the church; and they did so in the context of public, civic worship, in the gathered community of the church as a whole: male and female, young and old, lay and religious.[39] Unlike female deacons, their ministry was not defined as one by women for women. In fact, the development of these choirs during the fourth through sixth centuries coincided with the gradual demise in the larger ecclesiastical structure of other offices for women. This was the period that saw the slow disappearance of widows and deaconesses all across the Mediterranean, and the increasing confinement of

Christiana Analecta 229 (Rome, 1987), pp. 135-147; idem, 'Syriac Dispute Poems: The Various Types', in *Dispute Poems and Dialogues in the Ancient and Mediaeval Near East: Forms and Types of Literary Debates in Semitic and Related Literature*, eds. G. J. Reinink and H. L. J. Vanstiphout, Orientalia Lovaniensia Analecta 42 (Leuven, 1991), pp. 109-120.

[36] For discussion of how such performative variations affected the presentation, for example, of a figure such as the Virgin Mary, see S. A. Harvey, 'On Mary's Voice: Gendered Words in Syriac Marian Tradition', in *The Cultural Turn in Late Ancient Studies: Gender, Asceticism, and Historiography*, eds. Patricia Cox Miller and Dale Martin (Durham, NC, 2004), pp. 63-86.

[37] See the discussion in Harvey, 'Spoken Words, Voiced Silence' (see n. 2).

[38] A very helpful, annotated list of the extant Syriac dialogue hymns presently known may be found in the appendix to Sebastian P. Brock, 'Dialogue and Other *sughyotho*', *Mélanges offerts au Prof. P. Louis Hage*, ed. P. Ayoub Chahwan (Kaslik, 2008), pp. 363-384.

[39] A useful collection of Greek and Latin primary sources on early Christian teaching may be found in Robert Eno, *Teaching Authority in the Early Church*, Message of the Fathers of the Church 14 (Wilmington, DE, 1984). This particular aspect of choral responsibility seems not to have been considered by most historians of early Christianity, although I have tried to raise it on other occasions. See esp. my 'Revisiting the Daughters of the Covenant' (see n. 2).

nuns to enclosed convents rather than family households.[40] In Syriac communities, these offices seem to have survived for a longer period, perhaps because of the prominence of the women's choirs and their duties (which seem often to have included supervision or direction by a deaconess).[41] Ironically, then, during the period when other 'official' roles for women slowly diminished, the Syriac women's choirs grew in presence and authority. Moreover, in their designated task of singing the *madrashe*, these women seem to have carried a significance of ministry quite distinct for women in late antique Christianity, if not unique.

In what follows, I will argue that the performative aspect of these choirs contributed profoundly not only to their ritual function and meaning, but further even to the content of teaching which their singing provided.[42] These ancient choirs are anonymous in our sources: no singer is named, no choir specifically identified. Nor do any sources survive to us in Syriac written by women (at least, none of which we can be sure). We have no evidence regarding these choirs (or anything else, for that matter) from the women themselves. Yet the texts we have, written by the men who served with and heard these choirs, provide insightful reflection on their ritual functions, roles, and significance. To such comments we now turn.

2. The Choirs in Performance

In one of his Paschal hymns, Ephrem highlighted the women's choir: 'our ears are filled with the musical strains of virgins' (HPasch 2:7). For the Easter feast, he presented the image of the church in its gathered

[40] Extensive primary sources for women's offices in early Christianity are available in Ute E. Eisen, *Women Officeholders in Early Christianity: Epigraphical and Literary Studies*, trans. Linda M. Maloney (Collegeville, MN, 2000), and Kevin Madigan and Carolyn Osiek, *Ordained Women in the Early Church: A Documentary History* (Baltimore, MD, 2005). Neither includes any discussion of choirs. For the institutionalization of women's monasticism, see above all Susanna Elm, *'Virgins of God': The Making of Asceticism in Late Antiquity* (Oxford, 1994).

[41] See Brock, 'Deaconesses in the Syriac Tradition' (see n. 16); A. G. Martimort, *Les Diaconesses: Essai Historique*, Bibliotheca 'Ephemerides Liturgicae'. Subsidia (Rome, 1982), esp. pp. 21-54, 165-170; C. Robinson, *The Ministry of Deaconesses* (London, 1898), esp. pp. 169-196; S. A. Harvey, 'Women's Service in Ancient Syriac Christianity', in *Mother, Nun, Deaconess: Images of Women According to Eastern Canon Law*, ed. Eva Synek, Kanon 16 (Egling, 2000), pp. 226-241.

[42] In the following discussion, I am helped by issues raised in Richard D. McCall, *Do This: Liturgy as Performance* (Notre Dame, IN, 2007), as well as by the suggestive parallels from Goff, *Citizen Bacchae*, and Stehle, *Performance and Gender* (see n. 18).

wholeness. To the liturgy, he sang, all Christians brought a gift appropriate to their place; the collected beauty of the whole offering was the woven crown the church offered to God in thanksgiving.

'Let us plait a magnificent crown for Him…
The bishop weaves into it
   his biblical exegesis as his flowers;
the presbyters their martyr stories,
   the deacons their lections,
the young men their alleluias,
   the boys their Psalms,
the virgins their *madrashe*,
   the rulers their achievements,
And the lay people their virtues.
Blessed be the One who has multiplied victories for us.'[43]

Such was the clarity of place Ephrem identified for the women's choirs: a place defined amidst the ranks of worshippers from their different life stations, their different genders, their different liturgical duties, their different roles. The work of doctrinal presentation, of the *madrashe*, was theirs: a kind of teaching distinct from homily or sacred readings or songs of praise by others.

In some instances Ephrem addresses the women's choirs directly in his hymns. When he does, he points to the singing of the women's choir as instructive not only for the (correct) teaching proclaimed through their voices, but further by their example. He sees them typologically, as living icons of biblical figures, fulfilling particular roles from the biblical salvation drama. In the *Hymns on Virginity*, for example, the women's choir represents the type of the Wise Virgins from Matthew 25: 1-13, whose lamps stayed lit to receive their Heavenly Bridegroom: 'Since the time of the Bridegroom is not revealed to us, you virgins have become our Watchers/ so that your lamps might gladden, and your hosannas might glorify.'[44] Most often, however, Ephrem exalts the women's choir as consecrated virgins who stand as types for the Virgin Mary. Because of Mary, women's condition was transformed from the shame of Eve to a state of glory:

---

[43] Ephrem, *Hymns on Easter* 2: 8-9; trans. Sidney Griffith in McKinnon, *Music*, on pp. 93-94. The Syriac is edited by Edmund Beck, *Des heiligen Ephraem des Syrers Paschahymnen (de azymis, de crucifixione, de resurrectione)* CSCO 248 / Scr. Syr. 84 (Leuven, 1964).

[44] HVirg 5: 10; trans. McVey, *Ephrem*, 284 (see n. 3). The Syriac is edited with German translation by Edmund Beck, *Des heiligen Ephraem des Syrers Hymnen de virginitate*, CSCO 223-224 / Scr. Syr. 94-95 (Leuven, 1962).

'Let chaste women praise that pure Mary
Since in their mother Eve their disgrace was great,
behold in Mary their sister their triumph has been magnified.
Blessed is He Who shone forth from them!'[45]

Ephrem presents a pattern of recapitulation for which women's work in the image of Mary has undone that in the image of fallen Eve. Hence, Ephrem sings, the notion that women and music incited 'sinful' actions can now be replaced because of Mary.

'The unchaste dance pleased the tyrant. [cf. Mt 14:6]
May the chant of chaste women please You, my Lord,
May the chant of the chaste women dispose You, my Lord,
to keep their bodies in chastity.'[46]

But in Ephrem's Nativity hymns, the women's choirs do more than stand in Mary's place; they also sing in Mary's voice. Ephrem sets long passages in these hymns in imagined elaboration of Mary's words at the arrival of her divine Son.[47] He crafts Mary in wonder-struck prayer, or singing a lullaby to her newborn child, or prophesying across the vast arc of sacred time, from the biblical past to the liturgical present. The performative aspect of women's voices singing the voice of Mary is especially poignant in these verses, for Ephrem alludes frequently to the slandering of Mary by the women of her time — and to the slandering of the virgin choirs in his own. In various hymns, he presents Mary as scorned for her poverty, maligned for her lowly circumstances, and castigated for her misunderstood pregnancy.[48] Sung at the Nativity vigil, these hymns move delicately between the biblical narrative and the city beyond the church doors. Mary's vindication at the birth of the Savior becomes the vindication also of the widows and virgins who sing her voice as women's choirs in a society critical of their state.[49] For Ephrem trumpeted the valuation of consecrated virginity in the midst of a social order which, in the mid-fourth century, struggled with its consequences.[50] In Ephrem's hymns, women sang in the liturgy because God had worked

---

[45] HNat 22: N23; trans. McVey, *Ephrem*, 183.

[46] HNat 4: 62-3; trans. McVey, *Ephrem*, 93.

[47] See the discussion in Harvey, 'On Mary's Voice' (see n. 36).

[48] E.g., HNat 6: 4; 10; 12; 13: 13; 14: 11-3; 15: 2-3, 7; 25: 12.

[49] Especially HNat 12, in which the entire hymn is devoted to defending the reputations of the slandered virgins. See also HNat 17: 4-11, in defense of virginity.

[50] Well-captured in Peter Brown, 'The Notion of Virginity in the Early Church,' *Christian Spirituality, Vol. 1: Origins to the Twelfth Century*, eds. Bernard McGinn, John Meyendorff, and Jean LeClerq (New York, 1986), pp. 427-443.

salvation through a woman's body and a woman's voice: Mary's 'new song' (HNat 15:5) had heralded the new creation. Virginity marked its start.

Ephrem's alignment of the women's choirs with Mary's image (or type) is echoed repeatedly elsewhere in Syriac hymns.[51] Nonetheless, in Ephrem's hymns the women's choirs are addressed, held up, even glorified for their typological meaning. But they are not explained. In the sixth century, however, both the anonymous *vita Ephraemi* and Jacob of Serug in his verse homily, *On the Holy Mar Ephrem*, reflect at length on the Syriac tradition of women's choirs as one specifically inaugurated by Ephrem in order to teach doctrinal truth in the midst of heretical chaos. In the *vita*, as we saw earlier, this reflection comprised a (fairly) detailed description of the hymns and music, the choirs, the liturgical services, their times and locations. In Jacob, a lengthy *apologia* for the choirs and their work takes up fully one quarter of his panegyric in honor of Ephrem. Kathleen McVey has noted that such extended defense of these women most likely indicates a siege of criticism questioning their validity.[52]

Jacob admits that the practice of women's choirs differs from earlier custom as well as scriptural injunction.[53] He notes further that both the sight and the sound of the women's choirs are unnervingly bold: 'A new sight of women uttering the proclamation [*karuzutha*]/ and behold, they are called teachers [*malpanyatha*] among the congregations'.[54] Rather than mitigating the implications of such liturgical prominence for women, Jacob dramatically highlights its force, its unlikeliness, even its ability to shock by seeming to break social conventions. The women's

---

[51] E.g., Brock, *Bride of Light*, Anonymous Hymns 4 and 6 (see n. 3). Exhortation that the women should sing because of Mary's model also appears often in Jacob of Serug's verse homilies, as here: 'Let all the multitude of virgins praise Him with wonder/ because the great Savior shines forth from them to the whole world./ Let the voice of the young women be lifted up in praise,/ because by one of them, behold, hope is brought to the world.' *On the Mother of God* 3, trans. Mary Hansbury, *Jacob of Serug on the Mother of God* (Crestwood, NY, 1998), p. 83. Jacob, like Ephrem, also exalted the church as most glorious when the whole, in its ordered, gathered ranks, brought their gifts of voice in offering to God, that the liturgy might be fulfilled. That offering included 'the voice of handmaids grouped in choirs to make a joyful noise', and 'the voice of women who exalt Him with their hymns [*madrashe*]', (my trans.) *adv. Iud.* 7: 529-42, ed. and trans. Micheline Albert, 'Jacques de Saroug, Homélies contre les Juifs', *PO* 38 (Paris, 1976), pp. 216-217.

[52] McVey, 'Ephrem the Kitharode' (see n. 4).

[53] Jacob, 'Homily on Mar Ephrem,' vv 24, 40-43. My reading follows the edition and translation by Joseph Amar (see n. 4).

[54] Jacob, 'Homily on Mar Ephrem', v. 42, Amar p. 35.

choirs, he argues, were crucial components of Ephrem's efforts both to educate the church in right doctrine and to enact the redemption of God's salvific work through Christ, in the liturgy. God had made divine will a clear, present and active force in human history by offering typological models to the faithful. What Ephrem has done with these choirs, Jacob claims, is to fulfill what typology reveals.

Thus, Jacob declares, where Eve's disobedience had closed the mouths of women, Mary's obedient consent allowed them to be opened. Ephrem instructed the 'sisters' accordingly, and 'behold, the gatherings of the glorious (church) resound with their melodies'.[55] Indeed, Moses had led the Hebrew women in song at their deliverance from Egypt at the Red Sea; now Ephrem has led the Christian women to 'sing praises with their hymns', 'with sweet melodies' and 'joyful sound', for the deliverance from sin and death through baptism.[56] Finally, Jacob argues the power of sacramental soteriology: by one baptism are men and women baptized into Christ; from one chalice do they drink, from one loaf are they fed at communion. One and the same salvation is worked for men and women alike: both alike must sing God's glory! Just so, Jacob intones, did Ephrem summon his women: 'Uncover your faces to sing praise without shame/ to the One who granted you freedom of speech by His birth'.[57] Indeed, nowhere else in ancient Christian literature will one find such celebratory affirmation of the equality of women and men as in this extraordinary verse homily by Jacob of Serug. Yet, no less powerful is Jacob's insistence that this equality carries a necessary ethical mandate. Women must not only 'sing praises' like the men. They must also 'make their chants instructive melodies' (v. 114), that the battle against Satan's work might be won. Women's singing, Jacob implores, provides a teaching of God's truth — against heresy, but also about redemption, anthropology, and salvation — that cannot be taught in any other way.

3. Performance as Exegesis

Scholars of liturgical music will recognize in Jacob of Serug's typological casting an echo of a famous passage from the first-century Jewish philosopher, Philo of Alexandria. In Philo's description of the community

---

[55] Jacob, 'Homily on Mar Ephrem', vv. 41-44.
[56] Jacob, 'Homily on Mar Ephrem,' vv. 45-84.
[57] Jacob, 'Homily on Mar Ephrem', vv. 96-113.

life of the Therapeutae and Therapeutrides, the shared liturgical song of the male and female choirs is justified by reference to Moses instructing Miriam at the Red Sea to lead the Hebrew women in song. Moreover, the joyous song of the male and female choirs is shown to enact the ongoing fulfillment of God's redemptive work in the life of the worshipping community.[58] In fact, Philo's passage is the only parallel to Jacob's defense of women's singing to be found in ancient Jewish or Christian literature. It is certainly possible that Jacob knew the account via its transmission in Eusebius' *Ecclesiastical History*, a work already available in Syriac in Jacob's time.[59] His defense of the women's choirs might well be part of his anti-Jewish polemic (here supersessionist), no less than a strategy to instruct against heresy by insisting on orthodoxy displayed through liturgical practice.

The hymns and verse homilies composed by Ephrem and Jacob and their like must be analyzed with consideration of their literary forms and techniques. Yet I would argue that it is also critical to consider the performative requirements of the composer's chosen form, and how performance would have shaped presentation. How a biblical story was told, or how the dialogues were imagined, were aspects qualitatively changed by who said it, from what narrative perspective, in what ritual context, and with what performative features. The authority of the presentation could be heightened or diminished depending on whose voice presented it: the voice of the biblical character (male or female); that of the narrator, whether literary or performative; or that of the office through which it was spoken (priest, chanter, choir male or female, or congregation). Gendered voices sang these stories in worship services. This ritual element was indelibly part of the interpretation such poetry presented.[60]

As Ephrem had implied more than a century earlier, Jacob insisted that the women's choirs performed a musical ministry of teaching that instructed by substantive content no less than by liturgical example.

---

[58] Philo, *On the Contemplative Life*, 11.83-90, ed. and trans. F. H. Colson and G. H. Whitaker in *Philo: Works* (Cambridge, MA, 1941) vol. 9, pp. 164-169. On this passage, see the important discussion by Peter Jeffery, 'Philo's Impact on Christian Psalmody', in *Psalms in Community: Jewish and Christian Textual, Liturgical, and Artistic Traditions*, eds. Harold Attridge and Margot Fassler (Leiden, 2004), pp. 147-187; and also Stephen G. Wilson, 'Early Christian Music', in *Common Life in the Early Church: Essays Honoring Graydon F. Snyder*, ed. Julian V. Hills (Harrisburg, PA, 1998), pp. 390-401.

[59] The Syriac is edited and translated in William Wright and Norman McLean, *The Ecclesiastical History of Eusebius, in Syriac* (Cambridge, 1898).

[60] As in Harvey, 'Mary's Voice' (see n. 36).

These choirs must be *seen and heard* by the church as a whole for their instruction to be fully realized. Their teaching authority did not rest on the charismatic power of an exceptional individual (a female saint or holy woman; a holy man such as Ephrem or Jacob, or any particularly riveting singer). Rather, their authority stood on biblical example (typology) wedded to the collectively articulated, approved, and enacted doctrinal truth of the ecclesiastical institution. The position is clear: women's voices *as teaching voices* were necessary for the salvific work of Christian liturgy.

The history of these choirs represents an important, if often overlooked, tradition of women's contributions to Christian worship.[61] Their significance lies above all in their singing as liturgically performed: that is, the *content* of what they sang was profoundly shaped by its *context*. That context was spatial (within liturgical ritual, whether in a church building, in a procession, or at a shrine); and it was temporal (within the cycle of the ecclesiastical calendar). This context was further qualified in the *performance* itself: it was civic rather than monastic, and public rather than domestic. All of these contextual aspects contrast sharply with the frequent encouragement of Christian women elsewhere in late antiquity to chant Psalms in private, following the daily offices, or to chant them within the convent; or indeed, to keep silent.

There is much we do not know. In the late antique Eastern Mediterranean, societies granted exceptional importance to verbal performance in the civic context. Voice, gesture, posture, clothing, and style were crucial elements of such performance. Rhetoric, poetry, oratory, debate, theater, and entertainment of all kinds deeply infiltrated all aspects of civic community life.[62] These are the elements of which we have no knowledge in the case of Syriac women's choirs. Precisely *where* in the liturgy did they stand, for example? How did they stand — with what posture or attending gestures? What did they wear? How did they sing?

[61] Of great significance here is the work of Teresa Berger, *Women's Ways of Worship: Gender Analysis and Liturgical History* (Collegeville, MN, 1999).

[62] Consider, for example, the elements of civic life highlighted in Jaclyn Maxwell, *Christianization and Communication in Late Antiquity: John Chrysostom and his Congregation in Antioch* (Cambridge, 2006); Gregory S. Aldrete, *Gestures and Acclamations in Ancient Rome* (Baltimore, MD, 1999); Blake Leyerle, *Theatrical Shows and Ascetic Lives: John Chrysostom's Attack on Spiritual Marriage* (Berkeley, 2001); Dennis Potter, 'Entertainers in the Roman Empire', in *Life, Death and Entertainment in the Roman Empire*, eds. D.S. Potter and D.J. Mattingly (Ann Arbor, MI, 1999), pp. 256-325; Fritz Graf, 'Gestures and Conventions: The Gestures of Roman Actors and Orators', in *A Cultural History of Gesture*, eds. Jan Bremmer and Herman Roodenburg (Ithaca, NY, 1991), pp. 36-58.

With what tone and pitch, with what dynamics? For as much as we can know that these choirs mattered enormously, so much also do we simply lack the information needed to grasp the whole.

Epilogue

In recent years, Syriac churches of both the Eastern and Western Syriac traditions are reviving the practice of women's choirs in their parishes. In many churches now, one finds their place, presentation, and role significantly enhanced over what it was even a decade or so ago. Women's choirs now wear white robes, with white lace head scarves; sometimes they wear a single stole with the name of their parish. The women are generally younger, including young girls. They stand in front of the congregation on the left-hand side, facing the altar, balancing the (male) deacons on the right. They lead the congregation in singing the major Syriac hymns of the liturgy; they sing with bold, strong, full-throated voices. In Sweden and in Germany, annual competitions are now held between choirs, recorded on dvd for distribution among the communities.[63] The choir directors, or sometimes lead singers, may be tonsured or specially consecrated in some way. In May 2003, in Germany, a choir of seventy girls was consecrated by their bishop in a thrilling service of praise (available on videotape).[64] These choirs are greatly honored, with immense pride, among their people.

Much has changed, of course. The context for the Syriac-speaking communities in Europe and Scandinavia presently is one of intense focus on identity politics, as a recent, ongoing, and often well-educated immigrant population seeks to establish itself. Renewal of the women's choirs is part of a larger effort to preserve language, tradition, culture, and religion in wholly changed circumstances.[65] There is perhaps no greater

[63] E.g., 'Gesangswettbewerb der Kirchenchöre der syrisch-orthodoxen Kirche von Antiochien in NRW' (as recorded on 9 December 2006, Apostel St. Johannes Kirche, Rheda – Wiedenbrück).

[64] 'Weihe der Subdiakonen, Lektoren (*Qoruye*) and Messdienerinen am Weissen-Sontag dem 5. Mai 2003', St. Johannes Apostel Kirche, Rheda-Wiedenbrück.

[65] Önver Cetrez, *Meaning-Making Variations in Acculturation and Ritualization: A Multi-Generational Study of Suroyo Migrants in Sweden*, Acta Universitatis Upsaliensis: Psychologica et Sociologica Religionum 17 (Uppsala, 2005); Bas Ter Haar Romeny, 'From Religious Association to Ethnic Community: a Research Project on Identity Formation among the Syrian Orthodox under Muslim Rule,' *Islam and Christian-Muslim Relations* 16 (Oct. 2005), pp. 377-399.

measure of what has changed and what remains at stake for the Syriac
women's choirs, over the long duration of their history, than the simple
fact of the language that defines them. Today, these choirs sing the
ancient hymns in their original language — a language most often
unknown and unrecognized by those who sing, those who listen, or those
who join them in song. The teaching ministry of these choirs, in consequence, has taken a poignant, even haunting turn. In new homelands,
amidst new and varied cultures, languages, and religious communities,
the Syriac women's choirs now perform a ministry to teach an identity,
a language, a history, in addition to the doctrinal and biblical content of
their hymns. They perform, with ever changing ramifications.

THE CELEBRATION OF HOLY WEEK
IN EARLY SYRIAC-SPEAKING CHURCHES

Gerard ROUWHORST

In spite of numerous studies devoted to the celebration of Holy Week in early Christianity, the origins and earliest history of this celebration continue to pose a number of puzzling questions.[1] Thanks to Egeria's invaluable diary and the various versions of the Old Armenian lectionary and the Georgian lectionary of Jerusalem, we are exceptionally well informed about the way Holy Week was celebrated at Jerusalem from the end of the fourth century onwards.[2] It should also be emphasized that it is hardly possible to overestimate the importance of this very influential liturgical tradition. Nonetheless, it seems unlikely that the celebration of Holy Week as such has its origins in the stational liturgy of Jerusalem. Already Dionysius of Alexandria refers to some Christians extending the paschal fast to several days of the week preceding Easter.[3] At least some of these Christians appear to fast six days (this practice seems to be recommended by Dionysius). The *Didascalia Apostolorum* attests to a similar tradition.[4] Both of these sources date back to the end of the third or the beginning of the fourth century, a period in which the stational liturgy of Jerusalem had not yet come into existence. In fact, we find clear traces of a form of Holy Week that is both older than and different from the one celebrated at Jerusalem in a number of Syriac sources, the Syriac *Didascalia* being only one of them. In this article,

---

[1] See for a recent survey of the research on this issue: H. Auf der Maur, *Die Osterfeier in der alten Kirche: Aus dem Nachlaß herausgegeben von R. Meßner und W. Schöpf, mit einem Beitrag von Clemens Leonhard,* Liturgia Oenipontana 2 (Münster, 2003).

[2] *Ibid.,* pp. 136-155. See further: T. Talley, *The Origins of the Liturgical Year* (New York, 1986), pp. 42-54; K. Stevenson, *Jerusalem Revisited: The Liturgical Meaning of Holy Week* (Washington, D.C., 1988); S. Janeras, 'La Settimana Santa nell'antica liturgia di Gerusalemme', in *Hebdomadae sanctae celebratio: Conspectus historicus comparativus — The Celebration of Holy Week in Ancient Jerusalem and its Development in the Rites of East and West,* ed. A.G.Kollamparampil, Bibliotheca "Ephemerides Liturgicae". Subsidia 93 (Rome, 1997), pp. 51-65.

[3] *Letter to Basilides.* See PG 55, 519; L. Feltoe, *The Letters and other Remains of Dionysius of Alexandria* (Cambridge, 1904), pp. 101vv.

[4] Ch. 21. Edition and English translation: A. Vööbus, *The Didascalia Apostolorum in Syriac, II, Chapters XI-XXVI,* CSCO 407-408 (Leuven, 1979), pp. 206-214 (188-199).

I will try to reconstruct the development of this Syriac Holy Week, from the beginning of the fourth century until the end of the sixth century, when influences of the stational liturgy of Jerusalem have got the upper hand. In doing so, I will focus on two major aspects: a) the rather peculiar ways in which, in early Syriac sources, various moments of the Passion are associated with the successive days of Holy Week, more specifically the tendency to spread the whole Passion over the entire week, beginning with Monday instead of Maundy Thursday; b) the relationship that is established by several sources between Holy Week, on the one hand, and Jewish Passover and the Week of Unleavened Bread, on the other hand.

1. The Celebration of Passover in Early Syriac-Speaking Christianity

Before studying these two aspects, I want to make some preliminary remarks about the celebration of Passover/Easter in early Syriac-speaking Christianity that may be of some relevance, at least indirectly, for the origins of Holy Week. First, as I have tried to demonstrate in several other publications, there are very strong indications that prior to the Council of Nicaea the Syriac-speaking churches, as well as various Greek churches in the province of Syria, celebrated their Christian Passover in the night from 14 to 15 Nisan.[5] Second, contrary to what has been argued by several scholars, it seems that any sort of celebration of Pentecost, including Ascension and the feast of the fiftieth day after Easter, was unknown in the Syriac-speaking region until the end of the fourth century. (The introduction of these two days was almost certainly due to influences from the liturgical traditions of Jerusalem). I have dealt with this question in another article of mine[6] and I simply want to mention it here. Finally, it may be recalled — perhaps unnecessarily — that Lent did not yet exist, neither in the Syriac-speaking areas

[5] G. Rouwhorst, *Les hymnes pascales d'Ephrem de Nisibe: Analyse théologique et recherche sur l'évolution de la fête pascale chrétienne à Nisibe et à Edesse et dans quelques Eglises voisines au quatrième siècle*, Supplements to Vigiliae Christianae 7.1 (Leiden, 1989); *idem*, 'The Quartodeciman Passover and the Jewish Pesach', *Questions liturgiques* 77 (1996) 152-173.

[6] G. Rouwhorst, 'The Origins and Evolution of Early Christian Pentecost', *Studia Patristica XXXV: Papers Presented at the Thirteenth International Conference on Patristic Studies Held in Oxford 1999*, eds. M. Wiles and E. Yarnold (Leuven, 2001), pp. 309-322.

nor elsewhere, prior to the beginning of the fourth century. In the Syriac-speaking area it was probably introduced along with the custom of paschal baptism. It seems reasonable to assume that this happened in roughly the same period that the Quartodeciman Passover was abandoned and the paschal Triduum was introduced in its place.[7] All these changes may have occurred in the immediate aftermath of the Council of Nicaea.

2. The Chronology of the Passion of the Didascalia

Let us start with the commemoration of the various moments in the Passion on the successive days of Holy Week. The first document we will have to deal with here is the famous twenty-first chapter of the *Didascalia*, containing a rather curious chronology of the Passion. Although already a lot has been written about this chronology, I shall briefly sketch the order of events as presented by the author or redactor of the passage concerned.[8] Monday is the day on which the priests and the elders assembled and decided to put Christ to death. This day coincided with the tenth of Nisan, that is, the day on which, according to the book of Exodus, the paschal lamb was kept (imprisoned). The Last Supper and the imprisonment of the Lord took place on Tuesday. This means that Christ ate the Passover meal on the eleventh of Nisan, three days earlier than was prescribed by the Jewish Law. The author of the passage argues that it happened in this way because the priests and elders had consciously advanced the Passover meal by three days to be able to seize and imprison the Lord before the crowds had arrived at Jerusalem to celebrate Passover. One has to assume that, according to the author of the passage, Christ stayed in prison until Friday, but he does not provide any further detail about this question. In any case, Jesus was crucified on Friday.

As is well-known, this curious chronology of the Passion has given rise to rather wild speculations. Here, in particular, mention should be made of an hypothesis advanced by Annie Jaubert that the passage preserves historical information that would have been lost in the Synoptic Gospels: that Jesus would have celebrated Passover on Tuesday, as he

---

[7] Cf. Rouwhorst, *Les hymnes pascales* I (see n. 5), pp. 198-201.

[8] See above, n. 4. See also Rouwhorst, *Les hymnes pascales* I (see n. 5), pp. 171-173, 183-186.

would have followed an Essene calendar. According to this calendar the various feasts fell on fixed days of the week, and Passover was always celebrated on a Tuesday.[9] August Strobel has formulated an even more complicated hypothesis. I cannot present it here in all its details, but essentially, according to him, the chronology reflects the liturgical practice of so-called solar Quartodecimans, who would have celebrated Passover on the vernal equinox or fourteen days later and that date would have always fallen on a Wednesday. The author of the *Didascalia* would have then tried to harmonize the traditions of these solar Quartodecimans with the celebration of Sunday Easter and the paschal Triduum.[10]

As I have tried to demonstrate elsewhere these theories are unconvincing and, moreover, superfluous.[11] To understand the curious chronology, it is first and foremost important to keep in mind the author's major concern, that is, to support the practice of fasting a whole week, from Monday onwards. To legitimize this practice, he appeals to the fact that the paschal lamb was imprisoned on Monday and, still more importantly, that the apostles had started mourning and fasting from Monday onwards because on that day the Bridegroom had been taken away from them. Perhaps, this does not explain everything and it does not make the chronology proposed any less curious and unusual, but at the very least, it helps us to understand the purpose behind this unusual chronology, why it was constructed or invented.

3. Commemorating the Passion during Holy Week

Yet the *Didascalia* is not the only Syriac source that gives evidence for the tendency to extend the commemoration of the Passion to the entire Holy Week. Several other texts betray a similar tendency, even if they do not go so far as the *Didascalia* in bringing the chronological data of the gospels themselves in line with the order of the successive days of Holy Week and even if, for that matter, the chronologies given by these texts differ on many points from that of the *Didascalia*. It is striking that Jaubert herself pointed to the existence of some of these

---

[9] A. Jaubert, *La date de la Cène: Calendrier biblique et liturgie chrétienne* (Paris, 1957), pp. 81-91, 105-136.

[10] A. Strobel, *Ursprung und Geschichte des frühchristlichen Osterkalenders*, Texte und Untersuchungen 121 (Berlin, 1977), pp. 326-352.

[11] Rouwhorst, *Les hymnes pascales* I (see n. 5), pp. 171-173, including footnotes 61 and 62.

sources, in an article she published in 1966, after her book *La date de la Cène* had already appeared.[12] Moreover, to account for these traditions, she proposes a solution that is much more plausible than the one she offers for the chronology of the Passion of the *Didascalia*.

A long sermon ascribed to Ephrem the Syrian, whose relevance was noticed by Jaubert, is the first one deserving of mention.[13] Edmund Beck, who has published a critical edition of this text, has convincingly demonstrated, although Ephrem himself certainly was not the author of this text, that it presents a strong affinity with the authentic works of the deacon of Nisibis and Edessa and has been profoundly influenced by them. Most probably, as Edmund Beck has suggested, the author was a Syriac Monophysite of the second half of the sixth century.[14]

Apparently escaping Jaubert's notice is a very remarkable counterpart to the pseudo-ephremian sermon, an exceptionally long sermon (*memra*) of James of Sarug,[15] a well-known and very prolific Syriac author (equally a Monophysite), who lived in the sixth century. If Beck's attempt to date the pseudo-ephremian sermon is correct, both *memre* derive from the same period and the same Syriac-speaking region.[16]

These texts have two things in common: on the one hand, they deal with the full length story of the Passion, from the beginning of the Last

---

[12] A. Jaubert, 'Une lecture du lavement des pieds au mardi-mercredi saint', *Le Muséon* 79 (1966) 257-286.

[13] E. Beck, *Ephraem Syrus: Sermones in Hebdomadam Sanctam*, CSCO 412-413 (Leuven, 1979). Of course, Jaubert had not yet access to this edition. She based herself on the edition published by Th. Lamy, in *Sancti Ephraem Syri Hymni et Sermones* I (Mechelen, 1882), pp. 339-356.

[14] Cf. Beck's introduction to his German translation: CSCO 413 (see n. 13), pp. 1-12.

[15] Edition of the Syriac text: P. Bedjan, *Homiliae Selectae Mar Jacobi Sarugensis — Homilies of Mar Jacob of Serug* (Paris and Leipzig, 1905-1910; reprint Gorgias Press, 2006), vol. II, pp. 447-610.

[16] Apart from the pseudo-Ephremian sermon, Jaubert also makes mention of a series of 'strophes' (*bā'wāthā*, strophic prayers) transmitted by the ms British Library 14520 (ms of 8th or 9th century). See for the texts: Th. Lamy, *Sancti Ephraem Syri Hymni et Sermones* III (Mechelen, 1889), pp. XXIV-XXVIII; cf. Jaubert, 'Une lecture du lavement des pieds' (see n. 12), pp. 263-264. These prayers appear to contain extracts from Ephrem's *madrashe*. I believe it is very unlikely that they date back to an early period, for instance the 5th or 6th century. As has been noted by A. Baumstark, the type of *bā'ūthā* under consideration seems to date back to a rather later period, perhaps the 8th or 9th century. See A. Baumstark, *Festbrevier und Kirchenjahr der syrischen Jakobiten* (Paderborn, 1910), pp. 64-67; cf. *idem, Geschichte der syrischen Literatur* (Bonn, 1922), pp. 51-52. For that matter, the chronology of the Passion underlying these texts does not essentially differ from that of the Synoptic Gospels. At least, these texts do not refer to the celebration of the Last Supper or the Washing of the Feet on Tuesday or Wednesday. Therefore, I shall not take them into account.

Supper or even from some events that precede it and, on the other hand, are subdivided into sections attributed to the successive days of Holy Week. In doing so, they seem to ignore the existence of Maundy Thursday and let the story of the Passion begin on Monday, the first day of Holy Week. It may be interesting to compare the different ways in which these texts distribute the various episodes of the Passion over the successive days of Holy Week. Let us begin with the *memra* attributed to Ephrem.

According to its rubric the first section of this text, to be delivered on Monday at dawn (*d-nâgah*), is rather general in character. The main part of it consists of a sermon which Peter is supposed to have given in Rome, and which speaks about Christ, being the divine king who is dethroning earthly kings. This section apparently serves as a sort of introduction to the celebration of Holy Week, but most probably was added to the original *memra* itself. The opening sentence of the second section seems to confirm this; it situates the first event described at a specific place and a specific time, that is at Bethany and prior to the days of the Unleavened Bread. From a stylistic point of view a perfect sentence to start with! The central themes of this text are the anointing at Bethany, the preparation for the Passover by Simon Peter and John, the replacement of the old, Jewish Passover by a new Passover (the Eucharist). According to the introductory rubric, this section is intended for the night from Monday to Tuesday. The next section, which is intended for the night from Tuesday to Wednesday, is devoted almost entirely to the washing of the disciples' feet by the Lord. The final part of this section deals with Judas, at the moment when he is leaving the Upper Room to betray his Lord for blood money. The fourth section — to be read in the night from Wednesday to Thursday — contains a long passage in which Jesus explains the meaning of the washing of the feet (humility) and then deals extensively with the institution of the Eucharist, the new Passover. According to their rubrics, the two following parts (sections 5 and 6) are intended for the night from Thursday to Friday and for the morning of Good Friday respectively. They do not cause any surprise as far as their chronology is concerned; they are devoted entirely to themes that the gospels place on the Friday on which Christ was condemned and crucified. Remarkably, the sixth section dealing with the crucifixion is much longer than all the preceding ones. It ends with the scene of the burial and a description of the sadness and desperation of the disciples, who cannot believe that Christ will resurrect from the dead. As has been convincingly argued by Edmund Beck, this section constitutes the conclusion of the original sermon. The manuscripts add two further texts, one dealing with the resurrection from the tomb (it lacks a liturgical rubric connecting it with a specific day of the year) and the other with the apparition of the risen Lord to Thomas (a liturgical rubric indicates that it should be delivered on 'New Sunday', the Sunday after Easter). These two texts, however, are best regarded as independent entities, as complete sermons apparently added later. Therefore the long *memra* about the Passion of the Lord begins with the anointing at Bethany and ends with the burial of the body of Christ.

Globally, the content of the sermon of James of Sarug corresponds to that of Pseudo-Ephrem. After a long introduction, dealing with the ingratitude of the Jews among other things, it meditates and extensively comments upon the various moments in the story of the Passion. Unlike Pseudo-Ephrem, the sermon does not deal with the anointing at Bethany. Neither does it tell of the priests and the elders plotting against Jesus, which the *Didascalia* places at the beginning of Holy Week. Rather it starts with Christ setting off for the Upper Room to celebrate Passover.[17] Following this, James of Sarug describes and comments upon a series of moments of the Last Supper: Jesus' washing of the feet of the disciples,[18] Jesus eating of the Passover lamb and the bitter herbs together with His disciples,[19] His announcing of the betrayal by Judas,[20] His distribution of the bread and the wine that were His body and blood[21] and finally the departure of Judas leaving the Upper Room.[22] Next, Jacob meditates upon nearly all the details of the Passion: from the condemnation and the crucifixion[23] up to the resurrection on Sunday morning, on the third day (contrary to Pseudo-Ephrem, James does not conclude with burial, but with the resurrection).[24] The order of the events which the sermon describes and comments upon is hardly surprising. The only thing that deserves to be noted is the somewhat peculiar sequence of events during the Last Supper, with the washing of the feet preceding the Passover meal and the institution of the Eucharist. Apart from this fact, one is struck by the extreme length of the *memra*, even taking into

---

[17] Bedjan, *Homiliae selectae,* II (see n. 15), p. 455.
[18] *Ibid.,* pp. 456-468.
[19] *Ibid.,* pp. 468-470.
[20] *Ibid.,* pp. 471-482.
[21] *Ibid.,* pp. 482-488.
[22] *Ibid.,* pp. 493-496.
[23] *Ibid.,* pp. 504-593.
[24] *Ibid.,* pp. 601-610.

account James' verbosity and the length of the rest of his *memre*. What is perhaps even more remarkable is that, in all of the numerous manuscripts by which the sermon has been transmitted, the sermon is cut into sections that are intended for the successive days of Holy Week, not starting at Maundy Thursday but on Monday!

What liturgical tradition underlies these two sermons? What phase in the development of Syriac Holy Week do they reflect?

Before going more deeply into this question, this should be noted: it is practically certain that the division into sections, as well as their distribution over the various days of Holy Week, is not original. As has been clearly demonstrated by Edmund Beck, they were inserted into the pseudo-ephremian sermon at a later date. As for the sermon of James of Sarug, no two manuscripts divide the text in exactly the same way.[25] Thus, we have every reason to doubt the antiquity of any of these subdivisions and rubrics. Nonetheless, there are strong indications that one must have started making such subdivisions and rubrics at a rather early phase in the development of Holy Week in Syriac tradition. Agreeing that these divisions as such are not original, I would argue that they more or less faithfully correspond to the concept of Holy Week the sixth-century authors had in mind. It is not unreasonable even to hypothesize that the two *memre* were originally written for Holy Week, from Monday or Tuesday onwards. The following arguments may be adduced to bolster this hypothesis:

a. The subdivision of the texts does not fit well into the form of Holy Week which, due to the influences from the liturgical traditions of

---

[25] Basic information about these divisions is to be found in the catalogues of the British Museum and the Vatican by W. Wright and S.E. and J.S. Assemani where one can find the incipits of the various sections. See W. Wright, *Catalogue of the syriac manuscripts in the British Museum acquired since the year 1838*, 3 Parts (London, 1870); S.E. and J. S. Assemanus, *Bibliothecae apostolicae vaticanae codicum manuscriptorum catalogus in tres partes distributus* (Rome, 1758-1759). Cf. for the manuscripts in question and their contents: A. Vööbus, *Handschriftliche Ueberlieferung der Mēmrē-Dichtung des Jaʻqōb von Serūg*, CSCO 344-345 (Leuven, 1973). Unfortunately this work is not of any help in reconstructing the liturgical divisions of our *memra*.

Various divisions of the *memra* of James of Sarug are to be found in the following manuscripts: BL 14.585 (7th century; Wright, *Catalogue*, pp. 502-503); BL 12.162 (7th century; Wright, pp. 721-723); BL 17.198 (7th century; Wright, p. 503); BL 17.242 (11th or 12th century; Wright, p. 504); BL 12.165 (CE 1015; Wright, pp. 842-851); BL 17.249; Vat. Syr. 117 (12th or 13th century) and 118 (10th or 11th century). The division found in the edition of Bedjan (see n. 15) is the same as that of BL 12.162, and the one given by J.S. Assemani in his *Bibliotheca Orientalis* (Rome, 1719-1728) is the same as that found in the BL 17.242 (see *BO* I, pp. 324-325).

Jerusalem, gained an increasingly wide acceptance in Syriac-speaking Christianity, especially in the so-called Syrian Orthodox/West-Syrian tradition. (This development is, for instance, clearly attested by the list of pericopes transmitted by the BL 14528 and edited by F.C. Burkitt.)[26]

b. Several manuscripts (especially BL 12.162; BL 14.585; BL 17.198) containing the sermon of James of Sarug, which include rubrics for Holy Week and a subdivision of the text, date to the seventh century. They attest that one must have begun distributing the text over various days of Holy Week at a very early period.

c. Both the sermon of Ephrem and that of James of Sarug are much too long to be delivered on one occasion. (James of Sarug takes nearby two hundred pages of Bedjan's edition!) Moreover, they cover the entire story of the Passion. So it is impossible to think of them in relationship with one specific day of Holy Week, as it developed within the hagiopolite tradition.

d. At least half of the themes commented upon by both of the *memre* are closely connected with Maundy Thursday, as celebrated in most liturgical traditions. Still, among the very numerous sermons of James of Sarug that have been preserved, one will find none that appears to be specifically connected with themes related to 'our' Maundy Thursday. Strikingly, among the numerous sermons composed by the East Syrian author Narsai, one does not find any clearly intended for Maundy Thursday.[27] In my view this means that in the sixth century in large parts of the Syriac-speaking region, Maundy Thursday was still unknown.[28]

---

[26] F. Burkitt, *The Early Syriac Lectionary*, Proceedings of the British Academy X, 1923 (reprint: Analecta Gorgiana 62, [Picataway, NJ, 2007]).

[27] Cf. A. Mingana, *Narsai doctoris Syri Homiliae et Carmina*, 2 Volumes (Mosul, 1905). Cf. also the list of Narsai's *memre* which has been established by W. Macomber in: *id.*, 'The Manuscripts of the Metrical Homilies of Narsai', *Orientalia Christiana Periodica* 39 (1973) 275-306. The rubrics found in the manuscripts and in the edition of Mingana can be misleading in this respect. Thus, nr. 34 of Macomber's list (Mingana nr. 19, vol. I, 313-327) is according to its rubric intended for the Thursday of Passover, i.e. Maundy Thursday, but the strongly eschatological content of the sermon which is dealing with the coming of the Anti-Christ and the end of the world, clearly does not fit in with the liturgical character of that day. Fragments of this *memra* have been translated by Ph. Gignoux in his article 'Les doctrines eschatologiques de Narsai', *L'Orient syrien* 11 (1966), pp. 333-335, 342-343, 348-352, 462-463, 471-472, 475, 482-483, 486; *L'Orient syrien* 12 (1967), pp. 27-30, 32-34, 38-39, 53.

[28] The earliest example of a text or sermon intended for a Maundy Thursday is a homily by Cyrus of Edessa. Edition and English translation by W. Macomber, *Six Explanation of the Liturgical Feasts by Cyrus of Edessa*, CSCO 355-356 (Leuven, 1974).

e. The opening of the second section of the sermon of Pseudo-Ephrem, which actually begins the oldest core of the text, contains a clear allusion to the days of Unleavened Bread, more precisely 'not that of the Jews, but that of the Christians'.[29] This obviously has to be taken as a reference to Holy Week, given the fact that — in several sources derived from this region —Holy Week is considered as a counterpart of the Week of Unleavened Bread[30] or even straightfor-wardly called the 'Week of Unleavened Bread'.

f. Jaubert has rightly pointed out that numerous 'Nestorian' lectionar-ies, beginning with the seventh century, associate the reading of John 13 (Jesus' washing the feet of the disciples) with Wednesday of Holy Week.[31] This proves that it was not at all unusual to associ-ate this moment in the story of the Passion, which the gospels place on Thursday, with days falling earlier in Holy Week. It goes with-out saying that the well-known passage of the *Didascalia*, already mentioned earlier, gives evidence for the same tendency.

Taking into consideration all of these arguments, one cannot help but conclude that all of them point in the same direction. They strongly sug-gest the existence — from the fourth century onwards — of a form of Holy Week that was not yet familiar with the observance of Maundy Thursday and distributed the events that the gospels place on the eve of Good Friday, over the first four days of Holy Week. This tradition was only gradually supplanted by the hagiopolite one which concentrated the celebration of all of these events on Maundy Thursday.

4. The Origins of the Syriac Type of Holy Week

If there are strong and unambiguous indications that the type of Holy Week described was widespread in the Syriac-speaking region and was practiced at least from the fourth to the sixth century (the period from which the more recent strata of the *Didascalia* date), the question of course arises what was the origin of this tradition. When and why did it come into existence?

---

[29] Edition: Beck (see n. 13), CSCO 412, p. 7; 413, p. 24.
[30] See Aphraates, *Dem.* XII, 12. Edition: I. Parisot, *Patrologia Syriaca* I (Paris, 1894), pp. 535-536.
[31] Jaubert, 'Une lecture du lavement des pieds' (see n. 12), pp. 264-266.

Once more, I would like to argue that the whole theory, launched by Jaubert, of an Essene or vaguely heterodox Jewish 'Tuesday-Passover', which left traces in Syriac Christianity, has to be discarded. To begin with, the theory is extremely speculative. For the rest, apart from the weird chronology of the Passion of the *Didascalia*, in none of the oldest Syriac sources do we meet a clear allusion to Jews celebrating their Passover on a Tuesday. Instead of this problematic and speculative explanation, one can point to two facts that may lead to a less sensational, but more plausible solution. First, it is readily apparent from the *Didascalia* that its curious chronology serves a *liturgical aim*. It is used to legitimate a liturgical tradition, the observance of a liturgical practice, the observance of Holy Week which is, on the one hand, a fast and, on the other hand, a commemoration of the Passion of the Lord.[32] Secondly, apart from the curious chronology of the *Didascalia*, one of the most remarkable and widest attested characteristics of the chronologies of the Passion we have examined is that Jesus' washing of the disciples' feet described in the Gospel of John precedes what happened at the Last Supper, as recorded in the Synoptic Gospels. Actually, the fact that the foot-washing is commemorated on Tuesday or Wednesday — a tradition to which a large group of lectionaries attest — is but a natural consequence of this principle. It is precisely here that Jaubert made a very illuminating observation. This way of arranging the various moments in the story of the Passion corresponds exactly to that of the Syriac *Diatessaron*. She rightly points to the Arabic version of the *Diatessaron*, which is doubtless one of the oldest recensions of Tatian's work.[33] It may be added that the testimony of the Arabic version is confirmed by Ephrem's commentary on the *Diatessaron*, preserved in Armenian.[34] It therefore unmistakably represents a very ancient version of the *Diatessaron*, if not simply the original one. However, what is problematic in Jaubert's hypothesis is that she was not satisfied with this observation and refused to draw the rather obvious conclusion that

[32] Cf. Rouwhorst, *Les hymnes pascales* (see n. 5), pp. 171-173; *idem*, 'Liturgy on the Authority of the Apostles', in *The Apostolic Age in Patristic Thought*, ed. A. Hilhorst, Supplements to Vigiliae Christianae 70 (Leiden and Boston, 2004), pp. 63-85, on pp. 77-79.

[33] Jaubert, 'Une lecture du lavement des pieds' (see n. 12), pp. 276-277.

[34] See ch. XVIII, 22. Edition: *Saint Ephrem, Commentaire de l'évangile concordant: Version arménienne*, ed. L. Leloir, CSCO 137 (Leuven, 1953), pp. 267-268; cf. Ephrem de Nisibe, *Commentaire de l'évangile concordant ou Diatessaron: Introduction, traduction et notes par L. Leloir*, SC 121 (Paris, 1966), p. 330.

Tatian had tried to solve a purely exegetical problem, namely that of harmonizing the Johannine account of the foot-washing with the Synoptic tradition regarding Last Supper. Instead, she continued to search for a liturgical tradition underlying Tatian's harmonization and, in doing so, hypothesized the existence of an ancient liturgical celebration of foot-washing in Johannine circles, on Tuesday, the day on which formerly certain Jewish communities had celebrated their Passover![35] This explanation is very speculative and unnecessary. In my view, it would suffice to conclude that, at a certain moment, the Christians of the Syriac-speaking area decided to extend the paschal fast to one week. Perhaps, that may have occurred when the *triduum sacrum* was introduced in the place of the ancient Quartodeciman celebration. From that moment onwards, several attempts were made to bring the data of the gospels in line with liturgical practice. The curious chronology of the *Didascalia* was probably invented for that purpose (at least it was used to realize that aim). Another solution — which was less radical than the one proposed by the *Didascalia* and doubtlessly found a much wider acceptance — consisted of following the order of events described by the *Diatessaron* and commemorating first the washing of the feet before the Last Supper, either on Wednesday or on Tuesday.

5. A Christian Week of the Unleavened Bread?

But, perhaps this is not all that there is to be said. This brings me to the second aspect of the Syriac Holy Week as it was celebrated at this period: its relationship with the Jewish Passover and the Week of Unleavened Bread. As has already been mentioned in the preceding section, in several sources, Holy Week is not only regarded as the Week of the Passion, but also as that of 'Passover' and the 'Unleavened Bread'.

In some earlier publications, I have suggested the possibility that prior to the Council of Nicaea, Syriac Christians would not have simply celebrated their Passover on the Jewish date, but would have also continued celebrating it during the following week, that is, the Week of Unleavened Bread.[36] In that case, once the paschal triduum ending with the celebration of the resurrection had been adopted, celebrations in the

---

[35] Jaubert, 'Une lecture du lavement des pieds' (see n. 12), pp. 279-281.
[36] Rouwhorst, *Les hymnes pascales* I (see n. 5), p. 155, esp. note 20.

following week — which did not have the resurrection as their major theme — would have become a problem. But Holy Week preceding the triduum would have taken over the function of the older Week of Unleavened Bread. This theory has been questioned by Clemens Leonhard[37] who has raised three major objections against it: a) there is no unambiguous evidence available for the existence of a christianized Week of the Unleavened Bread in pre-Constantinian times;[38] b) all the evidence available strongly suggests that the Christian Week of Unleavened Bread was understood as a fast and this excludes the possibility that it was observed after the Quartodeciman Passover, because it is generally agreed that this ended in a joyful celebration of the Eucharist;[39] c) the Christian Week of Unleavened attested by the Syriac sources — which has the character of a fast — is basically different from the Jewish festival at that period which was not understood as a period of fasting and mourning.[40] On the basis of these arguments, Leonhard concludes that the Christian Week of Unleavened Bread did not exist in pre-Constantinian times and neither can have been inherited from Judaism. It was invented in the fourth century — after Holy Week observed before Easter Sunday had been introduced in the Syriac speaking region — by adherents to an especially biblicist approach to liturgical development who were constructing liturgies out of a biblical text.[41] Actually, it was a 'bookish innovation'.[42] The arguments adduced by Leonhard against the hypothesis I have formulated are definitely very much to the point. I readily admit that it is difficult to say anything with certainty about the pre-Nicene celebration of the Week of Unleavened Bread by Christians, supposing such a celebration existed. Personally, I think Leonhard's second objection is the strongest one. It remains difficult to explain why Quartodecimans would have fasted after Passover (even if it was less centred on the celebration of the resurrection than the dominical Pascha was). If they ever had been familiar with a christianized Week of the Unleavened Bread, at least it could not have had the character of a fast. However, the third objection seems to me the least convincing one. Assuming that Syriac Christians would have

---

[37] C. Leonhard, *The Jewish Pesach and the Origins of the Christian Easter: Open Questions in Current Research,* Studia Judaica 35 (Berlin and New York, 2006), pp. 205-230.

[38] *Ibid.,* p. 229.

[39] *Ibid.,* p. 209.

[40] *Ibid.,* especially pp. 214-215.

[41] *Ibid.,* p. 229.

taken over the Week of Unleavened Bread from Judaism, why would
they have limited themselves to taking it over or copying it? It appears
much more likely that they would have appropriated it in their own way
and perhaps even in an anti-Jewish way. The reason — or one of the
reasons — why they might have understood their Week of Unleavened
Bread as a fast, might have been precisely that they wanted to distinguish themselves from the Jews (who indeed must have passed this
week in a very different fashion). Next, the solution proposed by Leonhard according to which the Christian Week of Unleavened Bread was
merely a bookish innovation, an innovation based on the Old Testament, may provoke different objections as well. Is it likely that liturgical practices are merely invented out of biblical texts if there are no
other (non-biblical) reasons for doing so? Actually, there could have
been at least two non-biblical reasons why Christians in the Syriac-
speaking regions — or in the neighbouring parts of the Roman Empire
— might have been induced to observe some sort of christianized Week
of Unleavened Bread. First, once Holy Week had been introduced in
the third of fourth century for one reason or another, one might have
appealed to the Old Testament Week of Unleavened Bread to bolster
that practice. This might in itself provide a satisfactory explanation for
the fact that Holy Week was viewed as a Christian alternative to the
Old Testament Week of Unleavened Bread. In that case, contacts with
Jewish communities would not have played any role. However, this
explanation would leave unanswered the question of the origin of Holy
Week. Why Syriac Christians would have felt the necessity of extending the Quartodeciman paschal fast to one week? I therefore would like
to suggest that contacts between Jews and Christians *did* play a role in
this development. For the sake of clarity, I do not mean that Syriac
Christians of the fourth century would have per se preserved and
slightly adapted an ancient Jewish tradition that might go back to the
first or second century or even to Second Temple Judaism. It seems to
me that the explanation is rather to be found in the complicated and
often strained relations between Jews and Christians at a somewhat
later period, for instance during the fourth century.[43] We know for sure
that, in Syriac-speaking areas, Christians and Jews were living in close

---

[42] *Ibid.*, p. 214.

[43] Cf. for instance G. Rouwhorst, 'Christliche und jüdische Liturgie', in *Theologie des
Gottesdienstes*, eds. M. Klöckener, A. Häußling and R. Meßner, Gottesdienst der Kirche
2,2 (Regensburg, 2008), pp. 491-572, on pp. 563-565.

proximity to each other. Synods and church fathers warned Christians against participating in Jewish festivals. This may have led Christians to develop Christian alternatives to Jewish liturgical practices that would have had some elements in common with these traditions — otherwise, the strategy would not have worked at all —, but at the same time served to reinforce Christian identity over against the Jews. More in particular with regard to the festival of Unleavened Bread, it may be noted that both a canon of the Council of Laodicea (middle of the fourth century)[44] and one canon of the so-called 'Apostolic Canons' that have been incorporated in the eighth book of the Apostolic Constitutions,[45] explicitly forbid Christians receiving 'unleavened bread' from Jews![46] Taking into account these data, it does not seem too far-fetched to hypothesize that the Holy Week attested by the Syriac sources studied in this article was considered by the Christians of the Syriac-speaking regions — or at least by some of them — as a Christian alternative to the Jewish Week of Unleavened Bread which served to mark their identity over against the Jews. This might have been the case at least from Constantinian times onwards. Whether a christianized Week of Unleavened Bread existed in the pre-Nicene period — when those Christians celebrated Passover on 14 Nisan — remains very difficult to determine. In combination with other motives, this idea may even have been a strong stimulus for the coming into being and spread of Holy Week. Obviously, the Old Testament was used to bolster that liturgical tradition, but (polemical) interreligious interactions might have played an important role as well.

Conclusion

There are strong indications that, prior to the increase of liturgical influences coming from Jerusalem and its surroundings, Syriac Christianity was familiar with a type of Holy Week different from the hagiopolite.

---

[44] Canon 38. Edition: P.-P. Johannou, *Discipline Générale Antique (IV. e – IX. e. s)*, vol. I, 2: *Les Canons de Synodes particuliers*, Fonti Fasc. IX Pontificia Commissione per la Redazione del Codice di Diritto Canonico Orientale (Grottaferrrata and Rome, 1962).

[45] Canon 70. Edition: M. Metzger, *Les Constitutions Apostoliques*, vol. III, SC, 336 (Paris, 1985).

[46] These texts have been studied in detail by Elizabeth Boddens Hosang in her dissertation *Establishing Boundaries: Christian-Jewish Relations in Early Council Texts and the Writings of Church Fathers*, Jewish and Christian Perspectives Series 19 (Leiden and Boston, 2010), pp. 99-102, 120-122.

Liturgical practices of Jewish minority groups, such as the Essenes, did not play any role in the emergence of this liturgical tradition, but varying other factors did so.

BAPTISMAL LITURGY IN FOURTH-CENTURY JERUSALEM IN THE LIGHT OF RECENT SCHOLARSHIP

Maxwell E. JOHNSON

Introduction

It would be impossible to over-estimate the importance of Jerusalem in the development of Christian liturgy in the fourth and fifth centuries. Thanks to the multiple Hagiopolite liturgical sources we possess, namely, the *Baptismal Catecheses* of Cyril of Jerusalem (ca. 351),[1] the *Mystagogical Catecheses*,[2] attributed either to Cyril (in the late 380s) or to his successor John, the *Armenian*[3] and *Georgian Lectionaries*,[4] and, of course, the travel diary of the Galician pilgrim Egeria, the *Peregrinatio Egeriae*,[5] we have been able to reconstruct the liturgical practices in Jerusalem quite easily. This has been true especially with regard to the cathedral and monastic offices,[6] the rites of Christian initiation and the

---

[1] Greek text is in PG 33. For an English translation see the *Nicene and Post-Nicene Fathers*, 7, second series, ed. Phillip Schaff (Grand Rapids, 1971). A more recent translation of some of these lectures, including the *Mystagogical Catecheses*, is Edward Yarnold, *Cyril of Jerusalem* (London and New York, 2000).

[2] Critical edition in Greek with French translation is *Cyrille de Jérusalem: Catéchèses Mystagogiques*, ed. A Piédnagel, trans. Pierre Paris, Sources Chrétiennes (hereafter SC) 126 (Paris, 1966). For another Greek text with English translation see *St. Cyril of Jerusalem's Lectures on the Christian Sacraments*, ed. F.L. Cross (Crestwood, NY, 1977). Another English version is provided by Edward Yarnold, *The Awe-Inspiring Rites of Initiation: Baptismal Homilies of the Fourth Century – The Origins of the R.C.I.A.*, revised edition (Collegeville, MN, 1994), pp. 67-97.

[3] Athanase Renoux, *Le Codex armenien Jérusalem 121*, II (Turnhout, 1971).

[4] Michel Tarschnischvili, *Le grand lectionnaire de l'Église de Jérusalem* (Leuven, 1959).

[5] Critical edition in Latin with French translation is *Égerie: Journal de voyage*, ed. Pierre Maraval, trans. Manuel C. Diaz, SC 296 (Paris, 1982). For an English translation see John Wilkinson, *Egeria's Travels* (London, 1971).

[6] Paul Bradshaw, *Daily Prayer in the Early Church* (London, 1982), pp. 72-93; Robert Taft, *The Liturgy of the Hours in East and West: The Origins of the Divine Office and its Meaning for Today* (Collegeville, MN, 1986), pp. 48-56; Gabriele Winkler, 'Das Offizium am Ende des 4. Jahrhunderts und das heutige chaldäische Offizium, ihre strukturellen Zusammenhänge', *Ostkirchliche Studien* 19 (1970) 289-311; eadem, 'Über die Kathedralvesper in den verschiedenen Riten des Ostens und Westens', *Archiv für Liturgiewissenschaft* 16 (1974) 53-102. On Jerusalem liturgy in the fourth and fifth centuries in

catechumenate,[7] the liturgical year,[8] and, of course, the eucharistic liturgy and its anaphora.[9] It would be a mistake to assume, however, that
all of the questions with regard to this place and period have been
answered once and for all time. In the past few years, for example, at
least three significant studies related directly to our topic have been published, dealing either directly with the authorship of the *Mystagogical
Catecheses* or with the overall context and contents of liturgy there in
the fourth century and with potential wider liturgical influence. These
studies are: Alexis Doval, *Cyril of Jerusalem, Mystagogue: The Authorship of the Mystagogic Catecheses*;[10] Juliette Day, *The Baptismal
Liturgy of Jerusalem: Fourth- and Fifth-Century Evidence from Palestine, Syria and Egypt*;[11] and Abraham Terian, *Macarius of Jerusalem,
Letter to the Armenians (A.D. 335)*.[12] This short article, really a progress
report on a work in process, will offer a brief critical look at these studies in order to determine what light they may shed on especially Christian initiation and the eucharist in fourth-century Hagiopolite liturgical
practice and what avenues might be suggested for further research.

general see John Baldovin, *The Urban Character of Christian Worship: The Origins,
Development, and Meaning of Stational Liturgy*, Orientalia Christiana Analecta 228 (Rome,
1987), pp. 45-104; id., *Liturgy in Ancient Jerusalem*, Alcuin/GROW Liturgical Study, 57
(Bramcote, Nottingham, 1989).

[7] See Maxwell E. Johnson, *The Rites of Christian Initiation: Their Evolution and
Theological Interpretation*, revised and expanded edition (Collegeville, MN, 2007),
pp. 120-126; Bryan Spinks, *Early and Medieval Rituals and Theologies of Baptism:
From the New Testament to the Council of Trent* (Aldershot and Burlington, 2006),
pp. 38-42; Gabriele Winkler, 'The Original Meaning of the Prebaptismal Anointing and
Its Implications', *Worship* 52 (1978) 24-45 (reprinted in *Living Water, Sealing Spirit:
Readings on Christian Initiation*, ed. Maxwell E. Johnson (Collegeville, MN, 1995),
pp. 58-81).

[8] See Thomas Talley, *The Origins of the Liturgical Year*, second emended edition
(Collegeville, MN, 1991).

[9] See Emmanuel J. Cutrone, 'Cyril's Mystagogical Catecheses and the Evolution of
the Jerusalem Anaphora', *Orientalia Christiana Periodica* 44 (1978) 52-64; John R.K.
Fenwick, *The Anaphoras of St. Basil and James: An Investigation Into Their Common
Origins*, Orientalia Christiana Analecta 240 (Rome, 1992), pp. 36-45; Kent Burreson,
'The Anaphora of the Mystagogical Catecheses of Cyril of Jerusalem', in *Essays on Early
Eastern Eucharistic Prayers*, ed. Paul Bradshaw (Collegeville, MN, 1997), pp. 131-151.

[10] Alexis James Doval, *Cyril of Jerusalem, Mystagogue: The Authorship of the
Mystagogic Catecheses*, Patristic Monograph Series 17 (Washington, D.C., 2001).

[11] Juliette Day, *The Baptismal Liturgy of Jerusalem: Fourth- and Fifth-Century Evidence from Palestine, Syria and Egypt*, Liturgy, Worship and Society (Aldershot and
Burlington, 2007).

[12] Abraham Terian, *Macarius of Jerusalem, Letter to the Armenians (A.D. 335):
Introduction, Text, Translation and Commentary*, AVANT: Treasures of the Armenian
Christian Tradition 4 (Crestwood, NY, 2008).

1. A Summary of Recent Scholarship on the Authorship of the Mystagogical Catecheses

The authorship and date of the Jerusalem *Mystagogical Catecheses*, whether by Cyril of Jerusalem or his successor, the Origenist John of Jerusalem, have been long-standing scholarly debates ever since an important 1942 article by W.J. Swaans, in which Cyrilline authorship was questioned and Johannine authorship was defended.[13] Recently, two of the authors noted above, Alexis Doval and Juliette Day, have entered this debate and have come to opposite conclusions, based on somewhat differing methodologies.

1.1. Alexis Doval

Alexis Doval applies a three-fold methodological approach toward the resolution of the authorship question: 1) a study of authorship attributions in the manuscripts of the *Mystagogical Catecheses*, some of which do, in fact, refer to John of Jerusalem as author; 2) a study of the external evidence, namely, the date of Egeria's pilgrimage as well as the contents of *Armenian Lectionary* in relationship to Cyril's episcopate and the *liturgical* content of both the *Baptismal* and *Mystagogical Catecheses*; and 3) a detailed literary and theological study of the *Mystagogical Catecheses* in relationship to other extant texts by both Cyril and John. Like his dissertation director, Edward Yarnold,[14] Doval concludes that, similar to Cyril's own pre-baptismal catechetical lectures dated in the mid-fourth century, both the *Procatechesis* and the *Mystagogical Catecheses* 'ought rightfully to be included among the works of Cyril of Jerusalem'.[15] In arriving at this conclusion, Doval assumes that the oft-noted differences in liturgical practice between the *Baptismal Catecheses* and those of the *Mystagogical Catecheses* are to be explained simply in terms of liturgical developments or changes in the rites themselves during the years between them and, hence, there is no reason to assume that the *Mystagogical Catecheses* cannot belong to the later years of Cyril's own episcopate (ca. 387).[16] That is, certain differences need not

---

[13] W.J. Swaans, 'À propos des "Catéchèses Mystagogiques" attribuées à S. Cyrille de Jérusalem', *Le Muséon* 55 (1942) 1-42.

[14] See Edward Yarnold, 'The Authorship of the Mystagogic Catecheses Attributed to Cyril of Jerusalem', *The Heythrop Journal* 19 (1978) 143-161.

[15] Doval, *Cyril of Jerusalem* (see n. 10), p. 243.

[16] This was also the conclusion of Edward Yarnold. See n. 14.

be explained by pointing to different authors when another explanation is possible. In particular, Doval directs our attention to what appears to be a difference in the anointings between the *Baptismal* and *Mystagogical Catecheses*. According to him, while there was certainly a *pre-baptismal* anointing, and may have been already been a post-baptismal ('messianic' or 'christic') anointing in the Jerusalem initiation liturgy of the 350s, the *Baptismal Catecheses* indicate theologically that the gift and seal (*sphragis*) of the Holy Spirit was at that time associated with the immersion rite itself and not to the anointing(s).[17] And, together with various references to the laying on of hands associated with the Holy Spirit (*Baptismal Catecheses* 14.25, 17.25, and 16.26), only one of which (16.26) is related directly to baptism, Doval claims that the rite Cyril knew in the 350s was closer, at least theologically, to that of John Chrysostom in Antioch. By implication, this would also relate the rite of Jerusalem in the 350s to that which is assumed to be the case also in Cappadocia.[18] That is, while referring both to Moses laying on hands and Peter conferring the Holy Spirit by hand-laying, Cyril explicitly states that the 'manner' by which the Holy Spirit is given to the baptized cannot be discussed at this time but would have to wait until the proper season. Far from being a reference to a post-baptismal hand-laying for the gift of the Holy Spirit, Doval argues that:

> 'When Cyril says "but in what manner", this could be taken as indicating that the conferring of the Spirit will be done in a manner different from what has been the traditional way, that is, by some other way than a distinct laying on of hands. If ... all the events of the Jordan model are symbolized in the rite of immersion, then any laying on of hands for the giving of the Spirit would have happened there. Cyril speaks of an 'invocation of grace' over the candidates once they have gone down into the water ...; this could easily have involved a laying on of hands. Such a scene is exactly what is found in Chrysostom ....
>
> But by the time of *M* [the *Mystagogical Catecheses*]... the descent of the Spirit is ritualized in its own postimmersion rite. Now there would be no significance attached to the imposition of hands in the font ... A vestige of the laying on of hands still exists in the chrismation, but the *myron* alone suffices to convey the idea of being anointed by the Spirit.'[19]

---

[17] *Ibid.*, pp. 135-143.

[18] See the doctoral dissertation by my student, Nancy Johnson, *Living Death: Baptism and the Christian Life in the Writings of Basil of Caesarea, Gregory of Nazianzus, and Gregory of Nyssa* (Ph.D. Dissertation, University of Notre Dame, 2008), pp. 345-350.

[19] Doval, *Cyril of Jerusalem* (see n. 10), pp. 144-145.

Another important aspect of Doval's work is the attention he pays to the eucharistic liturgy and especially to its anaphora.[20] Although, and again like Yarnold,[21] Doval's primary concern here appears to be with establishing that the institution narrative was already part, or becoming part, of the Jerusalem anaphora in the *Mystagogical Catecheses*, he does note that the overall 'simplicity of the anaphora' would tend to place it earlier rather than later. A later date, such as the end of the fourth (John) or beginnings of the fifth century, would have necessitated a more developed anaphoral structure, more akin to the Anaphora of Saint James, than to the simpler form presumably in the *Mystagogical Catecheses*.

While Doval's approach and conclusions on Cyrilline authorship are rather compelling, he is a careful enough scholar to indicate potential problems with his conclusions. One in particular concerns his comparative (stylometric) analysis of the literary styles of both Cyril and John, a most difficult thing to do when it is considered that there is no extant catechetical work (like those of Cyril's pre-baptismal lectures) of John in Greek (or any other language)! Hence, if Doval has indeed made a strong case for Cyrilline authorship of the *Mystagogical Catecheses*, his conclusions can only be accepted as plausible but certainly not as definitive. Indeed, Cyril himself in the later years of his episcopacy may well have known the rites described in the *Mystagogical Catecheses* without being the 'author' of the document itself.

1.2. Juliette Day

Unlike Doval, whose method was primarily literary without ignoring the liturgical context, Juliette Day's approach to the authorship of the *Mystagogical Catecheses* is classic *Liturgiewissenschaft*. Her methodological question is not about authorship *per se* but about whether or not the baptismal liturgy in the Jerusalem *Mystagogical Catecheses* accurately reflects the time of Cyril, or whether it belongs to a period after that, namely, John, or possibly even later. The importance of an answer to this, of course, is that if the baptismal liturgy reflects a time later than Cyril, then the Jerusalem liturgy, including a strongly pronounced Romans 6 baptismal theology and a post-baptismal anointing, has itself been influenced from elsewhere and, as a consequence, the *Mystagogical*

---

[20] *Ibid.*, pp. 150-161.
[21] See Edward Yarnold, 'Anaphoras Without Institution Narratives?', *Studia Patristica* 30 (1997) 395-410.

Catecheses themselves can *not* be the source for similar liturgical development elsewhere. According to Day, the baptismal liturgy of the *Mystagogical Catecheses* can be no earlier than well *after* 397 (perhaps not yet even in Jerusalem until the end of the *fifth* century!), the year when Porphyrius, former senior presbyter at the Holy Sepulchre who, according to Day, did not know the baptismal rite of the *Mystagogical Catecheses*, left to become bishop of Gaza.[22] And, after a close comparative analysis of the sources for Christian initiation in the Syrian and Egyptian liturgical traditions, including the different rites apparently reflected in Cyril of Jerusalem's *Baptismal Catecheses* and that of the *Mystagogical Catecheses*, she concludes:

> 'In sequence, *MC* [*Mystagogical Catecheses*] resembles the Egyptian sources *CH* [*Canons of Hippolytus*] and *Ser.* [Sarapion of Thmuis], although there are some important distinctions between them, which indicate that *MC* was not *directly* influenced by these. It has become apparent that the two sources which lie closest to *MC*, both theologically and structurally, would appear to be those 'derived' from *AT* [*Apostolic Tradition*]. If *AT*, as reconstructed, lies behind *CH* and *AC* [*Apostolic Constitutions*], then the manner in which these two texts have interpreted their source is quite distinctive. It is possible, we suggest, that *MC* might be a hagiopolite interpretation of whatever source(s) — possibly even a version of *AT* — which lies behind the common sequence in *CH* and *AC*... [W]e suggest that the next stage of research into the liturgy of *MC* and Jerusalem needs to concern itself with what might have been the common source behind *CH*, *AC* and *MC*.'[23]

As we shall see below, Day's study offers, I believe, intriguing arguments both for new interpretations of the *Mystagogical Catecheses* and for new critical studies in the sources of Hagiopolite liturgy. If she is correct, her work would underscore one of the contemporary approaches in the study of early liturgy, namely, that Jerusalem, as a pilgrimage center, is just as much the *recipient* of new and innovative liturgical practices as it is the creator and exporter of new liturgical practices.[24] At the same time, her conclusions about authorship and date with regard to the baptismal liturgy would either be strengthened or weakened by a similar analysis of the eucharistic liturgy and anaphora in the *Mystagogical Catecheses*, such as attempted by Doval. Unless we are to assume that *Mystagogical Catecheses* 4 and 5 belong to a different stratum of

---

[22] Day, *The Baptismal Liturgy of Jerusalem* (see n. 11), p. 134.

[23] *Ibid.*, p. 138.

[24] On this, see Paul Bradshaw, *The Search for the Origins of Christian Worship*, revised and enlarged edition (London, 2002), pp. 113-117.

the document than 1-3, then it would seem that the dating of the eucharistic liturgy would be of great importance in resolving the question. Does the eucharistic liturgy reflect a mid- to late fourth-century or a later fourth and early fifth-century liturgical context? If later, then why do the *Mystagogical Catecheses* not contain an anaphoral text closer to that of *Saint James*? If the eucharist reflects the earlier context, which most scholars would assert, then why does the baptismal liturgy not reflect a similar overall context with the distinctions from the *Baptismal Catecheses* explained as being due to developments in the Jerusalem rite in the time of Cyril, as Doval concludes?

Similarly, Day's appeal to *The Life of Porphyrius* by Mark the Deacon, while logical in that Porphyrius was cross warden at the Holy Sepulchre in the 390s before his becoming bishop of Gaza in 397, is, by her own admission, not without its problems.[25] Not only are there serious literary problems with the text, including re-workings and historical inaccuracies, but the paucity of explicit baptismal references reduces the authority of the document often to an *argumentum ex silentio*. Further, in the context of the reception of heretics in the document, Day *does* note that there are references to the 'sealing' of those received which might have some parallel to the post-baptismal chrismation in Jerusalem. She writes:

> 'Porphyrius and the bishop of Caesarea receive an Arian boat captain by sealing him, praying over him and giving him the "divine mysteries" (eucharist) (*V. Porph.* 57). The spurious seventh canon of the Council of Constantinople (381) states that Arians were to be received by anathematising their heresy and then, "they are sealed or anointed with holy Chrism on the forehead, eyes, nostrils, mouth and ears. As we seal them we say, 'The seal of the gift of the Holy Spirit.'" If this canon is from within our time period, and we are mindful of Varghese's conclusion that it dates from the second half of the fifth century, then it may point to a ritual to complete baptism, which is not too dissimilar to that in *MC* 3.4. However, if this ritual is only for the reception of heretics and schismatics, then we cannot expect this episode to provide us with evidence of the normal post-immersion sequence in Gaza.'[26]

While Day is right to be cautious about this canon of Constantinople and the use of this rite for the reception of heretics, the parallels with the post-baptismal rites in Jerusalem are too strong not to be taken into consideration. Here, at least with regard to Constantinople, is a parallel ritual reference not based on silence.

---

[25] Day, *The Baptismal Liturgy of Jerusalem* (see n. 11), pp. 28-29.
[26] *Ibid.*, pp. 124-125.

2. The Liturgical Context Revisited: Macarius of Jerusalem and Abraham Terian

It is not very often in our field of early Christian liturgy that new documents are discovered, which necessarily compel us toward re-examining various scholarly presuppositions and conclusions. If Abraham Terian is correct in his analysis, however, this is precisely what has now happened with the document entitled, *Of the Blessed Macarius, Patriarch of the Holy City Jerusalem: Canonical Letter to the Armenians Concerning the Regulation of the Ordinances of the Catholic Church Which it is not Right to Transgress by Definition or Command*, and now published by him, as noted above, under the title of *Macarius of Jerusalem, Letter to the Armenians (A.D. 335)*.[27] That is, long thought to be a sixth-century document, thanks to the work of N. Akinian in the early twentieth century, who claimed that it was from Macarius II of Jerusalem (patriarch from 563-575), Terian argues convincingly that it should be dated A.D. 335. As such, the letter comes from Macarius I, who was patriarch from A.D. 314-335/6, during the time of the vast Constantinian building programs in Jerusalem and Bethlehem.

I shall leave it to others, who are experts in the field of Armenian studies, to evaluate what this document may have to say about the shape of Armenian liturgy in this time period,[28] but with regard to Jerusalem liturgy itself, especially with Christian initiation, this letter is a potential goldmine. If Terian's dating is correct, then it is highly significant that already in 335, several years before even the *Baptismal Catecheses* of Cyril, the baptismal rite of Jerusalem already included a period of catechesis, both pre- and post-baptismal anointing, and a Romans 6 paschal theological interpretation, along with an Epiphany Jordan-based, new birth interpretation and a Pentecost one, since all three of these feasts are described herein as regular baptismal occasions.[29] In other words, the

---

[27] See n. 12.

[28] Certainly the earlier dating of this document would strongly support the conclusions of Gabriele Winkler on the Armenian baptismal rites. See Gabriele Winkler, *Das Armenische Initiationsrituale: Entwicklungsgeschichtliche und liturgievergleichende Untersuchung der Quellen des 3. bis 10. Jahrhunderts*, Orientalia Christiana Analecta 217 (Rome, 1982).

[29] See Terian, *Macarius of Jerusalem* (see n. 12), pp. 121ff. It would be hard to reconcile the contents of Jerusalem liturgy reflected in this *Letter* with what is known of the shape and contents of Jerusalem liturgy in the sixth century or later. That is, a later date would undoubtedly reflect the more sophisticated theological interpretation we encounter in the *Mystagogical Catecheses*.

baptismal rite reflected in this *Letter of Macarius* has several parallels to the rite, if not yet the more sophisticated mystagogical interpretation, known to the author of the *Mystagogical Catecheses*. As Terian notes with regard to the use of Romans 6:

> 'The notion of baptism as participation in Christ's death ... goes back to Paul (Rom 6:4-5). While this notion was commonplace in the early churches in the West, it was not as common in the churches of the East, where the font and the water were perceived more as a womb or an embryonic sack ...The Letter of Macarius shows that the two notions were part of the baptismal theology of the Jerusalem Church *before Cyril*, but that it remained for the latter to articulate them in his exceptional way.'[30]

Further, even the way of administering the post-baptismal chrismation described in *Mystagogical Catechesis* III.4 on the forehead, ears, nostrils, and breast, seems to be paralleled by the statement in the *Letter of Macarius* that 'since they [the Armenians] do not have sufficient oil of sealing, which is from the Apostles and is kept here, they do not anoint the infant's entire organs of sense.'[31] Together with the *Canons of Hippolytus* in Egypt, the Greek original of which may well be in the 330s,[32] the *Letter of Macarius* would be then one of our first Orthodox witnesses to the post-baptismal anointing of the senses. But is this post-baptismal 'oil of sealing', which Terian interprets as the equivalent of *myron*, the means by which the Holy Spirit is bestowed on the baptized? There is some ambiguity here. For, on the one hand, Macarius can appear to associate the gift of the Holy Spirit with the baptismal immersion itself, writing that:

> '...forgiveness of sins and salvation of souls are granted out of the grace of the Spirit to those who are baptized in the holy font. And the Holy Spirit does not despise those who yearn for piety, but, bending low, descends and sanctifies through right confession of faith (and) *by means of the water of the holy font*.'[33]

---

[30] *Ibid.*, p. 123 [emphasis added].

[31] *Ibid.*, p. 105. On the post-baptismal sealing of the senses see the intriguing hypothesis of Alistair Logan, 'The Mystery of the Five Seals: Gnostic Initiation Reconsidered', *Vigiliae Christianae* 51 (1997) 188-206.

[32] On the dating of the *Canons of Hippolytus*, see C. Markschies, 'Wer schrieb die sogennante *Traditio Apostolica*? Neue Beobachtungen und Hypothesen zu einer kaum lösbaren Frage aus der altkirchlichen Literaturgeschichte', in eds. W. Kinzig, C. Markschies and M. Vinzent, *Tauffragen und Bekenntnis* (Berlin and New York, 1999), pp. 1-74. For relevant texts of the *Canons of Hippolytus* see E.C. Whitaker, *Documents of the Baptismal Liturgy* (hereafter, DBL), revised and expanded edition by Maxwell E. Johnson, Alcuin Club Collections 79 (London, 2003), pp. 129-132.

[33] Terian, *Macarius of Jerusalem* (see n. 12), p. 109 [emphasis added].

On the other hand, the bestowal of the Holy Spirit on the baptized is elsewhere connected to a post-baptismal context. In reference to baptism on Pentecost, Macarius writes:

> 'But on the grace-bestowing and sanctifying day of Pentecost was the luminous manifestation of the quickening Spirit, which, in the form of fiery tongues, descended on the Apostles, granting them that by laying hands on those who are being baptized (these shall) receive gifts from the grace of the Spirit. After the same pattern we also on the same day, bestow the same Spirit by laying hands on those who are baptized. We fulfill the pattern of this with unfailing care, that we may become perfect. And thus when we lay hands with right confession of faith the Holy Spirit is bestowed for our salvation, illuminating those who are called to adoption; and in faith *we are anointed with the oil of holiness*.'[34]

While Terian is probably correct here in interpreting the laying on of hands as related to the post-baptismal anointing itself and, hence, already associated with the 'seal' of the Holy Spirit in the Jerusalem liturgy, it is also possible that in these two references above we are dealing with a situation similar to that described by Doval for the rite known in Cyril's *Baptismal Catechesis* 16.26. That is, Macarius' references to the Holy Spirit descending and sanctifying 'by means of the holy font,' and to the Pentecostal apostolic laying on of hands *could* both be interpreted as referring to the baptismal immersion at the time of the 'right confession of faith'. At the same time, however, the fact that in this same context Macarius speaks of being 'anointed with the oil of holiness' does suggest that more is going on here than that. Might it be that this text actually helps us interpret Cyril's reference in *Baptismal Catechesis* 16.26 to the fact that, in spite of biblical references to hand-laying, he could not yet tell the catechumens 'what manner' in which the Holy Spirit would be given to them? And the manner he could not yet tell them was *not* the immersion, which may well have included a hand-laying at the time of baptismal confession and immersion, but a post-baptismal chrismation with the 'oil of holiness', *myron*. And, if so, just as it would have been up to the author of the *Mystagogical Catecheses* to articulate more strongly the womb and tomb theology of baptism, flowing now more decidedly from a Romans 6 approach, so too would it have been up to him to develop a more developed theology of the post-baptismal chrismation as, specifically, the conferral of the Seal of the Holy Spirit.

---

[34] *Ibid.*, pp. 125-126.

In this context, it is also important to note that the documents to which Juliette Day refers as somewhat parallel to the *Mystagogical Catecheses* are also, it now appears, somewhat parallel in baptismal structure to this *Letter of Macarius*. While the structure of the baptismal rite in *Canons of Hippolytus*, like its source, the so-called *Apostolic Tradition*, follows the post-baptismal chrismation with an episcopal hand-laying prayer and possible second anointing, with ambiguous pneumatic references,[35] only Prayer 16 in Sarapion's prayers, the prayer for what is clearly the consecration of the post-baptismal *chrism*, unambiguously refers to the baptized being 'sealed' by this chrism as they become 'sharers in the gift of the Holy Spirit'.[36] This is already the case in ca. A.D. 350, at least in Egypt! A similar parallel both to the *Letter of Macarius* and to, at least, the liturgical structure reflected in the *Mystagogical Catecheses*, appears, of course, in Book VII. 22 of the *Apostolic Constitutions*, where the following is stated:

> 'Beforehand you shall anoint with holy oil, then you shall baptize with water, and finally you shall seal with chrism, so that the anointing may be the partaking of the Holy Spirit, the water the symbol of the death [of Christ], and the chrism the seal of the covenants.'[37]

Hence, in the 330s (the *Canons*), the 350s (Sarapion), and the 380s (*Apostolic Constitutions*), we see structural liturgical parallels and some theological parallels with what is reflected in the *Baptismal Catecheses* and the *Mystagogical Catecheses*, as well as now in the *Letter of Macarius*. If the theology of the post-baptismal anointing is more developed in *Mystagogical Catechesis* III.1, 4, and 5 than it is in these other documents, with the notable exception of Sarapion of Thmuis, that is no reason whatsoever to assume a date any later than the final years of Cyril's episcopate for this interpretation. This, it would seem, is an *interpretation* of a rite, perhaps at least as old as the 330s in Jerusalem, not the development of a *new* post-baptismal ritual *after* the time of Cyril of Jerusalem himself!

---

[35] See DBL, p. 131. Like the Latin version of the *Apostolic Tradition*, the hand-laying prayer in the *Canons* seems to imply that the Holy Spirit has already been 'poured' out on the baptized: 'We bless you, Lord God almighty, for that you have made these worthy to be born again, that you pour your Holy Spirit on them, and to be one in the body of the Church not being excluded by alien works; but, just as you have granted them forgiveness for their sins, grant them also the pledge of your kingdom; through our Lord Jesus Christ, through whom be glory to you, with him and the Holy Spirit, to ages of ages. Amen.'

[36] Maxwell E. Johnson, *The Prayers of Sarapion of Thmuis: A Literary, Liturgical, and Theological Analysis*, Orientalia Christiana Analecta 249 (Rome, 1995), pp. 64-65.

[37] See DBL, p. 37.

3. Fourth-Century Jerusalem Baptismal Liturgy in Development

Having now looked briefly at these three recent important studies, it is important to ask whether we are today at a scholarly impasse, incapable of resolution with regard to the evolution of the Jerusalem baptismal liturgy, or if we are at present in a better position to suggest, at least in broad strokes, how those rites of Christian initiation evolved. If Terian is correct in his 335 dating of Macarius' *Letter to the Armenians*, then, since the rite known to the author of the *Mystagogical Catecheses* would have already been known earlier in Jerusalem, at least, in embryonic form, as well as in the time of Cyril's *Baptismal Catecheses*, Day's thesis that the rites of the *Mystagogical Catecheses* could not have been in Jerusalem until *after* 397 falls to the wayside. And, as such, one is led back to the plausibility of the theory of Cyrilline authorship held by Doval, and the most logical explanation for the differences between the *Baptismal* and *Mystagogical Catecheses* stem not only from further evolution in the rites over thirty years but in their theological interpretations, as well as from the fact that they are addressed to people at different stages within the initiation process.

Yet, at the same time, the most intriguing and promising part of Day's hypothesis on the development of the Jerusalem initiation rite are, I believe, the parallels she notes between the baptismal liturgy in the *Mystagogical Catecheses*, the *Prayers of Sarapion of Thmuis*, and in those documents derived from the so-called *Apostolic Tradition*, ascribed to Hippolytus of Rome, namely, *The Canons of Hippolytus* and the *Apostolic Constitutions*. What Day has done, in fact, is to re-open the question, earlier dealt with by Geoffrey Cuming[38] and Bryan Spinks,[39] on the question of the relationship and potential influence between Egypt and Jerusalem in the fourth century. By way of summarizing her conclusions she writes:

> 'Structurally, the rites of *CH* [*Canons of Hippolytus*, and *Ser.* [Sarapion of Thmuis] have much in common with *MC* [the *Mystagogical Catecheses*]: all contain a renunciation, adherence, pre-immersion anointing, immersion, and post-immersion anointing ... [W]e find that *CH* is closest to *MC* over the exorcistic pre-immersion anointing, although there it is described as the oil *of* exorcism rather than the oil which has been exorcised, and in *Ser.* we

---

[38] Geoffrey Cuming, 'Egyptian Elements in the Jerusalem Liturgy', *Journal of Theological Studies* 25 (1974) 117-124.

[39] Bryan Spinks, 'The Jerusalem Liturgy of the Catecheses Mystagogicae: Syrian or Egyptian?', *Studia Patristica* 18 (1989) 391-395.

noted a mixed interpretation, exorcistic and prophylactic, which ... could possibly be inferred from *MC* 2.3 ...
The only Egyptian elements, which Cuming identified in *MC* were the baptismal formula and the post-immersion anointing, but ... the pre-immersion rituals also have much in common with *MC*. Of all the sources discussed *MC* is closer to *CH* than any single other source, and that *CH* predates *MC* makes it a credible possibility that the former could have influenced the later. The lack of a theology of baptism in *CH* is a complicating factor, although the use ... of Romans typology in *Ser.* does suggest that a shift to this typology occurred in this province before Jerusalem. This can only indicate that the author of *MC* was possibly influenced by a rite, which was more like that of *CH* and *Ser.*, than that of Cyril [i.e., the *Baptismal Catecheses*] and Chrysostom, which is not to say that Jerusalem found a model for its rite in Egypt, but that *MC* may well have been subject to an influence from a source sharing similarities with *CH*.'[40]

For Day, this source, of course, might even be a version of the so-called *Apostolic Tradition* itself, which may well mean that together with the *Canons of Hippolytus* and the *Apostolic Constitutions*, the baptismal rite of the *Mystagogical Catecheses* may be yet one more redaction or derivative tradition in the overly complicated history of that document. In his study of baptism in the Alexandrian tradition some years ago Bradshaw suggested that the pre-baptismal exorcistic anointing entered the Egyptian rites via influence from the *Apostolic Tradition* and, as we point out in our recent commentary on that document, the process of 'daily exorcism' during the final preparation period of catechesis does have its closest parallel in Cyril's *Baptismal Catechesis* I. 5-6, and in Egeria's diary.[41] Further, if we are dealing with some kind of *Apostolic Tradition* type source behind the *Canons of Hippolytus*, the *Apostolic Constitutions*, and now, allegedly, the *Mystagogical Catecheses*, the fact that, together with Sarapion, only *one* post-baptismal anointing appears in the *Apostolic Constitutions* and the *Mystagogical Catecheses*, and that not all manuscripts of the *Canons* have a *second* post-baptismal anointing,[42] may also tend to confirm our hypothesis that the second post-baptismal anointing, reserved to the bishop in the *Apostolic Tradition,* is a later development in the textual history of that document and was not yet in the earliest version of the *Canons*.[43]

---

[40] Day, *The Baptismal Liturgy of Jerusalem* (see n. 11), pp. 137-138.
[41] Paul Bradshaw, Maxwell Johnson and L. Edward Phillips, *The Apostolic Tradition*, Hermeneia (Minneapolis, 2002), p. 109.
[42] DBL, p. 131.
[43] Bradshaw, Johnson and Phillips, *The Apostolic Tradition* (see n. 41), p. 133.

While Day is careful enough not to suggest direct influence from Egypt on the Jerusalem rites, the possibility of an indirect influence is certainly there and her thesis of the possibility of a version of the *Apostolic Tradition* is one I find rather compelling. With this possibility I remain intrigued by the old hypothesis of I.M. Hanssens[44] that the *Apostolic Tradition* itself had an Alexandrian or, at least, Egyptian origin. It may yet be that Egypt had an even stronger influence on the development of early Christian initiation rites than has been assumed up to now.

Whatever the influence of Egypt, direct or indirect, may have been, nothing of this part of Day's hypothesis necessitates a later date for the *Mystagogical Catecheses* than a date towards the end of Cyril's episcopate. In fact, Macarius' *Letter to the Armenians,* presumably in 335, already reflects the blessing of two different baptismal oils (an 'oil of holiness', consecrated by the bishop for the post-baptismal anointing, and another oil for use at the pre-baptismal anointing),[45] a baptismal theology based on Romans 6, but not exclusively, and a *Canons of Hippolytus* type post-baptismal anointing of the senses. Hence, along with Terian's now earlier dating of Macarius' *Letter to the Armenians*, the baptismal liturgies reflected in the *Baptismal Catecheses*, the *Mystagogical Catecheses,* the *Canons of Hippolytus*, the *Apostolic Constitutions*, and the *Prayers of Sarapion of Thmuis* need be nothing other than various fourth-century appropriations of common source material. Just as the dates of the other documents place us well within the mid to late fourth century, there is no reason to assume that the rites reflected in the *Mystagogical Catecheses* should be dated any later than them.

It is here, in this overall context of what one might refer to as the 'Egyptian connection' of Christian initiation in Jerusalem, that the eucharist, especially the anaphora, needs to be part of the discussion. Unfortunately, Macarius' *Letter* gives us next to no information about the eucharistic liturgy or the anaphora,[46] and, as noted, Day does not concern herself with this in her analysis of the baptismal rites. It would seem, however, that attention to recent scholarship on the anaphora in *Mystagogical Catecheses* V would be rather crucial in coming to a conclusion on the historical context of the Jerusalem liturgy reflected

---

[44] J.M. Hanssens, *La Liturgie d'Hippolyte: Ses documents, son titulaire, ses origins et son charactère,* 2nd edition, Orientalia Christiana Analecta 155 (Rome, 1965), pp. 463-470.

[45] Terian, *Macarius of Jerusalem* (see n. 12), pp. 104-106.

[46] *Ibid.*, pp. 131-136.

therein. Contemporary scholarship on the Jerusalem anaphora, in fact, may actually support that part of Day's hypothesis of some kind of, at least, indirect influence from Egypt. It is not necessary here to revisit all of this in detail,[47] but some treatment is important. Because the structure of the anaphora described in *Mystagogical Catecheses* V consists of dialogue, praise for creation (preface), sanctus, epiclesis, and intercessions, in that order, Geoffrey Cuming came to nuance his earlier position that there was *direct* Egyptian influence on Jerusalem and argued rather that such obvious parallels with an Alexandrian anaphoral pattern (e.g., Saint Mark, Der Balizeh, and the Louvain Coptic Papyrus) suggested some kind of common source, a source he identified as 'something very like' the fragmentary and controversial *Strasbourg Papyrus*. He wrote:

> '*St Mark* and *St James* probably had a common ancestor... If we had a papyrus fragment of *St James*, it would probably contain something very like the Strasbourg papyrus of *St Mark*. We do not have such a fragment, but we do have Cyril's *Catecheses*. If Sanctus and epiclesis are added to the Strasbourg anaphora, not at the end as in *St Mark*, but between the thanksgiving and the offering, the result is: thanksgiving – Sanctus – epiclesis – offering – intercessions; in fact, the exact sequence set out by Cyril. When the Jerusalem anaphora was merged with *St Basil* to produce *St James*, the first step would be the addition of institution narrative and anamnesis; then a christological section would take the place of the epiclesis, which would be moved to its Basilian position between the offering and the intercessions; the exact sequence of *St James*.'[48]

As is well known, this merging of the Jerusalem anaphora with *St. Basil* to produce *St. James* was part of the work of Cuming's student, John R.K. Fenwick in his study *The Anaphoras of St. Basil and St. James: An Investigation Into Their Common Origin.*[49] It is not my intent here to enter into this debate and try to solve these controversial issues about the origins of the Jerusalem anaphora itself but simply to draw attention to how the question of the anaphora and its contents may

---

[47] On this see especially Cuming, 'Egyptian Elements in the Jerusalem Liturgy' (see n. 38) and Spinks, 'The Jerusalem Liturgy of the Catecheses Mystagogicae' (see n. 39).

[48] Geoffrey Cuming, 'The Shape of the Anaphora', *Studia Patristica* 20 (1989) 333-345, on p. 341.

[49] Fenwick, *The Anaphoras of St. Basil and James* (see n. 9), pp. 36-45. For recent work on the Basilian anaphorae see Gabriele Winkler, *Die Basilius-Anaphora: Edition der beiden armenischen Redaktionen und der relevanten Fragmente, Übersetzung und Zusammenschau aller Versionen im Licht der Orientalischen Überlieferungen*, Anaphorae Orientales 2: Anaphorae Armenicae 2 (Rome, 2005); Achim Budde, *Die ägyptische Basilius-Anaphora: Text – Kommentar – Geschichte*, Jerusalemer Theologisches Forum 7 (Münster, 2004).

provide additional support for Day's hypothesis about a common source for Egyptian and Jerusalem initiation rites, if not a later date for the Jerusalem rites. While the *Canons of Hippolytus* contains no anaphora whatsoever (indeed, of the various 'versions' of the so-called *Apostolic Tradition*, only the Latin and Ethiopic do contain one), it was Gregory Dix, who suggested that the anaphora of *St. James* itself, at an earlier stage, would have been parallel in content to that of the anaphora in the *Apostolic Tradition*.[50] And in our commentary on the *Apostolic Tradition* we note that the *Strasbourg Papyrus* offers a model of a prayer that moves directly from 'praise through offering to petition'.[51]

It would seem, however, that, apart from any influence, direct or indirect, an issue with regard to dating the anaphora in *Mystagogical Catechesis* V, and, hence, the *Mystagogical Catecheses* as a whole, would be the presence or not of an institution narrative within it. Here, with the exception of Yarnold and Doval, both of whom assert Cyrilline authorship and the presence of the narrative, most contemporary scholars would argue that there was no narrative in the anaphora described in this text. Together with the recent conclusions of Gabriele Winkler on the 'missing' or interpolated institution narrative in Ethiopic anaphoras,[52] most scholars today would tend to put *Didache* 9 and 10, the *Strasbourg Papyrus*, and the anaphora of *Addai and Mari* together with the anaphora in *Mystagogical Catecheses* V as witnesses to an anaphoral pattern that did not yet contain this narrative.[53] Indeed, again in our own commentary on the *Apostolic Tradition*, we suggested that the institution narrative in the Latin and Ethiopic versions was quite likely a fourth-century innovation made at the time when the institution narrative was beginning to be added to anaphoral texts. Neither the presence nor the absence of the narrative of institution may be taken as absolute proof of the dating of the *Mystagogical Catecheses* in general. But it would seem that holding to a date *after* 397 would make the absence of such a narrative down right unthinkable, especially when the relatively complete

---

[50] Gregory Dix, *The Shape of the Liturgy* (London, 1945), p. 205.

[51] Bradshaw, Johnson and Phillips, *The Apostolic Tradition* (see n. 41), p. 46.

[52] See Gabriele Winkler, 'A New Witness to the Missing Institution Narrative', in *Studia Liturgica Diversa: Essays in Honor of Paul F. Bradshaw*, eds. Maxwell E. Johnson and L. Edward Phillips (Portland, OR, 2004), pp. 117-128.

[53] Cf. Emmanuel J. Cutrone, 'Cyril's Mystagogical Catecheses and the Evolution of the Jerusalem Anaphora', *Orientalia Christiana Periodica* 44 (1978) 52-64; Fenwick, *The Anaphoras of St. Basil and James* (see n. 9), pp. 36-45; Burreson, 'The Anaphora of the Mystagogical Catecheses of Cyril of Jerusalem' (see n. 9), pp. 131-151.

anaphora of *St. James* is itself dated to the end of the fourth century.[54] Sources and possible influences on the Jerusalem anaphora, yes; a later dating, presumably at the time when *St. James* would have already been in use, no. Even if Cyril himself is not the 'author' of the *Mystagogical Catecheses*, it would seem that either with an institution narrative or not in the text, *Mystagogical Catechesis* V would be inadequate as an exposition of a Jerusalem anaphoral shape *later* than the late fourth century, that is, quite possibly the later years of Cyril's episcopate.

4. Conclusion

In light of the foregoing overview and critique of recent scholarship, what might we say about the baptismal liturgy in fourth-century Jerusalem? I would suggest four tentative conclusions, all of which await much more detailed research:

a. The question of the authorship of the *Mystagogical Catecheses* remains unresolved, although there is no compelling reason to assert that Cyril of Jerusalem himself would not have known in the late 380s the rites as described therein.

b. If Macarius' *Letter to the Armenians* has been correctly dated and analyzed now by Abraham Terian, not only are Epiphany and Pentecost as baptismal days, along with that of Easter, confirmed for an early Jerusalem period, but the implication that Easter was not yet the *preferred* baptismal occasion in the 330s is also underscored.

c. Similarly, several other elements once thought later, now, thanks to Macarius' *Letter to the Armenians*, appear as part of the earlier Jerusalem tradition. Among them are: the use of a Romans 6 baptismal paradigm, the presence and use of two different oils for the pre- and post-baptismal anointings, and with the post-baptismal anointing itself, a signing or sealing of the senses.

d. While it is difficult, in light of a), b), and c), as well as issues related to the development of the Jerusalem anaphora, to support Juliette Day's thesis of the *Mystagogical Catecheses* coming from a time *after* 397, her hypothesis of indirect influence from Egypt on Jerusalem, or that Jerusalem and Egyptian liturgical texts had a common

---

[54] See Burreson, 'The Anaphora of the Mystagogical Catecheses of Cyril of Jerusalem' (see n. 9), pp. 166-167.

source behind them, perhaps even a version of the *Apostolic Tradition*, seems right on target and calls for additional detailed work in the sources themselves.

The study of the rites of Christian initiation in fourth-century Jerusalem remains a topic for which much more can and must be done. While the earlier dating of many elements afforded by Terian's edition and study of Macarius' *Letter* still enables us to view Jerusalem as the influential exporter, if not originator, of many standard aspects of fourth-century baptismal practice, Day's suggestion of influences and/or common sources also makes Jerusalem the potential recipient of ritual elements elsewhere. Day's suggestion 'that the next stage of research into the liturgy of *MC* and Jerusalem needs to concern itself with what might have been the common source behind *CH*, *AC* and *MC*,'[55] offers a solid starting point for the next step in research. Indeed, perhaps it is time for someone to re-visit the development of fourth-century Jerusalem liturgy especially in relationship, not only to the *Apostolic Tradition,* but to Egyptian liturgy in the same time period and so pick up the possible 'Egyptian connection' to Jerusalem also opened up again for us by Day and so begin where Geoffrey Cuming and Bryan Spinks left off in the 1980s.

---

[55] Day, *The Baptismal Liturgy of Jerusalem* (see n. 11), p. 138.

RESERVATION AND VENERATION OF
THE EUCHARIST IN THE ORTHODOX TRADITIONS

Robert F. TAFT

A. RESERVATION

I. Reservation Usage Today

Today in the Eastern Orthodox, Oriental Orthodox, and Assyrian Churches, only the Eastern Orthodox and Armenian Apostolic Churches always reserve in church a small amount of the eucharistic species.[1] But this is for communion in emergencies, and not with the idea of 'creating a sacramental presence', a notion that is a pure 'Latinism'. In Byzantine Orthodox usage it is customary to reserve at the Holy Thursday liturgy a portion of the consecrated Body intincted with the Precious Blood. This reserve, for use in emergencies, is generally kept for the whole year,[2]

---

[1] This paper is based on my Italian conference published in: 'Custodia e venerazione dell'eucaristia nelle tradizioni ortodosse', published in *Assemblea santa, Forme, presenze, presidenza: Atti del VI Convegno liturgico internazionale, Bose, 5-7 June 2008*, ed. G. Boselli (Bose, 2009), pp. 231-253. For a more detailed treatment of the topic see R.F. Taft, *A History of the Liturgy of St. John Chrysostom, vol. VI: The Communion, Thanksgiving, and Concluding Rites*, OCA 281 (Rome, 2008), chap. III and Excursus II.

Abbreviations used in the notes: BHG = F. Halkin, Bibliotheca hagiographica Graeca, Subsidia hagiographica 8a (Brussels, 1957³). CSCO = Corpus scriptorum Christianorum orientalium. CSEL = Corpus Scriptorum Ecclesiasticorum Latinorum. CSS = Cistercian Studies Series. DTC = *Dictionnaire de théologie catholique*. LBG = *Lexikon zur byzantinischen Gräzität besonders des 9.-12. Jahrhunderts*, Österreichische Akademie der Wissenschaften, Phil.-hist. Klasse Denkschriften 238 etc., Veröffentlichungen der Kommission für Byzantinistik, hrsg. von H. Hunger, Bd. VI/1- (Vienna, 1996-). OCA = Orientalia Christiana Analecta. ODB 1-3 = *The Oxford Dictionary of Byzantium*, eds. A. Kazhdan et alii, 3 vols. (New York and Oxford, 1991). PG = J.P. Migne, *Patrologia Graeca* (Paris, 1857-1866). PL = J.P. Migne, *Patrologia Latina* (Paris, 1841-1864). SC = Sources chrétiennes. ST = Studi e testi. TL = P.N. Trempelas, Αἱ τρεῖς Λειτουργίαι κατὰ τοὺς ἐν Ἀθήναις κώδικας, Texte und Forschungen zur byzantinisch-neugriechischen Philologie 15 (Athens, 1935).

[2] S. Alexopoulos, *The Presanctified Liturgy in the Byzantine Rite: A Comparative Analysis of its Origins, Evolution, and Structural Components*, Liturgia Condenda 21 (Leuven, 2009), p. 175, note 504.

which is why the host is sometimes desiccated by toasting it to prevent corruption,[3] a usage that goes back to at least the 13th century.[4]

II. Eastern Eucharistic Reservation in the Non-Byzantine Sources

The absence of reservation in the other Eastern Churches apart from the Byzantine and Armenian is not traditional, however, for we find evidence of reservation in numerous Late-Antique and Medieval sources.

1. Syria and Palestine

For Northern Syria, we learn from the late 5th c. Syriac *Vita of St. Symeon Stylites* (died 459), that the stylite had a niche on his column with a pyx in which he kept the reserved Eucharist.[5] And ca. 600 John Moschus (ca. 540/50-619), *Pratum spirituale* 48, recounts how at the shrine of the Holy Sepulchre a deacon was fetched at night to give communion in the Body and Blood to a woman converted from Severianism.[6] Note that communion was given *under both species,* and obviously from the reserve, since it was night. A similar anecdote at the same shrine in *Pratum* 49 seems also to illustrate communion under both species apart from the liturgy.[7] Conversion accounts in *Pratum* 29-30 also

---

[3] See R.F. Taft, *A History of the Liturgy of St. John Chrysostom, vol. V: The Precommunion Rites*, OCA 261 (Rome, 2000), chap. IX.

[4] See the euchology ms *British Library Harl. 5561* (f. 31ʳ). Some Byzantine Catholics also follow this custom of toasting the reserve and keeping it until the next Holy Thursday, others, more commonly, renew the reserved species from time to time, even weekly. In his regulations for the Italo-Greek Catholics, Pope Benedict XIV (1740-1758) in §§VI. iii-iv of his 26 May 1742 constitution *Etsi pastoralis* branded this an abuse and ordered the reserve renewed every eight or at least every fifteen days: Benedicti PP. XIV, *Bulla 'Etsi pastoralis' de dogmatibus et ritibus ab Italo-Graecis tenendis atque servandis* (Rome, Typographia Polyglotta Sacrae Congregationis de Propaganda fide, 1889), p. 12.

[5] H. Hilgenfeld, 'Syrische Lebensschreibung des hl. Symeon', in H. Lietzmann, *Das Leben des heiligen Symeon Stulites*, Texte und Untersuchungen 32.4 (Leipzig, 1908), pp. 103.1, 111.12, 165.5-13 = §§98, 112, and Appendix B in *The Lives of Simeon Stylites*, Translated with an Introduction by Robert Doran. Foreword by Susan Ashbrook Harvey, CSS 112 (Kalamazoo, 1992), pp. 171-172, 215, 181; cf. P. Canivet, *Le monachisme syrien selon Théodoret de Cyr*, Théologie historique 42 (Paris, 1977), pp. 131-132. For the date see P. Peeters, *Le tréfonds oriental de l'hagiographie byzantine*, Subsidia hagiographica 26 (Brussels, 1950), p. 113.

[6] PG 87.3: 2904-5; John Moschos (also known as John Eviratus), *The Spiritual Meadow (Pratum Spirituale)*, Introduction, Translation and Notes by John Wortley, CSS 139 (Kalamazoo, 1992), p. 39.

[7] PG 87.3: 2904-5; Wortley (see n. 6), pp. 39-40.

exemplify cases of communion outside the liturgy.[8] And *Pratum* 79 relates, again in the context of a miracle account, how the laity took the Holy Thursday eucharistic species home and kept it for over a year.[9]

In an anecdote from Palestinian lavriotic monasticism, Anastasius of Sinai (flourished 640-700), *Narrations* 30, recounts how three solitaries come frequently to communicate invisibly from the reserved Eucharist kept in a 'receptacle (σκευοφόριον)' in the monastery.[10] Here too, it is obvious that the reserve contained several portions of the presanctified eucharistic gifts, doubtless not just for emergencies but for monastic communion outside the eucharistic liturgy.

West-Syrian canonical sources also provide abundant evidence that the eucharistic species were reserved and sometimes used for communion outside the liturgy. The sources in question are not actual synodal canons but rather norms anthologized from responses to queries posed to Johannan bar Qursos, bishop of Tella, in the 6th c. and Jacob of Edessa in the late 7th, and other 'Oriental Fathers'. Especially interesting is canon 8 attributed to John of Tella:[11]

'We have heard that impudent and ignorant men, who have not learned to distinguish the sacred (from the profane), dare to bring to the altar loaves (in a quantity) more than required by the congregation of the church or of the monastery; and, also, the cup in the same manner. After the consecration and the distribution, they precipitate in the manner of animals without intelligence and eat the rest. They have prepared all this in advance in order to satisfy their ferocious passion. This is (a matter of) guilt and accusation against them for having degraded the spiritual nourishment to the nourishment of their bodies. Therefore I admonish you that you not be seized by this sin, but ascertain the number of persons who (want to) receive (communion) and consecrate only what is required of the loaves. Put into the cup half wine and half water. (Then) the little pearls[12] shall be prepared. When it happens that there are more fragments (left over) they shall be gathered carefully and collected and shall be given on other days.
Take care also in handling the cup so that nothing remains in it. For, if a little remains of the blood, and at that moment there is further need, it is always possible to add what is not consecrated to that which is in the cup and to give from it to those who wish to receive.'[13]

---

[8] PG 87.3: 2876-80; Wortley (see n. 6), pp. 20-22.

[9] PG 87.3: 2396-97; Wortley (see n. 6), pp. 63-64.

[10] F. Nau, 'Le texte grec des récits utiles à l'âme d'Anastase (le Sinaïte)', *Oriens Christianus* 3 (1903) 56-90, here pp. 77-78.

[11] A. Vööbus, *The Synodicon in the West Syrian Tradition,* vol. I, CSCO 367-368 = Scriptores Syri 161-162 (Leuven, 1975), vol. 368, p. 145. The material and references in this section I owe to Prof. Susan Ashbrook Harvey of Brown University.

[12] A common term in antiquity for consecrated particles of the eucharistic body.

[13] Note the practice of consecration by contact, on which see section IV below.

Numerous other Syriac canonical responses, especially of John of Tella, concerning deaconess, layman, or laywoman bringing the sacrament to the sick,[14] are also proof-positive that some of the eucharistic species could be reserved at the liturgy for this purpose, since none of these lay-ministers of Holy Communion were able to celebrate the Eucharist. One may infer the same from questions whether one may give the sacrament to those of another Christian confession or receive it from them,[15] from queries about stylites reserving the Eucharist on their columns,[16] as well as from the responses of Jacob of Edessa about bringing the Eucharist to the sick, about keeping the reserve for a year, about what to do if the sacred species spoil, etc.[17] None of this casuistry would have any relevance unless the Eucharist was in fact reserved at least on some occasions for these purposes.

2. Mesopotamia

For the Assyro-Chaldean tradition of Mesopotamia, there is evidence in the ancient Syriac manuscripts of a daily monastic office for the reception of the presanctified communion by solitary monks, which obviously necessitated reserving the consecrated gifts.[18]

3. Egypt

For Egypt, Sophronios (ca. 550-638), Patriarch of Jerusalem in 634-638, in his *Miracles of Cyrus and John* (BHG 477-479) XII, 14 and XXXVI, 14-19, recounts instances from the lives of these Alexandrian martyrs of communion outside the liturgy from the reserve kept in the baptistery (φωτιστήριον).[19]

---

[14] Vööbus, *The Synodicon in the West Syrian Tradition* (see n. 11), p. 159, canon 9; pp. 198-199: responses 8, 11 of John of Tella; pp. 202-203: responses 32, 36; pp. 226-227: response 3.

[15] Ibid., pp. 204-205: responses 42, 44.

[16] Ibid., p. 227: response 4.

[17] Ibid., p. 239: responses 26-27; p. 241: response 33.

[18] See J. Mateos, 'Les "semaines des mystères" du carême chaldéen', *L'Orient syrien* 4 (1959) 449-458, here pp. 453-456; T. Parayady, *A Communion Service in the East Syrian Church*, Pontifical Oriental Institute unpublished doctoral dissertation (Rome, 1980), pp. 57ff, 113ff.

[19] *Los «Thaumata» de Sofronio: contribución al estudio de la «incubatio» cristiana*, ed. N. Fernández Marcos, Consejo superior de investigaciones cientificas, Instituto «Antonio de Nebrija», Manuales y anejos de «Emerita» 31 (Madrid, 1975), pp. 268, 325-327. See also L. Deubner, *Kosmas und Damian: Texte und Einleitung*, BHG 385 (Leipzig and Berlin, 1907), pp. 118-119.

4. Armenia

Finally, an Armenian source, *Response 9* in a 7th c. collection of canonical queries attributed to John the Stylite or, in some mss, to Movsïs Xorenac'i ('Moyses chorenensis' (fl. 7/8th c.?),[20] with the accompanying responses of Catholicos Sahak III Jorap'orec'i (677-701) 'and of many of his fellow bishops (*ac eius coepiscoporum plurimorum*)', witnesses to the practice of reserving the host, but insists on its being renewed every Sunday and not kept for a year, as some do.[21] The same conclusion must be drawn from *Responses 10-11* in the same source, that deal with what prayers to say when Holy Communion is brought to those imprisoned, or when a stylite communicates in solitude.[22]

Though this evidence is sporadic and largely anecdotal, it is widespread enough to prove that the Eucharist was reserved in local traditions, especially monastic, throughout the Byzantine Empire and beyond.

III. Eucharistic Reservation in Byzantium

Since the later documentation is inevitably the richest for Byzantine Orthodoxy, by far the largest and most widespread Eastern Church, I shall focus my attention there. The evidence for eucharistic reservation in the Byzantine tradition dates from the earliest witness to the Lenten Presanctified Liturgy in AD 691/692, when canon 52 of the Quinisext Council 'in Trullo' orders its celebration on weekdays of Lent,[23] and such a service is found thereafter throughout the euchology ms tradition.

In addition to this Lenten Liturgy of the Presanctified, the Byzantine Horologion or Book of Hours has an office, known as the Typika (Slavonic Изобразительница or Обедница) used only on aliturgical days, i.e., days of fast and penance when the full eucharistic liturgy is not celebrated. Today this service is seemingly without purpose. But its earliest extant witness in the 9th c. Horologion ms *Sinai Gr. 863* shows

<hr/>

[20] See R.W. Thomson, 'Moses Xorenac'i', ODB 2, pp. 1417-1418.

[21] *Scriptorum veterum nova collectio e Vaticanis codicibus edita,* 10 vols., ed. A. Mai (Rome, 1825-1838) vol. X, part 2, pp. 301-302. I have been unable to locate the Armenian original of these canons, but Mai in a note ('Admonitio') at the end of the canons, ibid. p. 316, expresses his debt to a certain 'P. Arsenium Angiarakianum, monachum instituti antoniani asseclam', who translated them from the Armenian.

[22] Ibid.

[23] *The Council in Trullo Revisited,* eds. G. Nedungatt and M. Featherstone, Kanonika 6 (Rome, 1995), p. 133.

the Typika to have been originally a Palestinian monastic communion service to provide the monks and nuns an opportunity to communicate even on aliturgical days when the eucharistic sacrifice was not celebrated.[24] There was also communion from the reserved gifts at Byzantine imperial ceremonies such as coronations and the appointment of civil servants,[25] as well as at weddings both imperial[26] and common,[27] and possibly also at the cathedral hour of Trithekti or 'Terce-Sext'.[28] All these services obviously required the reservation of the consecrated eucharistic gifts.

Even apart from such services, the fact that in Constantinople at least some of the Eucharist was reserved and made available for communion outside the liturgy is proven by instances of communion administered by non-priests — hence apart from the eucharistic services, all of which required the ministry of one in priestly orders. For example, canon 58 of the Quinisext Council 'in Trullo' decrees that laypersons may not give themselves communion if a bishop, presbyter, or deacon is on hand to do so[29] — thereby implying that the laity could give themselves communion if these clergy were not available. Patriarch St. Photios (877-886), writing to archbishop Leo of Calabria in 885/886, permits even deaconesses to bring communion to Christians in captivity.[30] And as late as

---

[24] J. Mateos, 'Un Horologion inédite de S. Sabas: Le Codex sinaïtique grec 863 (IXᵉ siècle)', *Mélanges Eugène Tisserant* III: *Orient chrétien*, ST 233 (Vatican, 1964), pp. 47-76, esp. pp. 54-55; cf. id., *La célébration de la parole dans la liturgie Byzantine: Étude historique*, OCA 191 (Rome, 1971), pp. 68-71. For further sources of what Baumstark calls 'the Old Palestinian Melkite Rite' see A. Baumstark, *Comparative Liturgy* (Westminster, MD, 1958), pp. 223-224; R.F. Taft, *The Byzantine Rite: A Short History*, American Essays in Liturgy (Collegeville, MN, 1992), pp. 56-57 and the literature cited there, pp. 64-65, notes 26-31.

[25] See mss *Paris Cosilin 213* (AD 1017) and 13th c. *Grottaferrata Gb* I: M. Arranz, *L'eucologio costantinopolitano agli inizi del secolo XI: Hagiasmatarion & Archieratikon (Rituale & Pontificale) con l'aggiunta del Leiturgikon (Messale)* (Rome, 1996), p. 340; *Coislin 213: Euchologe de la Grande Église*, ed. J.M. Duncan, (Rome, 1983), pp. 56-57; cf. Alexopoulos, *The Presanctified Liturgy* (see n. 2), p. 78.

[26] See mss 8th c. *Barberini Gr. 336: L'Eucologio Barberini gr. 336*, eds. S. Parenti and Elena Velkovska, Bibliotheca "Ephemerides Liturgicae". Subsidia 80 (Rome, 2000²), §172.6; *Paris Coislin 213* (AD 1017) and 13th c. *Grottaferrata Γβ I*: Arranz, *Eucologio* (see n. 25) p. 329.

[27] Alexopoulos, *The Presanctified Liturgy* (see n. 2), pp. 78-80, summarizing the research on the topic by P. Skaltses, Γάμος καί Θεία Λατρεία. Συμβολὴ στὴν Ἱστορία καὶ τὴ Θεολογία τῆς Λατρείας (Thessalonica, 1998), pp. 194-265.

[28] Alexopoulos, *The Presanctified Liturgy* (see n. 2), pp. 90-94.

[29] Nedungatt-Featherstone, *Trullo* (see n. 23), p. 138.

[30] *Les Regestes du Patriarcat de Constantinople, I: Les actes des patriarches*, fasc. 1-3, ed. V. Grumel, Le Patriarcat byzantin, série I (Kadiköy-Istanbul, 1932, 1936; Bucharest, 1947); fasc. 1 (Paris, 1972²); fasc. 4, ed. V. Laurent (Paris, 1971); fasc. 5-7, ed. J. Darrouzès (Paris, 1977, 1979, 1991), §531 (4).

St. Symeon of Thessalonica (d. 1429), *Responsiones* 40, a deacon, in the absence of a priest, is allowed to give viaticum to one in danger of death.[31]

In all these instances where only a layperson, deaconess, or deacon was present we are dealing, obviously, with communion from the reserved species apart from the eucharistic liturgy, which only a bishop or priest can celebrate. This means that some of the leftover gifts must have been reserved for such emergencies when no presbyter or deacon was available.

IV. How Did the Byzantines Reserve the Eucharist?

In Byzantine Orthodox usage, rubrics for reserving the presanctified Eucharist were found, if at all, either in *diataxeis* or ordinals of the Presanctified Liturgy, extant from the 15th c. on,[32] or in mss of the Liturgy of St. Basil the Great, celebrated on the Sundays of Lent when the reserve had to be prepared for the celebrations of the Presanctified Liturgy that week.

As to exactly what was reserved, the evidence is ambiguous when not downright contradictory. The earliest available witness for Constantinople is St. John Chrysostom's AD 404 letter to Pope St. Innocent I (401-417) concerning the outrages that preceded Chrysostom's deposition and exile that same year.[33] In his letter, Chrysostom complains of the indignities and violence he and his followers were subjected to in the persecution preceding his exile. The incident that interests us occurred during Holy Week of 404: '...on Great [i.e., Holy] Saturday itself, towards evening, with the rest of the day almost over, a whole platoon of soldiers entered the church... The soldiers, some of whom, we learned, were not even initiated,[34] entered to where the holy reserve was

---

[31] PG 155: 889B. A. Almazov, *Тайная исповедь в Православной Восточной Церкви. Опыт внешней истории*, 3 vols. (Odessa, 1894), vol. II, pp. 116-126, cites evidence to show that such practices continued in some Byzantine Orthodox Churches up through the 17th century.

[32] Called *An Explanation of the Divine Liturgy of the Presanctified*, as in the 18th-c. ms *Athens Ethnike Bibliotheke 767*, TL, pp. 195-197; and in later printed editions, e.g., *Εὐχολόγιον τὸ μέγα* (Rome, 1873), pp. 112-114.

[33] On the history of these events and their sources, see G. Bertonière, *The Historical Development of the Easter Vigil and Related Services in the Greek Church*, OCA 193 (Rome, 1972), pp. 109-111.

[34] I.e., had not yet received the rites of Christian initiation: baptism, chrismation, Eucharist.

kept, and...amid such a tumult, the Most Holy Blood of Christ was spilled...'.[35] Exactly where the eucharistic species were reserved is not clear, though it must have been in what was the scenario of these events, the baptistery of the cathedral or 'Great Church' of Constantinople, inaugurated in 360 and burnt down by Chrysostom's supporters in 404 during these very disturbances.[36]

In present Byzantine liturgical usage, the consecrated prosphoras reserved for the Presanctified Liturgy are intincted with the Precious Blood before being placed in the tabernacle,[37] a usage witnessed to already in the 12th c.[38] The sources, however, betray a certain conflict concerning this practice of signing or intincting with the Precious Blood the consecrated prosphoras reserved for the Presanctified Liturgy,[39] and several later Byzantine texts forbid the practice — which of course only proves it was being done.

The issue in all this was not just a difference of usage but of theology, differences that still today divide Russian usage from that of the Greeks, Ruthenians, Ukrainians, and others, as to whether the chalice received at the Presanctified Liturgy holds unconsecrated wine, or whether the wine

---

[35] SC 342, pp. 82-87 lines 150-64 = PG 47:11, 52:533; cf. F. van der Paverd, *Zur Geschichte der Meßliturgie in Antiocheia und Konstantinopel gegen Ende des vierten Jahrhunderts: Analyse der Quellen bei Johannes Chrysostomos*, OCA 187 (Rome, 1970), pp. 533-534.

[36] On the various cathedrals of Constantinople before the still-standing Hagia Sophia of Justinian, see C. Mango, 'Hagia Sophia in Constantinople', ODB 2, pp. 892-895.

[37] Alexopoulos, *The Presanctified Liturgy* (see n. 2), pp. 153-157.

[38] See the Italo-Greek ms *Barberini Gr. 329* (f. 10ʳ) from the Rossano region in Calabria, cited Alexopoulos, *The Presanctified Liturgy* (see n. 2), p. 153. Only a very few late mss provide rubrics for this: e.g., Greek BAS in *Athos Esphigmenou 120* (AD 1602) and earlier Slavonic BAS in the 15th-c. ms *Sofija Slav 529,* M.I. Orlov, Литургия св. Василия Великаго (St. Petersburg, 1909), pp. 282-283. Similar rubrics are found in other late Greek mss like 18th-c. *Athens Ethnike Bibliotheke 767* (TL, pp. 195-196) as well as earlier and more frequently in Slavonic mss like 15th-c. *Sofija Slav 530,* 16th-c. *Sofija Slav 603,* 17th c. *Sofija Slav 5899,* from which they entered the printed editions like the 1602 and 1609 Moscow Sluzhebniki (Orlov, p. 283 apparatus), and the 1873 Roman edition of the Greek Euchologion, p. 112.

[39] That indefatigable Greek Byzantinist *ante vocabulum*, Leo Allatius (1586-1669), treats the question on the basis of primary ms sources, which he cites with the maddening insouciance customary at the time — '...Constantinopolitanus...Auctor in schedis meis (A Constantinopolitan [text]...the author [is indicated] in my notes)' — in his treatise *De Missa Praesanctificatorum apud Graecos dissertatione,* appended to his famous *De Ecclesiae Occidentalis atque Orientalis perpetua consensione, libri tres* (Cologne, 1648), pp. 1530-1599, esp. pp. 1591-1594, §§XIX-XX. M. Andrieu, *Immixtio et consecration: La consécration par contact dans les documents liturgiques du moyen âge*, Université de Strasbourg, Bibliothèque de l'Institut de droit canonique (Paris, 1924), chap. 8, pp. 196-215, esp. pp. 202ff, resumes all Allatius' texts.

is 'consecrated by contact' at the commixture of the presanctified Body of Christ,[40] an issue beyond the scope of our interests here.[41]

V. Where Did the Byzantines Reserve the Eucharist?

In the documentation examined above we saw that the Byzantines had more than one Greek term for what in the West one calls the eucharistic tabernacle.[42] The earliest Greek term we came across for a eucharistic receptacle is μουζίκιον,[43] used ca. 600 in John Moschus, *Pratum spirituale* 79, which Lampe translates 'a box inlaid with mosaic'.[44] This is a generic term with no sacral meaning.[45] Then ca. 700 in Anastasius of Sinai the name used for the eucharistic receptacle is σκευοφόριον, literally 'container', another non-sacral term. The next term to appear historically is περιστερά or 'dove', a term still in use today, as we shall see below. Also still in use is the term ἀρτοφόριον or ἀρτοφόρον,

---

[40] A. Raes, 'La communion au calice dans l'office byzantin de Presanctifiés', *Orientalia Christiana Periodica* 20 (1954) 166-174. Much of Raes' evidence, as he himself states (p. 170, note 1), is based on I.A. Karabinov, 'Св. Чаша на Литургии Преждеосвященных Даров', *Христианское Чтение* vol. 243 = year 95 (1915), pp. 737-753; vol. 244 = year 95 (1915), pp. 953-964.

[41] I have treated this question in R.F. Taft, 'Questions on the Eastern Churches, 1: Clergy Communion at the Byzantine Presanctified Liturgy', *Eastern Churches Journal* 8/1 (2001), pp. 125-126. On the whole issue of 'consecration by contact', see Taft, *The Communion, Thanksgiving, and Concluding Rites* (see n. 1), chap. III, sections F.III and F.IV.1, and Excursus II, section IV.4; idem, *Precommunion* (see n. 3), pp. 399, 419-420, 435-439, 459.

[42] On western receptacles for the Eucharist, see O. Nußbaum, *Die Aufbewahrung der Eucharistie*, Theophaneia 29 (Bonn, 1979), *passim;* S.J.P van Dijk and J. Hazelden Walker, *The Myth of the Aumbry: Notes on the Medieval Reservation Practice and Eucharistic Devotion with Special Reference to the Findings of Dom Gregory Dix* (London, 1957), pp. 27-41; J. Hazelden Walker, 'Further Notes on Reservation Practice and Eucharistic Devotion: The Contribution of the Early Church at Rome', *Ephemerides liturgicae* 98 (1984) 392-404, here pp. 398-404.

[43] J. Duffy and G. Vikan, 'A Small Box in John Moschus', *Greek, Roman and Byzantine Studies* 24 (1983) 93-99.

[44] G.W.H. Lampe, *A Patristic Greek Lexicon* (Oxford, 1961), p. 886; LBG, p. 1047.

[45] John Malalas (ca. 490-570's), *Chronographia* IX, 10, uses it for the 'mosaic boxes' in which ill-fated Cleopatra carried her fatal asps: *Ioannis Malalae Chronographia*, ed. J. Thurn, Corpus fontium historiae Byzantinae 35 (Berlin and New York, 2000), p. 167.33, *35. The mid-6th-c. *Vita I*, 42, of St. Matrona of Perge (ca. 430-510/515) testifies to its use for a chest in which valuables were kept: *Acta Sanctorum* (Société des Bollandistes, Antwerp, Paris, Rome and Brussels, 1643-1910), Nov. III: 809B; *Holy Women of Byzantium: Ten Saints' Lives in English Translation*, ed. Alice-Mary Talbot, Byzantine Saints' Lives in Translation 1 (Washington, DC, 1996), p. 56 and note 104; on the dates, see pp. 13-16.

literally 'bread holder', the most common Greek term for the eucharistic tabernacle today as well as in the euchology mss.[46]

The terms 'pyx', 'holy pyx' (πύξις, τὸ ἱερὸν πύξιον), are also found in late 12th c. sources. Though 'pyx' is a common term in western usage for small eucharistic containers, especially those used to bring communion to those unable to come to church services, it is a relatively rare term for a eucharistic vessel in Byzantine Greek and does not appear in this sense until late.[47] Small chests caskets, and pyx-shaped containers of precious materials abound in Byzantine art collections. These vessels could have been used for private reservation and communion, for bringing communion to the sick, for reserving it in church, for carrying it on journeys — all of which uses of the Eucharist are abundantly demonstrated in the sources. Which of these pyxes might actually have been destined for such use, however, we have no way of determining with any certainly. The monks and solitaries who were not priests certainly used other vessels, however. Byzantine monks did plenty of roaming around, at least until the 1340s,[48] and we know that Byzantine recluses brought the eucharistic species to their hermitages to have communion available during their seclusion.[49] But they certainly did not possess luxury items like the extant Byzantine ivory and silver pyxes. Furthermore, pyxes for church reservation were probably not of ivory, 'since ivory is not included in any church inventory in Byzantium'.[50]

[46] LBG, p. 207; mss in TL, pp. 196-199.

[47] Charles du Fresne du Cange, *Glossarium ad scriptores mediae et infimae graecitatis* (Lyons, 1688; reprint Graz, 1958), column 1274, gives only two instances, both from the 12th-c. Typikon of St. Nicholas of Casole.

[48] See A.E. Laiou-Thomadakis, 'Saints and Society in the Late Byzantine Empire', in *Charanis Studies: Essays in Honor of Peter Charanis*, ed. eadem (New Brunswick, NJ, 1980), pp. 84-114, here pp. 97ff.

[49] See R.F. Taft, 'Changing Rhythms of Eucharistic Frequency in Byzantine Monasticism', in *Il monachesimo tra eredità e aperture: Atti del Simposio 'Testi e temi nella tradizione del monachesimo cristiano' per il 50° Anniversario dell'Istituto Monastico di Sant'Anselmo, Roma, 28 maggio - 1 giugno 2002*, eds. M. Bielawski and D. Hombergen, Studia Anselmiana 140 (Rome, 2004), pp. 419-458, here pp. 437-445.

[50] S. Alexopoulos, 'A Short Note on the Liturgical Use of the Pyxides and Canon 101 of the Quinisext Council (691/2): Is There a Connection?' (Unpublished paper presented at the Annual Meeting of the North American Academy of Liturgy, 5-8 January 2006, in San Diego), p. 8 and note 22, citing Marlia Mundell Mango, 'Monetary Value of Silver Revetments and Objects belonging to Churches, A.D. 300-700', in *Ecclesiastical Silver Plate in Sixth-Century Byzantium: Papers of the Symposium held May 16-18, 1986, at The Walters Art Gallery, Baltimore, and Dumbarton Oaks, Washington, DC*, eds. Susan A. Boyd and Marlia Mundell Mango (Washington, DC, 1993), pp. 123-136 + 20 plates, here p. 124.

The only witness I know to what Byzantine-rite solitaries used for a eucharistic vessel, the *Vita* of St. Luke the Younger, who was not a priest, recounts how the saint asked the Archbishop of Corinth, who had stopped by the monastery on his way to Constantinople some time after 927, how to proceed in receiving the Eucharist in his hermit's cell. The prelate told Luke to take the consecrated particles from the vessel (σκεῦος) they were in and put them on a καλυμμάτιον.[51] Σκεῦος, like its English counterpart 'vessel', is an everyday generic term with no sacral meaning. It was also used for sacred vessels, in which case, however, it would usually be specified as a 'sacred (ἱερὸς)' vessel or a vessel 'of the liturgy (τῆς λειτουργίας)'.[52] As for the term καλυμμάτιον, not found in Lampe as Kazhdan notes,[53] it is the diminutive of κάλυμμα or veil,[54] the term still used today for the veils that cover the eucharistic gifts during Byzantine eucharistic services,[55] and probably refers to a small veil or cloth. This is not surprising, since we know that in the West it was customary for Christians to carry about with them the Eucharist in a small linen bag (*sacculum*) — so much so that it entered the Latin ordination ritual for acolytes.[56]

For a Byzantine tabernacle in the western sense of a visible structure in the sanctuary, we are on firm ground only with the περιστερά or dove-tabernacle. Bird-shaped tabernacles, occasionally in the form of a peacock, more frequently of a dove, were common in both East and West.[57] The earliest extant one is the 4/5th c. eucharistic peacock-receptacle found in the Byzantine gravesite of Umm-Thula near Bethlehem in Palestine.[58] For the Byzantine rite we have evidence from at least the

---

[51] *The Life and Miracles of Saint Luke of Steiris*, Text, Translation and Commentary, eds. Carolyn L. Connor and W. Robert Connor, The Archbishop Iakovos Library of Ecclesiastical and Historical Sources 18 (Brookline, MA, 1994), pp. 62-65.

[52] Lampe (see n. 44), p. 1236.

[53] Ibid., p. 699; A. Kazhdan, 'Hagiographical Notes III', *Byzantinische Zeitschrift* 78 (1985) 49-55, here p. 54.

[54] H.G. Liddell and R. Scott, *A Greek English Lexicon* (Oxford, 1966⁹), p. 871.

[55] L. Clugnet, *Dictionnaire grec-français des noms liturgiques en usage dans l'Église grecque* (Paris, 1895), p. 72.

[56] *Les «Ordines Romani» du haut moyen âge*, 5 vols., ed. M. Andrieu, Spicilegium Sacrum Lovaniense fasc. 11, 23, 24, 28, 29 (Leuven, 1956-1961), vol. III, p. 546 and note 3; vol. IV, p. 34 §8 line 23; cf. Walker, 'Further Notes on Reservation Practice' (see n. 42), p. 399.

[57] Nußbaum, *Aufbewahrung* (see n. 42), figs. 22-26, 39; van Dijk and Walker, *The Myth of the Aumbry* (see n. 42), p. 31.

[58] Nußbaum, *Aufbewahrung* (see n. 42), fig. 1; H. Leclercq, 'Paon', *Dictionnaire d'archéologie chrétienne et de liturgie* XIII.1: 1075-1097, esp. 1081-84 and fig. 9601.

12th c. of a golden dove hanging from the ciborium over the altar in Hagia Sophia. A cryptic passage in Michael of Thessalonica's mid-12th c. *Description of Hagia Sophia* 7, seems to refer to it: 'How should I not fall away from the mean, wishing also to describe the wings, truly golden, of the blameless dove (περιστερά) of the church? I mean that one, opposite to us; this one that is with us'.[59] Not long thereafter, Anthony of Novgorod saw it there on his pilgrimage to the holy shrines of Constantinople in 1200: 'In the great sanctuary on the high altar, in the middle of it, under the ciborium, is hung the crown of Constantine, and by the crown is hung a cross, and beneath the cross a gold dove'.[60] Whether this refers to the Byzantine eucharistic tabernacle in the form of a dove hanging over the altar from its ciborium, for which we have evidence later, seems probable if not certain.

Apart from this dove-tabernacle over the altar in the *bema* or sanctuary, there is almost no information whatever about just where the tabernacle with the eucharistic reserve was commonly kept. The most likely place was the *skeuophylakion* or sacristy to which the leftover eucharistic gifts were returned at the end of the liturgy. But as we saw above, the reserve was sometimes also kept in the baptistery in Palestine and, at least for the communion of the neophytes at the Paschal rites of Christian initiation, also in Constantinople.

B. Veneration

I. From Sacred Object to Divine Person: The Growth of Eucharistic Sensibility in East and West[61]

The historian of Christian worship and piety who sets out to study what Henri Bremond (1865-1933) would have called 'le sentiment religieux'[62] of the Christian East in matters like eucharistic worship cannot

---

[59] C. Mango and J. Parker, 'A Twelfth-Century Description of St. Sophia', *Dumbarton Oaks Papers* 14 (1960) 233-245, here 240, cf. 245.

[60] Книга паломник. Сказание мест сватых во Цареграде Антония Архиепископа Новгородскагои в 1200 году, ed. H.M. Loparev, Pravoslavn[y Palestinskiy Sbornik 51 = 17.3 (St. Petersburg, 1899), p. 9.

[61] Some of the material in section B was originally delivered as a public lecture at the Catholic University of America, Washington, DC, on 12 January 2006, and published in a slightly longer redaction in R.F. Taft, 'Is There Devotion to the Holy Eucharist in the Christian East? A Footnote to the October 2005 Synod on the Eucharist', *Worship* 80 (2006) 213-233.

[62] *L'histoire littéraire du sentiment religieux en France, depuis la fin des guerres de religion jusqu'à nos jours*, 11 vols. (Paris, 1916-1929).

but be struck by the extreme paucity of Byzantine witnesses to eucharistic devotion and practice, including eucharistic reservation, in contrast to the avalanche of available western evidence on all aspects of the issue. The classic studies on the question of eucharistic reservation by Freestone,[63] Maffei,[64] van Dijk and Walker,[65] and especially the monumental study of Nußbaum,[66] deal overwhelmingly when not exclusively[67] with western evidence, because by and large that is all there is. The reason why is obvious. Disputes and heresies caused questions of Eucharist and real presence to preoccupy the West and its theologians throughout the Middle Ages, while Byzantium, except for the occasional contretemps like the dispute over aphthartodocetism that raised its head again in the time of Nicetas Choniates (1155/7-1217),[68] went about its business blithely unconcerned by these issues,[69] leaving Byzantine eucharistic theology of the epoch strikingly unexplored in contrast to the reams of eucharistic treatises churned out in the Medieval West.[70] One finds no echo of any of this in Byzantine theology.[71]

---

[63] W.H. Freestone, *The Sacrament Reserved: A Survey of the Practice of Reserving the Eucharist, with Special Reference to the Communion of the Sick, during the first Twelve Centuries*, Alcuin Club Collections 21 (London and Milwaukee, 1917).

[64] E. Maffei, *La réservation eucharistique jusqu'à la Renaissance* (Brussels, 1942).

[65] Van Dijk and Walker, *The Myth of the Aumbry* (see n. 42).

[66] Nußbaum, *Aufbewahrung* (see n. 42).

[67] As does A.A. King, *Eucharistic Reservation in the Western Church* (New York, 1965).

[68] See Taft, *Precommunion* (see n. 3), pp. 468-472. Eucharistic theology in Byzantium remains one of many PhD dissertation topics in Byzantine studies screaming for attention. That a Christian tradition which prides itself on being a liturgical Church *par excellence* has, to the best of my knowledge, never produced a definitive work on this topic is simply stupefying. Still useful, however, is M. Jugie, *Theologia dogmatica Christianorum orientalium ab Ecclesia Catholica dissidentium,* 5 vols. (Paris, 1926-1935), vol. III, chap. 4; see also J. Meyendorff, *Byzantine Theology: Historical Trends and Doctrinal Themes* (New York, 1979), chap. 16, and the manual of P. Trempelas, *Dogmatique de l'Église orthodoxe catholique,* 3 vols. (Chevetogne, 1966-1968), vol. III, chap. 7. Most recently, see the lengthy new theological study of Michael Zheltov, 'Евхаристия', in the new and excellent multi-volume *Православная Енциклопедия* (Moscow, 2000-): the respective volume was not yet available to me.

[69] H.-G. Beck, *Kirche und theologische Literatur im byzantinischen Reich*, Handbuch der Altertumswissenschaft, Abteilung XII, II. Teil: Byzantinisches Handbuch, Bd. I (Munich, 1959), the standard handbook, has no entry whatever for 'Eucharistie' in the Table of Contents (pp. ix-xi), and in the index under 'Eucharistie' (p. 813) gives only eleven individual page references for a manual on Byzantine theology 798 pages long.

[70] F. Vernet, 'IV. Eucharistie du XIe à la fin du Xe siècle', DTC V.2: 1209-1233; J. De Ghellinck, 'V. Eucharistie au XIIe siècle en occident', ibid., 1233-1302; E. Mangenot, 'VI. L'eucharistie du XIIIe siècle au XVe siècle', ibid., 1302-1326.

[71] The later azyme and epiclesis controversies were not eastern heresies stimulating theological solutions. On those issues see Jugie, *Theologia* (see n. 68), vol. III, pp. 232-301; M.H. Smith III, *And taking bread... Cerularius and the Azyme Controversy of 1054*, Théologie historique 47 (Paris, 1978). On Orthodox opposition to Latin customs, see Tia

That is because in the pre-modern era theology was largely local. Theology may eventually move beyond its local origins to enter and influence the broader tradition. But it had local issues as its point of departure, and in the Middle Ages the Eucharist was largely a local western problem. So the Christian East was not wracked by the early medieval eucharistic heresies that riveted western attention to these matters, and that is why eucharistic real presence and reservation were not a major issue in Byzantium or beyond, as they clearly were in the Medieval West. It is also why extra-liturgical devotion to the real presence evolved in the West but not in the East.

II. Early and Late-Antique Christian Attitudes Towards the Eucharistic Species

Here, as with everything else, nothing can be understood apart from history. What history shows is that Early and Late-Antique Christian attitudes towards the eucharistic species and ways of handling them are startling to our modern sensibilities. In an earlier age, Christians of East and West used the eucharistic species as an amulet or talisman carried on their person for protection in times of danger,[72] as a relic to be applied to the senses to heal or protect or bless,[73] as a 'eulogy' or blessing sent to another as a sign of communion, as a vademecum travelers carried on

---

M. Kolbaba, *The Byzantine Lists: Errors of the Latins* (Urbana, Illinois, 2000); eadem, 'Meletios Homologetes "On the Customs of the Italians"', *Revue des études byzantines* 55 (1997) 137-168; eadem, 'Byzantine Perceptions of Latin Religious "Errors": Themes and Changes from 850 to 1350', in *The Crusades from the Perspective of Byzantium and the Muslim World* (Washington, DC, 2001), pp. 117-143.

[72] Ambrose, *De excessu fratris* I, 43, CSEL 73, pp. 232-233 = PL 16:1304B; cf. F. van der Meer, *Augustine the Bishop: The Life and Work of a Father of the Church*, trans. B. Battershaw and G.R. Lamb (London, 1978), p. 530.

[73] See the devotional gestures of the laity in the early rites of Holy Communion in the texts I cite in Taft, *The Communion, Thanksgiving, and Concluding Rites* (see n. 1), chap. III; also idem, 'The Communion of the Laity: The Ancient Ritual in the Mother Traditions of Syriac Christianity', in *Mélanges offerts à l'Abbé Jean Tabet*, ed. A. Chahwan, Publications de l'Institut de Liturgie à l'Université Saint-Esprit de Kaslik 34 (Kaslik, Lebanon, 2005), pp. 15-48. On this and the following questions treated here, see F.J. Dölger, 'Das Segnen der Sinne mit der Eucharistie: Eine altchristliche Kommunionsitte', *Antike und Christentum* 3 (1932) 231-244; also the recent study of G.J.C. Snoek, *Medieval Piety from Relics to the Eucharist: A Process of Mutual Interaction*, Studies in the History of Christian Thought 63 (Leiden, New York and Cologne, 1995), chaps. 2-3, which deals mostly with the western evidence, though not always well integratedly and systematically.

a journey as one would a relic or icon,[74] even as a poultice to cure an infection or wound.[75] In an extreme case of the latter, at the end of the 4th c. St. Gregory Nazianzen (d. 389) recounts, not without some embarrassment, how his seriously ill sister St. Gorgonia smeared her whole body with the eucharistic species and was cured:

> 'Having given up on all others, she fled to the Physician of all, and keeping watch until the dead of night when the disease gave her a little respite, she fell down before the altar with faith, and in a loud voice called upon Him who is honored upon it… Eventually she did something shamelessly devout. She imitated the woman who dried up her flow of blood with Jesus' hem [Mt 9:20-22, Mk 5:25-34, Lk 8:43-48]. And what is it she did? With a like cry she placed her head upon the altar and drenched it with abundant tears as the one who had of old drenched the feet of Christ [Lk 7:37-50; cf. Mt 26:6-13, Mk 14:3-9]. She threatened not to let go until she obtained her health. Next she smeared her whole body with her own medicine, something of the antitypes[76] of the precious Body and Blood that she treasured in her hand and mingled with her tears. Amazing! Conscious that she had been cured, she departed immediately, buoyant in body and soul…'[77]

In the West the eucharistic species were even built into the altar at the consecration of a church like a sacred relic.[78] Employing the Eucharist as a viaticum to be buried with the dead or even put into the corpse's mouth had to be condemned time and again in the 4/7th centuries — proof-positive that it was being done.[79] It is even said that the Precious

---

[74] Cf. J.C. McGowan, *Concelebration: Sign of the Unity of the Church* (New York, 1964), p. 15; R.F. Taft, 'One Bread, One Body: Ritual Symbols of Ecclesial Communion in the Patristic Period', in *Nova Doctrina Vetusque: Essays on Early Christianity in Honor of Frederic W. Schlatter, S.J.*, eds. Douglas Kries and Catherine Brown Tkacz (New York, 1998), pp. 23-50, here pp. 28-32; idem, *Precommunion* (see n. 3), pp. 404-412.

[75] Augustine, *Contra Iulianum opus imperfectum* III §162, CSEL 85.1, pp. 467-468; English trans. from van der Meer, *Augustine* (see n. 72), p. 530.

[76] The term ἀντίτυπος was commonly used for the consecrated eucharistic species in the earlier patristic period: cf. Lampe (see n. 44), p. 159 §6b.

[77] *Oratio 8*, 18, SC 405, pp. 284-286; trans. from Daniel Sheerin, 'Eucharist as Medicine of Body and Spirit' (unpublished lecture), p. 10. I am grateful to Prof. Sheerin of the University of Notre Dame for providing me a copy of his excellent paper.

[78] Walker, 'Further Notes on Reservation Practice' (see n. 42), pp. 394-395; cf. Freestone, *The Sacrament Reserved* (see n. 63), p. 100. This is attested by the 8th c. Latin *Pontifical of Egbert Archbishop of York* (d. 766): *The Pontifical of Egbert Archbishop of York*, ed. W. Greenwell, Publications of the Surtees Society 27 (London, 1853).

[79] Freestone, *The Sacrament Reserved* (see n. 63), p. 99. See for instance the III Council of Carthage (397), canon 6, and other North African canons in J.D. Mansi, *Sacrorum conciliorum nova et amplissima collectio*, 53 tomes in 58 vols. (Paris and Leipzig, 1901-1927), 3: 719, 881, 919.

Blood was used as ink to sign the condemnation of Patriarch Photios at the Eighth Ecumenical Council, Constantinople IV in 869-870.[80] Signing critical documents in blood is as old as writing — and what blood is more solemn than that of Christ? Historians may view the story with skepticism,[81] but it would not have been invented had it been considered unthinkable at the time.

Jean Carroll McGowan sums up how different things once were:[82]

'...historians of eucharistic doctrine and devotion assure us that this cultus of the eucharistic presence of Jesus did not exist during the first eleven centuries of the Christian era.[83] Thurston...tells us that in all the Christian literature of the first thousand years there is no clear evidence that anyone ever visited a church in order to pray before the Blessed Sacrament, and that there is no clear evidence of any other expression of a devotion to the abiding eucharistic presence earlier than 1100.[84] ... According to Freestone, the rudiments of a cultus of the reserved sacrament are to be found in the latter part of the eleventh century when such a cultus arose as a reaction against the Berengarian views of the sacrament.[85]

...as Thurston points out[86]...the eucharist was revered more as a thing than as a person. Great reverence was paid to this sacred thing, this Body of the Lord, as we know from the penalties for even accidental negligence in sixth century penitential canons,[87] but still this reverence was more a respect for a holy object than recognition of a divine person to be adored.'[88]

---

[80] Nicetas David Paphlagon (late 9th-early 10th c.), *Vita Ignatii archiepiscopi Constantinopolitani,* Mansi (see n. 79), 16: 264-65 = PG 105: 545CD.

[81] See J. Hergenröther, *Photius, Patriarch von Konstantinopel,* 3 vols. (Regensburg, 1867-1869), vol. II, p. 109; F. Dvornik, *The Photian Schism: History and Legend* (Cambridge, 1970), p. 149, note 4.

[82] McGowan, *Concelebration* (see n. 74), pp. 13-15. Notes within the citation are McGowan's, though I have corrected and updated them where necessary, and adapted their format to my stylesheet.

[83] Cf. J. de Ghellinck, 'V. Eucharistie au XIIe siècle en occident', DTC V.2: 1233-1502; Freestone, *The Sacrament Reserved* (see n. 63); P. Pourrat, *Christian Spirituality I* (Westminster, 1953); D. Stone, *A History of the Doctrine of the Holy Eucharist* (London, 1909); H. Thurston, 'The Early Cultus of the Blessed Sacrament', *The Month* 109 (1907) 377-390; idem, 'Notes to T.E. Bridgett, *History of the Holy Eucharist in Great Britain*' (London, 1908). To these still valuable older works which McGowan cites, add: N. Mitchell, *Cult and Controversy: The Worship of the Eucharist outside Mass* (New York, 1982), esp. chap. 4, part II.

[84] Thurston, 'Notes to Bridgett, *History of the Holy Eucharist*' (see n. 83), p. 170; E. Bertaud, 'Devotion eucharistique', *Dictionnaire de spiritualité* IV.2: 1621-1647, with substantial bibliography on columns 1635-1637.

[85] Freestone, *The Sacrament Reserved* (see n. 63), p. 258.

[86] Thurston, 'The Early Cultus of the Blessed Sacrament' (see n. 83), pp. 377ff.

[87] Bridgett, *History of the Eucharist* (see n. 83), p. 14.

[88] McGowan, *Concelebration* (see n. 74), p. 15. Regarding notes within the citation see n. 82 above.

III. The Eucharistic Presence 'Personalized'

But by the turn of the 4/5th centuries we already see the beginnings of a significant shift in eucharistic consciousness: what one might call the 'personalization' of piety toward the Divine Presence of Christ in the consecrated gifts of his Sacred Body and Blood. The first inkling I have found of this shift[89] comes from Theodore, Bishop of Mopsuestia in Cilicia Secunda north of Antioch[90] from 392 until his death in 428, where I believe he preached his homilies.[91] Theodore's *Hom. 16, 28* gives this description of what the communicant's devotional attitudes should be on receiving Holy Communion: '...after you have received it [the Body of Christ] in your own hands, you adore the Body... With great and true love you press it against your eyes and kiss it, and you offer your prayers to it as to Christ our Lord, who is now so close to you...'.[92] This is entirely new: prayer addressed directly to the Christ in the Eucharist, something extremely rare during the first millennium.

An even more striking example of the same is found in an instruction on the reception of communion by Philoxenus, from 485-519 Metropolitan of Mabbug (Hieropolis),[93] which describes communion prayers

---

[89] It is adumbrated somewhat earlier in St. Ephrem (ca. 306-373), though not in prayers addressed directly to the person of Christ in the eucharistic species: see *Hymni de fide* 85.8 (= *De margarita* 5.8): *Des heiligen Ephraem des Syrers Hymnen de Fide*, ed. E. Beck, CSCO 154-155 = Scriptores Syri 73-74 (Leuven, 1955), vol. 154, p. 261 (Syriac), vol. 155, p. 222 (translation); A. Cody, 'An Instruction of Philoxenus of Mabbug on Gestures and Prayer When One Receives Communion in the Hand, with a History of the Manner of Receiving the Eucharistic Bread in the West-Syrian Church', in *Rule of Prayer, Rule of Faith: Essays in Honor of Aidan Kavanagh, O.S.B.*, eds. N. Mitchell and J. Baldovin, A Pueblo Book (Collegeville, 1996), pp. 56-79, here p. 65; P. Yousif, *L'eucharistie chez Saint Éphrem de Nisibe*, OCA 224 (Rome, 1984), pp. 303-304.

[90] On Mopsuestia see G. Fedalto, *Hierarchia Ecclesiastica Orientalis, I: Patriarchatus Constantinopolitanus; II: Patriarchatus Alexandrinus, Antiochenus, Hierosolymitanus; III: Supplementum* (Padua, 1988, 2006), vol. II, pp. 770-771 §71.15.2; F. van der Meer and Christine Mohrmann, *Atlas of the Early Christian World*, trans. and edited by M.F Hedlung and H.H. Rowley (London, 1958), map 16a.

[91] See my remarks in R.F. Taft, *A History of the Liturgy of St. John Chrysostom, vol. IV: The Diptychs*, OCA 238 (Rome, 1991), p. 47. As I indicate there, others date the homilies to ca. 388-392, before Theodore's Mopsuestian episcopate. The issue is irrelevant in the present context, since both this and the following source cited were from within the Patriarchate of Antioch.

[92] R. Tonneau and R. Devreesse, *Les homélies catéchétiques de Théodore de Mopsueste*, ST 145 (Vatican, 1949), pp. 569-581; A. Mingana, *Commentary of Theodore of Mopsuestia on the Lord's Prayer and on the Sacraments of Baptism and the Eucharist*, Woodbrooke Studies 6 (Cambridge, 1933), pp. 110-114.

[93] A. de Halleux, *Philoxène de Mabbug: sa vie, ses écrits, sa théologie* (Leuven, 1963), p. 296; Cody, 'Philoxenus' (see n. 89), p. 59.

of the Syriac speaking centers of the interior like Edessa and Mabbug, beyond the Mediterranean littoral.[94] This text seems to be the earliest extensive witness to a tendency in Syriac Christianity to address the eucharistic Christ in prayer directly, a type of piety, later to become so common in second-millennium eucharistic devotion, especially in the Catholic West. It reads as follows:

> 'When you have extended your hands and taken the body, bow, and put your hands before your face, and worship the living body whom you hold. Then speak with him in a low voice, and with your gaze resting upon him say to him: "I carry you, living God who is incarnate in the bread, and I embrace you in my palms, Lord of the worlds whom no world has contained. You have circumscribed yourself in a fiery coal with a fleshly palm — you, Lord, who with your palm measured out the dust of the earth. You are holy, God incarnate in my hands in a fiery coal which is a body. See, I hold you, although there is nothing that contains you; a bodily hand embraces you, Lord of natures whom a fleshly womb embraced. Within a womb you became a circumscribed body, and now within a hand you appear to me as a small morsel.
>
> As you have made me worthy to approach you and receive you — and see, my hands embrace you confidently — make me worthy, Lord, to eat you in a holy manner and to taste the food of your body as a taste of your life. Instead of the stomach, the body's member, may the womb of my intellect and the hand of my mind receive you. May you be conceived in me as [you were] in the womb of the Virgin. There you appeared as an infant, and your hidden self was revealed in the world as corporeal fruit; may you also appear in me here and be revealed from me in fruits that are spiritual works and just labors pleasing to your will.
>
> And by your food may my desires be killed, and by the drinking of your cup may my passions be quenched. And instead of the members of my body, may my thoughts receive strength from the nourishment of your body. Like the manifest members of my body, may my hidden thoughts be engaged in exercise and in running and in works according to your living commands and your spiritual laws. From the food of your body and the drinking of your blood may I wax strong inwardly, and excel outwardly, and run diligently, and attain to the full stature of an interior human being. May I become a perfect man, mature in the intelligence [residing in] all [my] spiritual members, my head being crowned with the crown of perfection of all of [my] behavior. May I be a royal diadem in your hands, as you promised me (cf. Is 62:3), O hidden God whose manifestness I embrace in the perfection of your body"'.[95]

---

[94] Cody, 'Philoxenus' (see n. 89), p. 68. On Mabbug see Fedalto, *Hierarchia* II, 783 §73.1.17.

[95] Cody, 'Philoxenus' (see n. 89), p. 62-64.

Such devotional prayers addressed to the eucharistic Christ do not appear in the West, apparently, until the Middle Ages.[96] Note, however, that *these eastern prayers to the eucharistic Christ are always in the context of Holy Communion during the eucharistic liturgy.* So what is different about Eastern and Western Christian eucharistic adoration is not its presence or absence, but the fact that in the East it has remained where it was throughout pre-Medieval Christendom: *in the context of the eucharistic liturgy and not as something apart.* It is not worship of Christ in the Eucharist that distinguishes the West; *it is that worship outside the eucharistic liturgy and apart from Holy Communion.*

IV. Eucharistic Devotion in the Christian East

So forms of adoration of the reserved sacrament outside the context of the celebration of the eucharistic liturgy are not native to any authentic eastern tradition, even if in some cases Eastern Catholics may have borrowed them from the West.[97] In the Christian East today, as in antiquity, 'eucharistic devotion' means to receive Holy Communion. This was once true also in the pre-Medieval West. The idea that the reserved Eucharist was something one 'visited' or prayed to outside the context of Holy Communion was totally unknown throughout Christendom in the first millennium. The Christ to whom one prays is *everywhere present*; what is reserved in the tabernacle is the *sacramental presence* of his Body and Blood as spiritual food under the species of consecrated bread and wine, one of the many forms of Jesus' real presence among us — *but by no means the only one.* That is why Eastern Christians act in the same way upon entering a church regardless of whether or not the Eucharist is reserved. They make their reverences, visit and kiss the icons, say their prayers, because for the Eastern Christian every church is the house of God, a sanctuary made holy by its consecration, by its icons, its relics, by the liturgical celebrations and prayers that sanctify it day after day, and not just by the presence of the reserved Eucharist.

---

[96] Mitchell, *Cult and Controversy* (see n. 83), pp. 105-106.

[97] See for example S. Parenti, 'Una Diataxis inedita del XIV secolo per la solennità del Corpus Domini', in S. Parenti and E. Velkovska, *Mille anni di 'Rito Greco' alle porte di Roma: Raccolta di saggi sulla tradizione liturgica del Monastero italo-bizantino di Grottaferrata*, Ἀνάλεκτα Κρυπτοφέρρης 4 (Grottaferrata, 2004), pp. 149-170, here pp. 150-152, 169-170.

Present-day Roman Catholic devotional attitudes are quite different. The first thing Western Catholics will ask on entering a church is if the reserved Eucharist is present — as if they think God is somehow absent if it is not!

Is adoration of the reserved Eucharist foreign to the Christian East, then? In a passage from that 19th c. classic of Russian Orthodox spirituality, *The Pilgrim's Tale,* the pilgrim recounts for December 13, 1859, the following:

> 'Having traveled about ten kilometers I stopped to spend the night in a hamlet. In the overnight lodgings I saw a desperately sick peasant and advised those with him to have him receive the sacred mysteries of Christ. They concurred and toward morning sent for the priest from their village parish. *I waited so that I might reverence the Holy Gifts and pray before this great mystery.*'[98]

So the stereotypical western criticism that Eastern Christians are not devoted to the Eucharist is simply false. As I have shown elsewhere, Eastern Christians' profound devotion to the Eucharist is clearly demonstrated in a whole series of devotional practices surrounding the sacrament in the Christian East today.[99] One need only recall the full prostrations of both clergy and laity before the reserved sacrament that are scattered throughout the Liturgy of the Presanctified Gifts.[100] *The difference is that in the East this devotion has remained where it once was everywhere: in the context of the eucharistic liturgy and the reception of Holy Communion.*

[98] *The Pilgrim's Tale,* edited with an introduction by Aleksei Pentkovsky, translated by T.A. Smith, preface by J. Pelikan, Classics of Western Spirituality (New York and Mahwah, 1999), p. 91 (emphasis added). On this source see most recently Suzette Phillips, 'The Way of a Pilgrim: A Synopsis of Recent Scholarship on a Spiritual Classic', *Logos* 46 (2005) 525-542. For private eucharistic devotion in earlier, 16th-c. Slavonic mss in Russian collections, see D.V. Denisov, 'Практика личного благочестия на Руси в XVI в. Статьи, посвященные евхаристическое дисциплине и келейному правилу в рукописи РГБ. ТСЛ–осн. (f. 304 – 1). 793, XVI в.', Вестник ПСТГУ 1:14 (2005) 162-168.

[99] See Taft, *The Communion, Thanksgiving, and Concluding Rites* (see n. 1), chaps. II, V, and Excursus II.

[100] See the rite itself; also R.F. Taft, *A History of the Liturgy of St. John Chrysostom, vol. II: The Great Entrance. A History of the Transfer of Gifts and Other Preanaphoral Rites of the Liturgy of St. John Chrysostom,* OCA 200 (Rome, 2004⁴), pp. 213-214.

V. Conclusion

To conclude, East-West differences in eucharistic practice are the product of western developments during the Medieval and Baroque eras, when the West diverged from many usages of Early and Late-Antique Christendom still retained in the East. Christ's Church in East and West has always been eucharistic to its core. But earlier, this was manifested in the context of the eucharistic liturgy and in the reception of Holy Communion, not separately, as something apart. That is the ancient tradition of the Early Church; that is what still characterizes and shall continue to characterize the authentic eucharistic devotion in the Christian East, in faithful adherence to the ancient tradition once common to both East and West.

THE PROCESSIONAL APPENDIX TO VESPERS:
SOME PROBLEMS AND QUESTIONS

Gregory WOOLFENDEN

I wrote an article on the processional appendix to vespers in a recent
edition of *Worship*.[1] The article was inspired by some comments in
a review of my book on the offices, *Daily Liturgical Prayer*,[2] by
Fr. George Guiver CR.[3] Guiver took me to task for saying very little
about the processional elements concluding the major evening and morning offices, especially concluding vespers. While one reason for the
admittedly meagre treatment was the need to turn a doctoral dissertation
into a reasonably saleable book, another was the patchiness of the evidence I discovered. The latter consideration convinced me that I would
need to study this processional extension, in particular to the evening
service, in much more detail before I could come to any secure conclusions about it and its nature.

Those who have read this article may now discover that the more
I examine this question, the more it seems to escape easy categorization,
especially when we look carefully at the Eastern sources believed to lie
at the origins of these various devotional appendices to the evening service of prayer. Guiver stated the widely accepted proposition that the
procession '....is an ancient memorial of the crucifixion, later linked
with baptism, which only disappeared from service books at the time of
Vatican II but still survives in reduced form in Milan.'[4] While this statement is unexceptional, I would like to lay before a wider readership
some of the problems which appear to arise when examining this processional rite. The greatest problem of all being, how a procession to the
cross on Golgotha came to be, at least in some places, associated with
the baptistery. We will first examine the oldest evidence, that of the
Peregrinatio Egeriae, and then the likely Eastern developments of this

[1] 'The Processional Appendix to Vespers: Where and Why?', *Worship* 82 (2008)
339-357.
[2] (Aldershot, 2004).
[3] *Worship* 79 (2005) 287-288.
[4] *Ibid.*

procession at the end of vespers. In this article I am concentrating on the Eastern rites, especially those of Palestine and Constantinople, for I now suspect that the Western developments may have been the result of a somewhat different dynamic.

1. Egeria

In the well-known account of her fourth-century visit to the Holy Land, Egeria described the procession at the end of vespers in Jerusalem in the following terms: 'Then, singing hymns, they take the bishop from the Anastasis to the Cross (at Golgotha), and everyone goes with him. On arrival he says one prayer and blesses the catechumens, then another and blesses the faithful.'[5] The ritual was repeated behind the cross, as were the blessings. The description of vespers concluded with the words: 'So these are the services held every weekday at the Cross and at the Anastasis.'[6] This procession went from the church of the Resurrection (in modern western usage, the Holy Sepulchre) into the large open courtyard and, after the short open-air service, returned. Exactly what the positions 'before' and 'behind' the cross referred to is now probably beyond recovery, but it would appear that the rocky outcrop in the courtyard, believed to be Golgotha, the place of the crucifixion, was marked by a prominent cross. (We recall that both Egeria and St Cyril refer to the whole complex, not just the rock, as Golgotha.)[7] The cross on Golgotha was the focal point of a Good Friday observance, also described by Egeria, when the bishop's chair was placed 'behind the cross', and the box containing the true cross itself was brought to him for his, and the people's veneration. After that veneration, the bishop went 'before the cross' and a lengthy series of readings and chants followed, whatever the weather.[8]

This custom of going in procession each evening appears to have influenced other liturgical traditions and, originally, *followed* the final prayers of blessing of vespers and, we note, had its own blessings. What

---

[5] John Wilkinson, *Egeria's Travels*, 3rd edition (Warminster, 1999), p. 144. In *Egérie: Journal de Voyage (Itinéraire)*, ed. Pierre Maraval, Sources Chrétiennes 296 (Paris, 1982; réédition 1997), p. 240: 'Et postmodum de Anastasim usque ad Crucem [cum] ymnis ducitur episcopus, simul et omnis populus uadet. Ubi cum peruentum fuerit, primum facit orationem, item benedicet cathecuminos; item fit alia oratio, item benedicit fideles.'

[6] *Ibid.*: 'Haec operatio cotidie per dies sex ita habetur ad Crucem et ad Anastasim.'

[7] *Ibid.*, 22.

[8] *Ibid.*, 37.1 and 37.4 (pp. 155-156).

is absolutely clear though, is that the destination of the procession is the cross on Golgotha. This vespers procession appears to have been then, a Jerusalem tradition that was progressively adopted elsewhere. This leaves us with a question as to when and why this procession became associated, in some other places, with the baptistery.

We should mention in passing, that one of the problems that confronts anyone who tries to reconstruct the liturgical life of fourth-century Jerusalem, is that the exact location of the baptistery remains unclear, at least so far as the current extent of our literary and archaeological knowledge extends.[9] It appears that the baptistery may have been accessible from the courtyard in which the cross was situated, but does not itself appear to have been in any way closely connected with the cross. In the introduction to his edition of Egeria, John Wilkinson suggests parallels between the worship of the temple and that of the Constantinian complex. The basilica of the Anastasis and the courtyard are the Holy of Holies, the whole complex symbolizes the universe.[10] As to the act of worship itself, he suggests that the procession to the cross (the place of Christ's sacrifice) is paralleled by the procession of the temple priests from inside the temple to the altar outside for sacrifice, whilst the Levites sang.[11]

2. The Palestinian Monasteries

A later piece of Palestinian evidence, the ninth-century Saint Sabas Horologion (Book of Hours) edited by Mateos, makes the Trisagion ('Holy God, Holy mighty', etc.) the final element of vespers. This means that the *Aposticha*, the processional psalm which Mateos suggests is a remnant of the procession to the cross mentioned by Egeria, is entirely absent.[12] Similarly there is no hint that Abba John and Abba Sophronius missed this particular feature of what they were used to, when they visited Abba Nicon.[13] Even the Syriac Horologion edited by Matthew Black

[9] See Juliette Day, *Baptism in Early Byzantine Palestine 325-451*, Alcuin/GROW Joint Study 43 (Cambridge, 1999), pp. 18-27.

[10] *Ibid.*, p. 62.

[11] *Ibid.*, pp. 68-69.

[12] J. Mateos, (under the now rather inappropriate title:) *Un Horologion inédit de Saint-Sabas*, Studi e Testi 233 (Rome, 1964), pp. 75-76.

[13] A. Longo, 'Il testo integrale della "Narrazione deglo abato Giovanni e Sofronio" attraverso le "Hermineiai" di Nicone', *Rivista degli Studi Bizantini e Neoellenici* NS 2-3 (xii-xiii) (1965-66) 232-267.

and dated as late as 1188, makes no mention of *Aposticha* at either vespers or orthros.[14] All of this is somewhat complicated when we turn to the Georgian material recently edited by Stig Symeon Frøshov. The late tenth-century Georgian Horologion, ms Sin.Iber. 34, provides somewhat more conclusive evidence of a vespers procession in Sabbaite monasteries, a procession originally connected with devotion to the cross, like that described by Egeria.[15] After the litany, the synapte, and its conclusion, the order simply says: 'I lift up my eyes', which as Frøyshov says, best suits the first words of Psalm 120, 'I lift up my eyes to the hills'. There then follow five short hymns that might well be inserted between the psalm verses, but the fourth, 'Pray for us, holy martyrs...' is extremely close in wording to the similar one of the four troparia that now close a fasting day vespers. Then after 'Lord have mercy', five times, there is the title *Stikaroni* — none are given here, but they are given in the same place in other documents. The prayer of Symeon, Trisagion and Our Father follow, the normal ancient ending, but, with the addition of, under the heading *Litanisaj*, a prayer for pardon with 'Lord have mercy', fifty times, and concluding prayers.[16] (It should be noted that the way that the text is arranged, this whole appendix has no *necessary* connection with the vespers service that is placed before it.)[17] All this means that from the same monastery that is believed to be the source of the text edited by Mateos (see above), we have a development within a century of a further addition to the service of vespers that is beginning to look like the modern-day week-night *aposticha* psalm. Though in the contemporary office, that psalm is not 120, but 122 'To you have I lifted up my eyes, you who dwell in the heavens.'

Armenian vespers has a similar form of devotional appendix that has also come to be perceived as an integral part of the office. The trisagion is followed by some brief invocations and then the 'psalm of repose' 120 'I lift up my eyes to the mountains: from where shall come my help.' Here we have the same psalm as used by the Georgian documents. We need to ask if this was the original psalm at this point in the service, and if so, why did psalm 122 come to replace it in the developed forms that

---

[14] 'A Christian Palestinian Syriac Horologion', in *Texts and Studies* 1 (Cambridge, 1954), pp. 73-144.

[15] S. Frøyshov, *L'Horologe 'Georgien' du Sinaiticus Ibericus 34: Edition, traduction et commentaire* (Unpublished doctoral thesis Sorbonne, Paris, 2003), pp. 468-471 — in preparation for publication.

[16] *Ibid.*, vol 1, pp. 26-29.

[17] Clarification from Prof. Frøshov, September 2008.

we know now? The prayer that accompanies the psalm requests God to '... accept the supplications of thy servants in this evening hour', and for mercy on the afflicted, travellers etc.[18]

Psalms 120 and 122 both belong to the set of psalms known as the gradual psalms or psalms of ascent, associated with pilgrimage to Jerusalem. There could of course be a scribal mistake here, but maybe there was deliberate change. Psalm 120 prays to the Lord as the one who keeps His people by day and by night, and who will guard the going out and coming in of His people; it would seem more obviously suited to accompany a evening procession to the site of the Lord's crucifixion. Psalm 122 looks to the Lord enthroned in the heavens, and therefore could be said to relate more easily to Psalm 92, 'The Lord is King, with majesty enrobed', the text which comes to be associated with the Saturday night festal *aposticha* for Sunday.

Is it possible that the absence of any *aposticha* text from the St Sabas Horologion edited by Mateos, suggests that this austere monastic use did not provide for such a procession at this date; and further that this non-use continued in some settings, whereas, by the time of the Georgian Horologion, St Sabas monastery has begun to adopt from Jerusalem practice the psalm and what follows it, but as a devotional exercise, perhaps no longer connected with Golgotha, since Golgotha was indeed elsewhere? If this were so, then the change of psalm would be an almost unnoticed change to suit a different theological and ritual interpretation of this addition to main structure of vespers, perhaps, at this early stage, only used on specific occasions.

Egeria's description appears to be of a much more substantial liturgical unit, appended after vespers proper has been concluded, and having with its own prayers and dismissal ceremony, all of which would have been peculiar to the complex of the Anastasis basilica and its sacred sites. The later *Aposticha* is simply a psalm, into which verses come to be intercalated, verses that may or may not have anything to do with the psalm, now inserted before the conclusion of vespers, and having, in all probability, lost any memory of being processional.

If this is the case, then what about the *Lite*? The contemporary Byzantine Typikon, of the so-called neo-Sabbaite tradition, expects there to be a *Lite* procession on all Sundays and feasts.[19] Except amongst the

---

[18] *Rituale Armenorum*, eds. F. C. Coneybeare and A.J. Maclean (Oxford, 1905), p. 480.

[19] *Typikon* (reprint, Moscow, 1997), chapter 2.

Russian Old Ritualists, this practice is now largely confined to major feasts. The procession is to the back of the church, ideally to a narthex or porch, though it may go round the outside of the church.[20] The outdoor procession would appear to be closest to the original form, for although not found in the older documents associated with the monastery of Stoudion, this procession does appear in early redactions of the Sabbaite Typikon, which is the basis of the modern church Typikon. Some of these, from the 12th century, provide for a far more elaborate Lite which is really treated like a separate service of the all-night vigil, placed between vespers and matins. At Mar Sabbas itself, the procession might go first to the church of the Theoktistos, then to that of the Forerunner, where an anointing took place, and finally to the tomb of St Sabbas. During the procession *stichira* and litanies were sung, the diptychs were included in one of the latter, and there was an inclination prayer. At Sinai, the church of Moses and then St Symeon and, again, the tomb of the founder were the stations visited. A detailed note on one document requires a return to the katholikon in order that the *stichira* of Sunday be sung there; Arranz opines that this may have been a new usage.[21] In the tradition of Mar Sabbas then, the Lite was originally a procession to a subsidiary church, or churches, and ending in the narthex of the katholikon, the main church of the monastery.[22] In this latter case the *Aposticha* now seem to be envisaged as simply a unit of vespers, no longer in any way connected with a procession.

The Belarusian liturgical scholar M. Skaballanovich, perhaps rather fancifully, saw the procession to the narthex as an act of reaching out into the world outside. He also suggested that the appropriate *sticheron* for each church might have been sung in procession, a different set of the petitions being prayed in each church.[23] One might ask whether the lengthy series of *Kyrie eleisons* that still characterize this office, might have been sung while actually moving from one church to another, which might explain the different quantities of that response (currently, 40, 30, 50, 3 and 3).

---

[20] K. Nikolskyi, *Учебный Устав Богослужения* (= *Instructional Directory of Divine Services*) (reprint Moscow, 1999), p. 127, n. 1.

[21] Miguel Arranz, 'N.D. Uspensky: The Office of the All-Night Vigil in the Greek and the Russian Church', *St Vladimir's Theological Quarterly* 24 (1980) 83-113, 169-195, on pp. 175-177.

[22] *Ibid.*, p. 165.

[23] M. Skaballonovich, *Tolkovyi Typikon* (= *Analytical Typikon*) (reprint Moscow, 1995), pp. 163-165.

Some of the manuscripts mentioned by Uspensky had a *Lite* at matins as well. Later works, especially the Athonite Typika, show this procession as already being confined to the narthex, though some retained the reading of the diptychs. Later developments in Russia made it a popular devotional element of the vigil.[24] It seems though, that we may, in this case as well, conclude that the *Lite* was a separate and later development from that of the cross procession/*Aposticha*. However, further interesting questions are raised by what we find elsewhere, especially in the *Asmatikos* office of Hagia Sophia.

3. The Asmatikos Office in Constantinople

The rite of the *asmatikos* or 'chanted vespers' of Hagia Sophia appears to have acquired a processional coda at a late date, and then only on certain days. As a result, some of the oldest manuscripts do not include the prayers that appear to have accompanied this procession, and St Symeon of Thessalonica's 15th-century reference appears to be to an importation from the Palestinian office, as we shall see. Miguel Arranz enumerated four manuscripts that have the first prayer of the procession, and only two that contain the other prayer texts.[25] The two that contain the full range of texts are Coislin 213,[26] and Grottaferrata Gb1, both from the eleventh century.[27] The earlier euchologia, such as the eighth-century Barberini 336, do not include these texts, so it seems that we have here something introduced quite late in the history of these Constantinople vespers.

The first prayer, entitled 'of the "Katagyra"', (described as a word of uncertain meaning[28] — 'going down to make a circuit of some sort' seems a possible interpretation) prays that God, the giver of all good things, will regard the lowliness of His people, and make them serve Him as sanctified vessels.[29] That He may be for His people, the guide to

---

[24] Arranz, 'Uspensky' (see n. 21), pp. 178-182.

[25] M. Arranz, 'L'office de l'Asmatikos Hesperinos ('vêpres chantées') de l'ancien Euchologe byzantin', *Orientalia Christiana Periodica* 44 (1978) 107-130, 391-419, on pp. 125-129.

[26] *Coislin 213: Euchologe de la Grande Église*, ed. J. Duncan (doctoral dissertation Pontifical Oriental Institute, Rome 1983).

[27] Arranz, 'L'office de l'Asmatikos Hesperinos' (see n. 25), p. 112.

[28] Duncan, *Coislin 213* (see n. 26), p. 89, line 1, n. 3.

[29] Duncan, *Coislin 213* (see n. 26), lines 7-8.

go with them on their way in the hope of the eternal kingdom.[30] This could be seen as a prayer that reminds one of baptism, but it is to be said in the sacristy, the *skeuophylakion*.[31] This latter building also served as a treasury and depository for relics, including no doubt the holy lance that pierced Christ's side. The prayer is entirely suitable for such a location, but seems to draw most of its inspiration from the presence of the holy vessels, and we are also left with a question as to what sort of numbers could actually get into the building. A brief and rather general prayer 'at the bowing of heads' then follows, and then there was a station at the Great Baptistery. There is some dispute as to whether the surviving building at the south-west angle of the building was the Great or Little Baptistery, some holding that the Great Baptistery was on the same side as the *skeuophylakion*.[32] Here was said a prayer giving thanks for admission into the company of the saints in light after the vanquishing of the powers of darkness.[33] A further prayer 'at the bowing of heads' prays that we, the baptized, may remain faithful to the grace given us and that our souls and bodies will be illumined with the knowledge of God's truth.[34] This baptismal aspect of the vesperal service was emphasized by Uspensky,[35] who was also of the opinion that the procession served the same function as the procession to the cross in Egeria,[36] described above. However, one is left with the question as to why a procession relatively lately introduced to Constantinople, and that had once been a procession to Golgotha, should have become a procession to the baptistery. The relative inaccessibility of the ancient Jerusalem baptistery, and the accessibility of both at Hagia Sophia may have something to do with this. Is it not also possible, however, that this was a borrowing of the Sabbaite monastic *Lite*, adapted from the monastic setting to the cathedral complex of Constantinople?

[30] Arranz, 'L'office de l'Asmatikos Hesperinos' (see n. 25), p. 126; Duncan, *Coislin 213* (see n. 26), p. 89.

[31] Duncan, *Coislin 213* (see n. 26), p. 89.

[32] Arranz, 'L'office de l'Asmatikos Hesperinos' (see n. 25), p. 127, n. 55. For the position of the baptistery, see Rowland Mainstone, *Hagia Sophia: Architecture, Structure and Liturgy of Justinian's Church* (London, 1988), p. 124; Gabriel Bertonière, *The Historical Development of the Easter Vigil and Related Services in the Greek Church*, OCA 193 (Rome, 1972), pp. 132-133.

[33] Duncan, *Euchologe de la Grande Église* (see n. 26), pp. 89-90.

[34] Duncan, *Euchologe de la Grande Église* (see n. 26), p. 90.

[35] N.D. Uspensky, *Evening Worship in the Orthodox Church* (Crestwood, NY, 1985), pp. 50-54.

[36] Arranz, 'Uspensky' (see n. 21), p. 99.

St Symeon of Thessalonica, in his commentary on the *asmatikos* office, mentions a *Lite* procession in passing: 'Then the *Lite* is performed behind the Ambon to propitiate God on behalf of all the faithful. We sing the resurrection verses of the Apostichon.... Then intercession is made by the priest...'[37] He also describes the priest's processing behind the ambo at the dismissal hymn or *troparion*, when there is no *Lite*, as a 'type of the *Lite*'.[38] In this context, the *Lite* appears to be not only an importation from the Palestinian office that had by now largely taken over in most other churches, but one that had no real processional goal. By the time of St Symeon the cathedral office was largely confined to his cathedral (Hagia Sophia in Thessalonica), where the ancient baptistery on the south-east side of the church, may no longer have been in use by his time.[39]

4. Eastern Syria

Another interesting set of questions may be raised when we look at the evidence of a similar procession in the East Syrian/Chaldean tradition. At the end of the East Syrian vespers (*Ramsha*) is a complex appendix to the service which was already recognized as a later addition by the early seventh-century commentator, Gabriel Qatraya,[40] who explains its origin as being a Constantinopolitan procession from the church to the royal palace, in honour of the Christian king, and that this was done in memory of the conversion and victory of Constantine. It is known that the Katholikos (Patriarch) of the East, Mar Aba (536-552) visited the capitals of the Christian West and brought back texts and recollections of the ceremonies that were used there. It seems possible that the Chaldean rite received this processional observance then, in the late sixth century.[41] This would compel us to ask why there seems to be no such procession already well established in Constantinople. The memory of

---

[37] St Symeon of Thessalonike, *Treatise on Prayer: An Explanation of the Services Conducted in the Orthodox Church*, tr. H.L.N. Simmons, The Archbishop Iakovos Library of Ecclesiastical and Historical Sources 9 (Brookline, MA, 1984), p. 78.

[38] *Ibid.*

[39] Personal visit, and the scholarly guide of E. Kourkoutidou-Nikolaidou and A. Tourta, *Wandering in Byzantine Thessaloniki* (Athens, 1997).

[40] S.H. Jammo, 'L'Office du soir Chaldéen au temps de Gabriel Qatraya', *L'Orient Syrien* 12 (1967) 187-210.

[41] *Ibid.*, pp. 208-209.

the conversion and victory of Constantine, connected according to the well-known account of the sign in the sky 'in hoc signo, vinces!' would perhaps most obviously be connected with the Jerusalem procession to Golgotha, in Constantine's specially created Anastasis complex. Perhaps Mar Aba had the same sort of experience that we now associate with today's jet-lagged tourists, and simply mixed two places up? More sensibly, he could also have been thinking of a solemn visit to the imperial chapel to venerate its relics, not an uncommon practice at that date.

The East Syrian commentators normally interpret the procession as being in honour of the cross or of the victorious Christ.[42] This interpretation fits well with the idea that the real source of the rite is indeed the Jerusalem procession after vespers from the Anastasis to Golgotha.[43] In the writings of the later pseudo-George of Arbela, the procession is of the cross from the *bema* in the centre of the church to the sanctuary, but from Good Friday to Ascension the procession was to go outside the church, in order to represent the preaching of the apostles going out after the resurrection.[44] The processional route outside the church would be more in line with what we find in Jerusalem and might well be the older usage. A difficulty in either case would the Chaldean habit of referring to the table for the gospel and cross on the *bema* as Golgotha,[45] in which case the procession must be going the opposite way!

The first strophe of the processional hymn, *onita d-basaliqe*, is proper to the Sunday or feast, and on major feasts it has several strophes, indicating a much longer procession.[46] The second strophe is seasonal, and the prayer that introduces the procession is for divine assistance and that God will reveal Himself to save His people. After the hymn there is a custom in some places of reading the gospel of the day, thus making this processional appendix a form of vigil of preparation for the Sunday or feast.[47] The prayer after the hymn is variable. That for Advent, seasons of Epiphany and the Resurrection and all feasts of the Lord is more suited to a procession of the cross, representing the salvific work of Christ:

---

[42] Jacob Vellian, *East Syrian Evening Services* (Kottayam, 1971), p. 15.

[43] Jammo, 'L'Office du soir Chaldéen' (see n. 40), p. 209.

[44] Sylvester Pudichery, *Ramsa* (Bangalore, 1972), pp. 168-169.

[45] See, e.g., Robert F. Taft, 'Some Notes on the Bema in the East and West Syrian Traditions', *Orientalia Christiana Periodica* 34 (1968) 326-359, on pp. 334-335.

[46] Pudichery, *Ramsa* (see n. 44), p. 170.

[47] *Ibid.*, p. 42.

'To thy wonderful and unspeakable dispensation, O my Lord, which in mercy and compassion was perfected and completed and fulfilled, for the renewal and salvation of our nature, in the first fruits which were of us, we lift up praise and honour, and confession and worship, at all times, Lord of all...'[48]

The prayer is followed by an alleluia psalm or *shurraya*, which would have been added after the eleventh century. On weekdays instead of the *onita d-basaliqe* there is *the onita d-ramsha* ('of vespers'). Some of these latter texts appear to refer to communion, and may indicate that there was a communion at vespers on days when the full eucharistic service was not celebrated.[49]

This last chant is followed by yet another processional chant, the *onita d-sahde*, which praises the deeds of the martyrs and which was possibly connected with a procession to the *martyrion*, the place where relics were kept.[50] It seems that in earlier centuries, the Chaldean Christians kept relics of the martyrs in a building set well apart from the church, possibly in order to avoid offending the sensitivities of their Zoroastrian neighbours (who traditionally left bodies to be picked clean by carrion birds, neither buried nor cremated). The Church of the East commended the veneration of relics to the faithful, and a document believed by the Syrian scholar, George Khouri-Sarkis, to be directions for the reception of a sixth-century Chaldean bishop visiting a town, requires the bishop to venerate the place of the martyrs, '...if he finds one at the gate of the city...', by offering incense there.[51] Although not mentioned in the oldest sources, it is possible that this procession was not then originally associated with vespers.[52] If it were a free-standing devotion, this might also explain the often quite great length of these sets of chants.[53] Once again though, more questions are raised than answered.

---

[48] *East Syrian Daily Offices*, ed. A.J. Maclean (London: 1894; reprint Piscataway, New Jersey, 2003), pp. 80-81. In a footnote (1), Maclean explains that 'the first fruits that were of us' means human nature.

[49] Vellian, *East Syrian Evening Services* (see n. 42), pp. 28-29. E.g., Maclean, *East Syrian Daily Offices* (see n. 48), p. 11: 'The body of Christ and his precious blood are on the holy altar. In fear and love let us approach to it, and with the angels chant to him: Holy, holy, holy, Lord God.'

[50] Pudichery, *Ramsa* (see n. 44), p. 57; Vellian, *East Syrian Evening Services* (see n. 42), pp. 18-19.

[51] Lizette Larson-Miller, 'A Return to the Liturgical Architecture of Northern Syria', *Studia Liturgica* 24 (1994) 71-83, on pp. 78-80.

[52] Pudichery, *Ramsa* (see n. 44), pp. 196-197.

[53] See, e.g., Maclean, *East Syrian Daily Offices* (see n. 48), pp. 12-15.

5. Armenia

The Armenian vespers and its similar processional appendix were mentioned earlier. Psalm 120 was followed in Lent by the penitential prayer of Manasseh, and its 'proclamation', or prayer.[54] A very general evening prayer comes after these psalms on weekdays. That of Sundays is similar but invokes the protecting power of the cross, which leads naturally to the 'Proclamation of the Cross', involving a prayer for defence by the cross. There was then, it would seem, a procession to the church door with psalm 121 'I rejoiced when I heard them say, let us go to God's house.' Further prayers which mention Christ's resurrection[55] are followed by a return procession singing psalm 99 'Cry out with joy to the Lord' and concluded by a further prayer. However, while this Sunday version shows a much closer connection to the Jerusalem tradition of a procession to the cross at the end of vespers, the *Oratio Synodalis* of Yovhannes Ojnec'i of a much earlier date, expects vespers to finish with psalm 120: 'And thus singing the Psalm of Repose, they adjourn.'[56] The additional material was added by 1264[57] but was unknown to the eighth-century commentators who surely would have mentioned a procession to the cross at vespers, as they indeed do mention one in the morning.[58]

The final procession described by Coneybeare is similar in some ways to the modern Byzantine *Lite*, and may be a later borrowing. Overall then, in spite of the close connections with Jerusalem and Palestinian practices, it would seem that we cannot cite the Armenian service as very reliable evidence for the origins of a procession at the end of vespers.

6. Egypt, Ethiopia, and the West Syrians and Maronites

At vespers in the contemporary Coptic monastic rite, the common evening tradition of asking forgiveness of sins is present: 'Lord, I have sinned in thy sight like the prodigal son, but accept me, O Father, for

---

[54] Coneybeare and Maclean, *Rituale Armenorum* (see n. 18), p. 480.

[55] *Ibid.*, p. 482: '...Thy holy wondrous and victorious Resurrection we do laud...'

[56] Michael Daniel Findikyan, *The Commentary on the Armenian Daily Office by Bishop Step'anos Siwnec'i (+735)*, OCA 270 (Rome, 2004), pp. 490-491.

[57] *Ibid.*, p. 491.

[58] *Ibid.*, pp. 395-397.

I repent...' Interspersed with the poetic verses are verses from psalm 122, as in the *Aposticha* of the modern Byzantine rite.[59] Beyond this it is impossible to identify any processional appendix at vespers in Coptic Egypt, or, for that matter, in Ethiopia.[60] Similarly, there is no sign that the West Syrian and related Maronite offices ever possessed anything of this nature, in spite of their geographical proximity to Jerusalem.[61] Vespers or *Ramsho* usually concludes with the supplicatory chant called *Bo'utho* and the vestiges of a form of compline.

The evidence from the Christian East then is patchy. We are reliant upon what we can reconstruct of the Jerusalem rite, on the cathedral rite of Constantinople, and on the East Syrian rite. The important Coptic, Ethiopian and West Syrian traditions seem to know no such ceremony, nor originally, I would suggest, did the Armenians. What we do have would appear to indicate Jerusalem as the point of origin for processions at vespers. This Jerusalem tradition grew up as part of the daily veneration of the cross of Christ outside the basilica of the Resurrection. Later we have, what I now suspect, was a parallel development of a procession that went to other sites in monastic contexts. The only place in the Christian East from which we appear to have clear evidence for the procession to include a visit to a baptistery is eleventh-century Constantinople, and that too raises questions.

Conclusion

It will be apparent that I think that this whole subject could benefit from a much closer examination of the sources. It seems likely that a procession at the end of vespers, and sometimes also at the end of lauds/ matins, was, from the early Middle Ages, progressively adopted in many places (including Western Europe) in imitation of Jerusalem practice. This procession was primarily to the cross. Its extension to the baptistery (or baptisteries), a practice that seems more common in the western than the eastern sources, may be either because such buildings were ideal places to keep a relic of the cross, or, less hypothetically, because there

---

[59] See the appendix to John, Marquess of Bute, *Coptic Morning Service for the Lord's Day* (London, 1882), pp. 132-133.

[60] See Habte-Michael Kidane, *L'Ufficio Divino della Chiesa Etiopica*, OCA 257 (Rome, 1998).

was the other influential Palestinian custom of visiting other chapels or even churches to commemorate certain saints. Most baptisteries in Western Europe had an altar,[62] and might therefore have been treated as stational chapels for the purposes of these processions.

In the article in *Worship*, I highlighted my conclusion that only the ancient Easter vespers of the Roman Church appeared to have a primarily baptismal focus, as a service that processed to the font during, not after, vespers.[63] In *Daily Liturgical Prayer* I argued that a baptismal theology implicitly underlies all celebration of daily prayer, but one could also say that such a theology underlies many aspects of Christian life, including devotion to the cross of Christ. I am now even less certain that the baptismal memory could only be preserved by processing to a baptistery! Where I now think that we have a lot of work to do, is in re-examining these processional practices, especially in the Anastasis complex in Jerusalem and in the Sabbaite monasteries of Palestine. There may yet be more surprises to come.

---

[61] See, e.g., Bede Griffiths, *The Book of Common Prayer of the Syrian Church* (Vagamon, no date; reprint Piscataway, NJ, 2005).

[62] Such altars may be seen, e.g., at St John Lateran in Rome, in the Baptistery in Florence and in the Neonian (Orthodox) Baptistery in Ravenna.

[63] Described by S.J.P. van Dijk, 'The Medieval Easter Vespers of the Roman Clergy', *Sacris Erudiri* 19 (1969-70) 261-363, on p. 327.

UNSOLVED PROBLEMS CONCERNING THE BACKGROUND AND SIGNIFICANCE OF THE VOCABULARY OF PRAISE IN SOME OF THE OLDEST EUCHARISTIC PRAYERS

Gabriele WINKLER

The central aim of SOL is the investigation of primary sources, their edition and interpretation, including the presentation of solutions to hitherto unsolved problems, and/or overviews on new research projects. I shall attempt to follow this fundamental understanding of our newly established society in my present contribution.

First I shall present the sources to be investigated; then establish the location of the relevant vocabulary within the Anaphora, namely at the Initial Dialogue, before the Sanctus and before the Epiclesis; followed by a closer analysis of the vocabulary and a presentation of my results. My aim is to establish the theological origins of the various Verbs of Praise and to discuss their initial liturgical meaning, while offering some explanations of the Ethiopic vocabulary and modifying also prior retro-translations of the Syriac and Armenian verbs into Greek or translations into other languages.

Normally we no longer deal with retrotranslations of texts of the Christian Orient into Greek as was done, for example, by H. Engberding last century. Yet for the sake of clarity and in order to scrutinize more closely the vocabulary of praise in the various anaphoras of the Christian Orient, it was indispensable to procede as follows: (1) It all began by collecting on a systematic basis the Greek, Syriac, Armenian, and Ethiopic Verbs of Praise in the respective original languages. (2) In order to facilitate a comparison in greater detail, the relevant vocabulary was then retrotranslated into Greek. (3) This systematic collection and comparison allowed much greater precision and thereby several modifications of the prior Greek retrotranslation of the Syriac and Armenian vocabulary in H. Engberding's excellent publication, or the English translations offered by R.J. Ledogar in his otherwise valuable study of the Praise-Verbs.[1] (4) This procedure leads to several clarifications.

---

[1] See detailed overview in: G. Winkler, *Die Basilius-Anaphora. Edition der beiden armenischen Redaktionen und der relevanten Fragmente, Übersetzung und Zusammen-*

I. INTRODUCTION

While there are a number of important and extensive investigations concerning, for example, the various forms of intercessions, there are only very few studies which have addressed the formation and various shapes of doxologies, or the evolution and meaning of the vocabulary of praise in the context of the Anaphora,[2] more precisely before the Sanctus and Epiclesis.[3] In this context I had offered already modifications of past translations of the vocabulary by Ledogar and Engberding.[4] In this paper I shall once more address the tangled issue of the vocabulary of praise, its background and significance in some of the oldest and most remarkable Eucharistic formularies, such as the so-called 'Traditio Apostolica' (**TradAp**)[5] with its possible Alexandrian

---

schau aller Versionen im Licht der orientalischen Überlieferungen, Anaphorae Orientales 2. Anaphorae Armeniacae 2 (Rome, 2005), pp. 441, 443, 444-445.

[2] See the extensive study of R.J. Ledogar, *Acknowledgment. Praise-Verbs in the Early Greek Anaphora* (Rome, 1968); in addition H. Engberdings's Greek retrotranslation of the Syriac and Armenian texts of the Oratio ante Sanctus in the Anaphora of Basil in his famous dissertation: *Das Eucharistische Hochgebet der Basileiosliturgie. Textgeschichtliche Untersuchung und kritische Ausgabe*, Theologie des Christlichen Ostens. Texte und Untersuchungen (Münster, 1931); or the interesting observations of H. Cazelle, 'L'anaphore et l'Ancien Testament', in: *Eucharisties d'Orient et Occident* 1, Lex Orandi 46 (Paris, 1970), pp. 11-21.

[3] Cf. Winkler, *Basilius-Anaphora*, pp. 419-516, 758-774. For a more systematic investigation of the Praise-Verbs in the Ethiopian Anaphoras see now G. Winkler, 'Über das christliche Erbe Henochs und einige Probleme des Testamentum Domini', *Oriens Christianus* 93 (2009) 201-247.

[4] Cf. Ledogar, *Praise-Verbs in the Early Greek Anaphora*; and Engberdings's Greek retrotranslation of the Syriac and Armenian texts of the Oratio ante Sanctus in the Anaphora of Basil in his: *Das Eucharistische Hochgebet der Basileiosliturgie*; s. in addition Winkler, *Basilius-Anaphora*, pp. 424-451, 511 (in particular: 432-433, 435-439, *440-441*, *444-445*, 446-449).

[5] Among the recent publications concerning the so-called 'Traditio Apostolica' see next to the well known publications of G. Schöllgen ['Pseudoapostolizität und Schriftgebrauch in den ersten Kirchenordnungen...', *Jahrbuch für Antike und Christentum. Ergänzungsband* 23 (Münster, 1996)]; or W. Geerling [*Traditio Apostolica*, Fontes Christiani 1 (Freiburg, 1991), and the critique of Gerling's publ. by M. Metzger: 'A propos d'une Reédition de la prétendue *Tradition Apostolique*, avec traduction allemande', *Archiv für Liturgiewissenschaft* 33 (1991), pp. 290-294]; above all the extremely valuable contributions of B. Steimer, *Vertex Traditionis. Die Gattungen der altchristlichen Kirchenordnungen*, Beihefte der Zeitschrift für die neutestamentliche Wissenschaft 63 (Berlin/New York, 1992); and Ch. Markschies 'Wer schrieb die sogenannte *Traditio Apostolica*? Neue Beobachtungen und Hypothesen zu einer kaum lösbaren Frage aus der altkirchlichen Literaturgeschichte', in *Tauffragen und Bekenntnis*, eds. W. Kinzig – Ch. Markschies – M. Vinzent, Arbeiten zur Kirchengeschichte 74 (Berlin/New York, 1999), pp. 1-74. In connection with: *The Apostolic Tradition. A Commentary* by Paul F. Bradshaw, Maxwell E. Johnson, L. Edward Phillips, Hermeneia

ties, the East-Syrian Anaphora of the Apostles Addai and Mari (**syr Ap-An**)[6], and the Antiochene Liturgy of Basil (**Bas**).[7] Each one of these

(Minneapolis, 2002), see my review in the *Theologische Quartalschrift* 185 (2005) 323-326. For some important reflexions on editions, translations and appropriate introductions dealing with the necessary historical, philological, and theological considerations, cf. Ch. Markschies, 'Das Problem der *praefationes*', *ZAC* 8 (2004) 38-58.

I shall use the Ethiopic version, edited by H. Duensing, *Der aethiopische Text der Kirchenordnung des Hippolyt nach 8 Handschriften herausgegeben und übersetzt*, Abhandlungen der Wissenschaften in Göttingen. Philolog.-hist. Klasse. 3. Folge 32 (Göttingen, 1946); and the Latin version, edited by E. Hauler, *Didascaliae Apostolorum. Fragmenta Ueronensis Latina. Accedunt Canonum qui dicuntur Apostolorum et Aegyptiorum Reliquiae* (Leipzig 1900).

[6] Cf. W.F. Macomber, 'The Oldest Known Text of the Anaphora of the Apostles Addai and Mari', *OCP* 32 (1966) 335-371; *idem*, 'Anaphora of the Apostles' (1971) = Macomber, 'The Maronite and Chaldean Versions of the Anaphora of the Apostles', *OCP* 37 (1971) 55-84; *idem*, 'Anaphora of the Apostles' (1982) = Macomber, 'The Ancient Form of the Anaphora of the Apostles', in: N. Garsoïan – Th. Matthews – R. Thomson (eds.), *East of Byzantium: Syria and Armenia in the Formative Period* (Washington, 1982), pp. 72-88; A.Gelston, *The Eucharistic Prayer of Addai and Mari* (Oxford, 1992). For a more detailed recent investigation of various parts of Addai and Mari (= **syr Ap-An**) cf. Winkler, *Basilius-Anaphora*, pp. 291-297, 330-332, 342-348, 413-418, 431-440, 446-451, 491-494, 528-530, *etc.*; for further information cf. my index in *Basilius-Anaphora*, 890-891 (= **syr Ap-An**).

[7] For editions and extensive studies cf. Engberding, *Basileiosliturgie*; A. Budde, *Die ägyptische Basilius-Anaphora. Text – Kommentar – Geschichte*, Jerusalemer Theologisches Forum 7 (Münster, 2004); Winkler, *Basilius-Anaphora*. [Several studies, which appeared in English, such as J.R.K. Fenwick, *The Anaphoras of St. Basil and St. James: An Investigation into their Common Origin*, OCA 240 (Rome 1992) and several publications dependent on Fenwick, can be ignored; cf. review in: *Oriens Christianus* 78 (1994), pp. 269-277.] As is well known through Engberding's seminal study of 1931, the witnesses to the Anaphora of Basil fall into two large groups, a *short* and a *long* redaction. In his pioneering study of the Anaphora of Basil Engberding established for the first time the prominence of the four most important versions of this Anaphora: (1) The primary *short Egyptian* Anaphora of Basil (in Greek, Coptic, Ethiopic); (2) The secondary *longer* redaction based on a lost archetype Ω from which the first Armenian version emerged; (3) Dependant on Ω is also the lost archetype Ψ, from which the Syriac redaction derives; (4) The Byzantine-Greek version, also deriving from Ψ, is one of the youngest redactions according to Engberding. Some of Engberding's conclusions, such as the interdependance of the various redactions, or the primacy of the short Egyptian version, are no longer entirely tenable; cf. Winkler, *Basilius-Anaphora*, pp. 20, 568, 645-650, 666-668, 695, 726, 741, 749, 856-861, 878, 880; *eadem*, 'Fragen zur zeitlichen Priorität der ägyptischen Textgestalt gegenüber den längeren Versionen der Basilius-Anaphora', *Bollettino della Badia Greca di Grottaferrata* III/4 (2007) 243-273; *eadem*, 'On the Formation of the Armenian Anaphoras: A Completely Revised and Updated Overview', *Studi sull'Oriente Cristiano* 11/2 (2007) 97-130, here: p.106.

With regard to the internal structure and the various parts of the Anaphora it should be noted that the Anaphora of Basil seemingly contains building-blocks of different origin and diverging theological underpinnings. The high antiquity of several parts of this Anaphora on the one hand, and the past attribution to Saint Basil of Cappadocia on the other, moreover, the fact that this Anaphora has come down to us in virtually all languages of the Christian East, makes it one of the most venerable Eucharistic Prayers.

Eucharistic Prayers has its own well known characteristic traits: for
example, the striking absence of the Sanctus in the 'Traditio Apostolica' while offering the Institution Narrative at the same time, in contrast
to the pristine presence of the Sanctus (the Thrice 'Holy' of Is 6,3)
seemingly from the onset in both formularies,[8] **syr Ap-An + Bas**, while
the Institution Narrative is missing in **syr Ap-An**. Underneath these differences lie, of course, profoundly differing theological underpinnings
and the respective ritualization of these views.

All three formularies have the praise of God in common at the first
part of the Eucharistic Prayer, albeit giving this concept a widely differing emphasis and meaning. In the 'Traditio Apostolica' this praise
of God has a very brief and restricted form, being seemingly used as
a sort of transition to the credal statements concerning the Son, in contrast to the Anaphora of Basil where it is present in a most expanded
shape, forming the centre-piece of the 'Liturgy of the Angels' within
the Oratio ante Sanctus. Also in Addai and Mari this worship of God
is central, leading up to the climax with the 'Sanctus', the *'Qedušša*,
which even gave rise to the very name of the three East-Syrian 'Anaphoras'. In the manuscript tradition they are *not* referred to as *'Qurbana'*,
the Syriac equivalent term of *'Anaphora'* (*'oblatio'*), but referred to as
'Qedušša' (syr: ܩܘܕܫܐ/*'Quddaša'*): the *'Quddaša'* of the Apostles
(Addai and Mari), the *'Quddaša'* of Mar Theodore, the *'Quddaša'* of
Mar Nestorius.[9] Something similar is true for the older Ethiopian

---

In addition, the highly intriguing Christological formulae seemingly reflect the Christological position not so much of the great Cappadocian Saint, but of the Antiochene Synod
in 341 in the aftermath of the Nicene Council of 325. Thus this Eucharistic Prayer is
Antiochene in both, in its liturgical shape *and* in its Christology as well. This Anaphora
has obviously something to do with the struggle for orthodoxy and the Christological
disputes in the attempt to overcome Arianism, as was assumed already for quite some
time. However, the basic Christology in the various versions of the Anaphora of Basil
seems to be slightly earlier than the Christological tenets of Saint Basil himself, and they
apparently pertain not to Cappadocia but to the Antiochene struggle for orthodoxy in the
aftermath of the Council of Nicea. Cf. Winkler, *Basilius-Anaphora*, pp. 866-870, with
references to the respective detailed analysis of the vocabulary throughout my study;
eadem, 'The Antiochene Synods and the Early Armenian Creeds Including the "*Rezep-
tionsgeschichte*" of the Synod of Antioch 341 in the Armenian Version of the Anaphora
of Basil', *Bollettino della Badia Greca di Grottaferrata* III/3 (2006) 275-298.

[8] For the presence of the Sanctus in Addai and Mari from the onset cf. B.D. Spinks,
The Sanctus in the Eucharistic Prayer (Cambridge, 1991), pp.104, 108; for the Anaphora
of Basil and of Addai and Mari cf. Winkler, *Basilius-Anaphora*, pp. 281-283, 417-418.

[9] Cf. Macomber, 'The Oldest Known Text', pp. 342, 358; Gelston, *Addai and Mari*,
p. 47; S. Jammo, 'The Quddasha of the Apostles Addai and Mari', *Syriac Dialogue*
(Vienna, 1994), pp. 167-181, here: p. 168; Winkler, *Basilius-Anaphora*, pp. 349, 530-
532.

'Anaphoras', they are called: '*Qəddase*' (ቅዳሴ:), '*Qəddase*' of the Apostles (ቅዳሴ:ሐዋርያት:), '*Qəddase*' of the Lord (ቅዳሴ:እግዚእ:), *etc.*, and the 'Collection of Anaphoras' is referred to as 'Book of the *Qedušša*' (*Mäṣəḥafä Qəddase*).[10]

With this differing nomenclature: *Qedušša* (syr: *Quddaša*; ethiop: *Qəddase*) in contrast to 'ἀναφορά' ('*oblatio*', syr: '*qurbana*') we can detect already crucial differences in what is given preeminence in these Liturgical Prayers. Indisputable tensions surface thereby between the concept of 'εὐχαριστία' in connection with the 'ἀναφορά' on the one hand, and on the other the concept of 'εὐλογία' through the prominent inclusion and dramatisation of the Old Testament visions of the foremost prophets, the *merkava*-mysticism of Ezekiel (chap. 1+3+10), the vision of Isaiah (chap. 6) with the 'Heavenly Liturgy' of the highest ranks of Angels, culminating in the 'Thrice Holy' (Is 6:3), *watched and imitated by the faithful*. In the 'Traditio Apostolica' this 'Heavenly Liturgy' is totally absent while a crescendo via credal statements is leading up to the Institution Narrative, whereas in Addai and Mari and even more extensively in the Anaphora of Basil this vision of the 'Liturgy of Angels' is of paramount importance.[11]

For the sake of clarity let us begin by formulating some of the problems which need to be addressed and subsequently solved:

–   Where are these Verbs of Praise located in the Anaphora?
–   Who expresses the theme of 'Worship' and 'Thanksgiving'?
–   Where do the Verbs of Praise and Thanksgiving originally belong to?
–   What precise meanings do these verbs have?

---

[10] Cf. Winkler, *Basilius-Anaphora*, pp. 531-532.

[11] The Oratio ante Sanctus of the Anaphora of Basil in its present form shows a juxtaposition of: (1) the original nucleus of the Prayer before the Sanctus consisting of the 'Liturgy of the Angels', which in its pristine form is based on the grand prophetic visions of Ezekiel (chap. 1+3+10) and Isaiah (chap. 6), namely the worship of the Cherubim and Seraphim, culminating in the exlamation of the 'Holy', the Sanctus; (2) the later addition and evolution of an 'Oratio Theologica' with which the Prayer before the Sanctus now begins; (3) the juxtaposition of the 'Theme of Praise' with the Sanctus as high-point and the *Leitmotiv* of 'Thanksgiving' due to the increasing importance of the Institution Narrative, which brought about a reworking of the Initial Dialogue and other parts of the Anaphora. Cf. Winkler, *Basilius-Anaphora*, pp. 693-695.

II. THE LOCATION OF THESE VERBS WITHIN THE ANAPHORA

The themes of 'Worship', 'Praise', and 'Thanksgiving' occur:

(1) at the Initial Dialogue (**TradAp**; **syr Ap-An, Bas**);
(2) before the Sanctus (**syr Ap-An, Bas**);
(3) before the Epiclesis (**Bas, syr Ap-An, TradAp**).

The presence of the vocabulary of praise at the Initial Dialogue, immediately before the Sanctus and before the Epiclesis provides much food for thought: could it be that their location at these central parts of the Anaphora provide already a clue to the pristine and inherent relationship between the Initial Dialogue, the Sanctus, and the Epiclesis? It does seem to me that this question will be eventually answered in the affermative as we shall see.

1. The Praise-Verbs at the Initial Dialogue

As is well known, the Initial Dialogue consists usually of two parts, namely (1) the admonition of the deacon, (2) the Dialogue proper between the celebrant and the faithful:[12]

---

[12] With regard to the Opening of the Anaphora the following important overviews and studies of the various traditions should be consulted: H. Engberding, 'Der Gruß des Priesters zu Beginn der εὐχαριστία in den östlichen Liturgien', *Jahrbuch für Liturgiewissenschaft* 9 (1929) 138-141, with an important critique by A. Baumstark in his: *Comparative Liturgy* (London, 1958), pp. 82-83; C.A. Bouman, 'Variants in the Introduction to the Eucharistic Prayer', *Vigiliae Christianae* 4 (1950) 94-115; above all the highly significant analysis of W.C. van Unnik, '*Dominus vobiscum*: The Background of a Liturgical Formular', in: W.C. van Unnik, *Sparsa collecta. The Collected Essays of W.C. van Unnik* III, Suppl. to Novum Testamentum 31 (Leiden, 1983), pp. 362-391; for the Armenian evidence and a comparison to the Syriac tradition cf. Winkler, *Basilius-Anaphora*, pp. 279-350; also for the Armenian Opening: Feulner, *Athanasius-Anaphora*, pp. 230-254; for the Egyptian tradition cf. Budde, pp. 220-239; for the opening in the Anaphora of Addai and Mari cf. Macomber, 'Anaphora of the Apostles' (1971), pp. 55-84; *idem*, 'Anaphora of the Apostles', (1982), pp. 72-88; Gelston, *Addai and Mari*, pp. 118/119-122/123; for an extensive analysis of the opening in the Byzantine Rite cf. R.F. Taft, 'Textual Problems in the Diaconal Admonition before the Anaphora in the Byzantine Tradition', *OCP* 49 (1983) 340-356; *idem*, 'The Dialogue before the Anaphora in the Byzantine Eucharistic Liturgy I: The Opening Greeting', *OCP* 52 (1986) 299-324; *idem*, 'The Dialogue before the Anaphora in the Byzantine Eucharistic Liturgy II: The *Sursum corda*', *OCP* 54 (1988) 47-77; *idem*, 'The Dialogue before the Anaphora in the Byzantine Eucharistic Liturgy III: Let us give thanks to the Lord – It is fitting and right', *OCP* 55 (1989) 63-74; for the Ethiopian evidence cf. E. Hammerschmidt, *Studies in Ethiopic Anaphoras. Second Revised Edition*, Äthiopistische Forschungen 25 (Stuttgart, 1987), pp. 63-72; and Winkler, *Basilius-Anaphora*, pp. 316-328.

I. The Admonition of the Deacon (Στῶμεν καλῶς);
the old Armenian version (**arm Bas I**) adds:
'*Let us look* with attention' – '*To you*, o God'

II. The Dialogue proper (has 3 parts):
   – Blessing + response;
   – *Sursum corda/mentes* + response;
   – Admonition to '*give thanks*' (εὐχαριστήσωμεν)
   or: '*to praise*' + response.

The 'Traditio Apostolica' still provides only the second part in both versions (**eth TradAp** + **lat TradAp**[13]): the Blessing + response; Sursum corda + response; followed by the admonition: '*Gratias agamus domino*' (as in **lat TradAp**), whereas the Ethiopic text (**eth TradAp**) has here: ናአኩተ ፡ ለእግዚአብሔር ('*Let us laud/praise* the Lord').

The relevant verb አአኩተ ('*akkuətä*) in **eth Trad Ap** (here in the grammatical form of: ናአኩተ) primarily has to be compared to εὐλογεῖν (or δοξάζειν) and only secondarily to εὐχαριστεῖν as well. This verb አአኩተ ('*akkuətä*) with the noun አኩቴት ('*akkuätet*) is *unknown in other semitic languages*.[14] According to Dillmann this verb has the meaning of: '*laudibus celebrare, laudare, honorem reddere alicui*', as in Sir 35:13 አአኩተ: εὐλόγησον; in Dan 3:23 it translates ὑμνεῖν; in Mt 26:27 εὐχαριστεῖν.[15] For the noun አኩቴት Dillmann offers the following Latin translation: '(1) *laudatio, laus, gloria*; (2) *gratiarum actio, gratia, eucharistia*'.[16] In connection with the liturgical investigation of the Ethiopic vocabulary in my *Basilius-Anaphora*, I formulated:[17]

Insgesamt ist folgendes festzuhalten: Das Verb አአኩተ: (mit dem Substantiv አኩቴት:) steht zunächst dem εὐλογεῖν (bzw. der εὐλογία) und dem δοξάζειν bzw. δόξα) sehr nahe, erst in zweiter Linie ist der Gedanke der εὐχαριστία (bzw. εὐχαριστεῖν) einzubeziehen. Wenn dieses in den anderen semitischen Sprachen nicht bezeugte Vokabular im Zusammenhang äthiopischer Anaphoren auftritt, so muß die Nähe mit der εὐλογία (bzw. einem εὐλογεῖν) mitberücksichtigt bzw. mitgedacht werden, wenn dieses Vokabular mit εὐχαριστία bzw. εὐχαριστεῖν wiedergegeben wird.

---

[13] For the Ethiopic version (**eth TradAp**) cf. ed. Duensing, pp. 20/21; and the investigation in Winkler, *Basilius-Anaphora*, p. 326; for the Latin version (**lat TradAp**) cf. ed. Hauler, p. 106.

[14] Cf. A. Dillmann, *Lexicon linguae athiopicae cum indice latino* (Osnabrück 1970, photomech. reprint of the ed. of 1865), p. 785: 'rad. inus., neque in aliis linguis obvia; quod in gramm. [= first. ed. of 1857] p. 42 proposui etym., reprobandum est.'

[15] Cf. Dillmann, *Lexicon*, pp. 785-786.

[16] *Ibid.*, p. 786.

[17] Cf. Winkler, *Basilius-Anaphora*, pp. 323-328, citation: p. 324.

In this context we should also note the Syriac translation (*Vet Syr* + *Pəšitta*) of '*giving thanks*' in Jn 6:11. The Greek text says: ἔλαβεν οὖν τοὺς ἄρτους ὁ Ἰησοῦς καὶ εὐχαριστήσας ..., which in the Syriac text (*Vet Syr* + *Pəšitta*) is rendered, however, with ܘܒܪܟ ('et *benedixit*'). Likewise the *Pəšitta* text of 1 Cor 11:24:... ἔλαβεν ἄρτον καὶ εὐχαριστήσας is rendered in the *Pəšitta* with: ܘܒܪܟ ('et *benedixit*').[18] This means, the Greek text uses εὐχαριστεῖν, the Syriac text, however, has εὐλογεῖν. Also the evidence in the Syriac Acts of Thomas is here pertinent. G. Rouwhorst has shown in several important contributions that the concept of εὐχαριστία does not figure prominently in the Syriac original of these Acta.[19]

In the light of both, the earliest Syriac evidence, which seemingly favoured εὐλογεῖν over against εὐχαριστεῖν, and the Ethiopic vocabulary of አአኵቶ ('*akkuətä*) in **eth TradAp** with its primary tendency to express the concept of '*laudare*', we have to ask ourselves how we should render the verb አአኵቶ ('*akkuətä*) at the Initial Dialogue in **eth TradAp** and in all the other Ethiopic anaphoras. This verb, unknown in other Semitic languages, is not used, for example, in the Ethiopic Book of Enoch (**eth En**) in the context of the *Qeduššа* or other sections dealing with the praise of God. In **eth En** 9:4 the following two verbs are used: 'Your name is... *praised and glorified*' (ወበሩኽ : ወስቡሕ:);[20] likewise in the context of the *Qeduššа* of **eth En** 39:12 or other places. Hence in **eth En** the two verbs εὐλογεῖν ('to praise') and δοξάζειν ('to glorify') are very well attested. Given these facts I proposed to render the verb አአኵቶ ('*akkuətä*) with '*laudare*' (and the noun አኵቶት '*laudatio*') in order to distinguish the verb from εὐλογεῖν and δοξάζειν, which correspond to ܢܫܒܚ = '*glorificemus*' at the Initial Dialogue of **syr Ap-An**. Here is the respective overview concerning the vocabulary in

---

[18] Cf. G. Rouwhorst, 'Bénédiction, action de grâces, supplication. Les oraisons de la table dans le Judaïsme et les célébrations eucharistiques des chrétiens syriaques', *Questions Liturgiques* 61 (1980) 211-240, here p. 219; also my remarks in: *Basilius-Anaphora*, pp. 298, 325.

[19] Cf. Rouwhorst, 'Bénédiction, action de grâces', pp. 221-222; idem, 'La célébration de l'eucharistie selon les Actes de Thomas', in *Omnes circumstantes. Contributions Towards a History of the Role of the People in the Liturgy. Presented to Herman Wegman*, eds. Ch. Caspers – M. Schneider (Kampen, 1990), pp. 51-77, here: pp. 57-58, 66-67, 75; G. Winkler, 'Weitere Beobachtungen zur frühen Epiklese (den Doxologien und dem Sanctus). Über die Bedeutung der Apokryphen für die Erforschung der Entwicklung der Riten', *OC* 80 (1996) 177-200, here: p. 188; eadem, *Basilius-Anaphora*, p. 325.

[20] Cf. J. Flemming, *Das Buch Henoch. Äthiopischer Text*, TU 22 (Leipzig, 1902), p. 8 [herewith cited as: Flemming, *Henoch* (äth)].

Ethiopic, and how it corresponds to the Syriac and Greek, offering for the sake of clarity also the Latin equivalent:[21]

በረከ : (syr:[22])	εὐλογεῖν	*benedicere*	'to praise'
ሰብሐ : (syr: ܫܒܚ)	δοξάζειν	*glorificare*	'to glorify'
አሕመተ : (–[23])		*laudare*	
አሕምቶት :		*laudatio*	

So much for the interpretation of the pertinent vocabulary in the Ethiopic version of **TradAp**. With regard to the evidence concerning the Initial Dialogue of the East-Syrian Anaphoras, and in particular of Addai and Mari (**syr Ap-An**), which like the **TradAp** also testifies only to the second part of the Initial Dialogue, I refer to my detailed investigation of the evidence in my *Basilius-Anaphora*, pp. 279-285, 291-315. Here is a summary of my findings in regard to **syr Ap-An**:

(1) The established consensus is that the present wording of the Initial Dialogue in the Anaphora of the Apostles Addai and Mari does not reflect the original text.[24] Macomber showed via an investigation of the vocabulary that the early form of the Opening in **syr Ap-An** has been preserved in the Syriac Blessing of the oil.[25] According to Macomber, the relevant text in the Consecration of the oil was taken over from an older version of **syr Ap-An**.

(2) Macomber's observation is undoubtedly correct with two restrictions: first, it is highly unlikely that the verb ܐܘܕܝ (cf. εὐχαριστεῖν) and the noun ܬܘܕܝܬܐ (cf. εὐχαριστία) belonged in this context to the original text of **syr Ap-An**. This hypothesis is strengthened by the analysis of the Syriac Acts of Thomas and the translation of Jn 6:11 and 1 Cor 11:24 as we have seen already: the verb εὐχαριστήσας is translated with ܒܪܟ (*'benedixit'*) in these NT-texts.[26]

---

[21] Cf. Winkler, *Basilius-Anaphora*, p. 325.

[22] The original vocabulary (εὐλογεῖν) at the Initial Dialogue and the 'ante Sanctus' of **syr Ap-An** was *substituted by* ܫܘܒܚܐ (δόξα) or δοξάζειν; cf. Winkler, *Basilius-Anaphora*, pp. 296, 325, 432-433; likewise **arm Bas I** has at the Oratio ante Sanctus: փառաւորել (δοξάζειν) in the context of the praise by the faithful; at the praise *of the Cherubim* (and Seraphim) of **arm Bas I** and **II**, however: աւրհնել (εὐλογεῖν); cf. Winkler, pp. 442, 445, 446, and the overview below.

[23] The vocabulary is unknown in other Semitic languages.

[24] Cf. Macomber, 'Anaphora of the Apostles' (1971), pp. 55-84; *idem*, 'Anaphora of the Apostles' (1982), pp. 72-88; Gelston, *Addai and Mari*, pp. 118/119-122/123 (with pp. 76-80); Winkler, *Basilius-Anaphora*, pp. 291-315.

[25] Cf. Macomber, 'Anaphora of the Apostles' (1971), pp. 61-62; Winkler, *Basilius-Anaphora*, pp. 291-292-293.

[26] Cf. Rouwhorst, 'Bénédiction, action de grâces', pp. 221-222 (and p. 219); Winkler, *Basilius-Anaphora*, pp. 292-294.

The concept of εὐχαριστία and εὐχαριστεῖν is not given preference in **syr Ap-An** (with a striking parallel in **arm Bas**!), but rather
εὐλογία and εὐλογεῖν, which in most Syriac liturgical sources
became substituted by δοξάζειν[27], rarely also by the noun δόξα
(ܫܘܒܚܐ). This is clearly shown in the 'ante Sanctus' of **syr Ap-An**;
in Macomber's reconstruction the text begins with the *noun*: '*Glory*
be to you' (ܠܟ ܫܘܒܚܐ)[28] – in **arm Bas I** rendered with the *verb*
փառատրեմք (δοξάζειν).[29]

Second, Macomber had rearranged the sequence of the three parts of
the Opening by placing the reference to the 'Offering' at the beginning:[30]

(a) '*Oblatio* (ܩܘܪܒܐ) Deo omnium Domino offertur' (plus response:
   'Decens et iustum est');
(b) 'Sursum sint mentes vestrae' (plus response);
(c) *Gratias agamus*
   et adoremus
   et glorificemus Deum omnium Dominum.

Like Gelston, I also do not follow Macomber's rearrangement.[31]
I suggested the following original structure:[32]

(a) Blessing + plus response;
(b) Sursum sint mentes vestrae + plus response;
(c) ['*Gratias agamus*' = *secondary interpolation*], originally just:
   Adoremus et glorificemus (ܘܢܣܓܕ ܘܢܫܒܚ)
   Deum omnium Dominum.

[27] Cf. Winkler, *Basilius-Anaphora*, pp. 294, 416, 431, 433, 438, 439, 443 n. 60, 445,
446, 450, *762-763, 768, 771.*
[28] Cf. Macomber, 'Anaphora of the Apostles' (1982), p. 84.
[29] Cf. Winkler, *Basilius-Anaphora*, pp. 292-294, 348, 420, 435, 438-439, 442, 444,
446-451.
[30] Cf. Macomber, 'Anaphora of the Apostles' (1971), 61-62; *idem*, 'Anaphora of the
Apostles' (1992), pp. 84/86; Winkler, *Basilius-Anaphora*, p. 295.
[31] Cf. Gelston, *Addai and Mari*, pp. 118/119-122/123 (with pp. 76-80); Winkler,
Basilius-Anaphora, p. 295.
[32] Cf. Winkler, *Basilius-Anaphora*, pp. 295-296.

My hypothetical conclusion is based on a comparison to the praise of the Angels at the 'ante Sanctus', which undoubtedly inspired the text of the Initial Dialogue of **syr Ap-An**:

> Majestatem tuam, Domine,
> **adorant** mille milia supernorum…
> cum Cherubim et Seraphim sanctis
> nomen tuum **glorificant** …

The comparison between the verbs of the Initial Dialogue (*'adoremus et glorificemus'* = Syriac: ܢܣܓܘܕ ܘ ܢܫܒܚ) and those in connection with the praise of the Angels at the 'ante Sanctus' (*'adorant – glorificant'* = ܡܫܒܚܝܢ – ܣܓܕܝܢ) suggests that the verbs of the Initial Dialogue were clearly inspired by the verbs used for the Angels at the 'ante Sanctus': at the Initial Dialogue the faithful are admonished to imitate the worhsip of God by the Angels at the 'ante Sanctus'. This, of course, shows the intention to shape the Initial Dialogue and the 'ante Sanctus' as an inherent unity.

Originally neither the Anaphora of the Apostles Addai and Mari (**syr Ap-An**) nor the Anaphora of Basil (**Bas**) had here any reference to an *'oblatio'* (= ἀναφορά)![33] This immediately makes us wonder *what original function this Initial Dialogue once had* if any reference to an 'oblation' was originally missing in both formularies, **syr Ap-An** plus **Bas**.

Given the Armenian text (*'Let us look* with attention *– To you,* o God') and the originally missing allusion to the ἀναφορά we have to ask: What purpose this Dialogue serves? Is this Dialogue meant as an introduction to the 'ἀναφορά' as virtually all the publications on the subject have claimed, or is it the introduction to something else? Could it be that this Dialogue had originally in **syr Ap-An** plus **Bas** the function of introducing the theme of the 'Heavenly Liturgy of the Angels'? For we have to ask: What meaning does the 'Sursum corda/mentes' have? And what does the Armenian text mean: *'Let us look* with attention' – '*To you,* o God'? Could it be that we have here the traces of the original intention of this Dialogue, namely *to inaugurate* the 'Liturgy of the Angels in Heaven', which only later on became reworked by interpolating the theme of 'thanksgiving' for the ἀναφορά? The questions inherent in the Dialogue have to be answered: Why should we stand in fear and awe? *Why should we look* to God with attention? *Why should*

---

[33] For Addai and Mari (**syr Ap-An**) and also **syr TheoMop** + **syr Nest** cf. Winkler, *Basilius-Anaphora*, pp. 291-313; for **Bas** cf. *ibid.*, pp. 286-290, 313-315, 331.

we lift up our hearts? Because of the beginning of the ἀναφορά? Or rather because we should become aware of what is happening *above in heaven*: namely the Praise of God by the highest ranks of Angels? The admonition '*Let us lift up*' our hearts, in addition the admonition in the Armenian text: '*Let us look* with attention – *To you*, o God' fits much better the theme of beholding what is happening *above in heaven* (namely the worship of God by the Angels) than the theme of the ἀναφορά, the oblation of bread and wine *on the altar*.

The other East-Syrian Anaphoras of Nestorius (**syr Nest**) and of Theodore of Mopsuestia (**syr TheoMop**) offer a profound explanation of the meaning of the 'Sursum corda/mentes' by expanding the text with the following clarification:[34]

> *Above in the heavenly heights*, at the awesome place of glory,
> where there do not cease the flapping of the wings of the Cherubim,
> and the… sweet chanting of the holies of the Seraphim,
> *there* let your minds be!

This congruency between the Opening and the 'ante Sanctus' with its climax at the Sanctus suggests that the concept of the εὐχαριστία and '*oblatio*' became introduced only at a later stage. The inherent connection between the εὐχαριστία and the 'offering' (ܩܘܪܒܐ '*oblatio*') seemingly belongs to a later reworking of the initial opening of the Anaphora of the Apostles (**syr Ap-An**). Originally the Opening was intended as an introduction to the 'Heavenly Liturgy' of the Angels with its climatic highpoint in the *Qedušša*. This is certainly true not only for **syr Ap-An,** but also for **Ur-Bas**. But because of the increasing significance of the concept of the 'Offering' with its reference to the 'Institution Narrative' (the latter being absent in Addai and Mari), the Opening became reshaped by introducing the concept of '*Thanksgiving*' in reference to the '*Offering*', the '*Anaphora*'. Originally there was no mentioning of the offering, the '*oblatio*', at the Initial Dialogue. This is certainly true for **Bas**, and seemingly for **syr Ap-An** as well. Hence there was also no need for the vocabulary of '*giving thanks*' in reference to the '*oblatio*'.

One more detail of the Initial Dialogue begs for an explanation. It is the admonition in **arm Bas I**: '*Let us look* with attention' – '*To you*, o God'. The admonition 'to look/to see' is by no means restricted to the Armenian text of the Anaphora of Basil, but forms part of the Egyptian version as well. However, in the Egyptian version this admonition 'to

---

[34] Cf. Winkler, *Basilius-Anaphora*, pp. 298-300.

see' does not form part of the Initial Dialogue but is located in the Oratio ante Sanctus: Εἰς ἀνατολὰς βλέπετε ('Look to the East'), which is a peculiarity of the Egyptian tradition. Both traditions, the Armenian and the Egyptian versions, form a thematic unity and have to be compared with each other.

In the Egyptian tradition this admonition 'to look to the East' was placed in the 'ante Sanctus' and combined with two other admonitions:

> First admonition: 'Those who are sitting, stand up!'
> Second admonition: *'Look to the East!'*
> Third admonition: Πρόσχωμεν
> (**arm Bas I**: *'Let us look with attention!'* = at the Initial Dialogue))

With regard to the Πρόσχωμεν we should be mindful that already the Greek contains also the nuances of 'seeing' with the connotation of 'being aware' as I have explained in greater detail in connection with the analysis of the 'Sancta sanctis' in the various traditions, in particular the various versions of the Liturgies of Basil and James.[35] Hence the Armenian text: *'Let us look with attention!'* is not really a surprise.

Now it is highly interesting to investigate how these Egyptian admonitions were imbedded in the Oratio ante Sanctus:

(1) Just before mentioning the ranks of Angels and Archangels and in connection with the reference to 'The One who is sitting on the Throne of Glory' we find the first admonition: 'Those who are sitting, stand up!', which means: You who are sitting, stand up *before the One who is sitting on the 'Throne of Glory'*, whom the

---

[35] Cf. G. Winkler, *Die armenische Liturgie des Sahak. Edition des Cod. arm. 17 von Lyon, Übersetzung und Vergleich mit der armenischen Basilius-Anaphora*, Anaphorae Orientales 3. Anaphorae Armeniacae 3 (Rome, 2011) with the following chapters regarding the 'Sancta sanctis': Das Sancta sanctis und sein unmittelbares Umfeld; Einleitung: Die strukturellen Bestandteile des Sancta sanctis; 1. Die Proskynese; 2. Das Inklinations-Gebet des Priesters in der Basilius-Liturgie im Vergleich mit verwandten Texten und ihr Hintergrund: a. Die Oratio I (= Inklinations-Gebet): Δέσποτα Κύριε; b. Die Oratio II: Πρόσχες Κύριε; 3. Das Πρόσχωμεν im Kontext des Sancta sanctis; Über die Bedeutung des Πρόσχωμεν beim Sancta sanctis und seine syrische und äthiopische Übersetzung; 4. Die Oratio Πρόσχες Κύριε und ihre Bedeutung als Elevations-Gebet: a. Die Rubriken; b. Die Aussagen in der Oratio Πρόσχες Κύριε: (1) Die Gemeinsamkeit mit einer zentralen Aussage der Oratio ante Sanctus; (2) Die Gemeinsamkeit mit zentralen Verben der Epiklese; 5. Überleitung zum Sancta sanctis; 6. Das Τὰ ἅγια τοῖς ἁγίοις und seine Übersetzungen: a. Die armenischen Übersetzungen; b. Anmerkungen zur syrischen und äthiopischen Übersetzung; 7. Die Antwort des Volkes auf das Sancta sanctis: a. Die christologische Formulierung; b. Die trinitarische Formulierung; c. Die aus Εἷς ἅγιος hervorgegangenen Zeugen; *etc.*, Der Befund in den verschiedenen Redaktionen der Jakobus-Liturgie und seine wahrscheinliche Abhängigkeit von der Basilius-Liturgie, *etc.*

'heavenly powers' with the Angels and Archangels *are adoring* (προσκυνούμενος)';

(2) Then just before naming the *highest* ranks of Angels, namely the 'Cherubim and Seraphim' the second admonition is heard: *'Look* to the East!';

(3) And immediately before the Sanctus the Deacon shouts: Πρόσχω- μεν! (with the connotation of: *'Let us see!'*)

This suggests that all three admonitions are closely intertwined *with the Sanctus*. Moreover, they have the function of leading up to the cli- max, the Sanctus. The central admonitions, namely: *'Look* to the East!' and 'Let us be *attentive!'* have a direct parallel in the Initial Dialogue of **arm Bas I**: *'Let us look with attention!'*

Conclusions with regard to the Opening:[36]

(1) The older witnesses, **syr-Ap-An** and **TradAp**, only testify to the second part of the Dialogue with its centre-piece: 'Sursum corda/ mentes' (and variants thereof).

(2) The original intention of the 'Sursum corda/mentes' seemingly shows a considerable similarity with the descriptions of the Ascent to heaven of Enoch, or Rabbi Akiba, or for that matter, Saint Paul. We should lift up our hearts (or: minds) in order to witness how the highest ranks of Angels adore God, culminating in the exclamation of the 'Thrice-Holy', the Sanctus. With the admonition: 'Lift up your hearts (or minds)' we should begin our journey up into heaven in order to *'see'* and *'hear'* how the Angels adore and praise God.

(3) The reference to the 'oblatio' is placed outside of the actual Dia- logue in both versions of **TradAp**.

In **Bas** the concept of the 'offering' is still missing in the Egyptian version of **Bas**, as it very likely was also absent in **syr Ap-An**. The increasing importance of the theme of 'offering' and the Institution Nar- rative led to the adjustment of the Initial Dialogue: first the concept of *'thanksgiving'* referring to the ἀναφορά ('offering') was introduced. Thus the Initial Dialogue serves now as an introduction to the ἀναφορά, thereby obscuring the pristine intention of the admonition: 'Lift up your

---

[36] Cf. Winkler, *Basilius-Anaphora*, pp. 344-350.

hearts/minds!' Originally the 'Lift up your hearts/minds!' served as an admonition to ascend to heaven in order to witness the adoration and praise of God by the Angels. The analysis of the vocabulary and the investigation of their context, including a comparative study with related texts, seems to suggest that the *theme of thanksgiving for the offering*, the ἀναφορά of the gifts of bread and wine on the altar, was later on introduced with the result that the original intention of the Initial Dialoge, namely to lift up our hearts to what is happening in heaven and watching how the Angels worship God, became obscured.[37]

It may be helpful to remember: the concept of εὐχαριστία refers to the *Offering of bread and wine* culminating in the 'Institution Narrative' *for which we give Thanks*, whereas *the Angels* before the throne of God *do not give Thanks but worship Him by praising Him.*[38] Given the importance of this 'Heavenly Liturgy' in the Syriac liturgical texts, it is no longer so surprising that the three East-Syrian Anaphoras are not referred to as εὐχαριστία or ἀναφορά but called *'Qeduššа'* (syr: ܩܘܕܫܐ/*'Quddaša'*), whereby they refer primarily to the *'Thrice Holy'* of the Seraphim in Is 6:3.[39] Something similar is true for the older Ethiopian 'Anaphoras', they are called: *'Qəddase'* (ቅዳሴ :), and the 'Collection of Anaphoras' is referred to as 'Book of the *Qeduššа'* (*Mäṣəhafä Qəddase*).[40]

(For a detailed investigation of the Opening I refer to my analysis in *Basilius-Anaphora*, 291-347.)

2. *The Praise-Verbs in the Oratio ante Sanctus*

Since the **TradAp** has no Sanctus and hence also no section exclusively dedicated to the Praise of God, emphasizing instead the Christological aspects via credal statements, which lead up to the Institution Narrative, we have to turn our attention to the Oratio ante Sanctus of the East-Syrian Anaphora of the Apostles Addai and Mari (**syr Ap-An**) and the Antiochene Eucharistic Prayer named for Saint Basil (**Bas**).

---

[37] *Ibid.*, pp. 279-350.

[38] *Ibid.*, p. 298.

[39] Cf. Macomber, 'The Oldest Known Text', pp. 342, 358; Gelston, *Addai and Mari*, p. 47; S. Jammo, 'The Quddasha of the Apostles Addai and Mari', *Syriac Dialogue* (Vienna, 1994), pp. 167-181, here: p. 168; Winkler, *Basilius-Anaphora*, pp. 349, 530-532.

[40] Cf. Winkler, *Basilius-Anaphora*, pp. 531-532.

The lengthy Oratio ante Sanctus of the Anaphora of Basil consists of two larger sections: the 'Oratio Theologica', a later interpolation,[41] and the extensive theme of Praise in the context of the 'Heavenly Liturgy of the Angels'.[42] It is important to note that this theme of Praise falls into two parts in **Bas** (and in **syr-Ap-An** as well):

1. *the Praise of God by the Faithful*
   (consisting of a string of verbs in **Bas**,
   with one exception: **arm Bas I** has just 1 single verb (δοξάζειν);
   whereas **syr Bas** has 4 verbs, **byz Bas** 6).
2. *the Praise of God by the Angels*
   (with the following dominant verbs:
   προσκυνεῖν combined with εὐλογεῖν or δοξάζειν).

Given the division into the worship of God by the heavenly hosts and the praying community on earth, which precedes the Praise of the Angels in **syr Ap-An** and **Bas**, we have to ask:

(1) What is said by whom?
(2) Is there a correspondence between the Praise of the People and the Praise of the Angels? If we can answer this question affirmatively, then the question is: How close is this correspondence?
(3) Is it possible that there are regional differences in the usage of specific verbs?

In the Oratio ante Sanctus of both Anaphoras, **syr Ap-An** and **Bas**, the theme of praise is inaugurated with the worship of God by the Faithful, followed by the 'Heavenly Liturgy of the Angels' with its main protagonists, the Cherubim and Seraphim (in that order!). Our oldest witness for this Liturgy of the Angels is undoubtedly the East-Syrian Anaphora of the Apostles Addai and Mari (**syr Ap-An**).

With regard to the Praise of God we have distinguish the following string of verbs: (a) the relationship between εὐλογεῖν and δοξάζειν, (b) the προσκυνεῖν combined with εὐλογεῖν or δοξάζειν, (c) only in **Bas**: the secondary verbs of praise αἰνεῖν and ὑμνεῖν, (d) the interpolation of εὐχαριστεῖν.

---

[41] *Ibid.*, pp. 561-588.
[42] See my detailed investigation in *Basilius-Anaphora*, pp. 353-543.

Of prime importance seemingly are the following two verbs in both, the Anaphora of Basil (**Bas**) and in the East-Syrian Anaphora of the Apostles Addai and Mari (**syr Ap-An**):[43]

- 'to praise/bless' (εὐλογεῖν)
- 'to glorify' (δοξάζειν)

both combined with προσκυνεῖν.

(a) Some Preliminary Remarks concerning the Relationship between εὐλογεῖν and δοξάζειν

We begin with the analysis of the Verbs of Praise in the 'ante Sanctus' of the Anaphora of the Apostles Addai and Mari (**syr Ap-An**) and the striking parallel in **arm Bas I**.[44] According to Macomber's reconstruction, the Oratio ante Sanctus of **syr Ap-An** began with the glorification of God by using the *noun*: ܫܘܒܚܐ (δόξα), namly: '*Glory* be to you (ܠܟ ܫܘܒܚܐ)...'[45], whereas in **arm Bas I** the respective text begins with a *verb*: փառաւորել (δοξάζειν):[46] '... *to glorify* (փառաւորել) you...'.[47] It is quite likely that also **syr Ap-An** once had *n o t a n o u n, b u t the v e r b* '*to glorify*' (cf. δοξάζειν).[48]

Before we continue with the demonstration of the striking similarity between the vocabulary of praise in the 'ante Sanctus' in **syr Ap-An** and **arm Bas**, I want to point out the affinity of the Verbs of Praise, in particular εὐλογεῖν and δοξάζειν, in the Book on the Angels (the 'Wakeful

[43] For a more detailled analysis of the Praise-Verbs in the Ethiopian Anaphoras see now Winkler, 'Über das christliche Erbe Henochs und einige Probleme des Testamentum Domini' (as note 3 above).

[44] Cf. Winkler, *Basilius-Anaphora*, pp. 295-297, 348, 416, 420, 435, 438-439, 442, 444, 446-451.

[45] Cf. Macomber, 'Anaphora of the Apostles' (1982), p. 84/86; Winkler, *Basilius-Anaphora*, p. 432 with n. 29.

[46] Cf. Winkler, *Basilius-Anaphora*, pp. 294, 348, 420, 435, 438-439, 442, 444, 446-451.

[47] *Ibid.*, pp. 140/141, 294, 348, 420, 435, 438-439, 442, 444, 446-451.

[48] Cf. my detailed analysis in: *Basilius-Anaphora*, pp. 402-418, 431-439. In addition, I want to point out that in the Hymn of Thomas towards the end of the *syr Acts of Thomas* the verb δοξάζειν alternates with the singing of the "halleluja"; more precisely: the verb δοξάζειν is associated with the Father, whereas the "hallel"-chanting is connected with the Son; cf. W. Wright, *Apocryphal Acts of the Apostles Edited from Syriac Manuscripts in the British Museum and Other Libraries with English Translation and Notes* (London, 1871, photomech. repr. Amsterdam, 1968), pp. 179 ff (= syr. pag.)/245 ff (= engl. transl.).

Ones' or 'Those who do not sleep') in Enoch,[49] by making use of the Greek fragments (**gr En**) and the Ethiopic version of Enoch (**eth En**).[50]

In Enoch (**eth En**) the following Praise-Verbs play a dominant role[51] in connection with the *Qedušša* of 'those who do not sleep':[52]

eth Enoch 39:12
Flemming, 43:[53]

Those who do not sleep *praise* you
and they stand before your glory,
and *they praise* you (ወይባርኩ:)   cf. εὐλογεῖν/*benedicere*
and *they glorify* you (ወይሴብሕ:)   cf. δοξάζειν/*glorificare*
and *they exalt* you (ወያሌዕሉ:),   cf. *exaltare*
while they say:
Holy! Holy! Holy! is the Lord of Spirits,[54]
he fills the earth with spirits[55] [cf. Is 6:3].

The same verbs in that same sequence occur also in another chapter of **eth En** with the *Qedušša*:[56]

eth Enoch 61
Flemming, 70-71:[57]

9 ... they all will say with one voice
and *praise* (ወይባርኩ:)   cf. εὐλογεῖν/*benedicere*
and *glorify* (ወይሴብሕ:)   cf. δοξάζειν/*glorificare*
and *exalt* (ወያሌዕሉ:)   cf. *exaltare*
and *sanctify* (ወይቄድሱ:)   cf. *sanctificare*
the name of the Lord of Spirits.[58]

---

[49] Cf.Winkler, *Basilius-Anaphora*, pp. 425-431.

[50] For **gr En** cf. L. Radermacher in: J. Flemming, *Das Buch Henoch*, GCS 5 (Leipzig, 1901); M. Black, *Apocalypsis Henochi Graece*, Pseudepigrapha Veteris Testamenti Graece 3 (Leiden, 1970); for **eth En** cf. Flemming, *Das Buch Henoch (äth)*, p. 43.

[51] Cf. Winkler, *Basilius-Anaphora*, pp. 425-431. See now also Winkler, 'Über das christliche Erbe Henochs und einige Probleme des Testamentum Domini' (as note 3 above).

[52] For this specific category of angels cf. Winkler, *Das Sanctus*, pp. 175-191: 'Excursus III: "Wächter" oder "Wachende"? Die Kategorie dieser Engel in der Henoch-Überlieferung und den damit verwandten Texten'; for these and other categories of Angels cf. Winkler, *Basilius-Anaphora*, pp. 452-516.

[53] Cf. Flemming, *Henoch (äth)*, p. 43; Winkler, *Basilius-Anaphora*, pp. 323, 426.

[54] Cf. Winkler, *Das Sanctus*, p. 80 with n. 57.

[55] *Ibid.*, p. 80 with n. 58.

[56] Cf. Winkler, *Basilius-Anaphora*, pp. 427-428.

[57] *Ibid.*, pp. 427-428. Chap. 61 has not come down to us in the Greek fragments (**gr En**).

[58] The 'Lord of Spirits' occurs frequently in Enoch and serves as an equivalent to: 'Lord of hosts' of Is 6:3.

10 And the whole hosts of heaven...
the Cherubim, Seraphim, Ophannim...

11 At that day they will raise one voice
and *praise* (ወይባርኩ:)   cf. εὐλογεῖν/*benedicere*
and *glorify* (ወይሴብሑ:)   cf. δοξάζειν/*glorificare*
and *exalt* (ወያሌዕሉ:)...   cf. *exaltare*

12 All those shall *praise* Him,
who do not sleep...

All the saints shall *praise* Him...
and all the elected
and every spirit of light capable
to *praise*   cf. εὐλογεῖν/*benedicere*
to *glorify*   cf. δοξάζειν/*glorificare*
to *exalt*   cf. *exaltare*
and to *sanctify*   cf. *sanctificare*

And every flesh
that shall mightely
glorify   cf. εὐλογεῖν/*benedicere*
and *praise* your name...   cf. δοξάζειν/*glorificare*

These two passages in connection with the *Qedušša* testify to a string of verbs, which are repeated several times in the very same sequence: '*benedicere – glorificare – exaltare*', to which sometimes also the verb '*sanctificare*' is added.[59] Originally there were seemingly just two verbs, namely εὐλογεῖν/*benedicere* and δοξάζειν/*glorificare* as at the end of the citation. This hypothesis is further strengtened by Enoch 9:4, forming part of the so-called Book of the Angels (= the 'Wakeful Ones'), which has come down to us in Greek and Ethiopic (**gr En** + **eth En**):

äth Hen 9:4-5
Flemming, 8-9:[60]

(4) ወመንበረ : ስብሐቲከ :   And the *Throne of your Glory*[61]
ወ-ስተ : ኵሉ : ትዉ-ልደ: remains through all the generations
ዓለም: of the world.

[59] Cf. Winkler, *Basilius-Anaphora*, pp. 425-430. Moreover, the parallel with regard to 'benedicere – exaltare' in **eth En** 39:12; 61:9.11.12 and **syr Pet III** is noteworthy; cf. Winkler, *Basilius-Anaphora*, p. 437.

[60] Cf. Flemming, *Henoch (äth)*, pp. 8-9; Winkler, *Basilius-Anaphora*, pp. 375-376.

[61] Not only the reference to the '*Throne of Glory*' is also central to the Oratio ante Sanctus in the Anaphora of Basil, but the entire passage shows close parallels between the Egyptian Version of **Bas** and **gr En** 9: 4-5; cf. Winkler, *Basilius-Anaphora*, pp. 371-376, 385-387.

ወስምከ :　　　　　　　　And your name
ቅዱስ :　　　　　　　　　is holy,
ወቡሩክ :　　　　　　　　and *blessed* (cf. εὐλογεῖν)
ወስቡሕ :　　　　　　　　and *glorified* (cf. δοξάζειν)
ው-ስተ : ኵሉ- : ዓለም:　　in all eternity.
[ወቡሩከ : ወስቡሕ ::]⁶²　　　[*Blessed and glorified* are you.]⁶³
(5) አንተ : ገ በርከ : ኵሉ:　　　You have created everthing...

Here is the Greek text, including the variants in *Synkellos*:

griech Hen 9:4-5　　　　　　　*Synkellos*
Radermacher, 28:⁶⁴　　　　　　　Radermacher, 28:

(4) ὁ θρόνος τῆς δόξης σου　　　καὶ ὁ θρόνος τῆς δόξης σου
εἰς πάσας τὰς γενεὰς τοῦ　　　εἰς πάσας τὰς γενεὰς τῶν
αἰῶνος　　　　　　　　　αἰώνων,
καὶ τὸ ὄνομά σου　　　　　καὶ τὸ ὄνομά σου
τὸ ἅγιον　　　　　　　　ἅγιον
καὶ μέγα　　　　　　　　　　—
καὶ **εὐλόγητον**　　　　　καὶ **εὐλογημένον**
εἰς πάντας τοὺς αἰῶνας.　　εἰς πάντας τοὺς αἰῶνας·
(5) σὺ γὰρ ἐποίησας τὰ πάντα ...　σὺ γὰρ εἶ ὁ ποιήσας τὰ πάντα ...

It is noteworthy that the Greek version testifies to just *one* verb, namely εὐλογεῖν, in contrast to the Ethiopic version where two verbs, εὐλογεῖν and δοξάζειν, figure prominently. Both verbs, εὐλογεῖν – δοξάζειν, are also present in the Ethiopic version of the Anaphora of James, which is dependent on a Syriac text.⁶⁵ In the Ethiopic redaction the two verbs occur in the inversed and rare sequence δοξάζειν – εὐλογεῖν: 'We glorify you (ንሌብሕ :), we praise you (ንባርከ :)...'.⁶⁶

Throughout my systematic investigation of the vocabulary of praise in my *Basilius-Anaphora*, I have noticed that the Syrians replaced almost consistently the verb εὐλογεῖν with δοξάζειν in their liturgical texts.⁶⁷ (So far I have no explanation for this fact, as it also seems to me that the Ethiopic evidence, which witnesses both verbs, have to be investigated

---

⁶² According to Flemming, *Henoch (äth)*, 9, this is a later addition.
⁶³ Cf. previous note.
⁶⁴ For the Greek text cf. Radermacher, in Flemming, *Das Buch Henoch*, 28.
⁶⁵ Cf. O. Heiming, 'Anaphora syriaca sancti Iacobi Fratris Domini', in *Anaphorae Syriacae* II/2 (Rome, 1953), pp. 105-177, 110-111; see also my comentary on the Verbs of Praise in my: *Basilius-Anaphora*, pp. 424 with n. 9, 439.
⁶⁶ Cf. S. Euringer, 'Die Anaphora des hl. Jakobus, des Bruders des Herrn', *OC* n. S. 4 (1915) 1-23, here pp. 2-3.
⁶⁷ Cf. Winkler, *Basilius-Anaphora*, pp. 294, 416, 431, 433, 438, 439, 443 n. 60, 445, 446, 450, 762-763, 768, 771, 773.

more closely in this context.[68]) What seems to emerge here with considerable certainty is the observation that εὐλογεῖν and δοξάζειν have to be considered as synonyms in the Syriac (and Armenian) liturgical texts as we shall see momentarily. This cannot be said about the other verbs of praise (such as αἰνεῖν – ὑμνεῖν): they are *not* to be treated as synonyms of δοξάζειν or εὐλογεῖν, but have to be closely investigated with regard to their origin and meaning (*pace* Engberding and Ledogar).

(b) The εὐλογεῖν or δοξάζειν combined with προσκυνεῖν forming the Central Verb-Pair

As was stated already above, in both, the Anaphora of Basil (**Bas**) and in the East-Syrian Anaphora of the Apostles Addai and Mari (**syr Ap-An**), apparently the two verbs: *'to praise/bless'* (εὐλογεῖν) and *'to glorify'* (δοξάζειν) — combined with προσκυνεῖν — are of prime importance. In addition, the Syrians regularly replaced the verb εὐλογεῖν with δοξάζειν in liturgical texts. Hence εὐλογεῖν and δοξάζειν are synonyms, confirmed by the Armenian versions of the Anaphora of Basil, where these two verbs oscillate between εὐλογεῖν and δοξάζειν in combination with προσκυνεῖν.

The detailed analysis of the Praise-Verbs in the Oratio ante Sanctus lead to the following conclusions:

(1) In the Oratio ante Sanctus of the Anaphora of the Apostles Addai and Mari (**syr Ap-An**) and the Anaphora of Basil (**Bas**) *the community imitates the worship of the two main categories of Angels, namely the highest and lower ranks of Angels.* With regard to **Bas** the Angels closest to the 'Throne of Glory' of God, constituting thereby the highest ranks, it is *in particular the Cherubim* who are imitated: as the Cherubim *'praise* (cf. εὐλογεῖν)' God [as in **Ez 3,12**], so do the faithful: the same verb is used for both (in the genuine tradition of the Anaphora of Basil); in **arm Bas I** εὐλογεῖν is substituted by δοξάζειν, following here the Syriac tradition (*cf. infra*: comparison beteen **arm Bas I** and **syr Ap-An**).

(2) The other, lower ranks of Angels, namely the 'Angels and Archangels' (etc.), mentioned in all the versions of **Bas**, or the 'Upper beings', as they are referred to in **syr Ap-An**, *'adore/worship'*

---

[68] For the Ethiopian Anaphoras see now Winkler, 'Über das christliche Erbe Henochs und einige Probleme des Testamentum Domini' (as note 3 above).

(cf. προσκυνεῖν) God, imitated once more by the faithful (again in the genuine tradition of the Anaphora of Basil).

Hence these two verbs: δοξάζειν (in **syr Ap-An** substituting εὐλογεῖν) combined with προσκυνεῖν form the main vocabulary of Praise of the Angels and of the Community in the Oratio ante Sanctus not only of the Anaphora of Basil (**Bas**), but of the East-Syriac Anaphora of the Apostles (**syr Ap-An**) as well. They constitute a verb-*pair*: εὐλογεῖν/δοξάζειν plus προσκυνεῖν. This verb-*pair* was created in correlation with the two main categories of Angels, the highest ranks (= Cherubim and Seraphim), and the lower ranks. Both categories of Angels serve in their worship of God as a model for the Community of believers: as the highest ranks of Angels *'praise'* (or *'glorify'*) God and as the lower ranks *'worship'* Him so does the Community!

(3) The Byzantine version of the Anaphora of Basil (**byz Bas**) has a string of 6 verbs in connection with the Praise of the people in the following sequence: αἰνεῖν (*'to sing'*) + ὑμνεῖν (*'to laud'*), εὐλογεῖν (*'to praise'*) + προσκυνεῖν (*'to adore'*), εὐχαριστεῖν (*'to thank'*), δοξάζειν (*'to glorify'*).

Not all of these verbs in the Byzantine version belong to the original tradition of the Anaphora of Basil. I have placed the additions in the second column:

original verbs:	secondary additions:
εὐλογεῖν (*'to praise'*)	αἰνεῖν (*'to sing'*)
δοξάζειν (*'to glorify'*)	ὑμνεῖν (*'to laud'*)
προσκυνεῖν (*'to adore'*)	εὐχαριστεῖν (*'to thank'*)

(4) Of particular interest is the congruency between the East-Syrian Anaphora of the Apostles Addai and Mari (**syr Ap-An**) and the older Armenian version of the Anaphora of Basil (**arm Bas I**) as I found out to my greatest surprise. The affinity concerns not only the vocabulary of praise, but the allocation of the verbs to the respective category of Angels and to the Community of the faithful as well, as the following comparison shows:

According to Macomber's reconstruction, the Oratio ante Sanctus of **syr Ap-An** began with *'Glory* be to you (ܠܟ ܫܘܒܚܐ)...'.[69] Hence the glorification of God by the people is inaugurated with a *noun*:

---

[69] Cf. Macomber, 'Anaphora of the Apostles' (1982), p. 84/86; Winkler, *Basilius-Anaphora*, p. 432 with n. 29.

ܟܘܒܚܐ (δόξα), whereas in **arm Bas I** the respective text begins with a *verb*: փառաւորել (δοξάζειν):[70] '... *to glorify* (փառաւորել) you...'.[71] Very likely also **syr Ap-An** originally had in connection with the Praise of the faithful a *verb*, namely δοξάζειν, *not the noun* ܟܘܒܚܐ (δόξα).[72]

After the Praise by the Community of the faithful via the expression of ܟܘܒܚܐ (δόξα) in **syr Ap-An** follows the Praise of God by the lower ranks of Angels with the verb ܣܓܕܝܢ (προσκυνοῦσιν, '*they adore*'/'*worship*' God).[73] This has an exact parallel in **arm Bas I** (line 39): երկիր պագանեն (προσκυνοῦσιν).[74]

Turning to the Praise of God by the highest ranks of Angels, the Syriac text says that the 'Camps' and 'Servants' *with* the Cherubim and Seraphim[75] ܡܫܒܚܝܢ ('*they glorify*', cf. δοξάζειν) God, again with an Armenian parallel in **arm Bas I** (line 49) + **arm Bas II** (line 56): սրբել (εὐλογεῖν, '*to praise*').[76] Here we see the observation confirmed that δοξάζειν (in **syr Ap-An**) and εὐλογεῖν (in **arm Bas**) are synonyms. An overview on **syr Ap-An** and **arm Bas I** may help to demonstrate the striking affinity between **syr Ap-An** and **arm Bas I**:[77]

Anaphora of the Apostles Addai + Mari (syr Ap-An)	Armenian Anaphora of Basil (arm Bas I)
1. The Praise by the People:	
'*Glory*' (ܟܘܒܚܐ)	(δόξα δοξάζειν) '*to glorify*' (փառաւորել)[78]

---

[70] Cf. Winkler, *Basilius-Anaphora*, pp. 294, 348, 420, 435, 438-439, 442, 444, 446-451.

[71] *Ibid.*, pp. 140/141, 294, 348, 420, 435, 438-439, 442, 444, 446-451.

[72] Cf. my detailed analysis in: *Basilius-Anaphora*, pp. 402-418, 431-439.

[73] Cf. Winkler, *Basilius-Anaphora*, pp. 432-433.

[74] *Ibid.*, pp. 437-438.

[75] For the intriguing terminology for the Angels, namely the 'Camps' and the 'Servants', deriving probably from the Targumim, and forming thereby seemingly a duplication of the 'Cherubim and Seraphim', cf. Winkler, *Basilius-Anaphora*, pp. 432 n. 31, 433-434.

[76] Cf. Winkler, *Basilius-Anaphora*, p. 438.

[77] *Ibid.*

[78] Only **arm Bas I** has just one single Verb for the Praise of the Faithful! The other versions have a string of verbs: 4 verbs (= **syr Bas**) or 6 verbs (= **byz Bas**); cf. Winkler, *Basilius-Anaphora*, pp. 444-445. Before the immediate transition to the worship of the Angels **arm Bas I** (line 35) has further more: εὐλογεῖν, which precisely corresponds to δοξάζειν in **syr Bas**, and to προσκυνεῖν in **arm Bas II** (line 42), which is comparable to λατρευεῖν in **byz Bas**; cf. Winkler, *Basilius-Anaphora*, pp. 444-445.

2. The Praise-Verbs associated with the Angels:

a. the 'Upper beings'		**a.** the 'angels, archangels', *etc.*
'*adore*' (ܣܓܕ)	(προσκυνεῖν)	'*adore*' (երկիր պագանեն)[79]
b. the 'Camps' and 'Servants'		**b.**
with *Cherubim – Seraphim*		the *Cherubim – Seraphim*
'*glorify*' (ܡܫܒܚ)	(δοξάζειν = εὐλογεῖν!)	'*praise*' (պրծնեն)[80]

SANCTUS

No other redaction of Basil shows such close affinity with the East-Syrian tradition as the Armenian redactions. For the pecularities of the Egyptian version of **Bas** and the adaption of this Antiochene Anaphora to the liturgical customs of Egypt I refer to my other studies.[81]

(c) The Other Verbs: αἰνεῖν – ὑμνεῖν– εὐχαριστεῖν in **Bas**

(1) The verb-*pair*: αἰνεῖν ('*to sing*') + ὑμνεῖν ('*to laud*') is typical not for the genuine tradition of the Anaphora of Basil, but for the Egyptian tradition (cf. Serapion - Mark - Greg; and the Greek version of the Anaphora of James). This other verb-*pair* was introduced into the Anaphora of Basil only later on.

(2) The verb εὐχαριστεῖν ('*to thank*') is secondary: it did not belong to the original Praise verbs, but was included via the influence of the Institution Narrative. The theme of 'Thanksgiving' belongs to the Offering and to the Institution Narrative, not to the theme of worship: Angels do not thank God, but praise Him, and through the influence of the worship of the Angels the Community of the believers also worships God.

---

[79] *All* versions of **Bas** have in connection with the various ranks of the lower Angels προσκυνεῖν , with one exception: byz **Bas** has here αἰνεῖν; syr **Bas** has (according to the edition of Rahmani) several verbs, among them προσκυνεῖν; cf. Winkler, *Basilius-Anaphora*, pp. 444-445.

[80] In association with the highest ranks of Angels, the Cherubim and Seraphim, it is **arm Bas II** which has preserved just one verb, namely: εὐλογεῖν; **arm Bas I** has here 3 verbs, among them εὐλογεῖν; cf. Winkler, *Basilius-Anaphora*, pp. 444-445.

[81] Cf. my summary in, *Basilius-Anaphora*, pp. 877-879; *eadem*, 'Fragen zur zeitlichen Priorität der ägyptischen Textgestalt gegenüber den längeren Versionen der Basilius-Anaphora', *Bollettino della Badia Greca di Grottaferrata* III/4 (2007) 243-273, here: pp. 260-267.

Thus the later witnesses (**byz Bas** + **syr Ba**s) of this 'Heavenly Liturgy of the Angels', imitated by the Faithful according to the Anaphora of Basil, mirror — *like in the Initial Dialogue* — 'Janus-faced' intentions: one intention pertaining to the genuine theme of Praise *pointing toward the Sanctus*, the other *pointing to the Institution Narrative*:

In view of the Praise of the Angels + Sanctus:	In view of the Institution Narrative:
εὐλογεῖν ('to praise')	εὐχαριστεῖν ('to thank')
δοξάζειν ('to glorify')	
προσκυνεῖν ('to adore', 'to worship')	

So far we have dealt with some technical aspects and we have suggested that the themes of *'Praise'* and *'Thanksgiving'* became juxtaposed in the Initial Dialogue and in the Oratio ante Sanctus of both Anaphoras, **syr Ap-An** and **Bas**. But we can discover much more.

3. The Theological Significance of the Praise in **Bas** *and* **syr Ap-An**[82]

The investigation of the two Anaphoras, **syr Ap-An** and **Bas**, allows us to obtain a glimpse of the inner dynamics of these two Eucharistic Prayers.

According to these anaphoras, the two visions of the foremost Old Testament prophets, Ezekiel and Isaiah, form the absolute *centre-stage*: the movement does not go *toward* the Sanctus, but seemingly comes *from* the Sanctus. *From the Sanctus emerges what is said in the sections before the Sanctus.* This implies that the central part of the Oratio ante Sanctus (i.e. the Theme of Praise) presupposes the presence of the Sanctus!

(1) The exclamation of the 'Holy!', the *Qeduššа*, stands so to speak in the epicentre, and from the epicentre, the 'Thrice-Holy' moves outward into the cosmos in mighty waves and ripples:

The centre is constituted by the *Qeduššа* in its *twofold* shape:
– the *Cherubim* '*praise* (cf. εὐλογεῖν)' God
  according to the vision of Ez 3:12:
  '*Praised* (εὐλογημένη) be the glory of God...'
  ('*Benedicta* gloria Domini...')

---

[82] Cf. Winkler, *Basilius-Anaphora*, pp. 433-434, 446-451, 508-512.

– *combined* with the exclamation of the *thrice* ἅγιος!
by the Seraphim according to Is 6:3.

Consequently:
(a) the initially missing 'Benedictus' *following* the Sanctus!
    (NB: the verb εὐλογεῖν *precedes* the 'Sanctus'[ἅγιος]!)
(b) the initial sequence: *Cherubim and Seraphim* in that order:[83]
    the Cherubim who '*praise*' (εὐλογεῖν)
    and the Seraphim who exclaim: ἅγιος!

Moreover, originally the texts of the Eucharistic Prayers, the Anaphora of the Apostles Addai and Mari in particular and partially also the Anaphora of Basil, make it quite clear that it is not the people who shout 'Holy!' but that this prerogative is reserved for the highest ranks of Angels, the Cherubim and Seraphim. Both Anaphoras *narrate* what these Angels do! All versions of the Anaphora of Basil *describe* the Cherubim as multi-eyed (like in Ez 10:12), and the Seraphim are six-winged according to Is 6:2. Both Anaphoras *narrate* how *this pair* of Angels sing the *Qedušša*. The Anaphora of the Apostles Addai and Mari has even preserved the original text of Is 6:3: God is not yet addressed directly, but the text narrates how the Cherubim and Seraphim sing the *Qedušša*. According to the early understanding it is only in the 'Post Sanctus' that the Sanctus is *echoed* in the prayer.

(2) Further away from the epicentre, reserved exclusively to the Cherubim and Seraphim, stand the lower ranks, again in pairs[84] in the Anaphora of Basil: the Angels and Archangels, including the other pairs of Angels mentioned in **Bas**, which correspond to the 'Upper beings' in the Anaphora of the Apostles Addai and Mari. These Angels '*adore/worship*' God (cf. προσκυνεῖν).

(3) Further removed from these various lower ranks of Angels stand all human beings. Influenced by *what the Cherubim do*, namely '*praising*' (cf. εὐλογεῖν) God, they also '*praise*' or '*glorify*' (cf. εὐλογεῖν/δοξάζειν) Him.
    The verb εὐλογεῖν goes ultimately back to Ezekiel's vision of the praise of the *Ḥayyot* (= Cherubim) in Ez 3:12: '*Praised* (εὐλογημένη) be the glory of God...' ('**Benedicta** gloria Domini...').

---

[83] *Ibid.*, pp. 535-543.

[84] They form *pairs* not *triads* as was hitherto thought; cf. Winkler, *Basilius-Anaphora*, pp. 452-516, in particular, pp. 490-512.

This explains:
- the sequence: Cherubim (who *'praise'*/εὐλογεῖν)
  and Seraphim (who exclaim: ἅγιος)
  (in that order: Cherubim – Seraphim!)
- the initially missing 'Benedictus' *following* the Sanctus.[85]

(4) *After* the narration in the Anaphora of Basil of how the Seraphim shout the 'Thrice-Holy', that is *after* the Sanctus, the vocabulary 'Holy' is picked up in the 'Post Sanctus'.[86] This implies that human beings *echo* what is narrated of the Seraphim in the 'Ante Sanctus'. With the repetition of the 'Holy' of the Seraphim humans *echo* the Seraphim.

I cannot go into all the other details. For an in-depth analysis of the *Angels, who form* pairs *not triads*, and for the verb-pairs associated with these Angels, and what it all means I referr to my extensive study.[87]

A last remark: We have to realize that Jewish descriptions of the Heavenly Liturgy of the Angels are always preceded by the narration of an 'Ascent'. A Christian parallel to the Jewish descriptions of an 'Ascent' is perhaps the admonition: 'Sursum corda/mentes' at the Initial Dialogue, which precedes the narration of the Praise and Worship of God.[88] Yet this possible connection still awaits further scrutiny.

4. The Praise of God before the Epiclesis in the **TradAp**, **syr Ap-An**, *and* **Bas** *and the Meaning of* κατὰ πάντα *in the Anaphora of Basil*

We begin our analysis with both versions of the **TradAp**. The invocation of the Holy Spirit follows the Institution Narrative with the Anamnesis. At the end of the short Anamnesis there is a reference to the Offering, and as a transition to the Epiclesis both texts (**lat TradAp** + **eth TradAp**) repeat the theme of *'giving Thanks'* (= **lat TradAp**: *gratias tibi agentes*) respectively of *'Praise'* (= **eth TradAp**: ናአኩ፦ተከ :)[89]

---

[85] *Ibid.*

[86] *Ibid.*, pp. 550-560.

[87] Cf. Winkler, *Basilius-Anaphora*, pp. 446-451, 452-560; *eadem*, 'Fragen zur zeitlichen Priorität der ägyptischen Textgestalt gegenüber den längeren Versionen der Basilius-Anaphora', pp. 260-267.

[88] *Ibid.*, pp. 341-344, 451, 453.

[89] For the Ethiopic version (**eth TradAp**) cf. ed. Duensing, p. 22/24; for the Latin version (**lat TradAp**) cf. ed. Hauler, p. 107.

for having been made worthy to stand before God, establishing thereby a close connection with the *Vere dignum* of the Initial Dialogue. Both versions use here the very same verb as at the admonition of the Initial Dialogue: '*Gratias agamus*' (lat TradAp), whereas the Ethiopic text (eth TradAp) has here: ናአኵቶ : ('*Let us laud/praise*').[90]

The corresponding passage before the Epiclesis in syr Ap-An is also characterized by the vocabulary of Praise witnessing the following two main verbs:[91]

– ܡܫܒܚܝܢ ('*glorificantes*', cf. δοξάζειν)
– ܡܪܝܡܝܢ ('*exaltantes*').

(In this context we remember that δοξάζειν and εὐλογεῖν are synonyms and that the Syrians have regularely substituted εὐλογεῖν with δοξάζειν in their liturgical texts; *cf. supra*, text before n. 27 and n. 67.

These two main verbs at the Praise before the Epiclesis in syr Ap-An are also present at the two passages with the *Qeduššа* in Enoch (eth En 39:12 and 61:9.11.12) with the verbs '*benedicere – glorificare – exaltare*'[92] as we have seen above in connection with the analysis of the Praise-Verbs before the Sanctus.[93]

As the Praise of God *precedes the Sanctus*, so does God's Praise by the Community *precede the Invocation of the Holy Spirit* in syr Ap-An (and Bas as we shall see immediately), implying thereby a close relationship between the Epiclesis and the Sanctus![94] Once more the Praise-Verbs are of greatest interest because they reflect back primarily on the Praise-Verbs of the Oratio ante Sanctus (and secondarily of the Institution Narrative as well), and once more both Armenian versions (arm Bas I and arm Bas II) are of prime importance.

---

[90] See my commentary on the vocabulary of the Ethiopic version (eth TradAp) above in connection with the Initial Dialogue; moreover Winkler, *Basilius-Anaphora*, p. 326.

[91] The following string of verbs are used in syr Ap-An (I make use of Macomber's edition and Latin translation ['The Oldest Known Text', pp. 386-369]): '*laetantes – glorificantes – exaltantes*'; see also Macomber, 'Anaphora of the Apostles' (1982), p. 85/87; see in addition Winkler, *Basilius-Anaphora*, pp. 436-437.

[92] Cf. Winkler, *Basilius-Anaphora*, pp. 425-431, 437.

[93] For an analysis of the verbs in the Ethiopian Anaphoras see now Winkler, 'Über das christliche Erbe Henochs und einige Probleme des Testamentum Domini' (as note 3 above).

[94] For a detailed investigation of the testimony of the various redactions of Bas cf. Winkler, *Basilius-Anaphora*, pp. 753-774.

Here is the text of **arm Bas I**:[95]

1. Praise of the People:

In everything **you are** *praised*...	(cf. εὐλογεῖν)	= **Summary** of κατὰ πάντα! (in **byz Bas**: κατὰ πάντα καὶ διὰ πάντα 'According to everything and in view of everything')
We *praise* **you** we laud you we thank you	(= εὐλόγοῦμεν);; (= αἰνοῦμεν); (= εὐχαριστοῦμεν)	= **Praise-Verbs**
We implore you...	(= δεόμεθα)	= **Transition to Epiclesis**

[*Later interpolation*: Prayer of the celebrant for himself]

2. The Epiclesis: = **Epiclesis**

We implore you... (= δεόμεθα)

For the moment we leave aside the explanation of the κατὰ πάντα καὶ διὰ πάντα ('According to everything and in view of everything') in order to investigate exclusively the Praise-Verbs. For this purpose let us now turn to the text of **arm Bas II** and **byz Bas**,[96] comparing the Praise-Verbs *before the Epiclesis* to the Praise-Verbs *before the Sanctus* (– in order to facilitate the comparison I have translated the Armenian Praise-Verbs into Greek):

The Praise-Verbs

before the *Epiclesis*:		before the *Sanctus*:
byz Bas	**arm Bas II**	**arm Bas II**
Priest: κατὰ πάντα καὶ διὰ πάντα...	Priest: κατὰ πάντα...	
People: αἰνοῦμεν ('we laud')	People:	
εὐλόγοῦμεν ('we praise')	εὐλόγοῦμεν ('we praise') αἰνοῦμεν ('we laud') ὑμνοῦμεν ('we sing')	εὐλόγοῦμεν ('we praise') αἰνοῦμεν ('we laud')
–		
εὐχαριστοῦμεν	εὐχαριστοῦμεν	εὐχαριστοῦμεν

---

[95] *Ibid.*, pp. 759-760.
[96] For this comparison cf. Winkler, *Basilius-Anaphora*, pp. 760-763.

[absent in **arm Bas II**
but present in **arm Bas I**:
cf. προσκυνεῖν][97]   'we adore'
                   (cf. προσκυνεῖν)

—   'we glorify'
                   (cf. δοξάζειν)

NOTE: the **congruency of**:
- the **sequence** of the verbs
- the **grammatical construction!**

Commentary:

[For the time being I shall leave out the last two verbs (προσκυνεῖν and δοξάζειν) in **arm Bas II**].

(1) I used **arm Bas II** as a model to demonstrate the identity of the Praise-Verbs before the Epiclesis with those of the Prayer before the Sanctus.

The other versions of **Bas** do not show the same conspicuous congruency between the verbs before the Epiclesis and before the Sanctus. The similarity is there, but not to the same extent as in **arm Bas II**.

(2) Note the persistent sequence of the verbs εὐλογεῖν - εὐχαριστεῖν in **byz Bas** + **arm Bas (I+II)**. This verb-pair *echoes* the main verbs of the Institution Narrative: εὐλογεῖν for the bread, εὐχαριστεῖν for the wine.[98]

As the 'Thrice-Holy' of the Seraphim finds its echo in the 'Post Sanctus', so the verb-pair εὐλογεῖν - εὐχαριστεῖν has its echo in the Praise before the Epiclesis.

So far we have looked into the Armenian and Byzantine versions. How about the Egyptian version of the Anaphora of Basil? I shall use the Greek Egyptian text as a model:[99]

---

[97] *Ibid.*, p. 761 with n. 15.

[98] For an anlysis cf. Winkler, *Basilius-Anaphora*, pp. 699-700, 702-704, 706-708, *719-721*.

[99] Cf. Winkler, *Basilius-Anaphora*, pp. 764-767, 771-773, where also the Bohairic and Ethiopic texts are analysed.

The Praise-Verbs in the Greek Egyptian version

before the *Sanctus*:	before the *Epiclesis*:
1. Praise of the People:	
[absent!¹⁰⁰]	αἰνεῖν (*'to laud'*)
	εὐλογεῖν (*'to praise'*)
2. The Praise of the Angels:	
προσκυνεῖν (*'to adore'*)	προσκυνεῖν (*'to adore'*)
ὑμνεῖν (*'to sing'*)	

The missing Praise of the People is seemingly due to a secondary reworking of this Antiochene Eucharistic Prayer once it was taken over in Egypt. The possible reason for this secondary manipulation of the text has something to do with the fact that central theological aspects in the Egyptian version were shifted in a different direction and that the Heavenly Liturgy of the Angels and their imitation by the Community does not figure as prominently as it does in the other versions of the Anaphora of Basil.¹⁰¹

Let me summarize my findings in connection with the Praise-Verbs before the Epiclesis:

(1) In this presentation I did not go into the evidence of the Syriac, Coptic, and Ethiopic Praise-Verbs before the Epiclesis of the Anaphora of Basil;¹⁰² let me just sum up the evidence:
The Syriac tradition has once more replaced an original εὐλογεῖν (*'to praise'*) with δοξάζειν (*'to glorify'*). The verb δοξάζειν (*'to glorify'*) is also present in some of the Ethiopic manuscripts. Hence *all* versions of the Anaphora of Basil have the verb εὐλογεῖν (*'to praise'*) in common before the Epiclesis.

(2) This implies that it is above all the verb εὐλογεῖν that pertains to the original Praise-Verbs before the Epiclesis.
Neither the verb αἰνεῖν (*'to laud'*) of the Greek Egyptian and Armenian versions, nor the verb ὑμνεῖν (*'to sing'*) in **byz Bas +**

---

¹⁰⁰ For the striking absence of the Praise by the Community see my remarks in: *Basilius-Anaphora*, pp. 442, 444, 447, 771 n. 32; *eadem*, 'Fragen zur zeitlichen Priorität der ägyptischen Textgestalt gegenüber den längeren Versionen der Basilius-Anaphora', pp. 260-265.

¹⁰¹ Cf. Winkler, *Basilius-Anaphora*, pp. 442, 444, 447, 771 n. 32; *eadem*, 'Fragen zur zeitlichen Priorität der ägyptischen Textgestalt gegenüber den längeren Versionen der Basilius-Anaphora', pp. 263-265.

¹⁰² Here I refer to my, *Basilius-Anaphora*, pp. 763, 765-768.

arm Bas II belong to the original Praise before the Epiclesis. This is seemingly also true for the verb εὐχαριστεῖν in **arm Bas I+II** and **byz Bas**. This verb is still missing in the Greek Egyptian redaction of the Anaphora of Basil.

(3) *All* versions of the Anaphora of Basil have the verb δεόμεθα ('*we implore* [*you*]') besides the original εὐλογεῖν, that is also present in *all* versions. The verb δεόμεθα forms the transition to the Invocation of the Holy Spirit.

(4) Let me now briefly turn to the κατὰ πάντα καὶ διὰ πάντα ('According to everything and in view of everything') *at the beginning of the Praise-Verbs*.[103] The text of **arm Bas I** is of particular interest since it has substituted the κατὰ πάντα with: 'In everything you are *praised* (cf. εὐλογεῖν)', summarizing thereby already at the beginning the Praise-Verbs to come. It is also noteworthy that many versions of the Anaphora of Basil begin the Praise with the verb εὐλογοῦμεν.

(5) This verb εὐλογεῖν ('*to praise*') before the Invocation of the Holy Spirit has to be primarily compared to the εὐλογεῖν before the Sanctus. As the People *praise* God *before the Sanctus* (in imitation of the Cherubim), so do they again *praise God before the Invocation of the Holy Sprit*. With this parallelism the unity between the Sanctus and the Invocation of the Holy Sprit becomes apparent (which raises the possibility that not only the Epiclesis, but also the Sanctus is of Syrian origin).

(6) The inherent relationship between the Sanctus and the Epiclesis becomes further apparent with the verb προσκυνεῖν ('*to adore/to worship*') in both, the Praise before the Sanctus and the Praise before the Epiclesis: As the lower ranks of Angels and Archangels (etc.) '*adore/worship*' (προσκυνεῖν) God in connection with the Sanctus, so do the People before the Sanctus and before the Epiclesis.

(7) The increasing importance of the 'Offering' and the further reflexion on the two *central* words associated with the Institution Narrative,

namely εὐλογεῖν in connection with the bread
and εὐχαριστεῖν for the wine,[104]

---

[103] The κατὰ πάντα does *not* belong to the Anamnesis but to the 'Praise-Verbs' as was shown for the first time by A. Raes for the Syriac evidence in his ground-breaking contribution, 'ΚΑΤΑ ΠΑΝΤΑ ΚΑΙ ΔΙΑ ΠΑΝΤΑ. En tout et pour tout', OC 48 (1964), pp. 216-220; for the various redactions of **Bas** cf. Winkler, *Basilius-Anaphora*, pp. 729, 730, 733, 735, 753-774.

[104] For the central verbs in connection with the Institution Narrative in the various redactions of **Bas** cf. Winkler, *Basilius-Anaphora*, pp. 693-721, in particular, pp. 699-700, and their background: pp. 703-704, 706-708, 719-721.

seemingly led to the inclusion of the verb εὐχαριστεῖν before the Invocation of the Holy Spirit.

Thereby this Praise before the Invocation of the Holy Spirit *oscillates*, that is: *moves back and forth* – between reflecting back on the Liturgy of the Angels, imitated by the People in their Praise before the Sanctus, and moving forward to what is narrated in the Institution Narrative, echoing in particular the central vocabulary of the Institution Narrative:

the verb εὐλογεῖν spoken over the bread
and εὐχαριστεῖν spoken over the cup of wine.

(8) This verb-pair εὐλογεῖν - εὐχαριστεῖν appears persistently in that sequence, and is attested in all versions of the Anaphora of Basilius before the Epiclesis, with one significant exception: The Egyptian Greek version, which has just the two verbs αἰνεῖν (*'to laud'*) and εὐλογεῖν (*'to praise'*), emphasizing thereby the connection with the Heavenly Liturgy before the Sanctus.[105] We can even become more precise: εὐλογεῖν belongs to the genuine tradition of the Anaphora of Basil, whereas αἰνεῖν (*'to laud'*) [together with ὑμνεῖν (*'to sing'*)] seemingly are typical of the Egyptian (and Jerusalem) tradition.

To conclude, let me come back to the meaning and function of the κατὰ πάντα καὶ διὰ πάντα ('According to everything and in view of everything'), which has greatly mystified the scholars for a long time, leading thereby to imprecise translations.

Only the close scrutiny of the Praise-Verbs in their respective original texts enables us to understand the precise meaning and function of the κατὰ πάντα καὶ διὰ πάντα ('According to everything and in view of everything') *at the beginning of the Praise-Verbs*[106] before the Epiclesis:

This κατὰ πάντα ('According to everything and in view of everything') mirrors exactly:

–   what happend in connection with the Praise *before the Sanctus*;
–   what occured at the *Institution Narrative*
–   and what is happening now just *before the Epiclesis*!

---

[105] Cf. Winkler, *Basilius-Anaphora*, pp. 765-766, 771-773.

[106] As was stated already above, the κατὰ πάντα does *not* belong to the Anamnesis but to the 'Praise-Verbs' as was shown for the first time by A. Raes for the Syriac evidence in his: 'ΚΑΤΑ ΠΑΝΤΑ ΚΑΙ ΔΙΑ ΠΑΝΤΑ', pp. 216-220; for the various redactions of **Bas** cf. Winkler, *Basilius-Anaphora*, pp. 729, 730, 733, 735, 753-774.

These three sections of the Anaphora of Basil share the same verbs in a variety of combinations. The κατὰ πάντα καὶ διὰ πάντα ('According to everything and in view of everything') attempts thereby to encapsule the following reality:

- the Praise of God before the exclamation of the 'Thrice Holy';
- echoing the central verbs of the Institution Narrative;
- including the Praise of God before the Invocation of the Holy Spirit.

Thus the κατὰ πάντα καὶ διὰ πάντα is stating exactly what the words say: 'According to everything and in view of everything – *we praise* (εὐλογοῦμεν)...'.

Needless to say, this phrase, which we find in all the various versions of the Anaphora of Basil, has to be faithfully presented and translated by closely following the various original texts, for example:

Egyptian gr Bas:[107] Κατὰ πάντα καὶ διὰ πάντα καὶ ἐν πᾶσιν;

Bohairic Bas:[108] ΚΑΤΑ ϩⲰⲂ ΝΙΒⲉΝ : ΝⲉⲘ ⲉⲐⲂⲉ ϩⲰⲂ ΝΙΒⲉΝ: ΝⲉⲘ ϨⲉΝ ϩⲰⲂ ΝΙΒⲉΝ.
('According to everything and for everything and in everything');

Ethiopic Bas:[109] በኵሉ : ግብር ፤ በእንተ : ኵሉ : ግብር : ወወስተ : ኵሉ : ግብር ፨
('Through all things, because of all things, and in all things');

arm Bas I:[110] յամենայնի աւրհնեալ ես տէր
('In everything you are praised, o Lord');

arm Bas II:[111] ըստ եւ յաղագս ամենեցուն
('According and in view of everything');

byz Bas:[112] Κατὰ πάντα καὶ διὰ πάντα.

The analysis of the Praise-Verbs has shown that in early times there seemingly existed in the Antiochene regions and beyond an enormous wealth of expressions for articulating the interaction of the Divine with

---

[107] Cf. Budde, p. 158 (79); Renaudot I, p. 67; Winkler, *Basilius-Anaphora*, p. 774.

[108] Cf. Budde, p. 159 (79); Winkler, *Basilius-Anaphora*, pp. 774.

[109] Cf. Euringer, 'Anaphora des Basilius', p. 158/159 (39); Winkler, *Basilius-Anaphora*, p. 774.

[110] Cf. Winkler, *Basilius-Anaphora*, p. 774.

[111] *Ibid.*

[112] *Ibid.*

the hosts of Angels who worship God. Not so in the so-called 'Traditio Apostolica' with its sober Christological emphasis, expressed in credal statements leading up to the Institution Narrative: here the 'Heavenly Liturgy' with the Sanctus is absent, in contrast to the East-Syrian Anaphora of the Apostles Addai and Mari and even more so in the Antiochene Anaphora attributed to Basil, where the *Qeduŝŝa* of the Angels forms centre-stage.

The subtlety of the various expressions associated with the various ranks of Angels and the Community of the faithful and the precision with which the vocabulary was rendered in the various versions of the Anaphora of Basil allows us a glimpse of central aspects of this Heavenly Liturgy imitated by the Community on earth widely known in the Antiochene region including its hinterland and perceived as fundamental for the 'Eucharistic' gatherings.

Nothing is said here lightly or gratuitously. The investigation of the vocabulary demonstrated how in **syr Ap-An** and **Bas** the Initial Dialogue was originally intertwined with the Sanctus and how in **Bas** the Epiclesis and the Sanctus once formed an inherent unity. Due to the increasing significance of the role of the priest and associated with him the concept of 'Offering' with its high-point in the Institution Narrative, the original intent of the Dialogue, once inaugurating the imitation of the Liturgy of the Angels in heaven before God's throne in **syr Ap-An** and **Bas**, underwent considerable modification by introducing the theme of Thanksgiving in connection with the now paramount theme of 'Offering', once absent in both Eucharistic Prayers.

Concluding I present here the main vocabulary, its location in **TradAp**, **syr Ap-An**, and **Bas**, its original function and meaning:

I. Initial Dialogue:

Admonition to '*give thanks*' (εὐχαριστήσωμεν)
or: '*laudare*' (**eth TradAp**);
syr Ap-An: '*adoremus et glorificemus*' (ܣܓܘܕ ܘܢܫܒܚ).

a. TradAp:
lat TradAp: εὐχαριστεῖν ('to thank'); **eth TradAp:** '*laudare*!'
(no reference to the 'Oblatio' *at the Dialogue itself*)

b. syr Ap-An
(originally inauguration to the Heavenly Liturgy of the Angels):
vocabulary influenced by the Oratio ante Sanctus:
δοξάζειν ('to glorify')
προσκυνεῖν ('to adore/worship')

at Initial Dialogue repetition of these verbs from the Oratio ante Sanctus! (*cf. infra*)

later interpolation:
εὐχαριστεῖν ('to thank') in view of the '*Oblatio*'

c. Bas:
εὐχαριστεῖν ('to thank') / originally absence of concept of '*Oblatio*'! (cf. Egyptian version)
[add. in **arm Bas I**: 'Let us look with attention'!
cf. ante Sanctus in Egyptian version: Εἰς ἀνατολὰς βλέπετε + Πρόσχω-μεν];
in **arm Bas I** in particular, traces of inauguration to the Heavenly Liturgy of the Angels

II. The Praise before the Sanctus:

The Sanctus is absent in **TradAp**.
The Praise before the Sanctus consists of two parts in both, **syr Ap-An** + **Bas**.

a. syr Ap-An:
(1) *People*: δόξα (originally probably verb [not noun]:
δοξάζειν ('to glorify') as in **arm Bas I**!)
[later interpolation of the theme of εὐχαριστία, absent in **arm Bas I**!]

(2) *Angels*:
– lower ranks: προσκυνεῖν
– highest ranks: δοξάζειν

----
cf. main vocabulary in connection with the *Qedušša* in Enoch:
gr En: εὐλογεῖν ('to praise');
eth En: εὐλογεῖν + δοξάζειν (plus '*exaltare*')
----

b. Bas:
(1) *People*: δοξάζειν ('to glorify'); in **arm Bas I** this verb *only*!
 [in **syr Bas**: 4 verbs; in **byz Bas**: 6 verbs
(αἰνεῖν - ὑμνεῖν - εὐλογεῖν - προσκυνεῖν - εὐχαριστεῖν)
verb-*pair* αἰνεῖν - ὑμνεῖν belongs not to Antiochene but to Egyptian tradition;
 εὐχαριστεῖν was interpolated because of the influence of the Institution Narrative]

(2) *Angels*:
– lower ranks: προσκυνεῖν
– highest ranks: δοξάζειν

III. The Praise before the Epiclesis:

a. TradAp (repeats the vocabulary of the *Initial Dalogue*!):
lat: εὐχαριστεῖν ('to thank')
eth: '*laudare!*'

b. syr Ap-An (is influenced by the Praise of the People before the Sanctus):
syr Ap-An has the following two main verbs:
δοξάζειν (ܡܫܒܚ)
'*exaltare*' (ܡܪܝܡ; cf. testimony of *Qedušša* in Enoch above)

c. Bas (takes over the Praise-Verbs before the Sanctus in various formations):
verbatim in **arm Bas II**!

The κατὰ πάντα καὶ διὰ πάντα, which inaugurates the Praise-Verbs before the Epiclesis in the Anaphora of Basil, is stating exactly what the words say: 'According to everything and in view of everything – *we praise* (εὐλόγουμεν)...', referring thereby precisely to what was said in connection with (1) the Praise before the Sanctus, (2) the Institution Narrative and (3) what is now said at the Praise before the Epiclesis.

*   *
*

The following verbs belong originally to the Praise-Verbs of the Oratio ante Sanctus:

- εὐλογεῖν ('to praise')
- δοξάζειν ('to glorify')
- προσκυνεῖν ('to adore/worship').

More precisely: these verbs pertain to the Heavenly Liturgy of the Angels. The two verbs εὐλογεῖν ('to praise') and δοξάζειν ('to glorify') are synonyms forming a verb-pair with προσκυνεῖν ('to adore/ worship'). Also αἰνεῖν ('to sing') and ὑμνεῖν ('to laud') constitute a verb-pair belonging, however, not to the Antiochene but the Egyptian (or hagiopolite) tradition.

The verb εὐχαριστεῖν originally belonged to the Institution Narrative and in consequence to the '*Oblatio*' as well.

*   *
*

The pertinent Verbs of Praise and Thanksgiving concerning these three early Eucharistic formularies were for the first time investigated and interpreted on a systematic basis. With this analysis it was possible to demonstrate and explain:

(1) the ties between the Initial Dialogue and the 'ante Sanctus' and 'ante Epiclesis' (the **TradAp** shares the central verb of the Opening Dialogue and the Epiclesis);

(2) the overall significance of the 'Liturgy of the Angels in Heaven', being of such importance that it influenced the praise of the Community: the Faithful imitate the praise of the Angels in the East-Syrian Anaphora of the Apostles Addai and Mari and in the Anaphora of Basil;

(3) the initial tension between the *Qeduššа* of the Angels with its vocabulary of Praise as a central focus and the interpolation of the Institution Narrative and its ripercussion, namely the introduction of the vocabulary of Thanksgiving;

(4) the meaning of the κατὰ πάντα καὶ διὰ πάντα? which has greatly mystified liturgical scholars for a long time.

UNA CELEBRAZIONE LITURGICA TUTTA PARTICOLARE
A COSTANTINOPOLI NEL SECOLO SESTO

Sebastià JANERAS

Con questo titolo mi riferisco ai fatti che ebbero luogo a Costantinopoli i giorni 15 e 16 luglio del 518 e che condussero alla commemorazione liturgica del concilio di Calcedonia, fissata nel Typicon della Grande Chiesa il 16 luglio[1] e trasformata posteriormente in una commemorazione dei sei primi concili ecumenici il 13 luglio se è domenica, o la domenica susseguente.[2] La cronaca che racconta questi fatti offre elementi interessanti per la storia della liturgia bizantina, e credo che — tranne l'uno o l'altro aspetto — non siano stati mai esaminati globalmente. Ma per capirne tutto il significato, è opportuno inquadrare questo testo nel marco storico-politico-ecclesiastico in cui appare. Tracciarne cioè il *Sitz im Leben*.

Corre l'anno 512. Regge l'impero bizantino Anastasio I (491-518), di tendenze monofisite, e da un anno, la sede patriarcale di Costantinopoli è occupata da Timoteo I (511-518), anche lui monofisita. In questo stesso anno il 512, Severo, il grande teologo della corrente monofisita, è eletto patriarca di Antiochia. Ancora in quest'anno, nel mese di novembre, ci furono gravissimi tumulti a Costantinopoli a causa del Trisagio, cristologico in origine e così ritenuto dai severiani, trinitario invece per i bizantini.[3] Come si sa, il patriarca monofisita di Antiochia Pietro Fullone, nel 470, aveva aggiunto al Trisagio, per chiarirne il senso cristologico: Ὁ σταυρωθεὶς δι'ἡμᾶς: 'Tu che sei stato crocifisso per noi'. Questa frase sarà il nodo delle lotte tra calcedonesi e non calcedonesi. Ebbene, il 4 novembre 512, sull'ambone della chiesa di San Teodoro di

---

[1] J. Mateos, *Le Typicon de la Grande Église: Ms. Sainte-Croix nᴇ 40, Xe siècle*, I, OCA 165 (Roma, 1962), pp. 340-342. Nella domenica susseguente, secondo lo stesso Typicon (pp. 342-344), si commemora il sinodo di 536 contro Severo di Antiochia, di cui parleremo subito.

[2] Su questa commemorazione, cf. S. Salaville, 'La fête du concile de Nicée et les fêtes des conciles dans le rite byzantin', *Échos d'Orient* 24 (1925) 445-470; idem, 'La fête du concile de Chalcédoine dans le rite byzantin', in *Das Konzil von Chalkedon*, ed. A. Grillmeier e H. Bacht, II (Würzburg, 1953), pp. 667-695. Per la festa nel rito bizantino odierno, cf. Μηναῖα τοῦ ὅλου ἐνιαυτοῦ, 6 (Roma, 1901), pp. 108-121.

Costantinopoli, i monofisiti cantarono il Trisagio con l'aggiunta fullo-niana, mentre i calcedonesi contraposero loro il Trisagio senza l'aggiunta. Onde il clamore, il tumulto, le risse. Lo stesso accadde due giorni dopo nel Foro di Costantino. I fatti ebbero qui però come conseguenze persino incendi e morti.[4]

Nel 518 le cose cambiano. Il 5 aprile moriva il patriarca Timoteo e gli era succeduto, il 17 aprile, l'ortodosso Giovanni II. Due mesi più tardi moriva pure l'imperatore Anastasio, il 9 giugno, e saliva sul trono imperiale Giustino I, calcedoniano convinto. I calcedonesi prendevano così il sopravvento e un mese più tardi ebbero luogo i fatti che sono l'oggetto di questo articolo, i quali furono raccolti in una relazione, aggiunta poi agli atti del concilio di Costantinopoli del 536. Dobbiamo quindi seguire questa relazione.[5]

Il 15 luglio 518, domenica, quando il patriarca, insieme ai suoi presbiteri, si accingeva a celebrare la Divina Liturgia, il popolo si ribellò e cominciò a gridare, impedendo così l'inizio della liturgia. Ecco lo sviluppo dei fatti secondo la cronaca:

Εἰσόδου γινομένης κατὰ τὸ σύνηθες ἐν τῇ ἁγιοτάτῃ ἡμῶν μεγάλῃ ἐκκλησίᾳ ἐν ἡμέρᾳ κυριακῇ τῇ ιε᾽ τοῦ ἐνεστῶτος Ἰουλίου μηνὸς ... παρὰ τοῦ δεσπότου ἡμῶν τοῦ ἁγιωτάτου ἀρχιεπισκόπου καὶ οἰκουμενικοῦ πατριάρχου Ἰωάννου ... ἐν τῷ γενέσθαι αὐτὸν σὺν τῷ εὐλαβεῖ κλήρῳ περὶ τὸν ἄμβωνα, φωναὶ γεγώνασιν ἀπὸ τοῦ λαοῦ, λέγουσαι: ...

'Quando il nostro signore il santissimo arcivescovo e patriarca ecumenico Giovanni, la domenica 15 luglio, faceva il suo ingresso, secondo l'abitudine della nostra Grande Chiesa ...' (cioè, entrava a Santa Sofia venendo dall'esterno, come di abitudine), 'quando si trovava all'altezza dell'ambone,[6] il popolo cominció a gridare: ...'

---

[3] Sul Trisagio si veda S. Janeras, 'Le Trisagion: une formule brève en liturgie comparée', in *Comparative Liturgy Fifty Years After Anton Baumstark (1872-1948), Rome, 25-129 September 1998* ed. R. F. Taft e G. Winkler, OCA 265 (Roma, 2001), pp. 495-562.

[4] Si veda la narrazione di Marcellinus Comes, *Chronicum, ad annum 512*, PL 51, 937-938. Nell'anno 533, in occasione di un terremoto, il Trisagio sarà cantato di nuovo con l'aggiunta (Ὁ σταυρωθεὶς δι᾽ ἡμᾶς), secondo il *Chronicon Paschale*, PG 92, 889.

[5] Vedasi il testo in E. Schwartz, *Acta Conciliorum Oecumenicorum*, II, pp. 71-76. Anche, con traduzione latina, in Ph. Labbe, *Sacrosancta Concilia ad regiam editionem exacta*, vol. 5 (Venezia, 1728), cols. 1148-1157, e J. D. Mansi, *Sacrorum Conciliorum nova et amplissima collectio*, vol. 8 (Parigi, 1901; ristampa anastatica Graz, 1960), cols. 1058-1066.

[6] L'ambone era collocato in mezzo alla chiesa, con dei gradini dai due lati, cioè verso est, verso il santuario, e verso ovest, verso la porta. Se ne possono vedere alcuni esempi in S. G. Xydis, 'The Chancel Barrier, Solea and Ambo of Hagia Sophia', *The Art Bulletin*

E qui occorre pensare che vi era presente uno stenografo, che prendeva nota di tutto ciò che sentiva. Le grida, le acclamazioni, sono innumerevoli. Ne citerò soltanto alcune, poiché molte sono anche ripetizioni.[7] Frattanto, patriarca e clero rimanevano fermi presso l'ambone, senza poter avanzare verso il santuario, come dirà poi il patriarca. Quindi:

'Lunghi anni al patriarca! (Πολλὰ τὰ ἔτη τοῦ πατριάρχου!)
Lunghi anni all'imperatore! (Πολλὰ τὰ ἔτη τοῦ βασιλέως!)
Lunghi anni all'imperatrice! (Πολλὰ τὰ ἔτη τῆς Αὐγούστης!)
Perché rimaniamo senza comunione?
Perché non ci siamo comunicati per tanti anni?
Vogliamo ricevere la comunione dalle tue mani!
Ehi, sali sull'ambone! (Ἐὲς ἄνελθε εἰς τὸν ἄμβωνα!)
Ehi, convince il tuo popolo! (Ἐὲς πεῖσον τὸν λαόν σου!)
Sei ortodosso, di chi hai paura?
Degno della Trinità! (Ἄξιε τῆς Τριάδος!)
Scaccia Severo, il manicheo!
Degno della Trinità!
Sia subito proclamato il santo concilio!
Vince la fede nella Trinità! (Νικᾷ ἡ πίστις τῆς Τριάδος!)
Vince la fede degli ortodossi! (Νικᾷ ἡ πίστις τῶν ὀρθοδόξων!)
Santa Maria è Madre di Dio! (Ἡ ἁγία Μαρία Θεοτόκος ἐστίν!)
Regna un ortodosso, di chi hai paura?
Vince la fede dell'imperatore!
Lunghi anni al nuovo Costantino!
Lunghi anni alla nuova Elena!
Lunghi anni al patriarca!
Degno della Trinità!
Giustino augusto, vittoria! (Ἰουστῖνε Αὔγουστε, *tu vincas!*)
Proclama subito il concilio di Calcedonia!
Ti scongiuro, o proclami o vai via!
È la fede, non si può dubitare!
Fratelli cristiani, una sola anima! (Ἀδελφοὶ χριστιανοί, μία ψυχή!)
Se ami la fede, anatematizza Severo!
Ehi, a fe mia che ti trascino!
Ecco che chiudo le porte!
Chi non parla è manicheo!

29 (1947) 1-24. T. Mathews, *The Early Churches of Constantinople: Architecture and Liturgy* (London, 1980), pp. 123-124 cita il testo che ci occupa. Vedasi anche R. Taft, 'Ambo', in *Oxford Dictionary of Byzantium,* I, pp. 75-76. Nella chiesa di Kalambaka, ai piedi delle Meteora, nella Thessalia, Grecia, se ne conserva ancora uno del sec. XIV.

[7] Si potrà osservare in queste acclamazioni, come alcune vanno contro il patriarca, altre mostrano indifferenza o persino ignoranza, come nel caso di Nestorio. Lo stenografo annotava tutto quanto sentiva. Per alcune ne do anche il testo greco.

Fai subito la proclamazione!
Per il vangelo, non me ne va niente! (Μὰ τὸ εὐαγγέλιον, οὐδὲν παρ'ἐμέ!)
Fratelli cristiani, una sola anima!'

Dopo tutte queste grida, il patriarca Giovanni, secondo la cronaca, disse alla moltitudine dei fedeli:

Μακροθυμήσατε, ἀδελφοί, ἵνα πρότερον προκυνήσωμεν τὸ ἅγιον θυσιαστήριον, καὶ μετὰ τοῦτο δίδωμι ὑμῖν ἀπόκρισιν.

'Abbiate pazienza, fratelli, e lasciate che prima possiamo andare a prostrarci davanti al santo altare, e poi vi daremo una risposta.'

Ma appena il patriarca, con i presbiteri e i chierici, entrò nel santuario, il popolo riprese a gridare:

'Lunghi anni all'imperatore!
Lunghi anni all'imperatrice!
Ti scongiuro, non uscirai fin che non lanci l'anatema contro Severo!'

Allora il patriarca, salendo sull'ambone (καὶ λοιπὸν ἀνελθὼν ἐπὶ τοῦ ἄμβωνος ὁ ἁγιώτατος), fece una apologia e una professione di fede:

'Carissimi, conoscete le mie fatiche subite quando ero presbitero e quelle che devo subire ora, per causa dell'ortodossia, e quante ne dovrò subire ancora fino alla morte. Non è quindi giusto questo tumulto. La nostra fede non è stata per nulla trasgredita, neanche nessuno ha osato anatematizzare il santo concilio, bensì riconosciamo come ortodossi tutti i santi concili che confermarono il simbolo dei trecento diciotto padri riuniti a Nicea, e in particolare i tre santi concili, cioè di Costantinopoli, di Efeso e il grande di Calcedonia ...'

Ma il popolo non ne rimase contento e riprese le sue gride per lungo tempo (ἐπὶ πλείστας ὥρας):

'Non scenderai se prima non lanci l'anatema!
Lunghi anni al patriarca!
Degno della Trinità!
Lunghi anni all'imperatore!
Annuncia subito una sinassi in onore del concilio di Calcedonia!
Non me andrò finché non l'avrai annunciato! (Οὐκ ἀναχωρῶ, ἐὰν μὴ κηρύξῃς!)
Rimarremo qui fino alla sera. Annuncia la sinassi per domani!
Anuncia per domani la sinassi dei padri di Calcedonia!
Se oggi l'annunci, domani si celebrerà!
Se non ricevo una risposta, rimango qui fino alla sera!'

Prendendo la parola il patriarca disse al popolo che avrebbe fatto questa proclamazione solamente dopo aver chiesto il consiglio dell'imperatore. Ma il popolo non ne rimase soddisfatto e riprese a gridare di nuovo. Allora il diacono Samuele salì sull'ambone e fece quest'annuncio:

'Faciamo sapere alla vostra carità che domani celebreremo la memoria dei nostri santi padri e vescovi congregati nella metropoli di Calcedonia, i quali, insieme con i padri riuniti a Costantinopoli e ad Efeso, confermarono il simbolo dei santi padri congregati a Nicea. E faremo la sinassi in questo luogo.'

Ma neanche così si calmò il popolo, che continuò a gridare per lungo tempo (ἐπὶ πολλὴν ὥραν), chiedendo l'anatema contro Severo. Finalmente, il patriarca Giovanni, cedendo alle richieste, pronunciò la condanna di Severo:

'A tutti è manifesto che Severo, il quale si è separato da questa Chiesa, si è sottomesso lui stesso a giudizio. Seguendo quindi anche noi i divini canoni e i santi Padri, lo consideriamo estraneo e, condannato dai divini canoni per la sua bestemmia, l'anatematizziamo anche noi.'

La cronaca non dice più niente di questo giorno, domenica 15 luglio. Occorre pensare che la celebrazione della Divina Liturgia si sarebbe svolta senza più incidenti, nell'attesa della celebrazione dell'indomani.

L'indomani infatti, lunedì 16 luglio, si fece, come richiesto, la commemorazione dei Padri del concilio di Calcedonia. Dice la cronaca: Ἐπιτελουμένης τῆς μνήμης τῶν προλεχθέντων ἁγίων πατέρων ('celebrandosi la memoria...', che la versione latina rende: *finita memoria...*). Come nel giorno precedente, appena il patriarca, nel suo ingresso, raggiunse l'ambone (Πάλιν τῆς εἰσόδου γινομένης ..., εὐθέως ἅμα τῷ γενέσθαι αὐτὸν πλησίον τοῦ ἄμβωνος), la folla ricominciò a gridare con le solite esclamazioni:

'Lunghi anni al patriarca!
Lunghi anni all'imperatore!
Ἰουστίνε Ἄυγουστε, *tu vincas*!
Εὐφημία Αὐγούστα, *tu vincas*!
Siano esumate le ossa dei nestoriani!
Siano esumate le ossa degli eutichiani!
Chi sia Nestorio, non lo so.
Scaccia Severo, il nuovo Giuda!
Siano inviate subito a Roma le carte sinodali!
Lunghi anni al nuovo Giovanni!
Degno della Trinità!
Siano iscritti i nomi di Eufemio e Macedonio!
I quattro santi concilii siano iscritti nei dittici!
Sia iscritto nei dittici Leone, vescovo di Roma!
Siano proclamati sull'ambone i dittici!'[8]

---

[8] I dittici saranno proclamati dall'interno del santuario, non dall'ambone, come vedremo. Fuori del santuario erano proclamati i dittici dei vivi, non quelli dei defunti, d'accordo con lo studio di R. Taft, *A History of the Liturgy of St. John Chrysosostom*, IV, *The Diptychs*, OCA 238 (Roma, 1991).

Allora il patriarca fece (si suppone dall'ambone) una allocuzione al popolo ('Ieri abbiamo soddisfatto sufficientemente la vostra carità …'), manifestando la sua propria fede pienamente ortodossa, la sua adesione, conosciuta da tutti, ai concili e al simbolo di fede, 'nel quale tutti siamo stati battezzati', dice il patriarca. Perciò, conclude,

> 'mantenendo fermi questa fede, non dubitate gli uni degli altri, ma, rifiutando le parole vacue e le sottigliezze inutili, con una sola voce glorifichiamo la santa e consustanziale Trinità, la quale custodisca la vita dei nostri piissimi e amati di Dio imperatori e di tutti noi. Al Padre e al Figlio e allo Spirito Santo conviene la gloria ora e sempre e nei secoli dei secoli. Amen.'

Questa pietosa allocuzione non poteva soddisfare il popolo, il quale riprese le sue grida per molto tempo (ἐπὶ πολλὴν ὥραν):

> 'Se nessuno adesso esce, ti assicuro che chiudo le porte!
> Fratelli ortodossi, una sola anima!
> Fratelli nella fede, una sola anima!
> Ἅγιος, Ἅγιος, Ἅγιος! Ἡ Τριὰς ἐνίκησεν! (La Trinità ha vinto!)
> Degno della Trinità!
> Chi ama il concilio è onorato così!
> Vince la fede degli ortodossi!'

Il patriarca, una volta ancora, non si pronuncia apertamente e dice al popolo che occorre procedere canonicamente e, quindi, riunirà i vescovi e domanderà il parere dell'imperatore, al quale porterà tutte le acclamazioni. Ma come la reazione del popolo fu di chiudere le porte e di ricominciare a gridare (κλεισάντων αὐτῶν τὰς θύρας καὶ ἐπιμενόντων ταῖς αὐταῖς ἐκβοήσεσι), il patriarca finalmente prese i dittici e ordinò che vi fossero iscritti i nomi dei quattro concili (Nicea, Costantinopoli, Efeso e Calcedonia), così come i nomi degli arcivescovi di Costantinopoli Eufemio e Macedonio, e anche quello di Leone, arcivescovo di Roma. La cronaca prosegue con la celebrazione liturgica, ed è qui che ci troviamo davanti ad un testo rilevante per la storia della liturgia. Ma prima di farne il commento vorrei soffermarmi sul fatto delle acclamazioni e sul senso di alcune di esse in particolare.

Le acclamazioni popolari erano cosa comune nelle solennità, nelle grandi celebrazioni, negli atti della corte imperiale, ecc. Per queste ultime ocasioni basta percorrere le pagine del *Libro delle Ceremonie* di Costantino Porfirogenito (913-959).[9] Troviamo anche acclamazioni nel

---

[9] Cf. A. Vogt, *Constantin VIIe Porphyrogénète: Le Livre des Cérémonies,* I (Parigi, 1935), *passim.*

concilio di Calcedonia (451), alla fine della sessione ottava, quando i vescovi antiocheni gridarono:[10]

'Lunghi anni al senato!
Ἅγιος ὁ Θεός, ἅγιος ἰσχυρός, ἅγιος ἀθάνατος, ἐλέησον ἡμᾶς
Lunghi anni agli imperatori!
Questo è il vero sínodo!'

Troviamo la stessa pratica in Occidente,[11] dove appare spesso l'espressione *Exaudi, Christe*. Così quando Agostino anunciò al suo popolo che aveva scelto come successore Eraclio, il popolo proruppe in incessanti acclamazioni, tra le quali: *Deo gratias! Christo laudes! Exaudi, Christe! Augustino vita!* O pure nel concilio romano del 495: *Exaudi, Christe! Gelasio vita! Domine Petre, tu illum adiuva!* E non possiamo dimenticare le celebri *Laudes regiae* romano-gallicane, dove domina, ripetuto diverse volte, il versetto *Christus vincit, Christus regnat, Christus imperat!* che conoscerà una grande diffusione in Occidente.[12]

Ritorniamo ora al concilio di Calcedonia. In mezzo alle acclamazioni appare il Trisagio, ed è la prima volta che troviamo il testo di quest'inno, non però il suo uso nella liturgia, testimoniato già prima.[13] Un vestigio del canto del Trisagio in mezzo alle acclamazioni possiamo vederlo nella liturgia pontificale di rito bizantino, nella quale, alternando col Trisagio (non mi trattengo sulle diverse modalità) il diacono pronuncia queste parole: Κύριε, σῶσον τοὺς εὐσεβεῖς (cioè, gli imperatori), καὶ ἐλέησον ἡμᾶς. In slavo: Господи, спаси благочестивыя, и услыши ны! Nella relazione degli eventi di 518 a Costantinopoli non appare proprio il testo del Trisagio, ma vi è presente sotto la forma biblica: Ἅγιος, ἅγιος, ἅγιος. Anche nelle acclamazioni della corte imperiale troviamo diverse forme simili: Ἅγιε!, Τρισάγιε!, Ἅγιος, ἅγιος, ἅγιος!

Ricordiamo i fatti storici menzionati all'inizio. Siamo pienamente nel periodo postcalcedonese, nel periodo chiamato neocalcedonese.[14] Pochi

---

[10] E. Schwartz, *Acta Conciliorum Oecumenicorum*, II, 1,1, p. 195.

[11] Su questo tema cf. F. Cabrol, 'Acclamations', in *Dictionaire d'Archéologie Chrétienne et de Liturgie* I/1, cols. 240-265, e anche: Th. Klauser, 'Akklamation', in *Reallexikon für Antike und Christentum* 1, 1950, cols. 216-233.

[12] Cf. J. M. Hanssens, 'De laudibus carolinis', *Periodica de re morali, canonica, liturgica* 30 (1941) 280-302; 31 (1942) 31-53; E. H. Kantorowicz, *Laudes regiae: A Study in Liturgical Acclamation and Mediaeval Ruler Worship* (Los Angeles, 1946); B. Opfermann, *Die liturgischen Herrscherakklamationen im Sacrum Imperium des Mittelalters* (Weimar, 1953).

[13] Sulla storia del Trisagio vedasi il mio articolo citato nella nota 3.

[14] Su questo periodo si veda particolarmente Ch. Moeller, 'Le chalcédonisme et le néochalcédonisme en Orient de 451 à la fin du VIe siècle', in *Das Konzil von Chalkedon*, ed. A. Grillmeier e H. Bacht, I (Würzburg, 1951), pp. 637-720.

anni prima degli eventi del 518 assistevamo ad un certo dominio e
trionfo dei severiani. Ora, con l'imperatore Giustino e il patriarca Giovanni, i calcedonesi prendono la rivincita. I severiani, d'accordo con la
tradizione chiamata monofisita — e, in fondo, col senso primitivo e originale — indirizzavano il Trisagio a Cristo. Negli eventi del 518 i calcedonesi, fedeli alla loro interpretazione trinitaria del Trisagio, gridano
ora: 'Vince la Trinità!' e, rivolto al patriarca: 'Degno della Trinità!',
oltre gli anatemi lanciati contro Severo. È quindi certamente chiaro
che queste acclamazioni hanno a che fare con la questione del Trisagio
(cristologico o trinitario). Ho citato sopra alcune acclamazioni occiden-
tali. Non vi appare il Trisagio, ma sì altre acclamazioni, sempre cristolo-
giche: *Exaudi, Christe!*, *Christo laudes!*, e persino, nelle *Laudes regiae,*
alcune espressioni che non considero lontane dal Trisagio: *Fortitudo
nostra, Victoria nostra, Virtus, fortitudo et victoria.* Forse mi sono dilun-
gato un pò troppo (ἐπὶ πολλὴν ὥραν) nelle acclamazioni contenute nel
nostro testo, ma mi sembrano un capitolo interessante, anche per la liturgia comparata.

Vediamo ora come finì questa celebrazione tutta particolare. Dopo
che il patriarca ebbe fatto iscrivere nei dittici i quattro concili (Nicea,
Costantinopoli, Efesio e Calcedonia) e i nomi dei santi arcivescovi della
città imperiale Eufemio e Macedonio e dell'arcivescovo di Roma Leone,
come era stato richiesto dal popolo, questo esplose in un canto di azione
di grazie:

> Τότε φωνῇ μεγάλῃ πάντες οἱ τοῦ λαοῦ, ὡς ἐξ ἑνὸς στόματος
> ἐβόησαν: 'Εὐλογητὸς Κύριος ὁ Θεὸς τοῦ Ἰσραήλ, ὅτι ἐπεσκέψατο
> καὶ ἐποίησε λύτρωσιν τῷ λαῷ αὐτοῦ'. Καὶ πάλιν δεύτερον ἔκραξαν:
> 'Εὐλογητὸς Κύριος Ἰησοῦς ὁ βασιλεύς, ὅτι ἐπεσκέψατο καὶ ἐποίησε
> λύτρωσιν τῷ λαῷ αὐτοῦ'.

> 'Allora, con gran voce, tutto il popolo come una sola bocca, gridó: "Bene-
> detto il Signore Iddio d'Israele, perchè ha visitato e redento il suo popolo".
> E di nuovo gridarono: "Benedetto il Signore Gesù, il Re, perchè ha visitato
> e redento il suo popolo".'

Si tratta obviamente del cantico di Zaccaria, del *Benedictus.* E la narrazione dice che fu cantato a lungo a due cori, in forma antifonica: Ἐπὶ
πολλὴν δὲ ὥραν ἀντιφωνούντων ἑκατέρων τῶν μερῶν, καὶ
ψαλλόντων τὴν ψαλμῳδίαν ταύτην... Forse cantarono tutto il cantico,[15]

---

[15] Mateos, che cita questo testo, pensa piuttosto che si cantò il primo versetto: 'Le
peuple, rassemblé dans l'église, chanta, comme action de grâces à Dieu pour le triomphe

intercalandovi il primo versetto, il quale nella ripetizione acquista un senso cristologico: 'Benedetto il Signore Gesù, il Re ...' Questo versetto cristologico viene introdotto con le parole: 'E di nuovo gridarono' (καὶ πάλιν δεύτερον ἔκραξαν). Potrebbe ciò indicare forse che un coro rispondeva con il primo versetto e l'altro col versetto cristologico?

Troviamo un caso simile, ma riferito all'ὄρθρος ᾀσματικός, in Simeone di Salonicco.[16] Dopo i salmi 148-150, per i quali spiega il modo di cantarli e i versetti da intercalare, dice che si canta il cantico di Zaccaria: Εἶτα Εὐλογητὸς Κύριος ὁ Θεὸς Ἰσραήλ..., ecc. E dice che questo versetto è ripetuto dopo ogni versetto del cantico. Ma dopo il Δόξα Πατρί e dopo il Καὶ νῦν il versetto prende il senso cristologico: Εὐλογητὸς Κύριος Ἰησοῦς βασιλεύς, ὅτι ἐπεσκέψατο καὶ ἐποίησε λύτρωσιν τῷ λαῷ αὐτοῦ.

Nel caso riportato da Simeone di Salonicco si tratta dell'ufficio dell'orthros. Nei fatti del 518 a Costantinopoli invece il cantico di Zaccaria è cantato all'inizio della Liturgia eucaristica. Non conosciamo altri esempi di questa usanza, ma sotto questa luce possiamo forse capire una frase della preghiera del Trisagio della Liturgia di san Basilio nel codice Barberini (ora passata poi alla Liturgia del Crisostomo), ispirata quasi alla lettera nel cantico di Zaccaria:

Liturgia di san Basilio[17]	*Cantico di Zaccaria*
καὶ δὸς ἡμῖν	
ἐν ὁσιότητι λατρεύειν σοι	λατρεύειν αυτῷ ἐν ὁσιότητι
	καὶ δικαιοσύνῃ ἐνώπιον αὐτοῦ
πάσας τὰς ἡμέρας τῆς ζωῆς ἡμῶν	πάσαις ταῖς ἡμέραις ἡμῶν

Si tratta forse di un vestigio del canto del *Benedictus* all'inizio della Liturgia? Il cantico di Zaccaria tra i primi elementi della celebrazione eucaristica era certamente conosciuto in Occidente, concretamente nell'antica liturgia gallicana, la quale, così come la liturgia ispanica, possedeva parecchi elementi di origine orientale.[18] Dopo il canto *Ad*

---

de l'orthodoxie, le premier verset du cantique de Zacharie; les psalmistes ensuite, pour commencer la liturgie, entonnèrent le trisagion'. J. Mateos, *La célébration de la parole dans la Liturgie byzantine*, OCA 181 (Roma, 1971), pp. 26-27, 71-72.

[16] *De sacra precatione*, 351 (PG 155, 648). Cf. anche P. Trempelas, Μικρὸν Εὐχολόγιον, 2 (Atene, 1955), p. 200; I. Fountoulês, Τὸ λειτουργικὸν ἔργον Συμεὼν τοῦ Θεσσαλονίκης (Salonicco, 1966), pp. 156-157.

[17] S. Parenti e E. Velkovska, *L'Eucologio Barberini gr. 336*, Bibliotheca "Ephemerides Liturgicae". Subsidia 80, seconda edizione riveduta (Roma, 2000), p. 59.

[18] Cf. J. Quasten, 'Oriental Influence in the Gallican Liturgy', *Traditio* 1 (1943) 55-78; S. Janeras, 'Elements orientals en la litúrgia visigòtica', *Miscel·lània Litúrgica Catalana* 6 (1995) 93-127.

Praelegendum — equivalente all'introito romano —, il Trisagio (*Aius*)[19] e un triplice *Kyrie eleison,* seguiva la *Prophetia,* cioè il cantico di Zaccaria, concluso con l'orazione *Post prophetiam.* È interessante notare che lo Pseudo-Germano di Parigi, nella sua spiegazione di questo cantico, dice tra l'altro: 'Ideo prophetia quam pater eius ipso nascente cecinit, *alternis vocibus ecclesia psallit.*'[20]

Ritorniamo al testo della cronaca dei fatti di 518. Dopo aver detto che il popolo cantò a lungo, a due cori, il cantico di Zaccaria, aggiunge che i cantori poterono finalmente salire sull'ambone e intonare il Trisagio: οἱ ψάλται ἐπετράπησαν ἀνελθόντες εἰπεῖν τὸ Τρισάγιον. Qui appare — lasciato a parte il caso particolare del cantico di Zaccaria — il Trisagion come canto iniziale della Liturgia e intonato dal cantore dall'alto dell'ambone. Su questo fatto ne abbiamo altri testimoni. Per esempio, nel *Trattato sull'Incarnazione* del monaco Giobbe, del sesto secolo, che conosciamo attraverso il riassunto che ne fece il patriarca Fozio, si dice: 'Mentre i presbiteri si avvicinano all'altare, il cantore sacro proclama da un posto elevato: Ἅγιος ὁ Θεός, Ἅγιος ἰσχυρός, Ἅγιος ἀθάνατος, ἐλέησον ἡμᾶς.'[21] O pure nel *Typikon* della Grande Chiesa, il primo settembre: 'E i cantori, sull'ambone, intonano, come ritornello di processione, il Trisagio' (Καὶ ἄρχονται οἱ ψάλται ἐν τῷ ἄμβωνι ἀντὶ λιτῆς τὸ Τρισάγιον).[22]

Un altro punto interessante di questo passaggio è il modo di cantare il Trisagio. Infatti, dopo aver detto che i cantori salirono sull'ambone per cantare il Trisagio, aggiunge:

> Καὶ αὐτῶν ἀρξαμένων πᾶς ὁ λαὸς ἐπαύσατο καὶ ὑπήκουσε τοῦ Τρισαγίου.

> 'Appena i cantori incominciarono, il popolo cessò (cioè il canto precedente: il cantico di Zaccaria), e rispondeva al Trisagio.'

Qui abbiamo dunque un testimonio del Trisagio cantato in forma responsoriale. Purtroppo questa frase è stata parecchie volte interpretata

---

[19] Questo Trisagio era cantato in greco (e perciò *Aius*); dopo il vangelo invece si cantava il *Sanctus,* cioè lo stesso Trisagio ma in latino.

[20] E. C. Ratcliff, *Expositio antiquae Liturgiae Gallicanae,* I, 6, Henry Bradshaw Society 98 (Londra, 1971), p. 5. Il testo si può vedere anche in K. Gamber, *Ordo antiquus gallicanus: Der gallikanische Messritus des 6. Jahrhunderts* (Regensburg, 1965). Sullo Pseudo-Germano, cf. M. Smyth, 'La première lettre du Pseudo-Germain de Paris et la mystagogie', *Miscel·lània Litúrgica Catalana* 9 (1999) 51-71.

[21] Focio, *Bibliotheca,* 222, ed. R. Henry, vol. 3 (Parigi, 1962), p. 180.

[22] Mateos, *Le Typicon de la Grande Église* (vedi n. 1), p. 6.

e tradotta in maniera non corretta. La traduzione latina del Labbe ripresa dal Mansi, dice: *Totus populus quievit* (per επάυσατο), et *audiebat attentis auribus Trisagion*.[23] Salaville parafrasa e aggiunge elementi che non sono nell'originale: 'Puis les chantres reprirent le Trisagion, et le peuple se calma pour écouter l'hymne trinitaire (il testo dice semplicemente il Trisagio), l'Épître, l'Évangile'.[24] Persino uno studioso greco, Christos Tzogas, interpreta il verbo ὑπήκουσε nel senso di ascoltare, non di rispondere: Ὁ λαὸς δὲν ἐλάμβανε μέρος, ἀλλ'ἐτέλει ἐν πλήρει σιγῇ (così interpreta il verbo ἐπαύσατο) ἐπήκουσε τοῦ Τρισαγίου (quindi ascoltava in silenzio, poichè, come dice poco prima, il popolo non vi prendeva parte), e aggiunge: καὶ ἀφωσιοῦτο περισσότερον εἰς τὸν Θεόν.[25] Rimane chiaro che il verbo ὑπακούω significa 'rispondere', e corresponde al sostantivo liturgico ὑπακοή (*ibakoj* nella tradizione georgiana).

La cronaca prosegue:

Καὶ μετὰ τὴν ἀνάγνωσιν τοῦ ἁγίου εὐαγγελίου, ἐξ ἔθος τῆς θείας λειτουργίας ἐπιτελουμένης, καὶ τῶν θυρῶν κλεισθεισῶν, καὶ τοῦ ἁγίου μαθήματος κατὰ τὸ σύνηθες λεχθέντος...

'Dopo la lettura del santo vangelo, come è abitudine quando si celebra la Divina Liturgia,[26] e chiuse le porte,[27] e recitato come di abitudine il simbolo di fede ...'

Quest'ultima frase è importante. Innanzitutto, per il termine μάθημα riferito al simbolo di fede. Du Cange, nel suo *Glossarium*, raccoglie questo senso e cita appunto il testo che ci occupa;[28] ma si trova anche in alcuni manoscritti liturgici. E qui, una volta di più, la traduzione di Mansi è sbagliata: *Sancta lectione iuxta consuetudinem lecta*. Ma il fatto importante è che qui abbiamo il primo testimonio della recita del simbolo di fede nella Liturgia, e questa recita non è nuova, ma già abituale: κατὰ τὸ σύνηθες. Per l'introduzione del Credo nella Liturgia a Costantinopoli è solito citare il testimonio di Tedoro il Lettore, il quale dice che

---

[23] Labbe, col. 1155; Mansi, col. 1066.
[24] Salaville, 'La fête du concile' (vedi n. 2), p. 686.
[25] Ch. Tzogas, 'Ὁ Τρισάγιος ὕμνος', in *Θεολογικὸν Συμπόσιον* (Miscellanea P. Chrêstou), (Salonicco, 1977), pp. 277-286.
[26] Labbe e Mansi traducono: *ex more sacra missa finita*.
[27] Questa volta si tratta della chiusura liturgica delle porte dopo il congedo (non menzionato) dei catecumeni, non della chiusura fatta dal popolo nelle sue esigenze davanti al patriarca.
[28] C. Du Cange, *Glossarium ad scriptores mediae et infimae graecitatis*, I (Lione, 1688), col. 851.

fu introdotto dal patriarca monofisita Timoteo (511-518)[29], ciò che è
vero. Ma Teodoro scrive verso 550, mentre la cronaca di cui ci occu-
piamo fu scritta prima (518). Quindi si tratta del primo testimonio della
recita del Credo nella liturgia eucaristica a Bisanzio. Questa introduzione fu fatta certamente nei primi anni del patriarcato di Timoteo, poichè al tempo della cronaca era già una pratica abituale: κατὰ τὸ
σύνηθες.

La narrazione passa ora, senza citare altri elementi, al punto centrale
della discussione e delle esigenze del popolo, cioè, la proclamazione dei
quattro concili ecumenici e l'inclusione di certi nomi nei dittici:

> Τῷ καιρῷ τῶν διπτύχων, μετὰ πολλῆς ἡσυχίας συνέδραμον ἅπαν τὸ
> πλῆθος κύκλῳ τοῦ θυσιαστηρίου, καὶ ἠκροῶντο.

'Al tempo dei dittici, con grande silenzio, tutto il popolo accorse attorno al
santuario ed ascoltava.'

Ho tradotto θυσιαστήριον per 'santuario'. All'inizio della narrazione
vedevamo il patriarca dire al popolo: 'Lasciate che prima ci proster-
niamo davanti al santo altare' (ἵνα πρότερον προσκυνήσωμεν τὸ
ἅγιον θυσιαστήριον). Qui il termine θυσιαστήριον può essere tradotto adeguatamente per 'altare'; ma anche per 'santuario'. Infatti,
subito dopo il testo dice: Καὶ εἰσελθόντες εἰς τὸ ἅγιον θυσιαστήριον... ('ed entrando nel santo santuario...'). Nel passaggio relativo
ai dittici il termine θυσιαστήριον indica certamente il santuario e non
l'altare, poichè i fedeli non potevano accorrere attorno ad esso, dal fatto
che ai semplici fedeli non era dato di entrare nel santuario. Quindi i
fedeli si serrarono presso i cancelli, presso il τέμπλον, col fine di ascoltare meglio la proclamazione dei dittici, che il diacono faceva dall'interno del santuario, come spiega R. Taft.[30] Qui si tratta dei padri dei
concili, quindi di dittici dei defunti.

È da osservare ancora che il verbo usato qui per 'ascoltare' è ἀκροάω
e non ὑπακούω, che abbiamo trovato all'inizio e che non significa
'ascoltare', come alcuni hanno tradotto, bensì 'rispondere'.

Appena il diacono proclamò i santi concili e i nomi di santa memoria
di Eufemio e Macedonio e di Leone, dice il testo, μεγάλη φωνῇ ἔκραξαν πάντες: Δόξα σοι Κύριε! ('Tutti gridarono con grande voce:
"Gloria a te, o Signore!"'). E la cronaca conclude: Καὶ μετὰ τοῦτο,

---

[29] *Historia ecclesiastica*, 32, PG 86, 201.
[30] Taft, *The Diptychs* (vedi n. 8). Taft (pp. 102-103, 178-179) esamina proprio su
questo punto il testo che ci occupa.

μετὰ πάσης εὐταξίας ἐπληρώθη σὺν Θεῷ ἡ θεία λειτουργία ('Dopo di ciò, con pieno ordine si completò, con l'aiuto di Dio, la Divina Liturgia'). Si voleva, veramente!

Questi fatti succedettero il 15-16 luglio del 518. Il 20 si riunì un sinodo (σύνοδος ἐνδημοῦσα), con quaranta vescovi, nel quale fu letta una lettera dei monaci ortodossi, firmata da cinquantaquattro archimandriti, di cui i vescovi assunsero come proprie le domande. Questi testi, assieme ad altre lettere e alla cronaca dei fatti del 15-16 luglio, li troviamo tra gli atti del concilio posteriore del 536.[31]

Nel anno 527 Giustiniano saliva sul trono imperiale. Già prima, essendo associato al trono di Giustino, era intervenuto nell'affare dei monaci sciti e la loro celebre formula *Unus de Trinitate passus est,* tema di cui si occuperà ancora come imperatore teologo.[32] Calcedonese convinto, piano piano, grazie all'influsso dell'imperatrice Teodora, divenne incline verso i severiani e i monofisiti, cercando, nella linea religiosopolitica del neocalcedonismo, un avvicinamento tra calcedonesi e non calcedonesi. È così che nel 532 Giustiniano promovve a Costantinopoli una discussione tra le due parti, senza però nessun risultato. E i severiani guadagnavano di nuovo terreno nella capitale. Nel mese di novembre 533, secondo il *Chronicon paschale,* la città conobbe uno dei tanti terremoti che ebbe a subire.[33] Tutti gli abitanti della cità si riunirono nel Foro di Costantino, insonni, facendo delle preghiere e dicendo: Ἅγιος ὁ Θεός, Ἅγιος ἰσχυρός, Ἅγιος ἀθάνατος, ὁ σταυρωθεὶς δι'ἡμᾶς, ἐλέησον ἡμᾶς. All'alba tutti gridarono: Νικᾷ ἡ τύχη τῶν χριστιανῶν. Ὁ σταυρωθείς, σῶσον ἡμᾶς καὶ τὴν πόλην! ('Vince la sorte dei cristiani. Tu che sei stato crocifisso, salvaci, noi e la città!')

Dall'autunno 534 fino a febbraio 536 Severo si trovava di nuovo a Costantinopoli, accolto da Teodora. E nel 535 occupava la sede costantinopolitana un altro patriarca monofisita: Antimo. È proprio in questo periodo, sicuramente nel 535, e certamente prima di febbraio 536, che fu composto il celebre troparito Ὁ μονογενής, opera di Giustiniano

---

[31] Vedasi la bibliografia della nota 5. Nel Mansi (cols. 573-5766), troviamo un riassunto di questi fatti e un rinvio, per i testi, al concilio di 536 (cols. 1058-1066).

[32] Sugli sciti cf. E. Amman, 'Scythes (moines)', in *Dictionnaire de théologie catholique* 14, cols. 1746-1753; e particolarmente Ch. Moeller, 'Le chalcédonisme" (vedi n. 14). Su Giustiniano teologo, cf. M. Amelotti e L. M. Zingale, *Scritti teologici ed ecclesiastici di Giustiniano* (Milano, 1977); K. H. Uthemann, 'Kaiser Justinian als Kirchenpolitiker und Theologe', *Augustinianum* 39 (1999) 5-83.

[33] *Chronicon paschale,* 92, 889.

secondo i bizantini, o di Severo, secondo i siro-antiocheni, nel quale
però sicuramente intervennero tutti e due. Si tratta infatti di una formula
di conciliazione che divenne presto un canto iniziale della Liturgia in
quasi tutti i riti orientali.[34]

Nel febbraio 536, trovandosi il papa Agapito a Costantinopoli per
affari politici, depose il patriarca Antimo, e consacrò nel suo posto un
nuovo patriarca, Menna. Sotto la sua presidenza si tenne, nei mesi di
giugno-luglio (il papa era morto nella capitale il mese d'aprile), un concilio, nel quale fu letta la cronaca dei fatti occorsi il 15-16 luglio 518 e
gli altri documenti. In questo modo, anche se come semplice lettura,
risuonarono forse di nuovo a Santa Sofia le acclamazioni, le grida, gli
anatemi di diciotto anni prima. Il concilio condannò Severo, assieme ad
Antimo, Pietro e Zooras. Il 6 agosto, Giustiniano, oramai antimonofisita,
pubblicò una costituzione contro gli stessi personaggi.[35] Severo dovette
andare definitivamente in esilio e morì due anni dopo.

Questo è il *Sitz im Leben* che ci permette di capire meglio i fatti di
luglio del 518 e la cronaca che li racconta, ed è interessante per molti
versi per la storia della liturgia bizantina. Ecco per finire, in forma rias-
suntiva, gli elementi che possiamo rilevare da questa cronaca:

1. L'ingresso del patriarca nella chiesa all'inizio della Liturgia: dall'e-
    sterno, traversando la chiesa, passando accanto all'ambone fino al
    santuario.
2. Il caso particolare del canto, all'inizio della Liturgia, del *Benedictus*
    a due cori, in forma antifonica.
3. Il canto del Trisagio, intonato dai cantori dall'ambone e cantato in
    forma responsoriale col popolo.
4. La chiusura delle porte dopo il congedo (non menzionato) dei cate-
    cumeni.

---

[34] Sul tropario Ὁ Μονογενής, cf. J. Puyade, 'Le tropaire Ὁ Μονογενής', *Revue de
l'Orient chrétien* 7 (1912) 253-267; V. Grumel, 'L'auteur et la date de composition du
tropaire Ὁ Μονογενής', *Échos d'Orient* 22 (1923) 398-418; J. H. Barkhuizen, 'Justinian's Hymn Ὁ Μονογενής Υἱὸς καὶ Λόγος τοῦ Θεοῦ', *Byzantinische Zeitschrift* 77
(1984) 3-5; J. Breck, *The Power of the Word in the Worshiping Church* (Crestwood, NY,
1986), cap. VI, *Confessing the Monogenes, The Only-Begotten Son*; S. I. Nikitin, 'Еди-
нородный Сыне', in *Православная Энциклопедия* (Mosca, 2008) vol. 18, 51-54;
S. Janeras, 'Le tropaire Ὁ Μονογενής dans les liturgies orientales et sa signification
oecuménique' (con bibliografia più completa), in *Liturgies in East and West: Ecumenical
Relevance of Early Liturgical Development – Scholarly International Symposium Vindo-
bonense, Vienna, November 17-20, 2007*, ed. Hans-Jürgen Feulner (in stampa).

[35] Vedasi il testo in PG 86, 1095-1104, o pure in Mansi, 8, cols. 1149-1156.

5. La recitazione del simbolo di fede, prima testimonianza di una pratica già stabilita.
6. La proclamazione dei dittici dal santuario.
7. Anche l'uso dell'ambone per le proclamazioni, gli avvisi, ecc., non propriamente liturgici.

THE ADVENTURES OF A LITURGICAL COMMEMORATION:
THE SIXTH ECUMENICAL SYNOD
IN THE HEORTOLOGION OF THE BYZANTINE RITE

Chrysostom NASSIS

1. Introduction

The *heortologion* of the Byzantine rite is essentially a calendar of feasts that are to be kept in the Church throughout the liturgical year. The principal celebrations included in this calendar are of course the major dominical and Marian feasts. In its present form, it also includes the commemoration of saints: prophets and apostles, martyrs and confessors, ecumenical teachers and bishops, emperors and ascetics. No less, it records significant events in the history of the imperial city: the dedication of shrines, churches, and even Constantinople itself, the miraculous deliverance from the threatening advance of enemies, and rescue from potentially devastating natural forces. Furthermore, it references milestones in the life of the Byzantine Church, such as the translation of relics and the convocation of ecumenical synods. On the whole the *heortologion* is a coherently structured system with its own internal, logical composition. Nevertheless, historically speaking, like the gradual synthesis of the Byzantine rite, the *heortologion* followed its own evolutionary development, one that came to a head especially after the end of the second phase of iconoclasm. During this process, specific components of the *heortologion* were at times reduced, altered, confused, corrupted, or reconfigured, above all, when they were adopted from other local liturgical traditions. Similar phenomena can be noted in those instances whereby commemorations were adapted based on the liturgical needs of a specific cathedral, monastery, or oratory, the theological and historical sensitivities of a particular ecclesiastical center, and the initiatives or directives of an individual church leader or civil ruler influential in ecclesial affairs. These modifications can be identified when the feasts of the *heortologion* are both traced over an extended period of time and observed in multiple geographical regions. As a result of these variables, the *heortologion*, a compendium formulated primarily at the local level, is marked by a great deal of diversity. This is noted, for instance, in what

Jean-Baptiste Pitra calls the *Typicum Studitarum et Hierosolymitanorum*. According to the prefatory remarks of this *heortological* list:

> '... [T]here is no perfect agreement with regard to feasts ... but often those found in one work are not found in another. On this we learned that, in the place where these books are administered, they have a custom of celebrating the feast of [certain] saints; for this reason in each work, if they celebrate them as either major or minor observances, they enumerated them among the feasts.'[1]

The purpose of this article is to provide an example of the inner workings of the *heortologion* by looking at one particular feast. Specifically, examination will be made of the incorporation of the Sixth Ecumenical Synod into the *heortologion* of the Church of Constantinople and the subsequent developments related to this commemoration. I chose this topic that may seem secondary or peripheral at first glance because, in part, as we shall see, it coincides with the days on which the Rome congress of the Society of Oriental Liturgy is being held. More importantly, however, I chose it because I believe that this study may be linked to some of the broader issues that are currently being looked at by liturgical scholars with far greater attention to detail. These include matters such as the inner plurality of the monastic or cathedral liturgical sources and the critical evaluation of the *textus receptus* enshrined in liturgical books presently in use. During my research I examined various primary sources (lectionaries, *synaxaria*, *typika*, and *menaia*)[2] focusing on those originating in Constantinople or in regions that had come under the immediate influence of the liturgical practice of this primatial see of the East.

---

[1] Jean-Baptiste Pitra, *Spicilegium Solesmense, complectens sanctorum Patrum scriptorumque ecclesiasticorum anecdota hactenus opera selecta e graecis orientalibusque et latinis codicibus*, vol. IV (Paris, 1858; reprint, Graz, 1963), p. 452.

[2] On these sources, see Jacques Noret, 'Ménologes, synaxaires, menées: Essai de clarification d'une terminologie', *Analecta Bollandiana* 86 (1968) 21-24; Kônstantinos A. Manafês, Μοναστηριακὰ τυπικὰ-διαθῆκαι. Μελέτη φιλολογική, «ΑΘΗΝΑ» Σύγγραμα Περιοδικὸν τῆς ἐν Ἀθήναις Ἐπιστημονικῆς Ἑταιρείας. Σειρὰ διατριβῶν καὶ μελετημάτων 7 (Athens, 1970); Yvonne Burns, 'The Historical Events that Occasioned the Inception of the Byzantine Gospel Lectionaries', *Jahrbuch der österreichischen Byzantinistik* 32.4 (1982) 119-127; Robert F. Taft, 'Typikon, Liturgical', in *Oxford Dictionary of Byzantium*, vol. III, ed. Alexander P. Kazhdan (New York, 1991), pp. 2131-2132; Elena Velkovska, 'Lo studio dei lezionari bizantini', *Ecclesia Orans* 13 (1996) 253-271; Job Getcha, 'Le système des lectures bibliques du rite byzantin', in *La liturgie, interprète de l'Ecriture I. Les lectures bibliques pour les dimanches et les fêtes, Conférences Saint-Serge, 48e Semaine d'Etudes Liturgiques*, eds. A. M. Triacca and A. Pistoia, Bibliotheca «Ephemerides Liturgicae». Subsidia 127 (Rome, 2002), pp. 25-56.

2. The Introduction of the Feast into the Heortologion: Examining the Possibilities

There is no extant evidence that indicates precisely when the feast of the Sixth Ecumenical Synod was incorporated into the *heortologion* of the Byzantine rite. A plausible hypothesis is that it was introduced after the restoration of dyothelite Orthodoxy under Emperor Anastasius II (713-715). As is known, Philippicus Bardanes (711-713) unsuccessfully attempted to re-impose the monothelite doctrine upon the Church, especially by convoking and endorsing the synod held in the year 712.[3] After his deposition, along with the official reaffirmation of the Sixth Ecumenical Synod, an annual commemoration of Constantinople III may have been introduced into the Church's liturgical calendar so that a future heretical regression would be avoided. This may have been done at the initiative of Patriarch Germanus I of Constantinople (715-730), who even wrote a treatise *On Heresies and Synods* that ends with the Sixth Ecumenical Synod.[4] In any event, the feast was certainly in place by the ninth century, as documented in the early manuscripts of the text conventionally called the *Typikon of the Great Church*.

3. Inner Cathedral Rite Diversity and the Ensuing Distortion of the Commemoration

The day on which this feast was initially meant to be celebrated is equally problematic. When presenting a study on the 'theological feasts' of the Byzantine calendar at the 25th *Saint-Serge Conference* held in

---

[3] Rudolf Riedinger, *Concilium Universale Constantinopolitanum Tertium*, Acta Conciliorum Oecumenicorum, Series Secunda, II, part 2 (Berlin, 1992), p. 905.18-19. Philippicus-Bardanes also removed the icon of the Sixth Ecumenical Synod from the courtyard at Milion. He replaced it with one of himself and Sergius of Constantinople. See *ibid.*, pp. 899.15-24 and 900.30-38. On the religious policy of Philippicus-Bardanes, see Dorothy E. Abrahamse, 'Rebellion, Heresy, and Popular Prophecy in the Reign of Philippikos Bardanios (711-713)', *East European Quarterly* 13 (1979) 395-408.

[4] Mauritius Geerard, *Clavis patrum Graecorum*, vol. III, *A Cyrillo Alexandrino ad Iohannem Damascenum* (Turnhout, 1979), p. 8020; *PG* 98, 40A-88B = Geôrgios A. Rallês and Michaêl Potlês, Σύνταγμα τῶν θείων καὶ ἱερῶν κανόνων τῶν τε ἁγίων καὶ πανευφήμων ἀποστόλων καὶ τῶν ἱερῶν οἰκουμενικῶν καὶ τοπικῶν συνόδων καὶ τῶν κατὰ μέρος ἁγίων πατέρων, vol. I-VI (Athens, 1852-1856; reprint Thessalonica, 2002), here vol. I, pp. 339-369. Of course, the Seventh Ecumenical Synod was convened at a later date (787).

1978, Miguel Arranz noted the discrepancies in the primary material regarding the day on which the feast of the Sixth Ecumenical Synod was kept.[5] In order to make sense of this apparent inconsistency, one must begin by looking at the historical data of the Sixth Ecumenical Synod itself. According to extant sources, this synod was convoked 'at the directive'[6] of Emperor Constantine IV (668-685)[7] to oppose the previously imperially sanctioned monothelite teaching.[8] Its eighteen sessions were held in Constantinople, specifically, 'in the secretum of the divine palace, which is called Trullo'.[9] The first session of the synod took place on 7 November 680 and the eighteenth on 16 September of the following year.[10] The later, therefore, would be an appropriate date for an annual commemoration of the event. This is exactly what one finds in Constantinopolitan liturgical sources, such as ms *Metochion of the Holy Sepulcher* 426 (11th century).[11] According to the rubric notes found in this lectionary, all of the churches of Constantinople are to commemorate the Fathers of the Sixth Ecumenical Synod on 16 September.[12] The same note, however, mentions one exception to this common rule. In the Great Church of Hagia Sophia this celebration is to be held on the Sunday following the Universal Exaltation of the Precious Cross (14 September), that is, between 15-21 September.[13]

---

[5] Miguel Arranz, 'Les «fêtes théologiques» du calendrier byzantin', in *La liturgie expression de la foi, Conférences Saint-Serge, 25e Semaine d'Etudes Liturgiques*, eds. A.M. Triacca and A. Pistoia, Bibliotheca « Ephemerides Liturgicae ». Subsidia 16 (Rome, 1979), pp. 29-55, on p. 53.

[6] Rudolf Riedinger, *Concilium Universale Constantinopolitanum Tertium*. Acta Conciliorum Oecumenicorum, Series Secunda, II, part 1 (Berlin, 1990), p. 14.17-18 = Joannes D. Mansi, *Sacrorum conciliorum nova et amplissima collectio*, vol. 11 (Florence, 1765; reprint, Graz, 1960), 209B (see also 217B, 221D, and *passim*). For the imperial *Sacra*, see Riedinger, *ibid.*, pp. 2.1-12.25 = Mansi, *ibid.*, 195A ff.

[7] Commemorated on 3 September: Juan Mateos, *Le Typicon de la Grande Église: Ms. Saint-Croix n° 40 Xᵉ siècle*, vol. I, *Le cycle des douze mois*, OCA 165 (Rome, 1962), p. 14. For more, see Venance Grumel, 'Quel est l'empereur Constantin le Nouveau commémoré dans le synaxaire au 3 Septembre', *Analecta Bollandiana* 84 (1966) 254-260.

[8] Riedinger, ACO, Ser. Sec., II/1 (see n. 6), p. 14.2 = Mansi (see n. 6), 208D.

[9] Riedinger, *ibid.*, p. 14.17 = Mansi, *ibid.*, 209B.

[10] See Riedinger, *ibid.*, p. 14.13-14 = Mansi, *ibid.*, 209A and Riedinger, ACO, Ser. Sec., II/2 (see n. 3), p. 752.10 = Mansi, *ibid.*, 624D.

[11] For a description of the manuscript, see E. Iôannidês, Ὁ ἐν Κωνσταντινουπόλει Ἑλληνικὸς Φιλολογικὸς Σύλλογος 2 (1864), pp. 63 ff.

[12] Manouêl Gedeôn, Βυζαντινὸν ἑορτολόγιον, μνῆμαι τῶν ἀπὸ τοῦ Δ΄ μέχρι τῶν μέσων τοῦ ΙΕ΄ αἰῶνος ἑορταζομένων ἁγίων ἐν Κωνσταντινουπόλει, offprint of vol. 25 (1895) 121-160 and vol. 26 (1896) 144-320 of the periodical of the Greek Philological Society of Constantinople (Constantinople, 1899), p. 31.

[13] *Ibid.*

The distinction between the two major liturgical traditions of the Byzantine East, namely, the cathedral and the monastic rites, is a well-documented fact of liturgical history.[14] Indeed these two distinct rites coexisted in Constantinople up until the crusader conquest of the city in 1204.[15] While the distinctions among the various rites have been noted and studied extensively, the variety of liturgical practices within a single rite is something that is only now beginning to be appreciated, as references such as the one noted here are being given closer attention.[16] The commemoration of the Sixth Ecumenical Synod is but one such example that reflects the diversity of practice within a particular rite, in this case the cathedral rite. Simply put, what is going on in one church may be quite foreign to another right next door. This means the liturgical researcher must approach all sources with due caution, especially when attempting to draw conclusions broader than those explicitly supported in the documentary and other evidence preserved to our day.

The parallel commemoration noted in ms *Metochion of the Holy Sepulcher 426* is confirmed by the information found in other liturgical sources of Constantinopolitan provenance, such as the *Typikon of the Great Church*. In this text that reflects the 9th century cathedral rite of

---

[14] For a concise and helpful summary, see Alexander Rentel, 'Byzantine and Slavic Orthodoxy', in *The Oxford History of Christian Worship*, eds. Geoffrey Wainwright and Karen B. Westerfield Tucker (New York, 2006), pp. 254-306, on pp. 264-270.

[15] In other ecclesiastical centers these rites coexisted for an even longer period of time. In Thessalonica the cathedral office was known and used until that city fell to the Ottomans in 1430.

[16] In this respect, there is an interesting note in the *Euchologion* of Strategios written in 1027 that documents both the internal and external variety of the cathedral and monastic rites. See Miguel Arranz, *L'Eucologio Costantinopolitano agli inizi del secolo XI: Hagiasmatarion & Archieratikon (Rituale & Pontificale)* (Rome, 1996), p. 129. See also the *Synaxarion of the Monastery of the Theotokos Evergetis: Описание литургических рукописей, хранящихся в библиотеках Православного Востока*, Т. I: Τυπικὰ I, ed. A.A. Dmitrievskij, (Kiev, 1895), p. 544: 'Εἰς ... τὸν ὄρθρον εὐαγγέλιον οὐ λέγεται, καθὼς ἔθος τοῖς ἐν κόσμῳ (At orthros the gospel is not read, as is the custom of those in the secular churches)'. Nikon of the Black Mountain (c. 1025-1088) observes that there was variety in the rubrics of the monastic rite as well. See Vladimir N. Beneševič, *Тактикон Никона Черногорца: Греческий текст по рукописи N° 441 Синайского монастыря св. Екатерины*, Записки Ист–Филол. Факультета Петроградского университета 139 (Petrograd, 1917), pp. 21, 24-33; Theodôros X. Giangou, 'Νικὼν ὁ Μαυρορείτης. Βίος – Συγγραφικὸ ἔργο – Κανονικὴ διδασκαλία', in *Κανονικολειτουργικά*, Vol. I (Thessalonica, 1999), pp. 226-227, n. 13. English translation in Robert F. Taft, 'Mount Athos: A Late Chapter in the History of the Byzantine Rite', *Dumbarton Oaks Papers* 42 (1988) 179-194, on p. 179. Ms *Sinaiticus gr.* 436 (441), ff. 72v-73r; Giangou, *ibid.*, p. 226, n. 12 and *idem.*, ''Απόσπασμα ἀγνώστου 'Αγιορειτικοῦ Τυπικοῦ στὸ ἀνθολόγιο ''Ερμηνεῖαι τῶν ἐντολῶν τοῦ Κυρίου''', in *Κανονικολειτουργικά*, pp. 305-337, on pp. 313-314.

Constantinople, and specifically in ms *Jerusalem Hagios Stauros* 40, one finds the following note:

> 'On the same day, ... commemoration of the holy and blessed Fathers who were convened at the holy and Ecumenical Sixth Synod in the God-protected and imperial city, under the Emperor Constantine of pious memory. ... In the Great Church, the synaxis of the Fathers is held on the Sunday after the Exaltation (of the Cross)'.[17]

A similar *heortological* celebration is presupposed in the following 11th and 12th century lectionaries:[18] *Oxford, Bodl. Libr., Auct. T. inf. 2.7 = l.* 341[19], *Moscow, Hist. Mus. V. 21, S. 4, = l.* 59, and *Parisinus graecus* 294 = *l.* 83. As Theodoros Giangou states,[20] these lectionaries comparatively contain the most references to feasts or commemorations of patriarchs of Constantinople, something that betrays a pristine though developed Constantinopolitan tradition. Interestingly, in these lectionaries, as in the *Typikon of the Great Church*, the relative references are included not in the rubrics for 16 September or for the Sunday after the Exaltation of the Cross, as one might expect, although entries for those days do exist. Rather, according to Giangou's notes, they are placed on 15 September. This is the first possible date on which this commemoration could have been held.[21]

In another ms containing the *Typikon of the Great Church*, ms *Patmos* 266, a codex that predates ms *Jerusalem Hagios Stauros* 40 but considered less reliable,[22] it seems as though the feast of the Fathers is simply to be held on 15 September.[23] This is due to the omission of the

---

[17] Mateos, *Le Typicon de la Grande Église* (see n. 7), p. 34.

[18] Theodôros X. Giangou, "Ὁ κύκλος τῶν ἑορταζομένων ἁγίων καὶ οἱ κύπριοι ἅγιοι. Προσέγγιση τῆς τάξεως μὲ βάση τοὺς κανόνες καὶ τὰ λεξιονάρια', in *Κανόνες καὶ λατρεία*, 2nd ed., Κανονικὰ καὶ Λειτουργικὰ 1 (Thessalonica, 2006), pp. 93-162, on p. 129. On *l.* 59 now see, Georgios Andreou, *Il Praxapostolos bizantino del secolo XI, Vladimir 21/Savva 4 del Museo Storico de Mosca: Edizione e commento*, Excerpta ex Dissertatione ad Doctoratum (Rome, 2008), on pp. 214-215. To these manuscripts, one may add ms *National Library of Greece* 160 [22], f. 317: Basileios Giannopoulos, 'Αἱ Οἰκουμενικαὶ Σύνοδοι εἰς τὴν ὀρθόδοξον λατρείαν', *Θεολογία* 55 (1984) 402-434, 705-738, 1025-1071, on p. 729, n. 210.

[19] For the numeration, see Kurt Aland, Michael Welte, Beate Köster, and Klaus Junack, *Kurzgefasste Liste der griechischen Handschriften des Neuen Testaments* (Berlin and New York, 1994).

[20] Giangou, "Ὁ κύκλος τῶν ἑορταζομένων ἁγίων' (see n. 18), p. 121.

[21] According to contemporary practice the first Sunday after the feast of the Holy Cross must follow the first Saturday after the feast. This means that the Sunday after the feast of the Holy Cross is kept between 16 and 22 September. See Manouêl Gedeôn, *Ἑορτολόγιον κωνσταντινοπολίτου προσκυνητοῦ* (Constantinople, 1899), p. 113.

[22] Mateos, *Le Typicon de la Grande Église* (see n. 7), pp. viii-xviii.

[23] Dmitrievskij, *Описание* (see n. 16), p. 6. Notice here also the extensive reference and prominence of the commemoration of the feast of St Martin.

last phrase of the rubrics quoted above: 'In the Great Church, the synaxis of the Fathers is held on the Sunday after the Exaltation (of the Cross)'.[24] This marks a slight corruption with respect to the original dual Constantinopolitan commemoration. Of course, it is argued that ms *Patmos* 266 is of Palestinian origin, so divergences from the Constantinopolitan practice are to be expected. But this omission is especially noteworthy as there is evidence of a commemoration of the Fathers of Constantinople III on the Sunday following the Feast of the Cross in sources, such as the early Sabaitic *Typikon*, *Sinaiticus Graecus* 1094 (12th-13th century), which Dmitrievskij classified as belonging to the Jerusalemite redaction.[25]

An unequivocal 15 September commemoration of the Sixth Ecumenical Synod, such as that of ms *Patmos* 266, is to be found in numerous lectionaries from the 10th-14th centuries as well. These include the following mss:[26]

a) 10th-11th century:
   – *Moscow, Histor. Mus. V. 12, S. 225*, f. 393v = *l.* 49.
b) 11th century:
   – *Venice, Bibl. Naz. Marc. gr. Z. 549 (655)* = *l.* 108.
   – *London, Lambeth Palace 1190*, f. 200v = *l.* 165.
   – *Oxford, Bodleian Library, Auct. F. 6. 25* (year 1067) = *l.* 203.
c) 12th century:
   – *London, British Library Add. 22735* = *l.* 321.
   – *Sinai, St Catharine Monastery 289*, f. 90r = *l.* 1439.
d) 14th century:
   – *Ann Arbor, University Library 35*, f. 116v = *l.* 170.

---

[24] *Le Typicon de la Grande Église* (see n. 7), p. 34. As Mateos notes about this ms: '... il ignore l'usage de la Grande Église de transférer au dimanche les fêtes de certains saints importants, p. ex. Justinien et Théodora (14-XI), Théodore patriarche (28-XII), Flavien et Léon (17-II)' (*Le Typicon de la Grande Église*, p. ix). This is yet another such example.

[25] *Описание литургических рукописей, хранящихся в библиотеках Православного Востока*, Т. III: Τυπικὰ II, ed. A.A. Dmitrievskij, (Petrograd, 1917), p. 5. Cf. Mateos, *Le Typicon de la Grande Église* (see n. 7), p. 36.10-11. See also ms *Athos, Dochiarion 17*, (*l.* 623, 12th century), f. 164r.

[26] This information has been documented in Giangou, "Ο κύκλος τῶν ἑορταζομέ-νων ἁγίων' (see n. 18), pp. 110-111 and 129. In those cases where folia are given, I have been able to personally study the manuscripts. Giangou includes the 9th-century ms *Parisinus gr. 282* (*l.* 65) in this list. See, however, Georgios Andreou, 'Alcune osservazioni sul menologion del lezionario Paris Gr. 382 (X sec. *ex*)', *Bollettino della Badia greca di Grottaferrata*, III s. 2 (2007) 5-16, on p. 6, n. 5.

The mixed picture of the 'official' commemoration of the Fathers, that of Hagia Sophia, may also lie behind a parallel yet hidden Stoudite liturgical observance. In the *Synaxarion of the Monastery of Theotokos Evergetis* (c. 1055), a document that reflects the middle-Byzantine Stoudite liturgical practice,[27] there is no explicit reference to a commemoration of the Sixth Ecumenical Synod. Nevertheless, on 15 September, which this *Synaxarion* records as being the *apodosis* of the feast of the Exaltation of the Cross and the feast of the martyr Nicetas, one stumbles upon a puzzling *diataxis* that states the following: 'But if it (15 September) falls on a Sunday, … At the Liturgy, … the Apostle, to the *Hebrews*: "Brethren, remember your leaders" (see at 16 July)'.[28] The rubrics for 16 July in this *Synaxarion* shed no light on the above note. Apparently the directive given refers to finding the appropriate apostolic pericope in the *Praxapostolos* that was used at the Evergetis monastery.[29] Of course, the incipit makes it clear that, when 15 September falls on a Sunday, one of the apostolic readings was Hebrews 13:7-16, a pericope prescribed for feasts of church fathers. This is precisely the same reading given in the *Typikon of the Great Church*, when on this Sunday the Fathers of the Sixth Ecumenical Synod are commemorated.[30]

4. The Commemoration of the Synod and the Memory of Pope Martin I of Rome

The feast of the Sixth Ecumenical Synod, as Arranz notes, is also found in *Sirmondianus*.[31] Specifically, according to the *Synaxarium ecclesiae Constantinopolitanae*, a document compiled in the second half of the 10th century from earlier *synaxaria* and *menologia*,[32] the feast of

---

[27] For a detailed study of this *Typikon*, see the dissertation of John Klentos, *Byzantine Liturgy in the Twelfth-Century Constantinople: An Analysis of the Synaxarion of the Monastery of the Theotokos* (Notre Dame, IN, 1995).

[28] Trans. adapted from, *The Synaxarion of the Monastery of the Theotokos Evergetis*, vol. I, *September to February*, ed. and trans. Robert Jordan, Belfast Byzantine Texts and Translations 6.5 (Belfast, 2000), 71 = Dmitrievskij, *Описание* (see n. 16), p. 276.

[29] This case provides evidence on the early interrelationship between the *Synaxarion* and the *Praxapostolos*.

[30] Mateos, *Le Typicon de la Grande Église* (see n. 7), p. 36.

[31] See n. 5 above.

[32] Hippolytus Delehaye, 'Le Synaxaire de Sirmond', *Analecta Bollandiana* 14 (1895) 396-434; *idem.*, 'Prolegomena', in *Synaxarium ecclesiae Constantinopolitanae* (see below n. 33), pp. ii-vi; W. Vander Meiren, 'Précisions nouvelles sur la généalogie des synaxaires byzantins', *Analecta Bollandiana* 102 (1984) 297-301.

the Sixth Ecumenical Synod is to be kept on the Sunday after the Exaltation of the Cross.[33] In contrast to *Jerusalem Hagios Stavros* 40, however, in *Sirmondianus* this information is included along with the other entries of 18 September, which is exactly at the mid-way point between 15 and 21 September. Conversely, for 16 September the *Synaxarium* calls for the commemoration of the holy hieromartyr Martin, pope of Rome.[34]

Pope Martin I (649-653) suffered 'martyrdom' under the reign of Constans II (641-668), called 'the impious' due to his monothelite policy. It is well-known that Martin I of Rome categorically rejected the monothelite doctrine.[35] In fact, at the insistence of Maximus the Confessor,[36] he convoked the Lateran Synod of 649, during which the promoters of monothelitism, the *Ekthesis* of Heraclius and the *Typos* of Constans II, though not the emperors themselves, were formally anathematized.[37] On account of his theological position and actions, Martin

---

[33] *Synaxarium ecclesiae Constantinopolitanae e codice Sirmondiano nunc Berolinensi, adiectis synaxariis selectis*, ed. Hippolytus Delehaye, Propylaeum ad Acta Sanctorum, Novembris (Brussels, 1902; reprint, Wetteren, 1985), cols. 55-56: Μηνὶ τῷ αὐτῷ (Σεπτεμβρίου) ιη' ... Ἰστέον δὲ ὅτι Κυριακῇ μετὰ τὴν Ὕψωσιν μνήμην ἐπιτελοῦμεν τῶν ἁγίων πατέρων τῶν συνελθόντων ἐν τῇ ἁγίᾳ καὶ οἰκουμενικῇ ἕκτῃ συνόδῳ ἐν ταύτῃ τῇ θεοφυλάκτῳ καὶ βασιλίδι τῶν πόλεων ἐπὶ τοῦ ἐν εὐσεβεῖ τῇ μνήμῃ βασιλέως Κωνσταντίνου τοῦ Πωγωνάτου, υἱοῦ Κωνσταντίνου τοῦ δυσσεβοῦς, δισεκγόνου Ἡρακλείου, πατρὸς δὲ Ἰουστινιανοῦ τοῦ μικροῦ τοῦ τὴν ῥῖνα τμηθέντος, Γεωργίου τότε τὴν Κωνσταντινουπόλεως ἐκκλησίαν ἰθύνοντος καὶ Ἀγάθωνος τῆς Ῥώμης. Ἥτις σύνοδος συνηθροίσθη ἐν τῷ τρούλλῳ τοῦ παλατίου τῷ λεγομένῳ Ὠάτῳ, ἀναθεματίσασα καὶ ἀποβαλοῦσα Σέργιον καὶ Πέτρον καὶ Πύρρον καὶ Παῦλον, ἐπισκόπους γενομένους Κωνσταντινουπόλεως, Μακάριόν τε τὸν Ἀντιοχείας καὶ Κῦρον τὸν Ἀλεξανδρείας καὶ Ὀνώριον τὸν Ῥώμης, Στέφανόν τε καὶ τὸν Πολυχρόνιον καὶ τοὺς σὺν αὐτοῖς μίαν θέλησιν καὶ ἐνέργειαν τῶν δύο φύσεων τοῦ Χριστοῦ φρονοῦντας καὶ λέγοντας· ἥτις ἐπὶ μὲν Κωνσταντίνου συνηθροίσθη· ἡ δὲ τῶν κανόνων ἔκδοσις ἐπὶ Ἰουστινιανοῦ τοῦ υἱοῦ αὐτοῦ <γεγένηται>.

[34] *Ibid.*, cols. 49-50. Cf. Mateos, *Le Typicon de la Grande Église* (see n. 7), p. 38.

[35] John Duffy and John Parker, *The Synodicon Vetus*, Corpus Fontium Historiae Byzantinae, Series Washingtonensis XV (Washington, D.C., 1979), p. 117.

[36] Deno J. Geanakoplos, 'Some Aspects of the Influence of the Byzantine Maximos the Confessor on the Theology of East and West', *Church History* 38 (1969) 150-163.

[37] This synod opened on 5 October 649 and held five sessions. For its minutes, see Rudolf Riedinger, *Concilium Lateranense a. 649 celebratum*, Acta Conciliorum Oecumenicorum, Series Secunda I/2 (Berlin, 1984) = Mansi, vol. 10, 864B-1187E. The classical study of this synod remains that of Erich L. E. Caspar, 'Die Lateransynode von 649', *Zeitschrift für Kirchengeschichte* 51 (1932) 75-137. See also the dissertation by Johannes Pierres, *Sanctus Maximus Confessor, princeps apologetarum synodi Lateranensis anni 649 (Pars historica)* (Rome, 1940) and more recently Panteleêmôn G. Tsorbatzoglou, Ἡ σύνοδος τοῦ Λατερανοῦ (649 μ.Χ): σύγκλιση μετὰ τὴν σύγκρουση – Θεολογία καὶ πολιτικὴ τόν 7ο αἰώνα (Katerini, 2007).

was arrested and extradited to Constantinople. Once there he was con-
victed and condemned to death in a parody of a trial held on 20 December 653. This sentence, however, was not enforced. On the contrary, the
ailing monothelite patriarch of Constantinople, Pyrrhus, was able to
secure a reprieve for his Roman counterpart. As a result, Martin was
tortured and exiled to Cherson of Crimea where he died. Ancient witnesses offer conflicting information as to the date of the pope's death.[38]
According to the *Liber Pontificalis*, Martin was buried on 17 September
655.[39] It would be safe to assume, therefore, that the underlying date of
his death is the previous day, 16 September.[40] Nevertheless, according to
the late 7th/early 8th century Greek *Vita* of the saint, Martin fell asleep in
the Lord on 13 April.[41] There is a commemoration of Martin in the
Synaxarium ecclesiae Constantinopolitanae on that day as well.[42] Paul
Peeters, the editor of this Greek *Vita*, convincingly argues that it is
impossible to choose between the two dates.[43]

   The variance in the early sources with respect to the date of the death
of Martin of Rome and, as a consequence, his dual commemoration
in the *heortologion* of Constantinople, suggest that the Byzantine commemoration of Martin on 16 September may perhaps not originate
simply with the date of the pope's death. Rather, it is possible that this
date was established in the East as a day commemorating Pope Martin
because of his being a forerunner of sorts to the Sixth Ecumenical Synod.
As the feast of the Sixth Ecumenical Synod was celebrated on the
Sunday following the feast of the Cross, at least in the Great Church of
Hagia Sophia, it seems plausible that the commemoration of Martin was

---

[38] Bronwen Neil, 'The *Lives* of Pope Martin I and Maximus the Confessor: Some
Reconsiderations of Dating and Provenance', *Byzantion* 68 (1998) 91-109, on p. 107.

[39] *Le Liber Pontificalis: Texte, introduction et commentaire*, vol. I, ed. and trans.
Louis Duchesne (Paris, 1886; reprint, Paris, 1981), 388 = *PL* 128, 741.16-17: 'Depositus
sub die XVII mensis Septembris'.

[40] John N. D. Kelly, *Reclams Lexikon der Päpste* (Stuttgart, 1988), pp. 88-89.

[41] Paul Peeters, 'Une Vie grecque du pape S. Martin I', *Analecta Bollandiana* 51
(1933) 225-262, on p. 261: 'Τὸν ἀγῶνα τοίνυν τὸν καλὸν ἀγωνησάμενος καὶ τὸν
δρόμον τελέσας καὶ τὴν ἀληθῆ πίστιν τηρήσας, ἐκοιμήθη μηνὶ Ἀπριλλίῳ ιγ',
ἰνδικτιῶνος ιδ'' (13 April 656).

[42] Delehaye, *Synaxarium ecclesiae Constantinopolitanae* (see n. 33), cols. 599-602.
Cf. Miguel Arranz, *Le Typikon du Monastère du Saint-Sauveur à Messine: Codex Mess-
inensis Gr. 115 A.D. 1131*, OCA 185 (Rome, 1969), p. 145. See also the *Synaxarion of
the Monastery of the Theotokos Evergetis*, Dmitrievskij, Описание (see n. 16), p. 445,
and *Moscow, Hist. Mus. V. 21, S. 4*, Andreou, *Il Praxapostolos* (see n. 18), p. 347.

[43] Peeters, 'Une Vie grecque' (see n. 41), pp. 248-250.

fixed on 16 September in order to fill the lacuna created.[44] This hypothesis is corroborated by the content of the 16 September *hypomnema* on Martin in the *Synaxarium* of Constantinople. The emphasis there is on his trial, exile, and death as well as on his 'public denouncing' of Sergius of Constantinople, Cyrus of Alexandria, and Theodore of Pharan, as well as his activity at the Lateran Synod of 649.[45] The wording of the *synaxarion* in the Greek *menaion* currently used in the Orthodox Church also points to this conclusion. In it, specifically on 20 September,[46] there is a commemoration of 'Martin, the Pope of Rome, Maximus, and those with them'.[47] This citation apparently refers to the Martin in question, Maximus the Confessor, and other champions of the dyothelite cause. The wording of the *synaxarion* in the *menaion* is obviously related to the title of the *Hypomnesticon* or *Commemoratio*, a document edited in 668/9 by Theodore Spoudaeus recording the tribulations of Pope Martin I, Maximus the Confessor, Anastasius the Disciple, Anastasius the Apocrisiarius, Theodore, and Euprepius.[48] All of the figures mentioned

---

[44] The conception of such an arrangement is perhaps not unique to this case. A similar connection seems to be behind the feast of St Theophanes the Confessor (11 October), a key defender of the veneration of icons, and the commemoration of the Seventh Ecumenical Synod (Sunday between 11-17 October). Furthermore, as Eleonora S. Kountoura-Galaki has shown, St Euphemia (feast day 16 September) was a key symbolic figure in the exchange between popes of Rome and emperors of Constantinople. See her study, 'Ἡ ἁγία Εὐφημία στὶς σχέσεις παπῶν καὶ αὐτοκρατόρων', *Σύμμεικτα* 7 (1987) 59-75, especially on pp. 67-70. On the reference of the *Typikon of the Great Church* with regard to the 16 September feast of St Euphemia (arguably established in c. 680), see Cyril Mango, 'The Relics of St Euphemia and the Synaxarion of Constantinople', *Bollettino della Badia greca di Grottaferrata*, n.s. 53 (1999) 79-87.

[45] Delehaye, *Synaxarium ecclesiae Constantinopolitanae* (see n. 33), cols. 49-50. This is, of course, also the case in the 13 April entry; *ibid.*, cols. 599-602.

[46] For the 20 September commemoration of St Martin in eastern Greek sources, see Sôfronios Eustratiadês, *Ἁγιολόγιον τῆς Ὀρθοδόξου Ἐκκλησίας* (Athens, 1960), pp. 305b-306a. The transfer of the commemoration of St Martin to 20 September was fixed during the post-Byzantine period, when the feast of the Sixth Ecumenical Synod on the Sunday following the Exaltation of the Cross was forgotten and when 16 September was finally established as a feast of St Euphemia. At that time it seemed natural to couple the commemoration of Martin, Maximus, and the rest with that of the 'holy fathers and confessors Hypatius the bishop and Andrew the presbyter'. The later two were themselves forerunners of an ecumenical synod, the Seventh. Until 1969, in the Roman *kalendarium*, the feast of Pope Martin I was held on 12 November. Since then it has been restored to 13 April. See David Farmer, *The Oxford Dictionary of Saints*, 5th ed. (New York, 2004), p. 325: 'He died in exile on 13 April, the last pope to be venerated as a martyr. His name was recorded in the Bobbio Missal (8th century). Feast: in the East, 20 September; in the West, 13 April has been restored as his feast since 1969'.

[47] See also Gedeôn, *Ἑορτολόγιον* (see n. 21), p. 83.

[48] Robert Devreesse, 'Le texte grec de l'Hypomnesticon de Théodore Spoudée', *Analecta Bollandiana* 53 (1935) 49-80; Pauline Allen and Bronwen Neil, *Scripta saeculi VII*

here participated in the Lateran Synod of 649. This commemoration can be viewed, therefore, as a rare occurrence whereby a synod held in the West is mentioned, albeit indirectly, in an eastern liturgical source. If this is so, it means that the commemoration both of Martin I and of the Sixth Ecumenical Synod were incorporated into the *heortologion* sooner rather than later. After all, deference to the Lateran Synod of 649 played an important role in the initiative of Patriarch John VI of Constantinople (712-715) to restore the relations between Rome and Constantinople after Philipiccus Bardanes' failed monothelite regression.[49]

5. *Later Developments: Symeon of Thessalonica, the Feast of the Six Synods, and 14 September*

A later modification of the feast may be found in the *Διάταξις τῶν ἀκολουθιῶν*, written at the time and under the direction of Symeon of Thessalonica (1416/1417-1429).[50] This text is partially contained in ms *National Library of Greece* 2047, ff. 75r-274v.[51] According to the *Diataxis* of Symeon, on the Sunday after the feast of the Exaltation of

---

Vitam Maximi Confessoris illustrantia, una cum Latina interpretatione Anastasii Bibliothecarii iuxta posita, Corpus Christianorum, Series Graeca 39 (Turnhout, 1999), pp. 191-227; *Maximus the Confessor and His Companions: Documents from Exile*, eds. and trans. Pauline Allen and Bronwen Neil, Oxford Early Christian Texts (Oxford, 2002), pp. 148-171. See also Bronwen Neil, 'Narrating the Trials and Death in Exile of Pope Martin I and Maximus the Confessor', in *Byzantine Narrative: Papers in Honour of Roger Scott*, eds. John Burke, Ursula Betka et. al., Byzantina Australiensia 16 (Melbourne, 2006), pp. 71-83.

[49] See his letter to Pope Constantine I of Rome (708-715) in Riedinger, ACO, Ser. Sec., II/2 (see n. 3), p. 904.18-21.

[50] On this document, see Jean Darrouzès, 'Notes d'histoire de textes', *Revue des Études Byzantines* 21 (1963) 232-242; *idem*, 'Sainte-Sophie Thessalonique d'après un Rituel', *Revue des Études Byzantines* 34 (1976) 45-78; Iôannês Fountoulês, *Τὸ λειτουργικὸν ἔργον Συμεὼν τοῦ Θεσσαλονίκης. Συμβολὴ εἰς τὴν ἱστορίαν καὶ θεωρίαν τῆς λατρείας*, Ἴδρυμα Μελετῶν Χερσονήσου τοῦ Αἵμου 84 (Thessalonica, 1966), pp. 37-48; *idem*, *Ὁ ἅγιος Συμεὼν Θεσσαλονίκης συντάκτης Τυπικοῦ*, *Πρακτικὰ λειτουργικοῦ συνεδρίου εἰς τιμὴν καὶ μνήμην τοῦ ἐν ἁγίοις πατρὸς ἡμῶν Συμεῶνος ἀρχιεπισκόπου Θεσσαλονίκης τοῦ Θαυματουργοῦ (19-9-81)*, ed. Holy Metropolis of Thessalonica (Thessalonica, 1983), pp. 107-120; Panagiôtês Skaltsês, 'Τό τυπικό τῆς Ἁγίας Σοφίας Θεσσαλονίκης', *Πρακτικὰ Γ´ Διεθνοῦς Ἐπιστημονικοῦ Συμποσίου «Χριστιανικὴ Θεσσαλονίκη». Ἱστορία, λατρεία καὶ τέχνη τοῦ Ἱεροῦ Ναοῦ τῆς τοῦ Θεοῦ Σοφίας*, eds. Iôannês Fountoulês and Georgios Gavardinas (Thessalonica, 2007), pp. 81-92.

[51] Prof. Theodoros Giangou, Assist. Prof. Nikodemos Skrettas and I are currently working on an edition of this important late Byzantine liturgical ms.

the Cross,[52] the Sixth Ecumenical Synod is to be celebrated along with that of the Second Ecumenical Synod.[53] This is a *heortological unicum* that was most likely conceived of by Symeon himself. In contrast to the initial notice of the feast, the hymnographical material that follows does not refer directly to the Sixth Ecumenical Synod. The hymns extol rather the Nicene-Constantinopolitan Creed. Although there are some sporadic references to the theology of Constantinople III, the only direct reference to the Sixth Ecumenical Synod is to be found in the fourth troparion at the 'Lord, I have cried', of vespers. This troparion simply enumerates all seven Ecumenical Synods, as they all upheld the Symbol of Faith.[54]

Ultimately, neither 16 September nor the Sunday after the feast of the Exaltation of the Cross was able to consolidate the commemoration of the Fathers of the Sixth Ecumenical Synod. Liturgical sources contain alternative days on which the feast was to be kept. Sporadic commemorations of the Sixth Ecumenical Synod may be found on days such as the second Sunday following the feast of the Exaltation of the Cross[55] and 23 January.[56] Six months after the commemoration of

---

[52] The late professor of liturgics at the University of Thessalonica, Iôannês Fountoulês, argued that the feast of the Universal Exaltation of the Cross may have been the feast day of the church of Hagia Sophia in Thessalonica. See his study, ‛Ο ναὸς τῆς τοῦ Θεοῦ Σοφίας. Ἑορτολογικὰ προβλήματα', *Πρακτικά Γ' Διεθνοῦς Ἐπιστημονικοῦ Συμποσίου «Χριστιανικὴ Θεσσαλονίκη»* (see n. 50), pp. 57-80.

[53] Ms *National Library of Greece* 2047, f. 110v: 'Κυριακῇ μετὰ τὴν Ὕψωσιν ἑορτάζομεν τὴν ἕκτην σύνοδον, ἐν ᾧ καιρῷ καὶ ἡ δευτέρα προγέγονε σύνοδος'. On this celebration, see Iôannês Fountoulês, 'Περὶ συστάσεως ἑορτῆς εἰς μνήμην τῆς Β' καὶ ΣΤ' Οἰκουμενικῆς Συνόδου ἐπὶ τῇ 1600ῇ καὶ 1300ῇ ἐπετείῳ ἀπὸ τῆς συγκλήσεως αὐτῶν', *Γρηγόριος ὁ Παλαμᾶς* 64 (1981) 16-24 and *idem*, 'Ἡ μνήμη τῶν ἁγίων Πατέρων τῆς Β' Οἰκουμενικῆς Συνόδου στὸ ἑορτολόγιο καί στήν ὑμνογραφία', *Γρηγόριος ὁ Παλαμᾶς* 66 (1983) 61-79. In the *menaion* currently in use, the Second Ecumenical Synod is commemorated on May 22. Commemorations of Constantinople I in other sources include August 3, 4, and 25. For references, see Giannopoulos, 'Αἱ Οἰκουμενικαὶ Σύνοδοι' (see n. 18), p. 426.

[54] Ms *National Library of Greece* 2047, f. 111r: 'Σέβομεν καὶ κρατοῦμεν πιστῶς τὸ θεῖον σύμβολον, ὃ πρώτη ἐξέθετο συνόδων ἡ ἐν Νικαίᾳ καὶ ἡ δευτέρα σεπτῶς ἐν τῇ Κωνσταντίνου τετελείωκεν, ἡ τρίτη τε ἔστερξεν ἐν Ἐφέσῳ κηρύξασα τὴν Θεοτόκον, Χαλκηδόνος τετάρτη τε ἐβεβαίωσε, πέμπτη, ἕκτη, ἑβδόμη τε· τούτῳ οὐδὲν προστίθεμεν οὐδὲ ἀφαιρούμέν τι καὶ τοὺς ἁγίους τιμῶμεν τοὺς ἐκθεμένους καὶ στέρξαντας, αἱρετικοὺς πάντας ἀναθέματι διδόντες, Τριάς, καὶ σῶσον ἡμᾶς'.

[55] See Arabic ms *Balamand* 149, f. 15v (*Synaxarion*, dated 1556).

[56] Giannopoulos, 'Αἱ Οἰκουμενικαὶ Σύνοδοι' (see n. 18), pp. 728-729, lists the following mss of the National Library of Greece that contain a commemoration of the Constantinople III on this date: 552, 1029, 1034, 1035, 1037, 1038, and 2001. See also Delehaye, *Synaxarium ecclesiae Constantinopolitanae* (see n. 33), 'Synaxaria Selecta', Ian. 23.

23 January, there is yet another feast in the liturgical calendar that is related to Constantinople III. The original nucleus of this commemoration is, of course, the feast of the Fourth Ecumenical Synod,[57] or of the Four Synods,[58] kept on July 16. According to *Jerusalem Hagios Stavros* 40, on the Sunday after the feast of the Fourth Ecumenical Synod,[59] there is a commemoration of the Endemousa Synod of 536,[60] against Severus of Antioch.[61] This was later conflated with the Fifth Ecumenical Synod,[62] presumably because of the confusion caused by the relative reference in the *Oros* of the Seventh Ecumenical Synod. To this, the Sixth was added, and a new commemoration developed, namely, the feast of the Six (Ecumenical) Synods. This commemoration became fixed on the Sunday between 13 and 19 of July.[63] Later, Patriarch Anthimos IV, during his first patriarchal tenure (14 June 1840-6 May 1841), instructed Bartholomew Koutloumousianos to change the name of the

[57] See ms *Patmos* 266, Dmitrievskij, *Описание* (see n. 16), pp. 92-93. Cf. the 10th-11th century *Kanonarion* (ms *Sinaiticus gr.* 150), Dmitrievskij, *ibid.*, p. 219: '(Commemoration) of the 630 holy Fathers of the IVth Synod'. The feast for this synod was held for the first time on 16 July 518. For the account, see Eduard Schwartz, *Collectio Sabbaitica Contra Acephalos et Origeniastas Destinata. Insunt acta synodorum Constantinopolitanae et Hierosolymitanae a. 536*, Acta Conciliorum Oecumenicorum VI (Berlin, 1965), 71.30-76.25.

[58] Mateos, *Le Typicon de la Grande Église* (see n. 7), p. 340; James Rendel Harris, 'Cod. Ev. 561: Codex Algerinæ Peckover', *Journal of the Society of Biblical Literature and Exegesis* 6 (1886) 79-89, on p. 82.

[59] On the preceding Sunday the Tome of Union written in 920 under Constantine Porphyrogenitus is read (*l.* 341: 'Κυριακῇ πρὸ τῆς μνήμης τῆς Δ΄ συνόδου ἐπιτελεῖται ἡ ἕνωσις τῆς Ἐκκλησίας'). See Giangou, 'Ὁ κύκλος τῶν ἑορταζομένων ἁγίων' (see n. 18), p. 128; Rallês-Potlês, *Syntagma*, vol. IV (see n. 4), p. 104 and vol. VI, p. 159. The same information is given by Patriarch of Constantinople Nicholas III Grammaticus (1084-1111) in his canonical responses to the bishop of Zetounion. See Jean Darrouzès, 'Les réponses de Nicolas III à l'évêque de Zétounion', in *ΚΑΘΗΓΗΤΡΙΑ: Essays Presented to Joan Hussey for Her 80th Birthday*, ed. Julian Chrysostomides (Camberley, 1988), pp. 327-343, on p. 338. These responses were also published by Eleutheria Papagiane and Spiros Troianos, 'Die Kanonischen Antworten des Nikolaos III. Grammatikos an den Bischof von Zetunion', *Byzantinische Zeitschrift* 82 (1989) 234-250.

[60] Eduard Schwartz, *Collectio* (see n. 57), 25.28-189.17.

[61] Mateos, *Le Typicon de la Grande Église* (see n. 7), p. 342. James Rendel Harris, 'Cod. Ev. 561' (see n. 58), p. 83.

[62] See Dmitrievskij, *Описание* (see n. 16), p. 93.

[63] Gedeôn, *Βυζαντινὸν ἑορτολόγιον* (see n. 12), pp. 320-321. See ms *Ivan Dujčev Centre for Slavo-Byzantine Studies* 35 (1410/11 A.D.), ff. 121r-128v, Dorotei Getov, *A Catalogue of Greek Liturgical Manuscripts in the "Ivan Dujčev Centre for Slavo-Byzantine Studies"*, OCA 279 (Rome, 2007), p. 127. Ms *Benaki Museum* 68 (13th cent.), ff. 150v-154v. For an in depth analysis of the development of this commemoration, see Giannopoulos, 'Αἱ Οἰκουμενικαὶ Σύνοδοι' (see n. 18), pp. 706-720, 737-738, 1041-1051.

feast of the Six Synods back to that of the Fourth Ecumenical Synod.[64] This explains the discrepancy that exists between the *Horologion* published by Bartholomew in 1832 and his *Menaion* of 1843.

Besides these developments, a commemoration of the Sixth Ecumenical Synod is to be found on 14 September in numerous manuscripts,[65] such as ms *Oxford, Bodleian Library, Auct. E. 5.10* (dated 1329), one of the manuscripts Juan Mateos used in his edition of the *Typikon of the Great Church*.[66] Moreover, it is on this day that the printed editions of the *menaia* include a commemoration of the synod.[67] This must be viewed, therefore, as a further corruption of the earlier shift on 15 September of the Hagia Sophia celebration on Sunday following the feast of the Holy Cross. However, one cannot help but ask the question: Is this transfer simply another example of an arbitrary liturgical modification, or is there something else behind the relocation?

As it is known, the so-called monothelite compromise was devised by the Constantinopolitan prelate Sergius, 'under the auspices of Emperor Heraclius'.[68] It is this same Emperor, ὁ πιστὸς ἐν Χριστῷ βασιλεύς,[69] who won back from the Persians the relics of the passion of Christ, the Holy Sponge and the Holy Cross (and later the Holy Lance), which were exalted in a special ceremony at Constantinople on 14 September 629.[70] It is no wonder, therefore, that, throughout the centuries, 'Heraclius' reputation has undergone many vicissitudes'.[71] We have already mentioned that, although the *Ekthesis* of Heraclius was formally anathematized, the emperor himself was not. This allowed for subsequent attempts to rehabilitate the memory of Heraclius. By way of example we may

---

[64] Dêmêtrios Stratês, *Βαρθολομαῖος Κουτλουμουσιανὸς (1772-1851). Βιογραφία-Ἐργογραφία* (Mount Athos, n.d.), p. 375.

[65] For a select list, see Giannopoulos, 'Αἱ Οἰκουμενικαὶ Σύνοδοι' (see n. 18), p. 729.

[66] Mateos, *Le Typicon de la Grande Église* (see n. 7), p. 29.

[67] See, for example, the following pre-Bartholomew *menaia* printed in publishing houses of Venice where Greek liturgical books were systematically produced: Πιννέλου 1648, Ἰουλιανοῦ 1683, Σάρος, 1689, Γλυκῆ 1754, 1779, and 1798, and Θεοδοσίου 1760 and 1808.

[68] Allen and Neil, *Maximus the Confessor and His Companions* (see n. 48), p. 3.

[69] Joannes Konidaris, 'Die Novellen des Kaisers Herakleios', in *Fontes Minores V*, ed. Dieter Simon, Forschungen zur Byzantinischen Rechtsgeschichte 8 (Frankfurt, 1982), pp. 33-106, on p. 84. See Irfan Shahîd, 'Heraclius: Πιστὸς ἐν Χριστῷ βασιλεύς', *Dumbarton Oaks Papers* 34 (1980-1981) 225-237 and *idem.*, 'On the Titulature of the Emperor Heraclius', *Byzantion* 51 (1981) 288-296.

[70] Walter E. Kaegi, *Heraclius: Emperor of Byzantium* (Cambridge, 2003), p. 189.

[71] *Ibid.*, p. 3.

mention the fact that, in the extant Greek copies of the *Hypomnesticon* of Theodore Spoudaeus, the name of Heraclius is erased from the characterization of the monothelites as '*Ἡρακειανοκυροσεργιοπυρροπαυλοπετριτῶν*'. It is restored in the critical edition based on the early Latin translation of the text by Anastasius Bibliothecarius.[72] In addition, Michael Psellus referred to Heraclius as 'that excellent Emperor'.[73] Such examples may of course be multiplied. Could the 14 September commemoration of the Sixth Ecumenical Synod be yet another example of a late Byzantine attempt to salvage the memory of the conqueror of the Persians, Heraclius, at a time when another foreign threat was becoming all the more real?

In times past, the commemoration of the Sixth Ecumenical Synod included the reading of the Synod's *Oros*, which was read prior to the chanting of the *Trisagion* at the Liturgy.[74] Today, the commemoration has been reduced to a simple *hypomnema* of the *synaxarion* of 14 September in the *menaion*, a text not without problems of its own. The *textus receptus* is as follows:

> Τῇ αὐτῇ ἡμέρᾳ, μνήμη τῶν ἐν Ἁγίοις Πατέρων ἡμῶν, τῶν συνελθόντων ἐν τῇ ἁγίᾳ καὶ οἰκουμενικῇ ἕκτῃ συνόδῳ, ἐπὶ τῆς βασιλείας Κωνσταντίνου τοῦ Πωγωνάτου, *υἱοῦ* Ἰουστινιανοῦ *τοῦ δευτέρου, τοῦ καλουμένου* Ῥινοτμήτου, *Σεργίου* τὴν Ἐκκλησίαν Κωνσταντινουπόλεως ἰθύνοντος, καὶ Ἀγάθωνος τῶν Ῥωμαίων. Ἠθροίσθη δὲ ἐν τῷ τρούλλῳ τοῦ παλατίου, τῷ λεγομένῳ, ὤάτῳ, ἀναθέματι καθυποβαλοῦσα Σέργιον, καὶ Πύρρον, καὶ Πέτρον, καὶ Παῦλον, ἐπισκόπους γενομένους Κωνσταντινουπόλεως· *Μακρόβιόν* τε τὸν Ἀντιοχείας, καὶ Κύρον τὸν Ἀλεξανδρείας, καὶ Ὀνώριον τὸν Ῥώμης, Στέφανόν τε καὶ Πολυχρόνιον, καὶ τοὺς σὺν αὐτοῖς. Ἥτις ἁγία σύνοδος ἐπὶ μὲν τοῦ δηλωθέντος Κωνσταντίνου τοῦ Πωγωνάτου συνηθροίσθη· ἡ δὲ τῶν κανόνων ἔκδοσις ἐπὶ Ἰουστινιανοῦ *τοῦ υἱοῦ αὐτοῦ γέγονε.*

---

[72] Allen and Neil, *Scripta saeculi VII Vitam Maximi Confessoris illustrantia* (see n. 48), p. 223.

[73] The passage is given in Romilly J. H. Jenkins and Ernst Kitzinger, 'A Cross of the Patriarch Michael Cerularius with an Art-Historical Comment', *Dumbarton Oaks Papers* 21 (1967) 233, 235-240, 242-249, on p. 236.

[74] See *Τυπικὸν καὶ τὰ ἀπόρρητα* (Venice, 1545), p. 31: 'Κυριακῇ μετὰ τὴν Ὕψωσιν. Ἀναγινώσεται τὸ συνοδικὸν τῆς ς΄ Συνόδου ἐν τῇ Μεγάλῃ Ἐκκλησίᾳ'. See also the *Τυπικὸν τῆς ἐκκλησιαστικῆς ἀκολουθίας* (Venice, 1771), p. 22. This was dropped, however, before the first among the contemporary *Typika* of Constantinople was published, namely the *Typikon* of Kônstantinos Prôtopsaltês (Constantinople, 1838).

It has been noted that this text contains various historical inaccuracies found also in many manuscripts.[75] First of all, there is a discrepancy in the sources, including the *Synaxarium ecclesiae Constantinopolitanae*, as per the use of the epithet 'Pogonatus'. Is it supposed to belong to Constans II (who was also known as Constantine[76]), or to Constantine IV?[77] Leaving this question aside, the major problem with the text is that it presents the Constantine mentioned in the *hypomnema*, who of course is Constantine IV, as being both the father and the son of Justinian II Rhenotmetus. In truth, Constantine is Justinian's father.[78] This error is the result of an omission from the original text that reads, '...Κωνσταντίνου τοῦ Πωγωνάτου, υἱοῦ [Κωνσταντίνου τοῦ δυσσεβοῦς, δισεκγόνου Ἡρακλείου, πατρὸς δὲ] Ἰουστινιανοῦ τοῦ μικροῦ τοῦ τὴν ῥῖνα τμηθέντος'.[79] To my knowledge, the first person to explicitly point out this mistake is Giuseppe Simone Assemani, in his *Kalendarium Ecclesiae Universae*.[80] It is also corrected in the Συναξαριστής of Nicodemus Hagiorites.[81] This is particularly

---

[75] See Giannopoulos, 'Αἱ Οἰκουμενικαὶ Σύνοδοι' (see n. 18), p. 730.

[76] *PG* 98, 73, n. 63: 'Hic modo Constantinus dicitur, modo Constans in monumentis'.

[77] Constans II: Delehaye, *Synaxarium ecclesiae ·Constantinopolitanae* (see n. 33), cols. 47-49 and 887 (see also the Arabic *Synaxarion* ms *Hammatoura* 29, p. 21). Constantine IV: *ibid.*, col. 55. In canonical texts Constantine IV is usually referred to as 'Pogonotus'. See, for example, Nilus of Rhodes, Περὶ τῶν ἁγίων καὶ οἰκουμενικῶν συνόδων, Rallês-Potlês, *Syntagma*, vol. I (see n. 4), p. 392; Iôannês Zônaras, Περὶ τῆς ἕκτης συνόδου, Rallês-Potlês, *Syntagma*, vol. II, p. 293; Theodore Balsamon, Περὶ τῆς ἕκτης συνόδου, *ibid.*, p. 293. For more on this issue, see Ernest W. Brooks, 'Who Was Constantine Pogonatus?', *Byzantinische Zeitschrift* 17 (1908) 460-462 and Dêmêtrios Chatzêmichaêl', 'Τα παρωνύμια των αυτοκρατόρων του Βυζαντίου', *Βυζαντινός Δόμος* 16 (2007-2008) 111-150, on pp. 119-120.

[78] See, for example, Προσφωνητικὸς λόγος πρὸς Ἰουστινιανόν, Périclès-Pierre Joannou, *Discipline générale antique (IIe-IXe s.)*, Pontificia Commissione per la redazione del Codice di diritto canonico Orientale, Fonti – fasc. IX, vol. I/1: *Les canons des Conciles Oecuméniques*, (Rome, 1962), p. 107 = Rallês-Potlês, *Syntagma*, vol. II (see n. 4), p. 298. Duffy and Parker, *The Synodicon Vetus*, (see n. 35), p. 121, §143. Περὶ τῶν ἓξ οἰκουμενικῶν συνόδων, Rallês-Potlês, vol. 1, p. 373.

[79] For the entire text, see n. 33 above.

[80] Josephi Simonii Assemani, *Kalendaria ecclesiae universae: in quibus, tum ex vetustis marmoribus, tum ex codicibus, tabulis, parietinis, pictis, scriptis, scalptisve, sanctorum nomina, imagines, et festi per annum dies ecclesiarum orientis, et occidentis, praemissis uniuscujusque, ecclesiae originibus recensentur, describuntur, notisque illustrantur studio, et opera, tomus quintus. Kalendaria ecclesiae slavicae, sive graeco-moschae* (Rome, 1755; reprint Westmead, 1970), p. 241.

[81] Nikodêmos Hagioreitês, Συναξαριστὴς τῶν δώδεκα μηνῶν τοῦ ἐνιαυτοῦ, τόμος πρῶτος, περιέχων τοὺς τέσσαρας μήνας τοῦ Σεπτεμβρίου, Ὀκτωβρίου, Νοεμβρίου καὶ Δεκεμβρίου, ed. Maurikios Diakonos (Venice, 1819), p. 51, n. 1: 'Ἐσφαλμένως δὲ γράφεται ἔντε τῷ Μηναίῳ καὶ τῷ τετυπωμένῳ Συναξαριστῇ, ὅτι ὁ Κωνσταντῖνος

significant because Bartholomew Koutloumousianos systematically used this particular work of Nicodemus as a basis for his corrections of the twelve *menaia* that he had undertaken to re-publish at the behest of the Patriarchal Synod of Constantinople.[82] In this particular case, however, Bartholomew did not make the necessary amendment. Bartholomew's edition, with its faulty text at this point, has been republished consistently, and it is this edition that is in use even to this day. The only modern printed edition that is accurate in this regard is the so-called Patriarchal edition of 1843. This edition of the *menaia*, which was published only once, must not be confused with the Bartholomew edition, published

in Venice in the same year.[83] In the Patriarchal edition the contended text reads as follows: '... ἐπὶ τῆς βασιλείας Κωνσταντίνου τοῦ Παγωνάτου (sic), πατρὸς Ἰουστιανοῦ (sic) τοῦ μικροῦ, τοῦ ῥινοτμήτου'.[84] The dependency here on the note of Nicodemus' *Συναξαριστὴς* is more than evident. The Patriarchal edition, however, does not correct the other flagrant mistake in the *textus receptus* of the *hypomnema*, the result of a *lapsus calami*.[85] Neither does the Bartholomew edition for that matter. Specifically, the text presents Sergius as being the patriarch of Constantinople at the time of the convocation of the Sixth

Πωγωνάτος ἦτον υἱὸς Ἰουστιανοῦ (sic) τοῦ ῥινοτμήτου. Σημείωσαι, ὅτι ἡ Σύνοδος αὕτη ἑορτάζεται καὶ κατὰ τὴν δεκάτην ἕκτην τοῦ Ἰουλίου μήνα μετὰ τῶν ἄλλων πέντε Συνόδων'.

[82] Bartholomaios Kouloumousianos, 'Πρόλογος', *Μηναῖον τοῦ Σεπτεμβρίου* (Venice, 1843), p. ιβ′, §21; Stratès, *Βαρθολομαῖος Κουτλουμουσιανός* (see n. 64), pp. 364-366, 372-373. Bartholomew also based his work on Athos manuscripts, especially those of the Koutloumousion monastery, of which he was a monk. This error is to be found in two *Synaxaria* of Koutloumousion that I was able to study, namely mss *Koutloumousiou* 316 (copied in 1368), f. 141r and *Koutloumousiou* 314 (15th cent.), f. 52r. See also Athos mss *Konstamonitou* 8, f. 34r, *Iveron* 429, ff. 20v-21r, *Iveron* 430, ff. 14v-15r, and *Iveron* 432, f. 13r, the printed editions in n. 67 above, and ms *Benaki Museum* 39 (14th cent.), f. 23v.

[83] Contra Stratês, *Βαρθολομαῖος Κουτλουμουσιανός* (see n. 64), pp. 352-353, 387, 678. For more on this issue, see the remarks of Symeôn Paschalidês, 'Ἡ διόρθωση τῶν Μηναίων ἀπὸ τὸν Καισάριο Δαπόντε καὶ ἡ πατριαρχικὴ ἔκδοση τοὺς τὸ 1843', in the forthcoming edition *Τόμος τιμῆς εἰς τὸν μακαριστὸν καθηγητὴν τῆς λειτουργικῆς Ἰωάννην Φουντούλην*, eds. Panagiôtês Skaltsês and Nikodêmos Skrettas (Thessalonica, 2011).

[84] *Μηναῖον Σεπτεμβρίου* (Constantinople, 1843), p. 116. This must be the basis of the *September Menaion* published by the Holy Transfiguration Monastery (Brookline, 2005). See also the *Ἀνθολόγιον τῶν ἱερῶν ἀκολουθιῶν τοῦ ὅλου ἐνιαυτοῦ*, ed. Kônstantinos Papagiannês, vol. II (Thessalonica, 1993), p. 663.

[85] A third error is the name of the Antiochene prelate, who of course is Macarius (656-681), not 'Macrobius'.

Ecumenical Synod ('Σεργίου τὴν Ἐκκλησίαν Κωνσταντινουπόλεως ἰθύνοντος'.) This of course is not true. Sergius was patriarch of Constantinople from 610-638. As we have already mentioned, he was the theological mind behind the monoenergism-monothelitism adopted by Heraclius and expounded in the *Ekthesis*. In fact, during the Sixth Ecumenical Synod, George I (679-686) was at the helm of the Constantinopolitan see. Evidence shows that George and Sergius were confused from at least the early 11th century. Specifically, Peter of Antioch, in his letter to Michael Cerularius of Constantinople, written during the aftermath of the 1054 schism, mentions that, during his stay in Constantinople forty-five years earlier, at the recitation of the diptychs of the Liturgy, he heard both 'Sergius (sic) and the aforementioned pope (Agatho) referred to along with other patriarchs'.[86] Interestingly, this letter also offers an early account of the commemoration of the Sixth Ecumenical Synod held on the Sunday after the Exaltation of the Cross.[87]

6. Concluding Remarks

It has become evident that feast days may at times develop and become fixed in liturgical calendars in a circuitous and indirect manner. Moreover, they often are introduced or reconfigured on account of a particular theological controversy, historical circumstance, or ideological framework, a fact that reflects more on the later events than on the feast itself.[88] In our examination, as we have seen, the feast of the Sixth Ecumenical Synod, as found in the *heortologion* of the Byzantine rite, bears most of the characteristic trademarks of a *heortological* commemoration. The original inner diversity of the celebration in the cathedral rite was succeeded by a minor corruption with regard to the day the feast was to be kept (September 15). Later, other modifications and attempts at reconfiguring the feast followed (see the *Διάταξις* of Symeon of Thessalonica). Parallel adaptations also took place (e.g., the Feast of the Six Synods). Finally, today we are left with a reduction and a further shift with regard to the day on which the commemoration is to be kept (14 September) and a corruption in the *textus receptus* of the *hypomnema*

---

[86] *PG* 120, 800A.
[87] *PG* 120, 797C-800A.
[88] The same holds true for contemporary additions to or modifications of the liturgical calendar.

in the *synaxarion* of the September *menaion*. These make the feast of the Sixth Ecumenical Synod a fine example of the adventures particular liturgical commemorations of the *heortologion* may have over the course of time. By understanding these adventures we will be better equipped to reconsider, as necessary, the still many outstanding questions with regard to the church's rich life of prayer and worship and to reinforce the future of the church's liturgy.

EINIGE BESONDERHEITEN DER DEUTUNG DER VIERTEN BITTE DES VATERUNSERGEBETES DURCH MAXIMOS DEN BEKENNER IN IHRER ALTGEORGISCHEN GELATI-ÜBERSETZUNG (12. JAHRHUNDERT)

Nino SAKVARELIDZE

1. Die altgeorgische Übersetzung der exegetischen Schrift "Expositio Orationis Dominicae Brevis" Maximos des Bekenners aus der Gelati-Übersetzerschule, 12. Jahrhundert — Exkurs zum georgischen Gelaticorpus K 14

Die altgeorgische Übersetzung der *Expositio Orationis Dominicae Brevis* (*E.O.D.*; georgisch ლოცვისათჳს მამაო ჩუენოსა ქრისტეს მოყუარისა ვისმე მიმართ თარგმანებაჲ შემოკლებული) wird in der Gelati-Sammlung des Staatlichen Historisch-Ethnographischen Museums Kutaisi K 14 aufbewahrt. Die georgische Übersetzung wird in Clavis Patrum Graecorum unter Nr. 1691 angeführt.[1] Gleichfalls wird sie in Corpus Christianorum, Series Graeca, Band 23 erwähnt,[2] obwohl nur oberflächlich, denn es gab zur Zeit der *E.O.D.*-Edition durch CChr.SG 23 in Bezug auf die georgische Übersetzung des Werkes nur eine Handvoll Angaben.[3] K 14 gehörte ursprünglich dem Gelati-Kloster und ist nicht datiert; nach paläographischen Angaben lässt sich diese Handschrift in das 12. Jahrhundert datieren. Abgesehen von *E.O.D.* enthält die K 14-Sammlung die Werke *Ad Thalassium, Disputatio cum Phyrrho, Opuscula theologica et polemica, Epistulae XLV*.[4] Als Autor der Übersetzung wird in CChr.SG 23 Nikoloz Gulaberisdze bezeichnet, indem

---

[1] Clavis Patrum Graecorum (=CPG) III, ed. M. Geerard (Turnhout, 1979), 1691.

[2] *Maximi Confessoris Opuscula Exegetica Duo: Expositio in Psalmum LIX, Expositio Orationis Dominicae*, ed. P. Van Deun, Corpus Christianorum, Series Graeca (künftig *E.O.D.*, in: CChr.SG) 23 (Turnhout, 1991), *Introduction*, 142-143.

[3] Die Autoren verweisen auf Tarchnishvili (M. Tarchinišvili, *Die Geschichte der altkirchlichen georgischen Literatur*, 235-237) und M. Van Esbroeck (M. Van Esbroeck, 'Eutyme l'Hagiorite, le traducteur et ses traductions', *Bedi Kartlisa* (= Revue des études géorgiennes et caucasiennes) 4 (1988) 97.

[4] A. Chantladze und L. Choperia, მაქსიმე აღმსარებლის გელათური კრებული და მისი ბერძნული წყარო, *Mravaltavi* 21 (2005) 63-79.

man darin Kekelidze[5] und Tarchnishvili[6] folgt. Die Sammlungshand-schrift enthält keine Angaben zum Autor und wir wissen sehr wenig von der Übersetzertätigkeit von Gulaberisdze aus den alten Quellen. Daher soll die Frage der Autorschaft offen bleiben, solange wir nicht genügend Beweise besitzen. Bezüglich des Übersetzers ist eins ganz offensicht-lich: Wer er auch sein mag, er soll einer aus der hellenophilen Gelati-Schule gewesen sein. Der Autor der in der Sammlung K 14 enthaltenen georgischen Übersetzungen der Maximos-Werke bleibt daher anonym.

CChr.SG 23 kannte noch keine griechische Vorlage der georgischen Übersetzung.[7] Inzwischen kennt man eine: Dank der jüngsten For-schung durch georgische Wissenschaftler[8] ist eine dieser griechischen Vorlagen entdeckt worden. Diese ist Coislianus 90 (12. Jh., Lavra des Athanasios des Großen auf dem Berge Athos)[9], die in der Bibliothèque Nationale in Paris aufbewahrt wird.[10] Dies macht es nun möglich, die Beziehung der georgischen Übersetzung zum Stemma von Devreese zu bestimmen.[11] Der griechische Archetyp ist in drei Handschriften prä-sent: B (datiert ins 10. Jh.); E (10-11. Jh.); Taur. (Anfang des 11. Jh.).[12] Damit kann der terminus ante quem der *E.O.D.* festgestellt werden: 10. Jh. Dabei stammt die BE Gruppe aus einer und derselben Hss-Familie: *b*, während Taur. in die Hss-Familie *a* hineingehört.[13] Aus derselben Familie kommt auch die N-Handschrift oder Coislianus 90[14], die im Großen und Ganzen als Vorlage für die Gelati-Übersetzung diente. K14 folgt der Coislianus-Sammlung dem Bestand wie der Reihenfolge nach mit wenigen Ausnahmen. Im Unterschied zum Coislianus 90, die *Amb. Lib.* in lacunae enthält, findet sich diese in der georgischen Sammlung

---

[5] K. Kekelidze, უცხო ავტორები ქართულ მწერლობაში. ეტიუდები ძველი ქართული ლიტერატურის ისტორიიდან, Bd. *V* (Tbilisi, 1957), 96; ders., ძველი ქართული ლიტერატურის ისტორია, Bd. *I* (Tbilisi, 1980), 322. Kekelidze scheint hierin Tcitcinadze gefolgt zu sein. Siehe Z. Tcitcinadze, ქართული მწერლობა XII საუკუნეში (Tbilisi, 1887), 26-27. Das Werk von Tcitcinadze enthält aber viele fehlerhafte Angaben und ist deswegen nicht zuverlässig.

[6] Siehe oben, Anm. 3.

[7] *Introduction*, in: CChr.SG 23, 123.

[8] Die georgische Forschergruppe besteht aus Tamila Mgaloblishvili, Lela Choperia, Ani Chantladze und Nino Sakvarelidze.

[9] Dies bezeugen die Randbemerkungen, vgl. R. Devreese, *Bibliotheque Nationale, Catalogue des manuscrits grecs, vol. 2: Le fonds coislins* (Paris, 1954), 78-79.

[10] *Ibid.* Vgl. *Introduction*, in: CChr.SG 23, 33-34.

[11] *Introduction*, in: CChr.SG, 23, 138.

[12] *Introduction*, in: CChr.SG, 23, 85.

[13] *Introduction*, in: CChr.SG, 23, 106.

[14] *Introduction*, in: CChr.SG, 23, 33-34. Diese Hs wird beschrieben von Devreese, *Fonds Coislins* (siehe oben, Anm. 8), 78-79; *La Mystagogie de Saint Maxime le Confes-seur*, ed. Chr. G. Sotiropoulos (Athen, 2001), 146; Maximus Confessor: *Questiones ad Thalassium*, CChr.SG 7, ed. C. Steel und C. Laga (Turnhout, 1980), 54-56.

gar nicht. Auch manche am Schluß des griechischen Corpus angereihte Schriften sind hierin nicht enthalten. Dazu sei aber angemerkt, dass die georgische Sammlung nicht vollständig überliefert ist. (Sie endet mit der Schrift *Ad Catholicos per Siciliam consitutos*, N 8, K. Coislianus, ff249r-253r.)

Das Übersetzen der maximianischen Schriften ins Georgische hatte nicht erst im 12. Jh., d.h. in der hellenophilen Zeit, angefangen. Der erste georgische Übersetzer des hl. Maximos war der hl. Euthymios Athonites (955-1028), Hegumenos des Iviron-Klosters auf dem Berge Athos und Gründer der berühmten athonitischen Übersetzer-Schule. *E.O.D.* ist in der athonitischen Sammlung nicht enthalten. Dabei sei betont, dass uns alle in der Gelati-Sammlung überlieferten Übersetzungen nur in dieser einzigen Gelati-Hs überliefert sind. Die Gelati-Sammlung ist durch alle Merkmale der hellenophilen Epoche gekennzeichnet und unterscheidet sich sehr von der vorangegangenen euthymianischen Sammlung.

2. Das Vaterunser als gemeinschaftliches Gebet der Söhne Gottes, Symbol der Sohnschaft Gottes

Das Vaterunser ist das gemeinschaftliche Gebet ('Vater unser' – πάτερ ἡμῶν/'gib uns' – δός / δίδου ἡμῖν)[15] der Söhne Gottes der Gnade nach,[16] der Söhne, die, mit Gnade des Heiligen Geistes erfüllt, im Haus des Vaters wohnen.[17] Im Vaterunser rufen sie Gott als 'Abba,

---

[15] Die Pluralform des Possessivpronomens ('wir', 'uns') lässt vermuten, dass dieses Gebet ein gemeinschaftliches Gebet sein soll, ein Gebet, das wir alle für uns alle vor Gott, unserem Vater, beten.

[16] Vgl. Römer 8, 15. Hier wird der Geist der Sohnschaft (πνεῦμα υἱοθεσίας) dem der Knechtschaft (πνεῦμα δουλείας) gegenübergestellt. Im Georgischen: სული ოგი მგიოჲებისაჲ, 'Geist der Kindschaft', siehe auch Joh 1, 12: τέκνα θεοῦ. Derselbe griechische Begriff υἱοθεσία (υἱοθεσίαν ἐν χάριτι, *E.O.D.*, in: CChr.SG 23, 27-73, c. 81, S. 31; adoptionem in gracia, *E.O.D.*, in: PG 90, 875C) wird nun in der hellenophilen Übersetzung der *E.O.D.* mit ძეღ-ცაღებაჲ (ძეღ-ცაღებისაჲ მადლითა, მაქსიმე აღმსარებელი, ლომცვასაითა მამა ჩუჱნისა ჰრისტეს მოყუარისა ვისგე მიმართ თარგმანებაჲ მეჳელებელი, K 14, 153 v, künftig ლომცვასაითა მამა ჰჲჱნისა, in: K 14) übersetzt: ძეღ-ცაღებაჲ ist eine wörtliche Übertragung des griechischen Kompositums υἱο-θεσία. Damit wird die Sohnesgestaltung in uns, indem der Sohn Gottes Gestalt in uns annimmt, akzentuiert. (Neue Wortbildungen dieser Art sind für die hellenophilen Übersetzungen sehr charakteristisch). Mit Recht bemerkt Kardinal Daniélou, das Vaterunser sei ein Sohnesgebet. Siehe J. Daniélou, *Gebet als Quelle christlichen Handelns, mit einem Vorwort von Hans Urs von Balthasar* (Einsiedeln und Freiburg, 1994), 43.

[17] Vgl. Röm 8, 17: εἰ δὲ τέκνα, καὶ κληρονόμοι, κληρονόμοι μέν θεοῦ, συγκληρονόμοι δὲ Χριστοῦ (შვილ, მკჳღვცა, მკჳღ ღმრთისა თანა და თანა-მკჳღ

Vater' an; denn dieses ist das Gebet der Kinder Gottes, die in Erwartung
der Ankunft des Reiches Gottes zum Vater beten ('Dein Reich komme'
oder 'Dein Heiliger Geist'); die wollen, dass der Wille des Vaters
geschehe, im Himmel wie auf Erden; die als Söhne vom Vater das tägliche Brot, ἄρτος ἐπιούσιος, das 'wesentliche Brot', erbitten; die um
eine Allversöhnung und Verzeihung flehen und vom Bösen erlöst werden wollen.

Im Herrengebet, das Jesus Christus selbst gesprochen und uns gelehrt
hat, kann kein einziges Wort, kein Partikel überflüssig sein. So mögen
die Worte ἡμῶν (ჩუენი) und ἡμῖν (ჩუენ) im ersten Blick als Tautolo-
gie erscheinen, sie wollen aber in der Tat den gemeinschaftlichen Charakter des Gebetes hervorheben: Es ist unser gemeinsames Gebet, Gebet
der Gemeinschaft, der Versammlung, Versammlung der Einberufenen
(ἐκκλησία), das, was wir alle für alle vor Gott beten. Die ersten Kom-
mentatoren des Vaterunsers — die afrikanischen Kirchenväter Tertullian
(um 150 - um 230) und Cyprian (um 200/210-258) — beziehen das Pro-
nomen *nostrum* auf das betende Subjekt, nämlich auf die Kinder Gottes,
die nun das Gebet des Herrn aussprechen dürfen.[18] So ist auch die Brotbitte die Bitte um die Nahrung für die Kinder Gottes: Wir bitten um das
Brot, das uns, die wir Söhne Gottes geworden sind, dem Heilsplan Gottes nach, zur Erhaltung des Geistes wie des Leibes gegeben wird. Gott
gibt die Nahrung einem jedem je nach Bedarf und zur rechten Zeit.[19]
Deswegen sind wir als Söhne Gottes dazu berufen, uns nicht um Essen
oder Trinken zu sorgen, sondern vor allem das Reich und die Gerechtig-
keit Gottes zu suchen.[20] Auf diese Weise werden wir der Gnade der

---

ქრისტესა). Im Georgischen heißt მკჳდრ 'Bewohner', და-მკჳდრ-ება – 'behaust werden', 'ansässig sein'. Hierzu sei angemerkt, dass მკჳდრ auch andere Sinnesbedeutungen
hat und zwar 'fest' und 'eigen'. 'Gottes Erben und Miterben Christi' sind somit in der
georgischen Übersetzung diejenigen, die Gottes eigene Kinder geworden sind und mit
Christus eine feste Wohnstätte bei Gott gefunden haben.

[18] Tertullianus, *Libri Dogmatici: De Oratione* VI, PL 1, 1143A-1196D, 1160A =
Opera catholica ad Marcionem; De Oratione VI, ed. E. Dekkers, CCL 1, pars I (Turn-
hout, 1954), 257-274, 261; Cyprianus, *De Dominica Oratione* 18, CCL 3A, pars II, ed.
M. Simonetti und C. Moreschini (Turnhout, 1976), 325.

[19] Vgl. Ps 144 (145), 15-16: 'Alle Augen warten auf dich, und du gibst ihnen die
Speise zur rechten Zeit' (თუალნი ყოველთანი შენდამი ესვენ, და შენ მოსცი საზრ-
დელი მათი ჟამსა, აღებ შენ კელსა შენსა და განაძღებ ყოველსა ცხოველსა
ნებისაებრ).

[20] *E.O.D.*, in: CChr.SG 23, c. 585-587, S. 60-61: ζητεῖν τὴν βασιλείαν τοῦ Θεοῦ
καὶ δικαιοσύνην ὁ σωτήρ ἐνετείλατο; *E.O.D.*, in: PG 90, 898D: Sin autem solum
regnum Dei et justitiam ejus quaerenda Salvator jussit; vgl. მხოლოსა სამეფოსა
ღმრთისა და სიმართლსა მისისა ძიებაა ამცნო მაცხოვარმან, *ლოკვისათჳს მამაო
ჩუენრალ*, in: K 14, 162 r. Dies wird zu einem der Hauptmotive der Deutung des Vaterunsers schlechthin.

Sohnschaft Gottes[21] gewürdigt, so werden wir die Würde der Kindschaft Gottes anziehen dürfen. Es ist also von besonderer Bedeutung, dass jede einzelne Bitte wie auch das ganze Vaterunsergebet unsere Sohnschaft Gottes offenbart. Diese sei dessen Hauptziel und verborgener mystischer Sinn. Warum wird nun die vierte Bitte, die Bitte um das tägliche Brot, Mysterion der Teilnahme am ewigen Leben genannt?[22]

Gleich wie die Eucharistie der Mittelpunkt des heiligen Gottesdienstes, der heiligen Handlung ist, so stellt das Vaterunsergebet die zentrale Formel (Gebets- und Bittformel), das zentrale 'Wort' und Gebet (λόγος, εὐχή, προσευχή, δέησις, αἴτησις, αἰτητὸν, ἐπαγγελία) dieser zentralen Handlung dar. Die Brotbitte bildet den Mittelpunkt dieses zentralen Gebetes, in dem, mit Pavel Florenski, das Ende wie die Vollendung (τέλος) der gesamten heiligen Handlung gegeben ist.[23] Das Besondere und das Einzigartige an diesem 'Wort' ist, dass es von unserem Herrn, dem Gottessohn stammt und an unseren Vater gerichtet ist (Herrengebet, Vaterunser). Dieses Herrenwort an den Vater ist uns gegeben, damit auch wir es an unseren Vater richten. Allerdings kommt nicht jedes Wort vom Herrn, nicht jedes Wort ist eine Widerspiegelung des Himmlischen auf der Erde und nicht jedes Wort ist ein Gebet.[24] Dieses aber vom Gottessohn gesprochene und uns gegebene Wort ist jenes Wort, welches das Alltägliche und Gewöhnliche zum Besonderen und Ungewöhnlichen, zum Mysterion macht, das eine Handlung zu einer Sakralhandlung oder

---

[21] Vgl. Anm. 16.

[22] ἀϊδίου ζωῆς μετοχήν, *E.O.D.*, in: CChr.SG 23, c. 82, S. 31. სამართლისისა ცხორებისა ზიარქმნისაა, ღვიწისითი მამით რქენოსა, in: K 14, 153 v. Maximos spricht von sieben neuen Mysterien: ἑπτὰ τὸν ἀριθμὸν (*E.O.D.*, in: CChr.SG 23, c. 77-78, S. 30) / septem numero (*E.O.D.*, in: PG 90, 875C), denen wir durch Christus, den Selbstverwirklicher dieser Mysterien, im Gebet des Vaterunsers teilhaftig werden: 1. Gotteslehre; 2. Annahme an Kindschaft in Gnade; 3. Gleichrangigkeit mit Engeln; 4. Teilhabe am ewigen Leben (Brotbitte); 5. Wiederherstellung der Natur; 6. Aufhebung des Gesetzes der Sünde; 7. Befreiung von der Herrschaft des Bösen. καινῶν μυστηρίων αὐτουργὸς γίνεται καὶ διδάσκαλος...ὧν μυστικῶς περιέχει τὴν δύναμιν... τῆς προσευχῆς ὁ σκοπός θεολογίαν, υἱοθεσίαν ἐν χάριτι, ἰσοτιμίαν τὴν πρὸς ἀγγέλους, ἀϊδίου ζωῆς μετοχήν, φύσεως ἀπαθῶς πρὸς ἑαυτὴν νευούσης ἀποκατάστασιν, τοῦ νόμου τῆς ἁμαρτίας κατάλυσιν, καὶ τῆς τοῦ κρατήσαντος ἡμῶν δι' ἀπάτης πονηροῦ τυρραννίδος καθαίρεσιν (*E.O.D.*, in: CChr.SG 23, c. 76-77, S. 30, c. 80-85, S. 31)...; novorum mysteriorum ipse auctor atque opifex, doctorque exsistat,... quorum mystice vim,... complectitur scopus orationis: nempe, theologiam, adoptionem in gracia, parem cum angelis honoris sortem, sempiternae vitae societatem, naturae in seipsam nulla vitii labe aut libidine inclinantis in integrum restitutionem, legis peccati destructionem, ac nequissimi, qui nos seducendo addixerat, tyrranidis abolitionem (*E.O.D.*, in: PG 90, 875BC).

[23] P. Florenski, *Философия культа. Опыт православной антроподицеи. Соб. Соч. Философское наследие.* (Moskau, 2004), 397. Vgl. Passus über die Grundstruktur eines jeden christlichen Gebetes, *ebd.*, 382.

[24] *Ibid.*

einem Ritual werden lässt und das Sinnliche mit dem Noetischen, das Irdische mit dem Himmlischen verbindet. Dieses Wort also ist Gebet, da nur das Gebet es vermag, eine derartige Transformation zu bewirken. Und noch ein weiteres zeichnet dieses Wort aus: Wir, die wir von dieser Welt sind, bekommen kraft dieses Wortes, indem wir es aussprechen, Anteil an dem, was nicht von dieser Welt ist. Somit werden wir sogar aktive Teilnehmer am göttlichen Mysterion. Dieses göttliche Wort ist uns nämlich gegeben, und jedes Mal, wenn wir von diesem Wort, das nicht von dieser Welt ist, Gebrauch machen, beginnen wir zu handeln. Dies tun wir nicht aus eigener Kraft, sondern aus der Kraft Gottes.[25] So kann gesagt werden, dass das Gebet ein noetischer Opferdienst ist.[26] Das Wort wird uns vom Vatergott als seinen einzig-geborenenen Sohn, Logos Gottes, gesandt (κένωσις - Entäußerung im Fleische),[27] zugleich aber als Wort-Gebet, Logos des Gebetes, das uns der Logos und Sohn Gottes lehrt. Dieses ist das Wort, das vom Herrn herkommt und wieder zum Herrn zurückkehren soll. Das Herabsteigende trifft auf das Hinaufsteigende, die Menschwerdung Gottes auf die Vergöttlichung des Menschen. Es ist der Sohn Gottes, der uns das Wort Gottes überbringt bzw. uns über dieses Wort, über die Theologia, lehrt. Deswegen heißt er unser Lehrer des Gebetes (διδάσκαλος).[28]

Während das Mysterion des Wortes im gesamten Herrengebet verborgen bleibt, offenbart die vierte Bitte dieses Wort-Gebetes das größte Mysterion des Brotes und des Blutes. Einerseits ist es logos μυστικῶς κεκρυμμένον[29] (საიდუმლოდ დაფარული[30], 'auf mystische Weise verborgen'), andererseits, ἐμφανῶς κηρυττόμενον[31] (საჩინოდ ქადაგებული[32], 'geoffenbart verkündet'). Es wird geoffenbart, zugleich bleibt es aber verborgen. Während das Vaterunsergebet die zentrale Formel der Eucharistie darstellt, ist die Bitte um das tägliche Brot die zentrale Bitte

---

[25] θεουργοῦμεν, богодействуем, ebd., 382.

[26] Vgl.τῆς λογικῆς λατρείας, E.O.D., in: CChr.SG.23, c. 535-536, S. 58, dazu siehe unten, S. 8, 10-11.

[27] Dieser ist κενωθεὶς ὁ τοῦ θεοῦ Λόγος, E.O.D., in: CChr.SG.23, c. 66, S. 30 / კორცისა მიერ დაცალიერებული სიტყუაა, ლოგვისათვს მამაი ჩუენბოისა, in: K 14, 153 v. Auch im Georgischen wird hier die Entäußerung des Logos Gottes im Fleische betont (დაცალიერებული სიტყუა — 'das entäußerte, entleerte Wort'). Logos ist die Fülle, während die Fleischwerdung eine Entleerung, Entäußerung heißt.

[28] E.O.D., in: CChr.SG.23, c. 58-59, S. 30. Vgl. ვევედრები ლოგვისა ამის მასწავლელსა უფალსა, 'Ich bete zum Herrn, Lehrer dieses Gebetes', ლოგვისათვს მამაი ჩუენბოისა, in: K 14, 153 r. Christus als Lehrer ist ein geläufiger Topos.

[29] E.O.D., in: CChr.SG.23, c. 63, S. 30.

[30] ლოგვისათვს მამაი ჩუენბოისა, in: K 14, 153 r.

[31] E.O.D., in: CChr.SG.23, c. 64-65, S. 30.

[32] ლოგვისათვს მამაი ჩუენბოისა, in: K 14, 153 v.

dieser Gebetsformel, ihr Mittelpunkt und Sinn. So bitten wir darum, das eucharistische Brot, d.h. den heiligen Leib und das heilige Blut Christi verkosten zu dürfen. Hierbei gewinnt der Akt der Verkostung eine absolute Bedeutung. Die Eucharistie wird somit zur Grundlage und zum Ausgangspunkt des heiligen Kultes schlechthin, zugleich aber zu dessen Ziel und innerem Sinn.[33] Die Eucharistie ist damit unabdingbare Voraussetzung und Garant dafür, dass das gespaltene Wesen des Menschen zusammengeführt, die gefallene Natur des Menschen erneuert (vgl. die fünfte Bitte des Vaterunsergebetes als Wiederherstellung unserer Natur)[34] und das ursprüngliche Gleichgewicht zwischen den zwei Urelementen des Menschen — der Ousia und der Hypostase — wiederhergestellt wird.[35]

Die Verkostung vom täglichen Brot, d.h. Teilhabe am heiligen Leib und heiligen Blut Christi heißt somit Teilhabe am ewigen Leben. Dieses Brot ist das lebendige Wort Gottes, das durch Seine Entäußerung im Fleische (κένωσις)[36] auch uns die Fülle der göttlichen Gnade und des wahren Lebens, die Vergöttlichung schenkt; dieses Brot ist das Brot des Lebens (τῆς ζωῆς)[37], das in uns das unstillbare Verlangen nach Ihm selbst (bzw. nach dem Brot des Lebens, d.h. nach ewigem Leben) erweckt; dieses Brot ist die Erkenntnis, durch die auch wir erkennen, was wir vorher waren und zu was Christus uns gemacht hat, von woher und wohin Er uns durch die Macht Seiner menschenfreundlichen Hand hinaufgeführt hat; wir, die wir uns, durch das Gewicht der Sünde hinabgerissen, am alleruntersten Ort befanden, durch Ihn aber zu dem allerhöchsten gelangen.[38] Deswegen heißt dieses Brot auch das Brot der Erkenntnis (τῆς ἐπιγνώσεως).[39]

---

[33] Vgl. Florenski, *Философия культа* (siehe Anm. 23), 147.

[34] Siehe oben, Anm. 22.

[35] Florenski, *Философия культа.* (siehe Anm. 23), 147, 155, 156.

[36] *E.O.D.*, in: CChr.SG 23, c. 102, S. 32.

[37] *E.O.D.*, in: CChr.SG 23, c. 568, S. 60. Vgl. ცხორებისა, 'des Lebens', ლოცვისათჳს მამაო ჩუენოსა, in: K 14, 161 v. Dieses Leben ist das Leben in Christus. Deswegen steht ცხორება — 'Leben' so nah zu ცხონება — 'Erlösung'.

[38] *E.O.D.*, in: CChr.SG 23, c. 783-788, S. 71: Πρὸς τοῦτο δὲ τῆς θεώσεως τὸ μυστήριον βλέπων ἡμῖν ἔστω τῆς προσευχῆς ὁ σκοπός, ἵνα γνῶμεν ἀνθ' οἵων οἵους ἡ διὰ σαρκὸς κένωσις τοῦ μονογενοῦς ἀπειργάσατο, καὶ πόθεν ποῦ τοὺς τὸ κατώτατον τοῦ παντὸς εἰληφότας χωρίον, εἰς ὅπερ ἡμᾶς τὸ τῆς ἁμαρτίας βάρος κατέωσε, δυνάμει φιλανθρώπου χειρὸς ἀνεβίβασε...; *E.O.D.*, in: PG 90, 906D — 907A: Ad hoc autem nobis deificationis mysterium spectet orationis scopus, ut noverimus quales ex quibus Unigeniti nos per carnem exinanitio reddiderit, ac unde, quo (qui infimam rerum hujus universi sedem, gravi nos peccati onere deprimente, receperamus), benignissimae nos dexterae potentia evexerit... Siehe hier und unten die deutsche Übersetzung von Erzbischof Chr. Schönborn, *Maximos der Bekenner, Drei geistliche Schriften* (Freiburg i. Brsg., 1996).

[39] *E.O.D.*, in: CChr.SG 23, c. 568, S. 60. Vgl. მეცნიერებისა, 'des Wissens', 'der Wissenschaft', ლოცვისათჳს მამაო ჩუენოსა, in: K 14, 161 v.

3. *Grundzüge der georgischen hellenophilen Übersetzung der* E.O.D.

a. Der Charakter der Deutung der vierten Bitte des Vaterunsergebetes der *E.O.D.* darf als mystagogisch-eucharistisch bestimmt werden.
b. Die aus der hellenophilen Gelati-Schule[40] (12. Jh.) hervorgegangene altgeorgische Übersetzung dieser Schrift hat die Grundstimmung der maximianischen Deutung bewahrt.
c. Eine aus der hellenophilen Schule stammende Übersetzung lässt vermuten, dass es sich um ein mit allen Merkmalen der hellenophilen Übersetzungstradition ausgestattetes Werk handelt.
d. Daraus kann geschlossen werden, dass die altgeorgische Übersetzung auch auf der Wortebene, auf der morphologisch-syntaktischen Ebene die Art der maximianischen Auslegung beibehalten hat, was darauf hindeutet, dass der Übersetzer bei der Übertragung der Schrift die Übersetzungsprinzipien der formalen Äquivalenz angewandt hat.[41]

[40] Zu hellenophilen Tendenzen in der georgischen Geistesgeschichte siehe K. Kekelidze, 'მთარგმნელობითი მეთოდი ძველ ქართულ ლიტერატურაში და მისი ხასიათი', *Etiudebi* I (Tbilisi, 1956) 183-197; E. Metreveli, 'შავი მთის მწიგნობრული კერის ისტორიისათვის XI საუკუნის I ნახევარში', in *S. Janašias sax. Sak'. Sax. Muz. Moambe* XX-B (1959) 85-104; ders., 'ეფრემ მცირის ავტოგრაფი', in *Sak'. mec'nr. akademiis Moambe* 1 (1959) 115-125; K. Bezarashvili, ელინოფილური თარგმანის ჩამოყალიბების გზები და მიზნები, in A. Baramidze 100 (Tbilisi, 2002) 45-58; ders., 'ეფრემ მცირის მთარგმნელობითი ტენდენციებისათვის: დინამიკური ექვივალენტის ტიპის თარგმანი ელინოფილური მახასიათებლებით', *Logosi. Celicdeuli elinologiasa da lat'inistikashi* 1 (2003) 43-83; N. Doborjginidze, 'ენის გზით ნაციონალური იდენტურობისა და რელიგიური უნივერსალიზმის გამოხატვის ზოგიერთი ნიშანი ქრისტიანულ საუკუნეებში', *Ena da kultura* 1 (2000) 20-27; D. Melikishvili, 'ქართული მეცნიერული ტერმინოლოგიის ჩამოყალიბებისა და განვითარების გზები', *Mnatobi* 2 (1983) 156-172; ders., *გელათის სალიტერატურო სკოლა (XII) და ქართული ფილოსოფიური ენის (ტერმინოლოგიის) ჩამოყალიბების გზები,* Sadis. Našromi (Tbilisi, 1988); ders., 'გელათის სამონასტრო-ლიტერატურული სკოლა' (აკადემია), *Kut'aisis universitetis Moambe* 1 (1993) 6-24; 2 (1993) 5-25; ders., *ძველი ქართული ფილოსოფიურ-თეოლოგიური ტერმინოლოგიის ისტორიიდან* (Tbilisi, 1999); N. Melikishvili, 'რამდენიმე დაკვირვება ეფთვიმე ათონელისა და ეფრემ მცირის მთარგმნელობით მეთოდზე', *Macne (els)* 4 (1987) 119-128; ders., 'ზუსტი თარგმანის როლი ტერმინთა ჩამოყალიბების საქმეში', *Macne (els)* 4 (1991) 89-95; L. Menabde, *ძველი ქართული მწერლობის კერები II* (Tbilisi, 1980); E. Chelidze, *ძველი ქართულ საღმრთისმეტყველო ტერმინოლოგია I* (Tbilisi, 1996); A. Tchumburidze, *ქართულ-ბერძნული საღმრთისმეტყველო განმარტებანი ანგელოზურ ძალთა შესახებ* (Tbilisi, 2001); L. Khachidze, 'ეფრემ მცირის უცნობი თარგმანი', *Macne (els)* 1 (1991) 137-154.

[41] In der Regel wird zwischen zwei Übersetzungsmodellen unterschieden: a. adaptiv-modales Modell, das zu einer freien Übersetzung führt (inhaltliche Äquivalenz), b. strukturell-formelles Modell, welches eine wörtliche Übersetzung schafft (formale Äquivalenz). Siehe dazu E. Nida, *Towards a Science of Translating* (Leiden, 1964); E. Nida and

e. Die wortgetreue Übertragung des mystagogisch-eucharistischen Sinnes der Brotbitte lässt sich am besten auf der Ebene der Termini veranschaulichen.

f. Der Wunsch der hellenophilen Georgier, mittels terminologischer Genauigkeit und Gesetzmäßigkeit die griechische philosophisch-theologische Begrifflichkeit auch in der georgischen Sprache adäquat wiederzugeben und den feststehenden griechischen Begriffen auch im Georgischen eine entsprechende Festlegung zu verleihen, führte zur Entstehung einer authentischen georgischen philosophisch-theologischen Terminologie.

g. Diese Terminologie kann auf der einen Seite als wortgetreue Wiedergabe des griechischen Originals, d.h. als eine Innovation und Neuschaffung im Georgischen betrachtet werden, stellt auf der anderen Seite aber auch eine Intensivierung und Aktivierung der natürlichen Fähigkeiten der georgischen Sprache und des georgischen Denkens schlechthin dar.

h. Die altgeorgische Übersetzung der griechischen Schrift des hl. Maximos bildet den Auftakt zu einer theologischen Rezeption in einem vollkommen anderen Sprach- und Kulturraum.

4. Drei Perspektiven der Erforschung eines theologischen Übersetzungswerkes

Handelt es sich um ein theologisches Übersetzungswerk, so gerät als wichtiges Forschungsmoment die Frage der Beziehung zwischen dem Original und der Übersetzung in den Blick. Insofern die Übersetzung die grundlegende Basis einer derartigen Rezeption darstellt, sollte jede mit der Rezeption befasste Untersuchung mit der Erforschung der Übersetzungen beginnen. Die Beziehung zwischen dem Original und der Übersetzung ist eine durch Sprache vermittelte Beziehung, ein Sprache-zu-Sprache-Verhältnis, eine Begegnung zweier unterschiedlicher Sprachwelten auf der Ebene der Litera (literarisch), Laute (phonetisch) und logoi als Wörter (philologisch), in der ein Drittes und Neues geschaffen wird.[42] Mit dem dabei behandelten 'formellen' Aspekt wird

W.D. Reyburn, *Meaning Across Cultures* (New York, 1976); E. Nida and C.R. Tabor, *The Theory and Practice of Translation* (Leiden, 1964); S. Brock, 'Aspects of Translation Technique in Antiquity', *Greek, Roman and Byzantine Studies* 20/1 (1979) 69-87.

[42] Weiter unten werde ich versuchen, diese Begegnung vom hl. Maximos und dessen georgischen Übersetzer auf der sprachlich-terminologischen und theologischen Ebene zu erläutern.

aber nur ein erster Aspekt der Beziehung bzw. Rezeption zum Ausdruck gebracht. Neben diesem gibt es noch zwei weitere Aspekte der Begegnung von Übersetzung und Original: nl. auf einer geschichtlichen und auf einer theologischen Ebene. Logoi sind dabei nicht nur Wörter, sondern Sinnesinhalte des Ausgedrückten. Die Betrachtung und Behandlung eines theologischen Übersetzungswerkes kann demnach auf drei verschiedenen Ebenen unternommen werden: a) auf einer philologischen; b) auf einer historisch-kulturologischen und c) auf einer theologischen Ebene.[43] Anders gesagt: Aus der Betrachtung und Behandlung eines theologischen Übersetzungswerkes ergeben sich drei Hauptaufgaben bzw. drei fundamentale Aspekte der Erforschung einer theologischen Übersetzungstradition:

a)   eine philologische Erforschung des Übersetzungswerkes, die als vorbereitende Stufe und Grundlage für weitere theologische Untersuchungen dient und die untrennbare Verbindung zwischen philologischer und theologischer Wissenschaft verdeutlicht;

b)   eine historisch-kulturologische Erforschung, die ein theologisches Werk als historische Quelle und kulturologisches Phänomen darstellen will;

c)   eine Erforschung aus theologischer Perspektive, die die Übersetzung als theologisches Zeugnis betrachtet und ihren theologischen Gehalt prüft.

Die Betrachtung und Behandlung aller drei Dimensionen bildet den Kern einer jeden Wissenschaft, die sich mit der Übersetzung theologischer Werke befasst.

5. Einige Beispiele des Verhältnisses zwischen Original und Übersetzung auf der terminologischen Ebene

5.1. Gebet, Beten und Betender nach Maximos

Das Gebet[44] wird von Maximos als eine Bitte[45] definiert. Es ist die Bitte um das Gebotene,[46] um die göttlichen Güter[47] und Gaben.[48] Das

---

[43] Vgl. drei Aspekte einer liturgiewissenschaftlichen Methode: literargeschichtliche, liturgiegeschichtliche und liturgie-theologische Aspekte. Siehe R. Bornert, *Les commentaires byzantins de la divine Liturgie du VIIe au XVe siècle*, Archives de l'Orient Chrétien 9 (Paris, 1966), 32ff.

[44] προσευχή, *E.O.D.*, in: CChr.SG 23, c. 200, S. 38 oder *E.O.D.*, in: CChr.SG 23, c. 581, S. 60 / ლოცვა, ლოცვისათჳს მამა ჩუენისა, in: K 14, 155v oder K 14, 162 r.

Gebet ist somit die Bitte um die Güter, deren Selbstverwirklicher der menschgewordene Logos Gottes ist.[49] Das Gebet ist Gelübde und Versprechen, d.h. Verheißung.[50] Es ist ein Bittgebet,[51] das die opfernden Menschen Gott darbringen.[52] Der Betende wird als jemand dargestellt, der Gott das vernunftbegabte Opfer darbringt. Indem er seinen Opferdienst gemeinsam mit den Engeln vollzieht, ist er zugleich Darbringender und Mit-Darbringender.[53] In diesem Dienst wird sein Gebet frei von Begierde und Zorn.[54] Nach Maximos ist die Befreiung von den beiden

[45] αἴτησιν, E.O.D., in: CChr.SG 23, c. 200, S. 38 oder αἰτεῖν, E.O.D., in: CChr.SG 23, c. 581, S. 60/ თხოაა, ლოცვისათჳს მამაჲ ჩუენნალა, in: K 14, 155 v oder K 14, 162 r.

[46] Διὰ προσευχῆς γὰρ μόνον ἐστὶν αἰτητὸν τὸ κατ' ἐντολὴν ζητητόν, E.O.D., in: CChr.SG 23, c. 581-583, S. 60 / ლოცვის მიერ სათხოელ არს მცნებისაებრ ძიებუღთო მხოღოა, ლოცვისათჳს მამაჲ ჩუენნალა, in: K 14, 162 r.

[47] τῶν θείων ἀγαθῶν, E.O.D., in: CChr.SG 23, c. 604, S. 62/ სამრთითა კეთილთა, ლოცვისათჳს მამაჲ ჩუენნალა, in: K 14, 162 r.

[48] τῶν θείων δώρων, E.O.D., in: CChr.SG 23, c. 588, S. 61 / სამრთითა ნიჭთა, ლოცვისათჳს მამაჲ ჩუენნალა, in: K 14, 162 r. Vgl. auch E.O.D., in: CChr.SG 23, c. 197-198, S. 38.

[49] τῶν ὑπὸ τοῦ Λόγου σαρκωθέντος αὐτουργηθέντων ἀγαθῶν αἴτησιν εἶναι τὴν προευχήν, E.O.D., in: CChr.SG 23, c. 222-224, S. 40 / განკაცებულებულისა სიტყჳსა მიერ თჳთმოქმედებულთა კეთილთა თხოაა არს ლოცვა, ლოცვისათჳს მამაჲ ჩუენნალა, in: K 14, 156 r.

[50] τὴν εὐχὴν ὑπόσχησιν ἤγουν ἐπαγγελίαν, E.O.D., in: CChr.SG 23, c. 202, S. 38 / აღთქუმაა-მქადებღობაა ე.ი. აღმთქმელობაა, ლოცვისათჳს მამაჲ ჩუენნალა, in: K 14, 155 v. Alle drei hier verwendeten georgischen Begriffe wollen eben diesen Verheißungscharakter zum Ausdruck bringen.

[51] τὴν δέησιν, E.O.D., in: CChr.SG 23, c. 628, S. 63 / ძღიითი ვედღებაა, wörtlich: 'dringliches Beten', 'Beten mit Kraft'), ლოცვისათჳს მამაჲ ჩუენნალა, in: K 14, 162 v. Hier sei darauf hingewiesen, dass es im Georgischen den Zusatz "dringliches" oder "mit Kraft" gibt. Somit geht es hier um ein dringliches Beten mit Kraft. Diese Kraft wird uns von Gott gewährt. Dabei soll hervorgehoben werden, dass Georgisch ძაღი auch Logos bzw. Christus-Logos beinhaltet. Dieses Gebet, diese Deêsis ist somit logosbegabt und von Logos, von Christus selbst erfüllt.

[52] ὦν γνησίως λατρεύοντες θεῷ προσκομίζουσιν ἄνθρωποι, E.O.D., in: CChr.SG 23, c. 201-202, S. 38 / რომელთაჲ საკუთირად მკუთინვღენ კაცნი მიართუმებ ღმერთსა, ლოცვისათჳს მამაჲ ჩუენნალა, in: K 14, 155 v. Griechisch λατρεύοντες entspricht im Georgischen ein ebenso von კუთინკა (latreia, Opfer) stammendes Partizip Aktiv მ-კუთინვ-ელ-ნი, während προσκομίζουσιν mit dem Verb მიართუმებ, d.h. 'darbringen' wiedergegeben wird.

[53] ὁ …κατὰ μόνην τὴν λογικὴν δύναμιν… μυστικῶς προσάγων τῷ θεῷ τὴν λατρείαν…διὰ πάντων τοῖς ἀγγέλοις ὁμολάτρης, γενομένος καὶ ὁμοδίαιτος…, E.O.D., in: CChr.SG 23, c. 521-525, S. 57. Vgl. Qui sola rationis vi…mystice Deo cultum adhibet,…per omnia similis angelis adoratur, E.O.D., in: PG 91, 895AB / რომელმან მხოღოთა სიტყუჯეჲითა ძაღითა… საიღუმღოდ შეწიროს ღმრთისა მკუთინვეღღობაა თანამქცევ ანგეღოზთა და თანამკუთინვეღ ღმრთისა ქმნიღმან ყოველთა მიერ, ლოცვისათჳს მამაჲ ჩუენნალა, in: K 14, 161 r. Hier wird τὴν λατρείαν mit მკუთინვეღღობაა ('Opferdienst') übersetzt, während თანამკუთინვეღ ('Mit-Darbringende') eine wörtliche Übertragung von ὁμολάτρης darstellt.

[54] ἐπιθυμίας τε καὶ θυμοῦ κεχωρισμένην, E.O.D., in: CChr.SG 23, c. 521-522, S. 57/ გუღისათუმისა და გუღისწყრომისაგან განშორებუღნი, ლოცვისათჳს მამაჲ

Lastern der Begierde und des Zorns die erste Stufe der geistigen Askese, der erste Schritt hin auf dem Weg zur geistigen Vervollkommnung. Kraft dieses Gebetes, dieses vernunftbegabten Opferdienstes erfüllt sich der Wille Gottes auf der Erde und im Himmel gemäß der Ordnung der Engel,[55] womit unsere Nachahmung der himmlischen Ordnungen, unsere Angleichung an die Engel und unsere Bürgerschaft im Himmel betont wird. In Zusammenhang damit wird auf die dritte Bitte des Vaterunsergebetes hingewiesen und eine deutliche Verbindung zwischen der dritten und vierten Bitte hergestellt.

Der Betende ist für Maximos aber nicht nur derjenige, der ein unblutiges Opfer und einen vernunftbegabten Opferdienst vollzieht, sondern auch derjenige, der um das Brot der Erkenntnis, um die Gnosis bittet.[56] Diese Gnosis impliziert die Erkenntnis, wie süß der Herr ist.[57] Es ist die uns durch die Verkostung des heiligen Leibes und des heiligen Blutes unseres Herrn Jesus Christus verliehene Erkenntnis, dass wir essen, um zu leben, und nicht leben, um zu essen,[58] dass wir nicht bloß leben, sondern um Gottes willen leben.[59] Essen, um zu leben, bedeutet,

---

ჩუენთასა, in: K 14, 161 r. გულისთქუმა und გულისწყრომა sind feste georgische Entsprechungen für den griechischen Begriff ἐπιθυμίας τε καὶ θυμοῦ, die in der Askese häufig Verwendung finden. Es sei hervorgehoben, dass die beiden georgischen Termini mit გული, 'Herz' gebildet sind: გულისთქუმა, wörtlich: 'Wort des Herzens' und გულისწყრომა — 'Ärger des Herzens'.

[55] οὗτος ἐπὶ γῆς, ὡς ἐν οὐρανῷ τῶν ἀγγέλων αἱ τάξεις, τὸ θεῖον πεπλήρωκε θέλημα, E.O.D., in: CChr.SG 23, c. 52523-525, S. 57 / ამან ქუეყანასა ვითარცა ანგელოზებრთა წესთა ცათა შინა საღმრთოითა სრულყო ნებაა, ლოცვისათჳს მამთ ჩუენთასა, in: K 14, 161 r. სრულყო heißt 'vollenden' und entspricht an dieser Stelle dem griechischen πεπλήρωκε — der Wille Gottes wurde vollendet im Himmel wie auf Erden.

[56] ...τὸν γνωστικὸν ἄρτον αἰτῶν διακείσεται...προσευχόμενος, E.O.D., in: CChr. SG 23, c. 686-687, S. 66 / მეცნიერებითისა პურის მთხოელ არს მლოცველ, ლოცვისათჳს მამთ ჩუენთასა, in: K 14, 163 v.

Das Attribut des Brotes - τὸν γνωστικὸν wird ins Georgische mit მეცნიერებითი - 'gnostisches', 'wissendes' übertragen. მეცნიერება ('Wissen', 'Wissenschaft', d.h. 'göttliches Wissen', 'göttliche Wissenschaft') wird besonders in den hellenophilen Übersetzungen der Gelatischule zu einer festgelegten Entsprechung für das griechische γνῶσις.

[57] Vgl. Ps 33 (34), 9.

[58] τοῦ ζῆν ἕνεκεν δειχθῶμεν ἐσθίοντες, ἀλλὰ μὴ τοῦ ἐσθίειν χάριν ζῶντες ἐλεγχθῶμεν, E.O.D., in: CChr.SG 23, c. 612-613, S. 62 / prodamurque eo edere ut vivamus, non ut edamus vivere arguamur, E.O.D., in: PG 90, 899 C / სიცოცხლისათჳს მჭამელად ვიჩუენნეთ და არა ჭამისათჳს ცოცხალ ყოფად ვიმხილნეთ, ლოცვისათჳს მამთ ჩუენთასა, in: K 14, 162 v.

[59] არა რაისათჳს ვცოცხლებდეთ, არამედ რაითა ღმრთისად ვცოცხლებდეთ, ლოცვისათჳს მამთ ჩუენთასა, in: K 14, 162 v.

das Brot des Lebens, dieses uns heute und jeden Tag gegebene himm-
lische Brot zu verzehren und dadurch Anteil am ewigen Leben zu
erhalten.

Durch die Bitte um das tägliche Brot bezeugen wir vor Christus, unserem Lehrer des Betens, dass wir, indem wir über unser Leben philoso-
phieren, seinem Gebot folgend tagtäglich den Tod einüben.[60]

Das Gebet gebietet uns darum zu bitten, die Grenzen des Gebetes
nicht zu übertreten.[61] Dies bedeutet, dass wir einzig und allein um das
uns durch das Gebet verheißene tägliche Brot bitten sollen.[62] Diese Bitte
will uns zu Wächtern und Beschützern unserer Seele machen. Als solche
sollen wir unsere Seele bis zum Tod vor der Sorge um den Leib bewah-
ren, damit sie, ohne Beimischung von verderblichen Dingen,[63] fähig
wird, den Überfluß der göttlichen Güter zu erfahren.[64] Wir sollen Gott
bitten, dass er uns mit noetischen Augen ausrüstet und uns die gnosti-
sche, erkenntnisbringende Nahrung gibt, damit wir es vermögen, die
Liebe zur Materie wie Staub von unseren noetischen Augen zu wischen;[65]
damit wir unseren Leib zum Boten der Seele machen, die Seele aber

---

[60] ...καὶ δείξωμεν ὅτι φιλοσόφως κατὰ Χριστὸν μελέτην θανάτου τὸν βίον ποι-
ούμεθα, E.O.D., in: CChr.SG 23, c. 598-599, S. 61 / talesque nos ex Christianae philo-
sophiae norma exhibeamus, qui vitam mortis meditationem faciamus, E.O.D., in: PG 90,
899 A / ქრისტესმიერისა სიკუდილისა წურთითა ვფილოსოფოსყოფთ ცხორებასა,
ლოცვისათჳს მამაი ჩუენო, in: K 14, 162 r.
[61] Μὴ παρέλθωμεν τοὺς ὅρους τῆς προσευχῆς, E.O.D., in: CChr.SG 23, c. 593,
S. 61 / ნუ წარვხდებით საზღვარსა ლოცვისათა, ლოცვისათჳს მამაი ჩუენო, in:
K 14, 162 r.
[62] ἀλλὰ τὸν πρὸς ἡμέραν ἀπεριμερίμνως διὰ τῆς προσευχῆς αἰτήσωμεν ἄρτον,
E.O.D., in: CChr.SG 23, c. 597, S. 61 / მდღევარ ვითხოვთ ლოცვისა მიერი საზ-
რუნველოა პურსა, ლოცვისათჳს მამაი ჩუენო, in: K 14, 162 r..
[63] πρὶν ἐπιστῆναι τὸν θάνατον τῆς τῶν σωματικῶν μερίμνης τὴν ψυχὴν ἀποτέ-
μνοντες, ἵνα μὴ προσηλωθῇ τοῖς φθειρομένοις, E.O.D., in: CChr.SG 23, c. 602-603,
S. 61 / და პირველმოწევნადღე სიკუდილისა ზრუნვისაგან სხეულთასა გამოვჰ-
კუეთთ სულსა, რაჲთა არა შეემშჭუალოს განხრწნადთა, ლოცვისათჳს მამაი
ჩუენო, in: K 14, 162 r.
[64] μάθη πλεονεξίαν τῆς τῶν θείων ἀγαθῶν περιουσίας στερητικήν, E.O.D., in:
CChr.SG 23, c. 607-608, S. 61 / და ისწავოს ანგაჰრებაჲ საჲმრთოთა კეთილთა
ეუფმობისა განმლეველობითი, ლოცვისათჳს მამაი ჩუენო, in: K 14, 162 r.
[65] Φύγωμεν οὖν, ὅση δύναμις, τὴν φιλίαν τῆς ὕλης, καὶ τὴν αὐτῆς σχέσιν καθά-
περ κονιορτὸν τῶν νοερῶν ὀμμάτων ἀπονιψώμεθα, E.O.D., in: CChr.SG 23, c. 605-
607, S. 62. Vgl. Fugiamus ergo, quanta nobis facultas, rerum terrenarum amorem,
earumque procliviorem affectum instar pulveris ab animi occulis abstergamus, E.O.D.,
in: PG 90, 899 B / ვევლტოდი უკუჱ, რაოდენ გუეძლოს, სიყუარულსა ნივთისასა
და სქესი მისი ვითარცა მტუერი განვიყარით გონიერთა თუალთაგან, ლოცვისათჳს
მამაი ჩუენო, in: K 14, 162 r.

zum Verkünder Gottes;[66] damit wir unser irdisches Leben zusammen-
halten und es nicht bloß genießen.[67]

5.2. Gebet als noetischer Opferdienst, als noetische Darbringung des
Opfers, der Betende als der Mit-Darbringende, als jener, der
gemeinsam mit den himmlischen Engeln Gott das Opfer darbringt.

Unsere Aufmerksamkeit wendet sich nun einigen weiteren Termini
zu, die das maximianische Verständnis des Betens als noetischen
Opferdienstes zum Ausdruck bringen. Die Gleichrangigkeit des Menschen mit den Engeln (ἰσοτιμίαν τὴν πρὸς ἀγγέλους), die nach Maximos vor allem in der dritten Bitte des Vaterunsers ausgesprochen wird,
bedeutet nicht nur den Willen Gottes auf der Erde und im Himmel
geschehen zu lassen,[68] sondern auch die Engel in ihrer geistigen und
mystischen Opferdarbringung nachzuahmen, τοῖς ἀγγέλοις ὁμολάτρης (თანამკუთნვჱლ) und Mit-Darbringende zu werden.[69] Die
Menschen sind nicht nur λατρεύοντες (მკუთნვჱლნი), 'Darbrin-
gende',[70] sondern auch τοῖς ἀγγέλοις ὁμολάτρης, 'mit den Engeln
Mit-Darbringende'. Deswegen ist diese λατρεία eine λογικὴ λατρεία
(τῆς λογικῆς λατρείας[71]); im Georgischen wird an dieser Stelle das-
selbe Attribut wie im Griechischen სიტყვჱრი[72], 'logosbegabt'
gebraucht. Für das Griechische τὴν λατρείαν[73] wird im Georgischen

---

[66] ψυχῆς ἄγγελον τὸ σῶμα καθιστῶντες, λελογισμένον ταῖς ἀρεταῖς, καὶ
ταύτην θεοῦ κήρυκα ποιοῦντες, τῇ περὶ τὸ καλὸν παγιότητι πεποιωμένην, E.O.D.,
in: CChr.SG 23, c. 622-625, S. 63//corpus nimirum, virtutis probe rationibus institutum,
animae nuntium efficientes; animamque honesti constantia imbutam, Dei praeconem prae-
stantes, E.O.D., in: PG 90, 899 CD / ანგელობაცდ სულისა შემქმნელნი სხეულისა
საონოებათა მიერ სიტყვჱრ ქმნილისანი და მისნი ქადაგ ღმრთისა მყოფელნი
სიმტკიცითა კეთილისათა განჰრომელებთულისანი, ლოცვისათჳს მამთ ჩუჱნთაჳ,
in: K 14, 162 v.

[67] καὶ μόνοις ἀρκεσθῶντες τοῖς συνιστῶσιν, ἀλλὰ μὴ τοῖς ἡδύνουσιν ἡμῶν τὴν
παροῦσαν ζωήν, E.O.D., in: CChr.SG 23, c. 608-609, S. 61 / და მხოლონ შემამტკი-
ცებელნი ვიყვნჱთ და არა დამატკბომბელნი აქაისა ცხორებისა, ლოცვისათჳს
მამთ ჩუჱნთაჳ, in: K 14, 162 r.

[68] Siehe oben, Anm. 22.

[69] Siehe oben, Anm. 53. Dieser Gedanke spiegelt sich am besten im Cherubikon-
Hymnos der byzantinischen Liturgie wider.

[70] Siehe oben, Anm. 52.

[71] E.O.D., in: CChr.SG 23, c. 535, S. 58.

[72] ლოცვისათჳს მამთ ჩუჱნთაჳ, in: K 14, 161 r.

[73] Der griechische Begriff λατρεία bedeutet vor allem Dienst, besonders Gottesdienst
(im klassischen Griechisch auch Götzendienst), Kultstätte wie auch Sklavin und Magd.
Siehe W. Gemoll, Griechisch-Deutsches Schul- und Handwörterbuch, 9. Aufl. (München,
1991), 466; vgl. 'serve', 'be a slave', 'serve God', G. W. Lampe, A Patristic Greek

ein besonders interessanter Begriff, კუთნა oder მკუთნვლლობაᲓ[74] verwendet (vgl. auch ὁμολάτρης, თანამკუთნვლ), der aus dem Verb განკუთნა ('gehören', 'hingehören', 'gehörig sein') gebildet zu sein scheint.[75] Der Opferdienst ist somit das, was Gott gehörig und an Gott zu richten ist. Die Begriffe კუთნა und მკუთნვლლობაᲓ sind mit einem anderen Begriff, სა-კუთარ-აᲓ, 'eigen', 'eigentümlich' (griech. γνησίως)[76], der im gleichen Satz zusammen mit მკუთნვლნი (λατρεύοντες) gebraucht wird,[77] verwandt. Möglicherweise ist der georgische Übersetzer bei der Übersetzung von λατρεύοντες mit მკუთნვლნი und τὴν λατρείαν mit კუთნა vom griechischen Begriff γνησίως beeinflusst worden, indem er die georgischen Entsprechungen mit 'gehörig' in Verbindung stellte. An dieser Stelle sei daran erinnert, dass λατρεία neben προσκύνησις insbesondere die nur Gott gebührende Anbetung bedeutet (lateinisch ad-oratio).[78] Der Gebrauch des

---

Lexicon (Oxford, 1961), 793. Vgl. das Verb λατρεύω — 'um Lohn dienen', im NT 'gehorchen', 'huldigen', 'fröhnen', Gemoll, *Griechisch-Deutsches Wörterbuch,* 466; vgl. Lampe, *A Patristic Greek Lexicon,* 794. λάτριος - 'den Diener oder Dienst betreffend', Gemoll, *Griechisch-Deutsches Wörterbuch,* 466. Im christlichen Gottesdienst wird der Begriff öfters synonym zu προσκυνέω - 'an-beten' verwendet. Siehe dazu. Chr. Grethlein, *Religionspädagogik: Lehrbuch* (Berlin und New York, 1998), 353. Zu λατρεία in den Mysterienkulten und in der Liturgie siehe C. Colpe, 'Mysterienkult und Liturgie', in: *Spätantike und Christentum: Beiträge zur Religions-und Geistesgeschichte der griechisch-römischen Kultur und Zivilisation der Kaiserzeit,* ed. C. Colpe, L. Honnenfelder und M. Lutz-Bachmann (Berlin, 1992), 206. Dienen kann man Gott auf vielerlei Weise bis hin zur Darbringung von Opfer, Lobpreis oder ethisch vorbildlichen Taten, *ibid.*

[74] Zu diesem Begriff siehe I. Abuladze, ძველი ქართული ენის განმარტებითი ლექსიკონი (Tbilisi, 1973), 59, 205.

[75] Unter vielen Bedeutungen finden wir nach Angabe von Abuladze eine Vielzahl an Begriffen, die das Gehörige, das Eigene zum Ausdruck bringen (განკუთნებ: 'gehören', 'hingehören', 'angehören'; სა-კუთარება: 'Eigentum'; სა-კუთარ-აᲓ გახდომა: 'sich aneignen'; განსაკუთრებული: 'das Besondere', 'das Eigenartige', *ebd.,* 59. Es sei darauf hingewiesen, dass alle diese Termini auf die Wurzel კუთ(ნ) zurückgehen. Abuladze gibt auch andere Bedeutungen des georgischen Terminus wie განსაზღვრული: 'das Bestimmte'; გამორჩევა: 'auswählen'; განკუთეთა: 'reißen', 'spalten' an, *ebd.,* 59 und 205. Eine verbreitete Entsprechung für das griechische λατρεία im Georgischen stellt msaxureba ('Dienst') dar, vgl. Hebr. 9,14:…λατρεύειν Θεῷ ζῶντι /…მსახურებაᲓ Წმრთისა ცხოვლისა - 'zum Dienste des lebendigen Gottes' (dt. Übersetzung: '… damit wir dem lebendigen Gott dienen').

[76] 'unverfälscht', 'gehörig', 'rechtmäßig', 'vollbürtig', Gemoll, *Griechisch-Deutsches Wörterbuch* (siehe oben, Anm. 74), 174; vgl. 'belonging to the race', i.e. 'lawfully begotten', 'legitimate', 'genuine', 'authentic', 'true', bzw. 'legitimately', 'truly', Lampe, *A Patristic Greek Lexicon* (siehe oben, Anm. 74), 316, 317. Etymologisch stammt der griechische Terminus vom γνητ-ιος - 'Verwandter', Gemoll, *Griechisch-Deutsches Wörterbuch* (siehe oben, Anm. 74), 174.

[77] γνησίως λατρεύοντες, E.O.D., in: CChr.SG 23, c. 201-202, S. 38/ საკუთარᲓ მკუთნვლნი, ლოცვისათჳ მამაᲬ ჩუენჱსა, in: K 14, 155 v.

[78] Siehe dazu Grethlein, *Religionspädagogik* (siehe oben, Anm. 74), 353.

georgischen Terminus კულნზა soll deshalb auch den allein Gott gebüh-
renden Dienst betonen. Andere, den Opferdienst zum Ausdruck brin-
gende Termini wie მიართუმენ für προσκομίζουσιν[79] und მეწირის
für προσάγων[80] bedeuten wörtlich 'darbringen' und 'opfern'.

Es ist interessant, dass die lateinische Übersetzung der obengenannten
Stelle zwei verschiedene Begriffe für (προσάγων) τὴν λατρείαν und
ὁμο-λάτρης bietet: cultum (adhibet) und (similis)... adorator.[81] Ein und
derselbe griechische Terminus wird ins Lateinische zum einen mit cultum, zum anderen mit adoratio, adorare übersetzt. Letztgenannter soll
die in allem den Engeln gleichende (per omnia similis angelis) mensch-
liche Anbetung Gottes hervorheben.

Ferner ist es von Bedeutung, dass dieser Opferdienst gemäß der logosbegabten Kraft vollzogen wird. Dem griechischen τὴν λογικὴν δύναμιν[82] entspricht im Georgischen სიტყუერითა ძალითა.[83] Das Adjektiv
სიტყუერი geht, ähnlich wie das griechische λογικὴν, aus dem Nomen
სიტყუაჲ, Logos, Wort hervor und will den logosbegabten Charakter
des Gebetsdienstes betonen.

Das Brot, um das in dieser geistigen und mit Logos ausgerüsteten
Opferdarbringung von Engeln und Menschen gebetet wird, ist unser täg-
liches Brot, τοῦ ἐφήμερου[84] (მდღევრისაცა)[85], das uns zur tagtäglichen
Einübung in Christi Tod gegeben wird[86] und uns zu Teilhabern macht an
Christi Leib und Blut sowie an seinem Tod und seiner Auferstehung. Es
ist unser wesentliches (ἐπιούσιος) Brot (არსობისაჲ, 'des Wesens',[87]
არსობითისაჲ,[88] 'wesentliches')[89], das uns als Brot der Erkenntnis und
Gnosis gegeben wird,[90] auf das wir erkennen, wie süß der Herr ist.[91] Es

---

[79] Siehe oben, Anm. 52.
[80] Siehe oben, Anm. 53.
[81] *E.O.D.*, in: PG 91, 895 AB. Siehe oben, Anm. 53.
[82] Vgl. sola rationis vi, *E.O.D.*, in: PG 91, 895 A.
[83] Siehe oben, Anm. 53.
[84] *E.O.D.*, in: CChr.SG 23, c. 592, S. 61.
[85] ლოცვისათჳს მამაჲ ჩუენისაჲ, in: K 14, 161v.
[86] *E.O.D.*, in: CChr.SG 23, c. 597-602, S. 61.
[87] ლოცვისათჳს მამაჲ ჩუენისაჲ, in: K 14, 155 r.
[88] *Ibid.*
[89] Diese zwei georgischen Entsprechungen für das griechische ἐπιούσιος stellen zwei
verschiedene Wortbildungen ein und desselben dar: Eine ist die Nomenform im Genetiv,
die andere ist eine Adjektivform. Die Nomenform im Genetiv wird bereits in den ältesten
georgischen Übersetzungen bezeugt, während die Adjektivbildung erst ab dem 11. Jh.
zu finden ist. Es ist bedeutend, dass in der hellenophilen Übersetzung des 12. Jh. beide
Formen, sowohl die ältere als auch die jüngere, enthalten sind.
[90] *E.O.D.*, in: CChr.SG 23, c. 686-687, S. 66.
[91] *E.O.D.*, in: CChr.SG 23, c. 131-132, S. 34 / ლოცვისათჳს მამაჲ ჩუენისაჲ, in:
K 14, 154 v.

ist das Brot der Ewigkeit (სამარადისო[92]), das uns die Erkenntnis des ewigen Lebens[93] in Christus bringt. Christus ist der Logos, der die von Engeln und Menschen gemeinsam vollzogene und allein Gott gebührende Opferdarbringung und Anbetung leitet. Deswegen heißt er auch καθ' ἀληθείαν ἐστὶ χορηγός[94] / ჭეშმარიტებით მომნიჭებელ– wörtlich: 'wahrhaftig schenkend', 'indem er wahrhaftig schenkt'. Die hier verwendete georgische Entsprechung მომნიჭებელ für das griechische χορηγός ist eine Partizipialbildung vom ნიჭი, 'Gabe' (δῶρον).[95] Christus ist somit derjenige, der uns die Gaben Gottes schenkt. An einer anderen Stelle entspricht demselben χορηγεῖν ein anderer, dem Sinn nach 'der Gabe' nahstehender Begriff მიმადლებასა, 'Gnade schenken' (მადლი, 'Gnade').

Christus ist der Logos, der uns über das rechte Wort und das alleine Gott gebührende Gebet belehrt. Deswegen ist er auch unser Lehrer des Betens.[96] Christus ist das Wort, das unser Gebet und unsere Anbetung mit dem Logos erfüllt. Christus ist das Brot des Lebens und der Erkenntnis,[97] das uns Anteil schenkt am ewigen Leben und uns das erkenntnisbringende Brot darreicht (ὥστε τῇ γεύσει ταύτης τῆς βρώσεως εἰδέναι κατ' ἐπίγνωσιν ἀληθῶς[98] / ვინაცა გემო ეგევითარისა ჭამადისა არს შემეცნებითო ცოდნაჲ ჭეშმარიტებითო.[99] Christus ist unser tägliches Brot, das sich uns als tagtägliche Speise in der Eucharistie schenkt und uns so zu Teilhabenden am göttlichen Leben macht (ζωῆς δὲ θείας ποιεῖται μετάδοσιν, ἐδώδιμον ἑαυτὸν ἐργαζόμενος[100] / საზრთოსა ცხორებისასა ჰყოფს გარდმოცემასა საზუაგე მყოფელი[101]).

---

[92] ლოცვისათჳს მამაო ჩუენოსა, in: K 14, 153 v.

[93] E.O.D., in: CChr.SG 23, c. 82, S. 31 / K 14, 153 v.

[94] E.O.D., in: CChr.SG 23, c. 69, S. 30.

[95] Siehe oben, Anm. 48.

[96] E.O.D., in: CChr.SG 23, c. 66-67, S. 30.

[97] სიცოცხლისა და ძალისა პურად მყოფიცა და სახელდებული, ლოცვისათჳს მამაო ჩუენოსა, in: K 14, 154v oder E.O.D., in: CChr.SG 23, c. 555, S. 59 oder E.O.D., in: CChr. SG 23, c. 567-568, S. 60.

[98] E.O.D., in: CChr. SG 23, c. 130-131, S. 34.

[99] ლოცვისათჳს მამაო ჩუენოსა, in: K 14, 154 v.

[100] E.O.D., in: CChr. SG 23, c. 128-129, S. 34.

[101] ლოცვისათჳს მამაო ჩუენოსა, in: K 14, 154 v.

THE GEORGIAN WITNESS TO THE JERUSALEM LITURGY: NEW SOURCES AND STUDIES

Stig Simeon R. FRØYSHOV[1]

Introduction: The Liturgy of Jerusalem

The scholarly interest of the liturgy of Jerusalem[2] resides in at least three points. First, the Hagiopolite liturgy was central among the various rites observed in the ancient Church, thanks to the spiritual and ecclesiastical status of the holy city of Christendom, endowed with innumerable sacred sites. Secondly, the rite of Jerusalem lies at the roots of the Byzantine rite, together with that of Constantinople, as one of the two constituents of the Early-Byzantine liturgical synthesis that is usually called the Byzantine rite.[3] Thirdly, preserved sources of the Hagiopolite rite are comparatively numerous. While for the rites of the two most important political centres of the Roman Empire, Rome and Constantinople, few sources are available before the 8th century, for the rite of Jerusalem we dispose of a great number of excellent sources from Late Antiquity. Indeed, it might seem that the essential part of all pre-Islamic (before 638) liturgical books of Jerusalem have been preserved, although only very little in Greek, their original language. Taft's 'Law of the paradox of the conservative periphery' applies here.[4] Notably the Caucasian

---

[1] I wish to express my thankfulness to Fr. Andrew Wade for his generous aid in correcting and improving the English of this essay.

[2] I distinguish between 'Hagiopolite' (from Greek ''Η Ἁγία Πόλις', 'the holy city'), which denotes the liturgy of the city of Jerusalem, and 'Palestinian', which embraces all liturgical traditions of the region. Palestinian liturgy thus constitutes a liturgical family, of which the best known branches are the Hagiopolite and Sabaite ones.

[3] For the study of the latter, one of the major liturgical traditions of Christendom, the Hagiopolite rite is of primary importance, since three of six elements of the Byzantine rite come from Jerusalem: the Psalter, the Horologion, and the hymnodic genres as well as the oldest layer of hymnody. Byzantine liturgy can be properly understood only in the light of both branches of its roots.

[4] 'Local churches of the periphery ... tend to hold on to older liturgical practices long after they have been abandoned by the Mother Church' (Robert Taft, 'Anton Baumstark's Comparative Liturgy Revisited', in *Comparative Liturgy Fifty Years after Anton Baumstark (1872-1948)*, eds. Robert Taft and Gabriele Winkler, Orientalia Christiana Analecta 265 (Rome, 2001), pp. 191-232, on p. 214.

periphery, that is, the Armenian and Georgian[5] churches, has contributed the most to preserving the late Antique liturgy of Jerusalem.[6] Of these two, the Georgian witness is by far the most important, since while the Armenian witness is more or less limited to an archaic version of the Lectionary,[7] the Georgian one appears to cover all the liturgical books of Jerusalem. For the Jerusalem liturgy of the 9th and 10th centuries, the situation is different, like for most other rites, as the Georgian and Armenian source material is supplemented by Greek, Syriac, Syro-Palestinian and Arabic manuscripts.

In spite of the richness of the sources, the ancient liturgy of Jerusalem is still rather poorly known. There exists to this date no extensive general study of it; indeed, no such study could have been adequately written since major documents of this rite remain unedited or even unknown. Furthermore, the amount of unedited and unexplored sources has significantly increased through the New Finds of Sinai (1975)[8] and it will no doubt take time for these to undergo scholarly investigation. Finally, the linguistic variety of the source material makes the Jerusalem liturgy a demanding field of research.

This essay will deal with the particular Georgian witness to the Jerusalem liturgy. The time period covered naturally extends from the 5th century, when the Georgian Church seems to have started practicing the liturgy of Jerusalem, as well as translating[9] its liturgical

---

[5] For transliteration of the Georgian alphabet I shall here be using the international standard ISO 9984 (see http://en.wikipedia.org/wiki/ISO_9984). Authorship spellings of publications will be retained.

[6] The Syriac and Syro-Palestinian material still needs to be fully exploited. An example of its interest: Walter Ray has indicated that there is evidence suggesting that a 7th century Syro-Palestinian palimpsest Lectionary (lower text of palimpsest: *Codex Climaci rescriptus*, ed. Agnes Smith Lewis (Cambridge, 1909)) is even more archaic than the earliest Armenian version. See Walter Ray, *August 15 and the Development of the Jerusalem Calendar*, unpublished doctoral thesis (Notre Dame, IN, 2000), pp. 15-16.

[7] Other Armenian liturgical books, like the hymnal and the Horologion, show clear signs of connection with Jerusalem tradition, but they are not direct versions of Greek Hagiopolite originals.

[8] The catalogues of new Sinai manuscripts have appeared for all collections: Arabic (1985), Slavonic (1988), Syriac fragments (1995), Greek (1998), Georgian (2005, see n. 27), and Syriac (2008). The liturgical material of the Greek catalogue (*Tà νέα εὑρήματα τοῦ Σινᾶ*, eds. Archbishop Damianos et al., (Athens, 1998)) has been analysed by the present author in Paul Géhin and Stig Frøyshov, 'Nouvelles découvertes sinaïtiques: A propos de la parution de l'inventaire des manuscrits grecs', *Revue des études byzantines* 58 (2000) 167-184, on pp. 175-181.

[9] The Georgian monastery founded by Peter the Iberian in Jerusalem near the Zion Church, around the middle of the 5th century, could have been a major site for this translation activity.

books,[10] until the 10th-11th centuries, when the Georgian Church gradually replaced its Hagiopolite liturgy with a Byzantine one,[11] received through Iviron, the Georgian monastery of Mount Athos. The period in question is thus also called 'pre-Athonite'. After a few preliminary points, I shall endeavor to give a *status quo* of new[12] sources and studies[13] of most of the first millennium Georgian liturgical books.[14] Then I shall devote a chapter to the Georgian witness to some monastic peripheries of Jerusalem liturgy and, in conclusion, I shall discuss the value of Georgian liturgical books as a witness to the Hagiopolite rite.

1. Preliminary Points

1.1. Various Georgian Rites of the First Millennium

Initially it is worth making clear two simple facts: first, ancient Georgian liturgical documents are first of all Georgian. They are written in the ancient Georgian language and they constitute the books and texts of the early Georgian rite. Secondly, the pre-Athonite Georgian rite stood

---

[10] For a short overview of these Georgian texts, editions and translations as of 1993, see Bernard Outtier, 'Langue et littérature géorgiennes', in *Christianismes orientaux: Introduction à l'étude des langues et littératures*, eds. M. Albert et al. (Paris, 1993), pp. 261-296, on pp. 280-281 ('Traductions liturgiques'). A more recent overview is to be found in Heinzgerd Brakmann, 'Die altkirchlichen Ordinationsgebete Jerusalems: Mit liturgiegeschichtlichen Beobachtungen zur christlichen Euchologie in Palästina, Syria, Iberia und im Sasanidenreich', *Jahrbuch für Antike und Christentum* 47 (2004 [2005]) 108-127, on pp. 109-111 ('Die Quellen').

[11] Georgian manuscripts represent an important source also for the Byzantinising process affecting local liturgical traditions, but this topic is not included here (however, see 'Epilogue' below).

[12] The term 'new' in the title of this paper is of course relative. The sources are not new to the libraries in which they have been kept for centuries, neither do 'new' sources need to have been found recently (but some have been, cf. the Sinai New Finds of 1975); 'new' here signifies primarily newness to liturgical scholarship.

[13] I extend warm thanks to Shota Gugushvili for his never failing assistance in obtaining Georgian publications.

[14] I shall not include the Psalter and the Homiliary. Concerning the latter, Stéphane Verhelst's translation and commentary of the Lenten Sunday homilies of John of Bolnisi is forthcoming in 'Sources chrétiennes'. Significantly, Verhelst arrives at a more documented dating of this author: beginning of the 9th century. It should also be mentioned, even though it concerns the Byzantine rite rather than the Hagiopolite one, that the most ancient Georgian witness to the Sabaite Typikon, that of the Šio-Mĝvime monastery in the vicinity of Tbilisi, has recently been edited by Ek'vt'ime Kočlamazašvili and Elguĵa Giunašvili: ტიპიკონი მომმღვიმის მონასტრის, XIII ს. ხელნაწერის ტექსტი [*Typikon of the Šio-Mĝvime monastery: Text of 13th century manuscript*] (Tbilisi, 2005).

close to the Hagiopolite rite. These two facts correlate with two objects of research, between which we must also distinguish: a) the Georgian material as witness to the *Georgian* rite; b) the Georgian material as witness to the *Hagiopolite* rite.[15] This essay is concerned with the latter. To a large extent these two realities of Georgian liturgy were of course intertwined. Further, in a complex way they relate to yet another distinction, according to which three liturgical traditions of Palestine may be identified, all of them translated into Georgian to a lesser or greater extent:[16]

a) ქართული, *k'art'uli*, 'Georgian', which designates the Georgian version of ancient Hagiopolite liturgy, translated from Greek.[17] The content of the manuscripts of this 'Georgian' rite seems to be datable mainly to the 5th-6th century, that is, to the Byzantine, pre-Islamic period.[18]

b) საბაწმიდური, *sabacmiduri*, 'Saint-Sabaite', the Sabaite rite;

c) იერუსალჱმელი, *ierusalēmeli*, 'Jerusalemite', the later Hagiopolite liturgy (whose beginning we may tentatively place in the 7th-8th century).[19]

---

[15] Charles Renoux provides us with a salutary example of this methodology in his translation of the Sunday oktoechos of the Ancient Iadgari, calling this hymnography 'Les hymnes de la Résurrection: Hymnographie liturgique géorgienne'. While in the title Renoux designates it according to its immediate content, in the commentary he shows that this hymnography goes back to Greek Jerusalem and witnesses to Hagiopolite tradition.

[16] In *History of Ancient Georgian Literature* (Tbilisi, 1980; 1st ed. 1923), p. 579, Kekelije made the same distinction on the basis of data found in the famous Georgian 'Mc'xet'a Psalter, Tbilisi NCM A-38, probably to be dated to 1016 (ფსალმუნის ძველი ქართული რედაქციები X-XIII საუკუნეთა ხელნაწერების მიხედვით. I. ტექსტი *[The ancient Georgian redactions of the Psalter according to manuscripts of the 10th-13th centuries. 1. Text]*, ed. Mzek'ala Šanije (Tbilisi, 1960), p. 476). German adaptation-translation in *Geschichte der kirchlichen georgischen Literatur, auf Grund des ersten Bandes der georgischen Literaturgeschichte von K. Kekelidze*, red. and trans. Michael Tarchnišvili (Vatican City, 1955), pp. 443-444.

[17] For an overview of Georgian translations from the Greek, see Bernard Outtier, 'Traductions du grec en géorgien', in *Übersetzung-Translation-Traduction: An International Encyclopedia of Translation Studies*, vol. 2 (Berlin and New York, 2007), pp. 1186-1189. Whether Georgian sources also contain texts translated from Syriac or Armenian, or from Greek via one of these languages, constitutes a disputed question — see below.

[18] Some indications: The Georgian Lectionary in its most common redaction is basically a 6th century document; the Ancient stage hymnal (Ancient Iadgari) predates the new hymnographers of the 7th-8th centuries; the Horologion contains Ancient stage hymnography; the Psalter (60 antiphones, 20 kathismata) is used in the Horologion (see below under each liturgical book).

[19] A fourth tradition known by Palestino-Georgian monks of the 10th century was the Byzantine (which I label the 'Early-Byzantine liturgical synthesis').

Each of these distinct traditions was seemingly governed by a particular liturgical rule, sometimes named in the titles of liturgical books.[20] The question of the relationship of the Georgian versions to the Greek Hagiopolite books may, naturally, be treated more easily in cases where these Greek books have been preserved, that is, rites b) and c) above.

1.2. General Studies

Shorter general studies of the Jerusalem rite are beginning to appear. In a significant entry of the *Pravoslavnaâ Ènciklopediâ* (Moscow), the Georgian philologist and expert on ancient Georgian liturgical manuscripts, Lili Xevsuriani, offered in 2007 a first substantial summary on pre-Athonite Georgian liturgical history, to some degree taking into consideration also the Sinai New Finds.[21] Stéphane Verhelst published in 2006 a general article on the pre-Islamic Jerusalem rite in which Georgian sources play a significant role.[22] In 2003 the liturgiologist Ek'vt'ime Kočlamazašvili produced a Georgian liturgical dictionary.[23] The recent *Encyclopedical Dictionary of the Georgian Orthodox Church*[24] has valuable entries on liturgical themes. Tinatin Chronz has

---

[20] It seems that such a rule was not identical with a particular liturgical book; it is true that the Georgian title of the Lectionary is კანონი, *kanoni*, which could suggest that its Greek 'Vorlage' was κανών. But a perhaps more probable Greek 'Vorlage' is κανονάριον (the latter is the title of later Lectionary-Typika, as Sin. Gr. 150). The Hagiopolite and Sabaite rules were named at least from the 9th century in Greek κανών, cf. the Tropologion Sin. NE MG 56-5 (see below) and the Horologion Sin. Gr. 863 (see below), both in the title purporting to follow the κανών of the liturgical centre in question.

[21] 'Грузинская Православная Церковь. Богослужение ГПЦ [Georgian Orthodox Church. Liturgy]', *Православная Энциклопедия [Orthodox Encyclopedia]*, vol. 13 (Moscow, 2006), pp. 234-242, 250-252 (bibliography). Xevsuriani covers the pre-Athonite period, Shota Gugushvili the following periods till today.

[22] 'The Liturgy of Jerusalem in the Byzantine Period', in *Christians and Christianity in the Holy Land: From the Origins to the Latin Kingdom*, eds. Ora Limor and Guy G. Stroumsa (Turnhout, 2006), pp. 421-462. In addition come one monograph and a series of articles on the Hagiopolite rite of the Byzantine period, several of which concern Georgian sources. Verhelst's bibliography is given at this online address: http://fr.wikipedia.org/wiki/Utilisateur:Scholasate. Verhelst has composed a number of relevant entries of the French Wikipedia (listed on the above site address), among which certain represent valuable overview articles on Jerusalem liturgy ('Rite de l'église de Jérusalem', 'Lieux de station de la liturgie de Jérusalem', 'Année liturgique du rite de Jérusalem').

[23] 'ლიტურგიკული ლექსიკონი (მასალები) [Liturgical Dictionary (materials)]', *საქართველოს საკლესიო კალენდარი [Georgian Church Calendar]* (Tbilisi, 2003), pp. 280-340. A second, revised and extended edition is in progress.

[24] Enriko Gabajašvili et al., *საქართველოს მართლმადიდებელი ეკლესიის ენციკლოპედიური ლექსიკონი [Encyclopedic Dictionary of [the] Georgian Orthodox Church]* (Tbilisi, 2007), 1016 pp.

published a survey of the editions made by Georgians of Georgian liturgical sources, including those of Hagiopolite tradition.[25]

1.3. Sources: Old and New Collections of Sinai

While Georgian sources of the Jerusalem rite do exist in Georgia
itself, and to some extent in Europe and the USA, their great majority is
to be found at St. Catherine's Monastery on the Holy Mount Sinai,
whose library for this reason is of paramount importance for our topic.[26]
The ancient collection counts today 86 codices. It was photographed in
its entirety in 1950 by an expedition initiated by the American Library
of Congress.

A significant number of Georgian manuscripts were found among the
fragments discovered at Mt. Sinai in 1975, and the long-awaited catalogue of the New Georgian Finds of Sinai appeared in 2005.[27] Unlike the
three volume catalogue of the liturgical manuscripts of the old collection,
which was published only in Georgian, it is trilingual, adding Greek and
English translations to the original Georgian.[28] In addition to presenting
the entities of the New Finds, the catalogue in an informative introduction[29] provides an overview of both the study of the old collection and

---

[25] 'Editionen georgischer liturgischer Texte', in *Bibel, Liturgie und Frömmigkeit in
der Slavia Byzantina: Festgabe für Hans Rothe zum 80. Geburtstag*, eds. Dagmar Christians, Dieter Stern and Vittorio S. Tomelleri (Munich and Berlin, 2009), pp. 177-193.
This essay describes a significant part of the source material and edition history of the
Georgian manuscripts relevant for the present work. It also offers a helpful list of catalogues of Georgian manuscripts.

[26] On the Georgian manuscripts of Mt. Sinai, see Gérard Garitte, 'Les manuscrits
géorgiens du Sinaï', *La Nouvelle Clio* VII-VIII-IX (1955-56-57) 105-111 (old collection
only); the Introduction to the catalogue of the New Georgian Finds (below, n. 27).

[27] Zaza Aleksidze et al., *Catalogue of Georgian manuscripts discovered in 1975 at
St. Catherine's Monastery on Mount Sinai*, English tr. by Mzekala Shanidze (Athens,
2005).

[28] The accuracy of the Greek and English translations needs, however, to be reconsidered, as is clear from the following example. The Sin. N.58 has one section from the
Euchologion containing the burial rite. The English says that 'the rite follows the St. Sabas
ordination' (*ibid.*, p. 418), while the Greek, 'ἡ παροῦσα ἀκολουθία εἶναι τῆς
παραδόσεως τῆς Μονῆς τοῦ Ἁγίου Σάββα' ('the present office is of the tradition of
the monastery of St. Sabas'). These two phrases both translate the Georgian 'es gangeba
sabawmiduria', which literally means 'this rite is Saint-Sabaite'. The Greek translation is
here too approximate, while in the English translation the term 'ordination' is misleading,
signifying in a liturgical context ordination to holy orders.

[29] *Ibid.*, pp. 357-372. An article published a few years earlier has much of the same
scope as this introduction, while being less extensive: Mzekala Shanidze, 'Georgian
Manuscripts at St. Catherine's Monastery on Mt. Sinai', *The Kartvelologist* 9 (2002)
22-29.

the preparations for the new catalogue. The description of the manuscripts, however, is not nearly as detailed as that of the three volume catalogue of the liturgical manuscripts of the old collection, therefore representing rather an extended inventory. While the former provides a full description of content and constitutes a wonderful tool of research, the new catalogue specifies very little of the content of manuscripts.[30]

The new Georgian collection counts 142 entities, divided in three groups: 99 entities on parchment, 33 on paper, and ten scrolls (parchment and paper, all of liturgical content). This number is higher than that of the old collection (today 86), but it consists mostly of fragments. Only 17 codices count more than 100 folios, and its sheer quantity of folio is far less voluminous: little more than 4,000 folios versus about 18,000 folios.[31] Several fragments of the new collection belong to manuscripts of the old.[32] The Georgian New Finds of Sinai yield significant additional material to most Hagiopolite liturgical books; in the case of the Liturgy of St. James, their importance is capital.

2. Liturgical books of Jerusalem

2.1. Ancient Iadgari

Sources

Hymnographical creativity persisted in the Jerusalem liturgy throughout the first millennium,[33] so from one point of view it is correct to speak of a continuum of hymn writing. The Georgian version of the

---

[30] This may have to do with the fact that the writing of the new catalogue was based not on manuscript copies but on notes taken during four stays at the monastery from 1990 to 2002. See Alexidze et al., *Catalogue* (see n. 27), p. 371.

[31] In addition, the catalogue informs that the New Finds include no less than 1800 Georgian fragments which have not yet been examined. See Aleksidze et al., *Catalogue* (see n. 27), p. 362.

[32] In the case of hymnographical mss the following identifications have been made. *Ancient Iadgari*: N.29, 8 fol. (a KaO Heirmologion, fragment of O.40); N.36, 8 fol. + N.74, 7 fol. (of O.41). *New Iadgari*: N.2, 21 fol. (of O.65), N.5, 42 fol. (of O.59), N.73, 4 fol. (of O.1), N.95, 8 fol. (of O.64), N.97, 8 fol. (of O.49). The abbreviations KaO (Kanon Ordnung) and OdO (Oden Ordnung) are conventional designations of two types of Heirmologia. See *Die ältesten novgoroder Hirmologion-Fragmente*, ed. Koschmieder (Munich, 1952-1958).

[33] The existence of layers in the Ancient Iadgari is probably a sign of this. In that case the boundary between the Ancient and the New Iadgari should perhaps not be considered an absolute one.

hymnal of Jerusalem, called '*Iadgari*', is nevertheless known in two quite different stages: ancient and new. This distinction was drawn already by contemporaries, for instance Iovane Zosime[34] in explicatory notes to the 10th century Sin. Georgian O.34. The Ancient Iadgari was first published in a partial Russian translation in 1908[35] from a single manuscript, the codex Tbilisi National Center of Manuscripts (NCM) H-2123, then in its entirety in the original Georgian in 1977 on the basis of the same manuscript,[36] and finally in a critical edition in 1980 on the basis of seven witnesses, of which the same Tbilisi NCM H-2123 serves as primary witness.[37] The Sinai New Finds furnish one large and four smaller new fragments of the Ancient Iadgari.[38] This amounts to no sensation, but the new fragments add some new texts as well as new witnesses and variants to already edited material. The large fragment, Sin. N.56, copied by Iovane Zosime, has significance for the history of hymn books: according to the catalogue, it clearly seems to have been composed as a hymnal for the Paschal season ('Triodion') only, and not as a universal hymnal. Consequently it is the only preserved example of a splitting up of the universal Ancient hymnal.

Ancient stage hymnography is known in the form of a complete hymnal only in its Georgian translation. However, the Greek models of a certain percentage (more than a stipulated 5%)[39] of the Ancient Iadgari

---

[34] This Georgian monk worked in Palestine from about the middle of the 10th century until he died some time after 988. He stayed first at the Great Lavra of St. Sabas, then from the early 970s at the monastery of the Burning bush at Mt. Sinai. He was a great erudite of the period, heavily involved in copying, binding and annotating manuscripts. Liturgy was one of his great interests and his many and often long manuscript notes provide invaluable information on Palestinian liturgy.

[35] Korneli Kekelije, *Литургические грузинские памятники в отечественных книгохранилищах и их научное значение [Liturgical Georgian monuments in native libraries and their scientific significance]* (Tbilisi, 1908), pp. 351-372.

[36] A French translation of this manuscript is in progress by Renoux; the first volume has appeared (see n. 42).

[37] უძველესი იადგარი *[The most ancient Iadgari]*, eds. E. Metreveli, C'. Čankievi and L. Xevsurinai (Tbilisi, 1980). The codices used for the 1980 edition were the following (in the order of their importance): Tbilisi NCM H-2123, Sin. O.18, Sin. O.40, Sin. O.41, Sin. O. 34, Sin. O.26, Sin. O.20. The French summary of the commentary (pp. 930-939) was also published as E. Metreveli, C'. Čankievi and L. Xevsurinai, 'Le plus ancien tropologion géorgien', *Bedi Kartlisa* 39 (1981) 54-62.

[38] Sin. N.56 (103 fol., Paschal cycle only), Sin. N.38 (6 fol.) and 96 (1 fol.) (both Sunday Oktoechos), N.29 (8 fol., fragm of Sin. 40), N.36 (8 fol.) and N.74 (7 fol., the two latter being fragments of Sin. 41).

[39] Metreveli et al. 'Le plus ancien tropologion géorgien' (see n. 37), p. 58. In addition to the estimated 5%, Renoux is continuously identifying further Greek models in his translation in progress of the hymnal.

have been identified within the preserved Greek hymnographical corpus.[40] This has two implications: First, that a certain amount of Ancient stage hymnography was retained into the New stage and, second, that we know a small part of the Ancient *Greek* hymnal of Jerusalem.

Translations of the Ancient Iadgari into Western languages are beginning to appear. Charles Renoux has published a French translation of the Sunday Oktoechos hymnography according to Sin. Georgian O.18,[41] a great part of the movable (Paschal) annual cycle of Tbilisi NCM H-2123, and more is in preparation.[42] Hans-Michael Schneider has published a German translation of the Ancient Iadgari feasts of the incarnation[43] and other partial translations have appeared.[44]

Studies

Western and Georgian studies of the Ancient Iadgari

With both the critical edition and translations at hand there now exists an enormous material allowing for scientific scrutiny and increased

---

[40] About the Greek 'Textvorlage', see Hans-Michael Schneider, *Lobpreis im rechten Glauben: Die Theologie der Hymnen an den Festen der Menschwerdung der alten Jerusalemer Liturgie im Georgischen Udzvelesi Iadgari* (Bonn, 2004), pp. 21-32. Some of the best known hymns are the following (present Byzantine use in parenthesis): The Cherubic Hymn; 'Let all mortal flesh keep silent' (Liturgy of St. James); 'At your mystical supper' (Liturgy of Great Thursday); 'Now the powers of heaven' (Liturgy of Presanctified Gifts); 'Only-Begotten Son and Word of God' ('Ο Μονογενής), of the Divine Liturgy, traditionally attributed to Emperor Justinian); 'We have seen the true light' (Office of Pentecost and Liturgy of St. John Chrysostom); 'Receive our evening prayers, O Holy Lord' (Vespers, 'Lord, I have cried', mode 1); 12 troparia of Great Friday, now to be found as stichera idiomela in the four hours of the same day; 'Christ is risen from the tomb' (Paschal troparion); 'Your resurrection, Christ Saviour' (beginning of the Paschal vigil). But note that if a hymn figures in the Ancient Iadgari it does not necessarily mean that it is of Hagiopolite origin; it could be a loan from elsewhere. For instance, the 'Ο Μονογενής could be a loan from Constantinople.

[41] Charles Renoux, *Les hymnes de la résurrection. 1. Hymnographie liturgique géorgienne: Introduction, traduction et annotation des textes du Sinaï 18* (Paris, 2000). According to Renoux, *L'Hymnaire de Saint-Sabas* (see n. 42), n. 17, two more volumes will follow: vol. II for Sin. O.40 and O.41; vol. III for Sin O.34, O.20 and O.26.

[42] Charles Renoux, *L'Hymnaire de Saint-Sabas (Ve-VIIIe siècle): Le manuscrit géorgien H 2123. I. Du samedi de Lazare à la Pentecôte*, Patrologia Orientalis, 50:3 (Turnhout, 2008). This volume is numbered as the first; more volumes, consecrated to the rest of the hymnal, will follow.

[43] Schneider, *Lobpreis* (see n. 40). The feasts in question are: Annunciation, Nativity, Epiphany with octave, and Meeting of the Lord. See review article: Gabriele Winkler, 'Eine neue Publikation zum Iadgari', *Orientalia Christiana Periodica* 72 (2007) 195-200.

[44] Italian translation of the Ancient Iadgari feast of the Elevation of the Cross: Gaga Shurgaia, 'L'esaltazione della croce nello Iadgari antico', in *L'Onagro Maestro. FS Gianroberto Scarcia*, eds. Rudy Favaro et al. (Venice, 2004), pp. 137-188.

knowledge and understanding of the development of Hagiopolite hymnody and hymn books. After Andrew Wade's survey article of 1984,[45] from the 1990s onwards Western studies have begun to multiply, especially from the hand of Renoux.[46] A major drawback for most students of pre-Athonite Georgian liturgy is however that the 250 (large) pages commentary, composed by the editors, accompanying the text edition of the Ancient Iadgari are accessible only in modern Georgian. Even less known in the West, but accessible to more readers since it was written in Russian, is the 1984 unpublished doctoral thesis of Lili Xevsuriani, *The Structure of the Most Ancient Tropologion*.[47] Research on the Ancient Iadgari must imperatively take into account these works by scholars whose mother tongue is close to the sources and who know better than anyone else the manuscripts in question.[48]

[45] Andrew Wade, 'The Oldest *Iadgari*: The Jerusalem Tropologion, V-VIII c.', *Orientalia Christiana Periodica* 50 (1984) 451-456.

[46] Peter Jeffery, 'The Sunday Office of Seventh-Century Jerusalem in the Georgian Chantbook (Iadgari): A Preliminary Report', *Studia Liturgica* 21 (1991) 52-75; *id.*, 'The Earliest Christian Chant Repertory Recovered: The Georgian Witness to Jerusalem Chant', *Journal of the American Musicological Society* 47 (1994) 1-38; Charles Renoux, 'Le *iadgari* géorgien et le *šaraknoc'* arménien', *Revue des Études Arméniennes* 24 (1993) 89-112; *id.* 'Une hymnographie ancienne en géorgien conservée en géorgien', in *L'Hymnographie: Conférences Saint-Serge, XLVIᵉ Semaine d'Etudes Liturgiques* (Rome, 2000), pp. 137-151; *id.*, 'Les hymnes du Iadgari pour la fête de l'apparation de la croix le 7 mai', *Studi sull'Oriente Cristiano* 4 (2000) 93-102; *id.*, 'L'Hymne des saints dons dans l'octoéchos géorgien ancien', in Θυσία αἰνέσως, Mélanges George Wagner, eds. Job Getcha and André Lossky, Analecta Sergiana 2 (Paris, 2005), pp. 293-313; *id.*, 'Hymnographie géorgienne ancienne et hymnaire de Saint-Sabas (Ve-VIIIe siècle)', *Irénikon* 80 (2007) 36-69; Gaga Shurgaia, 'Formazione della struttura dell'ufficio del sabato di Lazzaro nella tradizione cattedrale di Gerusalemme', *Annali di Ca' Foscari: Serie orientale* 36 (1997) 147-168; *id.*, 'La struttura della liturgia delle ore del mattino della domenica delle palme nella tradizione di Gerusalemme', *Studi sull'Oriente christiano*, 1 (1997) 1-2, pp. 79-107; Stig Simeon R. Frøyshov, 'The Early Development of the Eight Mode Liturgical System in Jerusalem', *St. Vladimir's Theological Quarterly* 51 (2007) 139-178. A lengthy entry on the hymnody of Jerusalem, including the material of the Ancient Iadgari, has been prepared by this author for *Canterbury Dictionary of Hymnology* (forthcoming).

[47] Структура древнейшего Тропология [*The Structure of the Most Ancient Tropologion*], Academy of Science, Georgian SSR (Tbilisi, 1984), 181 pp. See also summary with identical title, also in Russian (*Avtoreferat* (Tbilisi, 1985) 28 pp.). Xevsuriani's latest contribution is found in the paragraphs on the two Iadgaris in her part of the entry 'Liturgy' (see n. 21), pp. 240-242.

[48] See also the chapter 'The Palestinian and Sinaitic hymnographic school' (in Georgian), in Nestan Sulava, ქართული ჰიმნოგრაფია: ტრადიცია და პოეტიკა [*Georgian Hymnography: Tradition and Poetics*] (Tbilisi, 2006), pp. 12-38.

Development of the Ancient Iadgari; Hymn Attributions

The historical development of the content of the two Iadgaris, and their relationship to their Greek 'Vorlage', is under scholarly debate. The earliest parts of the Ancient stage are thought to go back at least to the 4th century.[49] The presence in the New stage hymnography of trustworthy attributions to patriarch St. Sophronios (died 638)[50] and Sts. John of Damascus and Kosmas the Melodist indicates that the shift between the two stages took place around 600. Now, it is a fact that several stanzas attributed to New stage melodists figure already in the Georgian version of the Ancient Iadgari. The editors of Ancient Iadgari, followed by Schneider,[51] interpret this as if these stanzas were translated and added to the Georgian version of the Ancient hymnal, at a time preceding the Georgian translation of the whole New hymnal (Tropologion).[52] The prerequisite for this interpretation is the belief that the melodist attributions in question signify authorship.[53] However, ascriptions to hymn composers are in part notoriously untrustworthy, and here these melodists' authorship of the stanzas seems improbable. Another interpretation, perhaps more plausible, is the following: New stage melodists, in addition to writing new hymnography, employed some Old stage stanzas, possibly adorning them with a new melody, and incorporated them

---

[49] Cf. Renoux, *Les hymnes de la résurrection*' (see n. 41), pp. 49-57; *id.*, *L'Hymnaire de Saint-Sabas* (see n. 42), p. 353, n. 3.

[50] See my entry on this hymnographer in the *Canterbury Dictionary of Hymnology* (forthcoming).

[51] Schneider misunderstands the historical origin of the Ancient Iadgari, including the relationship between Ancient Iadgari manuscripts and the New Iadgari. In his work *Lobpreis* (see n. 40), p. 11 he believes that the witnesses Sin. O.18, O.40, O.41 and O.34, used for the Ancient Iadgari edition, belong to the 'zweite Version des Iadgari ... Diese Version wurde im Kloster des heiligen Sabas erstellt im Laufe des siebten und achten Jahrhunderts'. It is correct that these mss contribute to 'ursprünglichen vollständigen Form wiederherstellen' of the Ancient Iadgari, but this reconstitution does not involve the New Iadgari ('zweite Version') at all.

[52] 'En conséquence, dans la seconde couche poétique du Tropologion, à côté des tropaires poétiques anciens, on employait des traductions de stichères de mélodes byzantins célèbres' (Métrévéli et al., 'Le plus ancien tropologion géorgien' (see n. 37), p. 58. There does exist, however, a case which probably should be interpreted as a real example of such an inclusion: unlike the other edited Ancient Iadgari witnesses (Tbilisi NCM H-2123 and Sin. O.40), Sin. O.18 has as its Easter Canon that of St. John of Damascus ('This is the day of resurrection').

[53] Xevsuriani, 'Liturgy' (see n. 21), p. 241, col. B: 'В древнем Иадгари отражено развитие греческой гимнографии доиконоборческого времени: с образцов IV-V вв и до нач. VIII в. (In the Ancient Iadgari is reflected the development of Greek hymnography of the pre-iconoclastic period: with models of the 4th-5th cent. to beginning of 8th cent.).'

into a new corpus of hymnography. In this way they produced a mixed (old-new) hymnography, and the re-used ancient hymns became attached and ascribed to the melodist.[54]

2.2. New Iadgari

Sources

The Greek New Finds of Mt. Sinai include some Tropologia, including the spectacular fragments Sin. Greek NE MG 56 and 5, no doubt to be identified as one Tropologion[55] and dated to the 8th-9th century. The latter, and possibly other new fragments, represent redactions of the Greek annual hymnal of the Church of Jerusalem.[56] The Georgian version of the New Tropologion, the 'New Iadgari', is still inedited,[57] except for a few elements.[58] The source material of the New Iadgari is more extensive than that of the Ancient Iadgari, and it includes codices produced in Georgia, in addition to those of the old and new Sinai collections.[59] The significance of the Sinai New Finds for the New Iadgari

---

[54] The transfer from the Ancient to the New Iadgari is a rich subject. To take just one element of such a transfer: The Ancient Iadgari stanza at the washing of hands at the Eucharistic liturgy of Pascha (translation: Renoux, *L'Hymnaire de Saint-Sabas* (see n. 42), pp. 170,10-171,5) and also of the Oktoechos, mode 3 plagal (*ibid.*, pp. 121-122), became in the Byzantine rite the fourth Anastasimon sticheron at Lauds of the Sunday Orthros, also in mode 3 plagal (cf. *ibid.*, p. 170, n. 3).

[55] After having examined the two fragments, Sin. NE MG 56 and 5, in person at Sinai, I am still convinced of my initial identification of them on the basis of the data given by the catalogue, presented in Géhin and Frøyshov, 'Nouvelles découvertes sinaïtiques' (see n. 8), p. 179.

[56] For some information on the content of Greek Tropologia and related books of the Greek New Finds, see Roman N. Krivko, 'Синайско-славянские гимнографические параллели [Sinaitic-Slavonic Hymnographical Parallels]', *Вестник Православного Свято-Тихоновского гуманитарного университета [Messenger of St. Tikhon's University of Humanities]*, III: филология [Philology], 1(11) (2008) 56-102. The author treats of Sin. Gr. NE MG 4, 5, 15, 20, 24, 28, 37, 56, 80 and 84, which he has studied in person at Sinai.

[57] A criticial edition of the New Iadgari is said to be ready for publication in Tbilisi but has been delayed.

[58] Editions with translations of parts of the New Iadgari: Jean-Pierre Mahé, 'La fête de Melkisédec le huit août en Palestine d'après les *tropologia* et les ménées géorgiens,' *Revue des études géorgiennes et caucasiennes* 3 (1987) 83-125; Michel van Esbroeck, 'Ein georgischer liturgischer Kanon für Mariä Himmelfahrt', in *Lingua restituta orientalis: Festgabe für Julius Assfalg*, eds. Regine Schulz and Manfred Görg, (Wiesbaden, 1990), pp. 89-101.

[59] Overview of sources: *Old Sinai collection*: O.1, O.14, O.26, O.34, O.49, O.59, O.64-65. *New Sinai collection*: N.19 (61 fol., 980), N.34 (4 fol., part of OdO Heirmologion), N.39 (23 fol.), N.46 (8 fol.), N.64 (60 fol., OdO Heirmologion), N.69 (51 fol., Heirmologion), N.87 (8 fol.), the two scrolls Sin. N.2s and N.3s (both including

shows two similarities with the case of the Ancient Iadgari: first, while the three Heirmologion fragments may be important ones, the Sinai New Finds do not seem to provide substantially new material; secondly, as regards book history, a new example of segregation from the universal Iadgari is found: two 10th century Heirmologia of the New Finds seem to have been composed uniquely as such, separate from the Iadgari of which they otherwise constitute the first element.[60] It is also worth noticing the colophon by Iovane Zosime in Sin. N.19 (980), in which he explains that a new Oktoechos has recently been translated into Georgian at Cyprus, thereafter brought to Palestine and then included in New Iadgari collections.[61]

The Georgian Lectionary normally prescribes hymns of the Ancient Iadgari, but there is an example of a Lectionary incorporating in addition some New stage hymns.[62] In any case, it is clear that during the 10th century, Palestino-Georgian monks were increasingly occupied with the New Iadgari material. One fact indicating this is that Iovane Zosime, the key scribe and scholar of the second half of the 10th century, copied only New Iadgaris.[63]

---

hymnography of Kosmas). *Georgia*: Tbilisi NCM S-425 (Iadgari of Mik'ael Modrekili), Tbilisi NCM A-1562, Tbilisi NCM A-190 (fragment, 10 fol.), three Iadgaris of the Svanetian collection (Iadgaris of Ts'virmi, Ieli and Erušeni). The list of New Iadgari witnesses given by Xevsuriani in her *Orthodox Encyclopedia* article (see n. 21), p. 242, is erroneous, since it includes six Ancient Iadgari fragments (29, 36, 37, 38, 74, 96) and one liturgical collection (54).

[60] Sin. N.64 and N.69. For some details on these mss, see n. 59. With a similar move in another manuscript, Zosime also separated the Triodion from the Ancient Iadgari (Sin. N.56).

[61] This Oktoechos is also known from the old collection (Sin. O.26 and O.34). This Cypriote text is of evident interest for the question of Cyprus as a liturgical periphery of Jerusalem.

[62] The Lectionary Sin. O.37, copied in 982 by Iovane Zosime, includes the New hymnography of the Great Friday vigil (starting on Thursday night) as *sxuani*, 'others', having eleven stanzas instead of the former seven. See Sebastià Janeras, *Le vendredi-saint dans la tradition liturgique byzantine* (Rome, 1988), pp. 103-107. The text is edited by T'arxnišvili (see n. 100): GL, App. I, n° 99-157, with German translation in Helmut Leeb, *Die Gesänge im Gemeindegottesdienst von Jerusalem (vom 5. bis 8. Jahrhundert)* (Vienna, 1970), pp. 248-250. The Janeras hypothesis of a Sabaite origin of this hymnography (*ibid.*, p. 107) is contradicted by two rubrics: 'Others of the Agrypnia, Jerusalemite, eleven: you will find them after those of this [old] Agrypnia' (GL, App I, n° 59); 'Other, new eleven dasadebelni of the Agrypnia. Of the Agrypnia of Great Thursday, other in the Jerusalemite manner' (GL, App I, n° 99-100). These eleven stanzas therefore clearly are of the New Tropologion of Jerusalem.

[63] Sin. O.34, O.26, N.19 (Oktoechos), N.39, N.69 (Iadgari, KaO Heirmologion), N.87. The Sin. O.34, a 'Sabaite encyclopedia of the daily office' (see below), places the New Horologion and the New Iadgari before the old ones, and presents the Ancient Iadgari mostly by incipits.

Studies

So far Georgian scholars have done most of the investigation work on the New Iadgari. Profound studies on the New Iadgari were made half a century ago by Pavle Ingoroqva.[64] More recently, Lela Xač'ije has compared four Georgian translations of the Easter canon of St. John of Damascus, two of which belong to the New stage hymnography.[65] Recent studies include those of Eka Dugašvili[66] and Tinatin Chronz.[67] On the basis of Ingoroqva's achievements, Lili Xevsuriani has worked out an hypothesis on the historical formation of the Georgian version of New Tropologion:[68]

a) Approximately in the second half of the 9th c.: short constitution (Sin. O.34, O.26)

b) First half of the 10th c.: quite extensive form (Sin. O.1, O.14, Cvirmi Iadgari)

c) 950-960s: Great Lent is added (Sin. O.59, O. 64)

d) 970s: continued expansion (Sin. O. 49, O.59, N.39)

e) By 980: final form of full redaction of New Iadgari (Sin. O.64-65).[69]

This hypothesis certainly expresses an important aspect, that is, the ongoing translation process and its reflection in the production of new codices. But objections to such a synthetic view of the New Iadgari development may be raised, and will be set forth below.[70]

---

[64] Pavle Ingoroqva, გიორგი მერჩულე. ქართული მწერალი მეათე საუკუნისა [*Giorgi Merč'ule. Georgian author of the 10th century*] (Tbilisi, 1954); id., თხზულებათა კრებული, ტომი III (Complete works, t. III) (Tbilisi, 1965).

[65] Lela Xač'ije, 'წმ. იოანე დამასკელი "აღდგომის კანონის" ძველი ქართული თარგმანები [Ancient Georgian translations of St. John of Damascus' "Easter Canon"]', საღვთისმეტყველო-სამეცნიერო შრომები [*Scientific-Theological Works*] I (Tbilisi, 1999), pp. 31-45. As said in n. 52, one of the two early (pre-Athonite) translations figures in an Ancient Iadgari manuscript, but this obviously is the result of a Georgian redactor.

[66] Eka Dugašvili, student of E. Metreveli and L. Xevsuriani, wrote a doctoral thesis entitled *The Ancient Georgian translations of Kosmas of Jerusalem's hymnography (according to the 10th century Iadgari)* (in Georgian) (Tbilisi, 2001), in which she examines and compares various ancient Georgian translations of Kosmas.

[67] Tinatin Chronz, 'Das griechische Tropologion-Fragment aus dem Kastellion-Kloster und seine georgischen Parallelen', *Oriens Christianus* 92 (2008) 113-118.

[68] Xevsuriani, 'Liturgy' (see n. 21), p. 242, col. C.

[69] This ms, divided in two parts, dates from after 987, but its redaction was finished by 980. It needs to be explained how Sin. O.64 supposedly belongs to two different stages (c and e) at the same time.

[70] See below, 'Longer and shorter versions'.

2.3. Euchologion (კურთხევანი, *kurt'xevani*, 'Blessings')

Sources

In his well-known survey 'Les grandes étapes de la liturgie byzantine' Miguel Arranz stated: 'Nous ne connaissons pas l'Euchologe de Jérusalem de cette époque [pre-Byzantinising]. Il a dû exister un livre...'[71]. In fact, in 1975 we knew more than nothing about the Jerusalem Euchologion;[72] already in 1912 Kekelije had published what he labelled 'Ancient Georgian Archieratikon',[73] the pontifical Euchologion Tbilisi NCM A-86, containing the Liturgy of St. James and a series of ordinations. Soon after, this edition was published in an English translation by Conybeare and Wardrop.[74] Some years later, Kekelije in his monumental *History of Georgian Literature* wrote a paragraph on the ancient Georgian Euchologion, basing himself on earlier Georgian descriptions of Georgian manuscripts of Sinai.[75] He classified this Euchologion as belonging to an 'orientalische Typus'; what he was describing was the Hagiopolite Euchologion.

There exist Greek[76] and Syro-Palestinian[77] texts belonging to the Jerusalem Euchological corpus, but it is first of all the Georgian tradition that provides us with sources. These are for the most part preserved at Mount Sinai: Sin. O.12, O.54, O.66, N.26, N.53, and N.58.[78] All of these codices constitute what are usually labelled 'liturgical collections' or 'liturgical manuals', a type of liturgical book which, according to Xevsuriani and Šanije, most likely belongs to a Palestinian monastic

---

[71] Miguel Arranz, 'Les grandes étapes de la liturgie byzantine: Palestine-Byzance-Russie. Essai d'aperçu historique', in *Liturgie de l'église particulière et liturgie de l'église universelle*, Conférences Saint-Serge 1975 (Rome, 1976), pp. 43-72, on p. 49.

[72] The term εὐχολόγιον documented in the codex Jerusalem Holy Sepulchre 113 (fol. 212v), a late (1672) copy of the lacunary 9th c. Asketikon Athos Karakallou 251 (lacking this part).

[73] Korneli Kekelije, *Древнегрузинскій архіератиконъ* (Tbilisi, 1912), with an introduction in Russian, pp. I-XXX.

[74] Frederick C. Conybeare and Oliver Wardrop, 'The Georgian Version of the Liturgy of St. James', *Revue de l'Orient chrétien* 18 (1913) 396-410; 19 (1914) 155-173.

[75] Kekelije, *History of Ancient Georgian Literature* (see n. 16), p. 584; adaptation-translation in Tarchnišvili, *Geschichte* (see n. 16), p. 447.

[76] One of the New Greek Finds, the Sin. NE MG 53, may represent a redaction of the Jerusalem Euchologion, but only an edition and a full study of its text will confirm this. In addition, later Greek Euchologia contain many individual Hagiopolite prayers.

[77] London BL Or. 4951 (the so-called 'Rituale Melchitarum'); see study of this in Brakmann, 'Ordinationsgebete' (see n. 10; Brakmann erroneously indicates it as 4941).

[78] The only non-Sinaitic manuscript is the above mentioned Tbilisi NCM A-86, edited by Kekelije.

milieu.[79] In spite of flexibility in content, the first five of the above codices have the following common structure: a) a Euchologion section, consisting of Divine Liturgies (St. James, Presanctified Gifts of St. James),[80] litanies, dismissal prayers, sacraments and other prayers; b) a Lectionary section (see table 1).

Table 1: Comparative Table of the Content of Various Palestino-Georgian Liturgical Collections

Manuscript	Euchologion					Lectionary
	JAS (short or long version)	PRES-JAS	Litanies	Dismissal prayers	Sacraments and prayers	
Sin. O.12, 10c, 301 fol.	+ (short)	+	+	+	+	+
Sin. O.54+N.33, 9-10c, 184 + 2 fol.	+ (long)	+	+	+	+	+
Sin. O.66 + Mingana 1, 10c, 133 + 1 fol.	÷	+	÷	÷	+	+
Sin. N.26, 9-10c, 213 fol.	+ (long)	+	+	+	÷	+
Sin. N.53, 10c, 227 fol.	+ (short)	+	+	Diaconal diptychs	+	Lacuna
Sin. N.58, 9-10c, 98 fol.	+ (short)	Lectionary	Calendar	÷	+ (Sabaite Burial)	+ (Matins Gospel)
Sin. N.54, 10c, 129 fol.	+ (long) BAS, CHR	÷	÷	÷	÷	+ (Hagiopolite)
Sin. N.22, 10c, 79 fol.	+ (short)	÷	÷	÷	÷	+

Compared to the common structure, Sin. N.58 has a different make-up while Sin. N.54 and N.22 lack the Euchologion section with the exception of JAS.

---

[79] Eds. Khevsuriani et al., *Liturgia*, 'Introduction', pp. 11-37 (see n. 81).

[80] Except Sin. O.66 which, despite lacking its beginning, clearly never had any Liturgy at the beginning.

Edition of the Liturgy of St. James

Existing editions of the Georgian version of the Liturgy of St. James has now been replaced by a new critical edition[81] based on all known witnesses, including those of the Sinai New Finds.[82] The latter implies a huge expansion (thirteen witnesses) of source material, and one of the New Finds witnesses, the Sin. N.58, serves as main text of the new edition. This makes the St. James manuscripts the most important liturgical contribution of the Georgian New Finds of Sinai. There exist shorter and longer version of the Georgian St. James; according to the Georgian editors, the shorter is the more original and, further, the process of supplementing the shorter version may be seen as following two different lines.

Edition of Other Sacraments and Prayers

The two most important and complete sources of the non-Eucharistic part of the ancient Georgian Euchologion are the 10th-century codices Sin. O.12 and Sin. N.53. The latter is the longest (227 fol.) but is defective according to the catalogue, the lower half of the page being more or less illegible. The Sin. N.58 contains a burial rite following the Sabaite rite.[83] A full edition of the non-Eucharistic Jerusalem Euchologion material, as well as a study retracing both its roots and its survival in later Euchologion manuscripts, are definitely *desiderata* in liturgical science. However, parts of it have already been edited. First came, as already noted, the ordination prayers,[84] which have since then been the object of considerable study, notably an excellent recent article by Brakmann;[85] in addition there now exists a new edition of them by Čelije.[86] Further elements that have been published are the following:

---

[81] *Liturgia ibero-graeca sancti Iacobi Dei fratris: Georgian text edited and translated under the authority of the Institute of Manuscripts in Tbilisi,* eds. L. Khevsuriani, M. Shanidze, M. Kavtaria and T. Tseradze, with Greek retroversion and commentary by S. Verhelst, Jerusalemer Theologisches Forum 17 (Münster, 2011). I extend my sincere thanks to S. Verhelst and H. Brakmann, the series editor, for giving me access to a version of this publication.

[82] *Sinai Old collection*: O.12, O.53, O.54 (+N.33); *Sinai New collection*: N.22, N.26, N.31, N.33 (fragment of O.54), N.53, N.54, N.58, N.63, N.65, N.70, N.79, N.81, N.83; *outside Sinai*: Tbilisi NCM A-86 and Graz 2058/4 (+ the fragment Prague Lit. Mus. D I VI 1).

[83] On fol. 69v-85v (Aleksidze et al., *Catalogue* (see n. 27), p. 418).

[84] See n. 73.

[85] Brakmann, 'Ordinationsgebete' (see n. 10).

[86] Ed. Edišer Čelije, დიდი კურთხევანი I [*Great Euchologion I*], (Tbilisi, 2006), pp. 277-302. Čelije's edition improves and corrects the edition of Kekelije.

the so-called 'catholic' (major) litany,[87] the rite of marriage,[88] the rite of tonsure,[89] the burial rite,[90] the two first prayers of the rite of baptism,[91] prayers for the blessing of lamps,[92] as well as a dozen prayers from the daily office (of Sin. 12) included in the ancient Horologion of Sin. O.34.[93] The edition of the Ancient Georgian unction of the sick is announced[94] and that of the full rite of baptism is forthcoming.[95]

2.4. Lectionary (კანონი, *kanoni*)

Sources

The Lectionary[96] is perhaps the best known pre-Athonite Georgian liturgical book,[97] owing to its edition by Kekelije in 1912 (with Russian

---

[87] Bernard Outtier and Stéphane Verhelst, 'La *kéryxie catholique* de la liturgie de Jérusalem en géorgien (*sin.* 12 et 54)', *Archiv für Liturgiewissenschaft* 42 (2000) 41-64.

[88] Ek'vt'ime Kočlamazašvili, 'წინდობისა და ჯორწილის საეკლესიო რიტუალი უძველეს ქართულ "კურთხევათა" კრებულებში [The ecclesiastical ritual of betrothal and marriage in the ancient Georgian Euchologion collections]', *ქრისტიანულ-არქეოლოგიური ძიებანი (Investigations of Christian Archeology)* 1 (2008) 349-369 (Sin. O.12 and O.66 in parallel). Another edition is found in Čelije, *Great Euchologion* (see n. 86), pp. 69-79, but it has the text of Sin. O.12 only.

[89] Čelije, *Great Euchologion* (see n. 86), pp. 200-236, on the basis of Sin. O.12.

[90] Bernard Outtier, 'Der georgische Begräbnisritus', in *Liturgie im Angesicht des Todes: Judentum und Ostkirchen*, eds. Hansjakob Becker and Hermann Ühlein, Pietas liturgica, 9-10 (St. Ottilien, 1997), vol. I, pp. 573-579 (Sin.O. 12 and Sin 66); vol. II, 1996, pp. 1253-1261 (translation); vol. I, pp. 767-771 (commentary). In addition to the burial rite, Outtier includes the text and translation of the Ancient Iadgari office of the dead.

[91] Ek'vt'ime Kočlamazašvili, 'ჯრისტიანების წესი [The rite of Christianization]', *Religia* (Tbilisi) 7-8-9 (1999) 9-17 (pp. 16-17: German summary), here pp. 12-13 (Sin. O.12 and Birmingham Mingana Georgian 1, part of Sin. O.66).

[92] Ek'vt'ime Kočlamazašvili, 'ლამპრობის სულიერი შინაარსისათვის [On the spiritual content of Candlemas]', *Religia* (Tbilisi) 11-12 (1998) 12-24 (p. 24: English summary), on p. 17. Two different prayers are edited, one from Sin. O.54, another from Sin. O.12, the latter being partially identical to a similar prayer of the ancient Horologion of Sin. O.34.

[93] Edited in the doctoral thesis of this author: Stig R. Frøyshov, *L'Horologe 'géorgien' du* Sinaiticus ibericus *34. Edition, traduction et commentaire* (Paris, 2003). The publication of the Horologion is in preparation for the CSCO. Other prayers of this Horologion than those also found in Sin. 12 could belong to the Jerusalem Euchologion.

[94] In the doctoral thesis of Tinatin Chronz, under the supervision of Heinzgerd Brakmann, *Gottesdienst des heiligen Öles nach dem Jerusalemer Orolo* (Bonn, 2009) (in press).

[95] Ed. Ek'vt'ime Kočlamazašvili, to appear in Georgian in the journal *ქრისტიანულ-არქეოლოგიური ძიებანი [Investigations in Christian Archeology]*.

[96] There exist partial Greek witnesses to the Hagiopolite Lectionary, as the 8th century St. Petersburg RNB Greek 44 (common and Sunday Liturgies) and the NT Lection-

translation),[98] partially translated into German,[99] and edited with translation by T'arxnišvili in 1959-1960.[100] A list of sources of the Georgian Lectionary, not yet including the Sinai New Finds, was drawn up by Bernard Outtier in 1988.[101] The Sinai New Finds furnish altogether nine new sources of the Georgian Lectionary;[102] two of them comprise more than a hundred folios, which seems to represent a significant increase of source material. Whereas the most important witnesses to the Georgian Lectionary constitute separate codices, most of the Palestinian witnesses, including all of the Sinai New Finds as it seems, form part of

---

aries Sin. Arabic 116 and Sin. Greek 210, 211 and 212. It is noteworthy that the second edition (1994) of K. Aland's *Kurzgefasste Liste der griechischen Handschriften des Neuen Testaments* adds several codices of the Sinai New Finds to the hitherto known Greek sources of the Jerusalem NT Lectionary: *l* 2212-2217, of which the most significant in quantity is *l* 2213, the 9th century NE MG 11 of 125 fol. (Aland, p. 356; without photo in the New Finds catalogue). Sin. NE MG 11 is classified by Aland as '*l*sel', which designates selected Gospel lessons.

[97] For a presentation of the Jerusalem Lectionary, see Sebastià Janeras, 'Les lectionnaires de l'ancienne liturgie de Jérusalem', *Collectanea Christiana Orientalia* 2 (2005) 71-92; on the Georgian version, see pp. 76-79.

[98] Korneli Kekelije, *Іерусалимскій канонарь VII века (Грузинская версія) [Jerusalemite Kanonarion of the 7th century (Georgian version)]* (Tbilisi, 1912).

[99] Th. Kluge and A. Baumstark, 'Quadragesima und Karwoche Jerusalems im siebten Jahrhundert', *Oriens Christianus* N.S. 5 (1915) 201-233; Th. Kluge and A. Baumstark, 'Oster- und Pfingstfeier Jerusalems im siebten Jahrhundert', *Oriens Christianus* N.S. 6 (1916) 223-239; G. Peradze and A. Baumstark, 'Die Weihnachtsfeier Jerusalems im siebten Jahrhundert', *Oriens Christianus* 3. S. 1 (1927) 310-318.

[100] *Le grand lectionnaire de l'Eglise de Jérusalem (Ve-VIIIe siècle)*, ed. and transl. Michel Tarchnischvili, CSCO 188-189, 204-205 (Leuven, 1959-1960). This edition, here abbreviated GL, excludes the readings themselves (except incipits and desinits); a long term project of editing the full Lectionary text is in course at the National Centre of Manuscripts in Tbilisi. An online English translation by Kevin P. Edgecomb of T'arxnišvili's Latin translation of GL is available on http://www.bombaxo.com/georgian. html.

[101] Bernard Outtier, 'Essai de répertoire des manuscrits des vieilles versions géorgiennes du Nouveau Testament,' *Langues orientales anciennes: Philologie et linguistique* 1 (1988) 173-179, n° 47-89. Outtier has published a series of GL fragments: 'Deux fragments onciaux inédits d'un lectionnaire géorgien de Jérusalem (V)', *Xristianskij Vostok* 8 (2000) 220-226 (with ref. to the four preceding articles of this series in n. 1); 'Un nouveau fragment oncial inédit du *lectionnaire* de Jérusalem en géorgien', in *Pèlerinages et lieux saints dans l'antiquité et le moyen âge*, eds. Béatrice Caseau et al. (Paris, 2006), pp. 323-328 (this is number VI; VII is forthcoming).

[102] All are dated to the 10th century if not otherwise specified: N.10 (9 fol., 9th cent.), N.11 (7 f. + 3 small fragments), N.22 (fol. 21r-79v.), N.26 (fol. 97r-213v, 9th-10th cent.), N.31 (fol. 60r-256v, 9th-10th cent.), N.54 (fol. 109r-129v), N.58 (fol. 47r-58v: Burial rite, 9th-10th cent.), N.63 (fol. 65r-75v), N.70 (fol. 9r-12v), N.71 (8 fol: Index of gospel lessons, resembling that of Sin. O.38 (see n. 103), N.77 (2 fol., 9th-10th cent.), N.88 (2 fol.).

the Palestino-Georgian 'liturgical collections' (see above). In Palestine there also existed Georgian indices of readings.[103]

The Georgian Lectionary of Hagiopolite tradition is known in several chronologically succeeding redactions. For his edition T'arxnišvili used four 10th century manuscripts. He incorporated into his critical apparatus two older, fragmentary sources, witnessing to two more ancient redactions of the Georgian Lectionary. The oldest is the so-called 'xanmeti' Lectionary, preserved in four 7th century fragments, of which three belong to the same codex, constituting altogether 30 fol.[104] Slightly more recent is the so-called 'haemeti' Lectionary, preserved in the inferior text (dated to the 8th century) of a large codex of which only two fragments remain today, Tbilisi H-1329 and Q-333, comprising altogether 104 fol.[105]

Studies
Dating of the Georgian Lectionary

The 'Great Lectionary' (GL) edited by T'arxnišvili, that is, GL in its latest redaction, is usually dated to the period 5th-8th century.[106] This rather broad dating may probably be narrowed down. There are indications that the Georgian Lectionary basically reflects the liturgical situation of the 6th century:[107] a) the hymnography it prescribes is that of the pre-7th century *Ancient* Iadgari;[108] b) Verhelst, who has done extensive

---

[103] Gérard Garitte, 'Un index géorgien des lectures évangéliques selon l'ancien rite de Jérusalem', *Le Muséon* 85 (1972) 337-398 (Sin. O.38); Bernard Outtier, 'Un fragment d'index géorgien des lectures évangéliques selon l'ancien rite de Jérusalem', *Cahiers d'orientalisme* 25 (Geneva, 2005) 273-278.

[104] Graz Univ. Libr. 2058/1 (= Georgian 1), 28 fol., supplemented by Paris BN Georgian 30 (1 fol.) and Birmingham Mingana Georgian 7 (1 fol.) (Outtier, 'Répertoire', n° 47). According to Xevsuriani, 'Liturgy' (see n. 21), p. 237, L. K'ajaia has discovered that the lower text of Tbilisi NCM Q-999 (Outtier, 'Répertoire', n° 67) includes 3 fol. of a xanmeti Lectionary fragment of the 6th-7th cent. containing readings for Great Tuesday and Wednesday. To my knowledge this discovery has not yet been published.

[105] It is n° 48 of Outtier's 'Répertoire'. Description, partial translation and reference to partial Georgian edition in Michael Tarchnišvili, 'Zwei georgische Lektionarfragmente aus dem 5. und 6. Jahrhundert', *Kyrios* 6 (1942-1943) 1-28.

[106] Of course, each witness to the GL constitutes a proper redaction and, strictly speaking, each witness should be dated individually.

[107] This redaction has of course both more ancient and more recent elements.

[108] The Georgian monks of Palestine who, in the second half of the 10th century were keen on copying the New Iadgari, would certainly have effectuated a replacement in the Lectionary of the Ancient hymnography by the New, had not the Byzantine rite been introduced in this very period, eclipsing the relevance of such an operation. As seen above (n. 62), the Lectionary Sin. O.37 shows an example of the beginning of this.

studies of topographical[109] and calendar[110] aspects of the Georgian Lectionary,[111] has pointed out that very few holy places and persons in GL postdate 600.

Development of the Georgian Lectionary

The chapter on the Lectionary in the recent entry by Xevsuriani on Ancient Georgian liturgy resumes our present knowledge well. The development undergone by the Jerusalem Lectionary naturally included a progressive repletion of its calendar as well as changes and additions in the system of readings, both for the Greek original and the Georgian version, although not necessarily in the same way and with the same speed.

According to Xevsuriani[112], around 700 the 'extensive' (простран-ный) redaction was formed of the Georgian Lectionary, also called 'Great Lectionary (ჯანონი)'.[113] An early witness to the extensive redaction is the above mentioned 8ᵗʰ century 'hacmcti' Lectionary fragment. This fragment covers the period November 9 — December 1 and prescribes celebrations for nineteen out of twenty-three days.[114] In comparison, the 10ᵗʰ century GL manuscripts have festal arrangements for all days, a fact which indicates continuing repletion of feasts in the Georgian 'Great Lectionary' after 700.

The development of the system of readings is shown, according to Xevsuriani[115], for instance in that around the time of the apparition of the 'extensive' Lectionary readings were added on Mondays, Tuesdays

---

[109] Stéphane Verhelst, 'Les lieux de station du lectionnaire de Jérusalem. 1ère partie: Les villages et fondations', *Proche-Orient chrétien* 54 (2004) 13-70; *id.*, 'Les lieux de station du lectionnaire de Jérusalem. 2e partie: Les lieux saints', *Proche-Orient chrétien* 54 (2004) 247-289 (Wikipedia version: http://fr.wikipedia.org/wiki/Lieux_de_station_ de_la_liturgie_de_Jerusalem).

[110] Stéphane Verhelst, 'Le 15 août, le 9 avril et le Kathisme', *Questions liturgiques* 82 (2001) 161-191; *id.*, 'Histoire ancienne de la durée du carême à Jérusalem', *Questions liturgiques* 84 (2003) 23-50; *id.*, 'La place des prophètes dans le sanctoral de Jérusalem, *Questions liturgiques* 84 (2003) 182-203. See also the overview of Harald Buchinger, 'Das Jerusalemer Sanctorale: Zu Stand und Aufgaben der Forschung', in: *A Cloud of Witnesses: The Cult of Saints in Past and Present*, eds. M. Barnard, P. Post and E. Rose, Liturgia Condenda 18 (Leuven, 2005), pp. 97-128 (GL on p. 110-113).

[111] *Liturgia*, 'Conclusion: Vers une histoire de la liturgie eucharistique à Jérusalem', eds. Khevsuriani et al., p. 418; *id.*, 'The Liturgy of Jerusalem in the Byzantine Period' (see n. 22), p. 317.

[112] Xevsuriani, 'Liturgy' (see n. 21), p. 237, col. A.

[113] See n. 180.

[114] Tarchnišvili, 'Lektionarfragmente' (see n. 105), pp. 27-28.

[115] Xevsuriani, 'Liturgy' (see n. 21), p. 238, col. A.

and Thursdays of Great Lent, complementing the more ancient readings on Lenten Wednesdays and Fridays.

Verhelst finds 'reasons for thinking that the translation [of GL] was an evolving one, constantly being revised over the course of the fifth and the beginning of the sixth centuries'.[116]

GL and its 'Hymnographical Supplement'

It is sometimes thought that the Hagiopolite Lectionary provides the frame for other liturgical books. According to this theory, Ancient stage hymnography would have arisen within it as its hymnographical supplement,[117] eventually being extracted from it to form a separate book, the Ancient Iadgari.[118] Against this it may be objected that it is unlikely that the Lectionary ever contained hymnography to any considerable extent; the earliest, Armenian version of the Jerusalem Lectionary, the content of which is dated to the first half of the 5th century, contains extremely little hymnography, at a time when hymnography in all probability was already flourishing in Jerusalem. Neither is it likely that there was such a unique relationship between these two books. All of the liturgical books served a distinct purpose, and all of them adhered to and expressed the more or less 'abstract' liturgical canon of Jerusalem. It is true that Lectionary readings sometimes provided the themes expressed subsequently by hymnography connected to them. At the same time, however, the structure of the daily offices of the Ancient Iadgari was generally not given by the Lectionary, but by the Horologion (except for certain particular festal offices like vigils). This shows that the Iadgari was a 'hymnographical supplement', if one were to employ this term, not only to the Lectionary but also to the Horologion.[119] It would seem more proper to say that each liturgical book covered a particular part of the liturgical system, all governed by the canon.

---

[116] Verhelst, 'The Liturgy of Jerusalem in the Byzantine Period' (see n. 22), p. 430.

[117] E.g. Métrévéli et al., 'Tropologion' (see n. 37), p. 55.

[118] Renoux, Les hymnes de la résurrection (see n. 41), p. 31: 'Ces compositions hymnodiques s'acroissant considérablement par la suite, il fallut les séparer du Lectionnaire pour en faire un livre liturgique spécial, l'Hymnaire, dont la couche primitive était la partie hymnographique du Lectionnaire'.

[119] And the Lectionary itself could be termed a 'supplement of readings and responsorial chants' of the Euchologion ...

2.5. Horologion (ჟამნი, žamni)

Sources

Until very recently, knowledge of the daily office of the rite of Jerusalem could be gained only by gleaning data from secondary documents
like Egeria's journal, the Lectionary, the Iadgaris and the Narration of
John and Sophronios. However, it has now become clear that, among
the old liturgical books preserved by 10th century Georgian monks, the
ancient Jerusalem Horologion is counted. Together with a more recent
(and Sabaite) Horologion, both being of a 24 hour ordo, it is found in
the codex Sin. Georgian O.34, which in a remarkable section on the
daily office contains several, still unedited primary sources of both
Jerusalem and St. Sabas tradition.[120] The Catalogue of the New Finds
reports another Horologion of (originally) 24 hours, the defective Sin.
Georgian N.23, written in Constantinople in 986 by Iovane Meli, monk
of Iviron.[121] Only the twelve night hours survive today. Judging from
two remarks in the catalogue[122] it would seem that Sin. N.23 is closer
to the above mentioned Horologion of Sin. O.34 than to the Studite
Horologion.[123] The catalogue photo provides one element of the Horologion: Ps. 102, which most probably belongs to the nocturns/matins
Hexapsalm. But a close examination of the manuscript is of course necessary in order to evaluate its relation to the ancient Horologion of
Sin. O.34.

---

[120] About this manuscript and its daily office section, see further details below.

[121] Only gatherings 12-17 remain, followed by 6 fol. whose place within the original
manuscript has not yet been clarified. Thus the first eleven gatherings are missing and
only the twelve night hours have been preserved (54. fol.). The catalogue (Alexidze et al.,
Catalogue (see n. 27)) provides one photo of the ms, representing fol. 31v, whose text is
Ps. 102:5b-11a.

[122] The catalogue description remarks that the Horologion 'bears no resemblance to
the version of George the Hagiorite, which was compiled in the second half of the
11th cent. on the basis of the Greek Horologion (cf. Jer[usalem Georgian] 127)' (Alexidze
et al., *Catalogue* (see n. 27), 397). At the same time, 'the text differs considerably from
that of the old version of the Horologion found in Sin.Geo.O.34. (*ibid.*).'

[123] Further, the following interpretation seems to imply a contradiction: 'It would
seem that the text is part of an old translation of the Horologion following the Constantinopolitan traditions, which came into use in Georgian liturgical (Georgian original:
samonastro, 'monastic', instead of 'liturgical') practice in the second half of the 10th cent'
(pp. 396-397). These 'Constantinopolitan traditions' cannot be other than the Studite tradition, that is the 'version of George the Hagiorite', but with this, according to the remark
noted in the previous footnote, it 'bears no resemblance'.

Studies of the 'Georgian' Horologion of Sin. O.34
Horologion of the Cathedral of Jerusalem

In its preserved state, the ancient Georgian Horologion is not complete, since it lacks its beginning, but fortunately the most important daily offices have survived. It was copied by Iovane the Priest (or Elder) in the middle of the 10th century, either at the Šatberdi monastery in Tao-Klarjet'i or at the Great Lavra of St. Sabas. Later it was significantly revised[124] by Iovane Zosime.[125] This Horologion is labelled by the latter ქართული, *k'art'uli*, 'Georgian',[126] representing one of the few documents clearly identified as such. While included in a codex of strongly Sabaite character, its daily cursus of 24 hours celebrated in common is not particularly compatible with the lavriote organisation of St. Sabas. Strong indications in this document confirm the interpretation of 'Georgian' equalling 'ancient Hagiopolite': it contains prayers from the Georgian version of the Jerusalem Euchologion and hymns from the Jerusalem Ancient Iadgari.[127]

In the original codex, before the removal of a large number of folio, the 'Georgian' Horologion was preceded by another Horologion, called 'Sabaite'.[128] The latter includes hymnography from the *New* Iadgari, a fact which permits interpreting the two Horologia, in line with the perspective of the 10th century monastic redactor, as one Ancient and one New. With its public offices and its monastic intermediary hours,[129] the 'Georgian' Horologion seems to have been originally composed for a great church housing both a parish and a cenobitic community of ascetics or monks. Given the evidence of its Hagiopolite tradition, I consider this church to be the Resurrection cathedral of Jerusalem with its monastic *tagma* of Spoudaites (Σπουδαῖοι). It is particularly important to note that inasmuch as this 'Georgian' Horologion is the doubtless predecessor of the Sabaite and Byzantine Horologia, this shows that the latter have their origin in the Jerusalem cathedral (and not in any desert monastery as has sometimes been thought).

---

[124] More than 10% of it was erased and a great part of this rewritten.

[125] It seems, however, that these two Iovane are in fact identical. The question will be dealt with substantially in the publication of the Horologion in preparation.

[126] That is, one of the three Georgian rites as described above.

[127] But see the discussion below whether the Georgian versions are direct translations of Greek books or whether non-Hagiopolite elements have been included.

[128] See below.

Daily Cursus

In spite of the loss of its first gathering, containing hours 1-10 of the day, the preserved end shows that this Horologion originally had a daily cursus of 24 offices, twelve day hours and twelve night hours.[130] Ideally it prescribes one office per hour, in practice probably a *laus perennis*.

Table 2: The Daily Cursus of the Ancient Horologion of Sin. O.34
(P: public office; M: monastic office; ÷: lost)

HOUR	1	2	3	4	5	6	7	8	9	10	11	12	Outside cursus
DAY	÷	÷	÷	÷	÷	÷	÷	÷	÷	÷	P Vespers	P Communion (PRES)	P Meal
NIGHT	P Compline	M Midnight	M	M	M	P Nocturns	M	M	M	M	M	P Matins	

In Georgian sources a daily cursus of 24 hours is known also from the New, 'Sabaite' Horologion of Sin. O.34, from the Horologion Sin. N.23, and from the Typikon of Pakourianos (1083).[131] In Greek sources it is known from the Non-Sleeper ('Ακοίμητοι) tradition,[132] from certain Psalters and Horologia[133] as well as from the succinct Horologion of the 5th century Codex Alexandrinus, the twelve day psalms of which also figure on a papyrus of the second half of the 6th century found at the Egyptian lavra of Naqlun.[134] There is a partial identity between

---

[129] I call the latter 'very small' hours, the idea being that they are smaller than the 'Lesser hours' (first, third, sixth, and ninth hours).

[130] The night section bears the title Jamni Ramisani, 'The night hours' (fol. 6r1).

[131] *Typicon Gregorii Pacuriani*, ed. and transl. Michael Tarchnišvili, CSCO 143-144 (Leuven, 1954), p. 74, l. 25-26). Curiously the Greek version of this Typicon does not mention any Horologion. See the English version in *Byzantine Monastic Foundation Documents*, eds. John Thomas and Angela C. Hero (Washington, D.C., 2000), vol. 2, p. 553.

[132] *Vie d'Alexandre l'Acémète*, ed. E. de Stoop, PO VI.5 (Paris, 1911), ch. 30, p. 40.

[133] See E. P. Diakovskij, 'Последованіе ночныхъ часовъ ("Чинъ 12-ти псал-мовъ") [The office of night hours ("The ordo of the 12 psalms")]', *Труды Кіевской Духовной Академіи* (1909), pp. 546-595, on pp. 550-556 (ch. 'The plurality of daily cursus') and Georgi Parpulov, *Towards a History of the Byzantine Psalter*, unpublished doctoral thesis, University of Chicago (Chicago, 2004), app. C5 ('Psalms for the hours of the Day and Night, as Listed in some Greek Psalters'). While these daily cursus would include the 24 psalms or hours, the total cursus could reach a comprehensive size; the Horologion Sin. Gr. 868, for example, has no less than thirty-four daily offices. See Diakovskij, *ibid.*, p. 557.

[134] On the succinct Horologion of these two sources, see my 'The Cathedral-Monastic Distinction Revisited. Part I: Was Egyptian Desert Liturgy a Pure Monastic Office?', *Studia liturgica* 37 (2007) 198-216, on pp. 208-213.

the twenty-four psalm series of the latter and that of the 'Georgian' Horologion.[135]

The beginning of the 'Georgian' Horologion and its twenty-four hour cursus is thus the first hour of the day. The hour of prime also opens the 'Sabaite' Horologion of Sin. Geo. O.34 and Sin. Gr. 863. This correspondence shows that the first hour of the day was the beginning of the early Palestinian Horologion.

Two Distinct Types of Offices

As is clear from a rubric, all the twenty-four offices are meant to be celebrated in common by monks: 'About the ordo and the office of monks gathered together, observing the twelve hours of the day and the twelve hours of the night ...'.[136] It is clear from other rubrics, however, that while the actual redaction seems to have been in use in a monastery, the Horologion nevertheless distinguishes between two types of offices, one of which presupposing a people's community:

Table 3: Two Types of Offices in the 'Georgian' Horologion of Sin. O.34

'Public' Hour	'Very small' Intermediary Hour
Initial polypsalm (called 'extracted psalms')	One initial fixed psalm
Absence of continuous psalmody	One kanoni[137] ('kathisma' of the Psalter)
Variable hymnography	Responsorium: a c'ardgomay (hymnodic kathisma)
Halleluja-psalm (or stanza replacing it) at the bishop's entrance	Selected psalm verses
Fixed prayers	Fixed prayers
Prayer(s) from the public Euchologion	
Dismissal prayer said in the name of the Trinity (except at Compline)	A final prayer

---

[135] Some of the psalms are found at the same hours of the 'Sabaite' Horologion. I presume that the psalms of the 'very small' hours of this document are identical to the ones same hours of the 'Georgian' Horologion, since it seems unlikely that the 'Sabaite' Horologion should make new psalm choices at these hours. Most probably its 'very small' hours, absent in the otherwise very close Sin. gr. 863, are prolongations of the same offices of the 'Georgian' Horologion.

[136] წესიერებისათვს და ღმრთის-მსახურებისა ერთად შეკრებულთა მოწესეთა, რომელთა ათორმეტნი ჟამნი დღისა და ღამისანი ეპყრნეს (fol. 5v24-26).

[137] The term კანონი, kanoni, which designates the Lectionary, also signifies a kathisma of the Psalter.

The public offices, which include vespers, communion, nocturns, compline and matins, are all in some way or other characterised by the label საჶროჲ, *saeroy*, 'public'.[138] A *saeroy* office carries the features of what is commonly termed a 'cathedral' office: fixed and not continuous psalmody, celebration by bishop/priest, variable hymnography etc.[139] Vespers and matins are very close to the later and present Byzantine offices. The communion service, clearly intended for a Presanctified Liturgy, has unfortunately been almost completely erased. Compline closely resembles the first part of present Byzantine compline. The rest of the hours, to which the manuscript does not attach any label but which I call 'very small' hours, have for the most part a simple structure, their main characteristics being a fixed opening psalm and a Psalter unit (in later tradition termed 'kathisma'). They too carry some of the features of a 'cathedral' office (one fixed psalm, some hymnography, fixed times), but the prayers are not taken from the public Euchologion. The whole Psalter, divided into twenty *kanoni* ('kathismata') in the Hagiopolite manner, is performed daily, distributed over twenty offices. In principle, these hours are the 'very small' ones but, these being less than twenty, some public hours also have a kanoni. There is evidence, however, that the presence of a kanoni at public hours predates the elaboration of this 'distributed Psalter'.[140]

The Nocturns Office and Mateos' Hypothesis

One of the most surprising features of the 'Georgian' Horologion is the sixth hour of the night, which we may term 'nocturns'. This office has the Byzantine Hexapsalm and the classical night psalm 133. Their presence in a nocturnal office, separated from matins proper by five 'very small' hours with their continuous psalmody, elegantly confirms Juan Mateos' hypothesis[141] of the nocturnal beginning of Byzantine matins.[142]

---

[138] Some of them have particular titles, stemming from Zosime's rewriting: 'the 11th hour [of the day]: Vespers, public'; 'the 6th hour [of the night], public'. The term *saeroy* figures also, in one way or another, in the first lines of compline (original) and matins (rewritten). In addition, certain elements of the communion service indicate that it was a public office.

[139] For a summary of the features of the conventional cathedral and monastic rites, see my article referred to in n. 134, pp. 199-201.

[140] This concerns kanoni 18 at vespers and kanoni 17 at midnight, both of which have an anomalous place in the sequence of the twenty parts.

[141] Juan Mateos, 'Quelques problèmes de l'orthros byzantin', *Proche Orient chrétien* 11 (1961) 17-35, 201-220: 'Nous croyons que la première partie de l'orthros est un ancien office de minuit. Cet office comprendrait une partie introductive et une psalmodie nocturne' (p. 22).

[142] It is moreover a 'double' hour, in which a public first part (nocturns proper) is immediately followed by a 'very small' hour, undoubtedly in order to allow for the distribution of all twenty kathismata within the day and night.

3. Monastic Peripheries of the Jerusalem Liturgy

Georgian sources are of capital importance in our endeavour to delineate and identify the monastic rites of two great Palestinian monasteries, the Great Lavra of St. Sabas, founded in 483, and the cenobion of the Burning Bush at Mount Sinai (now dedicated to St. Catherine).[143]

3.1. St. Sabas

The rite of the Great Lavra constituted probably the most important liturgical periphery of Jerusalem, whether considered within a Georgian or a general context, destined to enjoy capital importance in later liturgical history. It is reasonable to presuppose, first, that from its foundation the Great Lavra in the main adopted and adapted the liturgy of the cathedral under the jurisdiction of which it was and with which it had close contacts[144] and, secondly, that in the course of time the Sabaite periphery took on the identity of a distinct rite, separate from its origin. Third, there are signs that the Sabaite rite in many respects was a conservative periphery of Jerusalem, preserving more ancient liturgical forms while the centre evolved.

Sinai Georgian O.34

A crucial source for the identification of first millennium Sabaite liturgy is the Sin. O.34. The redactor and main scribe of this composite, lacunary[145] codex[146] was the famous Iovane Zosime. At the Great Lavra,

---

[143] There also existed the very significant liturgical tradition of the Palestinian desert cenobion of St. Theodosios, possibly even lying at the roots of the Studite rite, and this tradition had its own liturgical relationship with the Jerusalem cathedral. There are to my knowledge no Georgian sources of explicit Theodosian character, but certain Georgian manuscripts of Sinaitic content (see below, ch. 'Sinai') may be implicitly Theodosian, since the Sinai rite may reflect the tradition of St. Theodosios. One indication of this is that the Typikon Sin. Gr. 1097 (AD 1214), which clearly reflects Sinai use, has at fol. 16r a second title: 'Τυπικὸν τῆς ἐκκλησιαστικῆς ἀκολουθίας τοῦ ὁσίου πατρὸς ἡμῶν Θεοδοσίου τοῦ κοινοβιάρχου'; see A. Dmitrievskij, Описаніе литургическихъ рукописей, t. II (Petrograd, 1917), p. 403.

[144] In addition there might of course have been particular influences from non-Palestinian monastic traditions through the presence of immigrant monks; it is well known that Palestinian monasticism was particularly international.

[145] As a result of thefts, or 'transfers', accomplished in the 19th century it consists today of 210 fol.; of the removed fragments 55 fol. have been identified while an unknown number of folios remains lost.

[146] See Lili Xevsuriani, 'Sin. 34-ის შედგენილობის საკითხისათვის [The Problem of the Composition of Sin. 34]', Mravaltavi 6 (1978) 88-123, and Michel van Esbroeck,

copying most of the codex himself but also gathering together material stemming from at least four other copyists, he finished its redaction in 965, after which he nevertheless continued to insert notes and texts into his old age. The manuscript stores as in an archive a vast series of elements, relevant and obsolete, in new and old versions, many of which are explicitly of Sabaite tradition.[147] Sin. O.34 has the following structure:

1. Documents on the daily office: mostly ordo documents (see next paragraph)
2. Calendar (edited by Garitte)[148]
3. Hymnography: the two redactions of the Hagiopolite hymnal (New Iadgari – full text, Old Iadgari – mostly incipits), including a KaO Heirmologion
4. Patristic reading: the Correspondence of Barsanuphius and John
5. Scripture readings (indices, lists and other information)
6. Chronological texts

All these sections, except the fifth, belong to the daily office. Given its distinct Sabaite character, the codex can be seen as an 'encyclopedia of the Sabaite daily office'. It does incorporate some Hagiopolite elements, for instance the 'Georgian' Horologion, but this is legitimate since in the Sabaite perspective the Jerusalem liturgy was the starting point.

Sabaite Daily Office According to Sin. O.34

The first section of the codex, devoted to the daily office, originally covered the six first gatherings; of these only 3-5 remain in the codex today. The order of the main elements of this first section may be plausibly reconstructed as follows.[149]

'Le manuscrit sinaïtique géorgien 34 et les publications récentes de liturgie palestinienne', *Orientalia Christiana Periodica* 46 (1980) 125-141.

[147] The most important of these are the following elements: a drawing representing St. Sabas; particular feasts of the Great Lavra included in the New Iadgari; the Sabaite layer of the calendar (one of its four models was Sabaite and Zosime marked off the feasts celebrated at the Great Lavra); a lost Sabaite Lectionary index; and many of the texts of the daily office section (1a, 1b, 1f, and 1g; see below).

[148] *Le calendrier palestino-géorgien du Sinaiticus 34 (Xe siècle)*, ed. Gérard Garitte (Brussels, 1958).

[149] Inverted commas (' ') indicate that the title figures in the manuscript, quotation marks (" ") that it is given by myself.

1a. "Rules for praying the seven daily hours in the cell" (1 page)

1b. 24 hour Horologion labelled 'Sabaite' (fragment (hours 1-5), 1 page)

1c. 24 hour Horologion labelled 'Georgian' (gatherings 3-5 of the codex, originally 2-5, incomplete)

1d. Alternative elements of the 'Georgian' Horologion (1/2 page)

1e. The 24 Egyptian psalms (part of page)

1f. "Sabaite Cell Horologion"

1g. 'Rule of St Sabas of Ordinary Chants'

1h. Minor supplements to the 'Georgian' Horologion

Among the identified fragments of Sin. O.34, belonging to removed gatherings of the daily office section, there are four documents (nos. 1a, 1b, 1f, and 1g of the above list) that shed a rare light on the 'pure', pre-Byzantinised Sabaite daily office.[150] Their Sabaite identity is clearly indicated either in their title or by their content.

'Sabaite' Horologion

The fragment of the New, so-called 'Sabaite' Horologion is very close to the Greek codex Sin. Greek 863, a mutilated uncial Horologion of the 9th century which according to its title follows the κανὼν (rule) of the Great Lavra of St. Sabas.[151] Both witnesses contain New stage hymnography. The difference between the two lies chiefly in the cursus of services: in addition to the quite regular cycle of hours of the Greek witness,[152] the Georgian one adds the 'very small' hours, which altogether results in the same 24 hour cycle as that of the Ancient, 'Georgian' Horologion. Another difference from the Greek witness is that the Georgian one indicates by incipit the prayer of the first and the third hours; these prayers are taken from the Georgian version of the Jerusalem Euchologion.

---

[150] I am preparing a monograph on the paleo-Sabaite daily office (roughly AD 500-1000), including the publication of these four texts.

[151] 'Un Horologion inédit de Saint-Sabas: Le Codex sinaïtique grec 863 (IXe siècle)', ed. Juan Mateos, in *Mélanges E. Tisserant*, vol. III, 1 (Vatican City, 1964), pp. 47-76. Sin. Gr. 863, mutilated at the end, is now to be supplemented by the fragment Sinai, Chest 1, no. 58 (identified by Parpulov, *Byzantine Psalters* (see n. 133), p. 61, n. 36, with summary of content). This fragment of 8 fol. represents the direct continuation of the codex, providing a large part of compline.

[152] That is, first, third, sixth, and ninth hours, communion, vespers, first hour of the night (compline). Matins without any doubt figured in the lost part of the codex.

Two Sabaite Texts on Daily Liturgical Prayer in the Cell

The purpose of these two texts seemingly was to serve as a cell supplement to the public Horologion of the Great Lavra. The first text, which I call the "Sabaite Cell Horologion", has two parts:

1) Title: 'The hesychast (*daqudebuli*) living in a cell at St. Sabas prays the seven hours thus, with three kanoni or five'.[153] The text prescribes the number and performance (prayers before and after, genuflexions) of the kanoni (kathismata) at the seven daily hours;

2) Title: 'The hesychasts thus keep vigil at the Agrypnias of the week'.[154] The text prescribes two Agrypnias on weekdays (the night before Thursday and Saturday), providing for them a summary ordo (of course lacking the Sunday nocturns part, the 'Resurrection Office').

The second text, which I call "Rules for praying the seven daily hours in the cell", placed by Zosime before the two Horologia as an introduction to the daily office texts, prescribes the use of the sign of the cross and genuflexions, the prayers before and after psalms and kanoni, and readings, as well as providing instructions about the inner disposition of the monk.

Evidently these two texts offer a precious view into the cell life of a Sabaite monk during the last centuries of the first millennium. They also shed light on the development of the Sabaite distribution of psalms. In these two documents the 'very small' offices of the 24 hour cursus have been abandoned, leaving a cursus of seven hours. While in the 'Georgian' Horologion the continuous psalmody was in principle a characteristic of the 'very small' monastic offices, in these two documents copied in the 10th century the kanoni have been relegated to the seven public hours. Further, for a 10th century Georgian monk of St Sabas the rules of daily psalmody were evidently not too rigid; according to the "Sabaite Cell Horologion", the third, sixth, and ninth hours and vespers had three kanoni, compline five, while matins had nine, twelve, fifteen kanoni or the whole Psalter, and the Agrypnia the whole Psalter in four sections of five kanoni each. Georgian Sabaite monks of the 10th century apparently still, ideally, read through the whole Psalter every day — or even more.

---

[153] დაყუდებული შინა-მყოფი საბაწმიდას შჳდთა ჟამთა ესრეთ ილოცვის, გ̄-გ̄-თა კანონითა, გინა ე̄-ე̄-თა.

[154] ხოლო კჳრიაკისა ღამისთევათა დაყუდებული ესრე ათევნენ.

'Rule of St. Sabas of Ordinary Chants'

Edited by Lili Xevsuriani,[155] this interesting document provides ordinary refrains for daily triodes, arranged as in Byzantine Lenten practice, and lauds (Pss 148-150), as well as for 'Lord, I have cried' (Ps 140 e.a.). These elements are those for which main hymnography was later composed. While some of the refrains are biblical, most of them are extra-biblical. For the ninth ode, the Rule prescribes particular extra-biblical refrains for each day. The Rule thus presents a simple, fixed ecclesiastical hymnody. Below are the refrains for Monday matins (rubrics in italics):

> Ode 1: Let us sing to the Lord, for he has been gloriously glorified [= biblical text].
> Ode 8: Let us sing to the Lord and exalt him above all to all ages [= biblical text in Georgian version].
> *'Glory' like this:* Let us bless the Father and the Son, with the Holy Spirit, let us sing to the Lord and exalt him above all for ever.
> *After 'Glory':* Let us sing to the Lord and exalt him above all for ever.
> Ode 9: Increase, o Lord, your mercy on us all.
> From 'Blessed be the God of Israel' [canticle of Zachariah]: Make your favour descend upon us all, o Lord.
> *From 'The oath which he swore' [v. 8 from the end]:* Make the light of your countenance shine upon us all, o Lord.
> *After 'To guide' [v. 3 from the end]:* Consubstantial Trinity, save our souls.
> Praises: To you song is due, o God.
> After 'Let us praise his name' [Ps 149:3]: Son of God, have mercy on us.
> After 'Praise Him for his mighty acts' [Ps 150:2] and 'Glory' and 'Now and ever': To you glory is due, o God.

A few times the Rule has the rubric 'change the *dasadebelni* [stanzas]', which seems to signify the insertion of variable hymnody. The Rule creates the picture of a liturgical practice in which variable hymnography destined to replace the refrains is minimal. This suggests that the Sabaite rite, contrary to what is often held, was reticent towards hymnography.

In spite of its title linking it to the desert Lavra of St. Sabas, the Rule seems ultimately to be of Hagiopolite origin;[156] thus the Sabaites would essentially have preserved an ancient Hagiopolite practice which, in a

---

[155] Xevsuriani, 'Composition of Sin. 34' (see n. 146), pp. 112-115.

[156] Psalmody with refrains points to a cathedral rather than to a desert monastery as its place of origin. Desert monks, especially those of a lavra who mostly stay in their cells, are not likely to have made their psalmody dialogical (by adding refrains) and needful of greater liturgical apparatus for its performance.

conservative periphery, in time got identified as the 'receiver' rather than the 'creator'.[157] The crucial question of the Rule's dating is complex; it may seem that it has layers of different age, the oldest parts possibly going back to the earliest times of the Great Lavra.

A Sabaite Witness of the Ancient Iadgari

Charles Renoux has reached the conclusion that the main witness of the Ancient Iadgari, the Tbilisi NCM H-2123, represents a Sabaite adaptation of a Hagiopolite Iadgari.[158] By a thorough examination of the liturgical structures of this Iadgari manuscript, he has identified eight arguments for claiming that this Iadgari reflects the Sabaite rite. The following arguments are the most important of these:[159] reduced quantity of hymnography, absence of certain processions, absence at certain matins services of chants preceding the gospel and therefore also of the gospel read by the bishop (indicating a community without a bishop), a more ancient stage of Iadgari development and continuous psalmody. None of Renoux' arguments *per se* points exclusively to the Great Lavra, but taken together the eight liturgical particularities may support his conclusion that the liturgical tradition reflected in the precious codex Tbilisi NCM H-2123 is indeed that of St. Sabas. The codex was kept at the Great Lavra before it was brought to St. Petersburg around 1850 and from there to Tbilisi in 1923. Renoux also affirms that it was copied at the Great Lavra,[160] which would enhance its connection with that monastery, but according to the catalogue description of the codex its Sabaite origin is only conjectural.[161]

---

[157] Just as Ancient Hagiopolite eventually was called *k'artuli*, 'Georgian', by the Georgians.

[158] Renoux, *L'Hymnaire de Saint-Sabas* (see n. 42), p. 28.

[159] *Ibid.*, pp. 9-18.

[160] *Ibid.*, p. 9: 'Le manuscrit a été copié à la laure de Saint-Sabas'.

[161] Cf. ქართულ ხელნაწერთა აღწერილობა. სინური კოლექცია, ნაკვეთი I [*Description of Georgian manuscripts. The Sinai collection, tome I*], eds. Eleni Metreveli et al. (Tbilisi, 1978), p. 230: 'გადაწერილი ჩანს საბაწმიდაში [It seems to have been copied at St. Sabas]'. An argument in favour of its having been copied elsewhere could be the fact that the codex was not taken to Sinai in the early 970s when the Georgian Sabaitic colony moved there, bringing their manuscript library with them; if the reason was not mere accident it could be that the ms, copied at another location, was brought to St. Sabas after the 970s.

3.2. Sinai

In the early 970s the Georgian community of St. Sabas moved to Mount Sinai, bringing their Georgian manuscripts with them. Their great erudite, Iovane Zosime, soon adapted to his new convent, attentive to and respectful of the community's proper liturgical tradition. In the late 970s he wrote some manuscripts that explicitly follow the local, Sinaitic rite.[162] Some examples from the hand of Zosime will show their interest for the identification of first millennium Sinaitic liturgy.

1. Oslo Schøyen Collection MS 035 (+ 129 fragments of the Russian National Library of St. Petersburg), 979, Sinai (formerly Tsagareli 81):[163] Lectionary index, Apostle and ascetic texts. In a note, Zosime explains that the index is კანონისაგან სინაჲმთიდისაჲ, 'of the kanoni of Holy Sinai', that is, following the Lectionary of the monastery of Mount Sinai.[164]

2. Sin. O.47 (+ Birmingham Mingana Georgian 6), 977, Sinai: The "Resurrection Office" of Sunday matins. In a note Zosime states that the resurrectional gospel readings in all eight tones are ვითარცა არს ბერძულად სინაჲმთიდას შინა, 'as it is in the Greek manner in Holy Sinai'.[165]

3. Notes in the Ancient Horologion of Sin. O.34. Long after having finished the redaction of Sin. O.34, Zosime, at Sinai, inscribes four short notes about liturgical practices at the cenobion of the Burning Bush.

---

[162] On the liturgy of Sinai, see Robert Taft, 'Greek Monastic Liturgy on the Sinai Peninsula in the First Millennium: Glimpses of a Lost World', Conference at the Symposium 'Holy Image – Hallowed Ground: Icons from Sinai', 26-27 January 2007, at the J. Paul Getty Museum (26 Jan.) and The Fowler Museum at UCLA, in press in the Symposium Acta.

[163] See Michel van Esbroeck, 'Les manuscrits de Jean Zosime Sin. 34 et Tsagareli 81', *Bedi kartlisa* 34 (1981) 63-75.

[164] R. Gvaramia et al., *ქართულ ხელნაწერთა აღწერილობა. სინური კოლექცია, ნაკვეთი III [Description of Georgian Manuscripts: The Sinai Collection, tome III]* (Tbilisi, 1987), p. 211.

[165] *Ibid.*, p. 55. See short description of this otherwise Sabaite manuscript in my forthcoming article 'The "Resurrection Office" of Hagiopolite tradition' (Festschrift Stefano Parenti).

4. Discussion: Do Ancient Georgian Liturgical Books Faithfully Reflect Greek Originals?

So how are we to evaluate these Georgian sources as witnesses to Hagiopolite liturgy and its monastic peripheries? This question proves delicate, especially in cases when Georgian sources are the only ones we have. We shall now discuss some aspects of it.

4.1. Additions Made in Georgia

Some non-Hagiopolite additions are found in manuscripts copied in Georgia itself, a fact suggesting that the additions in question were effectuated in Georgia. I shall give four examples:

1. The huge New Iadgari of Mik'ael Modrekili (Tbilisi NCM S-425), copied at the monasteries of Oški and Šatberdi in the late 10th century, includes much indigenous hymnography, added to the Hagiopolite Tropologion.[166]

2. In his dense study on the ordination prayers of Tbilisi NCM A-86, Brakmann gathers together demonstrations, made by himself or others, of textual loans, identifying three layers:[167]

   a) Main layer: prayers with uniquely Palestinian parallels. The main layer was extended by two additional layers:

   b) First additional layer: Prayers from the Testamentum Domini, a 4th-5th century church order.

   c) Second additional layer: Prayers used by the Mesopotamian Church of Selcukcia-Ktesiphon (East Syrian).

   The manuscript in question is Kartvelian, that is, it was made for the Catholicos of K'artli (Eastern Georgia), probably Symeon III (d. 1012). Brakmann opts for these supplements having been added in K'artli itself.[168]

---

[166] The hymnographers in question include Mik'ael Modrekili himself, Grigol Xandjt'eli, Iovane Minč'xi, Iovane Mtbevari, Iovane K'onk'ozisje and Step'ane Čqondideli. Cf. Michel van Esbroeck, 'L'hymnaire de Michel Modrekili et son sanctoral (Xᵉ siècle)', *Bedi Kartlisa* 38 (1980) 113-129, on p. 115. But note that the Ancient Iadgari Tbilisi NCM H-2123, seemingly written at St. Sabas, includes the feast of the Georgian martyr St. Abo (d. 786), as do copies of the Georgian Lectionary.

[167] Brakmann, 'Ordinationsgebete' (see n. 10), pp. 118-120: list of prayers and parallels.

[168] 'Offensichtlich wurde ein palästinensischer Grundbestand, wo auch immer, am ehesten wohl in Kaukasien, erweitert durch (a) pseudapostolische sowie (b) ostsyrische

3. The Ninevite fast, seemingly of East Syrian origin, but also common among West Syrians, is mentioned in the Palestino-Georgian calendar copied by Zosime in Sin. O.34.[169] In several New Iadgaris[170] the word 'Ninevites' is attached to Friday of Meatfare, but the ensuing hymnography belongs to a section ascribed to the Hagiopolite melodist Elias the Patriarch. It seems that in the calendar Zosime has included elements, brought from Georgia, of an originally East Syrian fast of which only a supplementary title remains in New Iadgaris copied in Palestine.[171]

4. Since the 'Georgian' Horologion may have been copied at Šatberdi, could it be that the 24 hour cursus was worked out in Georgia itself and not in Jerusalem, for instance by merging a twenty-four hour *Akoimêtos* tradition of Syrian origin with a Jerusalem cursus of seven hours? I do not think so, but it is worth considering the possibility.

4.2. Georgian Additions Made in Palestine?

The pre-Athonite Georgian Heirmologion, preserved both in Ode Order and Canon Order, differs from Greek and Slavonic witnesses by a particular feature: in all witnesses of both types, each heirmos is followed by a theotokion. The great majority of these manuscripts are Palestinian and, to my knowledge, no Greek equivalent has yet been found.

The New Iadgari, whose witnesses include two scrolls[172] of the Sinai New Finds containing hymnody of Kosmas the Melodist, offers a curious particularity that could have been a Georgian invention: A second ode has been added to some canons that originally did not have it.[173]

Gebete' (*ibid.*, p. 121). It should also be noted that a fairly recent study of the *Testamentum Domini* locates its origin not in Syria, as is usually held, but in Gaza. See Michael Kohlbacher, 'Wessen Kirche ordnete das Testamentum Domini Nostri Jesu Christi?', in *Zu Geschichte, Theologie, Liturgie und Gegenwartslage der syrischen Kirchen*, eds. Martin Tamcke and Andreas Heinz (Münster, 2000), pp. 55-137. But see Brakmann's reservations concerning this location in *ibid.*, n. 92.

[169] Garitte, *Calendrier* (see n. 148), pp. 115, 425.

[170] For instance Sin. O.1, O.34, and O.64.

[171] Some evidence could seem to point in the direction of a negative answer to the question of their faithfulness. In the composite codex Sin. Georgian O.34 the redactor Iovane Zosime includes three troparia composed by Symeon 'ant'iokeli', that is, Symeon the New Stylite (521-592). However, these stanzas, taken from a Georgian version of the Life of this Stylite, are not included in the liturgical books (Horologia or Iadgari).

[172] Sin. Georgian N.2s and N.3s.

[173] Sure evidence for an addition is found when the acrostic of the Greek original is complete without this ode, as in the Nativity Canon of Kosmas the Melodist (Χριστὸς γεννᾶτε, δοξάσατε).

However, very recently Roman Krivko has pointed out that the addition of a second ode, known also from Syriac and Slavonic versions, does stem from Greek tradition; it is found in no less a source than the 8th-9th century Jerusalem Tropologion Sin. NE MG 56-5.[174]

4.3. Have Elements of the Ancient Iadgari Been Translated from Syriac or Armenian?

The Ancient Iadgari constitutes a huge reservoir of theological expressions and a thorough examination of it against the complex background of first centuries' theological development may disclose evidence of the origin of some of the hymns. Gabriele Winkler has in recent studies[175] shown that Georgian translations in many cases deviate from Greek terminology, especially as regards incarnational terminology. She has further pointed out that the Georgian in these cases corresponds to Syriac and Armenian expressions, surmising that both translations have their roots in Syriac tradition. This makes Winkler voice the suspicion that a part of the Ancient Iadgari might have been translated from a language other than Greek.[176] Against this, Schneider points out that the Syriac expressions of the Incarnation found in the Ancient Iadgari, for instance

---

[174] Krivko, 'Sinaitic-Slavonic Hymnographical Parallels' (see n. 56), pp. 60-73, refers to three cases in this Tropologion of addition of a Second Ode.

[175] The following are the most important: 'Ein Beitrag zum armenischen, syrischen und griechischen Sprachgebrauch bei den Aussagen über die Inkarnation in den frühen Symbolzitaten', in *Logos: Festschrift für Luise Abramowski*, eds. H. Ch. Brennecke et al. (Berlin and New York, 1993), pp. 499-510; 'Der armenische Ritus: Bestandsaufnahme und neue Erkenntnisse sowie einige kürzere Notizen zur Liturgie der Georgier', in *The Christian East: Its Institutions and its Thought – A Critical Reflection*, ed. Robert Taft, Orientalia Christiana Analecta 251 (Rome, 1995), pp. 265-298; *Über die Entwicklungsgeschichte des armenischen Symbolums: Ein Vergleich mit dem syrischen und griechischen Formelgut unter Einbezug der relevanten georgischen und äthiopischen Quellen*, Orientalia Christiana Analecta 262 (Rome, 2000); 'Das theologische Formelgut über den Schöpfer, das ὁμοούσιος, die Inkarnation und Menschwerdung in den georgischen Troparien des *Iadgari* im Spiegel der christlich-orientalischen Quellen', *Oriens Christianus* 84 (2000) 117-177; 'Über die Bedeutung einiger liturgischer Begriffe im georgischen Lektionar und Iadgari sowie im armenischen Ritus', *Studi sull'Oriente Cristiano* 4 (2000) (= FS Metreveli) 133-154; 'Einige bemerkenswerte christologische Aussagen im georgischen *Iadgari*: Ein Vergleich mit verwandten armenischen Quellen', *Oriens Christianus* 91 (2007) 134-163.

[176] For instance: 'Mit dem Einbezug des syrischen und armenischen Formelguts in die Untersuchung georgischer Schlüsselbegriffe für das *homoousios* und die Inkarnationsaussagen lassen sich neue Zusammenhänge erschließen, wie sich auch neue Fragen ergeben, so z.B. bei der Annahme, dass es sich beim *Iadgari* angeblich ausschließlich um eine *Übersetzung griechischer Vorlagen* handelt, die großteils verlorengegangen sind.' See Winkler, 'Eine neue Publikation zum Iadgari' (see n. 43), pp. 198-199.

'to put on a body', are not only Syriac, but also typical of Greek and Latin texts, which are partly older than the Syriac ones.[177] Schneider even claims that the Syriac characteristic of embracing all salvation economy in clothing metaphors is *not* found in the Ancient Iadgari.[178] Renoux maintains the 'received' view that the Georgian witness to the Jerusalem rite reflects a Greek tradition only.[179]

4.4. Longer and Shorter Versions; Layers

A significant aspect of the Georgian sources of Hagiopolite liturgy is the distinction between shorter and longer redactions of liturgical books. This concerns both the Lectionary, the Iadgari,[180] and the Euchologion (including the Liturgy of St. James). How is one to interpret these variations? Are they chronological, geographical, or practical? Did Palestino-Georgian monks create their own types of books, different from Greek models?

The hypothesis of Xevsuriani, presented above, on the formation of the New Iadgari in five stages of increasing size has the weakness of excluding the possibility of short Iadgaris having been deliberately created. As a matter of fact, Xevsuriani herself elsewhere warns against interpreting hymnal size as a criterion of age.[181] The redactor might have simply omitted existing celebrations and hymns in order to create a particular hymn collection for a particular place and need. An example of this is probably the New Iadgari of Sin. O.34, whose short constitution is classified by Xevsuriani as representing a pristine stage (stage a. above), containing a little more than twenty larger feasts, plus common

---

[177] 'In den hier besprochenen Christusfesten aus dem Udzvelesi Iadgari finden sich alle auf die Inkarnation bezogenen Formulierungen wieder, die sich bereits im vierten Jahrhundert in den Texten der frühen Syrer, aber auch — zum Teil schon früher — bei griechischen und lateinischen Schriftstellern finden.' See Schneider, *Lobpreis* (see n. 40), p. 349.

[178] 'Das syrische Spezifikum, nämlich die ganze Heilsgeschichte in dieses Bekleidungsschema zu fassen, findet sich in den Inkarnationshymnen im Udzvelesi Iadgari nicht', *ibid.*, p. 349.

[179] Speaking about the Ancient Iadgari witness Tbilisi H-2123: 'Héritées de l'Église de Jérusalem, traduites du grec en géorgien et passées pour beaucoup d'entre elles dans la tradition byzantine, ces compositions hymniques …'. See Renoux, *L'Hymnaire de Saint-Sabas* (see n. 42), p. 24.

[180] GL (see n. 100), no. App. 6: 'and all other ordo which is lacking here, you shall find it in the "Great Kanoni" and the "Great Iadgari" ' (taken from Sin. O.37, copied by Zosime).

[181] See n. 186.

feasts (archangels, prophets, hierarchs, etc.). But, in view of its clear Sabaite identity,[182] could one not rather explain the brevity of this New Iadgari as being that of a lavriote community, in which cell dwellers quite rarely come together to celebrate common offices, rather than being an early one?

The various layers of the Ancient Iadgari, whose numbers vary from witness to witness and may amount to at least six,[183] raise several questions. Would the layers represent geographical variation, in that, for instance, Georgians composing their version would have added a layer of non-Hagiopolite origin, possibly from Caesarea, Antioch or Damascus? Or are all layers Hagiopolite but stemming from different periods? Does the presence of several layers in a Iadgari indicate that we are dealing with a 'compilation' and a not real codex? Renoux thinks so,[184] but such layers are found even today in Orthodox hymn books[185] and nothing prevents the interpretation that the choir was just meant to choose from a hymn material larger than what they strictly needed. The Ancient Iadgari witness Sin. O.40, on the other hand, has only one layer, which for the most part coincides with the first layer of the two main many-layered manuscripts (H-2123 and Sin. O.18). This first layer of these two manuscripts carries signs of being the most recent text.[186] Prudence

---

[182] There is a section of offices celebrating St. Sabas: Main feast on Dec. 5; the *oxitays* at the Sunday vigil litia to the grave of St. Sabas; an office written by a certain John, Bishop of St. Sabas; a secondary feast on Dec 9.

[183] High numbers of layers are particularly prevalent in the Sunday Oktoechos. The witness translated by Renoux (*Les hymnes de la résurrection*' — see n. 41), Sin. O.18, has up to four layers, while the Sin. O.41 has a maximum of six (for instance Metreveli et al, *Ancient Iadgari* (see n. 37), p. 414).

[184] 'Dans chacun de ces trois offices, de nombreuses სხუანი (*sxuani*), *autres* strophes, ont été ajoutées à celles propres à la liturgie du jour. Tel quel, le H 2123, comme les anciens hymnaires géorgiens, ne représente donc pas un hymnaire liturgique authentique et réel; c'est une compilation..'. See Renoux, *L'Hymnaire de Saint-Sabas* (see n. 42), p. 24.

[185] The cases of ἄλλος or ἕτερος hymns are innumerable and in contemporary Byzantine liturgical books they are meant to be sung.

[186] ‚Из списков Трополгия многослойность присуща спискам АВ. Из многослойных песнопений древнейшего Трополгия составитель списка С выбрал один слой, который в основном совпадает с первым слоем АВ, являвшимся в определенных случаях поздным пополнением Трополгия ([Ancient Iadgari, pp.] 849-851). [Among the witnesses of the Tropologion, "multilayeredness" is proper to the witnesses AB [Tbilisi NCM H-2123 and Sin. O.18]. Among the multilayered hymnography of the Ancient Iadgari the author of the witness C [Sin. O.40] chose one layer, which basically coincides with the first layer of AB, appearing in determined cases as a late addition to the Tropologion ([AI, pp.] 849-851).]' See Xevsuriani, 'Most Ancient Tropologion' (see n. 47), p. 94, n. without number.

is called for in interpreting Sin. O.40; as Xevsuriani warns, its shortness
does not imply antiquity.[187] This warning holds true in general when one
is dealing with varying sizes of liturgical books and with varying numbers of layers.

Conclusion of the Discussion

As a tentative conclusion of this inchoative discussion, it seems that
some non-Hagiopolite elements, whether indigenous Georgian, Syrian,
or others, have been added in Georgia. Further, it is not to be excluded
that some were added in Jerusalem before translation into Georgian or
by Georgians into their version. There is an East Syrian connection in
some Georgian material (ordination prayers, calendar) that is worth looking further into, and the theotokion particularity of the Georgian Heirmologion needs to be explained. On the whole, however, the material
here discussed does not generally call into doubt the Hagiopolite character of pre-Athonite Georgian liturgical documents copied in Palestine.

5. *Epilogue*

Georgian manuscripts constitute an essential, often unique, witness to
the first millennium liturgy of Jerusalem. While the old Sinai collection
of Georgian manuscripts was already spectacular, the Georgian New
Finds of Sinai add considerably to its richness. The philological ground-
work of edition and translation is needed for many Georgian sources to
become available to liturgical scholarship. Further, a broad examination
must be made of the question of whether or to what degree Georgian
witnesses have altered Greek originals. All in all, if Jerusalem liturgy
proves a rich field of research, this is thanks primarily to Georgian
monks of 9th-10th century Palestine, especially Iovane Zosime, and their
laborious copying of manuscripts.

In the second millennium, the Hagiopolite rite soon ceased to exist
as an independent rite. But it persevered on a partial basis, contained in
liturgical books of mixed tradition, that is, of the Early-Byzantine liturgical synthesis that was to become the Byzantine rite. The first signs of
Byzantinisation of the Georgian rite are found not in the Georgian

---

[187] Следовательно, краткость С нельзя рассматривать как признак древности
[Consequently, the shortness of C must not be considered a sign of antiquity] (*ibid.*).

monuments of the Athonite school, but in manuscripts written in Palestine in the last decades of the 10th century.

As signs of the gradual transfer from the Hagiopolite to the Byzantine rite we may highlight the following three examples: the liturgical collection Sin. Georgian N.54[188] has a Hagiopolite Lectionary but it also contains the Constantinopolitan Liturgies of Sts. Chrysostom and Basil; Iovane Zosime's calendar (in Sin. O.34), copied in the 960s, inserts a Constantinopolitan layer of celebrations into the basically Palestinian document; and finally, the Apostle Sin. Georgian O.58-31-60 + N.8, written in 977 at Sinai, mixes the Hagiopolite and the Constantinopolitan Lectionary systems. Also for the process of Byzantinisation of Jerusalem liturgy Georgian sources are of primary importance.

---

[188] See table 1 above.

TYPICA MANUSCRITS SABAÏTES DU 12ᴱ SIÈCLE
REFLETS D'UNE TRADITION COMPOSITE

André LOSSKY

Selon le modèle d'évolution liturgique formulé par le père Alexandre Schmemann, la synthèse byzantine est un processus considéré comme achevé vers le 14ᵉ siècle, période après laquelle le rite byzantin s'est peu modifié.[1] Schmemann fait entrer dans cette synthèse plusieurs couches ou éléments dont les influences se sont fait sentir à différentes époques. Avant le 14ᵉ s., on connaît plusieurs documents décrivant des liturgies locales au départ, mais qui comme on va le voir sont déjà des témoins de synthèses intermédiaires. Leur caractère composite se laisse observer au fait que la liturgie célébrée en leurs lieux ou régions d'élaboration a déjà intégré, avant le 14ᵉ s., des éléments de provenances ou d'époques diverses.

D'après les observations du regretté père Miguel Arranz, le rite byzantin s'est d'abord constitué à partir des liturgies de Jérusalem, puis de Constantinople, avec des influences réciproques à plusieurs époques[2]: stations de Jérusalem transposées à Mar Saba[3] et à Constantinople,[4] avec des adaptations différenciées, ou usages de la Grande Église de Constantinople repris et transformés par la tradition monastique studite, puis prépondérance, entre le 12ᵉ et le 14ᵉ s., des usages monastiques sabaïtes au détriment de la tradition studite, réputée moins stricte et moins propice à la spiritualité hésychaste.[5]

---

[1] A. Schmemann, *Введение в литургическое богословие* [*Introduction à la théologie liturgique*] (Paris, 1961), ch 4, pp. 169s., sp. 226-238.

[2] M. Arranz, 'Les grandes étapes de la liturgie byzantine: Palestine - Byzance - Russie, essai d'aperçu historique', *Liturgie de l'Eglise particulière et liturgie de l'Eglise universelle, Conférences S. Serge, XXIIe semaine d'études liturgiques* (Rome, 1976), pp. 43-72, ici pp. 45-47.

[3] Par convention, pour distinguer le lieu de son fondateur, «Mar Saba» désignera ici le monastère fondé en Palestine au 5ᵉ s. par Saint Sabas le Sanctifié.

[4] Cf. A. Lossky, 'La litie, un type de procession liturgique byzantine — extension du lieu de culte', *Les enjeux spirituels et théologiques de l'espace liturgique, conférences S. Serge, LIe semaine d'études liturgiques* (Rome, 2005), pp. 165-177 (plus bas: 'Litie...').

[5] Voir Arranz, 'Les grandes étapes' (voir n. 2), pp. 67-68. Sur le rôle de la tradition hésychaste dans l'évolution liturgique, voir aussi la thèse doctorale de l'archimandrite Job (Getcha), résumée: *La théologie liturgique du mouvement hésychaste*, Supplément au

Avant cette prépondérance de la tradition sabaïte, le rite byzantin a déjà connu une synthèse due à la tradition monastique de Constantinople, c'est-à-dire la liturgie studite, influencée à la fois par la Palestine et par le rite cathédral de la Grande Église.[6] L'évolution postérieure est qualifiée par le père Taft de synthèse néo-sabaïte, dans une analyse qui complète le modèle de Schmemann en y intégrant l'influence du Mont Athos et de la tradition hésychaste,[7] avec notamment le rôle de la *Diataxis*, un document liturgique attribué à Philothée Kokkinos et qui vient compléter les Typica sabaïtes.

Pour tenter de cerner de plus près divers éléments entrés dans la dernière synthèse liturgique, notre analyse va se concentrer sur quelques documents choisis parmi les témoins de la liturgie byzantine: ce sont les Typica byzantins manuscrits sabaïtes les plus anciens (12e s.), appartenant à la rédaction hiérosolymitaine distinguée par A. Dmitrievski.[8] Ces Typica offrent au moins deux caractéristiques: ils décrivent une liturgie locale, celle de leur région d'élaboration, à savoir la laure fondée par Saint Sabas au 5e s. au sud de Jérusalem, et d'autre part ils intègrent des usages liturgiques venus d'ailleurs que du désert de Palestine, ce qui en fait des documents décrivant une liturgie nettement composite à l'époque de leur écriture.[9] Quelques exemples: les stations hagiopolites transformées à Mar Saba pour devenir des lities pour les fêtes, le rite d'Exaltation de la Croix le 14 septembre, adapté depuis la ville sainte à Mar

---

Service orthodoxe de Presse 286 (Paris, 2004), pp. 11-14; repris dans: *La pensée orthodoxe* 7 (2009) 39-52.

[6] Le caractère composite de la tradition studite, ayant intégré avant le 12e s. des usages palestiniens dans un monastère de Constantinople, est montré dans l'analyse pertinente de Th. Pott, *La réforme liturgique byzantine* (Rome, 2000), pp. 108-113. Voir aussi R. Taft, 'Mount Athos: A Late Chapter in the History of the Byzantine Rite', *Dumbarton Oaks Papers* 42 (1988) 179-194, ici pp. 182, 186-187; N. Egender, 'La formation et l'influence du *Typikon* liturgique de Saint-Sabas', *The Sabaite Heritage in the Orthodox Church from the Fifth Century to the Present*, éd. J. Patrich, Orientalia Lovaniensia Analecta 98 (Leuven, 2001), pp. 209-216.

[7] Taft, 'Mount Athos' (voir n. 6), pp. 187-192.

[8] Cf. *Описание литургических рукописей хранящихся в библиотеках Православного Востока* [*Description des manuscrits liturgiques conservés dans les bibliothèques de l'Orient orthodoxe*], éd. A. Dmitrievski, t. III, *Τυπικά* 2 (Kiev, 1917, repr. Graz, 1965), pp. 1-70, où l'auteur regroupe les cinq Typica sabaïtes les plus anciens; sa classification est reprise par Arranz, 'Les grandes étapes' (voir n. 2), pp. 67-69, qui qualifie ce groupe de Typica manuscrits comme «les plus intéressants» pour cette tradition.

[9] La liturgie byzantine est déjà composite avant les premiers Typica sabaïtes parvenus: le témoignage de Nicon de la Montagne Noire (11e s.) montre la diversité des usages liturgiques à son époque. Cf. Arranz, 'Les grandes étapes' (voir n. 2), pp. 48, 60-62; Taft, 'Mount Athos' (voir n. 6), pp. 179, 186-187; Egender, 'La formation et l'influence' (voir n. 6), pp. 210, 213.

Saba, et décrit en détails par les Typica manuscrits sabaïtes, la Liturgie des Présanctifiés, un office de communion venu de Constantinople et passé de là à Jérusalem et en Palestine, et enfin la procession de la Croix le 1ᵉʳ août, un usage constantinopolitain qui commence à se propager au 12ᵉ s. dans les monastères de Palestine[10] et vers d'autres lieux.[11] Ces éléments importés ne sont pas tous d'origine monastique. A partir de ces quelques exemples au nombre volontairement limité ici, l'objectif de la présente étude est un bref parcours à travers les Typica sabaïtes manuscrits les plus anciens, pour caractériser le processus de transformation des usages liturgiques lorsqu'ils se trouvent intégrés depuis un lieu d'origine dans une autre tradition locale. Une conclusion montrera la place de ces Typica dans l'élaboration de la synthèse du 14ᵉ s.

1. Les Typica sabaïtes reflètent la tradition liturgique locale de Palestine

Parmi plusieurs usages liturgiques locaux, spécifiquement sabaïtes, on analysera ci-dessous la célébration de la Vigile nocturne (ou Agrypnie), et la description de la litie, un usage local par ses allusions topographiques précises.[12] La prière nocturne individuelle ou communautaire est une caractéristique de l'Église ancienne, selon plusieurs témoignages, parmi lesquels les apôtres Paul et Silas en prison (Act 16,25-34; cf. aussi Act 20,7-12)[13] ou Saint Jean Chrysostome qui loue ses fidèles pour leurs assemblées de prière nocturne, avec pour effet selon lui une abolition de

---

[10] Voir *infra*, n. 36.

[11] Voir *infra*, n. 37.

[12] Comme caractéristiques locales de Mar Saba, on pourrait encore évoquer des exemples d'éléments plus spécifiquement monastiques tels que la discipline quant à la prière en cellule (exposée dans le Typicon Sinaïticus gr. 1094, cf. déchiffrage intégral: A. Lossky, *Le Typicon byzantin: édition d'une version grecque (partiellement inédite) — analyse de la partie liturgique*, t. II, thèse dactylographiée (Strasbourg, 1987), p. 151), ou l'usage de l'eau (*ibid.*, p. 153), ou encore la manière de célébrer les complies (cf. par exemple dans les Typica Sinaïticus gr. 1094, Dmitrievski, Описание литургических рукописей, t. III (voir n. 8), p. 15 ou Lossky, *Le Typicon byzantin*, pp. 249-250 et Sinaïticus gr. 1096, Dmitrievski, Описание литургических рукописей, t. III (voir n. 8), pp. 58-59). Sur les prescriptions ascétiques dans les Typica sabaïtes, cf. A. Lossky, 'Le Typicon byzantin: une autorité dans la liturgie de l'Église?', *L'autorité de la liturgie, conférences S. Serge, LIIIe semaine d'études liturgiques* (Rome, 2007), pp. 123-126.

[13] Cf. N. Uspenski, 'Чин всенощного бдения (ἡ ἀγρυπνία) на Православном Востоке и в русской Церкви' ['Ordre de la vigile nocturne (ἡ ἀγρυπνία) dans l'Orient orthodoxe et dans l'Église russe'], Богословские труды [*Travaux théologiques*] 18 (1978), p. 9.

la différence entre nuit et jour.[14] Cette tradition est reprise de manière plus spécifique à Mar Saba et dans les monastères environnants, avec la Vigile nocturne organisée en une célébration rigoureusement structurée, devenue l'une des caractéristiques exclusives de la tradition sabaïte, non retrouvée en d'autres traditions liturgiques[15], mais qui par la suite s'est propagée depuis la Palestine vers d'autres régions du monde byzantin.

L'existence de Vigiles nocturnes à Mar Saba est d'abord attestée sans description, dans la *Vie* de Saint Sabas,[16] puis dans le *Testament* (*Typos*) qui lui est attribué.[17] D'après N. Uspenski, la Vigile sabaïte est une célébration qui s'enracine dans la pratique de l'Anastasis à Jérusalem, d'où elle est adaptée dans le désert de Palestine, avec des conditions topographiques différentes.[18] Par la suite, tous les Typica manuscrits et imprimés se réclamant de la tradition sabaïte commenceront leurs descriptions liturgiques par le déroulement détaillé de la Vigile des nuits du samedi au dimanche.[19]

Mais cette Vigile, tout en étant une caractéristique locale de Mar Saba, intègre aussi dès les premières descriptions du 12ᵉ s. un élément venu d'ailleurs: la litie est une procession tenant ses origines dans les stations de la liturgie de Jérusalem. Celles-ci sont connues et déjà décrites avec insistance par la voyageuse Égérie; elles sont au départ une caractéristique locale de la ville sainte. Leur exportation à Mar Saba

---

[14] Cf. *Homélie après séisme*, PG 50, 713-715, parmi d'autres témoignages rassemblés et étudiés par Uspenski, 'Чин всенощного бдения' (voir n. 13), pp. 11-12.

[15] Ni le rite cathédral de Constantinople, ni les Typica studites ne décrivent de vigile nocturne complète; le Typicon de Jérusalem écrit en 1122 (Hagios Stavros gr. 43), unique Typicon originaire de cette ville, décrit un usage qualifiable de mixte, associant des usages cathédraux, avec la présence active du patriarche, et monastiques, avec la participation d'une communauté de moines jouant un rôle non négligeable dans la célébration. Par exemple: Vigile des Rameaux, Ἀνάλεκτα Ἱεροσολυμιτικῆς Σταχυολογίας, éd. A. Papadopoulos-Kerameus (Saint-Pétersbourg, 1894), pp. 1-254, ici pp. 3 et 7, avec une partie de la célébration assurée par les moines Spoudaioi, ou celle du Grand Samedi, *ibid.*, pp. 161-162, avec à certains moments une forme liturgique monastique, caractérisée notamment par l'absence du patriarche.

[16] Ch. 32, *Kyrillos von Skythopolis*, éd. E. Schwartz, Texte und Untersuchungen 49,2 (Leipzig, 1939), p. 118; trad. A. J. Festugière, *Les moines d'Orient*, III,2, *Les moines de Palestine, Cyrille de Scythopolis, Vie de Saint Sabas* (Paris, 1962), p. 45.

[17] *Описание литургических рукописей хранящихся в библиотеках Православного Востока* [*Description des manuscrits liturgiques conservés dans les bibliothèques de l'Orient orthodoxe*], éd. A. Dmitrievski, t. I, *Τυπικά* 1 (Kiev, 1895), p. 222.

[18] *Ibid.*, p. 63.

[19] Les Typica dits sabaïtes mentionnent dans leur titre la laure fondée par Saint Sabas: c'est le cas pour près de 150 Typica manuscrits du 12ᵉ au 19ᵉ s., cf. par exemple Dmitrievski, *Описание литургических рукописей*, t. III (voir n. 8), pp. 1-2, 20-23, 68, 71, 81, etc. Cf. aussi Arranz, 'Les grandes étapes' (voir n. 2), p. 67.

peut s'expliquer par la forte influence de la liturgie hagiopolite sur les usages sabaïtes; l'adaptation ne s'y fait pas sans une transformation[20]: la laure de S. Sabas comprend plusieurs lieux de culte dès le début de sa fondation[21] et la communauté des moines de la laure, une fois constituée en assemblée liturgique, éprouve le besoin d'investir ces différents lieux en passant de l'un à l'autre durant la célébration, et d'y faire des prières d'intercession spécifiques ayant perdu le lien direct avec les lieux saints hagiopolites, pour en acquérir un autre en fonction des nouveaux lieux visités.[22] La liturgie stationale de Jérusalem a donc généré à Mar Saba la litie, une action liturgique accueillie et adoptée au point de devenir un usage local. Subsiste une caractéristique commune: à Mar Saba comme à Jérusalem, les déplacements liturgiques d'une station à l'autre se font au chant d'hymnes, et dans les points d'arrêt on prononce des prières.[23] Du caractère local de la litie témoignent les allusions topographiques précises dans l'un des Typica sabaïtes anciens.[24]

2. Les premiers Typica sabaïtes parvenus ont déjà intégré des éléments liturgiques venus d'autres lieux

Un autre élément importé à Mar Saba est le rite d'Exaltation de la Croix du 14 septembre, décrit en détail dans les Typica sabaïtes. On sait que ce rite s'enracine dans l'épisode de la découverte de la Croix à Jérusalem, attribué par certaines sources à l'impératrice Ste Hélène, épisode

---

[20] Voir aussi Lossky, 'Litie' (voir n. 4), p. 174.

[21] Cf. *Vie de Saint Sabas* (voir n. 16), ch. 18, pp. 101-102; trad. Festugière (voir n. 16), pp. 29-30; Lossky, 'Litie' (voir n. 4), p. 167.

[22] Sur les stations liturgiques et leurs différents sens, cf. J. Baldovin, *The Urban Character of Christian Worship: The Origins, Development, and Meaning of Stational Liturgy*, Orientalia Christiana Analecta 278 (Rome, 1987), pp. 36-37, 143-145, 258; voir aussi Lossky, 'Litie' (voir n. 4), pp. 165-166.

[23] Ex.: processions du dimanche des Rameaux à Jérusalem, au chant d'hymnes et d'antiennes, *Itinéraire* d'Égérie, 31,2; *Égérie, Journal de voyage*, éd. et trad. P. Maraval, Sources Chrétiennes 296 (Paris, 1982), pp. 274-275, ou usage similaire relevé pour le Vendredi Saint, *ibid.*, 36,1-2, pp. 280-281. Litie dans les Typica sabaïtes: Typicon Sinaïticus gr. 1096, Dmitrievski, *Описание литургических рукописей*, t. III, p. 22; voir aussi Lossky, 'Litie' (voir n. 4), pp. 169-170.

[24] Le lieu originel d'utilisation du Typicon Sinaïticus gr. 1096 semble bien être la laure de Mar Saba, à en juger par les allusions topographiques, mais des notes marginales, relevées par G. Bertonière dans le manuscrit, indiquent un réemploi du document en un autre monastère dédié aux saints martyrs Serge et Bacchus: cf. G. Bertonière, *The Historical Development of the Easter Vigil and Related Services in the Greek Church*, Orientalia Christiana Analecta 193 (Rome, 1972), p. 233.

relaté entre autres par l'historien Sozomène.[25] Le rite même de l'Exaltation fait partie des solennités des Encénies, relatées par Égérie comme
des célébrations très festives avec un grand afflux de pèlerins.[26] Ce rite
est mentionné à une date liturgique équivalente par le Lectionnaire
arménien (5e s.),[27] puis par S. Sophrone de Jérusalem (+638) dans un de
ses sermons.[28] Ces documents ne donnent pas de détails rituels. Les premiers Typica sabaïtes, de leur côté, décrivent pour cette Exaltation un
rite solennel qui correspond à la pratique susmentionnée de Jérusalem.
Parmi ces Typica, celui reflétant la pratique liturgique de Mar Saba[29] le
décrit de manière plus brève, et qui paraît plus archaïque qu'un autre,
appartenant à la même rédaction hiérosolymitaine, mais dont la pratique
n'est pas localisable.[30] Ce dernier offre un déroulement plus structuré,
décrit de manière plus précise et mentionnant davantage de pièces hymnographiques chantées en l'honneur de la Croix. La description d'une
même solennité se fait avec moins de détails dans le Typicon aux usages
localisables à Mar Saba, probablement plus ancien que le dernier mentionné ci-dessus: cette différence d'expression peut signifier le caractère
progressif de l'introduction de l'action liturgique originaire de Jérusalem
et importée de là en Palestine. Le fait que cette description soit aussi
précise dans les Typica sabaïtes traduit peut-être une certaine insistance
sur la nécessité de l'accomplir. L'absence de caractéristiques locales
proprement sabaïtes peut signifier que ce rite a été peu transformé lors
de son implantation depuis Jérusalem vers Mar Saba et alentours.

---

[25] Événement daté du début du 4e s., *Hist. Eccl.* II,1; *Sozomène, Histoire ecclésiastique, L. I-II*, B. Grillet, G. Sabbah (intr.), A.J. Festugière (tr.), Sources Chrétiennes 306
(Paris, 1983), pp. 226-233. Sur une attribution ou non à Hélène, voir discussion dans
H. Leclercq, 'Invention et exaltation de la croix' in *Dictionnaire d'archéologie chrétienne et de liturgie*, III,2 (1914), col. 3131-3139.
[26] *Itinéraire*, 49,3 (voir n. 23), pp. 318-319, avec des synaxes au Martyrium, les 1er et
2e jour. D'après la description, si le 1er jour célébrait la dédicace de cette église, le
2e comprenait probablement le rite d'Exaltation de la Croix.
[27] Fête de la Dédicace au 13 septembre, dans deux des trois mss édités: le 2e jour de
la fête, «on montre la vénérable croix à toute l'assemblée»; *Le codex àrménien Jérusalem 121, II, Edition comparée du texte et de 2 autres manuscrits*, éd. et trad. A. Renoux,
Patrologia Orientalis 36,2 (Turnhout, 1971), n° 168, p. 363 [225].
[28] Homélie sur la Croix, §3-4, *Sophrone, Fêtes chrétiennes à Jérusalem*, J. De La
Ferrière (intr.), M.-H. Congourdeau (trad.), Pères dans la foi 75 (Paris, 1999), pp. 26-27.
[29] Typicon Sinaïticus gr. 1096, f. 33, cf. Dmitrievski, *Описание литургических
рукописей*, t. III, pp. 29-30.
[30] Typicon Sinaïticus gr 1094, f. 19-20, passage non déchiffré par Dmitrievski.
Cf. Lossky, 'Litie' (voir n. 4), pp. 166-167.

De la même façon, on sait que la Liturgie des Présanctifiés en sa forme constantinopolitaine est venue à Jérusalem s'ajouter, sans l'évincer, à un ancien office de communion monastique palestinien.[31] Le fait que le *Typos* de S. Sabas ne mentionne pas de Présanctifiés, mais seulement les Typiques, forme palestinienne de l'office de communion, constitue un indice de plus en faveur de l'origine constantinopolitaine des Présanctifiés tels que les connaît la tradition sabaïte.[32] Les Présanctifiés se caractérisent à Constantinople par une entrée du patriarche, comme lors de toute célébration de Vêpres en cette ville,[33] alors que cette même entrée n'a lieu dans les monastères sabaïtes que les dimanches et fêtes.[34] La procession solennelle des Saints Dons présanctifiés, avec le chant «Maintenant les Puissances célestes…»[35] est aussi une caractéristique constantinopolitaine, importée ici sans beaucoup de transformation.

Le cas de la procession des reliques de la Croix le 1ᵉʳ août est différent, car on ne le trouve pas dans tous les Typica sabaïtes du 12ᵉ s. consultés ici d'après les descriptions laissées par A. Dmitrievski.[36]

---

[31] Le rite cathédral de Jérusalem connaît également des Présanctifiés en une adaptation différente de celle faite à Mar Saba: v. Typicon de 1122 (voir n. 15), pp. 49, 65, 82. Sur les deux sortes d'offices de communion byzantins, v. A. Lossky, 'Typiques et Présanctifiés, deux offices byzantins de communion', dans *Rites de communion, Conférences Saint-Serge, LVe Semaine d'Études liturgiques, Paris, 23-26 juin 2008*, Monumenta Studia Instrumenta Liturgica 59 (Vatican, 2010), pp. 255-266.

[32] Sur le *Typos* attribué à S. Sabas: cf. *supra*, n. 17; mention de la célébration des Typiques: Dmitrievski, *Описание литургических рукописей*, t. I, p. 223.

[33] Par exemple: entrée du patriarche «comme chaque jour», pour le 9 mars. Voir *Le Typicon de la Grande Église*, t. 1, éd. et trad. J. Mateos, Orientalia Christiana Analecta 165 (Rome, 1962), pp. 246-247.

[34] Ex.: Typicon Sinaïticus gr. 1096, fol. 5 (passage inédit, non déchiffré par Dmitrievski); Typicon Sinaïticus gr. 1094, Vêpres sans entrée les jours fériaux, Dmitrievski, *Описание литургических рукописей*, t. III, pp. 13-14, ou Vêpres solennelles, faisant partie de la Vigile, avec entrée, *ibid.*, p. 26.

[35] Première attestation de cette hymne dans les Présanctifiés à Constantinople au 7ᵉ s., d'après N. Uspenski, 'Литургия Преждеосвященных Даров. Историко–литургический очерк' ['La Liturgie des Dons Présanctifiés: Aperçu historico-liturgique'], *Богословские труды* [*Travaux théologiques*], 15 (1976), p. 146. Sur cette introduction, cf. R. Taft, *The Great Entrance*, Orientalia Christiana Analecta 200 (Rome, 1978), pp. 76, 85. L'auteur avance pour cette hymne une origine probablement constantinopolitaine, mais sans que l'on puisse déterminer si elle a connu une autre utilisation que dans la célébration des Présanctifiés. Voir aussi dans *Le Typicon de la Grande Église* (voir n. 33), pp. 246-247, l'utilisation de cette hymne à Constantinople aux Présanctifiés pour le 9 mars si jour férial de carême; autres occurrences: *ibid.* t. II, p. 308. Utilisation de cette hymne dans les Typica sabaïtes: Typicon Sinaïticus gr. 1096, f. 164 et Typicon Sinaïticus gr. 1094, f. 76, cf. Dmitrievski, *Описание литургических рукописей*, t. III, p. 14.

[36] Rite encore absent du Typicon Sinaïticus gr. 1096, mention du 1ᵉʳ août au f. 121, Dmitrievski, *ibid.*, p. 53; dans le Typicon Sinaïticus gr. 1094 (12ᵉ-13ᵉ s.), *ibid.*, p. 5,

A partir des passages qu'il a consultés et déchiffrés, on peut observer que l'introduction de cette procession dans les Typica sabaïtes est progressive, avec degré de solennité variable selon les documents.[37] La présence de cette solennité spécifique au 1er août et originaire de Constantinople n'est donc pas encore attestée dans toute la Palestine au 12e s., ce qui montre que le processus d'influence constantinopolitaine en cette région est encore inachevé à cette époque.

Les cinq exemples ci-dessus ont chacun des caractéristiques différentes: un usage local qui évolue (Vigile), un usage venu d'ailleurs et fortement transformé (litie) au point de devenir local, deux usages importés, probablement sans beaucoup de transformations (l'Exaltation de la Croix le 14 septembre et la Liturgie des Présanctifiés) ou enfin un usage en cours d'importation à l'époque des documents étudiés (procession et autres rites liés à la Croix le 1er août).

Conclusion: Facteurs de transformation des usages importés et élaboration de la synthèse byzantine

A partir de ces exemples, on peut admettre que les Typica du 12e s., tout en se réclamant de la tradition strictement sabaïte comme l'indique leur titre, recèlent déjà une synthèse liturgique intermédiaire car ils intègrent des éléments provenant de Jérusalem et de Constantinople, et plus ou moins transformés selon les cas. Le processus de transformation se fait sous l'influence de deux facteurs au moins, hypothétiquement formulables ainsi: la transformation d'un usage liturgique dépend d'une part de la topographie et d'autre part du type de communauté où est importé l'usage considéré.

mention: ordo selon le 3e dimanche de Carême, et renvoi *ibid.*, pp. 17-18; Typicon Sinaïticus gr. 1095 (12e-13e s.): même usage avec en plus une bénédiction des eaux, *ibid.*, p. 68; Typicon Sabaiticus gr. 312 (1201), fol. 76v-77, *ibid.*, p. 69, célébration avec avant-fête de la Croix le 31 juillet et rite de vénération le 1er août à la fin des Matines, puis procession en divers lieux du monastère.

[37] Attesté d'abord par le *Typicon de la Grande Église* (voir n. 33), t. I, pp. 356-357, à compléter par la description du *Livre des Cérémonies* de Constantin VII Porphyrogénète, I,31(22), avec mention de l'exaltation de la Croix sur l'ambon; éd. et trad. A. Vogt, t. I (Paris, 1935), p. 118. Ce rite se retrouve progressivement introduit non seulement en certains lieux de Palestine (voir n. 36) mais aussi au Sinaï, avec procession de la Croix et bénédiction des eaux (selon le Typicon Sin. gr. 1097 (1214), Dmitrievski, Описание литургических рукописей, t. III, pp. 416-417), en Asie Mineure (Typicon dit du Mont Galèse, Typicon Lavra 99 (13e s.), *ibid.*, p. 95), et dans la région de Trébizonde (Typicon Vatopedi 320 (1346), *ibid.*, p. 446, ici sans bénédiction des eaux).

La disposition géographique des lieux n'est pas sans influencer le déroulement d'une action liturgique: la rudesse du terrain à Mar Saba entraîne la naissance d'une nouvelle action liturgique, en l'occurrence la Vigile nocturne provenant des célébrations hagiopolites et devenant l'une des caractéristiques principales de la tradition sabaïte, y compris lorsque celle-ci sera transposée en d'autres parties du monde byzantin avec une topographie différente.

Dans le cas de la litie, envisagée ici comme adaptation de la liturgie stationale de Jérusalem, la caractéristique commune aux deux lieux reste le déplacement de l'assemblée au chant d'hymnes. L'objectif est de faire mémoire non plus des événements du salut là où ils se sont produits, mais du fondateur du nouveau lieu, là où repose son corps.[38] Les lieux de la Ville sainte sont remplacés par les lieux de culte du monastère de Mar Saba, d'où une transformation radicale, un changement d'objectif d'une action liturgique, la mémoire du salut étant remplacée par des prières d'intercession non seulement pour les saints fondateurs, mais pour tous les défunts de la communauté, et aussi, par extension, pour tous les besoins du monde. Le transfert d'un lieu à un autre s'accompagne d'une transformation de l'intention de l'action liturgique ainsi adaptée. A Jérusalem, la visite des lieux saints par les pèlerins s'enracine dans le besoin de faire mémoire, bien au-delà d'un simple souvenir, des événements du Salut, sur les lieux mêmes, réels ou présumés, où ceux-ci se sont déroulés. Communier à ces événements signifie participer toujours plus aux bienfaits qu'à travers eux Dieu a prodigué à l'être humain. A Mar-Saba, la visite des divers lieux de culte exprime d'abord la communion avec les fondateurs ou prédécesseurs, et la prière pour eux s'élargit en une intercession ou supplication, d'autant plus insistante que le lieu visité est lié à l'histoire de la fondation de la laure.

La communauté qui accueille un usage liturgique venu d'ailleurs diffère de celle d'où est issu cet usage. Ici, le lieu d'origine est la Ville sainte où affluent de nombreux pèlerins, avec des attentes liturgiques spécifiques, notamment le désir de visiter un grand nombre de lieux où se sont produits les événements du salut. Cette attente diffère de celle du lieu d'accueil, ici une assemblée composée non plus de pèlerins visiteurs occasionnels, mais de moines résidents, et qui élabore peu à peu une liturgie avec des exigences et des caractéristiques propres, comme par exemple l'intercession dans le cas de la litie. Ainsi, le fait qu'un élément

---

[38] Cf. Lossky, 'Litie' (voir n. 4), p. 169.

liturgique d'origine cathédrale ou séculière soit adopté par une communauté monastique entraîne inévitablement des transformations en fonction soit des besoins, soit de la vocation spécifique de la communauté
nouvelle. Dans le cas de cette communauté monastique prise comme
exemple, on peut songer avec la litie à une expression liturgique de la
vocation d'intercession pour le monde.

Les Typica sabaïtes byzantins les plus anciens parvenus (12ᵉ s.) ont
donc déjà intégré, à leur époque, des éléments qui les rendent liturgique-
ment composites. Ils sont témoins d'une évolution propre, accueillant
notamment et transformant plus ou moins des éléments liturgiques venus
d'ailleurs que de Palestine. Plusieurs éléments faisant partie de la synthèse proposée par Schmemann, et placée par lui au 14ᵉ s., sont déjà
présents, fût-ce en germe, dans nos Typica sabaïtes du 12ᵉ.

Après ces premiers Typica, il restera une dernière étape à cette évolution: c'est celle exprimée au 14ᵉ s. par plusieurs documents parmi lesquels d'une part les Typica sabaïtes postérieurs à la rédaction hiérosolymitaine, élaborés à partir du 14ᵉ s. et classés par Dmitrievski dans la
rédaction dite constantinopolitaine, et d'autre part la *Diataxis* du
patriarche de Constantinople Philothée Kokkinos,[39] qui tient compte du
grand courant spirituel que constitue la tradition hésychaste, laquelle a
débuté bien avant le 14ᵉ s. Étudier les transformations liturgiques du
14ᵉ s. sous l'influence hésychaste pourra aider à en dégager les prémices
décelables dans les Typica du 12ᵉ s.

Une des caractéristiques du rite byzantin est son adaptabilité en de
nouveaux lieux, sous l'influence non seulement de conditions topographiques différentes, mais aussi de types de communautés variables en
importance numérique et en qualité (moines, séculiers, pèlerins...), ou
de courants spirituels nouvellement exprimés. Ce phénomène d'adaptation s'est observé à plusieurs époques et n'est pas allé sans l'intégration
d'éléments liturgiques d'origines diverses, empêchant de considérer la
tradition liturgique byzantine comme monolithique. Avant la synthèse
considérée comme finale au 14ᵉ s., les Typica sabaïtes les plus anciens
parvenus constituent déjà des témoins non négligeables de cette riche
diversité liturgique.

---

[39] Sur ce document, cf. Taft, 'Mount Athos' (voir n. 6), p. 191; Schmemann,
Введение (voir n. 1), p. 238. Sur son évolution et sa relation avec les Typica sabaïtes,
v. N. Uspenski, 'Чин всенощного бдения' (voir n. 13), p. 89.

LA DISPOSITION INTÉRIEURE RÉDACTIONNELLE DES MANUSCRITS LITURGIQUES, PARIS, COISLIN 213; GROTTAFERRATA Γ. B. I; ATHÈNES, ETHNIKE BIBLIOTHÈKE 662

Panayotis KALAÏTZIDIS

Il est vrai que jusqu'à aujourd'hui le contenu de ces trois mss[1] a été assez bien étudié à plusieurs reprises par les chercheurs de la liturgie byzantine. De plus, le texte de ces deux mss a été édité, il y a beaucoup de temps;[2] par ailleurs une édition du troisième ms a vu le jour récemment.[3] Pourtant, ce qui n'a pas attiré beaucoup l'attention des chercheurs jusqu'à maintenant c'est la disposition intérieure du contenu de ces trois mss. Il y a un certain temps, nous avons effectué une recherche plus vaste et plus approfondie examinant ces trois mss justement de ce point de vue et nous sommes arrivés à des hypothèses intéressantes, voire des conclusions importantes.[4] Au cours de notre article, nous nous bornons à développer seulement deux sujets de l'ensemble de notre recherche: celui de la semaine sainte et celui de la conversion des hérétiques. Mais auparavant il faut dire un mot sur la méthode de notre étude.

---

[1] Nous utilisons ici les abréviations suivantes: STR pour le Paris, BNF, Coislin 213; BES pour le Grottaferrata Γ. β. I (sans contester les conclusions de la conférence des Parenti et Velkovska, présentée au cours du colloque de la SOL à Eichstätt, Allemagne, et publiée dans *Bollettino della Badia Greca di Grottaferrata*, III s., 4 (2007) 175-196, qui par ailleurs a jeté un nouveau jour sur l'histoire de ce ms); et EBE pour l'Athènes, Bibliothèque Nationale de Grèce 662.

[2] Sur le premier ms, voir James Duncan, *Coislin 213, Euchologe de la Grande Eglise*, Dissertatio ad Lauream, Pontificio Istituto Orientale [PIO] (Rome, 1983), (ff 3-101); Jósef Maj, *Coislin 213, Eucologio della Grande Chiesa*, Tesi di Laurea, PIO (Rome, 1990); *idem, Coislin 213, Eucologio della Grande Chiesa: manoscritto greco della Biblioteca Nazionale di Parigi (ff. 101-211)*, Excerpta ex Dissertatione ad Doctoratum, PIO (Rome, 1995). Sur le deuxième ms, voir Giovanni Stassi, *L'Eucologio Γ. β. 1 'Bessarione' di Grottaferrata*, Tesi di laurea, PIO (Rome, 1982); Miguel Arranz, *L'Eucologio costantinopolitano agli inizi del secolo XI: Hagiasmatarion & Archieratikon (Rituale & Pontificale) con l'aggiunta del Leitourgikon (Messale)* (Rome, 1996).

[3] Panaghiotis Kalaïtzidis, *L'Eucologio manoscritto 662 della Biblioteca Nazionale di Grecia*, Tesi di Dottorato, PIO (Rome, 2003); Παναγιώτη Λ. Καλαϊτζίδη, *Τὸ ὑπ' ἀριθμ. 662 χειρόγραφο - εὐχολόγιο τῆς Ἐθνικῆς Βιβλιοθήκης τῆς Ἑλλάδος*, Excerpta ex Dissertatione ad Doctoratum, PIO (Rome, 2004).

[4] *Idem*, 'Τρία χφφ «πατριαρχικὰ» εὐχολόγια: Coislin 213, Grottaferrata Γ. β. I, Ἐθνικῆς Βιβλιοθήκης τῆς Ἑλλάδος 662; ἱστορικοκριτικὴ προσέγγιση', à paraître.

Notre recherche se contente, en général, d'examiner les titres des offices sans aborder les questions de contenu des ces trois mss, sauf, si le cas échéant, cela est jugé nécessaire. Dans un premier temps, il fallait rédiger un tableau du contenu de ces mss selon leur ordre. Comme matériel de base nous nous sommes servi du πίναξ ἀκριβής, affiché dans les premières feuilles du premier et du troisième ms, en plaçant chaque office, selon leur ordre, à une cellule numérotée. Pour des raisons évidentes, s'agissant du premier et du dernier de ces mss cela n'a pas été difficile. Néanmoins parfois nous avons mis dans notre tableau aussi les titres qui se trouvent à l'intérieur de ces deux mss, car les variantes qui s'y trouvent suscitent un grand intérêt. En ce qui concerne le deuxième, le Grottaferrata Γ. β. I, vu son manque probable du πίναξ ἀκριβής, nous avons pris la liberté d'en rédiger un, en transcrivant les titres des offices qu'on trouve dans ses feuilles. Certes, parfois on encourt le danger de diviser des offices, qui dans la réalité représentent des offices unifiés, mais ce risque peut se rencontrer dans un nombre de cas très limité. En outre, on a écarté la discussion sur les diverses questions de chronologie, de provenance, d'écriture et de tradition de ces mss, etc.

En observant le contenu du STR nous nous apercevons qu'au commencement du ms se trouve un groupe de prières relatives à la fondation et à la consécration d'une église. Ensuite un deuxième groupe, de six chapitres, constitue la 'semaine sainte' de l'eucologe constantinopolitain, cc. 9-14:[5] Dépouillement du saint autel, Après le dépouillement, Lavement des pieds, Consécration du saint myron, Catéchèse du vendredi saint et une ''Ακολουθία ἑτέρα τοῦ νιπτῆρος'. Malheureusement, à cause d'une perte de huit feuilles, seulement la première de celles-ci nous a été parvenue intacte. Le mode de disposition de ces offices dans le codex a été conditionné probablement par le temps de leur célébration, qui s'accorde avec la pratique de la Grande Église, telle qu'elle nous a été connue par des sources du X-XIème siècle.[6] Et puisque

---

[5] L'abréviation c. ou cc. (cellule ou cellules) renvoie au tableau de trois mss placé en fin de cet article.

[6] Codex Sainte-Croix 40 (ms. H, selon son éditeur), Juan Mateos, *Le Typicon de la Grande Église: Ms. Sainte-Croix n° 40, Xe siècle*, vol. II, *Le cycle des fêtes mobiles*, Orientalia Christiana Analecta 166 (Rome, 1963), pp. 72^(26)-76^(14); Dresde 104, *Древньйшіе патріаршіе типиконы святогробскій іерусалимскій и Великой Константинопольской Церкви*, éd. Aleksej Dmitrievskij (Kiev, 1907), pp. 153, 127, 131, 124; Bibl. Marciana 13, XIème s., Elpidius Mioni, recensuit, *Codices graeci manuscripti: Bibliothecae divi Marci Venetiarum*, vol. I, *Thesaurus antiquus, Codices 1-299*,

ces sources en ce qui concerne le lavement des pieds, nous transmettent une τάξις sans prières,[7] nous croyons que aussi STR faisait de même. C'est pour cela qu'au c. 11 nous avons la leçon 'η´, Τάξις ἡ τοῦ νιπτῆρος', sans aucune allusion au nombre des prières, comme c'est l'habitude du STR pour le reste des offices, étant donné qu'à cette époque le patriarche répétait tout simplement l'action du Seigneur, pendant la lecture évangélique et avant la célébration de la liturgie. Le titre n° θ´, c. 12, ' Ἐπὶ ποιήσει μύρου τῇ μεγάλη Ε´ ὁμοίως εὐχαὶ β´', ne doit pas nous fourvoyer, parce que le mot ὁμοίως se réfère au jour et pas au nombre des prières. Pour cette raison, on rechercherait en vain des prières en cet endroit du STR. Les seules informations précises qu'il pourrait nous fournir, porteraient sur le temps exact de la célébration du lavement des pieds et aussi sur l'utilisation ou pas des diverses pièces hymnologiques, chose impossible aujourd'hui à cause de la perte des feuilles précitées. Pareillement, la place du 'ι´, Ἀκολουθία ἑτέρα τοῦ νιπτῆρος γινομένη ἐν τοῖς μοναστηρίοις ἔχουσα εὐχὰς γ´', c. 13, est intéressante. Bien que d'habitude la εὐχὴ ou τάξις ou ἀκολουθία ἑτέρα ou ἄλλη suivent exactement après la principale, ici le scribe l'a mise à la fin du jeudi saint, c'est-à-dire après la célébration de la messe, non comme une possibilité alternative ou un choix secondaire, mais à cause de sa célébration, selon l'ordre monastique, après la célébration de la liturgie. De surcroît, selon le titre du c. 174, le ms contient une autre série de prières concernant le lavement des pieds. Nous voyons, donc, la reforme liturgique, qui a eu lieu vers la fin de la période de l'iconoclasme et au-delà, dans des milieux monastiques,[8] frapper aux portes de la Grande Église et susciter l'intérêt des ses ministres.

[1981] p. 20; *Prophetologium*, Monumenta Musicae Byzantinae, *Lectionaria,* I, fasc. IV, éd. Castern Høeg et Günther Zuntz (Copenhague, 1960), pp. 380, 384-385, sigla V. La partie du ms qui concerne le Lavement des pieds est brièvement exposée par Mark M. Morozowich, *Holy Thursday in the Jerusalem and Constantinopolitan Traditions: The Liturgical Celebrations from the Fourth to the Fourteenth Centuries*, Excerpta ex Dissertatione ad Doctoratum, PIO (Rome, 2002), pp. 81-82. Aussi Pantéléemon 68, XIème s., *Описаніе литургическихъ рукописей хранящихся въ библіотекахъ православнаго востока*, vol. I, *Τυπικά,* éd. A. Dmitrievskij (Kiev, 1895), p. 129, n. 1.

[7] Contra Morozowich, *Holy Thursday* (voir n. 6), p. 81 et André Lossky, 'La cérémonie du lavement des pieds: Un essai d'étude comparée', dans *Acts of the International Congress, Comparative Liturgy Fifty Years After Anton Baumstark (1872-1948), Rome, 25-29 September 1998*, éd. Robert Taft et Gabriele Winkler, Orientalia Christiana Analecta 265 (Rome, 2001), pp. 813-814. Lossky souligne le fait que le Dresde 104 manque de prières (p. 812).

[8] A titre d'exemple voir Thomas Pott, *La réforme liturgique byzantine: Étude du phénomène de l'évolution non-spontanée de la liturgie byzantine*, Bibliotheca Ephemerides Liturgicae, Subsidia 104 (Rome, 2000), pp. 97-234; *idem*, 'Réforme monastique et

L'ordre de la disposition des chapitres déjà mentionnés de la semaine sainte des mss BES et EBE est changé, probablement à cause de l'ordre différent de leur célébration, résultat des remaniements liturgiques généraux, provoqués par l'expansion de l'office monastique depuis la fin de l'iconoclasme et de la prise de Constantinople par les Latins en 1204. La catéchèse du vendredi saint du BES, en particulier, c. 42, semble appartenir plutôt aux rites baptismaux et aux prières de l'office des Saintes Théophanies, cc. 31-41, qu'aux chapitres de la semaine sainte, cc. 43-46. Cette mise en rapport du c. 42 avec le baptême renvoie à la disposition du Barberini graecus 336, où l'''Απόταξις καὶ σύνταξις' se trouvent aussi en relation évidente avec le baptême.[9] EBE, d'autre part, dissocie totalement la catéchèse des cas précédents en la transférant 120 ff. après le baptême (cc. 8-15) et 116 après la semaine sainte (cc. 16-19), dans un lieu complètement isolé (c. 134), dans lequel avec le contenu de cc. 131-133, rassemble ce qui probablement ne faisait plus partie de la liturgie de son temps.[10] Du reste, les deux mss préfèrent un jeudi saint monastique, étant donné qu'ils transfèrent l'office du lavement des pieds après celui de la consécration du saint myron;[11] celui-là contient dorénavant

---

évolution liturgique: La réforme stoudite', dans *Crossroad of Cultures: Studies in Liturgy and Patristics in Honor of Gabriele Winkler,* éd. Hans-Jürgen Feulner, Elena Velkovska et Robert Taft, Orientalia Christiana Analecta 260 (Rome, 2000), pp. 557-589; Robert Taft, *The Byzantine Rite: A Short History* (Collegeville, MN, 1992), pp. 52-66.

[9] *L'Eucologio Barberini gr. 336,* éd. Stefano Parenti et Elena Velkovska, Bibliotheca Ephemerides Liturgicae, Subsidia 80 (Rome, 1995; seconda edizione riveduta con traduzione italiana: Rome, 2000), nn° 112-126 Baptême, 127-134 Théophanies, 135-139 Pannychis, 140-142 Consécration du nard, 143-145 Renonciation, 146-148 des hérétiques. Il serait intéressant si l'on avait connu le titre de la 'Catéchèse' contenue dans STR.

[10] Voir aussi Kalaïtzidis, *L'Eucologio* (voir n. 3), pp. XC, XCVI-XCVII.

[11] C'est-à-dire après la célébration de la liturgie, selon la tradition hiérosolymitaine mais aussi selon les témoignages d'une série de mss sabbaïtiques (type monastique de Sinaï 735, Xème s.), néosabbaïtiques (Vatopédiou 1488, XIème s., Laura Γ 67 et Γ 72 et en partie EBE 788, premier quart du XIème s., [Barbara Crostini Lappin, 'Manuscript: Brief Description of ms Atheniensis graecus 788', dans Robert H. Jordan, texte et traduction, *The Synaxarion of the Monastery of the Theotokos Evergetis: September to February,* Belfast Byzantine Texts and Translations 6.5 (Belfast, 2000), pp. xi-xii. Voir aussi Dmitrievski, I, Τυπικά, p. 438, Robert H. Jordan, texte et traduction, *The Synaxarion of the Monastery of the Theotokos Evergetis: March to August, the Movable Cycle,* Belfast Byzantine Texts and Translations 6.6 (Belfast, 2005), p. 62]) et enfin selon la tradition des mss studites (Bibliothèque Synodale de Moscou 330, XII-XIIIème s., Sainte Sophie de Kiev 1113, XIIIème s. Ces deux codices contiennent la traduction slave de l'original grec perdu, connu par ailleurs comme Typicon du patriarche Alexis Studite [1025-1043, Venance Grumel, *La Chronologie,* Traité d'Études Byzantines, éd. P. Lemerle, vol. I (Paris, 1958), p. 436]. Une présentation schématique du Lavement des pieds, d'après le premier ms est proposée par Morozowich, *Holy Thursday* (voir n. 6), p. 90. Traduction

des prières γινόμεναι ἐν τοῖς μοναστηρίοις, selon son titre.[12] Il faut noter que dans le pseudo-Kodinos, postérieur à BES et EBE, malgré la présence de forts éléments palestiniens, pénétrés dans la liturgie du palais impériale, souligne que ʿΠρὸ δὲ τῆς λειτουργίας τῆς αὐτῆς μεγάλης Πέμπτης γίνεται ὁ νιπτὴρ οὕτω ... καὶ μετὰ τοῦτο ἄρχεται ἡ λειτουργίαʾ, sans faire allusion à des prières.[13] La semaine sainte de ces deux mss nous permet de comprendre les modifications survenues, par rapport aux STR et au Typikon de la Grande Église, en raison des influences monastiques.

L'avant-dernière partie du STR est constituée, d'une part, des prières εἰς ἀνοίξια ἐκκλησίας profanée des diverses raisons, et d'autre part des chapitres concernant le mode d'admission dans l'Église des hérétiques et des apostats, et les prières respectives, cc. 148-167. Leur place dans le ms ne nous fournit pas des informations importantes. Ces chapitres se trouvent dans ce lieu, probablement à cause de la rareté de leur usage ou de leur constitution relativement récente.

Cet ensemble dans BES (cc. 52-65) se retrouve parmi les prières relatives d'une part à l'église et à l'autel et d'autre part aux prières du congé. Son scribe a choisi cette place en obéissant à la rubrique de la quatrième prière de ce groupe (c. 52): λεγομένη ἐν τῇ εἰσόδῳ πρὸ τῆς συνήθους.[14] De la sorte, il procède à une mise en rapport des chapitres concernant l'église avec ceux de sa réouverture. Puisque la plupart des cc. 52-65 avait comme prolongement naturel la célébration de la messe, c'est très probablement pour cette raison qu'à la suite de ceux-ci, nous avons les prières du congé.

Cependant dans EBE cette unité se présente divisée. Au début, précèdent les chapitres relatifs à la réouverture d'une église, εἰς ἀνοίξια ἐκκλησίας, cc. 122-125. Après cela, le scribe fait insérer un groupe de prières hétéroclite, cc. 126-135. La transposition remarquable des

---

anglaise du texte du Lavement des pieds de Sainte Sophie de Novgorod 1136 chez David M. Petras, *The Typicon of the Patriarch Alexis the Studite: Novgorod-St Sophia 1136*, Excerpta ex Dissertatione ad Doctoratum, PIO (Cleveland, 1991), pp. 73-78; voir et pp. 7-10. Le rédacteur du Typicon contenu dans ces deux mss slaves s'oppose explicitement à la célébration, après la liturgie, du Lavement des pieds, selon la tradition studite), Morozowich, *Holy Thursday* (voir n. 6), pp. 60, 67, 69, 72, 74-76, 87-88, 94.

[12] Cf. STR, c. 13.

[13] *Pseudo-Kodinos: Traité des offices*, introduction, texte et traduction Jean Verpeaux, Le monde byzantin 1 (Paris, 1966), pp. 228[(10-12)], 229[(19-20)].

[14] Arranz, *L'Eucologio costantinopolitano* (voir n. 2), p. 257; le titre est le même dans les STR, c. 151 et EBE, c. 125, la place qu'il y occupe est pourtant différente.

cc. 131-134, qui appartenaient à l'*asmatikos typos*, déjà en déclin à l'époque, ne doit pas être dictée par des besoins de nature liturgique. Le grand parcours de cette transposition trahit plutôt une mise en jachère de ces prières. Pour la même raison, le reste des chapitres pour les hérétiques peut être enlevé aussi, déplacé à cet endroit, cc. 136-148. D'ailleurs, au temps du copiage d'EBE le territoire de l'empire était tellement réduit et l'indépendance de la capitale même était mise en cause constamment, si bien qu'il serait une utopie de s'occuper de telles affaires, au moins non pas au même degré d'intensité que dans le passé. Il faut noter pourtant qu'entre les chapitres précités s'intercale la c. 135, c'est-à-dire les prières avant la communion, qui avaient déjà commencé à se développer et à se propager.

Voyons maintenant quelles autres informations peut nous fournir la disposition des chapitres précités. Les parties qui constituent cette unité sont les suivantes:

a)   les prières à la réouverture d'une église;
b)   dispositions sur les modalités d'admission des hérétiques à l'Église;
c)   la *Diataxis* du patriarche Méthode et les prières expiatoires des convertis;
d)   les anathématismes et des modalités d'admission des Hébreux, des Melchisédechites et des Sarrasins.

Le fait que les responsables de la profanation d'une église étaient des hérétiques ou des païens devient le lien joignant le a) et le b) et par extension le c) et le d).

Les a), b) et c) se disposent de la même façon dans tous les trois mss. L'ensemble des unités b), c) et d) a été complété jusqu'à fin du IXème siècle.[15] La place occupée par chaque chapitre à l'articulation de cet ensemble, pensons-nous, a été déterminée par le temps de leur insertion dans la praxis liturgique de l'Église. Ce qui présente des modifications, c'est l'unité d). BES en contient seulement la c. 56, Πῶς δεῖ δέχεσθαι τὸν ἐξ Ἑβραίων ...,[16] qui est placée en tête au chapitre pour les hérétiques, avant le b). Cette place particulière atteste soit l'ancienneté de

---

[15] Paolo Eleuteri et Antonio Rigo, *Eretici, dissidenti, musulmani ed ebrei a Bisanzio: Una raccolta eresiologica del XII secolo* (Venise, 1993), pp. 37-58, en particulier pp. 57-58.

[16] Sa rédaction remonte vers le milieu du IXème s. et en tout état de cause avant 878-879: Eleuteri et Rigo, *Eretici* (voir n. 15), p. 49.

son originale, étant donné l'absence du texte postérieur de l' Ἔκθεσις ἀκριβεστέρα,[17] STR c. 166 et EBE c. 146, soit la conviction que de toute l'unité d), le commanditaire du BES s'intéressait à l'époque de son copiage uniquement à cette question. Celle-ci coïncide avec les dernières tentatives de Théodoros II Laskaris (1254-1258)[18] en 1254[19] d'imposer le baptême aux Hébreux. Il a continué les mesures contre les Hébreux, prises par son père Iohannès III Batatzès (1222-1254)[20] en 1253.[21] Par conséquent, l'espace du temps entre 1253 et 1254 peut être considéré comme *terminus post quem* du copiage de BES. STR, en revanche, rassemble à la fin de cette unité trois chapitres pour les Hébreux, tandis que EBE, sans s'être beaucoup intéressé au noyau de la question, à cause de son archaïsme, copie exactement son original. Pour cette raison, la disposition de l'unité d), pensons-nous, se retrouvant dans le ms EBE, représente mieux que les deux autres, l'histoire de l'insertion des chapitres précités dans l'eucologe constantinopolitain.[22]

En examinant la disposition du contenu des ces trois mss dans sa totalité, comme dans les exemples qu'on vient d'exposer, nous avons constaté que ces trois eucologes se constituent en réalité des deux parties: l'une, la plus ancienne, c'est l'*archiératikon* ou mieux le *patriarchikon* étant donné qu'elle s'est développée dans l'Église Sainte Sophie; l'autre, plus récente, c'est le *hiératikon*.

Ce *patriarchikon* se développe dans STR, d'après des unités thématiques. La deuxième partie qui est constituée plutôt des prières isolées, se présente selon un ordre inhabituel, qui le rend plus utilisable. Sa structure trahit que son copieur n'était pas un scribe commun mais un connaisseur de la réalité liturgique de la Grande Église.[23]

---

[17] Sur sa datation, voir Eleuteri et Rigo, *Eretici* (voir n. 15), pp. 49-50.

[18] Grumel, *La Chronologie* (voir n. 11), p. 359.

[19] David Jacoby, 'Les Juifs de Byzance: une communauté marginalisée', dans Οἱ περιθωριακοὶ στὸ Βυζάντιο; Πρακτικὰ ἡμερίδας [9-5-1992], éd. Χρύσα Μαλτέζου (Athènes, 1993), p. 125 (= idem, *Byzantium, Latin Romania and the Mediterranean*, Variorum Collected Studies Series CS703 (Aldershot, Burlington, 2001), (III); Andrew Sharf, *Jews and other minorities in Byzantium* (Jerusalem, 1995), pp. 151-155.

[20] Grumel, *La Chronologie* (voir n. 11), p. 359.

[21] Peter Charanis, 'The Jews in the Byzantine empire under the first Palaeologi', *Speculum* 22 (1947), p. 75.

[22] Sur la disposition de b)-d) selon l'ordre d'autres mss mais aussi d'autres cas d'hérésies, voir Eleuteri et Rigo, *Eretici* (voir n. 15), pp. 21-31, 34-36.

[23] Voir Panaghiotis Kalaitzidis, 'Il πρεσβύτερος Στρατήγιος e le due note bibliografiche del codice Paris, Coislin 213', *Bollettino della Badia Greca di Grottaferrata*, III s. 5 (2008), pp. 179-184.

L'image que nous communique BES est aussi intéressante. Les premiers soixante titres, à peu près, de ce ms avec les μνῆστρα et les désignations constituent le *patriarchikon*. Si nous considérons que la place de la prière après la communion n'est pas accidentelle, cela signifie que les chapitres portant sur l'église jusqu'à la désignation du *basileus* s'articulent ayant comme centre la divine liturgie.

Pareillement, au début d'EBE nous retrouvons le *patriarchikon* selon une disposition différente de ses diverses unités, étant donné que sa mise en forme a été déterminée par les conditions de sa rédaction, qui ont influé sur la constitution du reste des chapitres.

Un examen minutieux d'un élément par excellence asmatique de l'euchologe, des *litai*, a démontré que BES et EBE procèdent à des omissions conscientes, qui peuvent être attribuées soit à leur rédaction ultérieure soit à leur utilisation monastique ou non constantinopolitaine. On a aussi constaté une ressemblance à la lettre quant à plusieurs titres de ces mss et quant à la disposition de la plus grande partie de leur *hiératikon*. Il en résulte que les mss en question puisent dans une source commune. Néanmoins, EBE adopte quelques fois une attitude ambiguë, parfois suivant BES en ce qui concerne la disposition, parfois STR en ce qui concerne le nombre des prières. Par ailleurs, tous les trois mss comprennent le même nombre de prières: en ce qui concerne la disposition, EBE s'accorde avec STR, mais en ce qui concerne le cadre de leur emplacement, il adopte le point de vue de BES.

Pour arriver, donc, à des conclusions plus probantes, il convient de procéder à une collation minutieuse du contenu des trois mss, qui nous permettra de constater leur parcours commun probable soit dans leur partie *patriarcale*, soit dans leur partie *hiératicale* et enfin, par conséquent, de déterminer la date de leurs sources.

Tableau comparatif de trois mss

STR		BES		EBE	
9	ϛ´ Εἰς τὴν ἀπαμφίασιν τῆς ἁγίας τραπέζης τῆς Μεγάλης Ἐκκλησίας γινομένη τῇ μεγάλῃ Ε´, εὐχὴ α´. Εὐχὴ ... τραπέζης τὴν γινομένην τῇ ἁγίᾳ Πέμπτῃ ὑπὸ τοῦ ἀρχιερέως μετὰ τὴν συμπλήρωσιν τῆς Τριτοέκτης. 23ʳ⁻ᵛ	41	μα´ Εὐχὴ ἑτέρα εἰς τὸ ὕδωρ τῶν ἁγίων Θεοφανίων λεγομένη ἐν τῇ φιάλῃ τοῦ μεσαύλου. 64ᵛ, Arranz, L'Eucologio costantinopolitano (voir n. 2), p. 205.	16	ιδ´ Εὐχὴ ἐπὶ ποιήσει μύρου γινομένη τῇ ἁγίᾳ καὶ μεγάλῃ Ε´. 95ʳ-96ᵛ
10	ζ´ Μετὰ τὴν ἔκπλυσιν εὐχὴ α´. Εὐχὴ μετὰ ... 23ᵛ⁻(...) ——8φφ	42	μβ´ Κατήχησις τῆς ἁγίας Παρασκευῆς. Ἀπόταξις καὶ σύνταξις γινομένη τῇ ἁγίᾳ καὶ μεγάλῃ Παρασκευῇ τοῦ Πάσχα. 64ᵛ-69ᵛ, pp. 206-215.	17	ιε´ Εὐχὴ εἰς τὴν ἀπαμφίασιν [τῆς ἁγίας τραπέζης]. ιε´ Εὐχὴ ... τραπέζης τὴν γινομένην τῇ ἁγίᾳ καὶ μεγάλῃ Ε´ ὑπὸ τοῦ ἀρχιερέως μετὰ τὴν συμπλήρωσιν τῆς Τριτοέκτης. 96ʳ-97ʳ
11	η´ Τάξις ἡ τοῦ νιπτῆρος.	43	μγ´ Εὐχὴ ἐπὶ ποιήσει μύρου γινομένη τῇ μεγάλῃ Ε´. 70ʳ-71ʳ, pp. 216-219.	18	ιϛ´ Εὐχὴ μετὰ τὴν ἔκπλυσιν τῆς ἁγίας τραπέζης. ιϛ´ Εὐχὴ ... ἔκπλυσιν. 97ʳ-98ʳ
12	θ´ Ἐπὶ ποιήσει μύρου τῇ μεγάλῃ Ε´ ὁμοίως εὐχαὶ β´.	44	μδ´ Εὐχὴ γινομένη εἰς τὰ ἀπαμφία τῆς ἁγίας τραπέζης τῇ ἁγίᾳ καὶ μεγάλῃ Ε´. 71ᵛ, p. 220.	19	ιζ´ Εὐχαὶ τοῦ ἁγίου νιπτῆρος ιζ´ Εὐχαὶ τοῦ ἁγίου νιπτῆρος γινόμεναι ἐν τοῖς μοναστηρίοις. 98ʳ-99ᵛ
13	ι´ Ἀκολουθία ἑτέρα τοῦ νιπτῆρος γινομένη ἐν τοῖς μοναστηρίοις ἔχουσα εὐχὰς γ´.	45	με´ Εὐχὴ μετὰ τὴν ἔκπλυσιν. 71ᵛ-72ᵛ, p. 221.	22	ρπη´ Εὐχὴ ἐπὶ ἀνοίξει ἐκκλησίας ὑπὸ αἱρετικῶν βεβηλωθείσης, Νικηφόρου πατριάρχου. 198ᵛ-200ʳ
14	ια´ Κατήχησις τῆς μεγάλης Παρασκευῆς. (24)-25ʳ	46	μϛ´ Εὐχαὶ τοῦ ἁγίου νιπτῆρος γινόμεναι ἐν τοῖς μοναστηρίοις. 72ᵛ-73ᵛ, pp. 222-224.	23	ρπθ´ Εὐχὴ ἑτέρα εἰς τὸ αὐτὸ Ταρασίου πατριάρχου. 201ʳ

	STR		BES		EBE
148	ριϛ´ Εἰς ἀνοίξιμα ἐκκλησίας βεβηλωθείσης ὑπὸ αἱρετικῶν, εὐχαὶ γ´. Εὐχὴ εἰς ... ὑπὸ αἱρετικῶν βεβηλωθείσης Νικηφόρου πατριάρχου. 118ʳ-119ᵛ	51	να´ Ἄλλη τάξις γινομένη ἐπὶ σαλευθείσης ἁγίας τραπέξης. 87ᵛ-88ᵛ, pp. 249-251.	24	ρκ´ Εὐχὴ ἐπὶ ἀνοίξι ναοῦ βεβηλωθέντος ὑπὸ Ἐθνικῶν. ρκ´ Εὐχὴ ἐπὶ ἀνοίξει ... Ἐθνικοῦ. 201ʳ-202ʳ
149	ριζ´ 2. Εὐχὴ ἑτέρα εἰς τὸ αὐτὸ Ταρασίου Πατριάρχου. 119ᵛ	52	νβ´ Εὐχὴ εἰς ἀνοίξιμα ἐκκλησίας ὑπὸ αἱρετικῶν βεβηλωθείσης, Νικηφόρου πατριάρχου. 89ʳ-90ᵛ, pp. 252-254.	25	ρκα´ Εὐχὴ λεγομένη ἐν τῇ εἰσόδῳ πρὸ τῆς συνήθους ἐπὶ ἀνοίξει ναοῦ, ἐν ᾧ συνέβη θανεῖν ἄνθρωπον βιαίως. 202ʳ-203ʳ
150	ριζ´ 3. Εὐχὴ ἐπὶ ἀνοίξει ναοῦ βεβηλωθέντος ὑπὸ Ἐθνικῶν. 120ʳ-ᵛ	53	νγ´ Εὐχὴ ἑτέρα εἰς τὸ αὐτὸ Ταρασίου πατριάρχου. 90ᵛ-91ʳ, p. 254.	34	ρλ´ Κατήχησις τῆς μεγάλης Παρασκευῆς τοῦ Πάσχα. ρλ´ Κατήχησις τῆς μεγάλης Παρασκευῆς τοῦ Πάσχα. Ἀπόταξις καὶ σύνταξις γινομένη τῇ ἁγίᾳ καὶ μεγάλῃ Παρασκευῇ. 212ʳ-218ʳ
151	ριη´ {ρη´} Καὶ ἑρμηνεία ἐπὶ ἀνοίξει ναοῦ, <ἐν> ᾧ συνέβη θανεῖν ἄνθρωπον βιαίως ἢ ζῷον ἄλογον καὶ ἀκάθαρτον ἔθανεν ἢ ἐγέννησεν, εὐχὴ α´. Εὐχὴ λεγομένη ἐν τῇ εἰσόδῳ πρὸ τῆς συνήθους ἐπὶ ἀνοίξει ναοῦ, ἐν ᾧ συνέβη θανεῖν{αι} ἄνθρωπον βιαίως. 120ᵛ-121ᵛ	54	νδ´ Εὐχὴ ἐπὶ ἀνοίξει ναοῦ βεβηλωθέντ<ος> ὑπὸ Ἐθνικῶν. 91ʳ-ᵛ, pp. 255-256.	36	ρλβ´ Ὅπως χρὴ δέχεσθαι τοὺς ἀπὸ αἱρέσεων τῇ ἁγίᾳ τοῦ Θεοῦ καὶ ἀποστολικῇ Ἐκκλησίᾳ προσερχομένους. 223ᵛ-225ᵛ
		55	νε´ Εὐχὴ λεγομένη ἐν τῇ εἰσόδῳ πρὸ τῆς συνήθους ἐπὶ ἀνοίξει ναοῦ, ἐν ᾧ συνέβη θανεῖν ἄνθρωπον βιαίως. 91ʳ-92ᵛ, pp. 257-258.	37	ρλγ´ Ὅπως χρὴ ἀναθεματίζειν ἐγγράφως τὴν αἵρεσιν αὐτῶν, τοὺς ἀπὸ Μανιχαίων προσιόντας τῇ ἁγίᾳ τοῦ Θεοῦ καθολικῇ καὶ ἀποστολικῇ Ἐκκλησίᾳ. 225ᵛ-233ʳ
		56	νϛ´ Πῶς δεῖ δέχεσθαι τὸν ἐξ Ἑβραίων τῇ τῶν Χριστιανῶν πίστει προσερχόμενον. 92ᵛ-94ʳ, pp. 259-261.		
		57	νζ´ Ἐκ τοῦ εὐχολογίου τοῦ πατριαρχικοῦ. Ὅπως χρὴ δέχεσθαι τοὺς ἀπὸ αἱρέσεων ἐν τῇ ἁγίᾳ τοῦ Θεοῦ καὶ ἀποστολικῇ Ἐκκλησίᾳ. 94ʳ-95ᵛ, pp. 262-267.		

STR		BES		EBE	
152	Τὰ περὶ αἱρέσεων. ριθ´ Περὶ τῶν ὀφειλόντων χρισθῆναι μύρον ἀπὸ πάσης αἱρέσεως ἐρμηνεία καὶ εὐχαὶ β´. Περὶ αἱρέσεων. Ὅπως χρὴ δέχεσθαι τοὺς ἀπὸ αἱρέσεων τῇ ἁγίᾳ τοῦ Θεοῦ καὶ ἀποστολικῇ Ἐκκλησίᾳ προσερχομένους, Περὶ ... μύρῳ. 121ᵛ-123ʳ				
153	ρκ´ Περὶ αἱρέσεων διδόντων λιβέλλους ἐρμηνεία. Περὶ ... λιβέλλους. 123ʳ				
154	ρκα´ Περὶ τῶν ἀναβαπτιζομένων ἐρμηνεία ἔχουσα εὐχὴν α´. Περὶ ἀναβαπτιζομένων. 123ʳ⁻ᵛ				
155	ρκβ´ Ὅπως χρὴ ἀναθεματίζειν ἐγγράφως τὴν αἵρεσιν αὐτῶν, τοὺς ἀπὸ Μανιχαίων προσιόντας τῇ Ἐκκλησίᾳ. Ὅπως ... τῇ ἁγίᾳ τοῦ Θεοῦ καθολικῇ καὶ ἀποστολικῇ Ἐκκλησίᾳ. 124ʳ-130ᵛ	58	νη´ Ὅπως χρὴ ἀναθεματίζειν ἐγγράφως τὴν αἵρεσιν αὐτῶν, τοὺς ἀπὸ Μανιχαίων προσιόντας τῇ ἁγίᾳ τοῦ Θεοῦ καθολικῇ καὶ ἀποστολικῇ Ἐκκλησίᾳ. 95ᵛ-102ᵛ, pp. 268-278.		
156	ρκγ´ Τάξις γινομένη ἐπὶ τοῖς ἀπὸ Μανιχαίων ἐπιστρέφουσιν ἔχουσα καὶ εὐχὴν μίαν, τὴν προγραφεῖσαν, καὶ ἑτέραν, τὴν λεγομένην εἰς τὸ ποιῆσαι κατηχούμενον, εὐχαὶ β´. Τάξις ... ἐπιστρέφουσι πρὸς τὴν καθαρὰν καὶ ἀληθῆ πίστιν ἡμῶν τῶν Χριστιανῶν. 130ᵛ-132ʳ	59	νθ´ Τάξις γινομένη ἐπὶ τοῖς ἀπὸ Μανιχαίων ἐπιστρέφουσιν πρὸς τὴν καθαρὰν καὶ ἀληθῆ πίστιν ἡμῶν τῶν Χριστιανῶν. 102ᵛ-104ᵛ, pp. 279-282.	38	ρλδ´ Τάξις γινομένη ἐπὶ τοῖς ἀπὸ Μανιχαίων ἐπιστρέφουσι πρὸς τὴν καθαρὰν καὶ ἀληθῆ πίστιν τῶν Χριστιανῶν. 233ʳ-235ʳ
		60	ξ´ Μεθοδίου, τοῦ ἁγιωτάτου πατριάρχου, διάταξις περὶ τῶν διαφόρῳ τρόπῳ καὶ ἡλικίᾳ ἐπιστρεφόντων. 104ᵛ-105ʳ, pp. 283-284.	39	ρλε´ Μεθοδίου, τοῦ ἁγιωτάτου πατριάρχου, διάταξις περὶ τῶν διαφόρῳ τρόπῳ καὶ ἡλικίᾳ ἐπιστρεφόντων. 235ʳ⁻ᵛ
		61	ξα´ Εὐχὴ ἱλασμοῦ εἰς τὸν ἀπὸ ἀρνήσεως ἐπιστρέφοντα πρὸς τὴν ἡμετέραν πίστιν. 105ʳ-106ᵛ, pp. 285-286.	40	ρλς´ Εὐχὴ ἱλασμοῦ εἰς τὸν ἀπὸ ἀρνήσεως ἐπιστρέφοντα πρὸς τὴν ἡμετέραν πίστιν. 235ᵛ-237ʳ
		62	ξβ´ Εὐχὴ ἄλλη εἰς ἱλασμὸν μετὰ τὸ εἰπεῖν ψαλμ(οὺς) ν´, λζ´, ρβ´. 106ᵛ-107ʳ, p. 287.	41	ρλζ´ Εὐχὴ ἄλλη εἰς ἱλασμόν. 237ʳ⁻ᵛ
		63	ξγ´ Εὐχὴ πρὸς Χριστιανοὺς ὑπαχθέντας δὲ καὶ τῇ Ἐκκλησίᾳ ἐθνικῇ πλάνῃ, ἐπιστρέψαντας καὶ τῇ Ἐκκλησίᾳ τοῦ Θεοῦ προσδραμόντας. 107ʳ⁻ᵛ, pp. 288-289.	42	ρλη´ Εὐχὴ πρὸς Χριστιανοὺς ὑπαχθέντας ἐθνικῇ πλάνῃ, ἐπιστρέψαντας δὲ καὶ τῇ Ἐκκλησίᾳ προσδραμόντας. 237ᵛ-238ʳ
		64	ξδ´ Εὐχὴ ἐπὶ ἀποστατήσαντος παιδὸς καὶ μαγαρίσαντος καὶ μετανοοῦντος. 107ᵛ-108ᵛ, pp. 290-291.	43	ρλθ´ Εὐχὴ ἐπὶ ἀποστατήσαντος παιδὸς καὶ μαγαρίσαντος καὶ μετανοοῦντος. 238ᵛ-240ᵛ
				44	ρμ´ Εὐχὴ εἰς τὸ ποιῆσαι Ἐθνικὸν κατηχούμενον. 240ʳ⁻ᵛ
				45	ρμα´ Πῶς δεῖ δέχεσθαι τὸν ἐξ Ἑβραίων τῇ τῶν Χριστιανῶν πίστει προσερχόμενον. 240ᵛ-242ʳ
				46	ρμβ´ Ἔκθεσις ἀκριβεστέρα περὶ τοῦ πῶς δεῖ δέχεσθαι τὸν ἐξ Ἑβραίων τῇ τῶν Χριστιανῶν πίστει προσερχόμενον. 242ʳ-247ʳ
				47	ρμγ´ Περὶ Μελχισεδεκιτῶν, τῶν καὶ Θεοδοτιανῶν καὶ Ἀθιγγάνων. 247ᵛ-250ᵛ

	STR		BES		EBE
157	ρκδ´ Μεθοδίου πατριάρχου διάταξις περὶ τῶν διαφόρῳ τρόπῳ καὶ ἡλικίᾳ ἐπιστρεφόντων. Μεθοδίου, τοῦ ἁγιωτάτου πατριάρχου, ... ἐπιστρεφόντων. 132ʳ-133ʳ	65	ξε´ Εὐχὴ εἰς τὸ ποιῆσαι Ἐθνικὸν κατηχούμενον. 108ᵛ-109ʳ, p. 294.	48	ρμδ´ Τάξις γινομένη ἐπὶ τοῖς ἀπὸ Σαρακηνῶν ἐπιστρέφουσι πρὸς τὴν καθαρὰν καὶ ἀληθῆ πίστιν ἡμῶν τῶν Χριστιανῶν. 250ᵛ-257ᵛ
158	ρκε´ Εὐχὴ ἱλασμοῦ εἰς τὸν ἀπὸ ἀρνήσεως ἐπιστρέφοντα, α´. Εὐχὴ ... ἐπιστρέφοντα πρὸς τὴν ἡμετέραν πίστιν. 133ʳ-134ʳ				
159	ρκϛ´ Εὐχὴ ἑτέρα ὁμοίως, α´. Εὐχὴ ἄλλη εἰς ἱλασμόν. 134ʳ-ᵛ				
160	ρκζ´ Ἑτέρα πρὸς Χριστιανοὺς ὑπαχθέντας ἐθνικῇ πλάνῃ, α´. Εὐχὴ πρὸς ... πλάνῃ, ἐπιστρέψαντας δὲ καὶ τῇ Ἐκκλησίᾳ προσδραμόντας. 134ᵛ-135ʳ				
161	ρκη´ Ἐπὶ ἀποστατήσαντος παιδὸς καὶ μαγαρίσαντος καὶ μετανοοῦντος εὐχαὶ γ´. Εὐχή ... μετανοοῦντος. 135ʳ-136ᵛ				
162	ρκθ´ Εἰς τὸ ποιῆσαι Ἐθνικὸν κατηχούμενον, εὐχαὶ β´. Εὐχὴ ... κατηχούμενον. 136ᵛ-137ʳ				

STR	
163	ρλ΄ Περὶ Μελχισεδεκιτῶν, τῶν καὶ Θεοδοτιανῶν καὶ Ἀθιγγάνων, ἑρμηνεία καὶ ὁ ἀναθεματισμός.
	Περί ... Ἀθιγγάνων. 137ʳ-140ʳ
164	ρλα΄ Τάξις γινομένη ἐπὶ τοῖς ἀπὸ Σαρακηνῶν ἐπιστρέφουσι καὶ ὁ ἀναθεματισμὸς αὐτῶν.
	Τάξις ... ἐπιστρέφουσι πρὸς τὴν καθαρὰν καὶ ἀληθῆ πίστιν ἡμῶν τῶν Χριστιανῶν. 140ʳ-145ᵛ
165	ρλβ΄ Πῶς δεῖ δέχεσθαι τὸν ἐξ Ἑβραίων προσερχόμενον καὶ ἀπόταξις.
	Πῶς ... Ἑβραῖον τῇ τῶν Χριστιανῶν πίστει προσερχόμενον. 145ᵛ-147ʳ
166	ρλγ΄ Ἔκθεσις ἀκριβεστέρα περὶ τοῦ πῶς δεῖ δέχεσθαι τὸν ἐξ Ἑβραίων προσερχόμενον καὶ ὁ ἀναθεματισμὸς αὐτῶν.
	Ἔκθεσις ... Ἑβραίων τῇ τῶν Χριστιανῶν πίστει προσερχόμενον. 147ʳ-151ᵛ
167	ρλδ΄ Ὁ λόγος Γρηγορίου τοῦ Νικαίας, ὅτι οὐ χρὴ ταχέως βαπτίζειν Ἑβραίους εἰ μή τις ἀκριβῶς τούτους πρότερον δοκιμάσει.
	Λόγος διαλαμβάνων ὅτι οὐ χρὴ ταχέως ἐπιτιθέναι χεῖρα βαπτίζουσαν Ἑβραίοις εἰ μή τις ... 151ᵛ-164ᵛ

THE RITE OF THE EUCHARISTIC LITURGY IN THE OLDEST RUSSIAN *LEITOURGIKA* (13TH-14TH CENTURIES)

Michael ZHELTOV

PRELIMINARY REMARKS

In this article I shall present the main results of my research of the prayers and other euchological elements peculiar to the oldest extant Russian Leitourgika (*Sluzhebniki*) manuscripts of the 13th-14th centuries. These antedate the Russian liturgical reform of the turn of the 14-15th centuries, when new translations of liturgical texts, including the *Diataxis* of Philotheos Kokkinos and corresponding new redactions of the eucharistic formularies, were introduced into Russian worship. One can find the details of this research in a series of my Russian articles: 'The Rite of the Divine Liturgy in the Oldest (11th-14th-centuries) Slavonic Euchologia'[1] (in this article one can also find a full bibliography on the topic), 'The Prayers During Clergy Communion in the Old-Russian Leitourgika',[2] 'The Priestly Prayers before the Beginning of the Divine Liturgy in the Old-Russian Leitourgika',[3] and 'Additional Prayers at the End of the Divine Liturgy According to the Slavonic Leitourgika of the 11-14th centuries'.[4] What follows is but a brief résumé of the results I reached in those studies.

There are thirty-two manuscripts of the oldest — I will call them pre-Philothean — Russian redactions of the eucharistic formularies of St Basil (BAS) and St John Chrysostom (CHR).[5] These exclude four

[1] M. Zheltov [М. Желтов], 'Чин Божественной литургии в древнейших (XI–XIV вв.) славянских Служебниках', *Богословские труды* 41 (2007) 272-359.

[2] *Idem*, 'Молитвы во время причащения священнослужителей в древнерусских Служебниках XIII–XIV в.', *Древняя Русь: вопросы медиевистики* 35 (2009) 75-92.

[3] *Idem*, 'Священнические молитвы перед началом литургии в древнерусских Служебниках' (in print).

[4] *Idem*, 'Дополнительные молитвы славянских Служебников XI–XIV вв. в конце литургии' (in preparation).

[5] A complete list of them is given in Zheltov, 'Чин Божественной литургии' (see n. 1), pp. 281-285. It counts 33 manuscripts, but two of them — *Saint-Petersburg, Russian National Library* O. п. I. 4 and *Baltimore, Walters Art Museum* W. 548, — as Anatoly Turilov has recently pointed out, are in fact just two parts of one and the same codex.

late-14th-century witnesses which already contain the *Diataxis* of Philotheos and any later manuscripts (though many of these could still preserve
this or that element of the pre-Philothean practice). What one finds in
these sources is by no means a pure Constantinopolitan redaction of the
liturgies of CHR, BAS and the Presanctified liturgy (PRES). Of course,
this classical set of the three liturgies still consists here of the same
prayers as everywhere — i. e., the Prothesis prayer, the prayer of the
first antiphon, etc. But the oldest Russian Leitourgika also contain many
other prayers, which are not to be found in the famous Constantinopolitan Euchologia. One could compare this phenomenon with other 'peripheral' redactions of CHR, such as the South Italian ones studied
by André Jacob, and, more recently, by Stefano Parenti.[6] Indeed, there
are some points of similarity between the South Italian sources and the
pre-Philothean Russian Leitourgika, but there are also many differences.

ALTERNATIVE PRAYERS OF SOUTH ITALIAN CHR IN THE OLD-RUSSIAN
BAS

As Jacob has shown, the most characteristic of the ancient South Italian redactions of CHR is the set of three prayers of Oriental provenance
which are used instead of normal Constantinopolitan prayers of, respectively: the Prothesis, the Trisagion and the Little Entrance.[7] Besides
these prayers, one often finds in the South Italian manuscripts of CHR
other alternative prayers, namely: of incense, of the *skeuophylakion* (at
the end of the liturgy), of the Great Entrance, of the Elevation, — as
well as many festal *opisthambonoi* prayers and additional prayers during
clergy communion.

According to Jacob, in the oldest stage of development of manuscript
formularies of CHR and BAS, it was BAS that was always written first
and in full. CHR was written after BAS and in the earliest manuscripts
was not a complete, but an abbreviated, formulary; it contained only

---

[6] See a survey of studies on the history of manuscript tradition of CHR and BAS,
which includes the works of the two mentioned as well as other scholars (Alexey Dmitrievsky, Sergey Muretov, Juan Mateos, Robert Taft, to name but a few), in: Zheltov,
'Чин Божественной литургии' (see n. 1), pp. 347-359.

[7] A. Jacob, 'La tradition manuscrite de la liturgie de saint Jean Chrysostome
(VIIIᵉ-XIIᵉ siècles)', in *Eucharisties d'Orient et d'Occident (Conférences Saint-Serge:
1ᵉʳ Semaine liturgique de l'Institut Saint-Serge)*, vol. 2, Lex Orandi 46 (Paris, 1970),
pp. 109-138. This article is a brief résumé of his unpublished and invaluable doctoral dissertation, defended in 1968.

those prayers that were peculiar to CHR. In Constantinople they just filled the lacunae in CHR with the corresponding prayers from BAS, but in South Italy they eventually filled the lacunae in CHR with some prayers taken from the Oriental liturgies of St Mark (MK) and St James (JAS). I have already mentioned that there were several such prayers, but the most prominent feature of the ancient South Italian redactions was the use of three Oriental prayers instead of the Constantinopolitan prayers of the Prothesis, the Trisagion and the Little Entrance in the rite of CHR.

These three prayers are presented in the pre-Philothean Russian Slu-zhebniki as well, but here they do not form a three-prayer set, belonging to CHR. Instead, two of these three prayers (those of the Prothesis and of the Trisagion) belong to BAS, not CHR. In BAS they form a four-prayer set, which also includes particular incense and *opisthambonos* prayers. So there is some resemblance between South Italian and Old-Russian traditions, but they are not identical.

I will give the Slavonic texts of these four prayers in full, providing the corresponding Greek texts and some comments. One should keep in mind that in the oldest Slavonic Leitourgika the texts are even less stable than in the Greek Euchologia. I will cite these and the other prayers according to the Leitourgikon *Jaroslavl' Museum* 15472, ca. 1328-1336 AD, which has never been published.

1. Alternative Prayers of Old-Russian BAS

1.1. Incense Prayer

ВЛАДКО ГН БЕ НАШЬ ·
ПРНИМЪИН АВЕЛЕВЪI ДАРЪI
· Н АРОНОВЪI Н НОЕВЪI ·
АВРАМОВЪI Н САМОНЛЕВЪI ·
Н ЗАХАРЬННЪI · Н ВСѢХЪ
СТЪIХЪ ТВОНХЪ · ТАКО Н
Ѿ РУКЪ НАШНХЪ ПРННМН
КАДНЛО СНК ВЪ ВОНЮ
БЛГООУХАНЬІА · Н ВЪ
Ѿ ДАНЬК ГРѢХОВЪ
НАШНХЪ · Н ВСѢХЪ
ЛЮДНН ТВОНХЪ · ІАКО
БЛГВНСА Н ПРОСЛАВНСА ·
ПРЕУ͠ТЬНОК Н БЕ ∴

The original Greek text (= one of incense prayers of JAS, MK and 11th-century Arabic version of CHR):
Ὁ Θεός, ὁ προσδεξάμενος Ἄβελ τὰ δῶρα, Νῶε καὶ Ἀβραὰμ τὴν θυσίαν, Ἀαρὼν καὶ Ζαχαρίου τὸ θυμίαμα, πρόσδεξαι καὶ ἐκ χειρὸς ἡμῶν τῶν ἁμαρτωλῶν τὸ θυμίαμα τοῦτο εἰς ὀσμὴν εὐωδίας καὶ ἄφεσιν τῶν ἁμαρτιῶν ἡμῶν καὶ παντὸς τοῦ λαοῦ Σου· ὅτι εὐλογημένος ὑπάρχεις καὶ πρέπει Σοι ἡ δόξα τῷ Πατρὶ καὶ τῷ Υἱῷ καὶ τῷ ἁγίῳ Πνεύματι, νῦν καὶ ἀεὶ καὶ εἰς τοὺς αἰῶνας τῶν αἰώνων. Ἀμήν.

1.2. Prothesis Prayer

ГꙊН ІСЕ ХЕ ХЛѢБЕ ЖНВОТНЫН
· ПРЕЛОЖНВЪН ВЪ ПРЕСТОН
СВОН ТѢЛО ХЛѢБЪ · Н
ПРЕꙊТУЮ СВОЮ КРОВЬ ВЪ
ВНЮ · ꙀА МНРЬСКЫН
ЖНВОТЪ · ВНОГРАДЕ
СВѢТЕ НСТННЬНЫН ·
ПРНꙀРН НА ДАРЫ СНꙖ ·
ПРНЮМН ВЪ НЕБЕСНЫН СВОН
ШЛТАРЬ ВЪ ВОНЮ
БЛꙖГООУХАНЬꙖ · ПОМАНН
ꙊЛѢКОЛЮБЬꙊЕ ПРНЮНЕСЪ-
ШАꙖ · Н ꙀА НАЖЕ СУТЬ
ПРНЮНЕСЛН · Н НАСЪ
НЕШСУЖЕНЫ СЪХРАНН ·
ꙖКО ШСТНСА Н
ПРОСЛАВНСА · ПРЕꙊТНОН
НМА ТВОН СО ШЦМЬ Н
СТЫНМЬ ДꙊХОМЬ Н НЫꙖꙀ :·

*The original Greek text (= Prothesis prayer in various Egyptian liturgies and in South Italian redactions of CHR. **NB:** known Greek redactions of the prayer differ substantially from the Old-Russian one; Coptic and Ethiopian redactions are noticeably closer):* Κύριε ὁ Θεὸς ἡμῶν, <Bochairic version of the same prayer: ⲚⲐⲞⲔ ⲄⲀⲢ ⲠⲈ ⲠⲓⲱⲓⲔ ⲈⲦⲞⲚϩ,> ὁ προθεὶς ἑαυτὸν ἀμνὸν ἄμωμον ὑπὲρ τῆς τοῦ κόσμου ζωῆς, ἔφιδε ἐφ᾽ ἡμᾶς καὶ ἐπὶ τὸν ἄρτον τοῦτον καὶ ἐπὶ τὸ ποτήριον τοῦτο, καὶ ποίησον αὐτὸ ἄχραντόν σου σῶμα καὶ τίμιόν σου αἷμα, εἰς μετάληψιν ψυχῶν καὶ σωμάτων. Ὅτι ἡγίασται καὶ δεδόξασθαι τὸ πάντιμον καὶ μεγαλοπρεπές·

1.3. Trisagion Prayer

СТЕ СТЫНХЪ БЕ НАШЬ ·
КДННЪ СТЪ НА СТЫНХЪ
ПОУНВАꙖ · СТЪ КСН НЖЕ
НЕНꙀМѢРНУЮ СЛАВУ СЕБѢ
СТАЖАВЪ · СТЫН БЕ НЖЕ
СЛОВОМЬ ВСАУЬСКАꙖ
СЪСТАВНВЪН · СТЫН БЕ
КГОЖЕ ꙊЕТВЕРОꙀРАꙊННН
ЖНВОТН НЕПРЕСТАНЬНОМЬ
ГЛАМЬ СЛАВАТЪ · СТЫН БЕ
НЖЕ Ѿ МНОЖЬСТВА
СТЫХЪ АНГЛЪ
НЕВНДѢНЬКМЬ ·
ТРЕПЕЩЮЩНМЪ ·
ПОКЛАНАКМЪ Н
СЛОВОСЛОВНМЪ · СТЫН БЕ
НЖЕ МНОГОУНТЫМН
ХЕРОВНМЫ НЕМОЛУЬНЫМН
ГЛАСЫ · НЕОУСЫПАЮЩНМЬ
ШКОМЬ · ПРНꙀНРАꙖ Н
ПРНКЛАНАꙖ ОУХО СВОН ·
СТЫН БЕ НА
ШЕСТОКРНЛАТЫХЪ
СЕРАФНМѢХЪ СѢДАН · Н
ОУДАРАЮЩЕ

The original Greek text (= prayer from the rite of sanctification of the Nile waters and a substitute Trisagion prayer in South Italian redactions of CHR): Ἅγιε ἁγίων ὁ Θεὸς ἡμῶν· ὁ μόνος ἅγιος καὶ ἐν ἁγίοις ἀναπαύομενος· ἅγιος ὑπάρχεις· ὁ τὴν ἀνυπέρβλητον δόξαν ἐν αὐτῷ κεκτημένος· ἅγιος ὁ Θεὸς ὁ λόγῳ τὰ πάντα συστησάμενος· ἅγιος ὁ Θεὸς ὃν τὰ τετράμορφα ζῷα ἀκαταπαύστῳ φωνῇ δοξάζουσιν· ἅγιος ὁ Θεὸς ὁ ὑπὸ πλήθους ἁγίων ἀγγέλων καὶ ἀρχαγγέλων ἀορασίᾳ τρεμόντων προσκυνούμενος καὶ δοξολογούμενος· ἅγιος ὁ Θεὸς ὁ τοῖς πολυόμμασιν χερουβεὶμ τῇ ἀσιγήτῳ φωνῇ τῷ ἀκοιμήτῳ ὄμματι ἐπιβλέπων καὶ ἐπικλίνων τὸ οὖς σου· ἅγιος ὁ Θεὸς ὁ τοῖς ἑξαπτερύγοις σεραφεὶμ ἐποχούμενος καὶ κροτούντων τὰς

свонмн крнлъı ·
повѣднүю пѣ поюще стъ
стъ стъ гь савашфъ
прнкмлан · стъ во ксн
бе нашь · н кмүже
начала н власти н
гьства на нбсн
покланаютса н на
землн человѣцн
хвалатъ н үтүть · тъı
самъ члбколювуе ·
прннмн ѿ оустъ насъ
грѣшнъıхъ · трестүю пѣ
прнносимүю · ѿ насъ ш
всѣхъ людехъ твонхъ ·
н послн намъ батъıа
млстн · н щедротъı
твоıа · млтвамн стъııа
бца н всѣхъ стъı ѿ
вѣка оугожьшнхъ тı ·

ἑαυτῶν πτέρυγας καὶ τὸν ἐπινίκιον
ὕμνον ὑμνούντων τό· Ἅγιος ἅγιος
ἅγιος Κύριος Σαβαὼθ
προσδεχόμενος· ἅγιος γὰρ εἶ ὁ
Θεὸς ἡμῶν ὃν ἀρχαὶ καὶ ἐξουσίαι
κυριότητες ἐν οὐρανῷ
προσκυνοῦσιν· καὶ ἐπὶ γῆς
ἄνθρωποι ἀνυμνοῦσιν καὶ
σέβουσιν· αὐτὸς φιλάνθρωπε
πρόσδεξαι καὶ ἐκ στόματος ἡμῶν
τῶν ἁμαρτωλῶν τὸν τρισάγιον
ὕμνον· προσφερόμενον παρ' ἡμῶν
καὶ παρὰ παντὸς τοῦ λαοῦ σου· καὶ
κατάπεμψον ἡμῖν πλούσια τὰ ἐλέη
καὶ τοὺς οἰκτιρμούς σου·
πρεσβείαις τῆς ἁγίας Θεοτόκου
καὶ πάντων τῶν ἁγίων τῶν ἀπ'
αἰῶνός σοι εὐαρεστησάντων· ὅτι
ἅγιος εἶ ὁ Θεὸς ἡμῶν καὶ ἐν
ἁγίοις ἐπαναπαύει καὶ σοὶ τὴν
δόξαν ἀναπέμπομεν·

1.4. Opisthambonos Prayer

Влко гн ісе хе бе нашь ·
съподобнвъıн нъı своеıа
славъı шбещннкомъ
бъıтн · прнчашеньемъ
стхъ твонхъ таннъ
жнвотворащнх · нхже
радн смрть твоıа н
воскрньıа · шбразъ
творнтн предалъ есн
намъ · тѣхъ радн н
насъ въ стнн твоен
съхранн · помннающнмъ
твою блгть вонну · тебѣ
жнвүщемү за нъı
оумершемү · н вставъшю
слүжнвъшю с намн · н
бжтвенъıмъ твонмъ
таннамъ
послүжнвъшнмъ · радъ
блгооустрон · н много
дерзновенье на
страшнемь твоемь
сүднщн · мнръ мнрови
твоемү даруıн · н

*The original Greek text (= an
opisthambonos prayer witnessed in
many mss of CHR and BAS (both
Constantinopolitan and non-
Constantinopolitan) and of JAS; the
prayer is widespread in the ancient
Georgian manuscript tradition):*
Δόξα σοι Κύριε Ἰησοῦ Χριστὲ ὁ
Σωτὴρ ἡμῶν· ὁ καταξιώσας ἡμᾶς
τῆς δόξης σου κοινωνοὺς
γενέσθαι· διὰ τῆς τῶν ἁγίων σου
μυστηρίων καὶ ζωοποιοῦ
μεταλήψεως· δι' ὧν τοῦ θανάτου
σου καὶ της ἀναστάσεως τύπον
τελεῖν παρέδωκας ἡμῖν· δι' αὐτῶν
καὶ ἡμᾶς ἐν τῷ ἁγιασμῷ σου
διαφύλαξον· μεμνημένους τῆς σῆς
χάριτος διὰ παντός· καὶ συνζῶντας
τῷ ὑπὲρ ἡμῶν ἀποθανόντι καὶ
ἐγερθέντι τοῖς συλλειτουργήσασιν
ἡμῖν· καὶ τοῖς θείοις σου
μυστηρίοις διακονήσασιν βαθμὸν
ἀγαθὸν περιποίησον· καὶ πολλὴν

цр҃квамъ твоимъ и
сщ҃енникомъ · и
блг҃овѣрнъімъ кнаꙁемъ
нашимъ · и҃ма · воимъ ·
и всѣмъ людемъ
твоимъ · тъі бо ѥси
истиннъіи б҃ъ н҃а ·
животъ вѣчнъіи · тебе
славу въꙁилаѥмъ оц҃ю ∴

παρρησίαν τὴν ἐπὶ τοῦ φοβεροῦ
βήματος σου· <*here comes an
insertion — a piece of the standard
opisthambonos prayer:* Εἰρήνην τῷ
κόσμῳ σου δώρησαι, ταῖς
ἐκκλησίαις σου, τοῖς ἱερεῦσι, τοῖς
βασιλεῦσιν ἡμῶν, τῷ στρατῷ καὶ
παντὶ τῷ λαῷ σου.> Σὺ γὰρ εἶ ὁ
ἀληθηνὸς Θεὸς ἡμῶν καὶ ζωὴ
αἰώνιος· καὶ σοι τὴν δόξαν
ἀναπέμπομεν·

Unlike the prayers of the Prothesis and the Trisagion, the prayer of the Little Entrance from the South Italian CHR is not used in the Old-Russian Leitourgika as an alternative prayer of BAS. Instead, it could be included either in CHR or BAS. And it does not function as an alternative, but as an additional prayer, i. e., it does not replace the corresponding Constantinopolitan prayer (as the four alternative prayers of BAS do), but is inserted into the formulary elsewhere and forms a completely new unit. Some manuscripts use this Little Entrance prayer at the beginning of the liturgy (in this case it is entitled, ꙁа вхⷪⷣащаꙗ въ цр҃къвь — '[A Prayer] for Those Entering the Church'); others attach it to the Great Entrance, but never use it to replace another prayer. It is, however, not characteristic of pre-Philothean Russian eucharistic practice; it is written in the manuscripts quite rarely, while the four prayers cited above are very common in the Old-Russian BAS.

Besides the four-prayer BAS set, in the pre-Philothean Russian Sluzhebniki there is only one prayer that could be used as an alternative one. It is the alternate prayer during the Great Entrance. It is a variant redaction of the Great Entrance prayer of JAS and is sometimes found in the South Italian manuscripts in the same function. Among the pre-Philothean Russian Leitourgika it is found in just two manuscripts, i.e. it is very rare.

ADDITIONAL PRAYERS OF THE OLD-RUSSIAN EUCHARISTIC FORMULARIES

But alternative prayers of BAS are by no means the most conspicuous feature of the pre-Philothean Russian Leitourgika. These manuscripts are overloaded with many additional prayers, inserted here or there and forming absolutely new yet stable units in the eucharistic formulary.

This is unparalleled in the South Italian witnesses. It should be noted that Greek originals of many of these additional prayers are unknown. These additional prayers of the pre-Philothean Russian Leitourgika are found in four places of the formulary:[8]

- before the liturgy [always];
- during the Great Entrance [sometimes];
- during clergy communion [always];
- at the end of the liturgy [nearly always].

There are also some festal *opisthambonoi* prayers (used indiscriminately in both CHR and BAS[9]), a couple of prayers intended for an episcopal liturgy (peculiarities of the episcopal rite are described in two of the extant pre-Philothean Russian Sluzhebniki), and a few prayers found in unique manuscripts only (either at the same positions as listed, or during the prothesis, or before the gospel reading[10]). Some of the additional prayers before and at the end of the liturgy, and during clergy communion are widespread, others are not. In general, contents of the Russian pre-Philothean Leitourgika are extremely variable. To a person accustomed to the standard printed editions of liturgical books this could even look like some sort of chaos. Nevertheless, there clearly are some patterns here.

Before discussing these patterns I should say a few words about the role of BAS in the Russian pre-Philothean Leitourgika. Here BAS is already a secondary formulary. Although in two manuscripts BAS comes first,[11] even here its secondary role is clear. In both manuscripts CHR is more complete than BAS, and instead of filling the lacunae in BAS the scribes just refer the reader to the formulary of CHR. One is tempted to

---

[8] One could note how astonishingly this confirms the idea of Robert Taft concerning the so-called 'soft points' of the Byzantine Eucharist: R. Taft, 'How Liturgies Grow: The Evolution of the Byzantine "Divine Liturgy"', *Orientalia Christiana Periodica* 43 (1977) 8-30.

[9] While the alternative *opisthambonos* prayer of BAS cited above is a fixed element of the formulary of BAS.

[10] Except the unique witness of *Moscow, State Historical Museum, Synodal Collection 598* (*datirovka*), pre-Philothean Russian Leitourgika do not contain a prayer before the gospel reading — as do not the Greek Euchologia prior to the turn of the 14-15th centuries. See J. Mateos, *La Célébration de la Parole dans la liturgie byzantine*, Orientalia Christiana Analecta 191 (Rome, 1971), pp. 139-140.

[11] Namely, *Moscow, State Historical Museum, Synodal Collection* 604 and *Saint-Petersburg, Russian National Library, Solovetskoje collection* 1017/1126. Both belong to the 13th century.

state that the secondary role of BAS hints that the Slavonic translation dates from the 11th century and not earlier, but that would not be correct: in the famous Glagolitic Sinai Leitourgikon,[12] — despite Nachtigal and others — BAS also comes after CHR,[13] and this witness contains a 10th-century Slavonic text. Rather, the secondary role of BAS means that the Slavonic translation of eucharistic formularies was of monastic origin: the monks could have already made CHR to be the first formulary in a translated text without touching their Greek models.[14] In the Old-Russian Leitourgika BAS often forms a block not with CHR, but with PRES. More precisely, besides the manuscripts containing the combination CHR+BAS+PRES, there are many which consist only of CHR, or only of BAS+PRES, and in a few CHR is separated from BAS+PRES by a number of non-eucharistic rites.

The secondary role of BAS resulted in abbreviating its written text. Sometimes it was copied in full, with all the standard prayers plus the additional ones, but more often the scribe provided only those prayers which differ from CHR, including the block of four alternative prayers described above, sometimes also abbreviated. Therefore I conclude that the absence of this or that additional prayer from an Old-Russian manuscript of BAS without CHR does not prove that this or that prayer was not in use. Moreover, many manuscripts are fragmentary, and their lacunae do not allow one to conclude that an additional prayer has or has not been present at the corresponding place of the formulary. Taking these two facts into account, I have noticed that while some non-standard additional prayers are found in the manuscripts inconsistently, others are found virtually everywhere.[15] While the

---

[12] I. e., a few Glagolitic folia from Sinai now kept at Saint-Petersburg (*Russian National Library, Glagolitic* 2 and *Library of the Academy of Sciences* 24. 4. 8). The handwriting is of the 11th century, but the philologists consider the manuscript's contents to be of the 10th century. The question of identity of the Sinai Glagolitic Leitourgikon with the Sinai Glagolitic Euchologion is an open one, but scholars often take them to be the parts of one manuscript.

[13] See T. Afanasyeva [Т. Афанасьева], 'К вопросу о порядке следования листов и составе Синайского глаголического Служебника XI в.', *Palaeobulgarica* 29: 3 (2005) 17-35.

[14] Concerning the probable reasons of giving CHR prevalence before BAS, see S. Parenti, 'La "vittoria" nella Chiesa di Constantinopoli della Liturgia di Crisostomo sulla Liturgia di Basilio', in *Comparative Liturgy Fifty Years After Anton Baumstark: Acts of the International Congress*, eds. R. F. Taft and G. Winkler, Orientalia Christiana Analecta 265 (Rome, 2001), pp. 907-928; S. Alexopoulos, 'The Influence of Iconoclasm on Liturgy: A Case Study', in *Worship Traditions in Armenia and the Neighboring Christian East*, ed. R. R. Ervine, AVANT Series 3 (New York, 2006), pp. 127-137.

[15] 'Virtually' here means that either a prayer is present, or there is a lacuna at its place, or what do we have is BAS, which is often abbreviated.

prayers found virtually everywhere should belong to the original core of the pre-Philothean Russian redaction of the eucharistic formularies, the others could have been added later, or were omitted from this core at an early date.[16]

2. Additional Prayers of the Old Russian CHR and BAS

2.1. Priestly Prayers before the Liturgy

Among the priestly prayers before the liturgy presented in the pre-Philothean Russian Leitourgika, two belong to the original core (there are three more, two of which could be also used in the context of the Great Entrance). Greek originals of both are unknown, here are the texts of them:

2.1.a

ВЛКО ГН ВСЕДЕРЖНТЕЛЮ · НЕ ХОТА СЪМРТН
ГРѢШНННКОМЪ · НО ѠБРАЩЕНЬН ДАВЪН НЪI · Н ПОКАЗА
НАМЪ ПУТЬ НОВЪ Н СТЪ · ѠБРАЗЪ ПОКАЗА ПОКАНАНЬЮ
ДРѢВНННМЬ БЛУДННКОМЬ · ДРЕВНННМЬ РАЗБОНННКОМЬ ·
ДРЕВЬНННМЪ МЫТОНМЬЦЕМЪ · ПОДАВЪ БЛУДННЦѢ
НСТОУНННКЪ СЛЕЗЪ · ТѢМЖЕ ВЛКО Н МЕНЕ СЪПОДОБН
· НЕ ПОМННАIА МОНХЪ БЕЩНСЛЕНЪIХЪ СОБЛАЗНЪ · НО
МНМОВЕДН МОIА ПРЕГРѢШЕНЬIА · НДННЪ БО НСН
БЕЗЪГРѢШЕНЪ · МЛРДЪ Н ПРЕМЛТНВЪ · КАIАСА Ѡ
ЗЪЛОБАХЪ УЛВѢЬСКЪIХЪ ПРННМЛА ПОКЛАНАНЬН Ѡ
ВСЕIА ТВАРН ХВАЛНМЪIН НЕПРЕСТАНЬНО · НЕБНЪIМН
СНЛАМН СТРАШЕНЪ СЪI ХЕРОВНМОМЬ Н СЕРАФНМОМЬ ·
Н Ѡ ТѢХЪ СЛУЖБУ НЕНЗРЕУЕННУ ПРННМЛА · Н
ПАКЪI НА ЗЕМЛН СОБОЮ ѠЦЮ ЖЕРТВУ ВЗНЕСЪ
ЗАКОЛЕНЬН ПРННМЪIН IАКО АГНА НЕЗЛОБНВО · Н
СВОНЮ КРОВЬЮ ѠСТЬ ВСЬ МНРЪ · Н ПОВЕЛѢВЪ НАМЪ
НЕДОСТОНННЪIМЪ · ТВОIА Ѡ ТВОНХЪ ТЕБѢ ПРННОСНТН
· ТЪI Н НЪINѢ ВЛКО · ПРЕЗРА МОIА ПРЕГРѢШЕНЬIА
РАЗЪДВНГНН ОУСТА МОIА · НСПОЛНН IА ТВОНГО
ХВАЛЕНЬIА · СРДЦЕ УТО СОЗНЖН ВО МНѢ · Н ДХЪ

---

[16] As a comparison with the South Slavonic sources shows, actually they should be later additions.

правъ ѿновн во оутробѣ моки · н прннмн ма
дерзающа входнтн въ стлнще твон · н вознестн
тебѣ твоıа ѿ твонхъ · ıакоже предалъ ıесн стмъ
твонмъ оучнкмъ · н мы ѿ тѣхъ прннмъше ·
таннѣ твон ѿбещнцн быванмъ · не по нашему
недостонньству · но твонго радн млрдьıа ·
ѿмын влко гнусъ ѿ душа мокıа · н всего ма
ѿтннудь ѿстн · снлою твоню невнднмою · н
дхвною десннцею твоню · нѣ бо вещн оутаıащнса
ѿ тебе но вса ѿбнажена ıак нага · предо
ѿчнма твонма суть · вѣдѣ же влко ıако
несдѣланныхъ монхъ зрнта ѿчн твон · н въ
кннгахъ вьса напнсаютсıа · тѣмьже не ѿмерзн
монго недостонньства · нн лнца твонго ѿвратн
ѿ мене · да не вращюсıа смѣренын посрамълкнъ
· н студенъ ѿ тебе · но сподобн ма поработатн
стмъ твонмъ таннамъ ·:· ıако подобакть тн
всака слава ѿцѣ н поклоненнк ·

2.1.b

Влко гн бе нашь · нынѣ хотаща прнступнтн
· къ чюднѣн сен н страшнѣн таннѣ · страхомь
ѿдержнм · не смѣю на нбо ѿчью възвестн · нн
рꙋ вздѣтн на высоту бню · нн оустну ѿверьстн
на млтву · нн вннтн в домъ бнн · во нже
кднн толнко нерен · кдною лѣта вхожаше
службу творнт · кмуже быхъ н азъ хотелъ
оуподобнтнса · но не съмѣю прнблнжнтн · къ
стѣн сен н страшьнѣн трапезѣ · на некже хощеть
взлещн · кдноуадын снъ бнн · гь нсъ хъ · н
раздробнтнсıа на оуды · подаıаса вѣрнымъ на
ѿставленьк грѣховъ · н на жнзнь вѣчную · но сего
радн дерзаю · на сню службу · понеже ты прнıа
влко блуднаго сна покаıавшаса · понеже прнıа
блуднцю раскаıавшюсıа · н слезамн ѿмывшн
скверны своıа · понеже прнıат разбоннка вопнюща
· поманн ма гн въ цртвнн твонмь · н ты не
поносн кму вьсѣ соблазнъ · но введе н в ран ·
да тѣмже млрдмь н намъ подан же свою млть
· н прннмн нынѣ хотащаıа прнчастнтнсıа стѣн
твонн жертвѣ · нн молю та влко ѿцтн преже

смꙑслъ мон · н ѿмꙑн гнꙋсъ ѿ дша мокꙗ · н
скверьнꙋ ѿ плотн мокꙗ · н всего мꙗ съпрославн
· н спроста ѡстн снлою твокю · да безъ ѡсꙋженьꙗ
твокго предъставъ · предъ лнцемь славꙑ твокꙗ
· неглн достоннъ бꙋдꙋ ѡкрнленьꙗ · кдннꙋꙗдаго
сна твокго ба нашего · кмꙋже кстъ слава съ
ѡцм н съ прстꙑмь блгнм ⁙

Additional prayers before or after the Great Entrance do not belong to
the original core of the pre-Philothean Russian eucharistic formularies.[17]

2.2. Additional Prayers During Clergy Communion

Among the additional prayers during clergy communion (twelve such
prayers are witnessed) there are four which belong to the original core.
Greek originals of three of them are not established, and I have discovered the original of the fourth one among the prayers of JAS. Here are
their texts:

2.2.a

Дан же намъ гн iсе хе бе · нзбавнтель рода
улвуа · стон тѣло н кровь · не въ сꙋдъ нн во
ѡсꙋженьк · но во ѿпꙋщеньк дшн мокн · ндеже
самъ жнвешн · н цртвꙋкшн со ѡцмь н стмь дхмь
н нꙑнꙗ н прн ⁙

2.2.b

Бꙋдн мнѣ гн во ѿданьк грѣховъ · ндеже стаꙗ
н прꙋта вошла сꙋть сщньꙗ · тꙋ нн кдннъ же
грѣхъ не ѡстанеть · млрдьꙗ радн бе · н
кдннꙋꙗдаго сна твокго га нашего iса ха · съ
ннмже блгвнъ ксн · съ престмь н блгнмь ⁙

---

[17] In the Russian 13-14th-century Leitourgika one can count four such prayers. They
form two stable pairs. The first one could also be placed among the priestly prayers
before the beginning of the liturgy, and includes a prayer which in the Greek sources is
known as an alternative Little Entrance prayer, and a prayer without a known Greek
original. The second one consists of a prayer from JAS (where it could be used in various
ways) and a prayer from the rite of 'reconciliation of the warring'.

2.2.c

ТѢЛО Н КРОВЬ ЮЖЕ ПРНІАХЪ ВЛ͠КО · ДАН ЖЕ ДА Н‘
БУДЕТЬ ВЪ ГРѢХЪ НН ВО Ѡ СУЖЕНЬ͠Е НО НА ПОТРЕБЛЕНЬ͠Е
ГРѢ͠ХОВЪ · Н НА Ѡ НЩЕНЬ͠Е Д͠ШН Н ТѢЛУ · ІАКО
ТВОІА ДЕРЖАВА Н ТВОЕ Ц͠РТВН͠Е · Н СНЛА Н СЛАВА
Ѡ͠ЦА ·:·

2.2.d

ВЪ МНОЖЬСТВЕ ГРѢ͠ХОВЪ
МОНХЪ · НЕ Ѿ ВЬРЬЗН МЕНЕ
ВЛ͠КО Б͠Е МОН · НЫНА БО
ПРНХОЖЮ КЪ УЮДЕСНОУ МОУ
Н НЕБ͠СНОМОУ ТАННЬСТВУ
НЕ ІАКОЖЕ ДОСТОННЪ СЫ ·
НО НА ТВОЮ ВЪЗНРАІА
ВЕЛНКОУЮ БЛГОСТЬ СНЮ ·
ПРОСТЬР͠Ъ ГЛАСЪ СВОН ·
НЕСМЬ ДОСТОННЪ
ВЪЗЬРѢ͠ТН НА ПОДОБНОУЮ
Н Д͠ХОВЬНОУЮ СНЮ
ТРАПЕЗОУ · НА НЕНЖЕ Б͠Ъ
НАШЬ · Г͠Ь Н͠С Х͠Ъ · Н
ЕДННОУАДЫН С͠НЪ · Н
ВСЕЮ СКВЬРНОЮ
Ѡ СКВЬРНЬШЮ МН СА ·
ТѢМЬЖЕ ЛЕЖНТЬ НА
ЖЬРТВОУ СДРОБЛЕНЪ ·
ТѢМЬЖЕ Н МОЛНТВОУ
ПРННОШЮ ТЕБЕ · Н ПРОШЮ
Ѿ СТАВЬЛЬННІА ГРѢ͠ХОВЪ ·
ДА БЫ МН ПРНШЬЛЪ
ОУ ТѢШНТЕЛЬ · Н
ОУ НСТЕЛЬ ГРѢ͠ХОВЪ МОНХЪ
· СНЛЬНЫН С͠ТЫН ТВОН
Д͠ХЪ · ОУКРЕПЛАІА МА Н
ОУ ТВЬРЖАІА · ДА Ѡ
УЮДНЕН СЛАВЬНЕН
ЖЬРТВѢ · ХВАЛОУ ТЕБЕ
ВЪСЫЛАЕМЪ ОЦ͠Ю Н С͠НОУ Н
С͠ТМОУ Д͠ХОУ І ·:·

Greek text (= priestly prayer in the beginning of JAS): Ἐν πλήθει ἁμαρτιῶν μεμολυσμένον μὴ με ἐξουδενώσῃ, Δέσποτα Κύριε ὁ Θεὸς ἡμῶν· ἰδοὺ γὰρ προσῆλθον τῷ θείῳ τούτῳ καὶ ἐπουρανίῳ μυστηρίῳ σου οὐχ ὡς ἄξιος ὑπάρχων, ἀλλ' εἰς τὴν σὴν ἀφορῶν ἀγαθότητα· ἀφίημί σοι τὴν φωνήν, ὁ Θεὸς ἱλάσθητί μοι τῷ ἁμαρτωλῷ· ἥμαρτον εἰς τὸν οὐρανὸν καὶ ἐνώπιόν σου καὶ οὐκ εἰμι ἄξιος ἀντοφθαλμῆσαι τῇ ἱερᾷ σου ταύτῃ καὶ πνευματικῇ τραπέζῃ, ἐφ' ᾗ ὁ μονογενής σου Υἱὸς καὶ Κύριος ἡμῶν Ἰησοῦς Χριστὸς ἐμοὶ τῷ ἁμαρτωλῷ καὶ κατεστιγμένῳ πάσῃ κηλῖδι, μυστικῶς πρόκειται εἰς θυσίαν. Διὸ ταύτην σοι τὴν ἱκεσίαν καὶ εὐχαριστίαν προσάγω τοῦ καταπεμφθῆναί μοι τὸ Πνεῦμά σου τὸ Παράκλητον ἐνισχῦον καὶ καταρτίζον με πρὸς τὴν λειτουργίαν ταύτην καὶ τὴν παρὰ σοῦ μοι τῷ λαῷ ἐπαγγελθεῖσαν φωνὴν ἀκατακρίτως ταύτην ἀποφθέγξασθαι καταξίωσον ἐν Χριστῷ Ἰησοῦ τῷ Κυρίῳ ἡμῶν, μεθ' οὗ εὐλογητὸς εἶ σὺν τῷ παναγίῳ, ἀγαθῷ, ζωοποιῷ καὶ ὁμοουσίῳ σου Πνεύματι, νῦν καὶ ἀεὶ καὶ εἰς τοὺς αἰῶνας τῶν αἰώνων. Ἀμήν.

2.3. Additional Prayers at the End of the Liturgy

Finally, the additional prayers at the end of the liturgy are somewhere after clergy communion; mostly, but not necessarily, after the *opistham-bonos* prayer. The Greek originals of these six prayers, when known, are invariably *skeuophylakion* prayers intended to be read in place of the standard one. But in the Russian sources they never replace the *skeuophy-lakion* prayer and form new units in the formulary instead. The Old-Russian Leitourgika have six such prayers,[18] two of which belong to the original pre-Philothean core. The Greek original of one of these two comes from JAS, whereas for the other one is not known. Here are the texts:

2.3.a

ГН БЕ НАШЬ · ПРИИМИ ОУМАЛЕНУЮ СИЮ НАШЮ
СЛУЖБУ И ХВАЛУ ІАКО РАБИ НЕДОСТОИНІ СУЩЕ ·
НЖЕ ТИ БѢХОМЪ ДОЛЖНИ ТВОРИТИ · СЪТВОРИХОМЪ
· ЗА НЕМОЩЬ НАШЮ · И ЗА ОУМНОЖЕНЬН ГРѢХЪ
НАШИ · НИКТОЖЕ БО НСТЬ ДОСТОИНЪ · ПО ЛѢПОТѢ
ТА ВОСХВАЛИМЪ · ТЫ БО НДИНЪ НСИ КРОМЕ ГРѢХА
· ТЕБѢ СЛАВУ ВСЬІ ⁘

2.3.b

ПРИХОДАЩАІА Ѿ СИЛЫ ВЪ
СИЛУ · МЫ ГРѢШНИИ · И
НЕДОСТОИННИ РАБИ ТВОН ·
ВОСПѢВАНМЪ ЦРТВИН
ТВОН ⁘

Greek text (= prayer in the end of JAS, widespread in South Italian redactions of CHR and BAS; the text of the prayer has many variations):
Ἐκ δυνάμεως εἰς δύναμιν πορευόμενοι ἡμεῖς οἱ ἁμαρτωλοὶ [ἔνθα τὰ ἅγια τῶν ἁγίων ἀποτίθονται] <ὑμνοῦμεν τὴν βασιλείαν σου> νῦν καὶ ἀεὶ καὶ εἰς τοὺς αἰῶνας τῶν αἰώνων. Ἀμήν.

[18] In a unique manuscript, *Moscow, Russian State Archive of Ancient Acts, Synodal Typography* 40, the liturgy ends with an additional prayer to the Mother of God, to be read before eating the *prosphora* which was offered in her name.

Pre-Philothean Russian Eucharistic Formularies: A Witness to Some Lost Greek Tradition?

To sum up, the pre-Philothean redactions of the Russian eucharistic formularies contain a number of peculiar prayers, most of which are used as additions to the standard formulary. In other words, only a few prayers actually replaced the standard ones; these are the four alternative prayers in BAS and the festal *opisthambonoi* prayers. All the others were inserted alongside the standard prayers and formed new units in the formularies. Many of these prayers were added around the turn of the 14th century.[19] But there is also a complex of prayers, consisting of four alternative prayers of BAS (which is already a secondary formulary) and eight additional prayers of both CHR and BAS: two before the beginning and two at the end of the liturgy, as well as four prayers during clergy communion. This complex of prayers was introduced into Russian practice not later than the turn of the 13th century.[20]

This Old-Russian distinguished prayer complex has some resemblance to the various South Italian Greek traditions, as well as to the Palestinian tradition (there are some prayers from JAS), but it is by no means identical to either. In Russian practice these peculiar prayers were used in a very special way, and a half of them are found neither in the South Italian Euchologia, nor in the manuscripts of JAS. The crucial question is: did this complex form within the Russian tradition itself, or did it originate elsewhere? To answer this question one must turn to the early South Slavonic sources.

The Glagolitic Sinai Leitourgikon and Other Pre-Philothean South Slavonic Sources

The Glagolitic Sinai Leitourgikon contains the oldest preserved text of a Slavonic translation of the Byzantine eucharistic formularies. This

---

[19] These are never present in the 13th-century manuscripts, but already appear in the Leitourgika of the first half of the 14th century. Interestingly, Greek originals of some of these are attested in the Athonite manuscripts. This localization together with the date of these additions suggests that they were an outcome of the liturgical activity of Serbs and Bulgarians on Athos in the second half of the 13th century. This needs further investigation.

[20] This is the date of the oldest preserved Russian Leitourgikon, *Moscow, State Historical Museum, Synodal* 604.

text represents the Bulgarian recension of CHR and BAS of the 10-11th centuries and goes back to the Bulgarian translations of the turn of the 10th century.

What does one find here? Here is the list of characteristic features of the eucharistic formularies in the Sinai Glagolitic Leitourgikon:

1. The primary eucharistic formulary is CHR; BAS is written after it.
2. BAS — and not CHR! — contains the same alternative Prothesis prayer as do the Old-Russian sources (the rest of BAS is lost).
3. CHR contains additional prayers in exactly the same positions as in the pre-Philothean Russian Sluzhebniki: an additional prayer before the liturgy and an additional prayer at the end of it (alas, the communion section is lost, but we can suppose again that it also contained the additional prayers).
4. Moreover, the prayer at the end of the liturgy is precisely the prayer 2.3.a from the Old-Russian Leitourgika cited above; the prayer in the beginning, though, is not the same as any of the Russian prayers, although it has some resemblance to the prayer 2.1.b.

Obviously, this is something very similar to the pre-Philothean Russian eucharistic formularies. Yet, the language and the wording of the extant parts of the anaphora of CHR in the Glagolitic Sinai Leitourgikon are somewhat different from the Old-Russian redaction. Still, despite the differences, the main features of the Glagolitic Sinai Leitourgikon and of the pre-Philothean Russian Leitourgika are the same. This means that the Russian pre-Philothean redaction is a descendant of the Bulgarian translations of the 10th century, but at some point the Russians edited and corrected them, most probably in the 11th century in Kiev.

The Glagolitic Sinai manuscript is the only South Slavonic Leitourgikon of the 11th century. There are five South Slavonic Leitourgika of the 13th century, and forty of the 14th.[21] Most of those from the 14th century date from the second half or even the last years of that century, and

---

[21] See the full list in: Zheltov, 'Чин Божественной литургии' (see n. 1), pp. 336-339. I should notice here that one manuscript in this list — *Belgrade, Patriarchal Library 365*, 14th century, — which I have not consulted until recently, is not a Leitourgikon, but contains only the rite of consecration of a church. It could be also noted that Radu Constantinescu mentions a few Slavonic Leitourgika of the 13-14th centuries which are not on my list. See R. Constantinescu, 'Euthyme de Tarnovo et la réforme liturgique au XIVe siècle', *Etudes balkaniques* 3 and 4 (1986) 62-78 and 53-80. However, his datings of these are not confirmed neither by their descriptions in the manuscript catalogues, nor by consulting them *de visu*.

they already contain the *Diataxis* of Philotheos. Most of the earlier manuscripts already show clear signs of standardization and 'constantinopolization' of the liturgy. But some earlier Bulgarian Leitourgika[22] still witness to the same peculiarities of the eucharistic formularies, which I have traced in both Old-Russian sources and in the Glagolitic Sinai Leitourgikon. This proves the Bulgarian origins of the Russian pre-Philothean complex of non-standard prayers of CHR and BAS. The same could be also shown on the rubrical and formulaic level: the Old-Russian Leitourgika contain a few very distinct rubrics and formulae, which are also found in the 13th-century South Slavonic sources.

CONCLUSIONS

According to the results of my research, the history of the Russian eucharistic formularies began with an acceptance of the 10th-century Bulgarian translation of CHR, BAS and PRES. In this translation CHR already was the primary formulary, in BAS some standard prayers were replaced by alternative ones, and in both CHR and BAS there were also additional prayers, which formed new units in the formulary. This happened at the end of the 10th century. In the 11th century, presumably, the Russians did their own re-working of the eucharistic formularies, which existed until the end of the 14th century. In the 13-14th centuries new additional prayers were added to the formularies, some of them coming from the South Slavonic milieu, others probably being added by the Russians themselves. Finally, by the end of the 14th century the Russians accepted a completely new translation of CHR, BAS and PRES, where CHR and BAS followed the *Diataxis* of Philotheos. All the peculiar prayers were gone.[23]

The peculiar features of the oldest pre-Philothean Slavonic redaction of the eucharistic formularies, which stand behind the Old-Russian and the most ancient Bulgarian manuscripts, are not attested in the classical Constantinopolitan sources. They bear some resemblance to the characteristic

---

[22] Namely, *Moscow, State Historical Museum, Khloudovskoye* 117 (13th c.), *Uvarovskoye* 46 (first half of the 14th c.), and *Synodal Greek* 484 (turn of the 13-14th centuries; here: fol. 1 and 314, used for binding a Greek manuscript).

[23] Yet in the 15-16th centuries this or that prayer from the ancient manuscripts accidentally happened to be introduced into the post-Philothean Russian Leitourgika. Only in the middle of the 17th century the Russian Sluzhebnik finally obtained its current form, based on the Ukrainian editions of the beginning of the same century. The latter, in their turn, were based on Greek editions printed in the 16th century in Italy.

features of the South Italian and Palestinian Greek traditions, yet they are different. Therefore, it is clear that the oldest Slavonic sources are witnesses to some other tradition, the corresponding Greek sources of which are lost (or, let us hope, have not been discovered yet). This should not be a surprise. Everyone knows that the ancient lectionary of Jerusalem is preserved only in Armenian and Georgian translations; the ancient Jerusalem Tropologion only in the Georgian manuscripts of *Udzvelesi Iadgari*; the Typikon of the Patriarch of Constantinople, Alexios the Studite, only in the Old-Russian translation, etc.

Concerning the tradition witnessed in the oldest Slavonic Leitourgika, it is not at all clear what ecclesiastical center it belonged to. I suggest that it was Thessalonica. First of all, it is natural to suppose that Bulgarian liturgical translations of the 10th century were made using the Thessalonian originals, because the Greek-Slavonic contacts at the time were the most intense exactly in the Thessalonian region. Secondly, Pentkovsky came to the same conclusions of a Thessalonian origin of the earliest Slavonic liturgy after he studied not the euchological, but the hymnographic and lectionary material.[24] Thirdly, even the late Thessalonian authors of the 14-15th centuries witness that the Thessalonian Church was observing its own distinct liturgical usages. St Nicholas Cabasilas even cites our prayer 2.3.b (this citation remained unnoticed by the editors of his commentary[25]).

If the Thessalonian theory is correct, then the oldest Slavonic Leitourgika present us with an invaluable picture of 9-10th-century Thessalonian eucharistic practice. But even if it is not correct, the oldest Slavonic material is a precious source for further study. In any case, the overall picture of Byzantine liturgical history is more complex than was thought of before. The so-called 'Byzantine rite' is not a single tradition, but a set of close traditions, both interfering with and/or originating from and influencing one another.

---

[24] A. Pentkovsky [А. М. Пентковский], 'Славянское богослужение и славянская гимнография византийского обряда в X веке', in *Liturgische Hymnen nach byzantinischem Ritus bei den Slaven in ältester Zeit*, eds. H. Rothe and D. Christians (Paderborn e.a., 2007), pp. 16-26; A. Pentkovsky and M. Yovcheva [А. Пентковский, М. Йовчева], 'Праздничные и воскресные блаженны в византийском и славянском богослужении VIII–XIII вв.', *Palaeobulgarica* 15: 3 (2001) 31-60; A. Pentkovsky and T. Pentkovskaya [А. М. Пентковский, Т. В. Пентковская], 'Синайский Апостол (Sin. slav. 39): История текста и история рукописи', *Лингвистическое источниковедение и история русского языка* 2002-2003 (Moscow, 2003), pp. 121-171.

[25] Cf. Nicolas Cabasilas, *Explication de la Divine Liturgie*, trad. et notes de S. Salaville, 2e éd. munie du text grec, revue et augmentée par R. Bornert, J. Gouillard, P. Périchon, Sources chrétiennes 4bis (Paris, 1967), p. 68.

THE 'DESCENT TO THE WEST' IN THE LITURGICAL COMMENTARIES OF SYMEON OF THESSALONICA

Steven HAWKES-TEEPLES

As Robert Taft and others have pointed out, the growth and development of liturgies is often quite similar to language growth, sometimes slower, sometimes faster, but with few sudden, dramatic shifts.[1] When one finds relatively swift changes, they deserve some attention. One such shift can be seen in the so-called 'Descent to the West' in the pontifical Divine Liturgy.

Between the time of Symeon of Thessalonica's commentaries and modern usage, this descent disappeared entirely. We do not have precise dates for Symeon's two commentaries on the Divine Liturgy. Symeon was probably born in Constantinople some time around 1384 by my calculations, based on correspondence with Makarios Makris.[2] He was archbishop of Thessalonica from 1416 or 1417 until his death in September 1429. On the basis of internal evidence, it is also clear that the independent work, Ἑρμηνεία περί τοῦ θείου ναοῦ (*Explanation of the Divine Temple*), predates the longer work, 'Περὶ τῆς θείας λειτουργίας' ('On the Sacred Liturgy'), which is one chapter of his voluminous Διάλογος ἐν Χριστῷ (*Dialogue in Christ*). That long rambling dialogue constitutes two-thirds of the Migne edition of Symeon's works.[3] Some or all of the more carefully crafted and structured *Explanation* may have been written while Symeon was still a monk in

---

[1] Abbreviations used in the notes: E = Ἑρμηνεία περί τοῦ θείου ναοῦ (*Explanation of the Divine Temple*), in a forthcoming edition by the author from the Pontifical Institute of Mediaeval Studies, Toronto and PG 155: 697-749. L = 'Περὶ τῆς θείας λειτουργίας' ('On the Sacred Liturgy') in a forthcoming edition by the author from the Pontifical Institute of Mediaeval Studies, Toronto and PG 155: 253-364. OCA = Orientalia Christiana Analecta. OCP = Orientalia Christiana Periodica. PG = J.P. Migne, *Patrologia Graeca* (Paris, 1857-1866).
    Robert F. Taft, *The Precommunion Rites: A History of the Liturgy of St. John Chrysostom, Vol. 5*, OCA 261 (Rome, 2000), pp. 46-53.

[2] Steven Hawkes-Teeples, *The Praise of God in the Twilight of the Empire: The Divine Liturgy in the Commentaries of St. Symeon of Thessalonika († 1429)* (Unpublished doctoral dissertation of the Pontifical Oriental Institute, 1997), pp. 11-13.

[3] PG 155: 33-696.

Constantinople. In both the Migne edition and Zagora 23, the most authoritative early manuscript,[4] one finds the correct, though nearly interminable, title, Ἑρμηνεία...περί τε τοῦ θείου ναοῦ καὶ τῶν ἐν αὐτῷ, ἱερέων τε πέρι καὶ διακόνων, ἀρχιερέων καὶ τῶν ὧν ἕκαστος τούτων στολῶν ἱερῶν περιβάλλεται, οὐ μὴν ἀλλὰ καὶ περὶ τῆς θείας μυσταγωγίας λόγον ἑκάστῳ διδοῦσα τῶν ἐν αὐτῇ τελοθμένων θείως, καὶ τοῖς ἐν Κρήτῃ εὐσεβέσι ζητήσασιν ἀποσταλεῖσα (An explanation... concerning the divine temple and what pertains to it, and also of the priests, deacons, and hierarchs, and the sacred vestments worn by each, as well as the divine mystagogy, giving an account of each of the rites divinely celebrated. <This explanation> was sent to the pious people of Crete, who requested it).[5] The later 'On the Sacred Liturgy' is longer, diffuse, and chaotic, interrupted by a number of excursus. Its scattered style would seem to suggest that it is the work of a busy bishop in besieged Thessalonica, dictating a few pages whenever time allowed. It focuses extensively on the prothesis, which was undergoing a great deal of rather chaotic development at the time.[6] Although Symeon composed a Διάταξις (still unedited)[7] with that name, a good deal of both commentaries are diataxal or prescriptive work dealing with how the liturgy should be celebrated and condemning errors, with which he was familiar.

I know of no solid evidence to demonstrate the diverse origin of the two works other than perhaps a rather more hierarchical tone in the later composition. Then again, Symeon never seems to have been greatly troubled by doubts about his conclusions. Nonetheless, the differing styles of the two works suggests that at least some of first draft of the earlier commentary was written by Symeon the monk and the later rambling chapter by Symeon the archbishop.

---

[4] Hawkes-Teeples, *Praise of God* (see n. 2), pp. 141-142; David Balfour, *Politico-Historical Works of Symeon Archbishop of Thessalonica (1416/17 to 1429)*, Wiener Byzantinische Studien 13 (Vienna, 1979), pp. 26-34; Basilius J. Groen, *Ter genezing van ziel en lichaam: De viering van het oliesel in de Grieks-Orthodoxe Kerk*, Theologie & Empirie 11 (Kampen and Weinheim, 1990), p. 40.

[5] E sect. 1 (paragraph-like sections of the forthcoming Hawkes-Teeples edition), PG 155: 697, and ms Zagora 23, f. 175, lines 1-7.

[6] Georges Descoeudres, *Die Pastophorien im syro-byzantinischen Osten: Eine Untersuchung zu architektur- und liturgiegeschichtlichen Problemen*, Schriften zur Geistesgeschichte des östlichen Europa 16 (Wiesbaden, 1983), pp. 111-126; Hawkes-Teeples, *Praise of God* (see n. 2), pp. 40-53.

[7] Ioannês M. Fountoulis, Τὸ λειτουργικὸν ἔργον Συμεὼν τοῦ Θεσσαλονίκης, Ἴδρυμα Μελετῶν Χερσονήσου Αἵμου 84 (Thessalonica, 1966) pp. 45-48.

For the most part, the difference between the Symeon's commentaries and present-day usage is not great. In Symeon's time most Orthodox bishops wore no miters,[8] the phrasing of commemorations in the prothesis was a bit different,[9] and so on. And Symeon was in no way restrained by modern ecumenical courtesy from bitterly denouncing and ridiculing the Roman Catholic and Armenian liturgies, rather more harshly in the later work.[10] He also has some fairly naïve notions that the Byzantine liturgy was the original liturgy of the primitive Christian Church.[11] So he is clearly not a modern writer, but for the most part the liturgy he describes closely resembles the modern liturgy.

It is no surprise, then, to find that Symeon re-emerges sometimes nearly verbatim in the early nineteenth-century commentary by Bishop Veniamin (Rumovskij-Krasnopevkov) of Nižnij-Novgorod, *Новая Скрижаль или объяаснение о церкви, о литургии, и о всех службах и утварях церковных* (*The New Tablet or an Explanation of the Church, of the Liturgy, and of Every Service and of Church Utensils*).[12] Because of the close similarity between the liturgy in Symeon and the liturgy Bishop Veniamin knew and celebrated, Bishop Veniamin could easily borrow Symeon's views and use them essentially without modification. Partly through Veniamin, and seemingly directly, Symeon also influenced one of the best known, though controversial, commentaries of the Byzantine Divine Liturgy, the *Размышления о божественной литургии* (*Meditations on the Divine Liturgy*) of Nikolai Gogol, published shortly after his death.[13] Since Gogol wrote much of the book in Italy and France where he lived for years, it should come as no surprise that Roman Catholic piety and theology left their mark. Nonetheless, its popularity has been enormous.

The *Explanation of the Divine Temple* begins with a general treatise on sacramental theology.[14] There follows a discussion of the symbolism

---

[8] E 41-42, PG 155: 716C-717B.

[9] L sect. 90 (paragraph-like sections of the forthcoming Hawkes-Teeples edition), PG 155: 284C.

[10] On Roman Catholics, L 35-60, PG 155: 265A-273C; on Armenians, L 64-78, PG 155: 276A-280C.

[11] E 11-12, PG 155:701A-B.

[12] Pub. Moscow, 1803; Eighteenth Russian edition, Moscow, 1999.

[13] Pub. Moscow, 1857.

[14] E 2-14, PG 155: 697-701D.

of the church building.[15] The following sections deal with the ministers, their vestments, and the preparatory rites.[16] After the description of vesting, and with no mention of the prothesis,[17] we find in the *Explanation* the following description.

Ὁ μὲν οὖν ἱεράρχης ἐν τῷ μέλλειν ἱερουργεῖν, κατελθὼν τοῦ θρόνου, ἐν ᾧ παρίσταται, τὴν πρὸς ἡμᾶς τοῦ Θεοῦ Λόγου δηλοῖ συγκατάβασιν. ἐνδυόμενος δὲ τὴν ἱερὰν στολὴν, τὴν παναγίαν αὐτοῦ σημαίνει σάρκωσιν. Κατερχόμενος δὲ ἄχρι καὶ τῶν τοῦ ναοῦ πυλῶν, τὴν ἐπὶ γῆς αὐτοῦ δηλοῖ παρουσίαν τε καὶ φανέρωσιν, καὶ τὴν μέχρι θανάτου καὶ ᾅδου κάθοδον. τοῦτο γὰρ δηλοῖ τὸ πρὸς δυσμὰς ἀπιέναι, καὶ μέχρι τῶν πυλῶν κατελθεῖν. τῆς ἱερᾶς δὲ ἀρξαμένης λειτουργίας, τοῦ ἀρχιερέως τὸν καιρὸν δεδωκότος· οὐ γὰρ δυνατὸν χωρὶς αὐτοῦ τι διενεργεῖσθαι· οἱ μὲν ἱερεῖς ἔνδον λέγουσι τὰς εὐχάς, τὰς οὐρανίους τυποῦντες τάξεις.[18]

'The hierarch, then, who is about to celebrate the sacred-service, descends from the throne where he was, representing the descent of God the Word to us. Putting on the sacred vesture, he represents His all-holy incarnation. Descending as far as the gates of the temple, he represents His appearance and manifestation on earth, and also His descent to death and to the underworld; for going to the west and descending to the gates show this. The liturgy is begun when the bishop indicates the moment. For it is not possible without him for anything to be carried out. The priests say the prayers inside, typifying the heavenly orders.'

So prior to the beginning of the Divine Liturgy, we find the bishop on a throne in the nave of the church. From there he descends from his throne and makes three reverences (προσκυνήσας τρὶς).[19] The bishop then vests. Deacons minister to him as he puts on the vestments. The bishop says a prayer, which Symeon describes as a prayer for 'the grace and power to accomplish the divine things, showing that he is a servant of God and that by His strength God serves His own <servants>.'[20] The prayer is almost certainly the present-day concluding prayer before the iconostasis, 'Κύριε, ἐξαπόστειλον τὴν χεῖρά σου ἐξ ὕψους κατοικητηρίου σου' ('Lord, extend your hand from the height of your

---

[15] E 15-23, PG 155:701D-708C.

[16] E 24-42, PG 155: 708C-717B.

[17] Some aspects of the prothesis are discussed at the very conclusion of the book, in E 106-110, PG 155:748B-749C.

[18] E 43, PG 155: 717B-C.

[19] L 8, PG 155: 256B.

[20] *Ibid.*: 'χάριν καὶ δύναμιν τοῦ ἐκτελέσαι τὰ θεῖα, δεικνὺς ὅτι δοῦλος Θεοῦ, καὶ τῇ αὐτοῦ ἰσχύϊ τοὺς αὐτοῦ ἐξυπηρετεῖ.'

abode'), which refers to being strengthened in order to complete the sacred-service.[21] The hierarch while standing blesses the deacons who assisted him.[22]

Having vested, the bishop then makes the κατάβασις πρὸς δυσμάς, or Descent to the West, going to the western doors of the nave of the church. Symeon notes that the bishop goes in silence (μετὰ σιγῆς). He is preceded by pairs of deacons. Arriving at the doors, he stands and awaits the moment for his entrance into the sanctuary.[23] From the back of the nave, he gives the signal to the first deacon for the moment when the liturgy is to begin. The deacon in turn calls on the priest at the altar to give the opening blessing. Interestingly, Symeon notes that the priest who intones the opening blessing at the altar is the one who completed the preparatory rite.[24] The priests say the prayers inside the sanctuary, ('ἔνδον λέγουσι τὰς εὐχας').[25]

Symeon served as archbishop of Thessalonica, but prior to his elevation he was a monk in Constantinople. Elsewhere he points out differences between Byzantine liturgical usages in Thessalonica, Alexandria, and Mount Athos.[26] Since he makes no such mention here, it is reasonable to suppose that the usage in Constantinople was at least roughly identical to that of Thessalonica.

For Symeon this procession to the doors of the nave has rich theological meaning. It is first and foremost a descent (κάθοδος, κατάβασις, συνατάβασις).[27] Consequently, it represents first Christ's descent to earth in the incarnation and also the Lord's descent to the dead after his death. Since the bishop is the preeminent image of Christ in the liturgy for Symeon, it is only fitting that his liturgical actions symbolize these two essential events of the life of the Lord. The deacons are an image of the angels as they minister to the bishop while he is vesting, just as angels assisted at the incarnation. Then in the procession to the west, the deacons are an icon of the apostles, who were sent out in pairs

[21] Frank E. Brightman, *Liturgies Eastern and Western*, 1 (Oxford, 1896), p. 354; Εὐχολόγιον τὸ μέγα, ed. S. Zerbos (Athens, 1986) p. 35.
[22] L 24, PG 155: 260D.
[23] *Ibid.*
[24] L 117, PG 155: 289D.
[25] E 43, PG 155: 717B-C.
[26] E 41-42, 716C-717B and L 116, PG 155: 289B-C.
[27] E 43, PG 155: 717B-C; E 46, PG 155: 720B; L 24, PG 155: 259D-260D.

before the passion. In following them, the bishop shows forth the humility of the Lord, who came as a humble man.[28]

The Descent to the West as described by Symeon also appears in the fourteenth-century *diataxis* of Demetrios Gemistos[29] and the fifteenth-century pontifical liturgy in the Athonite St. Andrew Skete codex,[30] as Sr. Vassa Larin pointed out to me.[31] Obviously, these two texts are roughly contemporaneous with Symeon. In particular the *diataxis* of Gemistos makes the patriarch's going to the western doors sound more like a simple functional walk, rather than a procession. After describing the vesting, it says simply, 'Καὶ εὐθὺς ὁ πατριάρχης κατέρχεται καὶ ἵσταται ἐν τῷ συνήθει τόπῳ τοῦ μέρους τοῦ δεξιοῦ τῶν βασιλικῶν πυλῶν τοῦ ναοῦ' ('And immediately the patriarch descends and stands in the customary place to the right of the royal doors of the church').[32] However at times the gradations between a simple walk and a procession can be hard to detect in the sources.

Such then is the 'Descent to the West'. What are its origins?

In the first two stages of the development of the Byzantine liturgy — the Paleo-Byzantine, and the Imperial eras, which is to say from 330 to about 650 — everyone including the imperial and patriarchal parties remained outside the basilica of Hagia Sophia until the doors were opened for the entrance.[33] The many doors on all sides of the basilica were opened and everyone poured in. The clergy put on liturgical wear outside the basilica and processed in fully vested.[34]

The third period, which has been called the Byzantine Dark Ages, was the period of officially sanctioned iconoclasm by both government and church. Things began to take on more limited dimensions. The sacristy

---

[28] *Ibid.*

[29] Alexander Rentel, *The 14th Century Patriarchal Liturgical Diataxis of Dimitrios Gemistos: Edition and Commentary* (Unpublished doctoral dissertation of the Pontifical Oriental Institute, 2003) p. 192.

[30] Aleksej Dmitrievskij, *Описаніе литургическихъ рукописей хранищахся въ библіотекахъ православнаго востока*, 1 (Kiev, 1895), p. 168.

[31] Barbara (Vassa) Larin, The *Hierarchal Divine Liturgy in Arsenij Suxanov's* Proskinitarij: *Text, Translation, and Analysis of the Entrance Rites* (Unpublished doctoral dissertation of the University of Munich, 2008) pp. 128-129.

[32] Rentel, *Diataxis* (see n. 29), p. 192.

[33] I use the historical divisions laid out in R. Taft, *The Byzantine Rite: A Short History*, American Essays in Liturgy (Collegeville, MN, 1992).

[34] Juan Mateos, *La Célébration de la parole dans la liturgie byzantine*, OCA 191 (Rome, 1971), pp. 71-90.

and preparation point for the Eucharistic gifts moved from the separated σκευοφυλάκιον (skevophylakion) building outside to a preparation altar or prothesis inside the church. In this framework, the bishop waits in the narthex, just outside the western doors of the nave — the Royal Doors, often confused with the Holy Doors of the sanctuary. Such is the situation we find in the twelfth-century *diataxis* in the codex *Brit. Museum Add.* 34060.[35]

With the collapse of iconoclasm, the Byzantine Empire, including the church, experienced one its most dramatic shifts. Not surprisingly it shows up in the liturgy. Indeed, a number of the most dramatic developments take place in the destitution of the iconoclastic clergy and the triumph of the heavily monastic, or monastic influenced, iconodule clergy.

In the fourth period of Byzantine liturgical history, the epoch of the Studites and the Middle Byzantine synthesis, we see the imperial liturgy of Constantinople shrink even further, becoming less and less a spectacle involving the whole city and more something contained within the confines of the church building, at least in part in imitation of the triumphant iconodule monks doing liturgy within the monastic enclosure and inside the monastic church.[36] For instance, the antiphons to be sung in procession on the way to church become the opening enarxis of the Divine Liturgy.[37]

It is a well known point that the bishop does not enter the sanctuary until the Little Entrance. This usage is a ritual reminder of the first and second periods of the liturgy, when it was the opening of the liturgy, when it was the entrance of everyone, and was anything but 'little.' At present, the bishop typically vests at his 'lower throne' in the nave and usually waits there until the clergy in the sanctuary comes to join him for the Little Entrance.[38]

Consequently, the Descent to the West is a penultimate stage in the development of the bishop's entrance. He no longer enters the cathedral from outside, coming in already vested. Rather, he vests at his throne in the nave. Then, in these fourteenth- and fifteenth-century texts, he goes

---

[35] Robert F. Taft, 'The Pontifical Liturgy of the Great Church according to a Twelfth-Century Diataxis in Codex *British Museum Add.* 34060', *OCP* 45 (1979), p. 284.

[36] Taft, *Short History* (see n. 33), pp. 56-61.

[37] Mateos, *Célébration* (see n. 34), pp. 42-45.

[38] Ἀρχιερατικόν, ed. Panteleêmôn Rodopoulos (Thessalonica, 2004), p. 20; Чиновникъ архіерейскаго священнослуженія Книга А. (Moscow, 1983), p. 62; Архиератиконъ или служебникъ святительскій (Rome, 1973), pp. 38-39.

to the western doors of the church. Clearly this preserves the bishop's entrance in church; he simply no longer starts from outside.

It is intriguing that such an entrance from the doors of the nave bears a resemblance to the opening entrance of either priest or bishop in the Roman Catholic mass. I don't think that there is any question of one liturgy influencing the other. At least, I know of none. Still, there is a certain curious similarity.

Am I suggesting that the Descent to the West be revived? Certainly not. What, then, are the concrete practical suggestions for the celebration of the liturgy that flow from these observations? There are none. The point is simply to understand more fully how our beautiful and glorious Divine Liturgy has grown and developed. For Symeon, the procession to the doors was an important part of the liturgy, full of theological significance. Today it doesn't exist. I am reminded of the Diptychs. At times in the past, cities and churches were ready to go to war over whom these lists mentioned or excluded. Now they are gone.[39]

My point would be that our liturgy does indeed change and grow. The Descent to the West is just one example of how it has changed. No serious participant-observer of the liturgy would suggest that changes should be made for light and trivial reasons. As a Greek-Catholic priest, I am often pained at how often individual priests make substantial modifications in the liturgy at their own initiative or personal whim. I don't value confrontation, but I was gratified a few years ago when an elderly parishioner reprimanded me for 'adding new prayers' when I read part of the anaphora aloud. I am glad that someone noticed and cared, even if there was hardly anything 'new' about the anaphoral texts I took aloud.

So our liturgy can and does change. That should neither frighten nor upset us. Our main task as laity, clergy, scholars and observers is to strive to make the changes good and helpful ones.

---

[39] Robert F. Taft, *The Diptychs: A History of the Liturgy of St. John Chrysostom, Vol. 4*, OCA 238 (Rome, 1991).

THE BISHOP AS MINISTER OF THE PROTHESIS?
RECONSIDERING THE EVIDENCE
IN BYZANTINE AND MUSCOVITE SOURCES

Vassa LARIN

1. Introduction[1]

In traditional Byzantine usage 'there is no question of [the hierarch] participating in the prothesis rite.'[2] Indeed, the earliest witnesses to the hierarchal rite usually have the hierarch already vested and entering the church only at the Little Entrance, the original beginning of the service, at which point his participation in the liturgy began: any rites preceding the Little Entrance, including the Prothesis and Enarxis, were later additions accomplished by lesser clergy.[3] This tradition is reflected in the

---

[1] The following abbreviations of ms locations, collections, and pressmarks are used in this paper:

Arxang. = Arxangel'skoe, of Arxangel'sk (BAN). Arxang. D. = Arxangel'skogo Drevlexranilišča, of the Arxangel'sk Collection of Antiquities (BAN). Arxang. Krasnogorsk. = Arxangel'skogo Krasnogorskogo Monastyrja, of the Arxangel'sk Krasnogorsk Monastery (BAN). Arxang. S. = Arxangel'skoj Seminarii, of Arxangel'sk Seminary (BAN). BAN = Biblioteka Akademii Nauk, St. Petersburg. Dmitr. = private collection of Prof. A. A. Dmitrievskij (BAN). GIM = Gosudarstvennyj Istoričeskij Muzej, Moscow. JMZ = Jaroslavl'skij Muzej-Zapovednik, Jaroslavl'. NBS = Narodna Biblioteka Srbije, Belgrade. NYPL = New York Public Library, New York. OSRK = Osnovnoe Sobranie Rukopisnoj Knigi, The Basic Collection of Manuscript-Books (RNB). RAIK = Russkogo Arxeologičeskogo Instituta v Konstantinopole, of the Russian Archaeological Institute in Constantinople (BAN). RGADA = Rossijskij Gosudarstvennyj Arxiv Drevnix Aktov, Moscow. *RGB = Rossijskaja Gosudarstvennaja Biblioteka*, Moscow. *RNB = Rossijskaja Nacional'naja Biblioteka*, St. Petersburg. *Rogož.* = *Rogožskogo Kladbišča*, of the Rogož Cemetery (RGB). *Sof.* = *Novgorodskogo Sofijskogo Sobora*, of the St. Sophia Cathedral in Novgorod (RNB). *Solovec.* = *Soloveckogo Monastyrja*, of Solovki Monastery (RNB). *Syn.* = *Sinodal'noe*, of the Holy Synod (GIM). *Syn. Typ.* = *Sinodal'noj Tipografii*, of the Moscow Synodal Printing-House (RGADA). *TSL* = *Troice-Sergievoj Lavry*, of the Trinity-Sergius Lavra (RGB). *Xlud.* = *Xludovskoe*, private collection of A. I. Xludov (GIM).

[2] R. Taft, *The Great Entrance: A History of the Transfer of Gifts and other Preanaphoral Rites. A History of the Liturgy of St. John Chrysostom II*, Orientalia Christiana Analecta 200 (Rome, 2004), p. 265.

[3] Cf. the 10th c. Pyromalus Codex, where the psaltai and people chant the synaptes before the entrance of the hierarch: J. Goar, Εὐχολόγιον *sive Rituale Graecorum*

earliest Greek *Archieratica*, in which the text of the hierarchal Divine Liturgy does not include the Prothesis rite save the Prothesis Prayer.[4]

In modern ms and printed *Archieratica* the Prothesis Prayer is almost invariably found before the beginning of the Enarxis, with no indication of exactly *when*, *where*, or even *who* is to read it.[5] To add to the confusion, some recent *Archieratica* have the bishop read the same prayer *again* before the Great Entrance, while others place it after the Great Entrance.[6] As Robert Taft has long ago explained, the presence of the Prothesis Prayer at the beginning of Divine Liturgy is 'a relic of the earlier rite as seen in *Pyromalus Codex* and the version of Johannisberg,'[7] in which the hierarch himself did the Prothesis in the outside skeuophylakion. With the disappearance of the outside skeuophylakion, the Prothesis came to be accomplished in the sanctuary area, which the hierarch traditionally only entered at the Little Entrance, making his participation in the preparatory rite of the Divine Liturgy physically impossible.

complectens ritus et ordines Divinae Liturgiae, officiorum, sacramentorum, consecrationum, benedictionum, funerum, orationum, &c. cuilibet personae, statui vel tempori congruos, juxta usum Orientalis Ecclesiae (Venice, 1730[2]; reprinted Graz, 1960), p. 153. In the 11th c. Arabic Liturgy of St John Chrysostom the bishop is already at his throne in the nave during the Enarxis, but does not participate in the celebration until the Little Entrance: C. Bacha, 'Notions générales sur les versions arabes de la liturgie de S. Jean Chrysostome suivies d'une ancienne version inédite', in *XPYCOCTOMIKA* (Rome, 1908), pp. 405-471, on p. 448. In the 12th c. pontifical of the Great Church, *Codex British Library Add. 34060*, the bishop is seated in the narthex, already vested, during the Enarxis: R. Taft, 'The Pontifical Liturgy of the Great Church According to a Twelfth-Century Diataxis in Codex *British Museum Add. 34060*', *Orientalia Christiana Periodica* 45 (1979) 279-307, on p. 284. In the pontifical of Gemistos (AD 1386) the hierarch is already in the nave at his stasidion if Orthros precedes the Divine Liturgy. He does not appear to take any part in the Prothesis, for which the priest and deacon do not request his blessing, although the entire rite is intriguingly included in this pontifical before the patriarch's vesting: see A. Rentel, *The 14th Century Patriarchal Liturgical Diataxis of Dimitrios Gemistos: Edition and Commentary*, Unpublished Dissertatio ad Doctoratum, Pontificio Istituto Orientale (Rome, 2003), pp. 177-184.

[4] Cf. *Washington Library of Congress Gr. 37* (ca. AD 1600), which begins with the concluding prayer of the Prothesis, read by the bishop: 'Ο Θεός, ὁ Θεὸς ἡμῶν... (f. 6v); the same is true of the 16th/17th c. Greek pontifical *BAN Dmitr. Gr. 15* (f. 5) and *BAN RAIK Gr. 189* (f. 3).

[5] See for example *BAN Dmitr. Gr. 15* (end of 16th – begin. of 17th c.), f. 5; *BAN RAIK Gr. 189* (AD 1623-1630), f. 3; *RNB Gr. 704* (AD 1635), f. 1; *BAN Dmitr. Gr. 24* (AD 1670), f. 1; *Archieraticon* (Venice, 1714), p. 1; *Archieraticon* (Constantinople, 1820), p. 1; *Archieraticon* (Athens, 1902), p. 3; *Archieraticon* (Thessalonica, 2004), p. 17.

[6] The *Archieraticon* of Thessalonica 2004 has the Prothesis Prayer both before the Enarxis (p. 17) and before the Great Entrance (p. 31). The Athens 1994 edition places the prayer *after* the Great Entrance (p. 19), but omits it before the Enarxis.

[7] Taft, *Great Entrance* (see n. 2), p. 270. See the entire discussion of the Prothesis in the pontifical liturgy, pp. 265-270.

Yet the Byzantine pontifical rite has retained Prothesis-elements, thus preserving the hierarch's role in the preparatory rite. What are the motivations for keeping the 'relic' of the Prothesis Prayer at the beginning of the pontifical Divine Liturgy a millennium after it lost its meaning? Concerning the 'pontifical Prothesis' before the Great Entrance, Taft has suggested that it may have been an extension of the *commemorations* that came to be attached to the Great Entrance.[8] However, the same explanation cannot hold for the presence of the Prothesis Prayer alone at the beginning of the pontifical Divine Liturgy, for this prayer is primarily offertory, with only a general commemoration: 'Μνημόνευσον, ὡς ἀγαθὸς καὶ φιλάνθρωπος, τῶν προσενεγκάντων καὶ δι' οὓς προσήγαγον· καὶ ἡμᾶς ἀκατακρίτους διαφύλαξον...'

This insistent preservation of Prothesis-elements in the Byzantine pontifical Divine Liturgy throughout the centuries warrants a reconsideration of the hierarch's 'traditional' role in the Byzantine Prothesis. In this article I shall attempt to unearth the liturgico-theological principle that motivated both the inclusion of the Prothesis Prayer at the beginning of the pontifical Divine Liturgy and the 'duplication' of the Prothesis at various moments of the pontifical celebration. For the Byzantine and Muscovite pontifical sources suggest that the Prothesis is not quite as 'apontifical' as we are wont to think.

2. The Hierarch's Participation in the Prothesis in Byzantine Sources

As has been noted by several liturgists,[9] one pre-12th century Constantinopolitan witness does *not* wholly exclude the hierarch from the activities of the lesser clergy before the Little Entrance. The Latin translation of the Liturgy of St Basil in the Johannisberg ms, which witnesses to the patriarchal liturgy of the Great Church in the 10th/11th c.,[10] has the

---

[8] *Ibid.*, 270.

[9] A. Jacob, *Histoire du formulaire grec de la Liturgie de Saint Jean Chrysostome*, Unpublished doctoral dissertation (Leuven, 1968), pp. 261-262; Taft, *Great Entrance* (see n. 2), pp. 267-270; idem, *A History of the Liturgy of St. John Chrysostom, VI: The Communion, Thanksgiving, and Concluding Rites,* Orientalia Christiana Analecta 281 (Rome, 2008), p. 551; G. Descoeudres, *Die Pastophorien im syro-byzantinischen Osten: Eine Untersuchung zu architektur- und liturgiegeschichtlichen Problemen*, Schriften zur Geistesgeschichte des östlichen Europa 16 (Wiesbaden, 1983), p. 113.

[10] On the origins and date of the Johannisberg version of the Liturgy of St Basil see R. Taft, '*Quaestiones disputatae:* The Skeuophylakion of Hagia Sophia and the Entrances of the Liturgy Revisited', *Oriens Christianus* 81 (1997) 1-35.

patriarch both *vest* and *take part in a Prothesis rite* in the skeuophylakion together with the concelebrating lesser clergy:

'Primum Patriarchę cum sequentis
ordinis Clero ecclesiasticis vestimen-
tis induto, offeruntur in Sacrario ab
oblationarijs, mundatæ ac compositæ
oblatæ, à populis susceptæ, quas ponit
in patenis, & adolens super eas incen-
sum, dicit hanc Orationem: Domine
Deus noster...'[11]

'To the Patriarch, [who] having first
vested with the accompanying clergy,
there are presented in the skeuophylakion by the oblationaries the pure
and arranged offerings received from
the people, which he puts on the pat-
ens and, burning incense over them,
says this prayer: O Lord, our God...'

After the patriarch completes the Prothesis Prayer, 'a priest and deacon enter the church' and celebrate the Enarxis 'before the entrance of
the hierarch' (*ante adventu Pontificis intrant Ecclesiam Presbyter &
Diaconus...*).

It is clear from the text that the offerings have already been 'arranged'
by the 'oblationaries' who are clearly not members of the concelebrating
clergy: the latter vest with the patriarch. Thus, although we do not know
what this 'arrangement' of the offerings by the 'oblationaries' consisted
of, it was not done by any of the concelebrants, and it did not include an
intrinsic component of any Prothesis rite such as the placing of the offerings on the paten(s). This is accomplished by the hierarch, along with
the incensation of the gifts and the reading of the Prothesis Prayer. It is
also clear that although the patriarch does not enter the church with the
priest and deacon who celebrate the Enarxis, he vests with the lesser
concelebrants and accomplishes the essential part of the Prothesis rite in
the skeuophylakion. As we shall see below, this tradition that preserves
a central role for the hierarch in the Prothesis is reflected in later Russian
practices.

Another 10th/11th c. source remarkably similar to the Johannisberg
version, the *Pyromalus Codex,* may presume a similar opening rite of
the pontifical celebration, but it unfortunately lacks the concise opening
rubrics of the Johannisberg version to confirm this supposition. But the
pontifical celebration described in the contemporaneous 11th c *Protheoria* (AD 1085-95) already clearly has a deacon do the Prothesis, after
which a *priest* reads the Prothesis Prayer.[12] The 11th c. Arabic pontifical

---

[11] *Liturgia S. Basilii Mag. Nuper e tenebris eruta, et in lucem nunc primum edita.
Cum Praefatione Georgij Vuicelij,* ed. G. Witzel (Mainz, 1546), f. b iiij.
[12] *Protheoria* §9, §10, ed. B. Dentaki, in *Anthologion Paterikôn Keimenôn* (Athens,
1974), pp. 307-330, on p. 312.

rite edited by Bacha also has the Prothesis Prayer said at the very beginning by a *priest*, not the bishop.[13] So the Byzantine hierarch might seem
to have given up his role in the Prothesis by this time.

3. The Hierarch's Participation in the Prothesis in the Slavonic Sources

In pre-Nikonian Russia,[14] however, a celebrating hierarch had more to
do with the Prothesis rite than 'traditionally' befits a hierarch of the
Byzantine rite. All the ms pontificals of the Muscovite tradition I have
had access to have the celebrating hierarch *in* church during the Prothesis, which usually commences after the bishop's vesting.[15] What is more,
the hierarch sometimes participated in the Prothesis: the earliest Russian
Orthodox pontifical, *JMZ 15472* (AD 1328-1336), has the 'святитель'
accomplish the Prothesis after vesting (по облеченьи) (f. 6v). It could
be argued that since the term 'святитель,' which today is always understood as 'bishop,' also meant 'priest' in 14th c. Slavonic,[16] we cannot be
certain as to who actually did the Prothesis in this case. Indeed, there is
a confusion of the terms 'попъ' (priest) and 'святитель' in the Liturgy
of St Basil of this very pontifical.[17] However, the same cannot be said of
the Liturgy of St John Chrysostom in the same ms, where the 'святитель'

---

[13] Bacha, 'Notions générales' (see n. 3), p. 442.

[14] I. e., before the mid-17th c. liturgical reforms initiated by Patriarch Nikon of Moscow (1652-1658).

[15] *JMZ 15472* (AD 1328-1336) (ff. 7-8); the two 16th c. pontificals *GIM Syn. 680
(366)* (ff. 16-23) and *GIM Syn. 909 (367)* (ff. 16v-23v), in which the 'святитель'
(usually meaning the hierarch) reads the conclusive Paschal troparia of the Prothesis
(Во гробѣ плотски, In the tomb in body…, f. 22v); the mid-17th c. *GIM Syn 690 (575)*
(f. 20); in the *Činovniki Uspenskogo Sobora* (AD 1622) [Ceremonials of Dormition
Cathedral in Moscow] the patriarch 'благословляетъ дѣйствовать надъ просви-
рами' ('blesses to act over the proshoras,' i.e., to do the Prothesis) after vesting and
lengthy 'молебенъ' or litany: *Činovniki Uspenskago Sobora (1622)*, ed. A. Golubcov,
*Čtenija v Imperatorskom Obščestve istorii i drevnostej rossijskix pri Moskovskom Univer-
sitete* 4 (1907) 1-312, on p. 71. In the later Serbian pontificals, *NBS Rs. 640* (AD 1688-
1705) (f. 19) and *NBS Dečani 135* (AD 1710-1720) (f. 34v), the bishop similarly blesses
the ministrants of the Prothesis after having vested.

[16] In the authoritative 27-volume *Slovar' Russkogo Jazyka XI-XVII vv.* [Akademija
Nauk SSSR, Institut Russkogo Jazyka, (Moscow, 1975-2006)], the meaning 'priest' is the
third possible definition for the word 'святитель,' whereas 'bishop' is the first (v. 23,
p. 207).

[17] For example, the 'святитель' says the Ekphonesis 'Яко подобаетъ' (For it is
meet…), f. 69v, while a 'попъ' says the Ekphonesis preceding the Cherubicon, 'Яко да
подъ державою' (For it is under Your power…), f. 70v; a 'попъ' recites the invitation
'Горѣ имѣимъ сердца' (Let us lift up our hearts) while a 'святитель' is reciting the
'secret prayers,' f. 74.

consistently functions as presider and accomplishes specifically 'pontifical' actions, like the incensation of the sanctuary 'with two candles' at the Little Entrance (f. 16v), while 'попове и діакони' (priests and deacons) are mentioned addressing the 'святитель' before clergy communion, wishing him 'Many years' (f. 45v). The strongest argument, however, for understanding the 'святитель' as 'bishop' in the Prothesis rite of *JMZ 15472* is the mere inclusion of the Prothesis rite in a pontifical euchology: this seems to show that the celebrating hierarch had some need for this text.[18]

In two 16th c. pontificals – *GIM Syn. 310 (377)* and *BAN 21. 4. 13 (Nov. 18)* – the hierarch, peculiarly, does the Prothesis immediately after the Little Entrance, before incensing the sanctuary and reciting the Trisagion prayer.[19] The Ruthenian-Catholic *Sipovič* pontifical is another anomaly: it has the hierarch accomplish the entire Prothesis just before the Great Entrance (ff. 28v-31v).

The mid-17th c. ms pontifical *GIM Syn 690 (575)* has the patriarch and concelebrating hierarchs read all the prayers of the Prothesis rite *outside* the sanctuary at their places in the nave before the beginning of the Divine Liturgy, while the actual Prothesis rite is being accomplished by lesser clergy in the prothesis chamber (ff. 20-26v). Having completed these prayers, the patriarch 'sends a subdeacon to the sanctuary to cover the Holy Vessels' (Таже патріархъ посылаетъ подъяка во святый олтарь, и повелѣваетъ покрывати святая), thus completing the liturgical action himself (f. 26). This presumably explains the rubric of the *Činovnik Novg. Sof.* (1629-1633), which prescribes that after vesting and a *moleben* 'the hierarch and bishops accomplish the Prothesis as usual' (святитель и власти дѣйствуютъ проскомидію по обычаю) (p. 18): evidently, the hierarchs said the prayers at their places in the

---

[18] See Nevostruev and Gorskij's comment on another pontifical, *GIM Syn. 370 (271)*, which does not contain the Prothesis rite: 'Проскомидія, *поелику совершается не архіереемъ*, опущена, кромѣ молитвы предложенія' ('The Prothesis is omitted, *since it is not accomplished by the bishop*, except for the Prothesis Prayer'): K. Nevostruev and A. Gorskij, *Opisanie slavjanskix rukopisej Moskovskoj Sinodal'noj Biblioteki* III, 1 (Moscow, 1917), p. 114. On the inclusion of the Prothesis in the pontifical of *Gemistos* see n. 20 below.

[19] *GIM Syn. 310 (377)*, ff. 216-217; *BAN 21. 4. 13*, ff. 3v-4v. The latter ms, *BAN 21. 4. 13*, apparently also has the lesser clergy accomplish the Prothesis before the beginning of the Divine Liturgy. Although this ms is missing the folia before the Enarxis, it becomes clear that a priest (and, perhaps, the protodeacon) have already done the Prothesis when at the Little Entrance the hierarch 'blesses the protodeacon and priest who slaughtered the Holy Lamb' (И благословляетъ протодіакона и священника заклавшему стй агнецъ), f. 3.

nave. The 17ᵗʰ/18ᵗʰ c. Serbian pontifical *NBS Rs. 640* indicates the beginning words of the Prothesis rite and prescribes with no ambiguity that these 'be recited in their entirety by the hierarch at his place, with the deacon' (Сіе же и святитель на своемъ мѣстѣ съ діакономъ глаголетъ въса пореду) (ff. 39-39v). Similarly, in the 16ᵗʰ/17ᵗʰ c. concelebration rites of *BAN Arxang. 219* the presider and concelebrants say the Prothesis prayers quietly while the 'second in seniority or lesser' priest (попъ подбольшій или меньшій) accomplish the rite (f. 251). This is probably one way the Russians interpreted the response of the Council of Constantinople in 1276 to the question of Theognostes of Sarai regarding who should do the Prothesis if a bishop is concelebrating: 'Let them all do it' (Да проскомисаютъ вси).[20]

4. The Hierarch's Blessing of the Prothesis in Greek Pontifical Usage

The Constantinopolitan pontifical ms tradition typically does not mention any blessing of the Prothesis rite or its ministrants by the celebrating hierarch.[21] Conversely, in his well-known commentary *On the Sacred Liturgy* Symeon of Thessalonica († 1429) is *insistent* on the hierarch's blessing of the Prothesis. As distinct from the Constantinopolitan pontificals cited above, the Thessalonian hierarchal celebration described by Symeon mentions the Prothesis rite *after* the vesting of the hierarch,[22] whose blessing is expressly requested by the minister of the rite. Symeon is at pains to stress the importance of this blessing:

[20] *Russkaja Istoričeskaja Biblioteka* VI, p. 134, question 14. Cf. Taft, *Great Entrance* (see n. 2), p. 268. Could the puzzling inclusion of the Prothesis rite in the 14ᵗʰ c. Constantinopolitan pontifical of *Gemistos* [Rentel, *Gemistos* (see n. 3), pp. 177-184] indicate that the Patriarch of Constantinople had some liturgical use for this text? Might he have read the prayers of the Prothesis from his place in the nave as did Russian and Serbian hierarchs? This seems rather implausible, but one does wonder whence the Slavs received the practice. For a discussion of other possible reasons for the inclusion of the Prothesis in *Gemistos*, cf. *ibid.*, pp. 34-37.

[21] For example, the 14ᵗʰ c. *Gemistos* [Rentel, *Gemistos* (see n. 3), p. 177] and the 15ᵗʰ c. *St. Andreas Skete* [A. Dmitrievskij, *Opisanie liturgičeskix rukopisej xranjaščixsja v bibliotekax pravoslavnago vostoka, I* (Kiev, 1895), pp. 168-169]. The pontifical of the Constantinopolitan Patriarch Athanasios Patellarios, introduced in the course of the Nikonian reforms as the official hierarchal rite of the Russian Orthodox Church, makes no mention of a Prothesis or its ministrants in either of its editions, *Patellarios Dejanija* [*Dejanija Moskovskix Soborov 1666 i 1667 godov*, ed. N. Subbotin (Moscow, 1893), ff. 42-62] and *Patellarios 1668* [*Čin arxierejskago dejstva* (Moscow, 1668)].

[22] As mentioned above, the pontifical of *Gemistos* (AD 1386) includes the entire Prothesis rite *before* the vesting of the bishop; see Rentel, *Gemistos* (see n. 3), pp. 177-184.

'The priest in the sanctuary, first having reverenced the bishop to display his subordination, and having been deemed worthy of a blessing, does the proskomide; for it is necessary that a prayer precede the divine actions and that permission be requested. Therefore, having first received a blessing and kissed the hand of the bishop, he goes off to celebrate the sacred service, as earlier the deacons did when they were about to put on their priestly vestments. All of them and the priests and bishops do so, as is suitable. They are bishops, priests, and clerics *by means of the hand of this first bishop*, that is, because they were ordained <by him>. They partake of his blessing and they maintain humility and order, because they come before God with blessing and permission, and because each comes to carry out his service with subordination and peace.'[23]

We find a similar practice among the Greeks in mid-17th c. Jerusalem. In Arsenij Suxanov's description of a Greek hierarchal celebration in Jerusalem (1652) as recorded in his *Proskinitarij* or Pilgrim's Report, the Patriarch of Jerusalem blesses the ministrants of the Prothesis in his quarters before they proceed to church.[24] Arsenij reports the same usage later in the *Proskinitarij,* where he describes the presbyteral celebration of the Divine Liturgy in Jerusalem, attended by a non-celebrating patriarch:[25] there the celebrating priest and deacon likewise receive a blessing from the patriarch at his quarters before proceeding to the church for the Prothesis. After the Prothesis, which is completed as usual with an Apolysis, they 'sit and await' the arrival of the patriarch.[26] After the patriarch arrives, blesses the people, and goes to his stasidion by the south wall of the church, the priest incenses the church and does a second 'Apolysis of the Prothesis' as he incenses. He exclaims 'Sofia,' the choir sings 'Axion estin' with the usual conclusion of 'Doxa...Kyrie eleison,' and the patriarch says the conclusive blessing from his stasidion. Arsenij notes that this blessing can also be said by the priest, apparently in the absence of the patriarch. This unusual 'Apolysis of the Prothesis' lends the preparatory rite of the liturgy a more 'public' character, bringing at least the end of the rite outside the sanctuary, where it receives a more solemn, 'public' blessing of the hierarch or other presider.

---

[23] *De sacra liturgia,* PG 155, col. 261. English translation from S. Hawkes-Teeples, *The Liturgical Commentaries of St. Symeon of Thessalonika (†1429): Edition of the text in Zagora Manuscript 23.* Unpublished version, Pontificio Istituto Orientale (Rome, 2002), pp. 14-16.

[24] *Proskinitarij Arsenija Suxanova, 1649-1653 gg.,* ed. N. Ivanovskij, *Pravoslavnyj Palestinskij Sbornik* 7.3 (1889), pp. 249-250.

[25] *Ibid.,* pp. 288-299.

[26] *Ibid.,* pp. 288, 293.

This hierarchal 'blessing' of the Prothesis in mid-17th c. Jerusalem may seem unusual, since the Jerusalem rite was essentially Constantinopolitan at this point, and could be expected to follow Constantinopolitan pontifical models.[27] As we have seen, Constantinopolitan pontificals typically do not mention a hierarchal blessing of, or participation in, the Prothesis. But the anomalous *Johannisberg* ms and Symeon of Thessalonica's insistence on the hierarch's blessing of the ministers of the Prothesis betray a liturgical principle also reflected, albeit in obscured form, in the later Byzantine pontifical tradition: like every other action in the Church, the Prothesis is ultimately done *by the means of the hand* of the bishop. The Jerusalem rite described by Arsenij Suxanov retains a trace of this principle in its own way, by providing the Prothesis with a hierarchal blessing.

5. *The Hierarch's Blessing of the Prothesis in Slavonic Pontifical Usage*

The Slavic branches of the Byzantine tradition are truer to this principle than their Greek counterparts.[28] In Pre-Nikonian Russian usage, the hierarch invariably blessed the Prothesis. Via elaborate ritualization, the Muscovites showed the great importance they attributed to the hierarch's

---

[27] On the Byzantinization of the rites of the Orthodox Patriarchates of Alexandria, Antioch, and Jerusalem, see R. Taft, *The Byzantine Rite: A Short History* (Collegeville, MN, 1992), pp. 56-57; cf. also A. Pentkovskij, 'Konstantinopol'skij i ierusalimskij bogoslužebnye ustavy', *Žurnal Moskovskoj Patriarxii* 4 (2001) 70-78; A. Dmitrievskij, *Drevnejšie patriaršie tipikony* (Kiev, 1907), chapter 3; A. Baumstark, 'Denkmäler der Entstehungsgeschichte des byzantinischen Ritus', *Oriens Christianus* series 3, vol. 2 (1927) 1-32; *idem*, 'Die Heiligtümer des byzantinischen Jerusalems nach einer übersehenen Urkunde,' *OC* 5 (1905) 227-289; J. Nasrallah, 'La liturgie des Patriarcats melchites de 969 à 1300', *OC* 71 (1987) 156-181; Ch. Hannick, 'Annexions et reconquêtes Byzantines: peut-on parler d'«uniatisme» byzantin?', *Irénikon* 66 (1993) 451-474; Kate Leeming, 'The Adoption of Arabic as a Liturgical Language by the Palestinian Melkites', *ARAM* 15 (2003) 239-246; K.-P. Todt, 'Religion und griechisch-orthodoxes Patriarchat von Antiocheia in Mittelbyzantinischer Zeit', *Byzantinische Zeitschrift* 94 (2001) 239-267.

[28] A. Pentkovskij, M. Iovčeva, and M. Želtov have recently suggested a possible Thessalonian source for the 9th/10th c. Bulgarian translations used in early Russian liturgy [M. Želtov, 'Čin božestvennoj liturgii v drevnejšix (XI-XIV vv.) slavjanskix Služebnikax', *Bogoslovskie Trudy* 41 (2007) 272-359, on pp. 346-347; A. Pentkovskij and M. Iovčeva, 'Prazdničnye i voskresnye blaženny v vizantijskom i slavjanskom bogosluženii VIII-XIII vv.', *Palaeobulgarica* 15.3 (2001) 31-60]. The curious similarity between Symeon's 15th c. Thessalonian and contemporary Muscovite usages regarding the hierarch's blessing of the Prothesis may support this hypothesis.

blessing of this rite:[29] even those Slavonic pontificals that do not have the hierarch doing the Prothesis himself still have him enter the prothesis chamber or 'small sanctuary' (малый алтарь) before vesting in order to kiss the Holy Vessels and bless the ministrants there with a cross in a rite of 'forgiveness.'[30] This rite is witnessed several times in Moscow's Dormition Cathedral by Paul of Aleppo in the mid-17th c.[31] In a later Serbian pontifical the bishop does not enter the prothesis chamber at this moment; he does, however, bless the ministrants of the Prothesis *twice*: at his residence before the beginning of the Divine Liturgy, and in church after he has vested.[32]

An additional 'blessing of the Prothesis' occurs in pontifical and presbyteral Muscovite euchologies at the Little Entrance, the traditional entrance of the bishop into the church. In the 16th c. pontificals *GIM Syn. 680 (366)* and *909 (367)* and in the mid-17th c. *GIM Syn. 690 (575)*, the deacon holding the Gospel approaches the hierarch just before the Little Entrance, saying 'Bless, master, this holy oblation' (Благослови владыко святое предложеніе се), to which the bishop answers, 'Blessed is the oblation of our Lord God and Savior Jesus Christ' (Благословено предложеніе Господа Бога и Спаса нашего Іисусъ Христа) and kisses the Gospel.[33] The significance of this exchange is unraveled in other 16th c. pontificals, *GIM Syn. 310 (377)* and *BAN 21. 4. 13*, where just before exiting the sanctuary for the Little Entrance, the concelebrating priests approach the prothesis altar and bless the oblation, saying: 'Blessed is the oblation of Your divine mysteries, now and ever and unto ages of ages' (Благословено предложеніе божественыхъ Твоихъ таинъ всегда и нынѣ и во вѣки вѣкомъ).[34] The same occurs in the later Serbian pontifical *NBS Rs. 640* (f. 50v). This 'blessing of the Prothesis' at the Little Entrance usually occurs in Muscovite presbyteral ms euchologies with an initial invitation of the deacon carrying the Gospel: he stops at the prothesis altar on his way out of the sanctuary and says to the priest: 'Bless, master, this holy oblation.' The priest then

---

[29] This moment is strangely omitted in the description of the pre-Nikonian hierarchal 'vstreča' (entrance into the church) in the *Pravoslavnaja Encyklopedia* [PE]: M. Želtov, 'Vstreča arxiereja,' PE IX, pp. 721-723.

[30] *Činovniki Uspenskogo Sobora* of AD 1622 (see n. 15), p. 71; the mid-17th c. *GIM Syn. 690* (f. 13).

[31] Paul of Aleppo, *Putešestvie Antoxijskogo Patriarxa Makarija v Rossiju v polovine XVII veka*, transl. G. Murkos (Moscow, 2005), pp. 299, 383.

[32] *NBS Rs. 640* (AD 1688-1705), ff. 30v, 39.

[33] *GIM Syn. 680 (366)*, f. 28v; *GIM Syn. 909 (367)*, f. 28v; *GIM Syn. 690 (575)*, f. 30v.

[34] *GIM Syn. 310 (377)*, f. 215v; *BAN 21. 4. 13*, f. 2v.

blesses the gifts with his hand, reciting the blessing cited above, 'Blessed is the oblation...,' the deacon responds 'Amen,' and the procession continues out the northern door of the sanctuary.[35] All the early Muscovite printed *Služebniki* included the blessing of the Prothesis at the Little Entrance,[36] while the early Ruthenian editions generally did not.[37]

This usage may stem from a time when the Proskomide or Prothesis could be performed by a deacon alone, save the Prothesis Prayer that was read by the priest.[38] With the development of the Prothesis rite and its 'consecratory' significance in popular Russian piety,[39] it is understandable that the deacon's authority to accomplish it came to be questioned. It is possible that the deacon's 'insufficient' Prothesis was first compensated by having the priest or hierarch read the Prothesis Prayer and the blessing at the Little Entrance, until the right to do the Prothesis was taken from the deacons altogether.[40] At this point the initial purpose

---

[35] Cf. the 15th c. *RGB TSL 216* (f. 11) *RNB Solovec. 1128/1238* (f. 13) and *BAN Arxang. D. 68,* where the blessing of the prothesis is added on the bottom margin by a later hand (f. 51v); the 16th c. *RGB Rumjanceva 402* (f. 76v); *BAN Arxang. D. 27* (f. 14v); *BAN Arxang. D. 66* (f. 14v); *BAN Arxang. D. 67* (f. 65v); *BAN Arxang. D. 67* (f. 47), and *BAN Arxang. D. 70* (f. 19); the 16th/17th c. *RNB OSRK 1256/Q1-60* (f. 76); the 17th c. *GIM Xlud. 115* (f. 131v); *GIM Xlud. 116* (f. 31v); *RNB Sof. 1027* (ff. 103v-104); *BAN Arxang. Krasnogorsk. 47* (f. 70); *RNB OSRK 1863/Q1-659* (53v).

[36] *Služebnik* (Moscow, 1602), no pagination; *Služebnik* (Moscow, 1616), no pagination; *Služebnik,* (Moscow, 1623), no pagination; *Služebnik,* (Moscow, 1630), f. 95; *Služebnik,* (Moscow, 1637), f. 100; *Služebnik,* (Moscow, 1646), f. 115v; *Služebnik,* (Moscow, 1651), f. 125.

[37] There is no blessing of the Prothesis at the Little Entrance in the Strjatin 1604, Kiev 1629 (P. Mohyla), and Kiev 1639 (P. Mohyla) *Služebniki*. It appears in the Lvov edition of 1637 (f. 31), but is then omitted in Lvov 1646.

[38] See for example *GIM Syn. 604 (343),* the 'Služebnik of Varlaam Xutynskij' (beginning of the 13th c.), f. 11, where the deacon accomplishes the Prothesis. On the ministrant of the Prothesis see M. Mandalà, *La Protesi della liturgia nel rito Byzantino-Greco* (Grottaferrata, 1935), pp. 73-96. On the sacerdotalization of the Prothesis in the Byzantine Rite in the 12th-14th c. see Descoeudres, *Pastophorien* (see n. 9), pp. 113-114. On deacons performing the rite in Slavonic sources cf. S. Muretov, *Istoričeskij obzor činoposledovanija proskomidii do „ustava liturgii" Konstantinopol'skago Patriarxa Filofeja* (Moscow, 1895), pp. 233-236; I. Mansvetov, *Mitropolit Kiprian v ego liturgičeskoj dejatel'nosti* (Moscow, 1882), pp. 137ff; A. Petrovskij, 'Histoire de la rédaction slave de la liturgie de S. Jean Chrysostome', in *XPYCOCTOMIKA* (Rome, 1908), pp. 859-928, on p. 863, and note 2; Taft, *Great Entrance* (see n. 2), p. 274.

[39] The very elaborate Prothesis rite in pre-Nikonian euchologies that resembled the consecration of the gifts at the anaphora could easily have encouraged the belief in the consecratory nature of the Prothesis rite. The prominent archpriest Avvakum († 1682), for example, believed the gifts were consecrated at the Prothesis. Cf. A. Šaškov, 'Avvakum,' PE I, p. 86.

[40] Deacons were forbidden to do the Prothesis alone already at the Council of Vladimir in 1274 [RIB (see fn 20) VI, pp. 96-97], although the usage survived until the 13th-14th centuries. Cf. M. Bernackij and M. Željtov, 'The Questions and Answers of Elias,

of the 'blessing of the Prothesis' at the Little Entrance was evidently forgotten: the erosion of the usage is most apparent in the 15th c. presbyteral euchology *BAN Arxang. D. 69*, in which the priest and deacon halt at the prothesis table on their way to the Little Entrance and the *deacon* recites, 'Blessed is the oblation of Your holy mysteries' (f. 57v), with no rubric instructing the priest to bless the gifts with his hand.

6. Concluding Remarks

Despite the disappearance of the outside skeuophylakion, which seems to have rendered the hierarch's participation in the Prothesis impossible, the Byzantine and Muscovite usages described above are at pains to *include* the hierarch in the preparatory rite in one way or another. These usages, ranging from a mere hierarchal blessing of the Prothesis' ministers to having the bishop recite the entire text of the rite in the nave as it is physically accomplished in the sanctuary area, imply that the hierarch's *hand* was perceived as necessary to truly 'complete' the initial action of the Divine Liturgy. As Symeon of Thessalonica said, everything accomplished in the Church by the lesser clergy is so done *by the means of the hand* of the bishop.[41] I believe it is this ecclesial principle that found expression in the curious preservation of Prothesis-elements in the Byzantine pontifical Divine Liturgy.

Metropolitan of Crete: A Testimony of Byzantine Liturgical Practice in the Beginning of the XIIth c.', *Vestnik Pravoslavnogo Svjato-Tixonovskogo Universiteta* 14 (2005) 23-53, on p. 27. See also Muretov, *Proskomidija* (see n. 38), p. 236.

[41] Cf. n. 23.

THE ADDITION OF SLAVIC SAINTS
TO SEVENTEENTH-CENTURY LITURGICAL CALENDARS
OF THE KYIVAN METROPOLITANATE

Michael PETROWYCZ

The young Church of Kyiv adopted the Byzantine calendar in a fully-developed form, but quite soon began adding its own characteristics. This development rather closely reflected the changing political configuration of the region. The influence of Kyivan commemorations (of saints and events) on calendars of other Rus' principalities and even Balkan was widest up to the 13th century, to the fall of Kyiv in 1240. In the following period of the fragmentation of Rus' principalities (13th-14th centuries) the initiative in adding saints passes to Vladimir-on-the-Klyazma and Rostov, and to a lesser degree to Novgorod.[1] An interesting characteristic of the earliest Rus' calendars, from the time, that is, of Kyivan influence, is a significant number of borrowings of saints from the Western churches, both Slavic and non-Slavic. This suggests an intense and positive level of ecclesial and cultural communication with these churches. After the fall of Kyiv, this Western presence in Rus' calendars all but disappears.[2]

In the 15th-16th centuries the main initiative for the development of Rus' calendars passes to Moscow, primarily in connection with the activity of Tsar Ivan IV (the Terrible) and Metropolitan Macarius of Moscow. At the prompting of the tsar, the metropolitan initiates the collecting of the *Great Reading Menaion* (Chetii-Minei), a vast collection of all available documentation about known Rus' saints, and at the Moscow Councils of 1547 and 1549 canonizes nine new saints and elevates twenty-one locally-venerated saints to the status of general commemorations (i.e. in the entire Moscow metropolitanate). The Russian church historian Evgenij Golubinskij brings these activities of the Muscovite Church in direct association with the growing influence of the theory of Moscow as the Third Rome and Ivan accepting the title of tsar, meaning

---

[1] О. В. Лосева, *Русские месяцесловы XI–XIV веков* (Moscow, 2001), p. 116.

[2] *Ibid.*, pp. 71-72; the full discussion is on pp. 63-75.

he considered himself to be the successor of the Byzantine emperors. In other words, the developed sanctorale shows that the new ecclesial mission of Moscow is manifested and confirmed by its fruitful sanctity.[3] Surprisingly, in spite of the solemn and official character of these decisions, over half a century passed before the new saints entered the liturgical calendars. In Moscow's earliest printed book, the 1564 epistle-book, we find only the prince-martyrs Borys and Hlib. In the second printing of the epistle-book thirty-three years later (in 1597) six Rus' saints are *added*: Grand-prince Vladimir, metropolitans Peter and Alexis, Leontii of Rostov and *hegumens* Sergius of Radonezh and Cyril of Belozersk. In the first Moscow printed Liturgicon (1602) there are already forty-five Rus' saints, and in the first Ustav of 1610 there are seventy-three.

The situation in the Kyivan metropolitanate see is somewhat similar and somewhat different. The difference is that up to the 17th century there were no numerous canonizations such as at the Macarian councils. The similarity is that up to the end of the 16th century the calendars had altogether few Rus' or Slavic commemorations. Typical examples would be the calendars of Lviv's earliest printed book, the 1574 epistle-book, with only Borys and Hlib,[4] the 1575 Vilnius gospel-book with only Vladimir, Borys and Hlib, and the 1581 Ostroh Bible, where in addition to these we find Metropolitan Peter, Theodosius of the Kyivan Caves, and Serbian saints Sava and Arsenius. A characteristic feature of the calendars of the Kyivan metropolitan see, mainly its south-western regions, wherein they differ from the Muscovite calendars of the time, is a noticeable presence of Southern Slavic saints (Serbian, Bulgarian and Romanian). For example, in the over eighty manuscript gospel-books of the 15th-early 17th centuries (primarily from the Pzremyśl, and partially the Chelm, Ruthenian eparchies), as recorded in Naumov's catalog, fifty have only Sava and Symeon of Serbia, thirteen have other combinations of only Serbian saints, two have Parasceve of Tarnovo; sixteen are without any Slavic saint. The anthologies of the same period have a slightly different preference, where Parasceve of Tarnovo is in eleven of the thirteen complete anthologies, Borys and Hlib are additionally only in four, and two anthologies have no Slavic saint.[5]

---

[3] Е. Е. Голубинский, *История канонизации святых в русской Церкви* (Moscow, [2]1903), p. 93, also pp. 94-95, 105-106.

[4] The same as in the 1564 Moscow epistle-book; the printer of both books was Ivan Fedorov.

[5] Alexander Naumow and Andzej Kaszlej, *Rękopisy cerkiewnosłowianskie w Polsce. Katalog* (Cracow, 2002), pp. 62-130, 260-303.

Seventeenth-Century Uniate Sanctorales

In considering the seventeenth-century sanctorale of the Kyivan metropolitanate, it is better to examine separately the situation of the Kyivan Uniate Church and that of the Kyivan Orthodox Church. The first Uniate liturgical book, the 1612 Ostroh Horologion,[6] has a calendar similar to that of the Ostroh Bible (1581), with the sole difference that instead of Sava of Serbia, there is John of Rila. The second Uniate liturgical book, the 1617 Vilnius Liturgicon, does not have a calendar to examine, nor are there any Slavic saints commemorated in the Proskomide of the Divine Liturgy or the petitions of the Litya, but in this it is similar to the 1604 Orthodox Stryatyn Liturgicon.

The next Uniate liturgical book that we have notice of is a Horologion mentioned by Metropolitan Havryil Kolenda in a report to Rome in 1671.[7] He claims that he prepared the calendar 'according to Greek menologia, eliminating the Ruthenian Kyivan saints which were unknown to the Holy Roman Church.' This certainly meant all except archbishop of Polatsk Josaphat, beatified in Rome in 1643. Kolenda notes that he petitioned Rome 'which of those in the lists [he] sent [to Rome] were saints.'[8] This was probably not a technical query as to whether the named persons should be considered 'saints' or 'beatified,' according to the new regulations introduced by Urban VIII several decades earlier. Kolenda had

---

[6] Although prince Constantine of Ostroh (d. 1608) was an opponent of the Union as it was realized at Brest in 1596, the internal evidence of the Horologion suggests that the publishers identified with the Union. There were two editions of the 1612 Horologion: with continual and with separate pagination. Pages 301r-302r of the edition with separate pagination contain a brief chronology of ecclesiastic history (beginning from Adam), which enumerates the seven (Ecumenical) Councils, naming the pope and the patriarch of Constantinople (starting from the Second Council) for each, followed by the Council of Florence (giving only the date, with no ordinal number). The chronology closes with the death of Prince Constantine, his burial in the cathedral of Ostroh, then: 'During his time there were two synods in Brest of Lithuania, of all the bishops and the metropolitan; the first in 1590 and the second in 1596.' The 1596 Brest synod that the metropolitan took part in was the one that ratified the Union with Rome. It is known that Constantine's son Janusz, who accepted the Roman rite, began in 1612 to introduce the Union in his principality. See Ярослав Ісаєвич, *Українське книговидання. Витоки, розвиток, проблеми* (Lviv, 2002) p. 136.

[7] *Vetera Monumenta Poloniae et Lithuaniae gentiumque finitimarum Historiam illustrantia*, 4 vols., ed. Augustinus Theiner (Rome, 1860-1864) vol. 3, pp. 598-599; quoted in Ivan Praszko, *De Ecclesia Ruthenica Catholica sede metropolitana vacante 1655-1665* (Rome, 1944) pp. 274-275. No copies of this Horologion have ever been described or found.

[8] Praszko, *De Ecclesia* (see n. 7), p. 275.

doubts about whether the named persons should be venerated at all, and, certainly referring to the Kyivan Caves saints, called it a superstition to consider the incorruptness of the bodies as a sign of the sanctity of the soul. It seems that he hoped Rome would support his doubt, and when this did not happen, he took it as a sign of tacit support: 'It does not seem a good idea to grant these persons a conditional cult, as if they were [true] saints; it is preferable that the decision on this matter remain perpetually suspended, rather than that the definitive sentence of the Holy See be made public.'[9]

The last Uniate publication of the 17th century is the 1692 Vilnius Liturgicon, printed by Metropolitan Kyprian Zhokhovskyj. The Liturgicon did not have the full approbation of the hierarchy, as was decided in a synod of the bishops of Ruthenia (1683), but the metropolitan again consulted with Rome about the inclusion of Rus' saints in the calendar. The metropolitan received a negative decision from cardinal Nerli, which (according to Prashko) he received 'with a heavy heart, since the Rus' Catholic Church, as is evident from manuscript liturgical books, has been including and venerating these saints for some time.'[10] As the example of Metropolitan Kolenda suggests, we should not conclude that the omitting of Rus' saints was only the work of the Roman authorities. The Bollandist Daniel Papebrochius, preparing the publication in the *Acta Sanctorum* of his commentary on a Rus' icon-calendar,[11] consulted on the matter with the Basilian archimandrite, Policarp Ohilewicz, considered to have been among the better educated of the Uniate clergy. The archimandrite responded that the Uniate Ruthenians were forced to use non-Uniate liturgical books, since they did not have their own, but that they were careful not to commemorate any saints they did not find in the Greek books (i.e. all Slavic saints), 'lest they commemorate as saints those who are actually schismatics'. Even though Papebrochius did not follow this advice (and concluded his study with a list of fifty 'saints proper to the Ruthenian Church'),[12] he published the content of

---

[9] 'Concedere autem cultum illorum sub conditione, nempe quatenus sunt Sancti, et hoc non videtur: satius aeterna suspensio decisionis circa hoc maneat, quam decisiva Sanctae Sedis propaletur sententia': *ibid.*, p. 275.

[10] *Ibid.*, p. 279. Praszko refers to F. Dobrjanskij, *Opisanie rukopisej Vilenskoj publ. Bibl. tserkovno-slavjanskich i russkich* (Vilnius, 1882), p. 323, n. 210 and p. 324, n. 211.

[11] Daniel Papebrochius, 'Ephemerides Graecorum et Moscorum, horum figuratae, istorum metricae, Latine redditae et observationibus variis illustratae', in *Acta Sanctorum. Maii tomus I* (Antwerp, 1680), pp. i-lxxvi.

[12] *Ibid.*, p. lxvii; he expressed uncertainty about the Rus' origin of twenty of these.

Ohilewicz's letter in his discussion of sources,[13] and Rome had some basis for its decision.

Seventeenth-Century Kyivan Orthodox Sanctorales

The development in the Kyivan Orthodox Church was altogether different. The first book the Kyivan Caves Lavra printed was the Horologion of 1616[14] which included an appendix of 'troparia and kondakia for Rus' saints' — Anthony and Theodosius, Vladimir and Olha, Borys and Hlib, and metropolitans Peter and Alexis.[15] Its separate place as an appendix is probably meant to emphasize the importance of the veneration of these saints.

The first *major* liturgical publication of the Lavra was the Anthologion of 1619. Much attention was put into this publication. The Preface mentions the names of three eminent scholars and churchmen of the time who worked on the edition: Yov Boretskyi,[16] Zakhariia Kopystenskyi,[17] and Pamvo Berynda.[18] The Slavic translations of the services were checked against a Greek text and many sections were translated anew.[19] For the Kyivan Church the sanctorale of the 1619 Anthologion was quite a novelty, in at least two respects. First, an additional Greek calendar was consulted and a versed Synaxarion (a short hagiographic note, usually two verses per saint) was borrowed from it. The additional saints were not added to the listing at the beginning of each service, but at the sixth ode of the canon, the customary place of the Synaxarion. This seems to imply that the saints were there to be simply commemorated, without the singing of their full service. This system discontinues after four months, at the month of December. Second, the sanctorale has about one hundred Slavic commemorations. At 7 September (John, archbishop of Novgorod), the second Slavic commemoration in the

---

[13] *Ibid.*, p. iii.

[14] Although after 1596 there was only a Ruthenian Catholic hierarch of Kyiv until the renewal of the Orthodox hierarchy in 1620, the Caves Lavra always opposed the Union, and therefore the pre-1620 editions of the Lavra should be seen as Orthodox publications.

[15] Ісаєвич, *Українське книговидання* (see n. 6), p. 169.

[16] Later Orthodox metropolitan of Kyiv, 1620-1631.

[17] Theologian and polemicist. He studied in Lviv, settled in Kyiv in 1617, was archimandrite of the Caves Lavra from 1624 until his death in 1627.

[18] Lexicographer. He worked in Lviv and Kyiv, died 1632.

[19] Ісаєвич, *Українське книговидання* (see n. 6), pp. 169-170.

Anthologion (after the Death of Hlib at 5 September), reference is made to 'the Typicon of Great Rus''.[20] This most likely refers to the 1610 Moscow Typicon, since this was the first Muscovite printed Typicon, and therefore would have commanded authority. This Typicon (as mentioned above) had a record number of Slavic (in fact all Rus', no Southern Slavic or Czech) saints: seventy-three, as compared to the forty-five in the first Muscovite printed Liturgicon of 1602. The Kyivan Anthologion borrowed most of these, adding eight Southern Slavic commemorations, and about two dozen Rus' saints not in the Muscovite list, including fifteen monks of the Kyivan Caves. The fact that there are separate days for the Caves saints indicates they may already have had a local veneration, most likely in the Lavra, but their inclusion in the Anthologion, a book for the wider ecclesial community, would normally have required some sort of hierarchical authorization in the form of a general canonization. Yevhen Kabanets views this lack as a breach of authority by the Lavra printers.[21]

Kopystenskyi seems to agree with this in his monumental apologetic work, the *Palinodia* of 1621,[22] even though he was one of the editors of the 1619 Anthologion. The work is a polemical response to the Uniate archimandrite Lev Krevza[23], and the abundant list of second-millennium Eastern saints that he quotes[24] has primarily an apologetic function — to prove the spiritual fecundity of the Eastern Orthodox Church after the separation with Rome. Nevertheless, while Kopystenskyi quotes post-schism Greek, Moldavian, Serbian and Bulgarian saints in a formal list, as liturgical commemorations, when he speaks of Kyiv, after naming Metropolitan Macarius (martyred in 1497), whose relics lie in the church

---

[20] The full text of the rubric reads: 'According to the Typicon of Great Rus' the service of Sozont martyr is sung at compline, or whenever the superior will decide. But since the service of the hierarch [John] is not printed here, [sing] first the *troparion* of the hierarch, then that of the martyr, [and after] the "Glory...now..." [the troparion of the] Forefeast [of the Exaltation]. If the Forefeast comes on a Sunday, leave one of the saints for another day, when the ecclesiarch will decide.' Thus the Slavic saint is given precedence over the Greek.

[21] Євген Кабанець, 'Петро Могила і печерська канонізація 1643 року' in *П. Могила: богослов, церковний і культурний діяч* (Kyiv, 1997), p. 152.

[22] A full English translation is available in *Lev Krevza's "A Defense of Church Unity" and Zaxarija Kopystens'kyj's "Palinodia"*, Part 1: Texts, Harvard Library of Early Ukrainian Literature, Translations 3/1 (Cambridge, Mass., 1995), pp. 157-911. Publication was planned for the year 1621, as appears on the manuscripts, but Kopystenskyi continued to write until 1624; *ibid.*, 157; xviii.

[23] *Obrona iednosci cerkiewnei*, published in Vilnius in 1617. See previous note.

[24] *Lev Krevza's "A Defense of Church Unity"* (see n. 22), pp. 609-624.

of Holy Sophia, and Princess Juliana Olshanska (died before 1540), whose relics were transferred to the Lavra's Dormition cathedral in 1624,[25] he mentions in general 'a great many saints' in the caves of Anthony and Theodosius, but does not name them separately, except for 'their pioneers' — Anthony, Theodosius, Sergius, Barlaam, Cyril, Demetrius, Dionysius, Abraham and Paul.[26] On the other hand, speaking of 'Great Rus'', Kopystenskyi quotes in full an extensive calendar, which clearly is a liturgical document, but not the 1610 Typicon.[27] The list of Rus' saints in this calendar, which he quotes as a separate document, apparently making no additions, differs from the 1619 Anthologion list: notably, there are no Caves saints (besides Theodosius; not even Anthony), and much fewer Serbian and Bulgarian saints. It is not clear why Kopystenskyi did not quote the Slavic commemorations from the calendar of the 1619 Anthologion, which would have bolstered his argument by a greater number of Rus' (including Kyivan) and Southern Slavic saints, and at the same time upheld the authority of the Lavra publication. By not doing so he indirectly admitted the less official character of the spontaneous Kyivan 1619 calendar vis-à-vis the Muscovite calendar, evidently approved by (Muscovite) patriarchal authority.[28] The list of Slavic saints of the 1619 Anthologion was never repeated in its entirety in liturgical editions of the Kyivan Church, with the 1680 Kyiv Common Menaion, and some Lviv publications (the Anthologia and the 1642 Horologion) listing the most.

The Kyivan Orthodox Canonizations of the 17th Century

As the sanctorale borrowings in the 1619 Anthologion and Kopystenskyi's *Palinodia* suggest, at the beginning of the 17th century the Kyivan

---

[25] *Ibid.*, p. 614, n. 1046.

[26] Kopystenskyi does refer the reader to the Kyivan Patericon, which at that time was only in manuscript. The first printed edition was in 1635 (in Polish), the first Slavonic printing was in 1661. See *ibid.*, pp. 610-615.

[27] Golubinskii surmises that Kopystenskyi borrowed a Muscovite list of saints similar to the 1621 manuscript Typicon of the Moscow Dormition cathedral which he himself published; *idem*, Исторiя канонизацiи (see n. 3), p. 427); sanctorale of Typicon described on pp. 412-424. Strumiński agrees on the Muscovite origin of Kopystenskyi's source; cf. *Lev Krevza's "A Defense of Church Unity"* (see n. 22), p. 616, n. 1051.

[28] Kopystenskyi's preference does not necessarily imply recognition of Muscovite patriarchal authority over Kyivan metropolitan authority: it might be the recognition of a lack of official approval of Kyivan authorities for the 1619 list.

Orthodox Church was impressed with the Muscovite canonizations of the past century, probably especially by their apologetic potential, and took measures to renew its own canonization practice.[29] Metropolitan Ilarion Ohienko counts four Kyivan Orthodox canonizations of the 17th century (besides the Mohylan canonization of the Caves monks): Iov, *hegumen* of Pochaiv (died 28 October 1651, canonized 28 August 1659 by Metropolitan Dionisij Balaban), Atanasij, *hegumen* of Brest (martyred by Poles 5 September 1648, canonized 20 July 1666, commemorated on both these dates), Macarius, *hegumen* of Ovruch (martyred by Turks 7 September 1678, canonized 1688, commemorated 7 September), and Athanasius, former patriarch of Constantinople, who died in 1654 at Lubny (near Poltava) while returning from Moscow to Moldavia (canonized 1662 or 1672, commemorated 2 May).[30] To these Vlasovskyi adds two: Juliana Olshanska, young noblewoman (buried in the Nearer Caves of the Lavra, canonized in the 17th century) and Macarius, metropolitan of Kyiv (martyred by Tartars 1497, canonized 1621 or 1622, commemorated 1 May).[31] Although Metropolitan Ilarion and Vlasovskyi give dates of commemoration for almost all the saints they quote, and speak of their veneration, these are not included in 17th-century Ruthenian Orthodox calendars.

The Canonization of the Caves Saints by Peter Mohyla

Many authors speak of Kyivan Metropolitan Peter Mohyla as having canonized a large group of the Kyivan Caves saints in 1643. Golubinskij claims as much, on the basis of Mohyla's commissioning the writing of the liturgical service for the saints with Meletios Syrigos, exarch of the Patriarch of Constantinople and noted theologian of his time.[32] Prior to this, at his initiative two important books appeared about the Caves saints: the first printed edition of the Kyivan Caves *Patericon* (1635)

---

[29] Митрополит Іларіон, *Канонізація святих в Українській Церкві*. Part 4 of *Українська патрологія* (Winnipeg, 1965), pp. 42-43.

[30] *Ibid.*, 47-49.

[31] І. Власовський, *Нарис Історії Української Православної Церкви*, 5 vols. (Kyiv, 1990, reprint), vol. 2, pp. 274-275.

[32] Голубинский, *История канонизации*, (see n. 3), p. 210. It was Syrigos who revised Mohyla's Orthodox Confession before it was approved by the Synod of Iasi in Romania (1642).

and the *Teratourgema* (1638),[33] a documented description, by the Lavra monk Atanasij Kalnofojskyj, of sixty-four miracles of the past four decades attributed to the saints of the Kyivan Caves. Shortly before his death in 1647, Mohyla also ordered from Athos a copy of Symeon Metaphrast's Menologion (Lives of the Saints), possibly intending to create a Kyivan Menologion, analogous to the Muscovite Macarian *Great Reading-Menaion*.[34] Nonetheless, this event is shrouded in many unanswered questions, starting with whether there was a canonization at all. The basic difficulty is the lack of documents concerning the canonization. From 1643 a general liturgical service to the Caves' and other Kyivan saints is printed in several Kyivan editions, but notably in those not based on a calendar: in a Psalter (1643-1644), in Akathist collections, (1663, 1677, 1693, and 1731) and finally in a Horologion (1753).[35] Unlike a regular canonization, the service lacked the indication of a date for the commemoration. Instead, it had the unusual indication that the service is to be sung 'whenever and wherever one wills'.[36] Mohyla did not include it in the calendar of his influential Euchologion (1646), which is noticeably sparse in Slavic saints, including, besides Borys and Hlib, Vladimir and Olha, Anthony and Theodosius, only Moses the Hungarian of the Kyivan Caves, and Sava the Serb.

The form Mohyla chose for the Caves saints' canonization raises several questions: Why, after an extensive preparation, did Mohyla establish a single common commemoration for seventy-four Kyivan saints, forty-one of which were monks from the Caves? Why did he not use the dates already published for many of these in the 1619 Anthologion? Why did he not appoint a date even for the single general commemoration, nor include it in the calendar of his 1646 Euchologion? Why did the Lviv liturgical publications, especially the Anthologia, show no changes to the Slavic sanctorale after 1643, not even printing the single common service as an appendix, as in the case of metropolitan Peter, Vladimir and Boris and Hlib? Yevhen Kabanets ventures a partial explanation in that Mohyla planned requesting for the large Kyivan group a general patriarchal (Constantinopolitan) canonization, which would grant the saints greater prestige and wider renown. When

---

[33] Both appeared in Polish. This is explained by the fact that even in Ruthenian circles, both Uniate and Orthodox, Polish was one of the current languages of educated circles, but also by the desire to make the books more accessible to non-Orthodox readers.

[34] Є. Кабанець, 'Петро Могила' (see n. 21), p. 154.

[35] *Ibid.*, p. 154.

[36] Іларіон, *Канонізація* (see n. 29), p. 46.

this was refused, we may conjecture, Mohyla canonized the group on his own authority, retaining the group character.

Kabanets states that dates for two Synaxes, or collective liturgical celebrations of the Caves saints were finally established by Metropolitan Varlaam Yasinskyi (1690-1707) 'on the basis of long-standing custom'.[37] From this it seems that the veneration of these saints must have indeed been firmly established even outside the Lavra, at least in the Kyiv area. By 1680, the *Common Menaion* printed in Kyiv again had fifteen Caves saints (although not the same as those of 1619), of a total of about seventy Rus' and Slavic saints.

After the Annexation of Kyiv to Moscow

After the annexation of the Kyivan Metropolitanate to the Patriarchate of Moscow (1686) there was only one separate canonization by the Kyivan metropolitan.[38] All subsequent canonizations of saints, including those of Ruthenian origin, were effected by the Moscow (and later Petersburg) authorities.[39] After that time the Ruthenian Orthodox sanctorales conformed even more to the Russian (Muscovite) sanctorales. In general, the Russian Church was slow to incorporate the Kyivan Caves saints into its own calendar. Golubinskij speaks of a 1762 'permission' and a 1775 'ruling' (repeated in 1784) to include the Kyivan saints into the general (i.e. Muscovite) calendars.[40] This reticence may be due to a preference to keep the Kyivan saints (except for the 10th to 11th-century

---

[37] Є. Кабанець, 'Петро Могила' (see n. 21), p. 154. The dates were the Saturday after 21 September (the Leave-taking of the feast of the Exaltation of the Holy Cross) for the saints of the Nearer Caves, and 28 August for the saints of the Farther Caves. The flexible date in September was changed to 28 September in 1886: С. В. Булгаков, *Настольная книга для священно-церковно-служителей* (1993 reprint of 1913 ed.), p. 389, n. 1.

[38] Macarius of Ovruch, canonized in 1688; cf. Іларіон, *Канонізація* (see n. 29), p. 48.

[39] For example, Dmytrij Tuptalo, archbishop of Rostov, died 1709, canonized 1757; Innokentij Kulchytskyj, bishop of Irkutsk, died 1731, canonized 1504. Metropolitan Ilarion points out that Feodosij Uhlytskyj, archbishop of Chernihiv, who served in a Ukrainian eparchy, encountered the greatest obstacles: died 1696, canonized 1896. See Іларіон, *Канонізація* (see n. 29), pp. 49-52.

[40] Голубинский, *История канонизации* (see n. 3), p. 202. Ohienko interprets this as a mutual reluctance to borrow commemorations, but this view is not tenable, seeing the large number of Muscovite saints in the 17th-century Ruthenian calendars. See Іларіон, *Канонізація* (see n. 29), pp. 51, 141.

saints) a 'provincial' phenomenon, rather than allotting them the general ('patriarchal') canonization Mohyla had hoped for, which, due to their large number, would have given them too prominent a place in the Russian calendar. However, by the end of the 18ᵗʰ century Kyiv was no longer an ecclesial competitor with Moscow, and the Kyivan saints could be incorporated into 'Russian Orthodoxy'.[41]

The Slavic Saints in Lviv

Lviv was not a center of canonization. It was, however a strong center of Slavonic book printing and Lviv printers thus showed their support for the Slavic canonizations of other centers. While the epistle- and gospel-books, which purportedly reflected the rhythm of celebration of the Divine Liturgy, retained a conservative restricted configuration of the Slavic sanctorale,[42] other liturgical books, based on the daily liturgical services, extensively borrowed Slavic commemorations from both Kyivan and Muscovite sources, but with their own criteria. The sanctorale of the Lviv Anthologia (1632, 1638, 1643, 1651, 1694)[43] included about forty commemorations of a variety of Slavic saints. This was more modest than the 1619 Kyiv Anthologion (the Lviv Anthologia included only four commemorations of the Kyivan Caves saints: Anthony, Theodosius, and Theodore and Basil), but also more balanced than the lists in *Palinodia* (with the Lviv editions including more Bulgarian and Serbian saints). Commemorated metropolitans of Kyiv are Peter, Alexis, Cyprian, Photius, and Jonas.[44] Besides them, the

---

[41] Notably, Golubinskij still treats the 'Kyivan saints' as a separate group, *after* his full description of the four periods of 'Russian Orthodox canonizations', but without explaining his reasons for doing so: *История канонизации*, pp. 202-223. Peeters also points out the inconsistency of this topographic addition to the general chronological structure of the study: Paul Peeters, 'La canonisation des Saints dans l'Église russe', *Analecta Bollandiana* 33 (1914) 380-420, on p. 384.

[42] The 1636 Lviv gospel-book (reprinted almost identically in 1644, 1665 and 1670) includes: metropolitans Peter and Alexis, Vladimir, Borys and Hlib (two commemorations), Theodosius (two commemorations) and Anthony of the Kyiv Caves — all with indications of a higher liturgical rank, and the Lithuanian martyrs, with a minor rank. The 1654 Lviv epistle-book, by contrast, has only Vladimir and Borys and Hlib.

[43] All printed by the Dormition Brotherhood. There are only slight variations in the Slavic sanctorale.

[44] Bulgakov explains that Jonas is designated as both 'metropolitan of Kyiv', since in 1443 he was indeed consecrated for the see of Kyiv, and as 'metropolitan of Moscow', because that is where he resided. See *Настольная книга*, p. 225, cf. p. 134. A more

Kyivan metropolitanate is represented by thirteen other saints: Borys and Hlib, Anthony and Theodosius, and Vladimir and Olha, Michael and Theodore of Chernihiv, the three Lithuanian martyrs and saints of Smolensk — Abraham and prince Theodore with sons. The Moscow metropolitan see is represented by ten saints,[45] and the Southern Slavs by seven.[46] As noted, it is curious that the Lviv Anthologia reveal no reaction to the canonization of Kyivan Caves saints by Mohyla in 1643: from 1638 to 1694 there were no significant changes in the Anthologia's Slavic sanctorale.

Another curious fact is that the sanctorale of the Lviv 1642 Horologion, printed by the same brotherhood, has a significantly more extensive list of Slavic saints than the Anthologia, including fifteen Kyivan Caves saints — *before* the canonizations of 1643. These fifteen only partially coincide with those of the 1619 Anthologion. This apparent lack of coordination between Lviv and Kyiv is difficult to explain, especially since in the 1640s the brotherhood appealed to Mohyla to support them in their efforts to limit the activity of Mykhail Sliozka, an independent printer in Lviv.[47]

In spite of all the questions that remain about the 17th-century Ruthenian Orthodox sanctorale, four conclusions may be ventured:

First, the formation of the sanctorales in 17th-century Ruthenian Orthodox printed liturgical books was still very much a spontaneous phenomenon, hardly regulated by the hierarchy. As such, it could include saints not formally canonized, or fail to include those already canonized. In this regard, they were similar to the Muscovite publications to the end of the 17th century.[48]

---

important justification of his Muscovite title is that it was under Metropolitan Jonas that the Northern Rus' hierarchy proclaimed in 1448 the autonomy (from Kyiv and Constantinople) of the metropolitan see of Moscow.

[45] Peter and Febronia of Murom, Sergius and Nikon of Radonezh, Stephen of Perm, Savvatij of Solovki, Isidore of Rostov, Macarius of Koliazin, Basil and Maxim of Moscow. It is noteworthy that the list contains saints both before and after the 1458 division of the Kyivan metropolitanate, including three 'fools for Christ' (Isidore, Basil and Maxim), a category of saints almost unknown in the early Kyivan tradition. Basil, the most recent, died in 1552, within a century of the first editions of the Lviv Anthologia.

[46] John of Rila, Parasceve of Tărnovo, Hilarion of Moglena, Simeon, Sava and Arsenius of Serbia, and the most recent — the New Martyr George of Bulgaria, martyred in 1515.

[47] Cf. Ісаєвич, *Українське книговидання* (see n. 6), p. 213.

[48] Golubinskij similarly speaks of the 'arbitrary' character of Muscovite sanctorales until the Typicon edited by Patriarch Yoakim in 1682: *История канонизации* (see n. 3), pp. 227, 257, 223-243.

Second, printers in Kyiv and in Lviv found it natural to incorporate saints from Muscovite sanctorales, at a time when the Muscovite sanctorales did not include the (more recent) Kyivan saints until over a century and a half later. In other words, as regards the saints, the Kyivan Church of the time felt and expressed a common heritage with the Muscovite Church, both before and after its separation from Kyiv, which was not the case vice versa.

Third, this incorporating of the Northern saints was most likely motivated by apologetic needs (as the *Palinodia* suggests), that is, the Kyivan and Lviv Orthodox intended to respond to Polish (and Uniate) polemical accusations against the Orthodox and their saints, by demonstrating a full hagiographic picture of the Rus' Church, as though it had not been divided.

Fourth, in spite of Uniate publications devoid of Slavic saints, there is evidence that in Uniate circles there was a variety of opinions on the matter, which in fact continued well into the 18th century.

THE RUTHENIAN HEIRMOLOGION IN THE HISTORY OF BYZANTINE LITURGICAL MUSIC: STATUS QUAESTIONIS

Šimon MARINČÁK

The original Byzantine-Ruthenian[1] liturgical music is spread today across Sub-Carpathian Rus', Slovakia, Hungary, Czech Republic, Croatia, USA and Canada, i.e. the archeparchies of Pittsburgh and Prešov, the eparchies of Mukačevo, Hajdúdorog, Križevac, Košice and Toronto, and the exarchate of Prague. The core music is contained in the book *Церковное простопѣніе* (henceforth the CP), published in Užhorod in 1906. Its idea, birth, distribution, and application in practice are a bit peculiar. Glorified and repudiated simultaneously, this book mirrors the *genius loci* and *genius populi* of the region.

The Birth of the Editio Princeps

The first stimulus for the book was given by the eparchial synod held in Užhorod in 1903, which recommended that Bishop Firczak begin the work on the improvement of the chant practice in his eparchy.[2] Bishop Firczak decided to prepare a collection of the local chants. The reason which led the synodal fathers to deal with the liturgical music undoubtedly was the poor status of its performance in the churches. The question is, however, why and how Bishop Firczak arrived at the idea of this kind of book. Extant artifacts and sources confirm that the chant of Lvov was in use in these lands, including the bishop's own eparchy. The first printed musical collection of Lvov chant appeared in 1700 (*editio princeps —*

---

[1] The word 'Ruthenian' has been widely used as the description of non-Russian ethnicity — mostly for the Ukrainians, but also for the Ruthenians themselves. Here, we refer to the people adhering to the Byzantine rite, living in the former Austrian Empire, Hungarian Kingdom, or later in the Austrian-Hungarian Empire.

[2] Athanasius Pekar, *Нариси історії церкви Закарпаття*. Том II. *Внутрішня історія*, Analecta OSBM (Lvov and Rome, 1997), p. 384. See also Athanasius Pekar, *The Bishops of the Eparchy of Mukachevo with Historical Outlines* (Pittsburgh, 1979), p. 51.

actually published in 1707), and was followed by numerous editions up to 1904. Many of them could be found in the parishes and churches throughout eastern Slovakia,[3] of which Užhorod was a part at that time. Extant manuscript sources attest the use of privately copied manuscript books of Lvov chant in the same territory as well. Were the cantors and people responsible for liturgical chant so uneducated musically that they distorted chant from its original form, even if they had published and manuscript musical books at their disposal? If this was the case, why did the bishop undertake the preparation of a new collection of chants, rather than to use existing Lvov books which he certainly had in his curia? Why did he not rather invest in the proper education of cantors? Was it perhaps a kind of his local patriotism to refuse books of Lvov and prepare his own edition? Or was he convinced that the local chant was genuine and particular to his eparchy, hence needed to be recorded in a printed form?

Despite the presence of books found in the examined Ruthenian territory suggesting that the chant of Lvov was used everywhere, another hypothesis has been advanced. It holds that while the eparchy of Prešov used the chant of Lvov, the eparchy of Mukačevo used its own local chant. However, so far we have found neither references nor sources supporting this notion.

The authors of the CP are the cantor of the Užhorod cathedral, Jozef Malinič, and the priest and musicologist, Ján Bokšaj. Jozef Malinič was born in the village of Radvanka near Užhorod. His birth date is unknown,[4] but we can make a rough estimate. He died in 1910,[5] and if he was then about sixty years old, his birth date could range from 1840 to 1860. He studied chant at the workshop organized by the Pedagogical Institute (the so-called *Preparandia*) in Užhorod. First he was a cantor in the village of Choňkovce (Sobrance district in Slovakia) and

---

[3] Witnessed by Ivan Alexejevič Gardner and Ivan Paňkevič. See Ivan Alexejevič Gardner, *Богослужебное пѣніе русской православной церкви*, II (Jordanville, NY, 1982), p. 102; Ivan Paňkevič, *Матеріали до історії мови південно-карпатських українців*, Vedecký zborník múzea ukrajinskej kultúry v Svidníku 4 (Prešov, 1970).

[4] Fr. Daniel Bendas from Vinogradiv mistakenly gives in his article Malinič's birth date as 1897. That would mean that Malinič must have been six years old when he sung for Bokšaj. Cf. Daniel Bendas, 'Життя і творчість о. Іоанна Бокшая', *Простопініе – наша спільна спадщина* (Užhorod, 2007), p. 69.

[5] Cf. *Irmologion — Ірмологіон: Grekokatolickij liturgijnyj spiv eparchiji Mukačevskoji — Gréckokatolícky liturgický spev eparchie mukačevskej*, eds. Štefan Papp and Nikefor Petraševič (Prešov, 1970), p. 190.

later in the cathedral of Užhorod. Probably he was also teaching music in the *Preparandia* in Užhorod, as suggested by the journal *Наука* [*Science*] in 1906: 'Fr. Ján Bokšaj, conductor of the cathedral choir, and Jozef Malinič, professor of the plainchant and the typicon at the Preparandia in Užhorod, wrote down our church plainchant...'[6] There is disagreement about the level of his education. Some authors today call him a great connoisseur of the local chants and a good singer.[7] However, Fedor Steško, quoting Bokšaj himself, says that Malinič was 'musically trained just a little bit', and that 'he could not read notes and was unable to sing from the notes'.[8] Joan Roccasalvo says that Malinič learned from memory, not only the melody lines, but also the details of the model heirmoi of each tone, which means that he possessed a phenomenal memory. However, as she says, he could not use printed heirmologia because of his inability to read music.[9]

Ján Bokšaj (1874-1940) was born in the city of Chust (Ukraine). He received elementary education in his native city, and later, in 1884, he studied at the Gymnasium in Užhorod, which he finished in 1892. Then he entered seminary and in 1898 was ordained a priest by Bishop Julius Firczak (1892-1912). During his later stay in Budapest in 1909-1911, he advanced his musical education at the Budapest Conservatory[10] (some authors say at the Budapest University,[11] or at the Budapest Musical Institute[12]). Ján Bokšaj died and was buried in Chust in 1940.

---

[6] *Наука* [Science — Journal published in Užhorod in the beginnings of the 20th century] 44, 1 November 1906. Our translation. It is also proved by *Schematizmus venerabilis cleri graeci ritus catholicorum dioecesis Munkacsiensis ad annum Domini 1908*, Ungvarini, Typis Typhographiae societatis comercialis 'Unio', p. 55, and *Schematizmus venerabilis cleri graeci ritus catholicorum dioecesis Munkacsiensis ad annum Domini 1915*, p. 33, both of which give also the names of those responsible for musical education at the seminary.

[7] Bendas, 'Життя і творчість о. Іоанна Бокшая' (see n. 4), p. 69.

[8] Fedor Steško, 'Церковна музика на Підкарпатській Русі', *Наук. зб. тов. 'Просвіта' в Ужгороді*, 12 (Užhorod, 1936), p. 126.

[9] Joan L. Roccasalvo, *The Plainchant Tradition of Southwestern Rus* (New York, 1986), p. 81 and n. 11 on p. 168.

[10] Bendas, 'Життя і творчість о. Іоанна Бокшая' (see n. 4), p. 70; Štefan Papp, 'Розвій церковного богослужбового співу (простоспіву) в Мукачівській епархії', in *Irmologion*, eds. Štefan Papp and Nikefor Petraševič (Prešov, 1970), p. 189; Steško, 'Церковная музика на Підкарпатській Русі' (see n. 8), p. 125.

[11] Roccasalvo, *The Plainchant Tradition of Southwestern Rus* (see n. 9), p. 21.

[12] Nikefor Petraševič, *Halіčská liturgická reforma liturgického spevu (Izidor Dolniczkij, 1894)*, Musica Byzantina-Slavica-Hungarica 8 (no data available).

Although we know who both of the authors of the book were, there still is disagreement on the process of their selection. According to Nikefor Petraševič, a competition was announced and Bokšaj won it, while Fedor Steško says that Bishop Firczak chose Bokšaj without competition, recognizing his musical abilities.[13] Several authors are wrong in their statement that Ján Bokšaj was selected because of his musical education in Budapest:[14] Bokšaj finished his editorial work in 1906, but studied music in the Budapest conservatory three years later, 1909-1911. However, his interest in church music, as well as his musical talent, certainly could have led Bishop Firczak to appoint him to such important task. Whatever the reason, Ján Bokšaj was given the task to work on the musical collection.

According to the sources, the procedure was simple: Jozef Malinič sang, and Ján Bokšaj set the music down on paper. He may have compared it with other heirmologia of that era, as some authors think,[15] although we consider this hypothesis quite improbable. After he finished his work, Ján Bokšaj submitted the manuscript to Bishop Julius Firczak, and, according to some authors, the bishop forwarded it without delay to the printing house.[16] Thus, the book did not undergo any editorial corrections. Although the reason for such precipitate procedure by the bishop is not known, one of the reasons admitted by some authors is the presupposed absence of anyone capable of such editorial work in the eparchy of Mukačevo at that time.[17] However, other authors think that the manuscript actually was reviewed by three eminent church musicians: Andrej Demjanovič (1836-1916), Emelian Żeltvaj (1860-1906), and Michail Medvid' (dates unknown) before its publication.[18]

---

[13] Steško, 'Церковная музика на Підкарпатській Русі' (see n. 8), p. 125. Cf. also Roccasalvo, *The Plainchant Tradition of Southwestern Rus* (see n. 9), p. 52.

[14] Štefan Papp, for example. See Papp, 'Розвій церковного' (see n. 10), p. 189. Joan Roccasalvo shares his opinion and quotes him in her dissertation. See Roccasalvo, *The Plainchant Tradition of Southwestern Rus* (see n. 9), p. 21.

[15] Papp, 'Розвій церковного' (see n. 10), p. 192; Bendas, 'Життя і творчість о. Іоанна Бокшая' (see n. 4), p. 69.

[16] Steško, 'Церковная музика на Підкарпатській Русі' (see n. 8), p. 126.

[17] Cf. *Ibid.*, p. 126.

[18] Cf. Bendas, 'Життя і творчість о. Іоанна Бокшая' (see n. 4), p. 69.

Cerkovnoje Prostopinije (CP)

Let us now make several preliminary observations. The CP is the *editio princeps* of the chant of the Mukačevo-Užhorod eparchy. The comparison of its content with similar collections of Lvov shows that the CP is a digest — it contains very little in comparison with the Lvov heirmologion. The selection of the melodies in the CP suggests that it is just an incomplete collection of the most frequent melodies. If we take into account the ambition of the CP to become the official collection of the Mukačevo and Užhorod chant, this book failed on all counts. Its content evokes a cantors' manual rather than an anthology of the vast repertory of chants of a single tradition.

Several authors have set out various hypotheses to determine more or less expertly the origin of the book and the provenience of its melodies. Most of them have tried to find a direct line from the Carpathian Ruthenian heirmologion (i.e. the chant of Mukačevo) via Lvov (with the interaction with Jerusalem) to Kiev, and concluding with the Russian lesser *Znamenny* chant as the archetype. They have demonstrated this on one single kind of the melodies: Joan Roccasalvo used *podobny* (idiomela) and *samohlasny* (automela);[19] Stephen Reynolds used *stichiry samohlasnyja*,[20] and Nikefor Petraševič and Daniel Pancza simply came out with this hypothesis, but offered no supporting evidence (in the published form at least).[21] Recently, Igor Zadorožnyj examined and compared the heirmoi of the Sunday canons of tones 1-4, canons of Nativity (Christmas), Theophany, and Presentation of the Lord (Meeting of the Lord),[22] and Daniel Pancza examined the canons of the three last mentioned feasts.[23]

The process necessary to locate chants of the CP will start with a preliminary comparison of the closest editions. The editions of 1906

---

[19] Roccasalvo, *The Plainchant Tradition of Southwestern Rus* (see n. 9), p. 51.

[20] Stephen Reynolds, *The Lesser Znamennyj and Kiev Chants and their Carpathian Counterparts: The Stichiry Samohlasnyja* (unpublished manuscript, no date available).

[21] Nikefor Petraševič, *História byzantinského liturgického spevu (8.-19. stor.) v Karpatsko-poddukelskej oblasti*, Musica Byzantina-Slavica-Hungarica 1 (no date available); David Pancza, 'Kánony sviatkov Narodenia, Bohozjavenia a Stretnutia Pána v Bokšayovom irmologione', *Простопініе – наша спільна спадщина* (Užhorod, 2007), pp. 183, 189.

[22] Igor Zadorožnyj, 'Ірмоси Простопінія: джерела, особливості мелодики', *Простопініе – наша спільна спадщина* (Užhorod, 2007), p. 104.

[23] Pancza, 'Kánony sviatkov Narodenia' (see n. 21), pp. 183-212.

(Mukačevo) and 1904[24] (Lvov) were published at the same time and represent neighboring traditions. Several representative songs of both editions have been chosen in this article:[25] (1) *Boh Hospod'*, (2) the Sunday troparia,[26] (3) the Sunday *prokeimena*, (4) the canons of matins, and (5) the *podobna*, in all eight tones. For the sake of brevity, the work sheets of this comparison are omitted from this article. As for the comparison, a similarity of the melodic line has been chosen as the basic criterion, and consequently, the similarity of the CP melodies to those of the Lvov heirmologion has been examined. In table 1 below, the word 'similar' stands for the least differences between the two melodies; 'bit similar' means that the melody in the CP shows some melodic similarity, although it has been changed to a certain degree. 'Dissimilar' means either that the melody is totally different in the two books, or there may be some tiny similarities, and the melody in the CP recalls the one of the Lvov heirmologion only at a few points. In all three groups, however, various degrees of similarity vs. dissimilarity have been detected.

Table 1

	Chant	CP 1906 p.	Lvov 1904 p.	Status
Tone 1	*Boh Hospod'*	1	20	Dissimilar
	Troparion	1	21	Similar
	Prokeimenon	1	30	Dissimilar
	Heirmos 1	2	31	Similar
	Heirmos 3	2	38	Similar
	Heirmos 4	2	44	Similar
	Heirmos 5	2-3	49-50	Similar
	Heirmos 6	3	55	Similar
	Heirmos 7	3	60-61	Similar
	Heirmos 8	3-4	66-67	Similar
	Heirmos 9	4	73-74	Dissimilar

[24] According to a note in the book, it has been printed only in 1906. Cf. *Ірмологіонъ содержащъ въ себѣ различная пѣнія церковная октоиха, минїи и трїодїоновъ, къ совершенному тѣхъ разуменїю, и согласію еже въ пѣнїи сличнейшему опасно по ексемпляремъ Греческимъ исправленная* (Lvov, 1904), p. 3.

[25] This selection has been made for the present article. Our research itself contains the comparison of all songs from the CP.

[26] Tones 3, 4, 6, and 8 have different melodies for the Kontakia in the CP. This practice has also been found in the reformed chant book by Isidore Dolnickij, published in Lvov in 1894, and in the Kiev Pechery Lavra chant.

	Chant	CP 1906 p.	Lvov 1904 p.	Status
	Podoben *Nebesnych činov*	5	80-81	Dissimilar
	Podoben *Prechvalniji mučenicy*	5	81-82	Dissimilar
	Podoben *O divnoje čudo*	5-6	82-83	Similar
Tone 2	Boh Hospod'	6	91	Dissimilar
	Troparion	7	91-92	Dissimilar
	Prokeimenon	7	101	Similar
	Heirmos 1	7	101-102	Similar
	Heirmos 3	7-8	107-108	Similar
	Heirmos 4	8	111	Dissimilar
	Heirmos 5	8	114-115	Dissimilar
	Heirmos 6	8	118	Similar
	Heirmos 7	8-9	122	Similar
	Heirmos 8	9	127-128	bit similar
	Heirmos 9	9	134-135	Similar
	Podoben *Jehda ot dreva*	10-11	142-143	Dissimilar
	Podoben *Dome Evfratov*	11	143	bit similar
Tone 3	Boh Hospod'	11	155-156	Dissimilar
	Troparion	12	156	Dissimilar
	Heirmos 1	12-13	167	Similar
	Heirmos 3	13	172	Dissimilar
	Heirmos 4	13	175	bit similar
	Heirmos 5	13	178-179	bit similar
	Heirmos 6	13-14	182	Dissimilar
	Heirmos 7	14	185-186	bit similar
	Heirmos 8	14	188-189	Dissimilar
	Heirmos 9	14-15	192-193	bit similar
	Podoben *Krasote devstva*	16	198	bit similar
Tone 4	Boh Hospod'	16	204	Dissimilar
	Troparion	16-17	204-205	bit similar
	Heirmos 1	17	218	bit similar
	Heirmos 3	17-18	226	bit similar
	Heirmos 4	18	231-232	Similar
	Heirmos 5	18	239	Similar
	Heirmos 6	18	246	Dissimilar
	Heirmos 7	18	251	Dissimilar

	Chant	CP 1906 p.	Lvov 1904 p.	Status
	Heirmos 8	19	256-257	Dissimilar
	Heirmos 9	19	266	Dissimilar
	Podoben *Jako dobl'a*	20	275-276	bit similar
	Podoben *Dal jesi znamenije*	20	276	Dissimilar
	Podoben *Zvannyj svyše byv*	21	276-277	Dissimilar
	Podoben *Udivisja Iosif*	21	N/A	N/A
Tone 5	*Boh Hospod'*	22	289-290	Dissimilar
	Troparion	22-23	290	Dissimilar
	Heirmos 1	23	302	Dissimilar
	Heirmos 3	23	304-305	Dissimilar
	Heirmos 4	24	306-307	Dissimilar
	Heirmos 5	24	308	Dissimilar
	Heirmos 6	24	310	Dissimilar
	Heirmos 7	24	312	Dissimilar
	Heirmos 8	25	313	Dissimilar
	Heirmos 9	25	216	Dissimilar
	Podoben *Radujsja živonosnyj*	26-27	318-319	bit similar
Tone 6	*Boh Hospod'*	28	327	Dissimilar
	Troparion	28	327-328	Dissimilar
	Heirmos 1	29	337	Dissimilar
	Heirmos 3	29	341-342	Dissimilar
	Heirmos 4	29-30	347	Dissimilar
	Heirmos 5	30	351-352	Dissimilar
	Heirmos 6	30	357-358	Dissimilar
	Heirmos 7	30	361-362	Dissimilar
	Heirmos 8	31	365	Dissimilar
	Heirmos 9	31	372	Dissimilar
	Podoben *Anhelskija pred idite*	32-33	378	Dissimilar
	Podoben *Vsju otloživše*	33	380	Similar
Tone 7	*Boh Hospod'*	33	401	Dissimilar
	Troparion	34	401-402	Dissimilar
	Heirmos 1	34	407	Dissimilar
	Heirmos 3	35	409	Dissimilar
	Heirmos 4	35	412	Dissimilar
	Heirmos 5	35	414	Dissimilar

	Chant	CP 1906 p.	Lvov 1904 p.	Status
	Heirmos 6	35-36	417-418	Dissimilar
	Heirmos 7	36	419	Dissimilar
	Heirmos 8	36	421	Dissimilar
	Heirmos 9	37	424-425	Dissimilar
	CP does not contain Podoben	N/A	427-428	N/A
Tone 8	*Boh Hospod'*	38	433	Dissimilar
	Troparion	38	433	Dissimilar
	Heirmos 1	39	445	Dissimilar
	Heirmos 3	39-40	453	bit similar
	Heirmos 4	40	458	Dissimilar
	Heirmos 5	40	462	Dissimilar
	Heirmos 6	40	466-467	Dissimilar
	Heirmos 7	40-41	472	bit similar
	Heirmos 8	41	477-478	Dissimilar
	Heirmos 9	41-42	483-484	Dissimilar
	Podoben *O preslavno čudese*	42-43	491-492	Similar
	Podoben *Čto vy narečem*	43	493	bit similar
Vsenoščnoje	Psalm 103	52	11-13	Dissimilar
	Kathisma	52	13-15	Dissimilar

This comparison shows that 63% of the selected chants are dissimilar, 20% are similar, 15% are a bit similar, and 2% are lacking either from the CP (*podobna* tone 7), or from the Lvov heirmologion (*podoben Udivisja Iosif*). Only a few of the compared chants are so dissimilar that they can be considered totally new and different chants. Similar to present results, the research of both Stephen Reynolds and Joan Roccasalvo also pointed to the very close relation of the CP to the chant of Lvov. My comparison and the comparisons by Stephen Reynolds and Joan Roccasalvo suggest with high probability that the chants of the CP could be derived from the chant of Lvov. The alterations could be a result of the oral transmission of chants, a process that has a certain 'freedom' in varying the original. Also the education of cantors, their ability or disability to sing correctly certainly played a role. Because Jozef Malinič learned to sing at the *Preparandia* in Užhorod, where the chant of Lvov had been taught, one expects to find Lvov chants in the book. But there are also chants in the CP which are very different from the Lvov tradition. Where did they come from? We read in the personal discussion of Fedor Steško with Ján Bokšaj (published by Steško) that Bokšaj put down most of the melodies as he heard them, and modified only a very few of chants.[27] Did Malinič alter these melodies, or did he sing what he had heard in his parish — some unknown local chant? Let us reverse this question and ask why, if Malinič sang the local chant of Mukačevo or Užhorod, are there chants in the book which are very similar to, even identical with, the chant of Lvov? Did the local chant contain just a few melodies? To explain the different melodies in the CP, Štefan Papp asserts that Jozef Malinič did not know the Lvov chant and was unable to read printed books, since he was illiterate (musically at least),[28] and Joan Roccasalvo shares this opinion.[29] However, about the education of Malinič, as well as his possible involvement with the educational process in the Preparandia, their opinion does not seem very reliable.

Sources

Since the comparison shows that the CP is a mixture of various chants, scaled from similar to dissimilar in comparison with the Lvov chant, we cannot consider it as a whole, but must have a close look at every single chant. Our examination will uncover their formal composition and will conclude with a comparison of the chants with their counterparts in the corresponding sources if there are any. Hence, the next step is the search for the sources in use in Slovakia as far to the past as possible.

The sources of the Mukačevo chant have not yet been discovered — neither the chants called 'of Mukačevo' nor the melodies themselves. The only resource remains the original CP, published in 1906. Hence, we will have to compare the music it contains with the closest neighboring tradition — that of Lvov — which is the most probable and logical source of influence. As is obvious from our investigation, the number of the manuscript sources in question is not great. An important reason for the lack of primary sources might be the regional poverty that impeded proper cultural development. Another cause could be that

---

[27] Steško, 'Церковная музыка на Підкарпатській Русі' (see n. 8), pp. 125-126.

[28] Cf. Papp, 'Розвій церковного' (see n. 10), p. 189.

[29] Roccasalvo, *The Plainchant Tradition of Southwestern Rus* (see n. 9), p. 168, note 11.

the South-Western Slavs adopted staff notation as late as in the 17th century,[30] and the very first published book with the staff notation appeared in 1700 (= Lvov). So, the time frame from the appearance of the first notated manuscript to the *editio princeps* was less than a hundred years — quite a short time to produce a huge number of manuscripts.

The selection of sources for our research is not very complex. The local origin, or contemporary presence of the primary sources can be taken as a proof that they have been used in the local church and that their content was known to the local people, even if it represents various and different musical traditions. The same applies to the sources of foreign origin, found in the local institutions. Our research permitted us to make a list of over forty manuscripts that suit to the chosen criteria. The sources must (1) contain melodies in use in the examined region; and/or (2) have local origin; and/or (3) be preserved in any of the local libraries, museums, and archives, as found in the local territory. The first information on most manuscripts was obtained from the comprehensive catalogue of the musicologist Jurij Jasinovskij. Most of the manuscripts were consequently examined and catalogued in our field research conducted in 2003, 2006 and 2007. The list of the selected manuscripts in the chronological order is listed in table 2. Manuscripts in square parenthesis are considered lost; we know them just from the references in the secondary sources.

Table 2

17th century	
■ Užhorod *KM Arkh. 8465*	2nd quarter of 17th century
■ Užhorod *НБУ Рук. 576*	last quarter of 17th century
■ Užhorod *KM I-465*..	end of 17th century
17th-18th centuries	
■ Eger *Archep. library T XIV, 14, 4044-I*	end of 17th and beginning of 18th centuries
18th century	
■ Užhorod *KM I-457*...	first half of 18th century
■ Užhorod *НБУ Рук. 577*	first third of 18th century
■ Manuscript of Michal Ternovskij (priv. coll. of M. Čarný, Bratislava)..	A.D. 1729

[30] Gardner, *Богослужебное пеніе русской православной церкви* (see n. 3), pp. 35, 123.

■ Lvov *ЦДІА ф. 201, оп. 4б, од. зб. 134/а*	beginning of 18th century
■ Užhorod *KM I-463/a*	beginning of 18th century
■ Užhorod *KM I-459*	2nd quarter of 18th century
■ Užhorod *KM Arkh. 8450*	2nd quarter of 18th century
■ Užhorod *KM I-463/b*	mid-18th century
■ [Manuscript of Bishop Manuil Olšavskij]........................	mid-18th century
■ Lvov *ЛНБ НТШ 272*..	2nd half of 18th century
■ Lvov *ЛНБ НТШ 323*..	2nd half of 18th century
■ Užhorod *НБУ Рук. 565*	2nd half of 18th century
■ [Manuscript of Ján Juhasevič]......................................	A.D. 1778-79
■ Lvov *ЛІМ Рук. 209*, Ján Juhasevič..............................	A.D. 1784-85
■ [Manuscript of Michail Rydzaj, d'ak Kojšovskij]	A.D. 1790
■ Lvov *ЛНБ НТШ 324*..	end of 18th century
■ Bratislava *SNM MUS I 229* (olim 527)........................	A.D. 1700-1800
■ [Manuscript of Ján Juhasevič]......................................	A.D. 1795
■ [Manuscript of Roztoka in Sub-Carpathian Rus']	ca. 1797
■ Bratislava *SNM MUS I 80*, Ján Juhasevič........................	A.D. 1800
■ Michalovce *ZM 356-74*	18th century
■ [Manuscript in the Užhorod НБУ]...................................	18th century
18th-19th centuries	
■ Bratislava *UK Ms 1084*	18th, or 18th-19th centuries
■ Bratislava *UK Ms 1099*	18th, or 18th-19th centuries
19th century	
■ Užhorod *НБУ Рук. 561*, Vasil' Kupa	A.D. 1804
■ *Ján Juhasevič* (priv. coll. of V. Ihnatišin, Užhorod)	A.D. 1806
■ [Manuscript of Ján Juhasevič]......................................	A.D. 1809
■ [Manuscript of Peter Kuzmiak (copy of Juhasevič 1809)].	A.D. 1841
■ Prague *NK XVII, L 16*, Ján Juhasevič	A.D. 1811-12
■ Užhorod *KM I-467*..	A.D. 1869
■ *Michal Kešel'ák*, (priv. coll. of P. Tremko, Snina)	A.D. 1878
■ Užhorod *KM I-469*..	end of 19th century
20th century	
■ Michalovce *materiál č. 12*, Mikuláš Ďurkáň	A.D. 1950-1951
■ Michalovce *materiál č. 13*, Mikuláš Ďurkáň	N/A
■ Michalovce *CHR*, Ján Ďurkáň..	A.D. 1968
■ Michalovce *materiál č. 14*, Mikuláš Ďurkáň	N/A
■ Michalovce *materiál č. 16*, Mikuláš Ďurkáň	A.D. 1969
■ Michalovce *materiál č. 17*, Mikuláš Ďurkáň	N/A
■ Michalovce *materiál č. 18*, Mikuláš Ďurkáň	N/A
■ Michalovce *materiál č. 19*, Mikuláš Ďurkáň	N/A
■ Michalovce *materiál č. 20*, Mikuláš Ďurkáň	N/A
■ Michalovce *materiál č. 22*, Mikuláš Ďurkáň	A.D. 1969-1970

Jurij Jasinovskij divides the sources into four types of structure:

a) Genre-thematic structure type. Usually older sources belong to this
    type. Their apparition is connected with the apparition of Russian
    'певческий сборник' (15th-16th centuries). Thus, a single book
    contains various chants selected from various liturgical books:
    Oktoechos, Sticherarion, Menaion, Liturgicon, Triodion and Heir-
    mologion. The usual provenience of these books is a monastery or
    cathedral church.

b) Calendar-menaion structure type. *Stichera* and *heirmoi* are to be
    found together within a single chapter of the book. It stands in the
    place of the Menaion and shows a tendency to strengthen the litur-
    gical role of the heirmologion. The book contains the most neces-
    sary repertory and reflects the customs of local usage (saints, feasts,
    etc.). The usual provenience of these books are small parish
    churches, and/or *d'ak* [cantor – singer] schools. This type was the
    most popular in the second half of the 17th century.

c) Tone structure type. This the most widespread type of the book.
    Selected chants from the Oktoechos and the *heirmoi* are organized
    according to the tone. The first manuscripts appeared in the begin-
    ning of the 17th century and soon became the prevailing type.

d) Greek structure type. This is organized after the canons (and not
    after the odes).[31]

The manuscripts are located in three museums, six libraries, one
archive, and in private collections.

The Geographical and Historical Museum in Užhorod (= KM –
Краэзнавчий музей) preserves nine manuscripts that meet our criteria.
Four of them belong to the Calendar-Menaion structure type. The oldest
one is ms *Arkh. 8465*. It is from the second quarter of the 17th century
and contains *heirmoi* and *stichera* for feasts, *heirmoi* on the resurrection,
chants of Great Lent, etc.[32] The second one is ms *I-457*, of the first half
of the 18th century. It contains resurrectional chants of the Oktoechos,
prosomoia, the Liturgy of the Presanctified Gifts, Lenten *koinonika*,
heirmoi, etc.[33] The third is ms *I-463/a*, written in the beginning of the

---

[31] Jurij Jasinovskij, *Українскі та білорускі нотолінійні Ірмолої 16-18 століть*
(Lvov, 1996), pp. 89-90.

[32] *Ibid.*, p. 114.

[33] Vasilij L. Mikitas, *Давні книги Закарпатського державного краэзнавчого
музею* (Lvov, 1964), p. 46; Jasinovskij, *Українскі та білорускі нотолінійні Ірмолої
16-18 століть* (see n. 31), p. 279.

18th century, which contains chants on the resurrection of the Oktoechos, *prosomoia*, and festal *heirmoi*.[34] The last is ms *I-463/b*, from the mid-18th century and is in a single volume with the heirmologion *I-463/a*. It contains chants on the resurrection of the Oktoechos.[35]

Manuscript *I-465*, written in the 17th century, belongs to the Tone structure type and contains *prosomoia*, *stichera*, and other chants.[36] Two manuscripts belong to the Greek structure type. They are ms *I-459*, from the second quarter of the 18th century, containing the Liturgy of the Pre-sanctified Gifts, Lenten *prokeimena* and *exaposteilaria*, *heirmoi* of the Oktoechos, *stichera* on the resurrection and *prokeimena* for the Liturgy of St Basil, etc.;[37] and ms *I-469*, copied toward the end of the 19th century, containing *heirmoi* for feats and on the resurrection,chants for the Liturgies of St John Chrysostom and the Presanctified Gifts, some Lenten chants, *prosomoia*, etc.[38] Furthermore, ms *Arkh. 8450*, from the second quarter of the 18th century, belongs to the Genre-Thematic structure type and contains Oktoechos with the *heirmoi* on resurrection, *prosomoia*, *heirmologion* in eight tones, etc.[39] Ms *I-467* was written in 1869 and contains *heirmoi* on resurrection and *prokeimena* in eight tones.[40]

The University Scholarly Library in Užhorod (= НБУ – Наукова бібліотека Університету) preserves four manuscripts of interest. There are two tone structure type manuscripts: ms *Рук. 576*, of the last quarter of the 17th century, containing hymns, *stichera*, *katavasias*, *prokeimena*, the Liturgy of the Presanctified Gifts, etc.,[41] and ms *Рук. 577*, written in the first third of the 18th century, containing *heirmoi* of the Oktoechos.[42]

The remaining manuscripts belong to the Calendar-Menaion structure type. Ms *Рук. 565* is from the second half of the 18th century and contains the Oktoechos with *heirmoi* on the resurrection, *prosomoia*, and

---

[34] Mikitas, p. 43; Jasinovskij, p. 296.
[35] Mikitas, p. 43; Jasinovskij, p. 413.
[36] Mikitas, p. 44; Jasinovskij, pp. 232-233.
[37] Mikitas, pp. 42-43; Jasinovskij, pp. 360-361.
[38] Mikitas, p. 46; Jasinovskij, p. 489.
[39] Jasinovskij, p. 361.
[40] Mikitas, p. 44; Jasinovskij, p. 489.
[41] Vasilij L. Mikitas, *Давні рукописи і стародруки наукової бібліотеки Ужгород-ського університету*, I (Lvov, 1961), p. 42; Jasinovskij, p. 202.
[42] Mikitas, I (see n. 41), p. 42; Jasinovskij, p. 286.

festal *heirmoi* and *stichera*.[43] Ms *Рук. 561* was written in 1804 by Vasil'
Kupar, when he was studying the chant with a certain Michail, who was
either the singer of Grebl'any, or his last name was Grebliansky (the
context makes both options possible). It contains Oktoechos with the
heirmoion the resurrection, the Liturgy of the Presanctified Gifts, *prosomoia, sedalna,* festal *heirmoi*, etc.[44]

The National Scholarly Library of the Ukrainian Academy of Sciences in Lvov (= ЛНБ – Львівська національна наукова бібліотека імені В. Стефаника Національної академії наук України)
contains three manuscripts of interest. All of them belong to the Calendar-Menaion structure type. Ms *НТШ 272* is from the second half of the
18th century and contains festal and other *heirmoi*;[45] ms *НТШ 323* was
copied in the second half of the 18th century and contains gradual antiphones, *heirmoi* of eight tones, *prosomoia*, and chants of the Presanctified Liturgy;[46] and ms *НТШ 324* is from the end of the 18th century and
contains chants of the Oktoechos, *prosomoia*, and various festal *heirmoi*.[47] According to the sources, the latter ms was found in the Sub-
Carpathian Rus'.

The State Central Historical Archive in Lvov (= ЦДІА – Цен-
тральный Державный історичный архів) preserves one manuscript:
Ms *ф. 201, оп. 46, од. зб. 134/а,* copied at the beginning of the 18th
century. It is a Tone structure type and contains *heirmoi* of the Oktoechos,
prosomoia, and festal *stichera*.[48] Marginal inscription is written in both
Ukrainian and Hungarian languages. This manuscript was found in Sub-
Carpathian Rus'.

---

[43] Mikitas, I (see n. 41), p. 42; Jasinovskij, p. 423.

[44] Mikitas, I (see n. 41), p. 46; Jasinovskij, p. 482.

[45] *Нотолінійні рукописи XVI-XVIII ст. Каталог*, ed. Jurij Jasinovskij (Lvov,
1979), p. 23; Jasinovskij, *Українскі* (see n. 31), p. 420.

[46] *Хроніка НТШ*, II (Lvov, 1911), p. 46; *Нотолінійні рукописи XVI-XVIII ст.
Каталог*, ed. Jasinovskij (see n. 45), pp. 26-27; Jasinovskij, *Українскі* (see n. 31),
p. 420.

[47] *Нотолінійні рукописи XVI-XVIII ст. Каталог*, ed. Jasinovskij (see n. 45), p. 27;
Jasinovskij, *Українскі* (see n. 31), p. 469.

[48] *Хроніка НТШ*, IV/56 (Lvov, 1913), p. 30; Jasinovskij, *Українскі* (see n. 31),
p. 296.

The Historical Museum in Lvov (= ЛІМ – Львівський історичный музей) preserves a very important manuscript for our research. The second known heirmologion of Juhasevič was written (copied) in 1784-1785 in the village Príkra for the church of the Archangel Michael. It belongs to the Greek structural type and bears the collection no. *Рук. 209*.[49]

The Slovak National Museum in Bratislava (= SNM – Slovenské národné múzeum) preserves two manuscripts. The first one was hitherto considered lost. It is a manuscript of Juhasevič, his fourth known. This was copied in 1800 in the village Nevické. Its last location would have been the Redemptorist monastery in Michalovce.[50] From 1950 until 2007 this manuscript was considered lost, but the author of this article identified it in the SNM in Bratislava under the coll. *MUS I 80*.

The second one is ms *MUS I 229* (olim 527), which has not been yet described. The catalogue classification gives its date as 1700-1800, provenience in the village Klenová. It contains 300 folios, its size is 180 × 155 mm, and it lacks the original binding (it has recently been rebound).

The University Library in Bratislava (= UK – Univerzitná knižnica) preserves two musical manuscripts, both belonging to the Calendar-Menaion structure type. The first one is the *ms 1084*, from the 18th, or 18th-19th centuries and contains resurrectional chants of the Oktoechos, *prosomoia*, and festal *heirmoi* and *stichera*.[51] The second is the *ms 1099*, from the 18th, or 18th-19th centuries and contains chants on the

---

[49] Jasinovskij, *Українскі* (see n. 31), p. 466; Jurij Jasinovskij, 'Мелодії минулих століть', *Жовтень* 3 (1984), p. 113; Jurij Jasinovskij, '3 історії музики західноукраїнських земель XVI-XVII ст.', *Українське музикознавство* 21 (Kiev, 1986), p. 113; Jurij Jasinovskij, 'Український нотолінійний Ірмолой як тип гимнографічного збірника: зміст, структура', *Записки НТШ* 226 (Lvov, 1993), p. 53.

[50] Jasinovskij, *Українскі* (see n. 31), p. 473; Paňkevič, *Матеріали до історії мови південно-карпатських українців* (see n. 3), p. 95; V. Hošovskij, 'Страницы истории музыкальной культуры Закарпатья XIX – первой половины XX в.', *Украинское музыковедение* 1 (Kiev, 1964), pp. 203-215; Jasinovskij, 'Мелодії минулих століть' (see n. 49), p. 113; Jasinovskij, '3 історії музики західноукраїнських земель XVI-XVII ст.' (see n. 49), p. 113.

[51] Imrich Kotvan, *Rukopisy univerzitnej knižnice v Bratislave* (Bratislava, 1979), p. 376; Jasinovskij, *Українскі* (see n. 31), p. 476; David Pancza, 'Rukopisy Ms 1084 (Rkp 964) a Ms 1099 (Rkp 978) v Univerzitnej knižnici v Bratislave', *Cyrilské a latinské pamiatky v byzantsko-slovanskom obradovom prostredí na Slovensku*, ed. Peter Žeňuch (Bratislava, 2007), pp. 107-128.

resurrection of the Oktoechos, *prosomoia*, the Presanctified Liturgy, and festal *heirmoi*.[52]

The Archiepiscopal Library in Eger preserves the ms *T XIV, 14, 4044-I*, written toward the end of the 17th and the beginning of the 18th centuries. It belongs to the Calendar-Menaion structure type and contains chants on the resurrection of the Oktoechos, *prosomoia*, all-night vigil, the Liturgy of St John Chrysostom, *theotokia*, *stichera*, *heirmoi*, etc.[53]

The National Library in Prague (= NK – Národní knihovna) preserves the last known heirmologion of Juhasevič, the seventh in succession, which was copied in the village Nevické in 1811-1812. It bears the collection no. *XVII, L 16*, belongs to the Calendar-Menaion structure type and contains chants on the resurrection of the Oktoechos, *prosomoia*, festal *heirmoi* and chants of the Triodion.[54]

We found three manuscripts in private collections. At the end of the 19th century, the fifth known heirmologion of Juhasevič, which was copied in 1806, probably in the village Nevické, could still be found there.[55] Since 1950, it had been considered lost. However, in 2005 or 2006, a

---

[52] Kotvan, *Rukopisy univerzitnej knižnice v Bratislave* (see n. 51), p. 380; Jasinovskij, *Українскі* (see n. 31), p. 476; Pancza, 'Rukopisy *Ms 1084* (*Rkp 964*) a *Ms 1099* (*Rkp 978*) v Univerzitnej knižnici v Bratislave' (see n. 51), pp. 107-128.

[53] Roman Baleckij, 'Эгерский рукописный ирмологий', *Studia Slavica Academiae Scientiarum Hungaricae*, IV (Budapest, 1958) 3-4, pp. 293-323; Béláné Pallagi and Ernőné Zbiskó, 'Az Egri Föegyházmeguei Könyvtár szláv anyagából', *Az Egri Tanárképző föiskola füzetei* 276 (Eger, 1962), pp. 608-616; Jasinovskij, *Українскі та білоруски нотолінійні Ірмолої 16-18 століть* (see n. 31), p. 270.

[54] Jasinovskij, *Українскі* (see n. 31), p. 485; Julian Javorskij, 'Карпаторусский художник-писец Иоанн Югасевич и его графически-художественные произведения и 22 снимков с его рукописей', Материалы для истории старинной песенной литературы в Подкарпатской Руси (Prague, 1934), p. 334; Papp, 'Розвій церковного богослужбового співу (простоспіву) в Мукачівській епархії' (see fn 10), pp. 185, 195-196; Jasinovskij, 'Мелодії минулих століть' (see n. 49), p. 113; Jasinovskij, 'З історії музики західноукраїнських земель XVI-XVII ст.' (see n. 49), p. 113.

[55] Jasinovskij, *Українскі* (see n. 31), p. 483; Alexej Leonidovič Petrov, *Матерiалы для исторiи Угорской Руси II. Приложенiе II* (Sankt Peterburg, 1906), p. 87; Javorskij, 'Карпаторусский художник-писец Иоанн Югасевич и его графически-художественные произведения и 22 снимков с его рукописей' (see n. 54), p. 334; Papp, 'Розвій церковного богослужбового співу (простоспіву) в Мукачівській епархії' (see n. 10), p. 185; Jasinovskij, 'Мелодії минулих століть' (see n. 49), p. 113; Jasinovskij, 'З історії музики західноукраїнських земель XVI-XVII ст.' (see n. 49), p. 113.

seminarian from Užhorod, Vladimir Ihnatišin, found it in the attic of the rectory in Nevické and keeps it in his private collection. The second heirmologion held in private hands, is the one written by Michal Kešel'ák in 1878, probably in the village Ol'šavica. It contains chant of Lvov and finds itself in the private hands of Peter Tremko in Snina.[56] The third manuscript is that of *Michal Ternovskij*, held in the private collection of M. Čarný in Bratislava. It was written in 1729.

Also important for our research is the collection found in the Monastic Library in Michalovce (Slovakia). The library was plundered in the 1950s by the Communist regime, and its contents were either taken to other libraries and archives or simply burned. The present-day collection of this monastery is of a newer origin. Among others, it preserves the heritage of two priests-musicologists: Mikuláš and Ján Ďurkáň CSsR.

The first pad (copybook, notebook) was edited by Mikuláš Ďurkáň while interned in Podolínec in 1950-1951 during the 'Action P' organized by the Communist regime. The music was written down as witness to the liturgy celebrated on the campus. He finished it on 1 October 1951 and entitled it the *Prostopiniálna služba Božia sv. Jána Zlatoústeho* [Plain Chant Divine Service of St John Chrysostom]. He describes it as the *Typus mukaczensis*. This manuscript includes the so-called *Prešovský dodatok* [Prešov Addition], where he noted chants which he heard in Prešov that are different from those of Mukačevo. The addition does not include the date of its origin. This manuscript is preserved in the monastery of the Redemptorists in Michalovce under the coll. *Materiál č. 12* [Item no. 12]. His second manuscript contains the Liturgy of St John Chrysostom. The notes are written in calligraphic style and for the text the typewriter has been used. Although the manuscript is not signed, its author appears to be Mikuláš Ďurkáň. The pad has been written after 1951; in the library it is located under the coll. *Materiál č. 13* [Item no. 13].

The third manuscript bears the title *Bohoslužba sv. Jána Zlatoústeho* [The Liturgy of St John Chrysostom]. It contains nine pages of musical notes, but the text is included only at the great synapte. Its date is unknown and in the library the manuscript is located under the coll. *Materiál č. 14* [Item no. 14]. The fourth manuscript does not bear any

---

[56] Šimon Marinčák, 'Ol'šavický Irmologion Michala Kešel'áka a jeho miesto v dejinách liturgického spevu na Slovensku', *Kalofonia* 4 (Lviv, 2008), 221-249.

title. It contains plainchant of the Chrysostom Liturgy in the Slovak language. Its author may be Mikuláš Ďurkáň, although the handwriting points to somebody else. It is located under the coll. no. *Materiál č. 17* [Item no. 17]. The fifth manuscript seems to be a copy of the previous Item n. 17. Its author is Mikuláš Ďurkáň, and the coll. no. is *Materiál č. 18* [Item no. 18]. The sixth manuscript is quite unique, because it contains the chants sung by the priest in Old Church Slavonic. The author is Mikuláš Ďurkáň, the date is not indicated, and the manuscript has the coll. no. *Materiál č. 19* [Item no. 19]. The seventh manuscript does not bear any title, or the author's name. It contains the Chrysostom Liturgy and other songs and devotions in the Slovak language, and has the coll. no. *Materiál č. 20* [Item no. 20]. The eighth manuscript contains several liturgical songs. The handwriting points to Mikuláš Ďurkáň as its author. The manuscript was probably written in 1969-1970 and it has the coll. no. *Materiál č. 22* [Item no. 22].

Along with his musical work, Ján Ďurkáň is the author of a manuscript containing the Chrysostom Liturgy. The manuscript is dated to 1968 and its title is *Svätá liturgia Jána Zlatoústeho* [The Divine Liturgy of John Chrysostom].

The last category concerns the lost manuscripts. Although they are lost now, here we list the following seven manuscripts to give a complete account. The first manuscript was written by Bishop Manuil Olšavskij. It is known from the letter of the bishop to the *hegumen* of the Mária-Pócs monastery (Hungary), Silvester Kovejčak. This manuscript can be dated to the mid-18th century.[57] The second lost source is the oldest known heirmologion of Juhasevič, written in 1778-1779. That manuscript was copied for the church of the Archangel Michael in the village Príkra in today's eastern Slovakia.[58] It was found by Ivan Paňkevič in 1946. Its last known location was the monastery of the Redemptorists in Michalovce. The next lost manuscript, again written by Juhasevič — his third known — was copied in 1795, probably by

---

[57] Antal Hodinka, 'Переписка М. М. Ольшавського з ігуменами ЧСВВ', *Записки ЧСВВ* VI (Lvov, 1935) 1-2, p. 257; Olexa V. Mišanič, *Література Закарпаття XVII-XVIII ст.* (Kiev, 1964), p. 36; Jasinovskij, *Українскі* (see n. 31), p. 419.

[58] Jasinovskij, *Українскі* (see n. 31), p. 463; Papp, 'Розвій церковного' (see n. 10), p. 185 (181-196); Paňkevič, *Матеріали до історії мови південно-карпатських українців* (see n. 3), p. 95; Jasinovskij, 'Мелодії минулих століть' (see n. 49), p. 113; Jasinovskij, 'З історії музики західноукраїнських земель XVI-XVII ст.' (see n. 49), p. 113.

then in the village Nevické in today's Sub-Carpathian Rus'. We know
of this manuscript from the biography of Ján Juhasevič, written by
Andrej Bukovský, the priest of the village Simirki.[59]

The fourth lost manuscript we know from the Catalogue of Jurij Jasinovskij. He states that the manuscript was written around 1797, and its
last known location was the village Roztoka in Sub-Carpathian Rus'.[60]
The fifth manuscript used to be preserved in the NBU in Užhorod. Jasinovskij dates it to the 18th century and says that it is now lost.[61] The
sixth manuscript is again that of Juhasevič — his sixth known — which
was copied in 1809 in the village Nevické. According to the sources, the
manuscript was to be found in the village Kajmonka (Kamionka?) in
Spiš.[62] This heirmologion has later been copied by Peter Kuzmiak in
1841 for the church in the village Stráňany (former name Fol'vark) in
Spiš.[63] Unfortunately the locations of these manuscripts are presently
unknown.

Concluding Remarks

While — metaphorically speaking — we can trace the political history of the Carpathian Mountains almost to the first chapter of the book
of Genesis, in liturgical terms, passing certain unknown points in the
medieval times, we can only reach as far as the 9th century. Musically
we already have to stop in the 16th-17th centuries. Although some authors

[59] Jasinovskij, *Українскі* (see n. 31), p. 472; Petrov, *Материалы для истории
Угорской Руси II. Приложение II* (see n. 55), pp. 87-88; Javorskij, 'Карпаторусский
художник-писец Иоанн Югасевич и его графически-художественные произведения и 22 снимков с его рукописей' (see n. 54), p. 334; Jasinovskij, 'Мелодії минулих
століть' (see n. 49), p. 113.

[60] V. Sachanev, 'Новый карпаторусскій эпиграфическій матеріалъ', *Наук. зб.
тов. 'Просвіта' в Ужгороді* IX (Užhorod, 1932), p. 82. Cf. Jasinovskij, *Українскі*
(see n. 31), p. 472.

[61] Mikitas, *Давні рукописи і стародруки наукової бібліотеки Ужгородського
університету*, I (see n. 41), pp. 42-43; Jasinovskij, *Українскі* (see n. 31), p. 475.

[62] Jasinovskij, *Українскі* (see n. 31), pp. 483-484; Javorskij, 'Карпаторусский
художник-писец Иоанн Югасевич и его графически-художественные произведения и 22 снимков с его рукописей' (see n. 54), p. 334; Papp, 'Розвій церковного'
(see n. 10), pp. 185, 195; Jasinovskij, 'Мелодії минулих століть' (see n. 49), p. 113;
Jasinovskij, 'З історії музики західноукраїнських земель XVI-XVII ст.' (see n. 49),
p. 113.

[63] Papp, 'Розвій церковного' (see n. 10), p. 185; Jasinovskij, *Українскі* (see n. 31),
p. 487.

go beyond this date and put forward various hypotheses, generally speaking, it is still *hic sunt leones* earlier than this date.

The CP provokes many questions today, some of which will probably remain unanswered. Its actual use in practice is unclear as well. As Fedor Steško pointed out, this book was published not only with the permission of the authorities, but even with their active support.[64] After the book was printed in the Užhorod publishing house 'Unio', every parish was obliged to purchase one — according to several authors, even two copies[65] — a fact that had to secure the unification of the chant practice in the eparchy. However, it soon became obvious that this book would not fulfill its ambition to become the official chant collection. According to a testimony of 1934, i.e. some three decades after its publication, cantors singing in church did not use it, and the chant heard in the church 'hardly recalled that of Bokšaj's book'.[66] Most cantors continued to sing by heart and used the CP only as additional resource for alternation of some melodies, or an addition to their local repertory.[67]

As our research proceeds toward conclusions, it seems that the CP is an authentic monument of the performance of liturgical chant at the time. The hitherto gained information does not support the hypothesis of local chant of Mukačevo partly recorded in the book of Malinič and Bokšaj. Rather it suggests that the chant of Lvov was modified to the shape found in the CP. There were several causes that probably effected such alteration. Among them we can mention the political and social conditions allowing incompetent cantors to sing and transmit the musical tradition, the lack of musical books, the expense of education precluding the education of the poor, etc. After years of mutating, the distorted chants were recorded by Ján Bokšaj. We can assume that the music recorded in the CP was highly affected by way Malinič sang as well.

The advertisement accompanying the publication of the CP, together with the opinion of scholars studying it, created the impression that the CP was the collection of official chants of the eparchy of Mukačevo. If that were true, it would mean that this chant was not very rich and contains few melodies. The question is, however, if Jozef Malinič sang

---

[64] Cf. Steško, 'Церковная музика на Підкарпатській Русі' (see n. 8), p. 120.

[65] Papp, 'Розвій церковного' (see n. 10), pp. 189-190; Roccasalvo, *The Plainchant Tradition of Southwestern Rus* (see n. 9), p. 21.

[66] Cf. Steško, 'Церковная музика на Підкарпатській Русі' (see n. 8), p. 122.

[67] *Ibid.*, p. 122; Papp, 'Розвій церковного' (see n. 10), p. 192.

everything he knew, or just the most well known chants. The conclusions of scholars (Reynolds, Roccasalvo, and Petraševič) who have examined Ruthenian chant are not necessarily wrong or incorrect as such. However, they cannot be applied to the entire CP as a model of decadence due to the corrector's input. So far the statement of Štefan Papp, who says that Jozef Malinič mistakenly sang and Ján Bokšaj erroneously wrote the music out, needs to be considered closest to the truth.

METROPOLITAN ANDREW SHEPTYTSKY
AND LITURGICAL REFORM
A CASE STUDY

Hlib LONCHYNA

The liturgical work of Metropolitan Andrew Sheptytsky (1865-1944) has never been adequately studied. Recently, however, a comprehensive thesis dealing with the subject has been published: Peter Galadza's *The Theology and Liturgical Work of Andrei Sheptytsky (1865-1944).*[1] Metropolitan Andrew is one of the most revered hierarchs in the Ukrainian Greek-Catholic Church and one of his greatest achievements is in the area of liturgy. Students are being directed to study the body of work of the great metropolitan.[2] One hopes that this tendency will continue to be encouraged. I have attempted to analyze Metropolitan Andrew's role in liturgical reform with my doctoral thesis on *The Trebnyk of Metropolitan Andrew Sheptytsky (Lviv, 1925-1926): An Attempt at Liturgical Reform.*[3] The publication of that *Trebnyk* was an extraordinary feat in the history of liturgical publications of the Ukrainian Greek-Catholic Church, especially due to the strong influence of Latinization in the preceding two hundred years. The reasons for this Latinization are fourfold: 1) most clergy were educated in Latin theological institutions because of a lack of Ukrainian seminaries and universities;[4] 2) Greek-Catholics lived side by side with the Latin-rite Catholics, often attending one another's services, especially on feast days; 3) a heavy polemical exchange between Orthodox and Catholics led Catholics to a defensive position in which they considered everything Latin as the gold standard of what was 'catholic', whereas their own traditions were 'orthodox' and

---

[1] Peter Galadza, *The Theology and Liturgical Work of Andrei Sheptytsky (1865-1944)*, Orientalia Christiana Analecta 272 (Rome and Ottawa, 2004).

[2] For example, Liliya Petrovych, *The Preservation of an Eastern Liturgical Tradition in the Context of the Question of the Union of Churches in the Correspondence Between Father Leonid Fedorov and Metropolitan Andrew Sheptytsky (1904-1917)* (in Ukrainian), unpublished licentiate thesis at the Ukrainian Catholic University's Institute of Ecumenical Studies (Lviv, 2008). All articles quoted are in Ukrainian, unless specified otherwise.

[3] Unpublished (Rome, 2001).

[4] In many places this is still the case.

perennially suspect; and 4) the traditions of the Christian East were often ridiculed and considered outmoded or impractical. This hybridism affected all areas of church life (theology, liturgy, monasticism, canon law, and even clerical garb[5]). My focus of interest here will be the liturgical field.

An important argument for the ratification of the Union of Brest was the preservation of the Byzantine tradition which is such a distinguishing mark of the Ruthenian (Ukrainian)[6] Church, particularly concerning the liturgy. But the history of one tragic development after another has shown that this principle was breached more than observed. In the course of time elements of the Latin liturgy and spirituality which did not suit the spirit of the Byzantine liturgical tradition were introduced into the Ruthenian liturgy. This process evaded almost any control, to the point that the Synod of Zamost in 1720 approved laws which did not conform to the requirements of the Union of Brest.[7] Thus these elements, often alien to the Byzantine spirit, became law by the authority of that synod. Since the Union of Brest liturgical reforms had been much discussed, and in the 17th century care was taken not to change the rituals so as not to lose the tradition held in common with the Orthodox Church, but in the 19th century liturgical 'reform' took on the significance of a 'return' to 'tradition' — meaning the Westernized forms of worship which followed the Synod of Zamost.[8] This becomes apparent in several editions

---

[5] The issue of clerical clothing still sometimes becomes overheated. In Poland, the traditional clergy dress of the Christian East became associated with serfdom and social disadvantage. As a result, Greek-Catholic hierarchs and clergy came to think that if they could dress up like Latins, they would automatically elevate their social position to match their clothes. Today, in many countries, it is no longer 'fashionable' for the clergy to wear any form of distinctive attire; on the other hand, some Greek-Catholic clergy for the past several decades have resumed the traditional clergy attire of the Orthodox, which can still provoke anger. It is not without reason that Fr. Peter Galadza compares the situation with the inner-city gang wars in which clothing often plays an important part. See Galadza, *The Theology and Liturgical Work of Andrei Sheptytsky* (see n. 1), pp. 246-247.

[6] I am using today's term 'Ukrainian' for what historically was called 'Ruthenian' even until the 20th century.

[7] The Synod of Zamost itself only approved five points which can properly be called 'Latinizations'. These are the requirement to commemorate the pope, the requirement to add the *Filioque* to the Symbol of Faith, the prohibition of the liturgical sponge, the prohibition of administering holy communion to infants and young children, and the prohibition of the zeon. However, this was seen, whether accurately or not, as opening the floodgates and more Latinizations followed. It became acceptable to claim the authorization of Zamost for many Latinizations; the use of 'Low Mass' is an outstanding example. Cf. the pastoral letter of Metropolitan Athanasius (Sheptytsky) issued May 5, 1738 demanding a variety of hybridisms allegedly in the name of Zamost.

[8] After the partitions of Poland most of the remaining Greek-Catholics lived in places where there was little contact with Eastern Orthodoxy.

of the *Trebnyk*. These opposing tendencies inevitably led to rivalry between the 'Easternizers' (*vostochnyky*) and 'Westernizers' (*zapadnyky*). But the official position of the church, as expressed by its hierarchy, definitely favored the Westerners and, because of this, official liturgical texts in the Ruthenian Catholic Church well into the 20th century carried an ever stronger influence of Latinization.

Metropolitan Andrew Sheptytsky

Adhering to the Byzantinizing tendency of the Ukrainian Greek-Catholic Church, Metropolitan Andrew led a massive effort to sensitize the bishops, the clergy and the faithful of his church to the value and the importance of tradition. This was not only a means of evangelization, but also of rapprochement with our Orthodox brethren with whom we share the same Constantinopolitan liturgical tradition.

As to the liturgical renewal which the metropolitan promoted, he was the first leader, after more than three centuries, to provide clear direction. He was not blindly attached to tradition for its own sake (or as a historic curiosity), nor did he consider every innovation or borrowing from the Latin West to be completely incompatible with the Constantinopolitan liturgical tradition.[9] In other words, he avoided extremes. He did not consider it proper to be attached to Latin tradition in order to maintain the Catholic faith, as had been the predominant opinion in the Ruthenian Church in the 18th and 19th centuries. In the restoration of the authentic liturgical tradition, he did not accept pressure to abandon the Catholic Church, as some had done in the 19th century,[10] but found wisdom in conserving the Constantinopolitan liturgical tradition without relinquishing Catholic communion. The great accomplishment of Metropolitan Andrew is that he provided leadership and the right direction on the right road. This road is *fidelity to tradition*. 'We need to adhere faithfully to all our ancient ritual and ecclesial traditions'.[11] The metropolitan

---

[9] Metropolitan Andrew's encouragement of devotion to the 'Sacred Heart' may serve as an example. This devotion was relatively recent at the time and had intruded itself into the Greek-Catholic Church only a few years before he became metropolitan. He realized its pastoral potential and endorsed it.

[10] The most important examples are Archbishop Joseph Siemashko, who headed the 'return to Orthodoxy' of 1839, and Fr. Marcel Popel, who led the Eparchy of Kholm into the Russian state church in 1875.

[11] 'Pastoral Letter ... on ritual matters' (13 April 1931), in: Metropolitan Andrew Sheptytsky, *Life and Activities, Church and Church Unity: Documents and Materials*

did not limit himself to liturgical services; his views were more global. In an earlier pastoral letter he wrote:

> 'I consider it indispensable that not only in the forms of church services, vestments, church instruments and everything that concerns liturgical practice, in the narrow sense of that word, but also in the style of church icons, and the building of God's churches, in the discipline of fasting, and in all other directions we adhere to — or rather return to — Eastern forms, to the Byzantine style of icons and churches and to the Eastern canonical discipline'.[12]

One must not consider Metropolitan Andrew's views a mere emphasis on Eastern forms. He saw spiritual significance in the keeping of rubrics and that is sincere worship. 'Everything that has to do with [liturgical] services is of great importance. Since a rubric relates to worship it is important'.[13]

The metropolitan was adamantly opposed to elements introduced into the divine services which had not been previously approved by a synod of bishops or, in the case of long-standing customs, at least tacitly approved by their silence. In the same pastoral he emphasized that,

> 'the will of individuals can in no way substitute for the church instruction in anything. What has been prescribed must be done according to instructions; no one is allowed to change or cancel the rubrics on his own'.[14]

The second reason for Metropolitan Andrew's emphasis on faithfulness to the Byzantine tradition was his desire to foster unity among Christians, primarily with the Orthodox. This was the *Leitmotiv* of the life and works of this great metropolitan. Like the fathers of the Union of Brest, he did not want to differ from the Orthodox Church in liturgical matters, lest we should become an alien church among the Orthodox.

1899-1944, vol. 1 (in Ukrainian) (Lviv, 1995), p. 223. Translations here and elsewhere are my own. A complete English translation of the text of this pastoral letter of 13 April 1931 appears in Galadza, *The Theology and Liturgical Work of Andrei Sheptytsky* (see n. 1), pp. 341-349.

[12] 'Gratitude to Jesus Christ' (Zhovkva, 1906), p. 9.

[13] 'Pastoral Letter on the Liturgical Life' (December 1934), to be republished.

[14] 'Pastoral Letter on the Liturgical Life' (December 1934), to be republished. Compare Vatican II, *Sacrosanctum Concilium*, art. 22 §2: 'In virtue of power conceded by the law, the regulation of the liturgy within certain defined limits belongs also to various kinds of competent territorial bodies of bishops legitimately established', and art. 22 §3: 'Therefore no other person, even if he be a priest, may add, remove, or change anything in the liturgy on his own authority'.

'In the matter of the attraction of our … brethren to the unity with the Universal Church, we must not only hold to the … real, profound, and holy ecclesial tradition through which the truths of faith are handed down to us, but also in this less important and holy, but still important and holy [matter], which are the services, customs, liturgical forms and everything which is our ecclesial and national physiognomy. There were times when we liked everything new and foreign. … Only after a number of years did we notice how unwisely we acted, and started returning to that which was old, which had been handed down by [our] parents'.[15]

Just how Metropolitan Andrew implemented these principles may be seen in the liturgical books he published. A case in point is the *Trebnyk* or *Euchologion*.[16]

Trebnyk, Lviv 1925-1926[17]

Editions of the *Trebnyk* in the Ruthenian Greek-Catholic Church had gone from traditional Byzantine to Latinized. Although there were a few attempts to revise the book in order to make it more traditional, the Latinized tendency prevailed. Metropolitan Andrew was the first to change that trend. I wish to illustrate this by using the example of the sacrament of matrimony, as presented in the Lviv *Trebnyk*. The rite of matrimony consists of two parts: the betrothal and the crowning. Since the Synod of Zamost, the first rite — the betrothal — had been conflated with the second, the crowning, into one service. Unfortunately, the betrothal was inserted after a prayer which asks the Lord to 'bless this marriage'; this prayer in turn is followed by a prayer asking the Lord only now to 'bless this betrothal'.

Metropolitan Andrew's *Trebnyk* restores the integral parts to the rite of matrimony: the rite of the exchange of rings and the rite of crowning. The 1925 *Trebnyk,* while maintaining the state of the customary service,

---

[15] 'Faithfulness to Tradition', in Metropolitan Andreas Szeptyckyj, *Opera (moralia et pastoralia)* (Rome, 1983), p. 96.

[16] The Church-Slavonic *Trebnyk* and the Greek *Euchologion* are not really the same book, although there is a considerable similarity in the contents. Especially since the seminal work of Metropolitan Peter Mohyla of Kyiv (Kiev) the Church-Slavonic *Trebnyk* includes much more material than the Greek *Euchologion*. On the other hand the Greek *Euchologion* includes the Divine Liturgy, but the *Trebnyk* does not.

[17] The editor of this *Trebnyk* was Fr. Titus Myshkovsky. He did this work on assignment from Metropolitan Andrew, who endowed the book with his own authority. The book was printed by the Stauropegion Institute in Lviv and is sometimes called the 'Myshkovsky *Trebnyk*'.

prints an addition with the entire rite of betrothal before the rite of crowning, but with a note indicating that the wedding ceremony *may* be preceded by the solemn betrothal, thus restoring a specific tradition. Besides this, Metropolitan Andrew's *Trebnyk* follows another peculiarity of the Ruthenian usage: the pronouncing of the vows and the 'sealing' of the vows by the priest with a formula lifted from the *Rituale Romanum* of Pius V. These elements were already in earlier editions of the *Trebnyk*.[18] Perhaps the metropolitan did not feel ready to remove them, or did not consider it necessary to remove them. Still, he restored a large part of the rite which had been abandoned for two centuries: the *aitesis* and the Lord's Prayer.

A prayer follows with the bowing of heads. This prayer was the subject of great controversy during the liturgical evolution of the Ruthenian Church. It is a prayer to bless the cup of wine which the spouses are to drink three times as a sign of the mingling of their lives, for better or for worse. Originally the spouses received holy communion from the presanctified gifts.[19] In later centuries the blessing of the cup of wine was added and, finally, just the cup of wine was exchanged. But due to a misinterpretation of the symbolism of the rite, mockery of the custom was such that Metropolitan Peter Mohyla removed the whole rite of the cup of wine from his *Euchologion* and replaced it with a prayer blessing the spouses. Most Ruthenian editions of the *Trebnyk* copied this. But the 1925 *Trebnyk,* even though it gives the prayer for the spouses, follows it with the note that according to the Greek liturgical tradition, the priest brings the cup [of wine], blesses it with the appropriate prayer, and gives it to the spouses to drink. This is another example of a neglected rite being restored to a liturgical book.

The troparia and a triple procession around the table (the so-called 'tetrapod' where the crowning is done) follow. All the editions of the *Trebnyk* have these troparia (with some textual variations), but the procession is another element which had been abandoned in the course of history. Metropolitan Andrew's *Trebnyk* restores this procession.[20] The blessing of the wine, the drinking of the wine, and the procession around

---

[18] The 'marriage vows' appear in the *Great Trebnyk* published by Metropolitan Peter Mohyla of Kyiv, 1646, pp. 416-417. The Roman 'Ruthenian Recension' edition prescribes that the vows are used 'if it is the custom'.

[19] In Greece the custom of giving holy communion from the presanctified gifts to the bride and groom at a wedding has also been forgotten — but the Greeks continue to put a piece of antidoron into the cup of wine, and to chant 'I will take the chalice of salvation and call upon the name of the Lord', which is clearly a remnant of the earlier practice of using the presanctified holy gifts.

[20] It is claimed that the use of the cup of wine and the procession fell out of liturgical practice because the Latins were mocking these practices. Perhaps that was true in the

the tetrapod did not survive the cut of the 'recensio ruthena' process. Thus they are also not included in Patriarch Joseph's Ukrainian translation of the *Malyy Trebnyk*.[21]

Metropolitan Andrew's *Trebnyk* also contains the ritual of removing the crowns eight days after the wedding — another example of a ritual which had been abandoned and is now restored. The marriage rite concludes with the blessing of the spouses. The examination of the liturgical ritual for the mystery of matrimony shows the same care of Metropolitan Andrew for the beauty of the service. It introduces the complete rite with the exchange of rings, and elements of the ritual of crowning which had been lost over the centuries: the *aitesis* and Lord's Prayer, the prayer of blessing of the common cup and the partaking of the cup, and the procession of the spouses.

Conclusion

The servant of God, Metropolitan Andrew Sheptytsky, is one of the greatest figures in the Ukrainian Greek-Catholic Church of the 20th century. As a pastor he guided his flock in the spirit of the gospel in its Byzantine-Slav enculturation. But his ideal went far beyond the confines of his own church. Deeply convinced that the divisions among the churches must be overcome to accomplish the will of Christ, he offered his life and all his strength to hasten the day of reconciliation — at least between Eastern Christians and the Apostolic See of Rome. He noticed an obstacle to this aim in the serious alienation of certain aspects of his church from the Eastern tradition, and the acceptance of Latin elements at the expense of the Byzantine tradition. He encouraged his own faithful to notice this, especially the clergy, the monks and nuns, the men and women religious, and strove to regain what had been lost over the centuries. One means of reaching this goal was liturgical renewal. The *Trebnyk* of 1925-26 was a critical feature of this task. The metropolitan published a book which retained in great part the elements introduced by way of illegitimate custom into the services. He was unafraid to restore elements which had been lost over the centuries, to make the ritual fully resplendent in all its beauty.

seventeenth century, but priests who retain these two elements report no difficulties or mockery today. Although the metropolitan had authorized the publication of the full marriage ritual in the *Trebnyk,* he discouraged or even forbade the use of these elements in liturgical practice. They are prescribed for use in the Ukrainian *Trebnyk* published in Lviv by the authorization of Patriarch Lubomyr in 2001.

[21] (Rome, 1973), p. 73.

THE STATE OF MODERN GREEK LITURGICAL STUDIES
AND RESEARCH: A PRELIMINARY SURVEY

Stefanos ALEXOPOULOS

'It is imperative that we consider and dare many things regarding divine worship. Time has attached much rust to the worship of the Church, and the easiest thing for us today is to attribute everything to tradition. This tradition is a very big trap for the Church and its life. After all, tradition is not something to be bounded upon and turn back, but a stepping stone to go forward. *Much study of things and knowledge is needed in order that we may dare to do what is needed*, not only because in this way divine worship may become modern and adjust to the current conditions of life, but also so that it may find again its true meaning and its discreet ecclesiastical countenance.'[1]

These words of Dionysios Psarianos, the late Metropolitan of the northern Greek city of Kozani, not only reflect the need for liturgical renewal but also point to the fact that the quest for liturgical renewal is the driving force behind modern Greek liturgical studies. From the very beginnings of the period that falls within the designation 'modern Greek liturgical studies', that is from the philokalic movement of the 18th century to this day, the need to renew, correct, and reform liturgical practice and all that it entails, has encouraged and promoted liturgical studies and research.

In surveying modern Greek liturgical studies and research I will proceed in the following way. In the first part, I will briefly and broadly review the history of Greek liturgical studies and research from its beginnings to the election of the late Archbishop of Athens, Christodoulos, in 1998. In the second part, I will cover the years from 1998 to the present (2008) and I will propose some thoughts, ideas, and hopes that I envision for the future. Because of limited time and space, here I will not cover the areas of Byzantine art and architecture and Byzantine music, related fields with significant contributions to Byzantine liturgical history.

---

[1] Dionysios Psarianos, 'To the Most Respected Hierarchs of the Church of Greece, Memo Regarding Divine Worship, that is on Some Necessary Reforms in the Holy Services and the Divine Liturgy' (in Greek, see n. 22), dated August 10, 1985, p. 2 (photocopied text).

I. Greek Liturgical Studies and Research in the Past

1. The Roots

The roots of the modern Greek liturgical studies and research lie, I believe, in the Philokalic movement of the 18th century. Frequency of communion, correction of liturgical books, and correction of ritual practice were among the liturgical issues promoted by the movement.[2] Spearheaded by St Nicodemus the Hagiorite, St Athanasios Parios, and St Makarios Notaras, the movement sought the renewal of liturgical life through a return to the authentic tradition. Although it began as a monastic movement aiming to the correction of certain practices of monastic liturgical life on Mount Athos, the expulsion of the Kollyvades from Mount Athos actually helped the dissemination of their ideas and started a movement of liturgical renewal among parishes throughout Greece. It was the first time in modern Greek times that current liturgical practices were questioned and answers were sought through the study of the history of liturgy and tradition.

2. The Beginnings

The first efforts to address parish worship lie in the early 1800s when the Patriarchate of Constantinople tried to amend and adjust the monastic neo-Sabbaitic liturgical practice to parish needs. The product of this effort was the publication of the *Typikon* of Constantinos Protopsaltis in 1838, revised by Georgios Violakis in 1888. It is this Typikon, with certain adjustments due to the calendar change in the 1920s, that regulates liturgical life in Greek parishes today. This first official liturgical reform brings forth the incompatibility between a monastic Typikon and a parish, even more so today, and points to the need to design a Typikon suitable for parish use. This realization that parish liturgical life needs adjustments, changes and reform is, I believe, the motive and moving force behind modern Greek liturgical studies and research.

---

[2] Constantine Karaisaridis, Ὁ ἅγιος Νικόδημος ὁ Ἁγιορείτης καὶ τὸ λειτουργικὸ του ἔργο (Athens, 1998); Amfilochios Rantovich (= Radović), Ἡ φιλοκαλικὴ ἀναγέννηση τὸν 18ο καὶ 19ο αἰ. καὶ οἱ πνευματικοὶ καρποί της (Athens, 1984); Soterios Kosmopoulos, ''Η λειτουργικὴ ἀνανέωση κατὰ τὸν ἅγιο Ἀθανάσιο τὸν Πάριο', Master's Thesis, University of Athens, 2000; Nikodemos Skrettas, Ἡ Θεία Εὐχαριστία καὶ τὰ προνόμοια τῆς Κυριακῆς κατὰ τὴ διδασκαλία τῶν Κολλυβάδων (Athens, 2004).

A brief look at the index of Greek theological bibliography of the years 1860-1960[3] reveals that a good number of studies on liturgical themes were published in those years: 393 articles listed under the title 'Liturgics,' including hymnology and ecclesiastical music. A separate study would be necessary to decode these articles and see where the interests of the period lay. As I went through the list my impression is that there is an emphasis on the liturgical books, tied with the effort to reform them as we shall see, and secondarily, on early liturgy. In addition, during the first part of this period (before the 1920s) most were published by the journals of the Patriarchates of Constantinople, Jerusalem, and Alexandria: *Ἐκκλησιαστική Ἀλήθεια* (1880-1923) of the Patriarchate of Constantinople, *Νέα Σιών* (1904-) of the Patriarchate of Jerusalem, *Ἐκκλησιαστικός Φάρος* (1908-1951) and *Πάνταινος* (1908-) of the Patriarchate of Alexandria. After the 1920s, periodicals published in mainland Greece take over the scene. Among the most important are *Γρηγόριος Παλαμᾶς* (1917-), *Θεολογία* (1923-) and *Ἀνάπλασις* (1887-).

Among the important personalities of this period I would like to point out the contribution of two scholars, protopresbyter Konstantinos Kallinikos, and the retired Metropolitan of Caesaria, Ambrosios Stavrinos. Kallinikos, a Greek Orthodox priest in Manchester, England, provided the Greek speaking world with essentially an 'introduction to liturgy' book that was well written and was a standard manual for many years. The book, *Ὁ Χριστιανικὸς Ναὸς καὶ τὰ τελούμενα ἐν αὐτῷ*, was first published in 1921 in Alexandria, and then repeatedly published in Greece. I would dare to call the retired Metropolitan Ambrosios Stavrinos the 'Greek Brightman.' He produced a two volume work titled *Αἱ Ἀρχαιόταται καὶ αἱ Σύγχρονοι Λειτουργίαι τῶν Κυριωτέρων τοῦ Χριστοῦ Ἐκκλησιῶν*, both volumes published in Constantinople in 1921 and 1922 respectively. The first volume is essentially an introduction to early liturgy, with a general introduction, and then introductory remarks and texts of the Liturgy of the Twelve Apostles, the Liturgy of Peter, the Liturgy of Mark, and the Liturgy of James. The second volume is dedicated to the liturgical traditions (in the sequence they appear) of the Armenian, Roman, Anglican, and Coptic Churches. For each liturgical tradition he provides the reader with an extensive introduction and then produces a Greek translation of the text of the Divine Liturgy of each tradition. According to the preface, the driving force behind writing these

---

[3] Charilaos Tzogas and P.S. Papaevaggelou, *Ἑλληνικὴ Θεολογικὴ Βιβλιογραφία τῆς Τελευταίας Ἑκατονταετίας (1860-1960)* (Thessalonica, 1963), pp. 377-399.

two volumes was twofold: inter-church dialogue and liturgical reform. For the author the two were interconnected. He noted emphatically:

> 'The Church, which boasts that it has kept the apostolic tradition unchanged ... out of respect for herself, ought to reject everything that reprehensible love for novelty, harmful vainglory and callous ignorance has attached to herself in older times, and appear among the sister churches with new clothing, but also portraying its ancient form.'[4]

This two volume work of Stavrinos was recently published again by the Patriarchal Institute of Patristic Studies in Thessalonica, at the proposal of the Patriarchal Committee of Dialogue with the Pre-Chalcedonian Churches, within the framework of the rapprochement between the two bodies and for the 'mutual knowledge and respect for the others and their liturgical wealth,'[5] pointing to the lack and therefore the urgent need of modern equivalent editions.

A brief note should also be made of the only two liturgical manuals that circulated in the end of the 1800s, the first modern Greek comprehensive introductions to liturgy that I know of, authored by two professors of liturgy at the School of Theology of the University of Athens: Panagiotis Rombotis (1830-1875) published his book in Athens in 1869, titled: *Λειτουργική* (Athens, 1869). It was published again in 1887 but edited by Ioannis Mesoloras (1851-1942) to be used in secondary education. In 1895, Ioannis Mesoloras published his own book, titled: *Ἐγχειρίδιον Λειτουργικῆς τῆς Ὀρθοδόξου Ἀνατολικῆς Ἐκκλησίας* (Athens, 1895). These were the standard manuals for several years.

Finally, mention should be made of polymath archivists who promoted liturgical studies by publishing valuable manuscripts and documents from the archives and libraries of the Eastern Patriarchates. Such figures were Athanasios Papadopoulos-Kerameus (1856-1912) and Manuel Gedeon (1851-1943).

---

[4] Ἡ Ἐκκλησία, ἡ ὁποία καυχᾶται ὅτι διετήρησεν ἀλώβητον τὴν ἀποστολικὴν παράδοσιν ... σεβομένη ἑαυτὸν ὀφείλει, ἀπορρίπτουσα ὅ,τι καινοσπουδία ἐπίμεμπτος, κενοδοξία κακόσινος καὶ ἀμαθία στυγερὰ εἰς χρόνους ἀρχαιοτέρους προσεκόλαψαν αὐτῇ, νὰ προσέλθῃ ἐν μέσῳ τῶν ἀδελφῶν ἐκκλησιῶν ἱματισμὸν νεότευκτον μέν, ἀλλὰ τὴν ἀρχαιότητα διαπλασθεῖσαν ἀπεικονίζοντα.' *Αἱ Ἀρχαιόταται καὶ αἱ Σύγχρονοι Λειτουργίαι τῶν Κυριωτέρων τοῦ Χριστοῦ Ἐκκλησιῶν*, Λειτουργικὰ Βλατάδων 4 (Thessalonica, 2001²), pp. 18-19.

[5] Stavrinos, *Αἱ Ἀρχαιόταται καὶ αἱ Σύγχρονοι Λειτουργίαι*, p. 10, n. 4.

3. The Patriarchal Committee – Panagiotis Trempelas

By the initiative of the Patriarchate of Constantinople, a patriarchal committee was established in 1932, having as its aim the correction and critical edition of the liturgical books of the Greek-speaking part of the Orthodox Church. Unfortunately, the life of this committee was very short, its work being interrupted by the Second World War, and never resumed. The committee included great ecclesiastical and academic figures of the time. Among them was Panagiotis Trempelas (1886-1977).[6] It is he that produced the first fruits of this committee in the publication of *Αἱ τρεῖς λειτουργίαι κατὰ τοὺς ἐν Ἀθήναις κώδικας* in 1935.[7] This pioneering book is the critical edition of the liturgies of St John Chrysostom, St Basil and the Presanctified Gifts according to the codices in the National Library of Greece, a work still of great value. The important contribution of Trempelas, but also the challenge for the new generation of Greek liturgists is reflected in a comment made by a colleague, namely that 'many of the codices in the National Library have not been looked at since Trempelas reviewed them for his book.'

Trempelas continued his work by publishing critical editions and studies of various sacraments and offices, gathered in two important volumes. The *Μικρὸν Εὐχολόγιον τόμος Α'* Athens 1950, dealing with the sacraments of marriage, baptism, unction, and ordination, and *Μικρὸν Εὐχολόγιον τόμος Β'* Athens 1955, dealing with the offices of the great and small blessing of the waters, dedication of churches, and the prayers of matins and vespers.[8] These important works were done within the framework of the patriarchal committee's vision and although outdated, maintain their value. Unfortunately, no one continued his work, nor did the official Church use his research in the various editions of liturgical books officially published since then.

Trempelas is also the author of the only comprehensive introduction to liturgical studies in the Greek language. His three volume work covers liturgy in the early Church (volume 1),[9] Eastern liturgical families

---

[6] For biographical information and a complete list of his publications see Nikodemos, Metropolitan of Patras, 'Φιλολογικὸν Μνημόσυνον Παναγιώτου Τρεμπέλα', *Ἐκκλησία* 45 (1978) 83-86, 118-120, 143-145, and Evaggelos Theodorou, 'Παναγιώτης Τρεμπέλας', *Ἐπιστημονικὴ Ἐπετηρὶς τῆς Θεολογικῆς Σχολῆς* 17 (1971), pp. vii-lxxiv (Greek numerals).

[7] Reprinted in 1982.

[8] These were originally published as a series of articles in the periodical *Θεολογία*.

[9] *Ἀρχαὶ καὶ Χαρακτὴρ τῆς Χριστιανικῆς Λατρείας* (Athens, 1962, reprinted in 1993).

(volume 2)[10] and Western liturgical families (volume 3).[11] This work, although outdated, is still a classic, the only reference in the Greek language for Western and non-Byzantine Eastern liturgical traditions. The lack of any comparable modern text led to its reprint in 1993.

Trempelas was critical of the Roman Catholic Church, but in the same time showed respect and admiration as regards its liturgical movement. He kept a close eye on the different stages of the movement, and saw it as an opportunity for the Orthodox Church to gain from the liturgical movement. As early as 1949 he published an offprint from a series of articles that appeared in the official periodical of the Church of Greece Ἐκκλησία, titled Ἡ Ρωμαϊκὴ Λειτουργικὴ Κίνησις καὶ ἡ Πρᾶξις τῆς Ἀνατολῆς. Through this study Trempelas addressed issues such as the participation of people in the liturgy and the audible recitation of the prayers of the liturgy, issues that occupied and still occupy Orthodox worship. Trempelas viewed the Roman liturgical movement favorably. He considered its purpose and its methods valid. Although he ended this small work with the affirmation that the Orthodox Church has kept the ancient character of worship, it is evident throughout his work that a renewal of Orthodox worship is needed.

I would call Trempelas the father of liturgical studies in modern Greece. He taught liturgy, wrote about liturgy, and lived the liturgy throughout his life. Trempelas supported the renewal of liturgy, wrote works still unsurpassed, and kept an open mind, looking both westwards and eastwards.

4. Academic and Ecclesiastical Figures after Trempelas – Transition to the Present Situation

Two academic figures that represent the transition from the past to the present and have in many ways influenced or even formed current Greek liturgical scholarship are the late Professor Ioannis Fountoulis and Professor Evaggelos Theodorou.

Professor Ioannis Fountoulis (1927-2007) was the person who continued the work of Trempelas, and established the School of Theology at the University of Thessalonica as the center of liturgical studies in

---

[10] Λειτουργικοὶ Τύποι Αἰγύπτου καὶ Ἀνατολῆς (Athens 1961, reprinted in 1993).
[11] Λειτουργικοὶ Τύποι τῆς Δύσεως καὶ Διαμαρτυρομένων Agenda (Athens 1966, reprinted in 1993).

Greece. He published numerous books and articles, produced many students and encouraged them to further their studies abroad. It is noteworthy that the majority of Greek liturgists have been at one point or another his students, and all Greek liturgists have been influenced by his work and thought. Among his publications I would point to his own 'Introduction to Liturgy', a book that was used as a manual for his liturgy course,[12] and the series *Κείμενα Λειτουργικῆς.*[13] He worked in the field in many capacities, not limiting himself to the pure academic study of liturgy, but also actively trying to disseminate historical and critical thinking and an awareness of international liturgical studies and research among clergy and laity. In this capacity he maintained a column in the periodical *'Εφημέριος* for a number of years titled ''Απαντήσεις εἰς λειτουργικὰς ἀπορίας.' These have been collected and repeatedly printed,[14] demonstrating their popularity and acceptance. In this column Fountoulis provided his readers (the clergy of the Church of Greece) with informed answers on liturgical issues, exposing them to current liturgical scholarship and the work of scholars such as Juan Mateos, Miguel Arranz, Robert Taft, and Sebastià Janeras. He also cultivated a shift in the mentality towards the study of liturgy, demonstrating by his work an attitude that critical liturgical research does not negate tradition and should not be feared. On the contrary, it respects and serves tradition.

Another important figure in liturgical studies in Greece is Professor Evaggelos Theodorou, who taught liturgy at the University of Athens from 1968 to 1988. His dissertation, written under Trempelas, was on the issue of ordination of deaconesses in the Orthodox liturgical tradition,[15] a work that stirred the waters and is considered one of the standard references on the topic. He also wrote a university manual for his liturgy class that is still in use today[16] and plethora of articles on a variety of issues.[17]

---

[12] *Λειτουργική Α΄: Εἰσαγωγή στή Θεία Λατρεία* (Thessalonica, 1995).

[13] This series is a collection of older publications of liturgical texts grouped into three volumes: *Κείμενα Λειτουργικῆς.* Τεῦχος Α΄: 'Ακολουθίαι του Νυχθημέρου; Τεῦχος Β΄: Θέματα Εὐχολογίου; Τεῦχος Γ΄: Θεῖαι Λειτουργίαι (Thessalonica, 1994).

[14] *'Απαντήσεις εἰς Λειτουργικὰς 'Απορίας* (Athens, 2006) in five volumes.

[15] *'Η Χειροτονία ἢ Χειροθεσία τῶν Διακονισσῶν* (Athens, 1954).

[16] *Μαθήματα Λειτουργικῆς* (τεῦχος Α΄) (Athens 1993⁶). The first edition was published in 1975, but in mimeographed form circulated in 1969.

[17] Among his most recent articles the following stand out: 'Τὸ σταθερὸ καὶ μεταβλητὸ στὴν 'Ορθόδοξη Λατρεία' *Θεολογία* 70 (1999) 7-55; 'Παράδοσις καὶ ἀνανέωσις στὴν Λειτουργικὴ Ζωὴ τῆς 'Ορθοδόξου 'Εκκλησίας' in «*Λατρεύσωμεν*

Note should also be made of two other figures, Dimitrios Moraitis (1896-1970) and Evaggelos Antoniadis (1882-1962). Moraitis taught liturgy at the University of Thessalonica (1942-1959), and then the University of Athens between the years 1959-1967. Among his works I would single out an introduction to early liturgy[18] and a monograph on the Presanctified Gifts liturgy.[19] Although Antoniadis was a New Testament scholar, his contribution to things liturgical should be mentioned as he published an important article on the cathedral rite of Constantinople, the first article in Greek, to my knowledge, that addresses in detail the distinction between the monastic and cathedral offices.[20]

As for ecclesiastical figures, the late Metropolitan Dionysios Psarianos of Kozani (1912-1997) was truly a visionary. In his capacity as the chancellor of the Archdiocese of Athens and then as bishop he systematically promoted a renewal of liturgical life and experience.[21] Mention should be made of his famous address to the members of the Holy Synod of the Church of Greece on August 10, 1985, titled: 'To the Most Respected Hierarchs of the Church of Greece, Memo Regarding Divine Worship, that is on Some Necessary Reforms in the Holy Services and the Divine Liturgy.'[22] This address is important because it is the first time that a member of the Synod so emphatically spoke about the necessity of renewal of liturgical life, identifying the Liturgy of the Hours, the Divine Liturgy, the language of divine worship, preaching, psalmody, and clergy vestments as the primary issues demanding attention, critical study and renewal. He also spoke of the necessity of scholarship in liturgical renewal. He wrote in that address: 'We try to be scientifically

---

εὐαρέστως τῷ Θεῷ» Τὸ αἴτημα τῆς λειτουργικῆς ἀνανεώσεως στὴν Ὀρθόδοξη Ἐκκλησία. Πρακτικὰ Β᾽ Πανελληνίου Λειτουργικοῦ Συμποσίου. Ποιμαντικὴ Βιβλιοθήκη 7 (Athens: Apostoliki Diakonia, 2003), pp. 41-58.

[18] Ἱστορία τῆς Χριστιανικῆς Λατρείας (α᾽-δ᾽ αἰών) (Athens, 1964).

[19] Ἡ Λειτουργία τῶν Προηγιασμένων (Thessalonica, 1955). More on Moraitis in the entry 'Μωραΐτης Δημήτριος' in Χριστιανικὴ καὶ Ἠθικὴ Ἐγκυκλοπαίδεια 9: 275-277.

[20] 'Περὶ τοῦ ἀσματικοῦ ἢ βυζαντινοῦ κοσμικοῦ τύπου τῶν ἀκολουθιῶν τῆς ἡμερονυκτίου προσευχῆς᾽ Θεολογία (1949-1951) 1-113. More on Antioniadis in the entry ''Αντωνιάδης Εὐάγγελος᾽ in Χριστιανικὴ καὶ Ἠθικὴ Ἐγκυκλοπαίδεια 2: 957-959.

[21] For a detailed account on his life, see Nicholaos Drosos, Metropolitan of Karpenisi, Ἐπίσκοπος Διονύσιος Ψαριανὸς (κατὰ κόσμον Νικόλαος) Μητροπολίτης Σερβίων καὶ Κοζάνης (Kozani, 1991).

[22] 'Πρὸς τοὺς Σεβασμιωτάτους Ἀρχιερεῖς τῆς Ἐκκλησίας τῆς Ἑλλάδος Ὑπόμνημα Περὶ τῆς Θείας Λατρείας, ἤτοι περὶ τινων ἀναγκαίων μεταρρυθμίσεων ἐν ταῖς ἱεραῖς Ἀκολουθίες καὶ τῇ Θ. Λειτουργίᾳ᾽ photocopied text, dated August 10, 1985.

informed on the issue of divine worship and we try to restore certain things as much as we can, not because we are ambitious to become reformers, but because we are forced by the needs of our times.'[23]

Also in 1985, the Metropolitan of Drama, Dionysios Kyratsos (1923-2005) initiated in his diocese an annual clergy conference with primarily liturgical themes, which took place every year until his death in 2005.[24] Although it was not set up as a scholarly conference, the participation of faculty from the University of Thessalonica and especially the presence and papers of Fountoulis from its very beginning set a good academic standard, preparing the way for the annual liturgy conferences initiated by the late Archbishop Christodoulos.

II. THE STATE OF MODERN GREEK LITURGICAL STUDIES AND RESEARCH AND ITS FUTURE

The late Archbishop Christodoulos proved to be a turning point for liturgical studies and research in Greece. With his encyclical on liturgical renewal[25] and the founding of the Special Synodical Committee on Liturgical Renewal[26] he initiated a renewed interest in liturgical studies fuelled by the ensuing discussion regarding liturgical renewal.[27]

---

[23] *Ibid.* p. 3.

[24] The acts of those conferences have been published but are hard to find. The themes of the conferences were (in chronological sequence): The pastoral work today (1985), Ecclesiastical Order (1986), Scripture in our faith and life (1987), Clergy and Laity as the Body of Christ (1988), Fasting and Spiritual Life (1989), The Christian Calendar (1990), Symbols and Symbolisms in the Orthodox Church (1991), The Mission of Orthodoxy in the Modern World (1992), The Parish as a Communion of Believers and Body of Christ (1993), The Liturgy of the Hours (1994), Psychological Problems of Modern Man (1995), Holy Baptism (1996), The Holy Sacrament of Matrimony (1997), The Divine Liturgy (1998), Priesthood according to the Church Fathers (1999), The Holy Sacrament of Unction (2000), Death Rites (2001), The Holy Sacrament of Confession (2002), Holy Eucharist (2003), Times of Prayer in the Church (2004), The Christian Temple (2005).

[25] 9/2292/16-10-1998.

[26] *Ἐκκλησία* 76.12 (1999) 270-272. The current (2008) committee members are: Chairperson: Metropolitan Daniel of Kaisariani. Members: Rev. Dr. Constantinos Karaisaridis, Rev. Dr. Dimitrios Tzerpos, Rev. Dr. Vasileios Kalliakmanis, Dr. Petros Vassiliadis, Dr Athanasios Vourlis, Dr. Georgios Filias, Dr. Panagiotis Skaltsis. Substitute Members are: Rev. Dr. Nicholaos Ioannides, Rev. Dr. Theodoros Koumarianos, Dr. Nicholaos Despotis. Secretary: Rev. Serapheim Kalogeropoulos.

[27] For a detailed critical presentation of the effort for liturgical renewal initiated by Archbishop Christodoulos, see Pavlos Koumarianos, 'Liturgical "Rebirth" in the Modern Church of Greece: An Ambiguous Effort for a Liturgical Reform', *Bollettino della Badia Greca di Grottaferrata* 4 (2007) 119-144.

The greatest contribution of that Synodical Committee is, I believe, the annual liturgy conference it organizes on specified themes. This annual liturgy conference has been a great opportunity for Greek liturgists to meet, discuss, initiate research and write papers. More importantly, the proceedings of each conference are available online[28] and are published by the Church of Greece and sent to all clergy, building a collection of scholarly liturgical volumes to be used as references, study, and guidelines for the clergy of Greece on various liturgical topics. To this day, ten such conferences have taken place with the following themes:

1. The Sacrament of Baptism (1999)
2. Liturgical Renewal (2000)
3. Divine Liturgy (2001)
4. The Sacrament of Marriage (2002)
5. Ministering the Gospel (2003)
6. Christian Worship and Idolatry (2004)
7. The Sacrament of Priesthood (2005)
8. The Christian Liturgical Year (2006)
9. The Sacrament of Death in the Worship of the Church (2007)
10. Health and Illness in the Liturgical Life of the Church (2008)

The Special Synodical Committee also organized an International Pan-Orthodox Liturgical Conference on Liturgical Renewal, originally planned to take place in August of 2007, but unfortunately it was cancelled due to the late Archbishop's illness. This would have been a significant conference addressing the issue of liturgical renewal at a pan-Orthodox level, but also bringing Orthodox liturgists from all over the world together, from the U.S.A. to the Middle East and Russia, in a first meeting of such a kind. Notwithstanding its cancellation, the planning and organization of this conference demonstrated Archbishop Christodoulos' will and determination to push the idea of liturgical renewal at a pan-Orthodox level, and to work towards a greater co-operation among Orthodox liturgists, something that is lacking in the Orthodox world and is desperately needed.

Here we have to point out the important role that the Greek theological journal *Synaxis* has played in the promotion of liturgical studies and

---

[28] www.ecclesia.gr/greek/holysynod/commitees/liturgical/liturgical.htm (September 14, 2008).

liturgical renewal. It is through the pages of *Synaxis* that the whole idea of liturgical renewal once more came to the forefront of theological debate and discussion in Greece, not only by regularly publishing articles of liturgical interest, but also by hosting the first liturgical conference in Greece in 1998 with the explicit theme of liturgical renewal. The proceedings were published in two consecutive volumes and stirred a lot of discussion.[29]

Who is Who in Greek Liturgical Studies

The people working in the field of liturgy in Greece today are not many. They could be placed in three categories: University liturgists having a university position teaching liturgy, independent-scholar liturgists having no academic position, but researching and publishing in the field of liturgy, and those who are not liturgists, but have a strong interest in liturgical matters. It should be noted that most people today working in the field of liturgy have had at least some of their formation, research, and/or writing in Italy, France, Germany, and the U.S.A.

Liturgy is taught at the School of Theology[30] of the University of Athens by Rev. Dr. Dimitrios Tzerpos[31] (Department of History) and the liturgy courses offered are Liturgics (History and Theology of Worship), Introduction to Divine Worship, Homiletics A and B.

In the School of Social Theology[32] liturgy is taught by Dr. Georgios Filias and the Rev. Dr. Theodoros Koumarianos (Department of Christian Worship, Education, and Pastoral Studies). The liturgy courses offered are Liturgics/Homiletics, Theology of Worship, Studies on Feast Days (Filias), History and Theology of Ecclesiastical Hymns, Hymnology (Dr. Athanasios Vourlis), Hagiology, Study of Rituals – Teleturgics (Rev. Dr. Constantinos Papadopoulos), Interpretation of the Divine Liturgy (Koumarianos).[33] Courses offered at the Master's level are: Sources

---

[29] The proceedings and discussion were published in 1999 in issues 71 and 72 of *Synaxis*.

[30] For the website of the School see http://www.theol.uoa.gr (last visited August 22, 2008).

[31] See http://www.theol.uoa.gr/index.php?id=207 (last visited August 22, 2008).

[32] For the website of the School see http://www.soctheol.uoa.gr/ (last visited August 22, 2008).

[33] For course descriptions in English see http://www.soctheol.uoa.gr/en/docs/guide 2007a.pdf (last visited August 22, 2008), p. 71f.

for Worship, Theology of Worship, Liturgical Year, Hymnology, Hagiology, Teleturgics, Theology of the Divine Liturgy, and Scientific Methodology. Right now there are five students working towards a Master in liturgy and three students working at the doctoral level. People who teach in related fields are the Rev. Dr. Constantine Papadopoulos (Hagiology) and Dr. Athanasios Vourlis (Hymnology).

Moving north to the University of Thessalonica, the following people teach liturgy: In the School of Theology,[34] (Department of Worship, Christian Education and Ecclesiastical Administration) Dr. Panagiotis Skaltsis and Dr. Dimitra Koukoura (Homiletics), and the liturgy classes offered are Introduction to Liturgy, Liturgics, Hymnology and Interpretation of Liturgical Texts (Skaltsis), Introduction to Homiletics and Communication, Homiletics, Hymnography and Preaching (Koukoura).[35] At the Master's level the following courses are offered: Topics from the Liturgical Year and Euchologion, Topics of Theology of Worship and Modern Liturgical Issues (Skaltsis), Methodology of Homiletical Texts, the Homiletic Dimension of Hymnography (Koukoura), Topics of Theology of Worship (Dr. Anestis Keselopoulos).[36]

In the School of Social Theology,[37] (Department of Worship, Archaeology, and Art) liturgy is taught by the Rev. Dr. Nikodemos Skrettas, the Rev. Dr. Konstantinos Karaisaridis, and in related fields Dr. Symeon Paschalidis (Hagiology and Hymnology). The liturgy classes offered are: Introduction to Divine Worship, the Byzantine Rite (Karaisaridis) Hagiology and Heortology, Hymnology (Paschalidis), Homiletics, Liturgy, Sources of Divine Worship, Teleturgics, History and Theology of Divine Worship (Skrettas). At the Master's level the following courses are offered: Interpretation of the Divine Liturgy, Temple — Liturgical Objects — Vestments, Modern Liturgical Issues (Karaisaridis), the Sacraments of the Orthodox Church, Interpretation and Theology of Prayers and Hymns, Liturgical Typika and Euchologia (Skrettas).[38]

---

[34] For the website of the School see http://web.auth.gr/theo/ (last visited August 22, 2008).

[35] For course descriptions in Greek see http://web.auth.gr/theo/proptyxiakes.htm (last visited August 22, 2008).

[36] http://web.auth.gr/theo/metaptyxiakes.htm (last visited August 22, 2008).

[37] For the website of the School see http://www.past.auth.gr/ (last visited August 22, 2008).

[38] For course descriptions in Greek see http://www.past.auth.gr/student%20 guide_2008.doc (last visited August 22, 2008).

People who are active in the field as independent scholars are the Rev. Dr. Pavlos Koumarianos who serves as a parish priest and teaches religion in secondary education; Rev. Dr. Themistokles Christodoulou who serves as a parish priest and is the director of the social ministry of the Archdiocese of Athens; Dr. Panayotis Kalaitzidis who teaches religion in secondary education; and Rev. Dr. Stefanos Alexopoulos who is a parish priest and adjunct Professor of Religion at the College Year in Athens Program, and also teaches at the Rome-Athens program of St. John's University, Collegeville, Minnesota.

Special note should be made of Dr. Cosmas Georgiou who has been teaching liturgy at the Ecclesiastical Academy of Athens for many years, and of two priest-scholars who have contributed in many ways to the field. These are Protopresbyter Konstantinos Papayiannis (retired priest - Thessalonica) and Archimandrite Patrikios Kaleodis (parish priest, head of Protocol at the Holy Synod of the Church of Greece - Athens).

Scholars in other fields with a strong interest in liturgy and contributions to the field include New Testament scholar Dr. Petros Vassiliadis and canonists Dr. Theodoros Giangou, and his student, the Rev. Dr. Chrysostomos Nassis, all three of the School of Theology of the University of Thessalonica.

Challenges for the Future

The challenges that lie ahead are great and many. The pioneers of liturgical studies have opened the way to the newer generation and have assisted in changing the attitude towards liturgy, liturgical studies and liturgical reform. More and more the field of liturgy is not seen as just the study of rubrics and ritual performance, but is seen as a field to itself, worthy of attention, study and research. The importance, effect and dynamics of liturgy in the life of the Church are acknowledged and the call to liturgical renewal has never been louder. It is now the time to invest and build upon this inheritance and upon the treasures housed in various libraries in Greece. The manuscript collections of the National Library in Athens, Mount Athos, Patmos, Mytelene (Leimon Monastery) and Meteora, the microfilm collection of the Sinai mss, and the smaller collections of the Byzantine Museum of Athens and the Benaki Museum alone may offer research opportunities and projects for generations of scholars to come.

Challenges for the Universities

1.   Course offerings should be expanded to include targeted electives on aspects of the Byzantine liturgical history, but also courses on the Western liturgical traditions (ancient and modern) and the Oriental liturgical traditions. Such an approach not only will improve the quality of liturgical scholarship, but will enable and enhance the inter-Christian dialogues that take place. The Orthodox need to be up-to-date with the liturgical traditions of the other Christian Churches in order to be able to have constructive discussions within the context of ecumenical dialogue.

2.   Course listings should also include a class on liturgical inculturation. Since most of the missions in Africa and Asia are supported by the Greek Church and Greek mission groups, and most of the missionaries come from Greece, there should be a conscious effort to inculturate the Byzantine liturgical tradition in the African or Asian settings, instead of transplanting modern Greek practice in the middle of Africa or in the Far East. By necessity, this would also involve related fields to liturgy such as architecture, art and music.

3.   Out of new course offerings research (dissertation projects) should be encouraged on topics related to the study of manuscripts housed in Greek libraries, the study of liturgy in the post-Byzantine times, the study of the 'Greek Liturgical Movement,' the study of Vatican II and its liturgical reforms, the study of the history of the liturgical books (mss and printing history), the study of significant personalities in Greek liturgical history, the study of liturgical inculturation, and the study of the Western and Eastern liturgical traditions.

4.   There is a desperate need for a good library collection of books on liturgy. This collection should be updated regularly with worldwide journals and publications on liturgy and related fields reflecting all liturgical traditions.

5.   The presence of faculty of the Theological Schools in international liturgical conferences is of paramount importance as in these venues their contributions in the field may be more widely acknowledged and Greek liturgical scholarship will gain from such an encounter.

Challenges for the Church

The presence of able young liturgical scholars (not only in liturgy but also in related fields) gives the Church the great ability to invest and use their scholarship and eagerness to contribute to the field. Since the Orthodox Church is a highly liturgical church, liturgy being its life and major expression, the Church should not be afraid to invest resources and people in the methodical study of liturgy. It is the Church that should spearhead the whole movement. The challenges for the Church would include:

1. The annual liturgical conferences should continue. They are a forum of discussion regarding liturgical issues, they give Greek liturgists the opportunity to meet, exchange ideas and present their work, they provide the incentive for research and papers, they expose clergy to liturgical scholarship and all that it entails, and they make their proceedings quickly and widely available both in print and on-line, thus disseminating knowledge and making the discussion public. I strongly believe that the discontinuation of these conferences would be a great blow and a major setback to the Greek liturgical movement.

2. In a broader level the Orthodox Church of Greece should organize and host an international pan-Orthodox liturgical conference every two-three years with the invited participation of non-Orthodox internationally renowned scholars in the field. The example and the success of the Fifth International Theological Conference of the Russian Orthodox Church on the Orthodox Teaching on the Sacraments of the Church, which took place in Moscow on 13-16 November 2007[39] and where major non-Orthodox scholars were also invited to participate, demonstrated in the best way the benefits of such events.

3. Systematically promote and permeate the idea of liturgical renewal at the parish level, but especially among the clergy. It is of paramount importance that the clergy are convinced as to the necessity of liturgical study and renewal. The Church should support and encourage clergy to continue their education and become scholarly involved.

4. Revise, correct, and edit the liturgical books. This is a huge topic, deserving particular attention and caution. Work should be systematic, scientific, and gradual. Liturgical books should be edited by a team of liturgical scholars dedicating their research and study to this object.

---

[39] www.theolcom.ru/ru/text.php?SECTION_ID=343 (last visited September 14, 2008).

5. Edit 'pew' editions of liturgical texts, especially services which are usually attended by non-church-goers such as baptisms, weddings, and funerals. These should include a short introduction and a translation of the pertinent service and should be available in parish churches for the faithful.

6. Organize and set into motion a project of translations of liturgical texts in Modern Greek aimed for future use in worship. I believe the use of Modern Greek in worship is a matter of time – reality will force this change, and the Church needs to prepare and be ready. There are some cases where this is already happening. Of course such an endeavor should be the work of a team of liturgists, philologists and poets in order to produce good translations for liturgical use, as the vast majority of the available translations are not intended for liturgical use.

7. Changes that affect the everyday liturgical life of the Church should be implemented gradually and slowly, only after the clergy and lay representatives of each parish have been exposed to the nature and reason for each change. For example, one reason among others why the measure promulgated by the late Archbishop Christodoulos to repeat the readings of the Gospel and Apostle in Modern Greek in the Divine Liturgy failed, is that there was not much effort placed in convincing the clergy of the parishes of the necessity and nature of this measure.

The Need of an Institute for Liturgical Study and Research

I would like to suggest the creation of an Institute for Liturgical Study and Research. This center will promote the scientific study of liturgy and connect it with the liturgical life of the Church. I believe that the existence of such an Institute is of paramount importance, something which I have discussed with other Greek liturgists, and there seems to be a consensus among us as to its necessity.[40] This Institute could be attached to the University or the Church but its academic independence and financial survival should be guaranteed.

---

[40] He has expressed the thought also in writing. See his article: 'Πρὸς μία ἀνανέωση τῆς λατρείας' in his book Λειτουργικὴ Ἀνανέωση. Δοκίμια λειτουργικῆς ἀγωγῆς κλήρου καὶ λαοῦ, Σύγχρονοι Λειτουργικοὶ Προβληματισμοὶ 2 (Athens, 2001), pp. 11-29, here p. 25.

Some thoughts about the function and nature of the proposed Institute for Liturgical Study and Research are:

1. Create and maintain an excellent reference liturgical library and maintain an online resource gate. All of us working in the field of liturgy in Greece live with the painful reality of poor liturgical libraries. The library of this Institute should heal this serious deficiency.

2. Oversee translations of 'classics' in Byzantine liturgical history and theology into Greek. For example, Robert Taft's books should be translated into Greek, an idea that the Archimandrite Patrikios Kaleodis has been promoting for some time and I believe all Greek liturgists are in agreement. Another such example is the translation of Hans-Joachim Schulz, *The Byzantine Liturgy: Symbolic Structure and Faith Expression* (New York, 1986) from the original German, *Die Byzantinische Liturgie* (Trier, 1980) into Greek by Dimitrios Tzerpos.[41] At the same time, good modern Greek liturgical studies should be translated into English making them available to a wider audience and giving publicity to the research and work of Greek liturgists.

   Attention should also be placed upon modern Russian liturgical scholarship, with translations in Greek of important articles and books.

3. Index and digitize the liturgical articles that appeared in hard-to-find Greek journals such as Ἐκκλησιαστικὴ Ἀλήθεια, Νέα Σιών, Ὀρθοδοξία, Γρηγόριος ὁ Παλαμᾶς, Πάνταινος, Ἐκκλησιαστικὸς Φάρος, one more idea of Patrikios Kaleodis, in a way creating the beginning of a Greek version of the ATLA database

4. Create and maintain a database of all liturgical manuscripts (the initial phase would include manuscripts housed in Greek collections), their location, call number, and if and where they have been published, microfilmed, or digitized.

5. Create and maintain a digital manuscript library with the assistance of centers with such an experience, such as the Center of Greek Medieval Studies and the Historical and Paleographical Archive of the Educational Foundation of the National Bank of Greece.

6. Create and maintain a database of dissertations on liturgical topics worldwide.

---

[41] Ἡ Βυζαντινή Λειτουργία. Μαρτυρία πίστεως καί συμβολική ἔκφραση (Athens, 1998).

7. Maintain an archive of syllabi of liturgy courses.
8. Encourage relations and facilitate contacts and cooperation between liturgists and experts in related fields.
9. Keep track of papers of liturgical interest delivered in liturgical and Byzantine conferences world-wide,[42] and catalogue paper topics submitted in these conferences.
10. Promote contact and co-operation among liturgists world-wide.
11. Become the contact-point for international liturgical scholars and researchers who want to work in Greece and support the work of young scholars working in the area of liturgy.
12. Publish a liturgical journal (which does not exist in Greece) and initiate a liturgical series of monographs.

Such a Center can also play an active and important role in the popular education of the clergy and the faithful regarding liturgical life and liturgical renewal. This could be done for example through pamphlets, open lectures and discussions and popular liturgical publications. Through its presence and work among clergy and laity this Institute could provide a popular forum of discussion, relieve the people of any wariness and distrust as to the nature, meaning, and purpose of liturgical renewal, and be a credible voice with convincing answers against the reservations, criticism and sometimes unfortunate slander voiced by some members of the Church arguing against liturgical renewal.

Important steps have been taken, new roads have been opened, new tools are available to us. Great challenges and a lot of work lie ahead of us. Inspired and guided by the pioneers of the Greek liturgical movement we need to work hard, dare, challenge, listen, understand, proclaim, teach, envision, pray, let the Holy Spirit guide our steps, since what we do is done for no other reason than to serve the Church.

---

[42] For example, conferences to keep track would be the following: the bi-annual international congress of the Society of Oriental Liturgies, the annual conference of the North American Academy of Liturgy, the bi-annual Societas Liturgica, the tri-annual Yale Worship Conference, the annual Semaine d'études liturgiques in Paris, the annual Byzantine Studies Conference (USA), the annual Συμπόσιο Βυζαντινής και Μεταβυζαντινής Αρχαιολογίας και Τέχνης, the Oxford Patristic Conference, the International Congress of Byzantine Studies (Belfast), the Byzantine Studies Spring Symposium (Dumbarton Oaks), and conferences with liturgical themes, such as the Vth International Theological Conference of the Russian Orthodox Church Orthodox Teaching on the Sacraments of the Church, (Moscow, 13–16 November 2007).

LITURGICAL RENEWAL MOVEMENT
IN CONTEMPORARY SERBIA

Nina GLIBETIĆ

Introduction[1]

When on June 5th, 2006, Bishop Jovan (Mladenović) issued an act in his diocese (Šumadija) instructing his presbyters to celebrate the Divine Liturgy with the holy doors open and to pronounce liturgical prayers aloud, he could not have predicted the far-reaching effect this document would have on the Orthodox Church in Serbia.[2] Not only did some of the faithful in his diocese, including clergy and monks, express great protest and dissidence,[3] but the Divine Liturgy became a key topic in the October regular Assembly of Bishops in Belgrade.[4] The discussions at the Holy Assembly resulted in the formation of the Committee for Research on Liturgical Questions, which includes members noted for contrasting views.[5] Until the findings of the Committee are accepted, the

---

[1] I would like to thank Gabriel Radle and Steven Hawkes-Teeples S.J., for their help in the writing and editing of this paper. I am also indebted to Professor Nenad Milošević who, through his lectures at the Theological Faculty of the Serbian Orthodox Church in Belgrade, was the first to inspire my curiosity on this subject. All translations from the Serbian original are my own.

[2] Jovan (Mladenović), Orthodox Bishop of the Šumadija Eparchy, document filed as E.br. 987, issued on 5 June 2006 in Kragujevac. The unpublished document instructs that all the prayers, from the First Prayer of the Faithful until the end of the Divine Liturgy, are said 'audibly, clearly and articulately'.

[3] Some disputes have been covered by the Press, for example: A. Milutinović, 'Истина о Венчанима и освећење темеља цркве светога Николаја у Тулежима', *Official Website of the Serbian Orthodox Church*: http://www.spc.rs/Vesti-2007/04/18-04-07-c.html#tul (accessed 24 January, 2009); M. Pešić, 'Ко навлачи завесу на црквене двери', *Politika Online*: http://www.politika.rs/rubrike/Drustvo/Ko-navlachi-zavesu-na-crkvene-dveri.sr.html (accessed 24 January 2009).

[4] Communications of Holy Assemblies are published in *Православље*, the bimonthly official newspaper of the Serbian Patriarchate. See 'Саопштење за јавност: редовно друго заседање Светог архијерејског сабора Српске Православне Цркве, одржаног у Београду од 4. до 8. октобра 2006. године', *Православље* 950 (Belgrade, 15 October 2006), pp. 2-3.

[5] The committee was formed on 6 October 2006. Its members are: the president, Metropolitan Jovan (Pavlović), Bishop Georgije (Djokić), Bishop Hrizostom (Stolić), Bishop Irinej (Bulović), Bishop Atanasije (Jevtić), Bishop Ignatije (Midić).

Holy Assembly has requested that the 'established, centuries-old' liturgical tradition of the Serbian Orthodox Church be maintained in every
diocese ['држати се устаљеног вековног поретка наше Цркве'].[6]
Bishop Jovan subsequently annulled his act and the tension in his diocese somewhat calmed. However, there soon emerged a challenge
regarding a larger liturgical question. Namely, it became clear that in
Serbia the Divine Liturgy is celebrated in different ways and the faithful,
including hierarchy and laity, are not always in agreement regarding
what constitutes 'the established, centuries-old' Serbian liturgical tradition.

At the risk of speaking too generally, one can discern two tendencies
in these debates with regard to the liturgical question. There are those
who want certain practices abandoned because they see them as contrary
to the Serbian, and more broadly, the Orthodox liturgical tradition
and there are those who oppose these changes, seeing them as contra-
dicting the established Orthodox liturgical tradition. The former have
spontaneously implemented reforms in worship on the parish level, a
move criticized by the latter as, among other things, betraying the tradition of the Serbian Orthodox Church. What lies behind these debates is
a tension between a spontaneous and still emerging liturgical movement
and a critical reaction against this movement. Our intention in the following pages is to offer a preliminary description. We will do so by
examining the general characteristics of this movement, the specific
liturgical reforms being implemented by it, and the historical circumstances that led to it. Lastly, we hope to show that the liturgical reforms
belong to an overall ecclesial renewal, one seeking a more authentic
expression of life in Christ.

1. Sources

Before describing the movement, some brief remarks about the
sources are in order. Because the liturgical movement in Serbia is contemporary to the writing of this essay, books and academic studies
on this subject are lacking.[7] In addition, unlike the liturgical rebirth

---

[6] 'Свети архијерејски сабор Српске Православне Цркве: саопштење за
јавност са редовног заседања одржаног у Београду од 14. до 25. маја 2007.
године', *Православље* 965 (Belgrade 1 July 2007), pp. 2-3.

[7] At the same time, the topic of liturgical renewal is not new in Serbia. For example,
see the discussions at the first and second *Catechetical Symposium* held in Belgrade in

movement in Greece described by Pavlos Koumarianos at the 2006 Society of Oriental Liturgies conference, the Assembly of Bishops of the Serbian Orthodox Church has not organized conferences nor published encyclicals on this subject and the Committee for Research on Liturgical Questions has yet to issue its findings.[8] For someone researching the movement, the sources are limited and often polemical, and the information is scattered. There are public debates, some of which have been published on-line or in various journals such as *Православље*, the official magazine of the Patriarchate.[9] Personal letters, usually of complaint, have been written and addressed to the Holy Synod.[10] One can find a growing number of articles and books published in Serbia dealing with the liturgy.[11] Finally, controversial brochure-type literature opposed to the renewal is easily available, ever proliferating

---

1980 and 1981: 'Парохиja као жива молитвена заједница: Први Катихетски Симпосион Архиепископије београдско-карловачке', *Теолошки Погледи* XIII (Belgrade, 1980) 3, pp. 73-161; 'Свете тајне и живот парохије: Други Катихетски Симпосион Архиепископије београдско-карловачке', *Теолошки Погледи* XVI (Belgrade, 1981) 1-3, pp. 1-79. For a more recent work discussing twentieth-century liturgical reform in Byzantine-rite churches see: Marcel Mojzeš, *Il movimento liturgico nelle chiese bizantine: Analisi di alcune tendenze di riforma nel XX secolo* (Rome, 2003). This book does not discuss the Orthodox Church in Serbia, but the recently published 3-volume work of the theologian and liturgist, Bishop Atanasije (Jevtić), does: A. Jevtić, *Христос – Нова Пасха: Божанствена Литургија*, 3 vols. (Belgrade-Trebinje, 2007-2008).

[8] Pavlos Koumarianos, 'Liturgical "Rebirth" in the Church of Greece Today: A Doubtful Effort of Liturgical Reform', *Bollettino della Badia Greca di Grottaferrata* III, 4 (2007) 119-144.

[9] For some examples, see the letter written by the editors of *Banatski Vesnik*: 'О Светој Литургији и променама у њој', *Банатски Весник* LXVI (Vršac, December 2006) 3-4, pp. 1-9, and the reply of Bishop Atanasije: A. Jevtić, 'О Божанској Литургији – Пасхи Господњој и нашој', *Православље* 961 (Belgrade, 1 April 2007), pp. 10-12.

[10] For example, see the letters of Bishop Jefrem (Milutinović) and Bishop Georgije (Djokić) addressed to the Holy Assembly of Bishops and published in *Православље*: J. Milutinović, 'Нарушавање богослужбеног поретка', *Православље* 968 (Belgrade, 15 July 2007), pp. 6-8; G. Djokić, 'Традиционално и савремено богослужење', *Православље* 968 (Belgrade, 15 July 2007, pp. 9-17. Bishop Atanasije replied to both these letters: A. Jevtić, 'О обнови литургијског живота, а не промени или реформи Литургије', *Православље* 968 (Belgrade, 15 July 2007), pp. 18-26.

[11] In recent decades, many works dealing with the history and theology of Orthodox worship have been published in Serbia. Primary source material important for the study of Christian worship has also been translated and issued. Additionally, one can find books opposed to the liturgical movement, for example: V. Dimitrijević, *Писма о литургијској обнови* (Gornji Milanovac, 2008); Grešni Miloje, *Не помичи старе међе: писма и разговори*, 2d ed. (Gornji Milanovac, 2008). The latter and similar works are almost always polemical in tone and content.

and triggering disagreements.[12] To comprehend more fully the situation as it emerges, one must also engage in active field work by attending local liturgies and in this way discover what the initiatives are first hand.

2. Description of the Movement

Contemporary liturgical renewal in Serbia is neither systematic nor an official, institutional undertaking. Despite some non-spontaneous elements, such as the previously described act issued by Bishop Jovan, it is a spontaneous movement, one without a clearly defined program of implementation.[13] This spontaneous quality is partly an outcome of contemporary historical circumstances. The Turkish and Austro-Hungarian occupations, the two world wars and the Communist era have for centuries created difficult situations for the Serbian Orthodox Church, leaving little room for mystagogical reflection. However, with the collapse of the Communist government and the growing interest in tradition and faith identity, the Church has begun to recuperate. In the words of Oliver Subotić, 'the time in which we live is characterized by a massive rejection of the previous atheistic ideology and by a great interest in ecclesial-liturgical life'.[14] This growing interest has created an impetus for theological reflection, which has in turn inspired liturgical reforms. Comparing the situation to the one after the Edict of Milan in 313, Subotić continues:

'The question which appeared then, and which also appears now, is the following: in what way can we preserve the authentic liturgical expression according to which the Eastern Church lives and breathes, but also satisfy the religious needs of the great number of the newly converted [нововеруjyħиx] who feel that their place is in the Body of the Church, but who still do not have the necessary spiritual sensitivity [истанчаност] relating to the Liturgy.'[15]

---

[12] Some examples are: V. Dimitrijević, *Хлеб небески и чаша живота* (Gornji Milanovac, 2007); *Посни Календар за 2008. годину* (Lipovac, 2008).

[13] For a discussion of 'spontaneous' and 'non-spontaneous' liturgical reform, see the excellent doctoral dissertation defended at the Pontifical Oriental Institute in Rome: Thomas Pott, *La réforme liturgique Byzantine: Etude du phénomène de l'évolution non-spontanée de la liturgie byzanine*, Bibliotheca 'Ephemerides liturgicae'. Subsidia 104 (Rome, 2000).

[14] O. Subotić, 'Повратак литургијској побожности', *Православље* 931-932 (Belgrade, 15 January 2006), pp. 28-29, on p. 28.

[15] Subotić, 'Повратак' (see n. 14), p. 28.

Alongside a dawning ecclesial movement is a growing number of Serbian people who identify themselves as Orthodox Christians but who have undergone little or no catechetical instruction. Their return is not infrequently accompanied by an overemphasized sense of national identity, and results in a narrowly conservative attitude, one aimed at preserving what they consider to be the authentic Serbian liturgical tradition. Because such a mentality is often paired with little theological education and infrequent liturgical participation, every perceived change in worship is experienced as a betrayal of the Serbian tradition and as a self-willed 'innovation' [новотарија], and rejected on these grounds.[16] This, at least in part, explains the controversies surrounding the liturgical movement.

Those involved in the movement have replied to these and similar accusations. According to them, the fundamental issue is not '"change" [промена] or "reform" [реформа] of the Holy Liturgy, but ... the renewal of us all in the Church through the renewal of our Christian, Orthodox, evangelical, liturgical life and existence'.[17] Or, in the words of Bishop Irinej (Bulović), what is at stake is 'our [personal] rebirth, the renewal of our own mind, heart and entire being'.[18] These writers avoid using the word 'reform' for seemingly two reasons: firstly, because it labels the liturgical movement as only implementing formal, structural changes in the liturgical action without taking into account its broader scope, including an overall ecclesial renewal.[19] Secondly, for the sake of dialogue, because the word 'reform' is regarded by many as designating an action that breaks away from the tradition of the Church.[20] The liturgical movement therefore – and the term 'movement' is here used loosely, to connote something not formally organized – has as its primary aim not the reform of worship but the renewal of Christian life. For this very reason, those involved in the renewal hold that the Liturgical

---

[16] For example: G. Miloje, *Не помичи* (see n. 11), p. 14.

[17] A. Jevtić, 'О обнови' (see n. 10), p. 18.

[18] See I. Bulović, Introduction to *На путу ка литургијском препороду*, by N. Balašov, trans. K. Končarević and K. Simić, 2 vols. (Novi Sad, 2007), vol.1, pp. 1-7, on p. 3.

[19] *Ibid.*, p. 3.

[20] The title of Bishop Atanasije's article is revealing. It translates as: 'The Renewal of Liturgical Life and Not Change or Reform of the Liturgy' (see n. 10). See the use of the word 'reform' by Bishop Georgije (Djokić): 'Традиционално' (see n. 10), p. 10. Though the word 'reform' is employed in this article, we use it to designate concrete, visible changes in the way worship is conducted. In other words, 'reforms' are a part of a larger movement, which in this case has as its aim the renewal of Christian life.

Committee can in fact come to a conclusion that a particular change in worship is desired. Such a change ought to be understood as a 'renewal' [обнова] of the 'forgotten, missed or suppressed centuries-old practice of ecumenical Orthodoxy' and not as a self-willed innovation.[21] The aim of such a change would be to bring the faithful closer to the truth on which the entire Orthodox tradition rests.

Despite its spontaneous quality, it is particular bishops who are at the center of the renewal, the majority of whom were educated in the Church Fathers as part of the broader Neo-Patristic movement. These include the retired Bishop Atanasije (Jevtić), from the Bosnian eparchy of Zahumsko-Hercegovačka. Primarily a patristic scholar, Bishop Atanasije is also a noted liturgical theologian and historian of the liturgy. He is the most vocal defender of the liturgical movement and has published extensively on the subject.[22] Another important figure is Bishop Irinej (Bulović) of the Bačka diocese and the dean of the Theological Faculty of the Serbian Orthodox Church in Belgrade.[23] His diocese, located in one of the most multi-cultural regions of Serbia, has seen a number of liturgical initiatives, including the translation and celebration of the Divine Liturgy into the Roma Gypsy language. Bishop Hrizostom (Stolić) of the historical diocese of Žiča also has an important role in this movement. His diocese is the seat of the first Serbian archeparchy, established by St Sava of the Nemanjić dynasty. Bishop Hrizostom is responsible for the writing and translation of important liturgical works and the publication of service books.[24] Though not as outwardly vocal as Bishop Atanasije, Bishop Hrizostom's diocese has struggled with the most protest and dissidence.[25] Another important figure is Amfilohije

---

[21] A. Jevtić, 'О обнови' (see n. 10), p. 18.

[22] Besides his already cited books and articles (see n. 7, 9, 10) consult: A. Jevtić, *О Цркви и Литургији* (Vrnjci, 2005); A. Jevtić, *Осам Предавања о Светој Литургији* (Vrnjci, 2008). In English: A. Yevtich, *Christ: The Alpha and Omega* (Vrnjačka Banja, 2007). The same work is available in Greek: A. Jevtić, Χριστός, Ἡ Χώρα τῶν Ζώντων (Athens, 2007).

[23] Consult: I. Bulović, 'Introduction' (see n. 18).

[24] H. Stolić, *Божанствена Литургија Светога апостола Јакова* (Belgrade, 1985); H. Stolić, 'О Хиландарском Типику', *Банатски Весник* 58 (Vršac, 1998) 1-2, pp. 11-13; *Литургија Апостолских Установа*, trans. and ed. H. Stolić (Kraljevo, 2004). Bishop Hrizostom has also initiated the publication of *Menaia* containing hymnographical texts for Serbian saints. For centuries and due to difficult historical circumstances, Serbia has been using Russian and Ukrainian *Menaia*. The Srbljak (in Serbian: *Србљак*), a supplementary book containing offices for Serbian saints, filled the gap.

[25] Liturgical reform was given as the reason for a 'hunger strike' by three priests from the small town of Čačak. The priests insisted that they were moved to a different parish

(Radović), the Metropolitan of Montenegro. He supports the liturgical movement and has replaced Patriarch Pavle during his long hospitalization.[26] This list is by no means exhaustive and the movement extends to include other people with diverse vocations in the Church, including laity, clergy, monks, students and professors.

One cannot talk about liturgical renewal in Serbia without mentioning the influence of the Theological Faculty of the Serbian Orthodox Church. The faculty was only in 2004 reintroduced into the University of Belgrade, following its exclusion by the Communists in 1952. At the faculty, the lectures on liturgics by Professor Nenad Milošević are some of the most popular and controversial, and always fill the lecture hall.[27] In addition to these lectures, Milošević has introduced the celebration of the complete daily liturgical cycle in the university chapel, a practice that has for many become the center of student life. These celebrations,

---

because they refused to celebrate according to the 'new rite' [нови обред]. See A. Arsenijević, 'Светосавље наспрам екуменизма', *Чачанске Новине* (Čačak, 5 February 2008), pp. 6-7; Н. Р., 'Свештеници прекинули протест', *Чачански Глас* (Čačak, 8. February 2008), p. 5; 'Саопштење за јавност Епархије жичке', *Чачански Глас* (Čačak, 8. February 2008), p. 5; S. Marković, 'Докле тако, Ваше Преосвештенство', *Чачанске Новине* (Čačak, 11 March 2008), pp. 10-11. In the small town of Duškovci, a group of people, protesting inside the church building during the celebration of the Divine Liturgy, attempted to physically prohibit Bishop Hrizostom (Stolić) from leaving. See B. Kerkezović, 'Истином на лаж', *Православље* 991 (Belgrade, 1 July 2008), pp. 12-13; Regent Archpriests of the Eparchy of Žiča, 'Саопштење Архиерејских намесника Епархије жичке', *Православље* 991 (Belgrade, 1 July 2008) p. 9; A. Jevtić, 'О пагубним новотаријама тзв. ревнитеља „старог начина служења"', *Православље* 991 (Belgrade, 1 July 2008), pp. 10-11.

[26] See his homily delivered in the Patriarchate chapel (Belgrade) and quoted on the Official Website of the Serbian Orthodox Church: 'О преовладавању суштине над формом у литургијском животу наше Цркве', 12. August 2008, *Official Website of the Serbian Orthodox Church*: http://www.spc.rs/sr/arhiepiskop_amfilohije_o_preovladavanju_sustine_nad_formom_u_liturgijskom_zivotu_nase_crkve (accessed 25 January 2009). (Patriarch Pavle died on 15 November 2009; note of the editors.)

[27] I provide here a partial bibliography of Milošević's works: N. Milošević, Ἡ θεία Εὐχαριστία ὡς κέντρο τῆς θείας λατρείας: Ἡ σύνδεσις τῶν μυστηρίων μετὰ τῆς θείας Εὐχαριστίας (Thessalonica, 2001); N. Milošević, 'Римска Литургија', *Богословље* (Belgrade, 2002) 1, pp. 19-37; 'Последовање тритекти или треће-шестог часа', *Богословље* (Belgrade, 2002) 2, pp. 69-89; 'Последовање панихиде', *Богословље* (Belgrade, 2003) 1-2, pp. 25-40; 'Света тајна исповести и покајања', *Беседа* (Novi Sad, 2004) 6, pp. 111-118; 'Протојереј Лазар Мирковић као литургичар', *Српска теологија у двадесетом веку* 1 (Belgrade, 2007), pp. 29-37; 'Епископ др. Сава Вуковић као литургичар', *Српска теологија у двадесетом веку* 2 (Belgrade, 2007), pp. 129-133; 'Евхаристиско богословље Светога Игнатија Богоносца на примеру тајне брака', *Видослов* 42 (Tvrdoš-Trebinje, 2007), pp. 109-114. I am grateful to Milan Jovanović, graduate student at the Theological Faculty of the Serbian Orthodox Church, who provided me with these bibliographical references.

including frequent all-night vigils, allow students to go beyond mere scholarship and enjoy a living understanding of worship. Another key initiative put forth by Milošević and inspired by his Greek mentor, Professor Ioannis Fountoulis, has been the weekly celebration of diverse liturgies found in history throughout the East, some of which are rarely or no longer celebrated by Christians today (an example is a reconstruction of the Divine Liturgy found in the *Apostolic Constitutions*). This initiative exposes Milošević's students to the dynamic pluralism found in liturgical practice and inspires a deeper reflection on the nature of Christian worship. Recently, and already celebrating in a spirit similar to the one existing at the Theological Faculty, a small chapel has been consecrated at the University of Belgrade's student Residence Hall. One must also mention the seminary in Kragujevac. Considering that youth make up by far the largest percentage of practicing Orthodox Christians in Serbia, the influence of these educational institutions is quite significant.[28] To the list we can also add specific monasteries, such as Žiča, Kovilj and Gradac, along with parishes throughout the country, where the liturgical life has been visibly affected by the renewal.

3. Specific Reforms

Having described in broad strokes some of the main characteristics of the liturgical movement, we now examine the specific reforms in worship which have already been implemented on the parish level. These reforms have been primarily restricted to the Divine Liturgy. Due to the spontaneous nature of the movement, they have not been introduced in a consistent manner but by partial implementation; various combinations of specific reforms are evident in actual practice.

a. Holy Communion

A central, visible change inspired by the liturgical movement is the frequent reception of holy communion. In his thirteenth-century partial translation of the Evergetis Typicon, from the Constantinopolitan monastery of the same name, St Sava, the first Serbian archbishop, upheld frequent communion as a Christian ideal.[29] Over the centuries however,

[28] Subotić, 'Повратак' (see n. 14), pp. 28-29.
[29] Saint Sava, *Хиландарски Типик Светога Саве*, trans. L. Mirković (Belgrade, 1935).

and especially during the Ottoman occupation, this practice fell into disuse. The contemporary liturgical movement encourages frequent communion, as is evident in churches affected by the movement.[30] Reminding that the Church is first of all a 'liturgical or an eucharistic community' ['литургијска или евхаристијска заједница'], Bishop Irinej (Bulović) cites the Gospel of John to show the centrality of communion in the Christian life: 'In all truth I tell you, if you do not eat the flesh of the Son of Man and drink his blood, you have no life in you' (John 6:53).[31] In Bishop Irinej's words: 'participating in the Eucharist and receiving [причешћивати се] the Bread of life and the True drink means having eternal life in the present and living in joyful expectation of the future resurrection'.[32]

Frequent communion is in contrast to common practices in the Serbian Orthodox Church, such as the faithful receiving only on Easter Sunday and Christmas, or clergy not allowing the faithful to receive outside the four major fasts. In churches affected by the renewal, communion always takes place at the time prescribed by the *Služebnik*, that is, following the communion of the clergy, and is never left for the end of the Divine Liturgy. The latter is an occasional practice in parishes throughout the country, especially during principal feasts.

b. The Relationship Between Fasting and Communion

Discussing different ways in which the relationship between fasting and communion is understood by the faithful, Patriarch Pavle writes: 'we must save ourselves from every extreme and every one-sidedness'.[33] The patriarch is referring to different practices evident in the Serbian Orthodox Church with regard to fasting in the preparation for holy communion. For example, in churches not affected by the renewal, it is common for a priest to question those approaching the chalice if they have prepared. This question refers to a week-long fast 'on water' ['на води'], that is, a week-long abstinence from any animal product and oil prior to communion. The practice seems to have become widespread in

---

[30] In some monasteries, such as Žiča and Gradac, the Divine Liturgy is celebrated every morning unless otherwise prescribed by the Typicon.

[31] *The New Jerusalem Bible: Pocket Edition* (New York, 1990).

[32] I. Bulović, 'Introduction' (see n. 18), pp. 1-2.

[33] Patriarch Pavle, 'О посту и причешћивању', *Православље* 953 (Belgrade, 1 December 2006), pp. 2-3, on p. 3.

the eighteenth century, though this has yet to be studied in a systematic way.[34] For now, we can hypothesize that the practice developed in order to enable those who attended the Liturgy infrequently to approach the sacrament by preparing in such a way. While exceptions are made due to illness or similar circumstances, the week-long fast is today considered a mandatory step in the preparation for holy communion by many Serbian faithful, even by those in church regularly. They defend the practice as a necessary ascetic dimension of church life.[35]

According to those involved in the liturgical movement, the week-long fast betrays the canons of the Orthodox Church, such as those of the Quinisext council, which forbid fasting on Saturdays and Sundays.[36] In parishes affected by the renewal, liturgically active faithful keep the regular fasts all the while receiving communion at every Divine Liturgy. Both fasting and communion may be occasionally restricted by the spiritual father or the parish priest, when a theologically sound reason presents itself.[37] In Metropolitan Amfilohije's words: 'who am I to deny the Lord to the one who fasts every Wednesday and Friday and all four annual fasts, who lives in the spirit of repentance and according to a Christian life?'.[38]

c. Marriage and Baptism Celebrated Within the Context of the Divine Liturgy

Insisting that marriage and baptism are not private but communal acts which involve the entire ecclesial body, when possible, churches affected by the liturgical movement celebrate both sacraments within the context of the Divine Liturgy. Their effort has not gone without criticism. Describing the two sacraments as a private family matter, Bishop Georgije (Djokić) asserts that their celebration within the context of the Divine Liturgy disrupts the communal prayer of the faithful.[39] His criticism seems to be motivated by an unfortunate pastoral reality: because

---

[34] V. Vukašinović, 'Библијско и светотајинско богословље у Карловачкој Митрополији XVIII. века' (Ph.D. diss., University of Belgrade, 2007), pp. 162-163.

[35] For example: V. Dimitrijević, *Хлеб небески* (see n. 12), pp. 29-33//54-56.

[36] A. Jevtić, 'Литургијски мир и јединство у нашој Цркви', *Православље* 973 (Belgrade, 1 October 2007), pp. 6-8, on p. 8; Jevtić, *Христос* (see n. 7), vol. 1, p. 23.

[37] Patriarch Pavle, 'О посту' (see n. 33), p. 3. Though Bishop Georgije (Djokić) is critical of the liturgical movement, on this subject he agrees: 'Традиционално' (see n. 10), pp. 15-16.

[38] A. Radović, 'О преовладавању' (see n. 26).

[39] G. Djokić, 'Традиционално' (see n. 10), p. 16.

many faithful do not personally know those being baptized or married, they do not experience the celebration of these sacraments within the Divine Liturgy as belonging to the entire ecclesial Body.

d. The Use of Holy Doors

We mentioned the debates over the use of holy doors in the introduction of this article, when describing the act issued by Bishop Jovan (Mladenović), in which he instructs the clergy of his diocese to keep the holy doors open throughout the Divine Liturgy. This seems to be the general practice in churches affected by the liturgical movement. Metropolitan Amfilohije (Radojević), in a homily delivered at the Patriarchate chapel, states: 'do not the closed doors and the silent reading of [liturgical] prayers keep the lay faithful from an essential understanding of the Holy Liturgy? If the curtain was torn in the Jewish temple at the moment of Christ's death, who are we to put it up again…?'.[40]

Contrary to the liturgical books of his day, the twentieth-century Serbian theologian, Justin Popović, spiritual father to many of the bishops involved in the contemporary renewal, does not mention the use of holy doors in his 1978 translation of the Divine Liturgy into Serbian, except at communion.[41] It was probably his intention to reduce rubrical instructions in Serbian liturgical books, because it is clear from video footage and photographs that he used the holy doors. Rubrics concerning the doors are listed in the 2001 Church Slavonic Moscow *Služebnik*, used in parishes throughout the country, whereas the 2007 *Služebnik* in Serbian does not mention them.[42] In churches unaffected by the renewal, doors and curtains are both employed in non-pontifical celebrations of the Divine Liturgy.

e. The Prothesis Rite and the Particles for the Holy Angels

In churches affected by the renewal, the practice of taking out particles for the Holy Angels in the prothesis rite has been restored. Justin Popović re-introduced the same in his translation, indicating the practice in older Slavic liturgical books and arguing that it ought to be used

---

[40] A. Radović, 'О преовладавању' (see n. 26).
[41] J. Popović, *Божанствене Литургије* (Belgrade, 1978), pp. 72//130.
[42] Holy Archiepiscopal Synod of the Serbian Orthodox Church, *Служебник* (Belgrade, 2007).

because it brings to light the cosmic dimension of Christian worship.[43] Bishop Atanasije shows that this practice fell into disuse in Serbia with the introduction of Russian liturgical books in the eighteenth and nineteenth centuries.[44]

f. Censing

Insisting on the importance for the faithful to hear biblical readings, those involved in the renewal encourage censing during the *Alleluia* and not during the Epistle reading.[45]

g. Liturgical Homily

Seeking to restore the traditional order of the Divine Liturgy, in churches affected by the renewal, the liturgical homily, when delivered, is always done after the reading of the gospel. This is contrary to the common practice of leaving the homily for the end of the Divine Liturgy. The latter is justified by those opposed to the reforms on pastoral grounds. For example, though Bishop Georgije (Djokić) does indicate that the homily was traditionally delivered after the gospel reading, he argues that for the sake of those arriving late to the Divine Liturgy it is best that it be left for the end.[46]

h. Litanies

In some though not all churches affected by the renewal, the litany for the catechumens and the dismissal that follows are no longer said.

i. The Reading of Liturgical Prayers in an Audible Voice

In churches where liturgical reforms have been implemented, the general practice is to pronounce liturgical prayers in an audible voice. A common exception is the so-called *Nemo dignus* prayer, considered to be a personal prayer of the celebrant. One of the effects of this reform is

---

[43] J. Popović, *Божанствене* (see n. 41), pp. 230-231.

[44] A. Jevtić, *Христос* (see n. 7), vol. 3, pp. 375//379. Also consult: V. Vukašinović, 'Библијско' (see n. 34), pp. 225-226.

[45] The same is encouraged by those opposed to the renewal: G. (Djokić), 'Традиционално' (see n. 10), p. 12.

[46] *Ibid.*, p. 12.

the return to only saying 'It is right and proper' at the opening dialogue of the anaphora, without the words 'to worship Father, Son, and Holy Spirit, Trinity one in essence and undivided'. Those involved in the liturgical movement argue that the audible recitation of liturgical prayers helps reveal the Eucharist as a sacrifice offered by the entire assembly. In Bishop Irinej's words, the faithful ought to be 'the royal priesthood and concelebrants', instead of mere 'passive observers'.[47] By pronouncing liturgical prayers aloud, it is thought that the occasional tendency toward clericalism evident among both laity and clergy in the Serbian Orthodox Church could at least partly be overcome.[48] Opponents of the practice hold that the silent reading of prayers can reveal the liturgy of the Church as a communal act which does involve the entire assembly. Bishop Georgije (Djokić) argues that praying the anaphora in an audible voice actually impedes the active participation of the lay faithful because it turns them into passive listeners.[49] It is preferable, he concludes, that the faithful participate in the Eucharistic offering by means of personal prayer or singing, while the celebrant silently reads these essentially private prayers of the clergy.[50] Similarly, Father Dušan Kolundzić argues that the reading of liturgical prayers in an audible voice does not solve the problem of clericalism. For him, only through catechetical instruction can the faithful develop an authentic understanding of their role in the Divine Liturgy.[51]

j. Troparia of the Third Hour

In churches effected by the renewal, troparia of the Third Hour are no longer said within the context of the Divine Liturgy. This is because they are seen as unnecessary fortifications of the epiclesis, interpolated into the Divine Liturgy for polemical reasons. However, even prior to the contemporary liturgical movement, there was a growing awareness of this problem. For example, in his 1942 translation of the Divine Liturgy into modern Serbian, Bishop Irinej (Dobić) shows a more critical

---

[47] I. Bulović, 'Introduction' (see n. 18), p. 2.

[48] S. Dobić, 'О Светој Литургији и читању литургијских молитава на глас', *Православље* 981 (Belgrade, 1 February 2008) pp. 6-9, on p. 9. See the reply of D. Kolundzić, 'О читању литургијских молитава на глас', *Православље* 984 (Belgrade, 15 March 2008), pp. 16-17.

[49] G. Djokić, 'Традиционално' (see n. 10), p. 14.

[50] *Ibid.*, pp. 14-15.

[51] D. Kolundzić, 'О читању' (see n. 48), p. 17.

assessment of the Serbian liturgical practice by indicating that these troparia are not said in the Greek Church.[52] Some years later, Justin Popović in his translation placed these troparia in brackets, reasoning that 'while it is not up to us at this time to omit them, it is also not up to us to include them without indicating their more recent introduction into the Liturgy'.[53] Today, Bishop Atanasije (Jevtić) argues that the use of these troparia within the Divine Liturgy is not witnessed in Serbian liturgical manuscripts and early printed books and is also not authentic to Orthodox liturgical theology.[54] For these reasons, he concludes, the troparia should be removed from both the Chrysostom and the Basil anaphoras.

Other practices seen as isolating one section of the anaphora as having particular consecratory power, have also been abandoned by those involved in the reforms. Some examples of these practices include the lay faithful kneeling during the Words of Institution and/or during the epiclesis, the ringing of small bells during the anaphora or the priestly gesture of blessing the holy gifts during the Words of Institution. However, these gestures were not universally present even before the reforms.

With all these reforms and various reactions to them, we can generally observe two tendencies being revealed in the Serbian Orthodox Church today. On the one side – and the word 'side' is here used reluctantly, for it is never helpful to speak about 'sides' when describing the Church – there are those who want liturgical reforms brought about because they see the reforms as authentic to Orthodox worship and theology. On the other side, there are those, such as Bishop Georgije (Djokić) and Bishop Jefrem (Milutinović), who describe the reforms as betraying the established Serbian Orthodox tradition. Both hold that they are abiding by the Holy Assembly's wish to celebrate in line with the spirit and centuries-old tradition of Serbian Orthodox Church.[55] How can this discrepancy be explained?

---

[52] *Недеља Свете Педесетнице: празничне службе*, trans. Bishop Irinej Ćirić (Ujvidek, 1942), p. 320.

[53] J. Popović, *Божанствене* (see n. 41), p. 229.

[54] A. Jevtić, *Христос* (see n. 7), vol. 2, pp. 134-148//360-373. Consult also Serbian manuscript evidence: V. Vukašinović, 'Библијско' (see n. 34), pp. 226-228.

[55] J. Milutinović, 'Нарушавање' (see n. 10), pp. 6-7; A. Jevtić, 'О обнови' (see n. 10), p. 18.

4. Metropolitanate of Karlovci

According to Bishop Atanasije (Jevtić), the most vocal supporter of the liturgical movement, what his critics consider to be the established liturgical tradition in Serbia is a more recent development in Serbian worship, which came about between the seventeenth and the nineteenth centuries.[56] This development, which was originally limited to the Metropolitanate of Karlovci, gradually became standard Serbian practice. Unfortunately, the changes in worship introduced at Karlovci, though explainable given the historical context in which they developed, have, according to Bishop Atanasije, led Serbian worship away from a liturgy that most authentically expresses the Orthodox faith. The transformation that he and others involved in the contemporary liturgical movement in Serbia are referring to will occupy us for remainder of this article. For without understanding this historical context, the liturgical renewal taking place in Serbia today cannot be understood.[57]

The history of the Metropolitanate of Karlovci, located in northern Serbia in the region today known as Vojvodina, is intimately connected to the large exodus of Serbs fleeing Ottoman rule following the Austro-Turkish war.[58] Though this migration began as early as the fourteenth century, it was in 1690 that Patriarch Arsenije III (Čarnojević, 1674-1706) led 40,000 people over the Danube River and into the Austro-Hungarian Empire. By that time, a significant number of Serbs were already living in that empire and this ethnic continuity allowed the refugees to adapt more easily to their new surroundings.[59]

However, the circumstances in which Serbs found themselves also brought new challenges. For the first time, the Serbian people were confronted with the ideas and prejudices of enlightenment rationalism and with the polemics of post-reformation Europe.[60] Deprived of their

---

[56] A. Jevtić, 'О обнови' (see n. 10), pp. 19-22; A. Jevtić, *Христос* (see n. 7), vol. 3, pp. 382-384. Consult also Bishop Atanasije's important article: A. Jevtić, 'Развој богословља код Срба', *Теолошки Погледи* XVI (Belgrade, 1982) 3-4, pp. 81-104.

[57] For a general study of Serbian Church history consult Dj. Slijepčević, *Историја Српске Православне Цркве*, 3 vols. (Munich, 1966). For a general history of Serbia, consult the well-known work: K. Juriček, *Историја Срба*, 2 vols., 2nd ed. (Belgrade, 1952).

[58] Dj. Slijepčević, *Историја* (see n. 57), vol. 1, pp. 373-374; V. Vukašinović, 'Библијско' (see n. 34), p. 7.

[59] V. Vukašinović, 'Библијско' (see n. 34), p. 7. For a general study on Serbs in Vojvodina prior to the 1690 migration, consult R. Grujić, *Духовни живот у Војводини: 1. до Велике Сеобе од 1690. год.* (Novi Sad, 1939).

[60] V. Vukašinović, 'Библијско' (see n. 34), pp. 7-12.

political and – with the cancellation of the Serbian patriarchate in 1766
– religious autonomy, they felt the need to defend their identity.[61] This
task was made especially difficult living in a heavily Catholic empire
and confronting explicit pressure toward union with Rome.[62] All these
circumstances resulted in what is sometimes described as a process of
'Russification' of Serbian Church and culture.[63] Realizing that the preservation of their spiritual identity demanded higher education, Serbs
turned to Russia for help.[64] Because even basic conditions for education, such as good schools, adequately trained teachers and books, were
lacking, Orthodox Russia, sharing a similar language and alphabet with
Serbs, was seen as an ideal ally.[65] Soon, promising students were sent
north, especially to Kiev, to study theology at the well-known Kievan
Academy.[66] By the eighteenth century this trend would result in the
systematization of Serbian education and the opening of the first 'Sla-
vonic-Latin' schools.[67] In 1727, Metropolitan Mojsije (Petrović) opened
a new primary school [основна школа] and the Russian Maxim Suvo-
rov, sent by the Synod of the Russian Orthodox Church, became its first
teacher.[68] Six years later, Metropolitan Vikentije Jovanović opened a
High School [средња школа, or гимназија] leaving another Russian,
Emmanuel Kozačinski, in charge.[69] The primary schools opened during
this period taught the Slavonic alphabet along with fundamentals such
as arithmetic, grammar and simple spiritual works.[70] In the High
Schools, students were taught theology from the so-called 'Slavonic-
Latin' manuals and catecheses, brought to Serbia from the east.[71]
Russian works, including liturgical books, were imported and already

---

[61] A. Jevtić, 'Развој' (see n. 56), pp. 97-98.

[62] Dj. Slijepčević, *Историја* (see n. 57), vol. 1, pp. 414-429.

[63] V. Vukašinović, 'Библијско' (see n. 34), p. 198.

[64] Ibid., pp. 8//197-200. For a general historical discussion on Serbian-Russian relations, consult Dj. Slijepčević, *Историја* (see n. 57), pp. 402-414.

[65] V. Vukašinović, 'Библијско' (see n. 34), p. 198; A. Jevtić, 'Развој' (see n. 56),
p. 100.

[66] Dj. Slijepčević, *Историја* (see n. 57), p. 412.

[67] V. Vukašinović, 'Библијско' (see n. 34), pp. 201-211. For an overview of education at Karlovci, see R. Grujić, *Српске школе у Београдско–карловачкој митрополији*
(Belgrade, 1908).

[68] Dj. Slijepčević, *Историја* (see n. 57), p. 412; R. Grujić, *Духовни живот* (see
n. 59), pp. 31-41.

[69] V. Vukašinović, 'Библијско' (see n. 34), p. 201.

[70] *Ibid.*, p. 201; R. Grujić, *Духовни живот* (see n.. 59), pp. 82-90.

[71] V. Vukašinović extensively discusses the history, contents and use of catecheses:
'Библијско' (see n. 34), pp. 50-91.

by the middle of the eighteenth century – a relatively short amount of time – the Russian version of Church Slavonic, today simply known as Church Slavonic, had replaced the previously used Serbian recension in worship.[72] The wide-spread introduction of Russian liturgical books, such as the *Minej*, *Trebnik* and *Službenik*, meant also the introduction of liturgical elements specific to Russia, such as feasts commemorating Russian saints, or peculiarities in the celebration of the Divine Liturgy previously unused in Serbia.[73] A parallel process of Russification was evident also on the level of general culture, where Russian literature, art and music quickly began to dominate.

5. Contemporary Renewal Movement

Until recently, most historians described the above-mentioned period in the history of the Serbian Orthodox Church in positive terms. The so-called process of 'Russification' was seen as the only way Serbia would be able to overcome pressures toward union with Rome.[74] Russian presence at Karlovci was seen as inspiring a new intellectual dynamism in a culture severely weakened by the Ottoman conquest and by the exile into a foreign empire.

However, in the twentieth century and especially during the Communist era, the Serbian theological community initiated what would become a widespread theological awakening. This awakening led to a critical re-examination of the changes brought about at Karlovci and has resulted in the contemporary liturgical movement. Like well-known Neo-patristic theologians in both East and West, Serbian theologians gradually became disillusioned with the manualist tradition that had been introduced at

---

[72] Ksenija Končarević, 'Лингвистички коментар' in Балашов, *На путу* (see n. 21), vol.1, pp. 259-285. Consult also J. Milanović, 'Богослужбени језик Српске Цркве: савремено стање и перспективе', *Логос* (Belgrade, 2006), pp. 189-208. For a discussion on the use of the vernacular in Serbian Orthodox worship, see R. Bajić, *Богослужбени језик у Српској православној цркви: прошлост, савремено стање, перспективе* (Belgrade, 2007).

[73] V. Vukašinović, 'Библијско' (see n. 34), pp. 215-240. A well-known work dealing with the history of Serbian literature including liturgical works is by D. Bogdanović, *Историја српске књижевности* (Belgrade, 1980).

[74] For example, see: Dj. Slijepčević, *Историја* (see n. 57), p. 415. Vukašinović challenges this assumption: 'Библијско' (see n. 34), p. 3. He cites the following work: I. Tarnanidou, *Τὰ προβλήματα τῆς μητροπόλεως καρλοβίκων κατὰ τὸν ιη' αἰῶνα καὶ ὁ Jovan Rajić 1726-1801* (Thessalonica, 1972), p. 170.

Karlovci. It was notably Bishop Nikolaj (Velimirović. 1880-1956), and especially Archimandrite Justin Popović (1894-1979), who turned to the Church Fathers in search of a more authentic expression of Orthodox theology[75]. In an article published in *Православље*, Sava Dobić writes:

> 'The two of them [Nikolaj Velimirović and Justin Popović] have started a general spiritual-ecclesial renewal, whose fruits we are reaping today and which is crowned by the liturgical renewal. Their work demands that we not discontinue this renewal.'[76]

Besides writing numerous books, including theological, historical and poetical works, Nikolaj Velimirović was the spiritual leader of an earlier existing Serbian renewal movement, the so-called Bogomoljci [Бого-мољци], meaning the 'God-Beseechers'.[77] An indirect relationship could possibly be established between this lay movement and the contemporary liturgical movement, though we leave this task for another time.[78] For now it suffices to say that the writings of Bishop Nikolaj continue to inspire Serbian theology, and in this way also the liturgical movement.[79]

Justin Popović is more directly related. In his theological writings, we see a clear return to the Fathers, and a strong influence of Neo-patristic authors.[80] His search for a more authentic theological expression also inspired him to introduce concrete liturgical reforms. These include translating the liturgies into modern Serbian, re-introducing particles for the holy angels in the prothesis, placing Third Hour troparia in brackets,

---

[75] Bishop Atanasije mentions others who have contributed to the overall renewal, such as Radoslav Grujić, Lazar Mirković and Dragi Anastasijević. He also indicates the theologians connected with the following Serbian periodicals: *Богословски гласник, Хришћански живот, Хришћанско дело, Богословље, Гласник Патријаршије, Хришћанска мисао, Светосавље*. See A. Jevtić, 'Развој' (see n. 56), p. 102.

[76] S. Dović, 'О Светој Литургији' (see n. 48), p. 9.

[77] For a study on the Bogomoljci movement and Nikolaj Velimirović, see D. Subotić, *Епископ Николај и Православни Богомољачки Покрет* (Belgrade, 1996). Bishop Nikolaj also wrote a book on the Bogomoljci: *Диван: наука о чудесима* (Munich, 1953).

[78] For some initial discussions on the influence of Bogomoljci on Serbian worship, see D. Kapisazović, 'Певање богомољачких песама у храмовима' *Весник* 392 (Belgrade, 15 October 1965) p. 3; S. Ratković, 'Певање богомољачких песама у храмовима', *Весник* 395-6 (Belgrade, 1-15 December 1965), pp. 3-4; D. Kapisazović, 'Одговор', *Весник* 397 (Belgrade, 1 January 1966), p. 8; A. Jevtić, *Христос* (see n. 7), vol. 3, p. 382.

[79] A. Jevtić, 'Развој' (see n. 56), pp. 102-103.

[80] An English bibliography of Father Justin's works is available in *Човек богочовека Христа: споменица 110-годишњици блаженог преставовења Преподобног Оца Јустина Новог Ћелијског*, ed. A. Jevtić (Belgrade, 2004), pp. 352-382.

and insisting that it is 'people' and not 'choirs' who ought to sing liturgical responses.[81] Both his theological writings and his liturgical initiatives influenced the current liturgical movement. This is especially evident when one takes into account that Justin Popović was the spiritual father to the most active bishops involved in the renewal, such as Irinej (Bulović) and Atanasije (Jevtić).

When reading the writings of Father Justin's disciples, one often encounters the concept of 'pseudomorphosis' [псевдоморфоза], used to describe the developments at the Metropolitanate of Karlovci we examined earlier.[82] According to these authors, the theological-liturgical life at Karlovci during the eighteenth and nineteenth centuries underwent a process similar to the 'pseudomorphosis' described by Georges Florovsky, a father of the Neo-patristic movement in the East.[83] Generally speaking, what is meant by the use of this word in the Serbian context is the visible transformation of Serbian theology, worship and popular liturgical piety. This transformation came about especially through the introduction of Russian theological and liturgical books, heavily influenced by Moghilan Kiev and the theology of the "Manualist" School.[84] For example, referring to those opposed to the liturgical movement, Jevtić writes:

> 'For some of them, the 'centuries-old tradition' is in fact... the Karlovci practice, introduced a few centuries ago, not witnessed in our manuscripts and first printed *Službnici*... but appearing through [those books] brought from Kiev, Lvov, Vilnius and Moscow, or in those reprinted at Karlovci...'[85]

---

[81] J. Popović, epilogue to *Божанствене* (see n. 43), p. 232. I hope to soon publish an English translation of this text, important as it is for the study of twentieth-century worship in the Serbian Orthodox Church.

[82] For example: A. Jevtić, 'Развој' (see n. 56), pp. 98-101; A. Jevtić, Epilogue to *Велики пост* by A. Schmemann, trans. J. Olbina (Vrnjačka Banja, 1999), pp. 164-174, on pp. 164-165; A. Jevtić, 'О обнови' (see n. 10), pp. 19-22; V. Vukašinović, 'Библијско' (see n. 34), p. 61. Bishop Irinej (Bulović) alludes to this process: 'Introduction' (see n. 21), pp. 1-7. Consult also S. Dobić, 'О Светој' (see n. 48), pp. 7-8.

[83] See G. Florovsky, 'Westliche Einflüsse in der russischen Theologie,' *Procès-Verbaux du Premier Congrès de Théologie Orthodoxe à Athènes,* ed. H. S. Alivisatos (Athens, 1939), pp. 212-232; G. Florovsky, *Collected Works,* 4 vols. (Belmont, Mass., 1975), pp. 157-182.

[84] Theological books introduced during this period, the so-called 'confessions of faith' [исповедања вере] and similar works, are described in: V. Vukašinović, 'Библијско' (see n. 34), pp. 56-61.

[85] A. Jevtić, 'О обнови' (see n. 10), p. 19.

Even though we may attribute the adoption of this predominantly late Scholastic theology[86] to historical circumstances, Jevtić indicates that Neo-patristic theologians, such as Justin Popović, have already exposed this theology as an inadequate expression of the Christian ethos, both eastern and western. It follows that this theology, and the liturgical reforms implemented under its influence, should be abandoned.

However, those involved in the contemporary liturgical movement do not seek reforms simply to rid the Serbian liturgy of Russian or Roman Catholic influences that came about at Karlovci. Neither do they seek to return Serbian worship to an imagined, idealized liturgy as once celebrated 'by the Fathers'.[87] Rather, the re-discovery of a theology centered on the liturgical dimension of *ecclesia* has prompted an evaluation of established Serbian liturgical practices, which in turn inspired concrete reforms in worship. For example, in his epilogue to the Serbian translation of Father Schmemann's *The Great Lent*, Jevtić agrees with Schmemann's criticism of the Scholastic tradition. However, he reminds that "Manualist" theology, and its adoption by the Orthodox, is an expression of a more profound crisis, and one repeatedly witnessed in Christian history; that is, it is a crisis of faith.[88] The solution, therefore, is not simply to abandon practices in the celebration of the Divine Liturgy because they have come about in more recent centuries, and in this case, also under foreign influence. The implemented reforms, and the theology from which they derive, instead seek a more authentic epiphany of the Christian life of faith in Christ. Although patristic theology is a sure test of profound and authentic theological expression, 'the Fathers' are not limited to a particular historical epoch. One can speak of twentieth-century Fathers, for example Popović and Velimirović. It is Christ who

---

[86] We specify 'late Scholastic' so as not to disregard the entire Scholastic philosophical-theological tradition, but to refer to a particular development within this tradition, and one that has been heavily criticized by Orthodox and Catholic theologians alike. This specification is our own.

[87] We write this partly in response to the following important essay, which criticizes the use of the concept of 'pseudomorphosis' by Orthodox and Catholic theologians alike: Dorothea Wendebourg, '"Pseudomorphosis": Ein theologisches Urteil als Axiom der kirchen- und theologiegeschichtlichen Forschung', in *The Christian East: Its Institutions and its Thought. A Critical Reflection*, ed. Robert F. Taft, *Orientalia Christiana Analecta* 251 (1996), pp. 565-589. In English: '"Pseudomorphosis": A Theological Judgment as an Axiom for Research in the History of Church and Theology', trans. Alexandra Riebe, *The Greek Orthodox Theological Review* 43 (1997) 321-342. I am indebted to Sister Vassa Larin and Father Robert Taft who showed me this article and inspired a more critical evaluation of this concept.

[88] A. Jevtić, 'Epilogue' (see n. 82), pp. 165-166.

is the true source of theological reflection and of the Church's liturgy, and He promised to be with His Church in every epoch.

Conclusion

Although we have examined some of its main characteristics, introduced the persons most intimately involved, listed concrete reforms being implemented, and described the broader historical context, our study of the current liturgical movement in Serbia has only touched the surface. Not only would we have to follow up with a more systematic, historical examination of Serbian worship, but more importantly, we would have to seek a deeper understanding of the theology on which this movement rests. Alexander Schmemann rightly notes that 'the Church's *leitourgia*... is the full and adequate "epiphany"... of that in which the church believes'.[89] The deepening in faith and in theological understanding that has accompanied the Serbian Church in recent decades has begun to manifest also in the liturgical life of the Church. Given the especially difficult political and social circumstances in recent Serbian history, it is remarkable, or perhaps only natural, that a search for Orthodox faith and its genuine expression in worship should arise. This search was especially inspired by the Neo-Patristic movement, and in particular by the writings of Nikolaj Velimirović and Justin Popović.

However, spiritual renewal is never an easy task, and resistance, *искушење*, is always encountered. There are radical differences among the Serbian faithful on the level of education, exposure to other cultures and liturgical traditions, in theological understanding and in the experience of *ecclesia* and it is here, more than anywhere else, that we find our explanation for the criticism the movement has received. Here we also discover an explanation for the divergences in liturgical practice evident in the Serbian Church today. In the words of Emilianos Timiadis, worship too 'bears the seal of history, that of the pilgrimage of the chosen and redeemed people struggling to remain loyal to their Savior and to participate in His glory'.[90] Historical tensions have a way of showing their face in the liturgy of the Church. At the same time, liturgical divergences

---

[89] A. Schmemann, 'Liturgical Theology, Theology of Liturgy, and Liturgical Reform', *Saint Vladimir's Theological Quarterly* 13 (1969) 217-224, on p. 218.

[90] E. Timiadios, 'The Renewal of Orthodox Worship', *Studia Liturgica* 6 (1969) 95-115, on p. 95.

ought not to be feared, for diversity in liturgical practice has always been present in the life of the Church.

The Serbian liturgical movement is a new movement, one still predominantly acting on an intuition, albeit one rooted in vigilant theological reflection. Though this intuition has judged particular historical developments in Serbian worship critically, more detailed historical analysis has yet to substantiate these assumptions. While a distanced evaluation of the fine points must still stand the test of time, the current situation should be seen as expression of hope. This is because it reveals our liturgy as indeed living, and us, pilgrims, as struggling to remain true to our Lord.

CHANTING AND CHILDREN
AT ST. MARK'S COPTIC ORTHODOX CHURCH, JERSEY CITY

Margot FASSLER

1. An Introduction to St. Mark's: Christmas, 2006

David Labib and Steve Soliman, both singers in St. Mark's Coptic Orthodox Church, Jersey City, are setting up the altar behind the iconostasis, a wooden screen that separates the sanctuary from the nave and displays the icons of Jesus, Mary, and the saints.[1] As is customary, they have taken off their shoes and stowed them away beneath the choir benches in front of the screen; the sanctuary behind the iconostasis is the location of the altar, a holy place, not to be approached wearing shoes. Dave Labib will serve in his customary role later this evening at the Christmas mass as a major singer, leading the chant from a position near the door of the altar screen. He has recently graduated from law school and started his first job as a lawyer. In spite of the pressures of his professional life, Labib continues to teach singing at St. Mark's as well as to play a leadership role in its liturgical song. Although Steve Soliman is trained in finance, what he loves is not money, but chant. He once told me that his ideal occupation would be to sing the Coptic hymns from early morning until late at night.[2]

---

[1] The Coptic Network (http://www.coptic.net/ypages/Churches.html) lists many of the Coptic congregations in the USA and throughout the world, including St. Mark's church in Jersey City. This is the oldest Coptic congregation in the USA and was founded in the 1960s. Its church building, purchased from the United Methodist Church, is surrounded by other houses which the congregation has purchased for its extensive Sunday schools and other activities. At present there are two sanctuaries in the church to accommodate the needs of this immigrant population and their children and grandchildren: downstairs, the liturgies are in Coptic and Arabic; upstairs they are prayed in Coptic, Arabic, and English. The 'upstairs-downstairs' feature of the chant and liturgy would make a fascinating subject for study, and will probably remain as long as there is still a major contingent of worshippers who have come directly from the homeland.

[2] One day in Lent, as we were preparing to shoot the morning liturgy on a grey and drizzly day, a sole choir member began to sing up before the icon of the Virgin by the door of the iconostasis. He was offering an early doxology of praise, while cameras were being set up and the sound crew worked on adjusting the boom. The singer was Steve

While Labib and Soliman are readying the wine and altar vessels for the Christmas liturgy, Mina Gergis arranges the powerpoint for two large screens hanging high on the iconostasis, one on each side: in a display created by deacons at St. Mark's, all liturgical texts will be transmitted to the congregation in one of three languages: Coptic, Arabic, and English, and most often in some combination, and with the occasional use of Greek texts as well.[3] The visuals at St. Mark's offer the ancient styles of Coptic icons alongside digital technology and telecommunication; over the heads of singers will be cameras, and to the far right, two sound guys are setting up a boom and stringing microphones on a wire, these latter courtesy of our own production studio. Gergis, one of numerous men and boys who form the choir singing in front of the iconostasis at every feast, is a student in electrical engineering at Rutgers University. He keeps strong ties with the church in which he has been raised in the midst of these undergraduate years. He chants, continues to study Coptic, works with the media for the church, and often keeps an eye on one of his younger brothers, who entertains our film crew with inside stories, and gives us quizzes on how to pronounce his Arabic name. We are outsiders, trying to learn about this young immigrant community that has grown considerably since the mid-1960s when Copts first began to migrate to the USA and Canada in significant numbers.[4] The attraction for us is the chant, which is powerfully rhythmic, highly inflected, and in the process of being "trilinguated" in some cases, as the powerpoint presentation testifies, as do the lives of the musicians who sing it today at St. Mark's church.[5] Westerners tend to think of monophonic chanting as something belonging only to the choir

Soliman, who had come to begin the morning office, and who was gradually joined by others. This was one of those times when you say 'if I only had a camera': the sound and sight revealed his piety and the need to express it in song.

[3] The ancient Coptic liturgy survives in the Coptic language, which exists today only as a liturgical and literary language, and so it is like Ge'ez, the liturgical language of the Ethiopian Orthodox church, or like Latin, the liturgical language of the Roman Catholic church.

[4] The Immigration Act of 1965 changed earlier more restrictive policies dramatically, opening up the USA to peoples who had not been admitted before in great numbers, most notably large numbers of men and woman from Asia, Africa, and the Near East. In a short number of decades the demographics of many large urban centers have been transformed through new immigrant groups, who have brought cultures, languages, and religions not previously known in major concentrations in North America.

[5] Tasbeha.org offers an example of the richness available for the study of the Coptic tradition, its liturgy and music, on the web. Many of the materials available there, including services and chants, were produced at St. Mark's Coptic Church in Jersey City.

or to soloists, but Coptic chanting belongs to three groups: priests, 'deacons' (as the choir members are called regardless of actual rank), and to the congregation, each having their own role to play in the singing. All three know significant amounts of repertory from memory. We record what the priests, singers, servers and congregants tell us about their identities; what interests us is what various members of the community think about their history and how music serves in understanding, studying, and retaining the past. In general we have learned that Coptic music praises God, but in ways that allow Copts today to join voices with Copts in Egypt and all over the world, and to proclaim their history as a people and as a faith tradition.[6]

This particular article is about the teaching of chant in this church, by the men mentioned here, and the several ways in which the chant is a reflection of a spirituality that is shaped by the music. Chant is taught as a part of a larger mission to help children understand theology, and also prepare for lives in which God will have 'his time', as Mary Sleman put it in one interview.

Dave Labib, Steve Soliman, and Mina Gergis are involved in an ancient process that has taken place over centuries within the musical traditions of the Coptic Orthodox Church, constantly adapting the music to new conditions while preserving its melodies as they have been learned from teachers, or in recent generations through recordings as well. Coptic chant had no written tradition until the nineteenth century, so it is hard to say how old the music actually is, and scholars struggle with this question. It is clear, however, that the texts are ancient, and that the music was passed down within tightly knit communities, from cantor to cantor, musicians who until recently were usually blind, allowing for a unique focus on sound.[7] The views of Coptic cantors concerning the

---

[6] The footage shown in the clips was gathered at St. Mark's church by our studio at the Yale Institute of Sacred Music, in collaboration with St. Mark's church, and supported by a grant from the Lilly Foundation to make documentary films for classroom teaching of repertories of sacred music. We are grateful to Father Abraham Sleman for his permission to film within the church, and for his kind support during 2006-2009, the years during which we have been filming at St. Mark's.

[7] See the article on blind cantors by Ragheb Moftah and Martha Roy, 'Coptic Cantors, their role and musical training', in A.S. Atiya, ed., *The Coptic Encyclopedia* 6: 1736–1738 (New York, 1991). The article offers an account of the training and practice of blind cantors who take a leading role in religious ceremonies of the Coptic Church, a tradition dating from early Christianity, reflecting the much earlier participation of blind musicians in Egyptian court ceremonies, and continuing to the present in Egyptian Coptic church life. David Labib says the demand for teaching by blind cantors in the Coptic Church is now breaking down.

music they sing and its age and source materials is crucial to the self-understanding possessed by the community as a whole, especially in the work of restoration and preservation taking place in the last century. A quotation from the obituary of Ragheb Moftah (1898-2002), who worked tirelessly to find cantors throughout Egypt to tape for an enormous project now stored in the Library of Congress, offers an outsider's summary of music's importance in expressing identity among Copts today:

> 'It is a personal conviction that it is in playing Coptic Orthodox music that we come close to the inner reality of Coptic liturgical life. It is essential to be aware of the public setting of Coptic Music whilst affirming the value of individual experience. All religious music, and especially Coptic music in this context, can be experienced at once as inward and intimate, communal and educational. There is nothing so evocative of the Coptic experience as the enigmatic melisma (a melodic extension of a vowel); the long unison phrases (the music is monophonic); and the measured metrical scanning of the verses of Coptic liturgical music, pointed by the metallic ring of the lonely naqus (a pair of small hand cymbals) or the trianto (triangle).'[8]

Copts look behind the apostle Mark in the first century CE to the traditions of the pharaohs, and worship following a calendar based upon the ancient Egyptian civil year, with its subdivision into the three seasons, four months each, and a first day timed to the highest point of the Nile flood in Memphis, south of Cairo. 'This subdivision is maintained in the Coptic Calendar. The three seasons are commemorated by special prayers in the Coptic Divine Liturgy.'[9] Easter is calculated differently

---

[8] John H. Watson, the author of the obituary, identifies himself as follows: 'an Anglican priest who has been writing the fortnightly Coptophile Column for Watani International since 2002. He is the author of several books including *Among the Copts* (2000), *Christians Observed* (2004), and *Listening to Islam* (2005).'

[9] 'Historically, ancient Egyptians initially used a civil calendar based on a solar year that consisted of 365 days only, without making any adjustment for the additional quarter of a day each year. However, in the mean time, they knew an astronomical calendar which is based on an astronomical concept, namely the heliacal rising of a bright star called Sirius 'Canis Major', the 'Dog Star' at the dawn of the eastern horizon. The day on which the heliacal rising of Sirius occurs marks the first day of the year. Sirius (or Spdt in ancient Egyptian) is characterized by high luminosity and is a member of the constellation Canis Major. It lies about 8.6 light years from earth. The first day coincides with the arrival of the highest point of river Nile flood at Memphis, south west of Cairo, the capital of Egypt during the early dynastic period of the old kingdom.' From an on-line discussion written by Deacon Dr. Medhat R. Wassef of St. Mark's Coptic Orthodox Church, Jersey City, at http://www.copticchurch.net/easter.html. (accessed January, 2009).

from Western-rite churches, and Coptic Christmas is celebrated on January 7; the service begins in the early evening of January 6, and continues on into the night, with a celebration after midnight. Like many members of Oriental Christian churches, Copts are a minority group in their country of origin and have suffered centuries of persecution; today they have spread out over the United States and Canada, and have major communities in Australia and Europe as well. The head of the Coptic Orthodox Church, Pope Shenouda III, is a scholar and theologian with strong ecumenical interests, and was the first Coptic Pope to visit the Vatican in over 1500 years.[10] The old and the new are mingled in his character: His Holiness' background is monastic, and this is reminiscent of the history of the Coptic Orthodox Church and of Egypt, the cradle of Christian monasticism; but he is also a dynamic leader for the Coptic Orthodox Church today, and an outspoken believer in dialogue and outreach to other Christian traditions.[11]

2. The Journey of the Bread: The Liturgical Ambience of Coptic Chant

While some of our crew sets up in the sanctuary and films the work of three deacons there, another cameraman is down in the basement of the church complex in the baking room called 'Bethlehem', where other preparations are taking place. 'In Bethlehem', with its ovens and other equipment, Sami Gergis, Mina's father, bakes 'the bread that will become the body of Christ'.[12] Sami Gergis speaks to us in Arabic through a translator, describing the actions of mixing flour, water, and yeast to

---

[10] Under the leadership of His Holiness, the Coptic Orthodox Church is a full member of the World Council of Churches, the Middle East Council of Churches, the All-African Council of Churches, the National Council of the Churches in Christ in the U.S.A., the Canadian Council of Churches, and the Australian Council of Churches. In May 2000, he established the first ecumenical office, in the Archdiocese of North America.

[11] Almost all the men of the community of St. Mark's have made pilgrimages to monasteries in Egypt, and two Coptic monasteries have been started in the USA since the 1960s, one in California and the other in Texas. *The Holy Family in Egypt* (St. Mina Monastery, 2000) provides a pictorial introduction to Coptic monasteries in Egypt and their histories, following what Copts believe was a three-year period of travel by Mary, the baby Jesus, and Joseph, and tracing their route through the land. Many monasteries take their foundation stories from this contact with the holy family.

[12] There are several men who are bakers at St. Mark's, and others are training to learn the ritual of baking. On one morning, usually Friday, women come to bake the small loaves that are distributed to the people as sacramentals on Sunday, and for which a small offering is given.

make the traditional loaves, each of which is marked with an antique wooden bread stamp, and pierced five times. Each loaf of holy bread must be perfect, and Gergis shapes and reshapes the loaves removing all roughness with his skilled hands. As he stirs and shapes, he prays, sometimes consulting a small prayer book open before him; psalms and hymns come softly from a tape player above his head; loaves rise with one blessing; they go into the ovens with yet another. Hours later, Sami Gergis will bring five loaves of holy bread up into the nave during the Christmas mass. The five loaves, in their elaborately dressed basket, will then be solemnly processed from the back of the church, and at the end of the procession, the priest will choose one of them, the one he deems without blemish, and mark it with wine for consecration on the altar.

The hours of bread making in Bethlehem demonstrate the interplay between the old and the new. Bread is baked with traditional ingredients to ancient prayers; but a shining bread machine stirs the dough before it is shaped and baked. Copts prize their Egyptian traditions and desire to preserve them, tracing their brand of Christianity back to the Apostle Mark, whom they believe established Christianity in Egypt in the first century CE. But they do not attempt to freeze time, nor become slaves to traditional ways that will not answer for modern needs. Mina Gergis' texts in English pop up on his powerpoint screens during the service, and are stored on the internet so all who wish can read them as well. His work with texts and chants resembles his father's work with flour and yeast in the bread machine: old materials adapt to new modes of treatment so more can be served. Sami Gergis makes enough bread so other Coptic churches in the region can have the traditional loaves they need; Mina Gergis sends Coptic liturgical texts throughout the world.

Theological understanding in this religious community has correspondences with the nature of the liturgical chant and the baking of the bread: all three involve taking what is ancient and keeping it, but remaining open to transformation and fresh interpretation. Copts are Oriental Orthodox Christians, a group that also includes Armenians, Ethiopians (Abyssinians), and Syriac and Malabarese Jacobites. The fine points of the theological differences between these churches and their Eastern Orthodox brethren often center on Christology as defined in the Council of Chalcedon (451), an Ecumenical Council not accepted by the Orientals (who are also often called non-Chalcedonian or, more pejoratively, Monophysite); as can been seen from reading contemporary Coptic theology, this branding is not something that Copts accept, and they believe that their position at Chalcedon was misunderstood in the fifth century and mistakenly portrayed ever since.[13] The Christology of Oriental Christian Churches is very high, a point reflected in the treatment of the holy bread and in the long periods of preparation and sanctification required to receive the divine presence within community. An outline of the Christmas service demonstrates the focus upon preparation for the divine presence within the mysteries and then receiving them into one-self through the act of communion. Because Christmas is a major feast, and celebrated at night as several of them are, it is more elaborate in some aspects than others, still the basic shape of this feast is followed on all major feast days and on Sundays as well.[14] The Liturgy of St Basil, one of three followed by the Coptic Church, and sung throughout most of the year today, consists of the following sections and is divided basi-cally into two times of experiencing the presence of God, one in the long service of the word, which begins with the church nearly empty as the deacons sing prayers and praise, and leading up to the readings of the gospel, by which time most people have gathered in the church. There is much coming and going in Orthodox liturgies; they are very long, community affairs, and this is a part of the tradition of holiness. Yet the structure demonstrates the importance of the bread/body and of the use of the senses to understand and be embraced with the mysteries.[15]

[13] The on-line Coptic Encyclopedia offers a good summary of the position: The Cop-tic Church has never believed in Monophysitism the way it was portrayed in the Council of Chalcedon. In that Council, Monophysitism meant believing in one nature. Copts believe that the Lord is perfect in His divinity, and He is perfect in His humanity, but His divinity and His humanity were united in one nature called 'the nature of the incarnate word', which was reiterated by St Cyril of Alexandria. Copts, thus, believe in two natures 'human' and 'divine' that are united in one *without mingling, without confusion, and without alteration'* (from the declaration of faith at the end of the Coptic Divine Liturgy). These two natures *'did not separate for a moment or the twinkling of an eye'* (also from the declaration of faith at the end of the Coptic Divine Liturgy)…. the Coptic Church has always felt a mandate to reconcile 'semantic' differences between all Christian Churches. This is aptly expressed by the current 117th successor of Saint Mark, Pope Shenouda III: *'To the Coptic Church, faith is more important than anything, and others must know that semantics and terminology are of little importance to us.'* For further reading, see 'Mono-physitism: Reconsidered', by Fr. Matthias F. Wahba.

[14] *The Coptic Liturgy of St. Basil in Pictures* (Marriout, Egypt, 2000) by Dr. Usama Azmy, St. Mary Coptic Orthodox Church, Lancaster, England, provides an excellent introduction for newcomers to the study of this liturgical tradition. In the preface to this book Azmy says 'Our Coptic Orthodox Church looks like the Old Testament Tabernacle of meeting, which was covered from outside with tanned rams' and goats' skins but from inside, it was made of gold (Exodus 39:34). Our church can't be recognized by looking at her from the exterior, but only by going deeper, and experiencing her dogmas, rites and traditions.'

[15] The liturgy takes from three to five hours, depending on the feast: Part I. Prepara-tion and Liturgy of the Word: 1. Raising of the incense in preparation for meeting God,

People start with the smelling of incense and close with the taste of
bread dipped in wine; they are surrounded throughout by icons of saints,
by chant and by elaborate ceremony, all of which has layers of meaning.
In Sunday school, children discuss the meanings of the liturgy with a
sophistication that astounds the non-Coptic observer: each child must
become something of a theologian. We are now finishing a film on
St. Mark's Coptic Orthodox Church. The presentation below offers
some of our work, related to, but not directly a part of, the documentary
film itself, which we hope to have finished by the end of 2011.

*3. Narrative for the film clips (Rome, 2008): Teaching the Chant at
   St. Mark's Coptic Orthodox Church*

To the reader of this article: what follows is essentially the text I read
in conjunction with film clips. In an envelope to the back of this book a
DVD is attached. You can get something of the same experience by
playing the clips in order and reading the text. I have also provided short
synopses of what is on the clips for those readers who do not have a way
to play the clips. The talk has six sections, labeled A-F.

3.1. Introduction to Musical Life at St. Mark's

Synopsis of clip 1 and text: Scenes of St. Mark's church establish the
setting. 1 minute. Over this plays the music from the Doxology for
St Mark, sung at vespers as part of the Verses of the Cymbals:

> 'O Mark, the apostle: and the evangelist, the witness to the passions: of the
> Only Begotten God.
> You have come and enlightened us: through your gospel, and taught us
> about the Father and the Son: and the Holy Spirit...
> All the tribes: of the earth were blessed through you, and your sayings
> reached: the ends of the world.'

---

2. The choosing of the Lamb, the loaf of bread to be consecrated, 3. The readings, each
of which is prefaced and punctuated by chanting: from the Pauline Epistles, from the
Catholic Epistles, from the Acts of the Apostles, from the lives of the Saints, and from the
Gospel. Part II. The Liturgy of Communion: 4. The Orthodox Creed and the prayers of
reconciliation and the Anaphora, the great prayer of consecration, which includes the
prayer of the invocation of the Holy Sprit, at which point the elements are transubstanti-
ated to the body and blood of Jesus Christ, 5. The Fraction, the breaking of the bread, and
the distribution of communion followed by the final prayer of thanksgiving.

Spoken Presentation began after clip 1: The praise of Mark the Evangelist has special resonance in St. Mark's Orthodox Coptic Church, Jersey City. He is the patron saint of this, the oldest Coptic Church in the USA, and also, of course, the Apostle to Egypt, said to have been martyred in Alexandria. 'All the tribes of the earth were blessed through you, and your sayings reached the ends of the world.' This doxology sung at vespers during the Verses of the Cymbals accompanies the large numbers of Copts who have emigrated from Egypt to North America since the 1960s, bringing their musical and liturgical traditions with them as central components of their culture. St. Mark's Coptic Church is located not far from the Hudson River in Jersey City, where bread to be consecrated is now made from local waters, and a prayer at the eucharistic service that once pleaded for the rising of the Nile, now refers to all rivers.

This presentation focuses on two aspects of the musical and liturgical life of St. Mark's church, and each concerns the old and the new, bringing forth ideas of what it means to adjust and adapt, to transform only to better preserve. We begin with the ways the church is structured to offer support to the community, and especially the role of music within it, ending with the attitudes of those who actually teach chant to Coptic children today and their thoughts about what they do and why they do it. A sidebar to this discussion references the role of technology in the transmission of ancient musical practices, not only in communities of North American Copts, but throughout the Coptic diaspora and in Egypt itself. Secondly we analyze actual teaching within a hymn class at St. Mark's church, taught by subdeacon and cantor David Labib. We conclude with two clips of this singer/teacher from St. Mark's chanting the gospel for Christmas Day, demonstrating his adaptation of older modes of intoning the text to the language of the community's new homeland: English. I am grateful to co-producer Jacqueline Richard and shot coordinator and sound engineer Sachin Ramabhadran for their work with me on this presentation, as well as for the advice of professor Peter Jeffery, David Labib, and Steve Soliman. These clips are not part of our actual film in progress, but rather were put together solely for the SOL conference in Rome.

3.2. Chant and Community

Synopsis of clip 2: An introduction to the role of the Coptic church within the immigrant community, and to the importance of the hymnody within it, is provided first by Father Marcos Ayoub, one of the three priests of St. Mark's church, and then by David Labib's mother Adail Labib, and his sister Carol Labib Doss, who remembers her brother as a boy, studying the hymns with hundreds of tapes. In another part of her interview, Carol talks about trying to give the tape player away, or throw it out the window, it was such an intrusive member of the Labib household.

Father Marcos emphasizes the range of services offered by the church, and Dave's mother gets specific: you cannot expect the kids to care about the church unless they understand what is going on, so you teach them the hymns, and they start to love them, and they start to understand. Carol describes her mother's persistent efforts to take them to activities in the church, and encourage them to enjoy the kinds of things Father Marcos describes as essential. Among the several educational programs at St. Mark's today, this presentation includes only the Sunday school and the teaching of Coptic hymnody to the youth and children of the church. The Sunday school, open to all the children of the community, is an enormous enterprise. The church has expanded by purchasing nearby many houses, and then remodeling them for community use; in these houses the teachers meet hundreds of children per week. In the other program, boys and young men form a liturgical choir, trained in the traditional repertory of Coptic hymnody by Dave Labib and other experienced members of the choir. These youths and men are referred to as 'deacons' and their service to the church continues from early childhood to old age in many cases. Girls and young women learn the hymns as well, and they have recently formed a choir; at present their liturgical role is within the congregation; the congregation plays a powerful role in the Coptic liturgical tradition.

I played clip 3 as I talked

Our team has been deeply impressed with the vitality of the teaching by the men and women in school, who use many of the same techniques of rote memorization and repetition in the teaching of texts and ideas that David Labib uses when he teaches chant. But both kinds of 'servants' – deacons and Sunday school teachers – emphasize theological understanding of what is learned, so that Coptic children are often able to hold their own in conversations about why things are done in the liturgy and what they mean and have a sophisticated understanding of Coptic ecclesiology and the role of music within it. Music defines a person's and a community's relationship to God, and the two are constantly interactive through communal song.

3.3. David Labib and Steve Soliman: A Philosophy of Teaching

In the next series of clips, we hear Dave Labib discuss his own understanding of the work of Coptic cantors from ancient times and cantors today, and then we hear from Labib's star pupil, Steve Soliman, who is now a leading singer and himself a teacher of hymns at St. Mark's. David Labib knows the entire repertory he sings by heart, and he teaches it from the rich and complex storehouse of his own memory. He may supply a class with a text, as you will later see him do, but never with a notated melody. When we asked him in an interview for an example of the kind of melody he first teaches to children, he immediately offered the gospel response in Coptic, with the melody used for the Liturgy of St Basil on Sundays of the year, a piece that is sung so often that it is a good place to begin; once his classes know this melody, he then adds other basic chants to their repertory, each chosen for a reason. And we hear him sing it in this clip, with the Coptic text alliterated and the English, showing how useful video might be for teaching this particular repertory. It is to be noted that there are six 'tones' or 'tunes' used for the Coptic liturgy, but each of these is really a set of melodies appropriate to a particular feast, season or sets of circumstances.[16]

Synopsis of clip 4: In this clip Dave speaks about beginning to teach with this melody because it is sung throughout the year on ordinary Sundays.

The text in alliterated Coptic, for the purpose of following the sound of the text:

> 'Oa oo ni atoo khen oo methmee:
> ni ethowab ente pai eho oo:
> pi owai pi owai kata pef ran:
> ni menrati ente Piekhristos.
> Ari epresvevin e ehree egon:

---

[16] As David Labib explains the six tones:

1. First there is the tone that is used throughout the year – the regular tone.

2. There is also the joyous tone, the tone used for the feasts (either the seven major feasts or the seven minor feasts)

3-4. There is a tone that is used for great Lent and that tone is also used for Jonah's fast – but even in Great Lent there are two different tones: one that is used during the weekdays and another that is used on Saturdays and Sundays.

5. There is also a tone that is used for great Advent.

6. There is also a tone that is used for Palm Sunday and also used for the feast of the cross.

O ten chois en neeb tiren ti Theotokos:
Maria ethmav em Pensoteer:
entef ka nen novi nan evol.'

('Blessed are they, in truth,
the saints of this day,
each one by his name,
the beloved of Christ.
Intercede on our behalf,
O lady of us all, the Mother of God,
Mary, the Mother of our Savior,
that He may forgive us our sins.')

It is important to Dave that he is heir to an ancient line of Coptic cantors, who traditionally were blind; even the musicians of the pharaohs were blind. There has never been a role for musical notation in this tradition. Though transcriptions into staff notation have been made by twentieth-century ethnomusicologists, most cantors still do not use available scores. Instead the memory has to be carefully developed to learn the chant. It does not matter to Dave Labib that he does not read music, or that most of the other deacons in the church do not either; they have other ways of learning. Steve Soliman describes how he writes out shapes to help him remember the contours of the melodies, emphasizing that each person adapts his own notes to his own needs and memories. The notes help him fix the melodies in his mind as he goes over them again and again until he has them by heart; he clearly uses this same technique in imparting the music to others.

Synopsis of clip 5: Steve Soliman describes the various notes he takes to help him fix the chants in his mind and speaks about how every person who learns the chant has their own way of making these guides.

3.4. Technology and Transmission

The hymn texts of the Coptic liturgy have been transmitted in writing for centuries. Aside from papyri, the best known early parchment manuscripts are two ninth-century collections in the Morgan Library in New York. Complete copies of the repertory in its classic form only date from the Ottoman era (mid-fifteenth-nineteenth centuries). And the study of this repertory has not progressed much since O. H. E. Burmester wrote, seventy years ago, that 'Coptic hymnography is a vast virgin forest, beyond whose confines no Coptic or liturgical scholar has as yet penetrated.'[17] The same is true of the melodies: Since they were handed down orally from the beginning, it is difficult at present to say when they originated or what historical or chronological layers there may be in the tradition. The articles on hymnody and music in the *Coptic Encyclopedia* provide good recent introductions in English; most of the scholarship is in Arabic and in French. Ernest Newlandsmith's transcriptions made in the 1930s are still unpublished. Ragheb Moftah, long-time director of the Department of Music and Hymns at the Coptic Institute of Higher Studies in Cairo, assembled a bank of recordings of Coptic cantors, and then worked with ethnomusicologist Margit Toth and Coptic scholar Martha Roy to produce a hefty volume of transcriptions of *The Coptic Orthodox Liturgy of St. Basil*, published in 1998. Significant collections of Coptic recordings also exist at Harvard University and at the Library of Congress. Marian Robertson-Wilson, the scholar who prepared the index for Ragheb Moftah's vast collection of tapes and other materials at the Library of Congress, addresses the problem of the historical nature of Coptic chant:

> 'The Coptic rites developed gradually, with the alleluia, Sanctus and psalms among the earliest texts to be set to music. The Divine Liturgies, translated from their original Greek counterparts, became fixed in the 4th and 5th centuries. One melody, a *lahn ma'rūf* ('familiar melody'), which is still sung today, probably dates from the 7th century or even earlier. Long-enduring archetypal melodies have also been identified in the Anaphora of St Basil. Controversy exists as to whether there is a connection between simple Coptic melodies and the folksongs of Egyptian peasants (Arabic *fallahīn*). The music, in fact, probably derives from many regions of Egypt and from various centuries, and at the very least is a reflection of its ancient past. Certain practices appear to have persisted from ancient Egypt, such as the employment of professional blind singers, the use of percussion instruments echoing the sound of ancient sistra and bells, antiphonal singing, and the unusually long vocalises reminiscent of the 'hymns of seven vowels' sung by Pharaonic priests.'[18]

Coptic singers today are increasingly reliant on commercial recordings released by the leading cantors, many of which can be found on the website Tasbeha.org, which also features live broadcasts from St. Mark's

---

[17] Quoted in Leslie MacCoull, 'Oral-Formulaic Approaches to Coptic Hymnography', *Oral Tradition* 14/2 (1999) 354-400, on p. 356.

[18] Marian Wilson-Robertson, from the article 'Coptic Church Music', in *Grove Music Online* (Oxford University Press, 2007-2008), accessed January, 2009.

Orthodox Church in Jersey City, with members of the community, especially youth, from this church playing major roles in the maintenance of the site and in adding materials to it. Both Dave Labib and Steve Soliman are serious students of early recordings and often make musical decisions based upon their knowledge of them.

Hegumen Abraam Sleman of St. Mark's church is credited as one of the first Coptic priests to stress the importance of the use of the internet as a medium to reach Copts. He created one of the first Coptic online publications, 'Voice of the Bible', which was later expanded to be www.SaintMark.com and has now evolved into www.CopticChurch. net. It now interfaces with Tasbeha.org and together they form one of the largest Coptic resources on the internet. Thus modern technology has become central in sustaining a musical tradition that was established and transmitted orally for centuries. North American Copts are not afraid to use recorded audio technology, or software programs like PowerPoint, in their teaching of liturgical practices or within liturgies themselves. Mary Sleman, Father Abraam's daughter said in an interview that she can pray the liturgy better with the screen than with a book. St. Mark's church is well-equipped electronically to provide these aids for worship and some of the younger choir members have recently set up a film and media studio to help with this part of their mission. The Coptic technicians have been adding film clips to their site in recent years, and these are very useful for study.

Clip 6: Here we showed a clip of media and powerpoint as I said the following:

At Saint Mark's church, there are two services going on simultaneously every Sunday and on major feast days: downstairs the liturgy is primarily in Arabic; upstairs it is mostly in Coptic and English with only occasional Arabic. Both liturgies use powerpoint slides with parallel texts in two and three languages. Young boy 'deacons' run the powerpoints as part of their liturgical duties, but have been known to fall behind the actual progress of the service, only to be urged on by older youths and adults.

3.5. Scenes from the Classroom

Both David Labib and Steve Soliman talk about the importance of learning the hymns so they can be prayed, and of understanding the theological meanings of the sung texts so the prayer of the liturgy (which is completely sung) makes sense, from beginning to end. Both Dave and Steve spend hours a week in church working on the music, yet both of them have demanding jobs, Dave as a beginning lawyer (who works in the same firm as his sister Caroline). When David Labib began the hymn class we filmed in 2006, he started with prayer before the image of Mary and Jesus on the iconostasis. He opened by leading the students in the singing of Nicherobim, an Aspasmos sung by the congregation that introduces the Greek Sanctus. Margit Toth has transcribed this melody in her edition of the liturgy of St Basil and I will play it as sung in Coptic by Ibrahim Ayad, which is another version of the melody transcribed from earlier recordings by Toth. (On the recording posted on the Tasbeha website, this melody is labeled as from the liturgy of St Gregory.) This congregational hymn of praise was well-chosen for opening the class, then, both because it would serve to remind the students of the importance of the material, set as it is in the heart of the greatest liturgical mystery and also because it glorifies God, joining human song to that of the angelic hosts. So, the melody first in Coptic and then we hear and see yet another version of it in English sung by children in a hymn class at St. Mark's church.

Synopsis of clip 7: the clip shows the students and Dave singing at the opening of their class. The music as transcribed by Toth was handed out during the presentation before the sound clip.

A response of the people sung as part of the Liturgy of the Believers (St Basil). Opening of the response is in Coptic, followed by the Greek Sanctus, showing the way the two languages are sometimes juxtaposed in liturgical texts. I also played the chant as sung by Ibrahim Ayad.[19]

> 'Ni Sheroubim se oo osht emmok:
> nem ni Serafim seti oa oo nak:
> ev osh evol ev go emmos:
> Je agios agios agios:
> Kerios saba oth:
> epliris o ooranos ke ee gee:
> tis agias soo doxis.'

---

[19] Text and audio file are available on http://tasbeha.org (accessed March, 2009). This is a good piece to use as an exercise for finding Coptic chants on Tasbeha: first use the URL to access the site. Then click on 'media', and 'hymns', and 'annual'; then click on 'congregational responses', and on 'Ibreham Ayad'. The 'Parts' take you through the liturgy, and to find this hymn you need Part 4, and then 'Nisherobim – Gregorian'. If you then click on that you will hear the hymn, and can follow the text (http://tasbeha.org/mp3/Hymns/Annual/Congregation_Responses/Ibrahim_Ayad/part4.html).

('The Cherubim worship You,
and the Seraphim glorify You,
proclaiming and saying:
"Holy, holy, holy,
Lord of hosts.
Heaven and earth are full
of Your holy glory".')

Dave Labib has strategies for teaching liturgical chant that Steve Soliman and others are carrying out as well. In general, the children should be taught by teenagers, and young men like Steve and Dave should teach the teens. In that way, each group is taught at least some of the time by the ones they most look up to, and when you observe Dave's little group, you can see these same children later in church being tended to by the young 'deacons' that Dave teaches in another class as they sing alongside Dave and Steve. The children learn by rote, section by section, and they learn the pieces in both Coptic and in English, and occasionally even in Greek or Arabic. Steve says when he teaches he tries to get the children to make each section or portion 'perfect' and he says he is quite hard on them until they have it. In this clip, Dave teaches the communion response for the Feast of Pentecost.[20]

The strategy operates in the liturgy as well, where boys of all ages are featured in a variety of roles, learning how to scrub down the thuribles, how to vest properly, how to hold candles, and manage the books and powerpoints. It is more difficult to appreciate the work of the girls and young women unless one observes that they are instrumental in keeping the congregational song going, which is such an important part of the Coptic liturgy. Food and fasting, both of which are crucial to Coptic religious life, are also managed primarily by the women (although certainly not exclusively). In St. Mary's and Archangel Michael's Coptic Church in Hamden, Connecticut, where Dave sometimes also teaches, two girls have begun to sing with the 'deacons', from the front row of the congregation. It seems clear that if a musical role is not given to women, and if their knowledge of the hymnody and singing of it is not encouraged, it will be much harder to keep the musical tradition alive.

Dave works section by section in the class, and he usually sings with the children two or three times, then has them sing alone. Sometimes he

---

[20] For audio of the entire piece and the text in translation, see http://tasbeha.org/media/index.php?st=Hymns%2FMajor_Feasts_of_the_Lord%2FPentecost%2FHigher_Institute_of_Studies%2F19-Asomen.1240.mp3 (accessed in March, 2009).

changes the pitch of the song if he thinks it is too high or too low for them. He is most concerned in his work that he pitch the music to encourage congregational participation, and the same principle holds when he teaches.

Synopsis of clip 8: David Labib is teaching 'Asomen', the communion response from the feast of Pentecost; he teaches from his memory, with no cues, and he works portion by portion.

The use of English is a real concern for the singers at St. Mark's, especially given that the Coptic language is built into the structure of the music. Steve Soliman discusses this aspect of his memorization, and, in doing so, underscores the importance of keeping the Coptic texts, in parallel with the English. Dave Labib has tried to adapt Coptic texts to English, and when he does, he attempts to keep the rhythm and to place the melismas on the same words they have in the originals.

Synopsis of clip 9: Steve discusses the importance of Coptic in the sound and structures of the musical tradition.

Immediately after this hymn class, Dave Labib took the children to vespers, and you can see him after having moved from the classroom to the liturgy itself. He leads one side of the choir, and Steve leads the other, while the girls sing from the congregation on the women's side of the nave. Dave and Steve put their work in the classroom into practice: cajoling, pointing out the texts, keeping everything moving smoothly. Teens assist with younger ones. As the service goes on, more and more people join in, older men coming from work, and bringing their children, step into the choir, while women, children, and other men enter the congregation. It is completely in character in a Coptic service to have choir members holding their children and babies in their arms as they sing. A new energy comes into the singing when in an actual service, as can be seen in the singing of this child, who was observed earlier as a member of Dave's hymn class:

Synopsis of clip 10: close up of a child singing a verse with enthusiasm and understanding (play twice, as the clip is very short).

3.6. Conclusion: Observations on the Gospel in English

Clip 11 begins with the preface 'Stand up in the fear of the Lord' and continues to the first few sentences of the gospel text which mentions

Herod. The reading of the gospel is the last of several scriptural readings in the Liturgy of the Word in the Coptic Eucharistic service. David Labib's reading is in English in this Christmas service, and he sings to the melody that is used for the gospel throughout the entire church year, except for readings at Holy Week. Each cantor has many choices to make regarding pitch, which he sets, and most importantly which words to emphasize in the reading. Whereas every cantor will use the same melody, every individual will bring the reading to life in a unique way, looking at the text alone, and singing in accordance with his own interpretations.[21] You can hear just a few of the ornaments Labib has chosen for his highly dramatic rendering of the Christmas text, first in the preface (clip 11) and then in a bit of the reading itself contained in clip 12.[22]

The ancient hymnody of the Coptic Church has survived migration to the new world, the social changes of modern society, the invention of audio technology and the emergence of the internet, not by shunning modernization but by embracing it. It is a liturgical practice and a chant in transition: this is an ideal time to study it and record it for posterity. Surely it will not remain the same, even in the immediate future, as new cantors, deacons, priests, and Sunday school teachers shape the lives of an emerging immigrant church within the confines of the old and the demands of the new. But fixity will be encouraged by the use of technology and the recordings that circulate widely today. The energy with which the Copts preserve their chant repertories is part of their inheritance; if communities do not work to remember music transmitted by an oral tradition it dies. There is much for musicians who practice within a written tradition to learn from the singers of St. Mark's Coptic Orthodox Church, Jersey City.

---

[21] You can hear a version of this gospel text sung in Arabic at http://tasbeha.org/mp3/Hymns/Major_Feasts_of_the_Lord/Nativity/2005_Liturgy_at_Cathedral.html (accessed, March, 2009); there is a version in Coptic on this same section as well.

[22] When a reading is sung in English, the singer faces west, out to the people; when the reading is sung in Coptic, the singer faces east, toward the altar. Early in our project, we were going to film David Labib singing the gospel, and so we set up the cameras to get this moment in the service, working from the congregation side of the altar. Then, just as we were rolling, he turned and faced East, as he was singing in Coptic on that particular Sunday. We filmed the back of his head.

INTRODUZIONE ALLA TEOLOGIA E SPIRITUALITÀ DEI *KATANYKTIKA* DELL'*OKTŌĪCHOS*

Marcel MOJZEŠ

Introduzione

Alcuni anni fa (2005) ricevetti una proposta, sia dalle suore basiliane che dalle suore Serve dell'Immacolata, di iniziare una mistagogia sulla liturgia bizantina.[1] Risposi loro: 'Partiamo dai testi liturgici che voi pregate ogni giorno dell'*Oktōīchos*' (soprattutto le basiliane). Inizia, allora, una riflessione sui testi dell'*Oktōīchos* (Ὀκτώηχος) e rimasi molto impressionato dalla loro profondità. In questo articolo vorrei comunicare parte della mia esperienza e di questa mia riflessione, cercando di fare una introduzione alla spiritualità e alla teologia dei *katanyktika* dell'*Oktōīchos*. Sono consapevole del fatto che, per far ciò, è necessario avere un metodo. È esperienza già dei Padri della Chiesa la consapevolezza della necessità di introdurre fedeli nell'esperienza liturgica, nel mistero celebrato. Essi lo facevano attraverso il metodo di *mistagogia*,[2] che di per sé rimane sempre attuale. Oggi sappiamo che per spiegare bene un testo liturgico serve una buona ermeneutica. Ma è vero anche che negli studi liturgici orientali, per quanto è di mia conoscenza, non sono stati ancora sufficientemente studiati i principi e metodi dell'ermeneutica di un testo liturgico, sebbene sia lecito attendersi che non saranno molto diversi dall'ermeneutica di un testo biblico. Lo studio di base che fino a oggi può essere preso in considerazione è quello di René Bornert, *Les commentaires byzantins de la Divine Liturgie*.[3] Il fatto, però, della mancanza di uno studio completo sui principi dell'ermeneutica orientale del testo liturgico non può e non deve impedire il tentativo di fare una mistagogia. I Padri della Chiesa non si chiedevano prima *come* fare la

---

[1] Questo articolo riassume una parte delle conferenze date dall'autore nel monastero delle suore basiliane a Presov (Slovacchia) nel 2005.

[2] Cf. Enrico Mazza, *La mistagogia: Le catechesi liturgiche della fine del quarto secolo e il loro metodo*, Bibliotheca "Ephemerides Liturgicae". Subsidia 46 (Roma, 1996).

[3] René Bornert, *Les commentaires byzantins de la Divine Liturgie du VIIe au XVe siècle*, Archives de l'Orient Chrétien, 9 (Parigi 1966).

mistagogia o *come* spiegare il testo liturgico. Guidati dallo Spirito Santo sentivano soprattutto il bisogno di *fare* mistagogia per il bene dei fedeli, per educarli alla scuola della preghiera. Come sottolineava il servo di Dio Giovanni Paolo II nella sua lettera apostolica per il terzo millennio *Novo millennio ineunte* (2001), 'le nostre comunità cristiane devono diventare autentiche scuole di preghiera.'[4] In ogni scuola c'è bisogno non solo di studenti o di discepoli ma anche di insegnanti. Certo, alla scuola di preghiera l'insegnante *par excellence* è Gesù Cristo stesso. Gli apostoli stessi gli hanno chiesto: 'Signore, insegnaci a pregare' (Lc 11,1). Ma possiamo anche dire che maestri della preghiera lo sono pure tutti i santi, con le loro vite e le loro esperienze di cammino verso Dio. Queste esperienze di preghiera sono conservate nella tradizione liturgica dalla quale vorrei attingere. Giovanni Paolo II nella sua lettera apostolica *Orientale Lumen* (1995) ha scritto: 'La ricchissima innografia liturgica, della quale vanno giustamente fiere tutte le Chiese dell'Oriente cristiano, non è che la continuazione della Parola letta, compresa, assimilata e finalmente cantata: quegli inni sono in gran parte delle sublimi parafrasi del testo biblico, filtrate e personalizzate attraverso l'esperienza del singolo e della comunità.'[5]

1. Katanyktika

Cerchiamo di introdurci almeno nelle linee principali della teologia e della spiritualità dei *katanyktika* dell'*Oktōīchos*. Il nostro obiettivo non è quello di analizzare tutto l'*Oktōīchos* (cosa impossibile in un singolo articolo), piuttosto invece vorremmo scavare la profondità dei singoli στιχρὰ κατανυκτικά e studiarne la teologia e la spiritualità. Cercherò, inoltre, di mostrare l'ispirazione biblica del testo liturgico e i legami con la teologia della tradizione della Chiesa.

Con il termine κατανυκτικά sono chiamati, nei libri liturgici bizantini, tutti gli στιχρά il cui contenuto viene legato al termine greco κατάνυξις, uno dei termini più importanti nella spiritualità orientale[6], di

---

[4] Giovanni Paolo II, *Novo millennio ineunte*, 33, http://www.vatican.va/holy_father/john_paul_ii/ apost_letters/documents/hf_jp-ii_apl_20010106_novo-millennio-ineunte_it.html.

[5] Giovanni Paolo II, *Orientale Lumen*, 10, http://www.vatican.va/holy_father/john_paul_ii/apost_letters/ documents/hf_jp-ii_apl_02051995_orientale-lumen_it.html.

[6] Cf. Tomas Spidlik, *La spiritualità dell'Oriente cristiano: Manuale sistematico* (Roma, 1985), p. 173.

non facile traduzione. Si tratta di un atteggiamento del cuore che esprime la compunzione, il desiderio di conversione e la penitenza. Secondo San Basilio il Grande la '*katanyxis* è un dono di Dio'.[7] Innanzitutto comparare le tematiche degli *stichīra* dell'*Oktōīchos* nei giorni feriali, (dal lunedì fino al venerdì) durante il vespro e l'*orthros*, ossia il mattutino (oltre agli *stichīra* dedicati alla Madre di Dio – *theotokia* che si cantano al *Gloria* e *ora e sempre* oppure all'*Ora e sempre*). Visualizziamo questa comparazione con l'aiuto di una tabella.

	lunedì	martedì	mercoledì (= venerdì)	giovedì
Vespro: *Kyrie ekekraxa*	*katanyktika* + agli angeli	*Katanyktika* + a Giovanni Battista	alla Croce + a Madre di Dio	agli apostoli + a San Nicola
stichīra aposticha	*katanyktika*	*katanyktika*	alla Croce	agli apostoli
Orthros: kathisma	*katanyktika*	*katanyktika*	alla Croce	agli apostoli
canone	*katanyktikos* + agli angeli	*katanyktikos* + a Giovanni Battista	alla Croce + a Madre di Dio	agli apostoli + a San Nicola
stichīra aposticha	*katanyktika*	*katanyktika*	alla Croce	agli apostoli

Per ogni giorno vediamo una struttura simile. Abbiamo, prima di tutto, un tema principale: *stichīra katanyktika* (lunedì, martedì), *stichīra* alla Croce (mercoledì, venerdì) o *stichīra* agli apostoli (giovedì). Al tema principale si uniscono ancora altri *stichīra*: agli angeli (lunedì), a Giovanni Battista (martedì), alla Madre di Dio (mercoledì, venerdì) e a San Nicola (giovedì). Qui analizzeremo gli *stichīra katanyktika*, che si trovano nell'*Oktōīchos* per il lunedì e il martedì. Seguiremo la traduzione italiana, così come anche la terminologia liturgica, dell'*Anthologion* italiano, pubblicato dal Centro Aletti a Roma.[8] Iniziamo con il primo tono.

2. Katanyktika *del lunedì del primo tono*

Iniziamo con il primo *kathisma* (сѣдалєнь in paleoslavo) dell'*orthros*, che appartiene ai cosiddetti *kathismata katanyktika*. Prima di passare al testo può essere utile riportare alla coscienza la situazione nella quale, di

---

[7] Citato secondo Geoffrey W. H. Lampe, *A Patristic Greek Lexicon* (Oxford, 1961), p. 713.

[8] *Anthologion di tutto l'anno, I-IV* (Roma, 1999-2000).

solito, si trovano l'uomo o la donna il lunedì mattina quando si recano a pregare l'*orthros*: È l'inizio di una nuova settimana, forse si sta sperimentando una certa amarezza per il fatto che il fine settimana è ormai finito e molti doveri si profilano davanti. Nasce allora la domanda: come iniziare la settimana nel modo migliore? (Per il cristiano, e l'*Oktōīchos* ce lo insegna perfettamente, la settimana dovrebbe cominciare il sabato sera con il vespro, che di nuovo invita ogni fedele ad immergersi nel dogma della resurrezione di Cristo, e così sperimentare di nuovo anche la nostra resurrezione in Cristo e con Cristo: cf. Rm 6,4-11; Col 2,12-13. La domenica stessa era il primo giorno della settimana: cf. Mt 28,1; Mc 16,2; Lc 24,1; Gv 20,1.[9] Nonostante ciò, di fatto molti cristiani oggi considerano il lunedì come l'inizio della settimana, poiché allora hanno inizio i giorni lavorativi.)

Il primo *kathisma* allude all'*inizio*: 'Concepito nelle iniquità...'[10]. Si tratta del versetto salmico (Sal 50,7). La settimana può essere iniziata in vari modi, compreso nelle iniquità, nei peccati, ma questa strada non conduce verso una meta favorevole. Il *kathisma* prosegue: 'Concepito nelle iniquità, io, il dissoluto...' Il paleoslavo al posto di dissoluto ha la parola блѫдьныи che si potrebbe tradurre anche come *colui che non ha una meta*, che va qua e là, senza una direzione. In greco troviamo la parola ἄσωτος, cioè colui che è senza la salvezza, cioè che è senza Cristo. Dunque, l'inizio di questo *kathisma* ci dice già una grande verità, fornisce un grande aiuto per iniziare la settimana nel modo migliore: Chi non comincia con Cristo, non sa dove andare, perché non ha una meta nella sua vita. Il *kathisma* continua con le parole: 'non oso fissare le altezze del cielo'. Questa è la descrizione della situazione dell'uomo dopo il peccato: L'uomo si vergogna così tanto che non osa nemmeno guardare verso Dio. Il *kathisma*, però, non finisce qui, ma continua: 'confidando nel tuo amore per gli uomini grido: O Dio, siimi propizio e salvami (σῶσον με).' Questo *kathisma*, quindi, non è un inizio della settimana pessimista. Al contrario, esso offre una continuazione dell'esperienza della Pasqua di Cristo (celebrata la domenica) nella vita dell'uomo: un *passaggio* dal constatare ciò che è avvenuto nel passato: 'Concepito nelle iniquità...' fino alla richiesta: 'O Dio,... salvami'. Si tratta di un *passaggio* da uno sguardo orientato verso se stessi (io,

---

[9] Per la teologia della domenica cf. Giovanni Paolo II., *Dies Domini*, http://www. vatican.va/holy_father/john_paul_ii/apost_letters/documents/hf_jp-ii_apl_05071998_dies-domini_it.html.

[10] *Anthologion di tutto l'anno*, I (Roma, 1999), p. 192.

dissoluto) a uno sguardo orientato verso Dio che salva. Possiamo osservare che anche alcuni altri seguenti *kathismata* finiscono con le parole: 'salvami'.[11] Tutto questo (cioè il cambiamento della direzione dello sguardo, la Pasqua) si realizza attraverso l'amore di Dio verso gli uomini. È questo amore in cui possiamo confidare subito, fin dall'inizio di una nuova settimana, come dice il *kathisma*: 'confidando nel tuo amore per gli uomini'. Dunque, nonostante il fatto di una situazione di 'figlio dissoluto', proprio a causa dell'amore di Dio ogni cristiano può iniziare la settimana con il grido: 'O Dio,...salvami'.

Il secondo *kathisma* ha una tematica simile: 'Se il giusto a stento si salva, dove mi presenterò io, il peccatore? Non ho portato il peso e il calore del giorno: annoverami tra quelli dell'undicesima ora, o Dio, e salvami.'[12] Si tratta di una parafrasi di un testo biblico, la parabola degli operai nella vigna (Mt 20,1-16). In questo senso vediamo confermate le parole di Giovanni Paolo II sul fatto che l'innografia liturgica altro non è che 'delle sublimi parafrasi del testo biblico' (vedi sopra). Che cosa dice questo *kathisma* all'inizio di una settimana lavorativa? In breve, possiamo vederci una preghiera in questo senso: 'Signore, il mio lavoro non è un granché, ma tu mi salvi.' Sicuramente il testo liturgico non parla soltanto di un lavoro fisico o psichico, bensì soprattutto del lavoro sulla propria salvezza. Come dice San Paolo nella lettera ai Filippesi: 'Adoperatevi al compimento della vostra salvezza con timore e tremore' (Flp 2,12). Il testo del *kathisma* non parla di un uomo perfetto, ma di un peccatore che si trova già in un atteggiamento di *katanyxis*. Si rende conto che non ha lavorato secondo la volontà di Dio: 'Non ho portato il peso e il calore dei giorno'. Però, nonostante ciò, si affida al Signore e gli chiede di salvarlo: 'Annoverami tra quelli dell'undicesima ora, o Dio, e salvami.' Il testo liturgico esprime dunque una totale dipendenza dell'uomo dalla grazia e dalla misericordia di Dio.

Al tema degli operai nella vigna è legato ancora uno *stichīron* del lunedì del primo tono. Si tratta del secondo *stichīron apostichon* delle lodi dell'*orthros*: 'Non respingermi, o mio Salvatore, sono prigioniero della mollezza del peccato. Solleva il mio pensiero al pentimento (διέγειρόν [sveglia completamente] μου τὸν λογισμὸν πρὸς μετάνοιαν) e rendimi operaio provato nella tua vigna, accordandomi la mercede dell'undecima ora e la grande misericordia.'[13] È interessante notare

---

[11] Cf. *ibid.*
[12] *Anthologion, I* (cf. n. 10), p. 192.
[13] Cf. *Anthologion, I* (cf. n. 10), p. 195.

il modo in cui viene descritto lo stato del peccatore: 'sono prigioniero della mollezza (ῥαθυμία) del peccato.' Nel vocabolario patristico, la parola ῥαθυμία significa indifferenza, indolenza, ma anche desiderio, passione.[14] A causa di questa indifferenza verso le cose di Dio, legata al desiderio per il peccato, l'uomo non va a lavorare nella vigna del Signore, ossia non va a lavorare per la sua salvezza. Per poter cominciare a lavorare nella vigna del Signore bisogna che qualcosa cambi nel modo di pensare del peccatore. Perciò lo *stichīron* dice: 'Solleva il mio pensiero al pentimento'. Riguardo alla parola διέγειρον è da notare che nei vangeli la risurrezione viene spesso chiamata in greco con la parola ἔγερσις (cf. Mt 27,53; Lc 24, 6 e 34).

Prendiamo adesso un altro *kathisma* nel quale risuona il tema del figlio prodigo, cioè un figlio (o una figlia) senza la salvezza, (ἄσωτος). Questo *kathisma* si canta anche all'inizio dell'ufficio dei voti monastici (l'incipit paleoslavo: 'Ѡбіатнꙗ ѻтча')[15]: 'Affrettati ad aprirmi le tue braccia paterne: da dissoluto (ἄσωτος) ho consumato tutti i miei beni, volgendo le spalle all'inesauribile ricchezza delle tue compassioni, o Salvatore: non disprezzare ora un cuore impoverito. Compunto (ἐν κατανύξει) a te grido, Signore: Contro di te ho peccato, salvami.'[16] Un altro *kathisma* che riprende lo stesso tema: 'Stoltamente mi sono allontanato da te, o pietosissimo, e nella dissolutezza ho consumato i miei beni, servendo di continuo alle passioni irrazionali: ma tu per intercessioni degli angeli accoglimi, o Padre tenerissimo, come già il figlio dissoluto (ἄσωτος), e, te ne prego, salvami.'[17] Quali sono queste 'passioni irrazionali' (ἄλογοι) di cui la liturgia dice che l'uomo serve 'di continuo'? Nella teologia del Vangelo secondo Giovanni, lo stesso Gesù Cristo viene chiamato Λόγος. Dal punto di vista cristiano dunque potremmo dire che le passioni ἄλογοι sono quelle che sono vissute senza Cristo. Lo scopo di una vita spirituale non è di non avere le passioni, ma di essere libero dalle passioni. Cristo è venuto 'per proclamare ai prigionieri la liberazione' e 'per rimettere in libertà gli oppressi' (Lc 4,18). Dunque anche se arriva una qualche passione, con Cristo possiamo vincerla e rimanere in libertà dei figli di Dio. E non solo il lunedì, ma durante tutta la settimana.

---

[14] Cf. Lampe, *Patristic Greek Lexicon* (cf. n. 7), p. 1215.
[15] Cf. Послѣдованіе иноческагѡ постриженіꙗ (Roma, 1952), p. 16.
[16] *Anthologion, I* (cf. n. 10), p. 192.
[17] *Ibid.*, 192-193.

3. Katanyktika *del martedì del primo tono*

Il tema della partenza del figlio prodigo dal Padre risuona anche in alcuni *stichira katanyktika* del martedì. All'*orthros* si ripete il *kathisma* del lunedì 'Affrettati ad aprirmi le tue braccia paterne'[18] in cui si parla di 'un cuore impoverito' dell'uomo nel contesto della richiesta: 'O Salvatore: non disprezzare ora un cuore impoverito'. Il *kathisma* seguente cerca di spiegare come si è arrivati all'impoverimento del cuore. Questo *kathisma* non si trova nell'attuale testo greco,[19] ma soltanto in quello paleoslavo. In italiano si potrebbe tradurre così: 'Quando il nemico dei giusti vide la ricchezza delle virtù di Giobbe, cercava di minarla e di rubarla. Rovinò la forza del corpo, ma non poteva rubare la ricchezza spirituale, perché l'anima dell'immacolato l'ha trovata armata. Me stesso, però, spogliò e derubò. Prima che arrivi la fine, liberami, o Salvatore, dal bugiardo e salvami.'[20] Una delle immagini che in questo *kathisma* descrive lo stato dell'uomo dopo il peccato è che il nemico 'mi spogliò'. In queste parole risuona lo stato di Adamo ed Eva dopo il primo peccato nel paradiso: 'Allora si aprirono gli occhi di tutti e due e si accorsero di essere nudi; intrecciarono foglie di fico e se ne fecero cinture. Poi udirono il Signore Dio che passeggiava nel giardino alla brezza del giorno e l'uomo con sua moglie si nascosero dal Signore Dio, in mezzo agli alberi del giardino. Ma il Signore Dio chiamo l'uomo e gli disse: 'Dove sei?'. Rispose: 'Ho udito il tuo passo nel giardino: ho avuto paura, perché sono nudo, e mi sono nascosto'(Gn 3,7-10). Nel paradiso, il bugiardo (per usare le parole del *kathisma*) ha ingannato Adamo ed Eva dicendo loro che quando avessero gustato dall'albero di conoscenza del bene e del male, sarebbero divenuti come Dio. Ma gli uomini erano già come Dio: creati a Sua immagine e somiglianza (cf. Gn 1,26-27). Per convincerli, il bugiardo, sotto forma di serpente, iniziò la sua tentazione con un dubbio: 'È vero che Dio ha detto: Non dovete mangiare di nessun albero del giardino?'(Gn 3,1). Ogni peccato comincia in modo simile, con un dubbio e con una menzogna su Dio, nel senso che si fa apparire Dio come colui che vuole limitare l'uomo e, quindi, probabilmente non lo ama poi così tanto. Dopo il peccato l'uomo si è reso conto che era nudo, ha avuto paura di Dio e si è nascosto. Ma Dio non ha cessato di cercarlo e gli fa una domanda: 'Dove sei?' (Gn 3,9).

---

[18] *Anthologion, I* (cf. n. 10), p. 192.
[19] Cf. *Παρακλητική*, (Atene, 1994), pp. 59-60.
[20] Октωнχъ сноⷬ҇чь осмогласникъ, гаⷧсы а–д (Mosca, 1996), p. 85.

Questo sforzo di Dio alla ricerca dell'uomo è espresso anche nell'*orthros* del Sabato santo: 'Sulla terra sei disceso per salvare Adamo, e non avendolo trovato sulla terra, o Sovrano, sino all'ade sei disceso per cercarlo.'[21] Una rappresentazione iconografica di questa continua ricerca dell'uomo da parte di Dio è possibile vederla nell'icona bizantina della Risurrezione, chiamata in paleoslavo Соⷲⷷⷷⷷⷷⷷⷷ (Discesa agli inferi). Dio è sceso fino all'ade per cercare l'uomo e per prenderlo per mano. Secondo alcuni teologi, questa ricerca dell'uomo da parte di Dio cominciò ancor prima della cacciata dell'uomo dal paradiso. Infatti, Dio diede ad Adamo e a Eva le tuniche di pelle. Queste hanno un senso doppio. Rendono simile l'uomo agli animali (come conseguenza del peccato), ma lo proteggono pure dal freddo, ossia, anche se gli uomini hanno perso la vita di Dio, possono sopravvivere. Dio non crea il male, ma nel suo immenso amore *tollera* questo nuovo stato dell'uomo dopo il peccato e lo trasforma in benedizione. Così le tuniche di pelle sono da una parte la conseguenza del peccato, ma dall'altra rappresentano una benedizione, una medicina (φάρμακον), cioè la possibilità di sopravvivere e di trovare una vita più degna e più simile a Dio.[22]

Dio, però, non si limita a dare all'uomo le tuniche di pelle, ma fa molto di più. Nel secondo troparío della terza ode del canone *kananyktikos* del martedì mattina leggiamo: 'Guarda la mia incapacità, tu che l'hai indossata, guarda la mia anima che non ha una forma (ἀμορφία; amorfo è ciò che non ha una ferma struttura interna) e ascolta la mia voce, misericordioso Cristo e trasforma, o Salvatore, la non bellezza della mia anima ad una buona forma (εὐμορφία).'[23] Il troparío menziona l'incapacità dell'uomo. Secondo il teologo bizantino medievale Nicola Cabasilas (1322-1391) la situazione dopo il peccato era la seguente: da una parte, c'era l'uomo che aveva bisogno di pagare il debito verso Dio, ma non ne era capace; dall'altra, c'era Dio che non aveva debiti nei confronti di alcuno, ma poteva fare tutto. Per risolvere questa situazione era necessario, secondo Cabasilas, che le nature di entrambi (uomo e Dio) si unissero in una persona.[24] Con queste parole, Cabasilas esprime il mistero dell'incarnazione di Dio, di cui parla anche il sopramenzionato

---

[21] *Anthologion di tutto l'anno, II* (Roma, 2000), p. 1117; cf. Трⷷⷷⷷ свⷷⷷ Трⷷⷷⷷ. Трⷷⷷⷷ постнаⷷ (Mosca, 2000), p. 469ʳ.

[22] Cf. Panayotis Nellas, *Voi siete dei: Antropologia dei Padri della Chiesa* (Roma, 1993), pp. 70-73.

[23] Cf. Окⷷⷷⷷ (cf. n. 20), p. 87.

[24] Cf. Nicola Cabasilas, *La vita in Cristo* (Roma, 1994), p. 89.

tropario quando dice: 'hai indossato la mia incapacità'. In un altro luogo dell'*Oktōīchos*, il mistero dell'incarnazione viene espresso similmente attraverso l'immagine dell'indossare (la natura umana). Nel *theotokion* dopo gli *aposticha* del sesto tono del vespro del sabato sera leggiamo: 'Il mio Creatore e Redentore, il Cristo Signore, procedendo dal tuo grembo, o tutta pura, rivestendosi di me ha liberato Adamo dalla maledizione antica...'[25] Si tratta di parole concrete ('rivestendosi *di me*') che invitano ad una profonda esperienza personale con il mistero dell'incarnazione. L'uomo si unisce a questo mistero in un modo particolare nel battesimo, quando la liturgia, insieme a San Paolo, dice: 'Quanti siete stati battezzati in Cristo, vi siete rivestiti di Cristo (Gal 3,27).' Noi possiamo essere battezzati, cioè 'rivestiti di Cristo' soltanto perché lui stesso da primo si è rivestito di noi.

Finiamo con il tropario seguente dello stesso canone *katanyktikos*: 'Salva (σῶσον), Gesù, il dissoluto (ἄσωτος), salvami (σῶσον με), perché solo io ho trasgredito i tuoi comandamenti salvifici (σωτήριοι) e in modo irrazionale (ἀλόγως) ho commesso ogni peccato e sono stato guidato via da te, o Buono, dai pensieri (λογισμοί), i quali mi hanno fatto straniero.'[26] È interessante come spesso, in un tropario *katanyktiko*, risuonino parole come 'salvifico', 'senza salvezza' (ἄσωτος) e 'salvami'. In questo modo la liturgia ci insegna che ogni vera compunzione o penitenza (κατάνυξις) ci conduce a Cristo e alla richiesta della sua salvezza.

Ancora più interessante è l'interpretazione della parabola sul figlio prodigo (Lc 15), soprattutto in quanto si parla delle motivazioni della partenza del figlio prodigo dalla casa del Padre: 'Sono stato guidato via dai pensieri (λογισμοί), i quali mi hanno fatto straniero.' Nella spiritualità orientale il termine λογισμοί si usa spesso per vari pensieri che non conducono a Dio.[27] Infatti, questi pensieri, se l'uomo rimane immerso in essi, lo rendono straniero alla vita di Dio e alla casa del Padre. Vediamo che questo tropario è un altro esempio del fatto che l'innografia liturgica è spesso 'una sublime parafrasi del testo biblico, filtrata e personalizzata attraverso l'esperienza del singolo e della comunità'.[28]

---

[25] *Anthologion, I* (cf. n. 10), p. 405.
[26] Cf. Октшнхъ д–д (cf. n. 20), p. 87.
[27] Cf. Spidlik, *Spiritualità dell'Oriente cristiano* (cf. n. 6), pp. 207-212.
[28] Cf. Giovanni Paolo II, *Orientale Lumen*, 10 (cf. n. 5).

Conclusione

Abbiamo analizzato otto *katanyktika* dell'*Oktōīchos*. In questi *stichīra* si è potuto notare una dinamica del *katanyxis* simile, che consta di due parti:

a)   descrizione della situazione dell'uomo peccatore;
b)   richiesta di salvezza, di liberazione, di azione di Dio.

Alla fine possiamo riassumere entrambe le parti di questa dinamica:

a)   Situazione dell'uomo peccatore:
   – concepito nelle iniquità
   – dissoluto (ἄσωτος, senza la salvezza, senza il Salvatore)
   – non osa fissare le altezze del cielo
   – prigioniero della mollezza del peccato
   – ha volto le spalle alla ricchezza di Dio
   – ha il cuore impoverito
   – si è allontanato da Dio
   – serve di continuo le passioni irrazionali
   – è stato spogliato e derubato dal nemico
   – è incapace di salvarsi da solo.

b)   Che cosa chiede l'uomo da Dio?
   – essere salvato
   – essere liberato
   – essere annoverato tra gli operai nella vigna dell'undicesima ora
   – la grazia di sollevare il pensiero al pentimento
   – che si aprano le braccia paterne.

Si vede dunque che un vero κατάνυξις non è solo un'enumerazione delle difficoltà e delle conseguenze del peccato, bensì è al contempo pieno di speranza in Gesù Cristo, il quale 'ha indossato la mia incapacità' e 'si è rivestito di me'. Gli *stichīra katanyktika* diventano così una buona scuola di preghiera, di spiritualità e, infine, anche di teologia. Come diceva Evagrio: 'se sei teologo, preghi veramente; e se preghi veramente, sei teologo.'[29]

---

[29] Citato secondo Edward G. Farrugia, *Introduzione alla teologia orientale* (Roma, 1997), p. 91.

THE ALTAR IN THE ETHIOPIAN CHURCH:
HISTORY, FORMS AND MEANINGS

Emmanuel FRITSCH

Central in every church building of any traditional Christian church is the altar, the concrete focus of the celebration, especially of the Eucharistic liturgy.[1] Unique as it may be, the forms of the altar, its number, size, understanding etc. are varied, and it is important to account for these differences insofar as that can be done.

In the Ethiopian context, the observers' experience can often be confused, first of all because of the many terms employed regarding the altar while secrecy surrounds it, with connotations of a sometimes exotic nature, especially when it comes to the holy *tābot*. We wish, therefore, to show in a first part what the Ethiopian tradition understands as the altar, both through the vocabulary used and through the way two authoritative liturgical-canonical writings discuss the altar.

We shall dwell in the body of this article on the peculiar developments which we have found took place in Lālibalā in the first part of the 13th century, namely the phenomenon of the multiplication of altars and, more important, of the possibility that certain altars may have been made complete so that they would have been used without the addition of an altar-tablet (*tābot*). The monumental rock-altars that appeared in the 14th century, in sharp contrast with the comparatively modest realizations known previously, make us wonder if they were ever consecrated. We shall also investigate the nature of the cavity observed in many altars, address the mystery of those altars lacking a proper table, and see whether it is possible to know how relatively light altar-tables were supposed to be positioned in the church.

[1] I am very grateful to Ugo Zanetti, Habtemichael Kidane, Claire Bosc-Tiessé, Marie-Laure Derat and Michael Gervers, who kindly proposed several improvements to this study. Professor Gervers also kindly provided me with pictures illustrating this study. I owe a debt of gratitude to the Centre français des études éthiopiennes (C.F.E.E.), Addis Ababa, and its director François-Xavier Fauvelle-Aymar, who has enabled me to pursue the indispensable systematic visits to churches.

In order to provide for a context to our reflections, I shall present in the Appendix an overview of the development of the altar through history in correlation with the development of the churches themselves. In a previous study conducted with Michael Gervers on 'Pastophoria and Altars', we have tried to present a provisional chronology of the development of the Ethiopian altars.[2] In this Appendix, I attempt to go somewhat further, exploiting data which were not available at the time. These data have been gathered both through field investigation and through a method we have developed and will introduce below. The resulting overview of the inter-related history of churches and altars is organized into four major phases. The first phase begins with the earliest altars available up to the turn of the 13th century at Lālibalā. The altars of a second period in Lālibalā will form the object of the second phase. Our overview will continue from the 13th to the 15th century and we shall discover that, while a more traditional form of altar went on even through creative realizations, a totally new type of altar, monumental ones, appeared in the 14th century. We shall end our overview with a look at altars from the 16th century and to the present. Naturally, the chronology below is open to challenges and comments. If at this point we have acquired some idea regarding the development of the Ethiopian altar, we have surely also opened more questions.

How does one proceed in order to situate the altars in time, to ascribe a date, at least a relative one, to the altars found in Ethiopian churches? We propose that the following elements are likely to provide dates with some degree of reliability. We suggest associating the altars with the churches in which they are found and ascribing to them the contextual and chronological elements which are manifested through the development of church architectonics, an aspect related to the evolution of the liturgy. This approach supposes that a certain clarity has been obtained about the development and chronology of churches, rarely dated, in the first place. We propose then to review a number of altars after having provided some background on the churches in which they are found, although not in great detail due to the nature of our topic. In this way we attempt to provide a relative time-frame of the churches-altars classification.

---

[2] Emmanuel Fritsch and Michael Gervers, 'Pastophoria and Altars: Interaction in Ethiopian Liturgy and Church Architecture', *Aethiopica* 10 (2007) 7-50. Since then, I published 'The Churches of Lalibäla (Ethiopia): Witnesses of Liturgical Changes', *Bollettino della Badia Greca di Grottaferrata* 5 (2008) 69-112.

Our approach assumes that the altars are normally stable in the sense of not leaving the churches for which they were made. Of course, unless they are rock-hewn, altars do have a degree of mobility and may be destroyed and replaced. We shall see below that church tradition makes it unlikely for altars to leave the place where they were installed at the blessing or consecration of the church, although it is not totally excluded that an altar may be moved to another location.[3] Besides, considering the way the altars are stored in churches or sacristies, both conservatively and carelessly, it appears that moving them around definitely is not customary. There is, therefore, no apparent reason why the altars should be dissociated from the churches they are found in. There is, however, one significant exception. Although it is by no means general,[4] it is a documented fact that new churches are sometimes dedicated by introducing into them altar-tablets already consecrated and hitherto belonging to another older church. For example, the 15th century Chronicle of Ba'eda Māryām tells how this king 'made a (new) tabernacle (saqalā) and made many *tābotāt* come from Marḥa Bētu and he introduced (them) into it and named it Meshala Māryām'.[5] But in fact, it is sometimes possible to tell where altars come from, as is the case in the text quoted, and to obtain various indications from the context, for example, that we must be in a period when there would have to be several altars, or that, the term used being *tābotāt*, they would consist of altar-tablets placed on supports called *manāberta tābotāt* (see below) etc. But not every altar in a church always has its story readily available. Such difficulties are

---

[3] The particular case reported by Alvares in connection with the travels of the royal court (see below) does not represent a real objection to the general stability of the altars. See *The Prester John of the Indies: A true relation of the lands of Prester John, being the narrative of the Portuguese embassy to Ethiopia in 1520 written by Father Francisco Alvares*, translation of Lord Stanley of Alderley (1881) revised and edited with additional material by C.F. Beckingham and G.W.B. Huntingford, The Hakluyt Society, nº 114 (Cambridge, 1961), 2 vols., here vol. II, p. 518.

[4] As the Life of Samuel of Dabra Wagag shows, who made new altar-tablets from doors, brought them to the metropolitan for him to consecrate them, and only then introduced them into newly constructed churches. See Stanislas Kur, *Actes de Samuel de Dabra Wagag*, CSCO, 287-288, Scr. Aeth. 57-58 (Leuven, 1968), p. 43 (text), p. 33 (version). This document was written in the first half of the 16th century. A similar story is presented by Getatchew Haile in the Ethiopian Manuscript Microfilm Library (EMML, Collegeville, Minnesota), ms 7506, ff. 199v-200v, 'On the House of Lasta from the History of Zena Gäbrə'el', *Proceedings of the 9th International Congress of Ethiopian Studies*, vol. 6 (Moscow, 1988), pp. 7-21, on pp. 11-12 (text) and 15 (translation).

[5] Jules Perruchon, *Les chroniques de Zar'a Ya'eqob et de Ba'eda Mâryâm rois d'Éthiopie de 1434 à 1478 (Texte éthiopien et Traduction)* (Paris 1893), p. 127 (my translation) and 121. See also below the discussion of S. Munro-Hay's question, n. 66.

increased by important limitations on research in the Ethiopian context, for it is not possible to investigate systematically the altar-tablets because of their sacrosanct character. However, damaged *tābotāt* are discarded and it (occasionally) is possible to examine them,[6] a work that we have not undertaken yet. Even though the critical scope is sometimes limited, it is often possible to go farther than to draw a few conclusions from the observation of the *manbara tābot* in its relationship to the altar-tablet. In any case, this phenomenon follows the multiplication of altars and, in a second phase, the multiplication of just the altar-tablets. However in some cases the term *tābot* may stand for both the *manbara tābot* and the *tābot* as one object even if in two parts, or one object altogether (see 2, below). Doubts arise when these or other unexpected things occur, and explanations for them will have to be sought.[7] Otherwise, we may assume that, by and large, altars belong where they are found today.

In a number of cases, epigraphy and history of art, as well as pictures engraved or painted, may be important resources, but few concrete details are given in literary sources. A relative chronology can also be attempted by a comparison of one altar with others. Such a comparison between the relative chronology of churches and that of altars either confirms or calls into question the reliability of the chronology.

The discussions proposed below are new and, although the propositions offered are not definitive, they represent an effort to increase the understanding of the relationship between the churches of Christian Egypt and Ethiopia, of the evolution of the liturgy and, as a consequence, of the evolution of the buildings erected or hewn in order to house it, and, finally, to allow for a better grasp of the altar itself, which is a crucial element in the church's worship, both in the physical arrangement of the churches and in terms of the altar's meaning.

---

[6] A number of *tābotāt* can be seen under 'alabaster' and 'altar' in 'Mazgaba Seelat' (MS), a website database on Ethiopian material (Deeds, Toronto), eds. Michael Gervers and Ewa Balicka-Witakowska (URL http://ethiopia.deeds.utoronto.ca. User ID & Password: 'student'; into the box to the right of 'Quick Search' and click on 'Quick Search').

[7] For example, it will be the case below, when five differently made altars are found in the pre-13th century church of Dabra Salām Mikā'ēl. Certain situations remain puzzling: for example, how should one sort out the number and variety of altars found at Gʷāhegot or Masqala Krestos (near Saqoṭā)?

1. The Altar

1.1. The Vocabulary

In the Ethiopian context, the notion of altar is covered by several terms, which are: *tābot, ṣellāt, meśwā', manbar, manbara tābot.*[8]

a) The terms *tābot* and *ṣellāt*. The noun *tābot*, lit. 'box', or *tābota ḥeggu [la-Egzi'abehēr]*, lit. 'coffer of the law [of God]' (Rev. 11:19), or *tābota Musē*, the 'coffer of Moses' (cf. Mt. 24:38), refer specifically to the Ark of the Covenant while designating the altar-tablet. *Ṣellē*, lit. 'tablet, board' of any kind, has taken a specialized sense and, in its plural form of *ṣellāt*, has become the equivalent of *tābot* in reference to the tablets of the Ten Words given by God to Moses. The two terms of *tābot* and *ṣellāt* are both equally employed.

Concretely, the *tābot/ṣellāt* is a tablet made of hard wood or some kind of marble (*'ebna barad*) measuring more or less 30 × 25 cm. It is engraved with a cross and the name of the mystery or saint to whom it is dedicated[9] and consecrated (in private) by the bishop according to

---

[8] We have left aside the term *mā'ed* (or *mā'ed '*), the 'table' of the altar. To be complete, the way the different terms regarding the altar are used in the liturgical books of the *Maṣḥafa Qeddāsē* or Missal and the *Maṣḥafa Pāppās* or Pontifical, should also be the object of a survey, but this is outside the possibilities of this article and, although useful, would not add to the discussion which follows.

[9] Kidāna Wald Keflē, *Maṣḥafa sawāsew wa-geśś wa-mazgaba qālāt ḥaddis – Nebābu bu-ge'ez, fečew bāmāreññā* ('A Book of Grammar and Verb, and a New Dictionary: Ge'ez Entries with Amharic Definitions') (Addis Ababa, 1948 E.C., 1956 A.D.) pp. 755, 892. See pictures in David Buxton, *The Abyssinians* (New York, 1970) plates 100-101; J.M. Hanssens and A. Raes, 'Une collection de tâbots au Musée chrétien de la Bibliothèque Vaticane', *Orientalia Christiana Periodica* 17 (1951) 435-450; Jacques Mercier *et al.*, *L'Arche éthiopienne, art chrétien d'Éthiopie*, Pavillon des Arts, 27 septembre 2000-7 janvier 2001 (Paris, 2000), p. 26. One may also usefully refer to Appendix III, 'The Tābot', in *The Prester John of the Indies* (see n. 3), here vol. II, pp. 543-548. Sometimes, painted *tābotāt* are found, so far undocumented. From the pontificate of H.H. Abuna Takla-Hāymanot († 1988 A.D.), modern altar-tablets are much larger than earlier ones and are engraved in a more complex manner. First of all, the face of the tablet includes the image of the Holy Trinity above whom the phrase *ḥebu' semu [la-Egzi'abehēr]* ('hidden [is] the Name [of God]') is carved. Underlining the character of the altar-tablet as throne of God, its corners are occupied by the Four Living Creatures. Below, a representation of the mystery or saint to whose name the *tābot* is dedicated is found. In between, the names of the five nails and wounds of the Passion are inscribed, while Michael stands on the left side near the letters *Alfā wa-'O* (for *alpha* and *omega*) and Gabriel on the right side near the letters *Yeweṭā wa-Bētā* (for *iota* and *beta*) (*iota* is the first letter of Jesus' name and, since its numerical value is 10, stands for *the* Word manifested in the Ten Words written by God's finger). A cross adorns the back of the tablet, on which additional data may be carved.

the specific 'Rite of the Metropolitans' contained in the Coptic ritual translated into Ge'ez.[10] As many of the *tābotāt* of the collection of the Vatican show, there may be several names sharing the same tablet.[11] The *tābot* is counted among and as the first of the *newāya qeddesāt*, i.e. the 'sacred vessels' consecrated with holy Chrism.[12] During the services, the *tābot*, wrapped up in a small cloth (*māgonaṣafiyā*) and covered with a larger one (*māgonaṣafiyā* or *qaṣalā*), rests on the *manbar*, lit. the 'seat', more precisely the *manbara tābot*, lit. the 'seat of the *tābot*'.

b) The term *meśwā'*, 'altar', comes from the root *śewwā'*, 'to sacrifice' which Dillmann 256 describes: 'root *śawwe'a*, I,1 I, 1 [primitus incendere et comburere...] 257: *meśwā'*, 1) altare.' Here, Dillmann quotes the Synodos, noting that it prescribes to have both a mobile altar and another one, fixed (alterum fixum), and the *Faus Manfasāwi* 29, 2 (sic). Dillmann continues: '2) sacrarium, adytum, locus altaris. 3) sacrificium.'[13] The Amharic for *meśwā'* is *meśewiyā*, a word quite used in the liturgy. As we shall see again below, the *meśwā'* is, in principle, a

---

[10] *Śer'āta p̣āp̣p̣āsāt*, a phrase found in Getatchew Haile, 'On the House of Lasta from the History of Zena Gäbrə'el' (see n. 4), pp. 11-12 (text) and 15 (translation). See Abba Mārqos of Dabra Bizan, Bishop of Eritrea, *Maṣḥaf za-śimata kehnat: maṣḥaf śer'āta śimat za- śeyumāna bēta krestiyān ityop̣eyāwit*, ms., Maggābit 1933 E.C. [1941 A.D.] under *re'es beḍu'ān* Yoḥannes, *liqa p̣āp̣p̣āsāt za-Ityop̣eyā* 'Book of the Ordination of the Priesthood: Book of the Order of the Ordination of the Selected Persons of the Ethiopian Church' p. 108-111. On p. 110, a second title reads: *Ba-'enta ṣalot za-burākē tābot em-maṣḥafa śer'āt za-Gebṣāweyān* 'About the Prayer of Blessing of the Tābot, from the Book of the Order of the Egyptians'. See also *L'Ordinamento Liturgico di Gabriele V, 88° Patriarca Copto (1409-1427)*, ed. and trans. Alfonso 'Abdallah, in *Studia Orientalia Christiana*, Aegyptiaca, Centro Francescano di Studi Orientali Christiani (Cairo, 1962) 54-55, 437-438, 440-459, var. from 'Abdallah 1962: 440-459, *The Service for the Consecration of a Church and Altar according to the Coptic Rite, edited with translations from a Coptic and Arabic Manuscript of A.D. 1307 for the Bishop of Salisbury*, ed. and trans. Georges Horner (London, 1902) and Oswald Hugh Ewart Khatzis-Burmester (O.H.E. KES-Burmester), *The Egyptian or Coptic church: a detailed description of her liturgical services and the rites and ceremonies observed in the administration of her sacraments*, Publications de la Société d'Archéologie Copte, 'Textes et Documents' (Cairo, 1967), pp. 236 ff. See the remark by Coquin about a longer and shorter consecration of the altar, in 'La consécration des églises dans le rite copte: ses relations avec les rites syrien et byzantin', *L'Orient Syrien* 9 (1964) 160-161.

[11] When it is a secondary one.

[12] Maṣḥafa Qeddāsē (Missal), Ch. I. Chrism should be used, although it has hardly been possible to really do so in much of the Ethiopian history. See Emmanuel Fritsch, 'Mèron et chrismation dans la liturgie éthiopienne moderne', in: *Chrismation et confirmation: Questions autour d'un rite post-baptismal, LIVᵉ Semaine d'Études Liturgiques, Paris, juin 2007* (Rome, 2009), pp. 253-263.

[13] Wolf Leslau disagrees with this third meaning (entry 'məśwā'' in *Comparative Dictionary of Ge'ez: Ge'ez-English/English-Ge'ez* (Wiesbaden, 1987) p. 538, used by Getatchew Haile to translate *manbara məśwā'*, in fact an equivalent to *manbara tābot* (see below), in ms 7506, ff. 199v-200v, 'On the House of Lasta from the History of Zena Gäbrə'el' (see n. 4), pp. 10 (text) and 15 (translation).

fixed altar, established in a church through consecration, while the *tābot* is a small and mobile tablet.

c) The term *manbar* or *manbara tābot* refers to the table of different sizes and styles made in a way congruent with the holy *tābot* it carries during the liturgical services. While the proper term means 'seat' or, more precisely, 'seat of the *tābot*', many people call this table 'altar'. The *manbar* or *manbara tābot* is anointed when the *tābot*, normally already consecrated, is brought into a new church.

From this initial examination, we see that *tābot/sellāt* is not always, but may be, synonymous with *meśwā'*.[14] Both are forms of the altar, and the *manbar* or *manbara tābot* is a table which supports the *tābot/sellāt*. Each is expected to have a specialised sense as we are going to examine further now.

1.2. The Usage in the Liturgical-Canonical Literature

Among the books having authority, only two, it seems, mention both the *tābot* and the *meśwā'*, namely the much revered *Mashafa Sēnodos* and the famous later *nomocanon* of the *Fetha nagaśt*. They contain passages which are helpful to sort the notions out.

The first passage which concerns us here is found in the *Letter of Peter*, no 44, incorporated in the *Mashafa Sēnodos*.[15] We quote the following lines, which we already met in Dillmann's quote above:

p. 298 (44) *Ba-'enta qeddāsē tābot. Wa-qaddes kwello tābota hegg wa-hetemo ba-māhetama Egzi'abehēr za-we'etu mēron qeb'a tefśehet... wa-hetem tābotāta wa- meśwā'āta ba-māhetama Egzi'abehēr kama yerkab ba-za yeqēddesu lā'elē-hu mekha Egzi'abehēr.*

Translation: 'About the consecration of an altar-tablet (*tābot*). Consecrate every altar-tablet (*tābot*) of the law and sign it with the stamp of God, that is to say the chrism, the oil of gladness ... and sign the altar-tablets (*tābotāta*) and the altars (*meśwā'āta*)[16] with the seal of God in order to find the glory of God in what they (the priests) sanctify on them.'

---

[14] It is the case in the phrase *manbara məśwā'*, Getatchew Haile, 'On the House of Lasta from the History of Zena Gäbrə'el' (see n. 4), pp. 10 (text) and 15 (translation).

[15] We are using the edition of Alessandro Bausi, *Il Sēnodos etiopico*, C.S.C.O. vol. 552, t. 101 (text) (Leuven, 1995). The translation, however, is ours as we have attempted to capture the notions found in the texts more accurately than produced hitherto. The Letter of Peter to Clement 'è di origine melchita ed è fatta unanimemente risalire al sec. VIII', A. Bausi, *Il Sēnodos etiopico*, C.S.C.O. vol. 553, t. 102 (Leuven, 1995), xxi.

[16] Wilhelm Riedel, *Die Kirchenrechtsquellen des Patriarchats Alexandrien* (Leipzig, 1900) has: 'Bezeichne den Altar und die Kirchen mit dem Siegel des Herrn...' (p. 172, 27).

p. 300 (52) *Ba-'enta śer'āta meśwā'. Wa-yeqaddesu qwerbāna diba
meśwā' za-ḥetum ba-mēron...* (53) *Wa-yekun westa kwellu bēta maqdas
kele'ētu meśwā' haḥada za-yeṣawerwo emmakān* |p. 301| *westa makān
kama ebna daqiqa Esrā'ēl za-kona ba-gadām yeṣawerwo emmakān westa
makān wa-kāl'o za-'iyeṣawerwo emmakānu.* (54) *Wa-la'emma tasabra
meśwā' za-'iyeṣawerwo aw anqalqalo sab' emmakānu za-taqaddasa
a'emmer kama atata qeddesennā-hu emnē-hu ba-kama atata qeddesennā
daqiqa Esrā'ēl em-weludu wa-yedallu yeqaddese-wo dāgema.*

Translation: '(52) About the order of the altar. Let them (the priests) consecrate the offering on an altar that is signed with the chrism ... (53) And
let there be in every sanctuary (*bēta maqdas*) two altars (*meśwā'*): one
which moves from place to place like the stone of the children of Israel
which was in the wilderness moved from place to place, and a second one
which will not move from its place. (54) And if the altar which does not
move from its place be broken, or if someone has taken it away from its
place which is sacred, realise that its holiness has left it as the holiness of
the children of Israel left their children and it should be consecrated again.'

We find here a distinction between two sacred objects which are
equally 'altars', one type being meant to be moveable and the other
fixed. Both need a consecration with the chrism, a re-consecration being
necessary whenever the fixed altar is damaged or carried away. This
means that a fixed altar could physically be removed from one place and
be brought to another, but that was not allowed.

This source has partly been incorporated into the *nomocanon* of the
Fetḥa nagaśt, also of great authority, which was compiled only in 1238
by Aṣ-Ṣafī Abū l-Faḍā'il Ibn al-'Assāl in Egypt and was introduced into
Ethiopia around the 16th century,[17] long after the coming to existence of
the ancient churches and altars. A provision of the First Chapter of the
Fetḥa nagaśt reads as follows: [18]

*Wa-la'emma tasabra meśwā' aw falasa yeqaddesu dāgema, wa-yekun
tābot ba-za-yefales emmakān westa makān kama ebna daqiqa Esrā'ēl za-
falasa emmakān westa makān.*

Translation: 'If the altar breaks or is transferred elsewhere, it shall be consecrated again, and the *tābot* shall be such that it can be transferred from
one place to another like the stone of the children of Israel which could be
transferred from one place to another.'[19]

---

[17] Paulos Tzadua, entry 'Fetḥa nagaśt', in *Encyclopedia Aethiopica*, II, ed. Siegbert
Uhlig (Wiesbaden, 2005), p. 534.

[18] We are using the Ge'ez-Amharic edition of the Patriarchate of Addis Ababa, *Fetḥa
nagaśt. Nebāb-ennā tergʷāmēw* (Addis Ababa, 1962 E.C. [1970 A.D.]), p. 21. The translation is ours.

[19] Paulos Tzadua, *The Fetha Nagast: The Law of the Kings translated from the Ge'ez*
(Addis Ababa, 1968), p. 11; Ignazio Guidi, *Il 'Fetha Nagast' o 'Legislazione dei Re'*,

The term used for altar here in the first part of the sentence is *meśwā'*, like the one employed in the Ethiopian *Sēnodos*, primarily but not exclusively designating a fixed altar. Here, it refers to the fixed altar because, although its meaning would cover the qualities of the *tābot* insofar as it is consecrated and expected to be consecrated anew if broken or moved, this canon is made to contrast with what is said of the mobile *tābot* in the second part of the sentence.

In the following case, the *Fetḥa nagaśt* has a development from the *Maṣḥafa Sēnodos*, again taken from the passage of the *Letter of Peter* we already read (no 44):

> *Wa-yāḥetewu ba-sam' wa-qandil gizē yeqēddes episqoppos tābotāta meśwā' wa-yahallewu meselē-hu gizē qeddāsē-hā sab'atu qasāwest wa-yeḥetem kiyāhā ba-mēron za-we'etu qeb'a tefśeḥet esma māḥetama Egzi'abeḥēr we'etu; yedallu kama yeqaddesu ba-westētā.*

> Translation: 'Let them illuminate with wax tapers and candles when the bishop consecrates the tablets of the altar and let seven priests be together with him at the time of her (the church) consecration and let him sign her with chrism, that is the oil of gladness, for it is the seal of God; it is fitting for them to celebrate mass inside her (the consecrated church).'[20]

In this case, *tābotāta* is in both the plural and construct state. But in reality *meśwā'* qualifies the tablets, with which the text is concerned according to the reading that, 'when the bishop consecrates the tablets of the altar', it is the tablets which are the altar, or the 'altar-tablets' which are meant. This construct state is in fact epexegetic: it is not a question of the unlikely situation of having several tablets attached to one (consecrated) altar (*meśwā'*) or the notion of altar-tablets meant to remain on a fixed (consecrated) altar. In the original situation, it would have made no sense to identify mobile altars with fixed altars, as concrete objects, and no bishop would go systematically around a large country in order to consecrate fixed altars when he could consecrate light mobile altar-tablets and, in normal circumstances, no one would have brought to him from afar altars meant to be fixed altars.

Pubblicazioni scientifiche del R. Istituto orientale di Napoli, tomo III, vol. I (text) (Rome, 1897), p. 16; Guidi, *Il 'Fetha Nagast' o 'Legislazione dei Re'*, Pubblicazioni scientifiche del R. Istituto orientale di Napoli, tomo III, vol. II (translation) (Rome, 1899), p. 19: ch. I: 'Se si rompe l'altare o vada altrove [note 6: according to the vocalisation to be given to the Arabic = 'o sia trasportato'], si consacri di nuovo'.

[20] Cp. Guidi, *Il 'Fetha Nagast'* 1899 (translation), ch. I, p. 19. The *Fetḥa nagaśt* contrasts with both the *Letter of Peter* found in the Ethiopian *Maṣḥafa Sēnodos* and the Arabic source edited by Riedel (see above n. 16) which mention both altar and church.

In conclusion, there is no mention here of a fixed altar, only of mobile ones. We can also understand that the textual alteration reflects a situation whereby the multiplication of mobile altar-tablets has already taken place after the distinction between mobile and fixed altars had disappeared as irrelevant or inapplicable (see below, 2).

Already in 15th-century Ethiopia, King Zar'a Yāʿeqob had quoted the same no 44 of the *Letter of Peter* and mentioned the *tābot* only.[21] Today still, the *tābot* or altar-tablet has kept the character of the mobile altar, Coptic in origin,[22] and is the only type of altar known. So the available Pontificals contain a rite for the consecration or re-consecration of a *tābot*, but do not mention a fixed altar as far as we can determine. It is this mobile type of altar which is referred to in the ancient representations of the giving of the law to Moses by God, or that we read about when, in the lives of saints or marginal notes in Four-Gospel books, the making of *tābotāt* or the consecration of new churches is discussed.[23] Among others, the noun *tābot* translates in the Prayer of the Prothesis the Greek τράπεζα already used in all the sources of the Liturgy of Saint Mark.[24] The mention of 'the stone of the children of Israel', naturally authorises the making of an altar-tablet of stone[25] but, more importantly, it establishes a relationship between the altar-tablet and the Ark of the Covenant on account of their mobility. Once the relation is established it opens wider correspondences. Further, several churches, even Western ones, have established analogies between Moses' Ark and the altar, particularly when mobile. The mobile altar allows people to use it outside a

---

[21] 'Il libro di re Zar'a Yā'eqob sulla custodia del mistero', ed. and trans. Carlo Conti-Rossini, *Rassegna di Studi Etiopici* XXI, Anno III, Numero II, Maggio-Agosto 1943, text on p. 151-152; translation on p. 160.

[22] See Hishmat Messiha, 'Portable Altars: Luxor Treasure (1893)', *Bulletin de la Société d'Archéologie Copte* 31 (1992) 129-134 and pl. xvii-xix. However, it is not certain that what is described here as altars actually are such. See Dominique Bénazeth, *Catalogue général du Musée Copte du Caire, 1. Objets en métal*. IF 873 MIFAO 119 (2008²), pp. 383-384; Abdallah, 1962: 55; Abu l-Makarim fol. 97b; Evetts (1895) 269; Alfred J. Butler, *The Ancient Coptic Churches of Egypt*, vol. II (Oxford, 1884, reprint: Gorgias Press, 2004), ch. I; *Paulos Tzadua, The Fetha Nagast – The Law of the Kings translated from the Ge'ez* (Addis Ababa, 1968), p. 11.

[23] E.g. in Kur, *Actes de Samuel de Dabra Wagag* (see n. 4), pp. 43 (text) and 33 (version).

[24] Ṣalota ʿenforā, Maṣhafa Qeddāsē, ch. III, # 47; in Marcos Daoud, *The Liturgy of the Ethiopian Church* (Cairo, 1959), p. 29, n° 47. See Geoffrey Cuming, *The Liturgy of Saint Mark*, Orientalia Christiana Analecta 234 (Rome, 1990), pp. 4, 86. How it happened and which languages channelled such texts are still open matters.

[25] Usually a kind of marble (*'ebna barad*), as in Getatchew Haile, 'On the House of Lasta from the History of Zena Gäbrə'el' (see n. 4), pp. 11 (text) and 15 (translation).

permanent setting in order to focus on the permanent presence of God in the midst of the community at worship, even outside a permanent framework.[26]

1.3. The Manbara Tābot

One relatively difficult element of the discussion is the status of the *manbara tābot* already mentioned above. In itself, it is only a support of the consecrated mobile tablet, which is the actual altar. However, the tablet without it would be of little use and significance, because it needs to be carried for its raison d'être as an altar to be operative. Besides, the bishop says a *Ṣalot ba-'enta burākē manbar wa-albāti*, 'Prayer for the Blessing of the *Manbar* and her Clothes',[27] and also anoints the *manbar* when he dedicates a new church. This liturgical rite confers on the *manbar* a certain level of consecration and, therefore, calls for an appropriate reverence. Such reverence would be expressed in reference to the prescriptions concerning the altar, including its normal immobibility. The 16th-century priest-traveller Alvares noted in the end of his diary something interesting:

> 'When the Prester John and all his people travel, the altar and the altar stone on which mass is said all go on the shoulders of the priests as on a litter, and eight priests go with each altar by turns, that is, four and four: and a priest goes in front of them with a thurible, and further in front a deacon ringing a bell, and all the people go away from the road, and those that are on horses dismount, and show reverence to the altar stone or altar.'[28]

This witness distinguishes the altar stone or altar tablet from what he calls the altar, which, properly speaking, was a *manbara tābot*. Yet, reverence is paid to the whole, even as it is travelling and when, therefore, one could have been more casual with the *manbar* dissociated from the *tābot*. The *manbar* itself is the object of reverence.

For the sake of simplification of language in our study, and, aware that the *manbara tābot* may fully constitute an altar only when the *tābot* rests upon it, even if it shares something of the sacrality of the altar, we shall simply refer to the *manbar* as the 'altar', whether complete or not, and will specify when clarity demands it.

---

[26] On altars and mobile altars in the Western context, see Éric Palazzo, *Liturgie et société au Moyen Âge*, Aubier, collection historique (Paris, 2000), pp. 71-77 and 128-139.

[27] Abbā Yā'eqob, Bishop, Dabra Libānos (*ad usum* Abuna Zakkāryās, Arba Minch 1988), p. 171. This prayer is lacking in Mārqos, *Maṣḥaf za-śimata kehnat*, 1933 E.C. [1941 A.D.] (see n. 10), pp. 108-111.

[28] *The Prester John of the Indies* (see n. 3), vol. II, p. 518.

2. Questions Raised by Facts at Lālibalā (First Part of the 13th Century)

2.1. The Multiplication of the Altars

Whereas some of the monolithic churches of Lālibalā (Bēta Māryām, Bēta Madḥanēʿālam, Bēta Amānu'ēl) follow the plan of older churches (see Appendix, 1), other monolithic or semi-monolithic churches (Bēta Rufā'ēl-Gabre'ēl, Bēta Masqal, Bēta Marqorēwos, Dabra Sinā, Bēta Golgotā, Bēta Danāgel, Bēta Giyorgis, Śellāsē) show marked differences.[29] There, the abundance of shrines is matched by an over-abundance of altars of a kind found in Lālibalā itself but also at Zoz Ambā, Ṭerā Asfari Esṭifānos, Bilbālā Giyorgis and as far as Dabra Maʿār in Gar'āltā (East Tegrāy): they are not restricted to Lāstā.

At Lālibalā in the first part of the 13th century under King Lālibālā, we find a relatively short period of transformation of the initial part of the Eucharistic liturgy. This change was a sequel to a movement in the Coptic Church whereby people wanted to respond to their felt need to dedicate churches to more saints. Unable to build new churches because of adverse circumstances, they erected new altars dedicated to these saints in the *pastophoria*, where hitherto the preparation of bread and wine was taking place prior to the Eucharistic liturgy. These rooms were therefore transformed into as many additional sanctuaries. The new altars are of a type which, generally, allows them to be easily introduced into places not originally planned for such use. Hence, it is not surprising to find several of them in a given place. They confirm that the new order may have begun in the churches of the older order in the Lālibalā area. Their table is only large enough to receive an altar-tablet (the *tābot*), which in turn could support just the paten and chalice. The missal and other paraphernalia for the Eucharistic celebration would have been borne by attendants. As a result, the *prothesis* rite was no longer done in a *pastophorion*, but at the altar itself. The doors of the new sanctuaries were adapted to the new functions of the place and the presbyterium (*hurus*) was transformed or simply abolished.

This movement progressed in Egypt from the 10th to the early 13th century. I should like to consider a double hypothesis as to its beginnings in Ethiopia. A first moment may have been isolated at

---

[29] See Appendix, 1. This matter is the subject of the study: Fritsch, 'Liturgical Changes' (see n. 2).

The altars were multiplied and introduced in the *pastophoria* which were ipso facto turned into additional sanctuaries. New churches were made either like wide open halls (Lālibalā Dabra Sinā), or on the contrary kept a sanctuary of the former proportions but without side-rooms (Lālibalā Bēta Giyorgis), or often kept seeming *pastophoria* which were in fact sanctuaries from their inception as at Gannata Māryām.[32] Certain older churches like Gundefru Śellāsē (Tegrāy) were adapted to the new order.[33]

2.2. Authentic Consecrated Altars without Altar-tablets?

A number of altars in Lālibalā are intriguing because of the specific type of inscriptions they bear (Fig. 1). The documents have been brought to the light by Stanisław Chojnacki and partly presented by Stefan Strelcyn, then more abundantly by Gigar Tesfaye.[34] Our own research in the larger region has brought about a few more elements. As an example amongst the inscriptions collected, King Lālibālā wrote on the altar of Madḥanēʿālam 3 (pl. XIII):

> 'This is the *tābot* that I caused to be made, I King [Lālibālā, by the name][35] of the cherubs, of the holy angels who have many eyes, so that they may beseech compassion and mercy for me before God.'[36]

[32] Fritsch and Gervers, 'Pastophoria and Altars' (see n. 2), p. 37. Gannata Māryām and contemporaneous Emmakinā Madḥanēʿālam represent a *terminus ante quem*, since they display the transformations we are describing in the years following 1270.

[33] See Appendix, 1. We shall not develop this topic here, since it has been already treated in: Fritsch and Gervers, 'Pastophoria and Altars' and Fritsch, 'Liturgical Changes' (see n. 2).

[34] Gigar Tesfaye (avec la collaboration de Jacqueline Pirenne), 'Inscriptions sur bois de trois églises de Lalibala', *Journal of Ethiopian Studies* 17 (1984) 107-126, 17 plates, states in his first paragraph: '… Trois de ces objets avaient déjà été vus et photographiés par S. Chojnacki en 1964, et furent publiés par S. Strelcyn.1 voir ici sous Mädhane Aläm 2, gabriel 4 et gabriel 5' (*sic*). See Stefan Strelcyn,'Quelques inscriptions éthiopiennes sur des 'mänabərt' des églises de Lalibäla et de sa région', *Bibliotheca orientalis* XXXVI, 3/4 (1979) 137-156, LMA2 (= Lālibalā Madḥanē'ālam), LM2 (= Lālibalā Māryām) and LM3 (p. 138) and, in addition, LMA1, LGa (= Lālibalā Gabre'ēl), ṬE (= *Ṭerā Asfari Esṭifānos*, of Mercurius) (p. 138) as well as LM1 and again ṬE (= of the *Arbaʿetu Ensesā*) (p. 155), which Gigar Tesfaye has not made use of. Unfortunately, the documentation is incomplete, but it has had the merit of revealing an important source for philology, history, history of art, theology and liturgy.

[35] The name of *Lālibālā* has been added by the editor as well as the words *[ba-sem] omu*, 'by the name…' probably on the grounds of consistency with the other altars found in the area where King Lālibālā's name is quoted as author, consistency with the *formulae* employed elsewhere as well as the space needed for the letters proposed.

[36] Gigar Tesfaye, *Inscriptions* (see n. 34): Madḥanēʿālam 3 (pl. XIII) p. 123, partly Golgotā 4 (pl. VIII-X).

Fig. 1: Altar in Bēta Rufā'ēl-Gabre'ēl (Gigar Tesfaye's 'Gabriel 4', face 3),
Lālibalā (Photo: Emmanuel Fritsch)

In this case, it is first of all remarkable that the king describes the object he writes on as a straightforward *tābot* when we are used to speak in such case of a *manbara tābot*. It may only be a question of vocabulary, since *tābot* means chest and it is a chest. But hardly just so since the object appears to be dedicated in the same way an altar-tablet is, and in this case it is dedicated to the cherubim.

The text engraved on the altar Golgotā 1 (pl. IV)[37] reads:

'... I [Lālibālā] made [this] *tābot* and gave her the name of Sanbata krestiyān,[38] putting my trust in her...'

'... And I, putting my hope in your mercy, engraved this *tābot* and named her Sanbatiyān;[39] may your mercy be here where this *tābot* dwells...'

In Bēta Madḥanēʿālam 2 (pl. XII), we find this dedication:[40]

'King Lālibālā [dedicates this *tābot*] in the name of the 24 priests of heaven, so that they pray to God that he may remit my (sic!) sin and my (sic!) iniquity. Amen and amen.'

We observe further that, besides dedicating the *tābotāt* to the cherubs or the Sunday, Lālibālā has added a prayer to them. We remember that it is the altar-tablets or *tābotāt* that are dedicated, not just their supports or *manāberta tābotāt*. In the present case, however, the king put his request of intercession in the indirect form only, which may create an uncertainty as to the rapport between the patron or 'owner' of the *tābot*, as the Ethiopians say about the person to whom it is dedicated, and the altar. However, the direct form is even more frequent, like in the following examples of Golgotā 2 (pl. V) and 3 (pl. VI-VII), respectively:

'Melchisedek, priest of the Lord, pray and beseech for me, for Lālibālā the sinner and guilty one, so that he may have mercy on me and forgive me. Amen.'

'Pray for me, Children Ananya and Azarya and Misael, martyrs of Christ, because of God the Father, because of Christ the Son, and because of the Paraclete the Holy Spirit, so that you may obtain compassion and mercy for the servant of God Lālibālā forever. Amen.'

---

[37] Gigar Tesfaye, *Inscriptions* (see n. 34), faces 1 and 2, pp. 115-116 (text) and 117-118 (version).

[38] Lit. the 'Sabbath of the Christians', i.e. the Sunday, often personified (e.g. in the Anaphora of Athanasius N° 56-69; 172-176) and to whom are dedicated altars and confraternities (*māḥbarāt*). Here, the gender of *tābot* is feminine.

[39] A contraction of *Sanbata krestiyān*, i.e. the Sunday. See the previous note.

[40] Gigar Tesfaye, *Inscriptions* (see n. 34), pp. 122-123; Strelcyn, *Mänabərt*, LMA2 (see n. 34), p. 138.

One detail in the above quotes is intriguing: the pious king asks for God's mercy in his favour and is, therefore, concerned with his personal salvation. Does this feature describe his spirituality or the altars as such? Possibly more the former than the latter. The case of this altar of Mary, easy to find in Lālibalā Bēta Gabre'ēl wa-Rufā'ēl, different because the prayer is uttered by a community but similar in content, shows that the point is irrelevant:[41]

> 'O Mary, pray and beseech your good Son our Saviour in our favour, so that he may have mercy on us and be compassionate to us and forgive our sin through the abundance of his mercy for ever. Amen and amen.'[42]

We further note that all the dedications and invocations which we have been able to see are addressed to one name only, whether of one person or of a group of persons seen as one.[43] These altars, like the authentic altar-tablets, are "monosemic".

The small cross-shaped altar Golgotā 4[44] has its sides engraved as follows:

> 'One of them the face of a man; and one the face of an ox; one the face of an eagle and one the face of a lion (...) because of the living Lord, the Almighty, who spread their wings, the Four Animals of the one God, Christ, so that he may have mercy upon the servant of God Lālibālā.'

This altar is therefore dedicated to the Four Living Creatures (*Arbā'etu Ensesā*, the 'Four Animals').[45] But the conventional *tābota...* in the construct state does not precede the ascription as it did in the first examples quoted above or as it would in: *Tābota Arbā'etu Ensesā*. The ascription is neither direct nor complete, but the invocation survives, if somewhat unclear.

---

[41] Gabriel 5 in Gigar Tesfaye, *Inscriptions* (see n. 34), pp. 124-125 (pl. xvi); Strelcyn, *Mänabərt*, LM2 (see n. 34), p. 138; Alessandro Augusto Monti della Corte, *Lalibala: Le chiese ipogee e monolitiche e gli altri monumenti medievali del Lasta* (Rome, 1940) p. xxxix, top left.

[42] According to Ugo Zanetti, it is likely that such a Marian prayer may have been a conclusive prayer.

[43] This has been verified in Gigar Tesfaye, *Inscriptions* (see n. 34), Strelcyn, *Mänabərt* (see n. 33), and the altars we have seen in person. When there are several names, they belong to a group such as the Three Children of Babylon, the Twenty-four Priests of Heaven, the Cherubim. They should be considered as one dedication.

[44] Gigar Tesfaye, *Inscriptions* (see n. 34), pp. 120-121, pl. VIII, IX, X.

[45] Commemorated on Ḥedār 8.

The church of Zoz Ambā Giyorgis[46] offers similar examples of the same phenomenon. The altar dedicated to Gabre'ēl[47] does bear his name written on the cross carved on its table: *Gabre'ēl mal'ak*, 'Angel Gabriel'. In addition, a prayer is carved on one side: *se'al ba-'enti'a-na*, 'Pray for us'. The pattern of the cross, the name of the person to whom it is dedicated, i.e. in a permanent manner, not just as a piece of furniture, only meant to receive any *tābot* consecrated to any saint, and the prayer, all these details suggest that this piece of furniture was made not just as a *manbara tābot* but as a *meswā'*, an altar proper which does not need the addition of a separate *tābot* in order to be the site of the liturgy (Fig. 2).[48]

There remains a question, however, as to the way such an altar should be named. It is more than likely that it would have been named *tābot*, as a simple altar-tablet, because its first meaning of 'chest' makes it naturally congruent with the object, in contrast with *ṣellāt* which refers to a flat tablet, but especially because this is the way we see it called by king Lālibālā in the engravings quoted above. *Meswā'* may also be used, but hardly with the specific connotation of a real, complete, stable altar: the limited size of most of our altars does not exclude the notion since the *Sēnodos* established the rule: '... if someone has taken it away from its place...',[49] but we have not yet come across texts which would speak about consecrated altars with another name but *tābot*[50] and have observed above how the original notion does not match any reality.

---

[46] Monument visited with Claire Bosc-Tiessé on 11th February 2008 in the context of a mission facilitated by the Centre français des études éthiopiennes (CFEE), Addis Ababa.

[47] We saw two ancient monoxyle altars in the area nowadays used for the ablutions, apparently the same as those described by Claude Lepage et Jacques Mercier, 'Une église lalibelienne: Zoz Amba', *Annales d'Éthiopie* 18 (2002) 151-153, here on p. 153, who mention the presence of three monoxyle altars in the church, although their report, as ours, only concerns two of them. We were not able to measure them or view them under their different angles at the time. We have obtained the measurements of two altars by kindness of Ewa Balicka-Witakowska, to whom I am grateful. See 'Mazgaba Seelat' (see n. 6), photograph 2006.067:016-31 by Michael Gervers. The impression obtained on the spot as well as from the photographs is that their size, which corresponds to the volume of the central sanctuary and side-rooms, permits their use as adequate altars. This fact as well as the fact that the two altars are very similar in style, which suggests the one intention of furnishing the same church, suggests in turn that the church did have three altars.

[48] A similar text is carved on the altar of Zoz Ambā dedicated to Mary: *Māryām walādita Amlāk se'ali ba-'enti'a-na*, 'Mary Mother of God, pray for us'. See 'Mazgaba Seelat', picture 2006.067:016-31 (see n. 6).

[49] See our first part above.

[50] E. g. Perruchon, *Les chroniques de Zar'a Ya'eqob et de Ba'eda Māryâm rois d'Éthiopie de 1434 à 1478* (see n. 4), pp. 81, 121, 127.

Fig. 2: Altar of Gabre'ēl, Zoz Ambā Giyorgis,
with text reading opposite to cavity (Photo: Michael Gervers)

At Māwerē Ṭerā Asfari Esṭifānos,[51] three out of the four altars seen bear a cross on their table and are dedicated in the same way to Marqorēwos, Esṭifānos, or *Arbāʿetu Ensesā* (Fig. 3).[52] A fourth *manbar* bears the inscription: *Ze-tābot Ṗarāqliṭos za-yered la-na*, 'This *tābot* [is of the] Paraclete; may he descend to us'.[53] The surprise is that the table-top has a frame obviously meant to hold an altar-tablet (Fig. 4), and the reason for this must be that this particular altar was not a consecrated *tābot* but was meant to be the *manbara tābot* permanently associated with a certain *tābot* of the Paraclete and no other.

At Emmakinā Madḫanēʿālam,[54] a church which belongs to the period following 1270, an altar bears a dedication engraved on its feet. It reads: *Arbāʿetu Ensesā*, the 'Four Animals'. The conventional *tābot*a... in the construct state could have preceded the ascription as in: *Tābota Arbāʿetu Ensesā*. As in many other earlier cases (Golgotā 4, Ṭerā Asfari Esṭifānos etc.) there is no apparent reason to see a problem in this shortening.[55] A detail may be of relevance: in contrast with the other larger altar of the church, the top of this small cross-shaped altar makes it difficult to lay directly upon it safely a paten and a chalice, because the hollow part between the edge and the narrow cross in the middle seems too wide, even if covered by a cloth, unless another flat surface, that of a *tābot* proper, was placed over the whole *manbar*, expectedly (Fig. 5).

The phenomenon described finds a literary echo in the following text:

> *Wa-ʾādi mahara·kama iyerasseyu wa-iyānberu aḥada tābota za-ʾenbala kelʾētta tābotāt; aw za-yebazeḫ; wa-ʾemuntu-ni tābotāt iyekunu ba-bāḥetitomu; enbala yedammeru tābota Māryām māʾekalēhomu.*

> '[King Zarʾa Yāʾeqob] also taught that one was not to set up and place one unique *tābot* but rather two *tābotāt* or [*tābotāt*] which would be many, and that these *tābotāt* were not supposed to be on their own, but one was to add the *tābot* of Mary between them.'[56]

---

[51] Monument visited by Claire Bosc-Tiessé, Marie-Laure Derat and Martin Tiessé during a mission of the French Centre for Ethiopian Studies (CFEE), Addis Ababa, in March 2008. They were kind enough to let me avail of their photographs.

[52] These have been noted for their beauty since Gerster, *Churches in Rock* (see n. 29), pp. 141-142, photos 209-211, fig. 123. Other altars are stored in the treasury of the church but are never shown.

[53] Lit.: 'This *tābot* the Paraclete who-may he descend to us'.

[54] Monument visited by the author during a mission sponsored by the French Centre for Ethiopian Studies (CFEE), Addis Ababa, in May 2008.

[55] See Gigar Tesfaye, *Inscriptions* (see n. 34), p. 121.

[56] Perruchon, *Les chroniques de Zarʾa Yaʾeqob et de Baʾeda Mâryâm rois d'Éthiopie de 1434 à 1478* (see n. 4), p. 81 (my translation).

Fig. 3: Altars at Māwerē Ṭerā Asfari Esṭifānos
(Photo: Claire Bosc-Tiessé)

Fig. 4: *Manbara tābot* of the Paraclete at Māwerē Ṭerā Asfari Esṭifānos
(Photo: Claire Bosc-Tiessé)

Fig. 5: Altars of Emmakinā Madḥanēʿālam (Photo: Emmanuel Fritsch)

This 15th century report states that:

a) It is becoming a norm to have several *tābotāt* in a church, although there are still cases when one only is found, hence the regulation.

b) We are at this stage, therefore, still close enough to the frame of mind which triggered the multiplication of the *tābotāt* as a consequence of the cult of saints, since several altars are established simultaneously.

c) This, in turn, suggests that the relationship *tābot-manbara tābot* is stable. We are still far from the simplification whereby several *tābotāt* are placed in turn on the same *manbara tābot*, dissociated from any particular *tābot*.

d) The several *tābotāt* are expected to be placed together in the same location, not in different sanctuaries, which supposes that a large type of sanctuary such as the one which developed in the 'hall churches'[57] be in favour.

---

[57] E.g., see the churches of Dabra Sinā and Golgotā at Lālibalā, of Dabra Ṣeyon, Abbā Yoḥanni *etc.*, Appendix 2 and 3.1.a, d, e, respectively and 3.2.b, c and d.

e) The *tābot* ascribed to Mary seems to be placed on a *manbara tābot* which is in the middle of the others, hence in the centre, and only on that one — unless this notion squeezes the text too much, for a consequence may be that all churches would then be named after their main altar, that of Mary.

f) If this is true of Mary's *tābot*, there is no reason why it would not be true for the other *tābotāt*, which are expected to be placed always on the same *manbara tābot*, at the side of the other altars.[58]

2.3. Dedication of Altars and Remarks

As we observed in the beginning, a *tābot* is characterised by a cross and a dedication, e.g. *Tābota Māryām*, '*Tābot* of Mary'. Here, we have the name *tābot*, the cross and the dedication. The latter is sometimes reinforced with a request for intercession. The dedication engraved on an altar is always the only one on this altar. A practical detail is that, in general and in contrast with the *manāberta tābotāt* which have a frame around their tops clearly meant to receive a *tābot*, the top surface of these altars is levelled, despite the fact that a cross and various motives are engraved on it. It follows that it would be somewhat perilous to place a *tābot* on top of such altars, because it might easily slip and slide even though, and perhaps because, it is expected to be wrapped up in a textile. These details lead us to think that these are complete consecrated altars.

The fact that a precise dedication is carved on a table equipped with a frame meant that: a) the table is in fact a *manbara tābot* made to receive an altar-tablet, and b) the altar-tablet should always be the same *tābot*, precisely one dedicated to the same mystery or saint as named by the name engraved on the *manbara tābot*, to the exclusion of any other altar-tablet.

So far, such "monosemic" dedicated altars have been found in Lālibalā, Māwerē Ṭerā Asfari Esṭifānos and Zoz Ambā Giyorgis, which are all neighbouring areas. They are in groups, which situates them in the

---

[58] This is the way the sanctuary was eventually arranged at Lālibalā Golgotā (17th century): an altar (not a 'shrine') was installed on each side of the altar with a ciborium; see Getatchew Haile, 'On the House of Lasta from the History of Zena Gäbrə'el' (see n. 4), p. 11 (text) and p. 15 (translation). The text explicitly mentions that the *manbara tābot* installed on the tomb of saint Lālibālā is of the holy archangel Michael; it follows that only the *tābot* dedicated to Mikā'ēl is to be used there. This is why the church is known as 'Golgotā-Mikā'ēl'.

period when altars were systematically multiplied, that is the first half of the 13th century.[59] This dating agrees with the presumed authorship of the engravings signed with King Lālibālā's name and, interestingly, may provide external support to their authenticity. In our survey of the following periods, such altars will not be met again. Thus, they may be ascribed to the initiative of a certain metropolitan, likely the first successor to Mikā'ēl II, i.e. Kîl al-Mulabbas, previously bishop of Fuwā, who served too short a period and too early (1200-1205, deposed 1210) in relation to Lālibālā to have been involved in this. We, therefore, suggest abuna Yeshaq (ca. 1209-?) as the person who may have consecrated not just light, mobile altar-tablets as hitherto or thereafter, but also full *tābot*-altars, complete from mensa to feet. This course of action may also have been started or continued by the metropolitan following Yeshaq, Giyorgis (1225-?),[60] whose dates may fall during the final years of King Lālibālā's reign (the date of his death is unknown), when he is more likely to have completed a number of his churches and, perhaps, when the changes involving the multiplication of altars also had time to gain momentum. Although the phenomenon reached the post-1270 Emmakinā Madhanēʿālam's church, we saw that it is likely that a *tābot* was used with the altar in question (see above).

In contrast, a particular altar in Lālibalā presents interesting material. It is the *manbar* Golgotā 5,[61] on which sides are engraved in low relief

---

[59] It is difficult, however, to appreciate the nature of the altars at Māwerē Ṭerā Asfari Esṭifānos because of their number in such a remote and small place as well as because of the striking difference between the high quality of the altars on the one hand and the poor monastic cave-church on the other hand. Claire Bosc-Tiessé suggests that the remote monastery may have been used to shelter these precious objects from looting (March 2008). Might the altar dedicated to St Stephen (see below) point to such a thing, when special links are said to unite Ḥayq Esṭifānos and Ṭerā Asfari Esṭifānos, as often suggested orally?

[60] The first successor to Kîl, Yeshaq, is mentioned in the *History of the Patriarchs of the Egyptian Church*, III/2 (see n. 31), pp. 191-193; Perruchon, 'Notes pour l'histoire d'Éthiopie: Abba Jean' (see n. 31), p. 84. Giyorgis II, his second successor, is mentioned in a feudal act dated 1225 in connection with a land-grant effectuated by Lālibālā (Conti-Rossini, 'L'evangelo d'oro di Dabra Libanos', *Rendiconti della Reale Accademia dei Lincei* 10, ser. 5 [1901] 189-191), which documents that both this king and this metropolitan were flourishing at this time. It is stated in the colophon of the *Kebra nagast* (C. Bezold, *Kebra Nagast: Die Herrlichkeit der Könige*, [Munich, 1905], p. 138) that that book was translated from Coptic into Arabic in 1217 E.C. (1224-25 A.D.) during the reign of Lālibālā and the metropolitanate of Giyorgis II. See Salvatore Tedeschi, 'Ethiopian Prelates', in *The Coptic Encyclopedia*, ed. Aziz Atiya (New York, 1991), vol. 4, pp. 1007-1009; Stuart Munro-Hay, *Ethiopia and Alexandria: The Metropolitan Episcopacy of Ethiopia*, I (Warsaw, 1997), pp. 189-190.

[61] Gigar Tesfaye, *Inscriptions* (see n. 34), p. 122, pl. XI.

the images of King Lālibālā and his wife Masqal Kebrā. An inscription, at times difficult to decipher, reads as follows:

ሳሊባላ፡ ንጉሥ፡ ዕጉሥ፡ ወቅዱስ፡ እግዚአብሔር፡ [...] እ፡ ዕሴቶ፡[...]⁶²

Lālibālā, neguś 'eguś wa-qeddusa Egzi'abeḥēr [...]e 'essēto [...] 'Lālibālā, king, patient and saint of the Lord... his reward...'

መስቀል፡ ክብራ፡ ንግሥት፡ ቅድስተ፡ እግዚአብሔር፡ ዘነረያ፡ ክርስቶስ፡እምኵሎን፡ አንስት፡⁶³

Masqal-Kebrā negeśt qeddesta Egzi'abeḥēr za-ḥaraya Krestos em-kwellon annest.
'Masqal-Kebrā, queen, saint of the Lord, whom Christ chose from among all women.'

Many other *manāberta tābotāt* at Lālibālā have been engraved with texts ascribed to the living King Lālibālā himself. In the present case, one deciphers on Gigar Tesfaye's (bad) photographs (pl. XI) that they bear a nimbus. Besides, the king and the queen are not asking the intercession of anyone as they did in the other cases, and mention is made of Lālibālā's reward (*'essēto*) in the third person. What is written about the king and queen has therefore been done by other persons. We further observe that no invocation is addressed to them, like at least 'Pray for us' and, therefore, the adjective *qeddus* ('holy, saint') is probably not used in the sense that a *tābot* would already be dedicated to Lālibālā and Masqal-Kebrā. Finally, we observe that this *manbar* is found in the Golgotā church, where tradition says that both Lālibālā and his queen have been laid to rest. They must have died by then. In this case, the *manbar* clearly is not a *tābot*; it is commemorative of Lālibālā and Masqal-Kebrā and is a *manbara tābot* only.⁶⁴

The proposition that there were fully consecrated altars in the area of Lālibalā in the first half of the 13th century is reinforced by the correlation between this possibility and the proximity in time of the original situation which triggered such a development: the wish to build more

---

⁶² According to the transcription of the inscription given by Gigar Tesfaye, *Inscriptions* (see n. 34), p. 122. He translated: 'Lālibālā, le roi patient et saint, le Seigneur [...] sa rétribution'.

⁶³ Gigar Tesfaye, *Inscriptions* (see n. 34), p. 122, pl. XIa et b = 'Golgotha 5'.

⁶⁴ There may be in this some valid elements to contribute to the understanding of the caption *qeddus* (saint) *Iyasus Mo'a* in the gospel book ordered by this abbot for his monastery of Ḥayq Esṭifānos. See Claire Bosc-Tiessé, 'Sainteté et intervention royale au monastère de Saint-Étienne de Ḥayq au tournant du XIIIᵉ et du XIVᵉ siècle: L'image de l'abbé Iyasus Moa dans son Évangile', forthcoming in *Oriens Christianus*.

altars for more saints. As the need was felt by Copts in the first place and as they brought their solution to Ethiopia — a country where there was no difficulty in building new churches —, it comes as no surprise that the changes adopted a Coptic form at the start: additional (in the present case, consecrated) altars dedicated to specific saints were introduced into the *pastophoria*, from which the preparation of the Eucharistic gifts was removed to be accomplished directly on the altar at which mass was to be celebrated. The *pastophoria* became new sanctuaries. As time went on, the *pastophoria* were never restored as such. However, side sanctuaries looking like *pastophoria*, developed. In terms of altars, the Ethiopian solution eventually became the multiplication of the altar-tablets so that a given tablet could be used for the liturgical services celebrated in commemoration of a saint to whose name an altar has been dedicated. That use would have been reserved for the day of the saint's commemoration. As for the *manbar*, it eventually became unique again and not fully consecrated, just blessed. The polysemic *tābotāt*, as those of the collection of the Vatican Museum show,[65] may have appeared only later, as a solution to a demand to honour numerous saints by having a very large number of altar-tablets.[66]

[65] See *tābotāt* 1 (which bears 35 names!), 2, 3, 4, 6, 7 and 8 in J.M. Hanssens and A. Raes, 'Une collection de tâbots' (see n. 9), pp. 435-450. The *tābot* 5 has one dedication only. Today at least, such altar-tablets are used as additional (*dabbāl* or *derreb*) *tābotāt*, not as the main *tābot* of a given church.

[66] Stuart Munro-Hay correctly wrote 'Dedications of churches may not always have been the same as they are today in either Aksum or Lalibela'. He then added: 'The wooden altars that have been found there (in Lalibela) with inscriptions apparently dating them to the time of Lalibela and his queen, Masqal Kebra, do not, by and large, share the present dedications of the churches. They might have been *debalat*; alternatively, the dedications might have changed with time'. See Stuart Munro-Hay, *Ethiopia the Unknown Land: A Cultural and Historical Guide* (London and New York, 2002), p. 191. The fact is that the altars mentioned are each real and dedicated to one saint. Of course, one altar had to be the main one, by which the church was named, the others being secondary altars (i.e. *debbālāt*, 'companions'). But which was which is hard to tell since we have no access to these altars or altar-tablets and are only in possession of the partial, though precious, information provided by S. Chojnacki and Gigar Tesfaye. The fact that there have been churches with one *manbara tābot* with its *tābot* (or a fully consecrated altar instead) in the first place, then several real altars, probably secondary, then again a disaffection for the additional altars and possibly the original main one as well, makes it difficult to know which *tābot* was originally the main one. At Lālibalā Madḥanēʿālam, however, one could argue that the Lord's image engraved on a large altar of the church bearing the same name supposes that the dedication of the church is ancient and that that altar was or is the main one. See Gigar Tesfaye, *Inscriptions* (see n. 34), fig. xvii, and Gigar Tesfaye, 'Découverte d'inscriptions guèzes à Lalibela', *Annales d'Éthiopie* 14 (1987) 75-79, fig. 2.

Mikā'ēl Ambā (Wembartā, East Tegrāy) and a real beginning may have taken place at Lālibalā. Mikā'ēl Ambā is vindicated as a realisation of Metropolitan Mikā'ēl dated 1150.[30] Built on the model of Abrehā wa-Aṣbehā with *pastophoria*, this church presents significant re-workings. Its sanctuary has been deepened and a rock-altar reserved there. The doorway between the southern *pastophorion* and the sanctuary has been enlarged into a passage. The western walls of the *pastophoria* are built, which suggests they were destroyed in the first place. A triple chancel barrier has been made which suggests that three sanctuaries were made at a time when this item was still in use — possibly the end of that type of equipment. This hypothesis needs verifications that are difficult to make, especially in order to identify the extent of the work carried out on all the doorways of the *pastophoria*-sanctuaries. As to the real turn, it may have taken place in the pontificate of Kîl (1200-1205), since the monument which best matches his tragic story[31] is Bēta-Rufā'ēl-wa-Gabre'ēl. Bēta-Rufā'ēl-wa-Gabre'ēl is, in fact, similar to an ancient stronghold in which the northernmost room — and only that room — distinctly is the chapel. This chapel, which has never been described so far, is made up of two parts: first, a raised area eastwards, lit by three narrow windows visible from the courtyard; the northernmost window is a little apart and opens on a slightly wider area of the sanctuary, possibly allowing for either a second altar or storage; then, westwards, the small nave without aisles. Steps which rise under a rough triumphal arch allow the two areas to communicate. There are neither presbyterium or *hurus* or any other platforms at all. The chapel is accessed through a door hewn out of the northern wall of the hall. As a private chapel of the metropolitan, it did not have to depend on the general progress to be arranged in this fashion but, rather, may have been imitated later on since that was the trend developed in the Coptic Church.

---

[30] According to a note in a gospel book in the possession of the monastery.

[31] See the story of Pope John VI of Alexandria (1186-1216) in the *History of the Patriarchs of the Egyptian Church, known as the History of the Holy Church* ascribed to Sawīrus al-Muḳaffa', Bishop of al-Ašmunīn, eds. and trans. Aziz Suryal Atiya, Yassa 'Abd al-Masih and O. H. E. Khs.-Burmester: II/1 (1943), II/2 (1948), II/3 (1959); III/1 (1968), III/2 (1970), III/3 (1970) (up to 1894 A.D.); IV/1 (1974), IV/2 (1974), Société d'archéologie copte (Cairo), on III/2, pp. 188-189; Jules Perruchon, 'Notes pour l'histoire d'Éthiopie: Extrait de la vie d'Abba Jean, 74ᵉ patriarche d'Alexandrie, relatif à l'Abyssinie', *Revue sémitique*, 'Notes et Mélanges', VI (1898), pp. 267-271, 366-372 (Arabic text); VII (1899), pp. 76-88, on p. 81; Claude Lepage, 'Un métropolite égyptien bâtisseur à Lalibäla (Éthiopie) entre 1205 et 1210', communication, in *Comptes-rendus de l'Académie des Inscriptions et Belles-Lettres*, fasc. 1 (Paris, January-March 2002), pp. 141-174, on p. 169.

2.4. Making Sense of Small Altars

One of the things that is puzzling about Ethiopian altars is the variety of their sizes, above all when they are very small: how might it be possible to use them for mass at all? An altar at Bilbālā Qirqos, a possibly mid-thirteenth century church in the surroundings of Lālibalā, provides us with a model showing the way such altars were and sometimes may still be used. The use of stones as stilts adding their length to the feet of a small altar convincingly demonstrates the way in which small *manāberta tābotāt* could have been used as altars despite their size.[67]

3. Were the Large Rock-Altars Consecrated?

We saw above that it is quite possible that altars — not just altar-tablets — may have been consecrated during the first part of the 13th century. This fact suggests that, while hitherto altar-tablets only were consecrated by the metropolitans, a development was possible and stable altars could be consecrated as a whole, should they exist. This would only conform to the prescriptions of the *Maṣḥafa Sēnodos* and to a lesser extent the *Fetḥa nagaśt*. The fact is that stable altars have existed, at least since the apparition of the monumental rock-hewn altars in the 14th century.

When one is aware of the importance of the Coptic impact in Ethiopia, one expects possibly to find there something which may match what has been noted in Egypt, such as Butler's remarks: 'The Coptic altar is a four-sided mass of brickwork or stonework, sometimes shallow, sometimes nearly solid throughout, and covered with plaster. It approaches more nearly to a cubical shape than the altars of the western churches. It is never built of wood, nor upheld on pillars .... The top does not differ from that of the side walls, but contains an oblong rectangular [depression] about an inch deep, in which is loosely fitted the altar-board — a plain piece of wood carved with the device of a cross in a roundel in the centre ....'[68]

The 'oblong rectangular [depression] about an inch deep, in which is loosely fitted the altar-board' which Butler mentions has been observed

---

[67] See a picture in: Fritsch and Gervers, 'Pastophoria and Altars' (see n. 2), p. 17, Fig. 1.

[68] Butler, *Coptic Churches,* II, p. 3 (see n. 15).

in the form of the frame in which the *tābot* is fitted on wooden altars, but we have not yet been able to verify the fact on high rock altars. Again like some wooden altars (e.g. the small additional altars at Dabra Salām Mikā'ēl), side rock-altars often have an edge all around their table but no other depression. This fact matches two realities: the existence of similar ancient altar tables in Egypt as elsewhere in the Mediterranean world and the fact that a consecrated altar does not need an altar-tablet. It follows that the absence of a place to fit a *tābot* on a rock-altar would be an indication that such tablet is unnecessary, because the whole altar would be consecrated. However, this indication is close to the argument drawn from silence. Still the conclusion cannot be rejected because there were hardly any bishops to go around and consecrate fixed altars.[69] Furthermore the area where we observe their presence is not huge, they are spread over some time, and the places are generally important ones. Rather, it could be thought that the altar can hardly be seen as consecrated, if the modern Ethiopian high-altar, which has prevailed to our days and is the heir of the tall rock-hewn altar, always features a place to lodge an altar-tablet. Positive facts must be obtained in order to resolve this ambiguous situation. Such facts perhaps may be obtained from the existence, unlikely but yet to be investigated, of a Pontifical including the consecration of altars differing from the consecration of a *tābot*. Allusions may also be read in *vitae* or royal chronicles.

4. Questions on Morphology and Sense

4.1. The Cavity of the Altars: What Was it For?

Regarding the morphology of altars, we have already observed that they are made of a table which is often the top part of a chest supported by feet and in which a cavity is accessible through an opening sometimes equipped with a small door. This empty space is found even in

---

[69] In the 14th and 15th centuries, the metropolitans were Yoḥannes II (*ca.* 1310-1330), Yā'qob (sent back in *ca.* 1345), Salamā II *Matarg^wem* 'the Translator' (*ca.* 1346-1388), Bartolomēwos (*ca.* 1390-1435), Mikā'ēl III (*ca.* 1438/9-1450) together with Gabre'ēl until Mikā'ēl died, then Gabre'ēl alone (*ca.* 1438/9-1458), Metropolitan Yesḥaq II (1481/2-*ca.* 1500) together with Mārqos, his named successor (*ca.* 1481/2-1530), and auxilliaries Mikā'ēl and Yoḥannes, plus another Yā'qob.

small or tiny altars as at Lālibalā.[70] Scholars of Ethiopian studies have often tried to interpret this feature and often suggested that it should be a place to store the altar-tablet, but the tiny size of many altars precludes this possibility.[71] However, the lighter and older altars of earlier periods, such as Agewo Qirqos, do not seem to have had a cavity. It is impossible to say from the mortises in the ground at Gundefru or Degum. The similarity between the relic at Zāramā and the altar at Agewo do not allow to expect one at Zāramā. Elsewhere, e.g. at Dabra Salām Mikā'ēl, the frame and cavity occur when there are several altars. We may, therefore, associate the feature with the type of altars which prevailed when altars multiplied, i.e. during the first part of the 13th century. Several rock-hewn altars — whether of the canopy type or not — have been equipped with a similar opening. It gives access to a cavity which may range from shallow to very deep in depth. Never does a door shut it.[72] In this case, the cavity is eastwards and therefore invisible from the west where the faithful stand.[73] The difference with the previous type of wooden altars is that the rock-hewn altars were not made with feet, understandably, no more than their Coptic parents.[74]

The last detail concerning the presence or absence of feet may be related to the cavity. Commenting on Coptic altars, Alfred J. Butler wrote: 'On the eastward side in every altar, level with the ground, is a small open doorway showing an interior recess or cavity.... There is in no case any sign of the opening ever having been blocked or closed... The cavity is of varying size; but very often it is nearly co-extensive with the altar ...'[75] Grossman adds his interpretation: '... In the back of

---

[70] There is no available description of any sort documenting the eastern side of the rock-altars in the Śellāsē crypt, and therefore we do not know about the presence or absence of such a cavity there.

[71] The cavity is visible as a distinct detail on an early 15th century painting accurately showing the altar, supporting correct understanding of this representation of Mary as *tābot* sitting on the *manbara tabot* with her child on her lap — propitiatory between the cherubim. See Jacques Mercier, *L'Arche Éthiopienne: art chrétien d'Éthiopie* (Paris, 2000-01), p. 59. A similar representation is the 15-16th century illumination from Gunda-Gundē (Agāmē). See, e.g., *L'Art en Éthiopie*, ed. Walter Raunig (2005), p. 209, Fig. 169.

[72] Unless such device has been fitted recently, and with cement, like at Dabra S'eyon (Garʿāltā).

[73] Except at Gabre'ēl Weqēn (Dabra ʿĀsā, Tembēn). Fig. 18 in Fritsch and Gervers, 'Pastophoria and Altars' (see n. 2), p. 30, shows such a niche in the east side of the southern (finished) altar of the church of Abbā Yoḥanni.

[74] Feet, however, are represented in the carving of the altars in the Śellāsē crypt of Lalibala, but they imitate in every point the usual wooden altars.

[75] Butler, *Coptic Churches*, II (see n. 15), p. 5.

the [Coptic] altar, facing the east, a small but relatively deep cavity like a niche is left open close to the floor; this must be regarded as the last vestige of the original table-shaped form of the altar. Today the consecrated oil is frequently kept in it.'[76] Having personally seen many Coptic altars, I am able to confirm that, very often, the intervals between the feet of a wooden altar as well as the niche within are rather wide and the whole area under or within the altar often is available for the storage of all kinds of paraphernalia.

In conclusion, we may state that originally the cavity was a storage place.[77] When feet are still present, the cavity amounts to a doublet, a redundancy or tautology of sorts. As many concrete altars do not allow much storage if at all, due to their tiny dimensions, the cavity, then, amounts to a relic, a formal vestige which marks the authenticity and manifests the faithfulness of the Ethiopian Christians to the models provided by the Alexandrian mother-church.[78] But its basic nature as a storage place has not been forgotten: the Ethiopian clergy calls this cavity the *karśa ḥamar*, i.e. literally the 'womb of the ship', in reference to the ark of Noah, ark of salvation (cf. 1 Pet 3:20-21). Indeed, the noun of *tābot* first means a chest and a chest is a hollow container with a means of access into it. *Tābot* also means chest in the sense of the ark of Noah (*tābota Noḥ, ḥamara Noḥ*) and, since the time of the systematic development of the tall altar which has become usual today, the inside of the chest has regularly been divided into three shelves, precisely because of the divisions found in Noah's ark (Gen 6:16).

4.2. Altars Without a Mensa?

Curiously enough, a series of rock-altars appear to have their east side open from their backs to their tops. They are, therefore, deprived in various degrees of a table or mensa which would be expected to cover the entire horizontal surface available. It is the case for Māryām

---

[76] 'Altar', under 'Architectural Elements of Churches', *Coptic Encyclopedia*, I (see n. 59), pp. 106-107.

[77] The top shelf is traditionally and in principle used to store the altar-tablet(s) between the liturgical services, the middle one for the sacred vessels and the bottom for the books and other paraphernalia.

[78] This is an attitude similar to the one expressed by Heinzgerd Brakmann in conclusion of 'La *Mystagogie* de la liturgie alexandrine et copte', in *Mystagogie: pensée liturgique d'aujourd'hui et liturgie ancienne, Conférences Saint-Serge, 39ᵉ Semaine d'Études Liturgiques, Paris 1992*, eds. A. M. Triacca and A. Pistoia (Rome, 1992), pp. 55-65.

Dengelāt's only altar (near Edagā Ḥamus, Hārāmāt, East-Tegrāy) (Fig. 6) and for the southern altars of Enda Iyasus Seharti (near Guǧat, South-West of Makale), Dabra Ṣeyon (Garʿāltā), Mikā'ēl Bārkā (near Aṣbi)[79] etc. All the cases seen happen to belong roughly to the same time-frame and the Region of Tegrāy. Māryām Dengelāt's altar is totally hollow, open eastwards and above; an additional structure has been affixed to it in order to obtain a mensa.[80] Dabra Ṣeyon (see above): the southern altar, approximately cubic (H: 92 cm, W: 100 cm), has an eastern cavity which, beginning 30 cm above the floor, goes up right to the mensa of that altar, made without surrounding rim around it. The dimensions of the cavity being modest (50 cm high, 50 cm wide, 11 cm deep) there is still ample surface to do the ablutions there after communion. Yet, it is a strange thing. At Seharti Endā Iyasus (near Guǧat, Tegrāy), also attributed to Abuna Abrehām, the architectonics of altars are unusual. In particular, two side rock-altars have been preserved in the eastern end of the north and south aisles on either side of the *qeddest* area, outside the sanctuary proper. While the north altar is very low (ca. 45 cm) and flat, the south one is ca. 110 cm high and is characterised by a depression which occupies the central part of its east side to its top (Fig. 7). How to explain this unlikely phenomenon of an altar without a top or with a much reduced one?

In Ethiopia, we have come across monoxyle 'mobile' altars in the probably 14th-century parallel rock-churches of Yačirā Madḫanēʿālam (near Kon, Wādlā, North Wallo) which could be illuminating.[81] In the

---

[79] See Jean Gire and Roger Schneider, 'Étude des églises rupestres du Tigré: Premiers résultats de la mission 1970', CNRS, *Travaux de la Recherche Coopérative sur Programme RCP 230: Documents pour servir à l'histoire des civilisations éthiopiennes*, fasc. 1 (Paris, 1970), pp. 73-79, on p. 74, plan 3.

[80] The cliff face having collapsed, the church is abandoned. We owe information and pictures to the kindness of Michael Gervers and Ewa Balicka-Witakowska, who have visited it since. Michael Gervers, 'Two late sixteenth-century Roman engravings from the rock-cut church of Maryam Dengelat (Haremat, Tigray)', in *Ethiopian Art: A Unique Cultural Heritage and a Modern Challenge*, eds. Walter Raunig and Prinz Asfa-Wossen Asserate, Bibliotheca nubica et æthiopica 10 (Lublin, 2007), pp. 160-184. The ground plan Fig. 2 shows the altar and its peculiar shape in the centre of the sanctuary. We call *mensa* the horizontal superior surface of the altar, its 'table', whether it is the altar-tablet or the wholly consecrated altar, and even, for commodity sake, the *manbara tābot*. See a picture of the altar *in situ* in Fritsch and Gervers, 'Pastophoria and Altars' (see n. 2), p. 29, fig. 16.

[81] The foundation of these three churches roughly hewn side by side with internal connections (Madʿanēʿālam, Arsimā, Egzi'abeḫēr Ab) is ascribed to the still mysterious figure of an abuna Musē (reportedly the fifth abbot of Ḥayq Esṭifānos and 4th successor of St Iyasus Mo'a, who died at Yadiba Māryām, *ca.* 5 km from Kurbā, 50 km south-west of Kon, seat of the Dāwent *waradā.*

Fig. 6: Altar without *mensa* at Māryām Dengelāt (Photo: Michael Gervers)

second church, dedicated to Arsimā, there is a very small "monoxyle" altar, out of use, measuring 50 cm (total height) × 22 cm (height of chest) × 22 (length) × 21 cm (width). The horizontal opening on the table of the altar is practically square and measures 8 × 8 cm. It is positioned 4 cm from the closest edge above the vertical opening to the cavity, 6 and 7 cm from the two other [N] and [S] edges respectively. The vertical opening to the cavity is practically square (7 H × 8 wide and positioned 4,5 cm from the top). It provides access to an inner cavity (a tiny *karśa ḥamar*) 12 cm deep, horizontally. This altar shows interesting details: there are two openings, one as usual on the side of the chest, the other one on the horizontal table itself, but closer to the edge above the side opening, not right in the middle — which indicates the orientation of the altar (the celebrant must have been standing eastwards, opposite the openings, which we assume to be on the east side); the feet are worn out, a sign of a regular use. In the treasure, a second altar was shown, again with two openings accessing the same cavity: the opening placed vertically on the side of the chest has a wider frame (14,5 horizontally × 17 vertically) and an inner one (10 horizontally × 13 vertically). The opening placed horizontally on the top of this *manbar* has a wider frame of 24,2 [N-S] × 21,7 [E-W] cm. The inner ledge (1,8 cm) is

Fig. 7: Cavity in southern altar of Seharti Endā Iyasus
(Photo: Emmanuel Fritsch)

just appropriate to fit a *tābot* inside its frame.[82] The depth up to the first edge is of 25 cm. This altar too has been used much (Fig. 8).[83]

Since the cavity-niche is a Coptic feature, we may search for precedents in Egypt. But while the niche or hollow within altars has countless examples, could we find Coptic altars without the surface upon which the altar table or tablet may be placed? As it happens, a dig in the Wadi n'Natrun has recently brought to light the church of Saint John the Short's monastery and its altar (Fig. 9).[84] This brick altar is still standing in the old sanctuary. It is totally hollow, with two large semi-circular openings providing access to the inside: one is east of the altar and represents the normal access to the internal storage place; the second is in the centre of the table and was meant to be closed with a semi-circular altar-slab (Fig. 10).[85]

In conclusion, the absence of a proper table rules out the possibility that such monoliths were ever consecrated as altars. They were always meant to be completed by an altar-tablet — a *tābot* — which must have been rather large, comparatively. This feature has to do with the depression prepared on Coptic altars and the frame found on Ethiopian wooden altars to receive the altar-tablet. However, a study of the evolution of the Coptic altar is needed in order to document the usage of marble mensae in relation to the wooden altar board (*lawh al-muqaddasah*) which is the norm today, but has not entirely replaced the former. In this case as in others, a Coptic precedent has been identified although, as often, the temporal discrepancy between an ancient model and a later Ethiopian application makes it difficult to retrace the intermediate links.[86]

---

[82] Total height: 64,5 × height of chest 32,5 × length 29,5 × width 27,5 cm.

[83] The fact that we did not see the third church prevents us from drawing conclusions as to the existence of other altars, or as to the place they occupied when in use.

[84] See www.website1.com/odyssey/week4/NewsFlash02b.html 'Odyssey in Egypt. Egypt and Archaeology through Cyberspace - Week Four - Discovery of the Altar'; Yale Egyptological Institute in Egypt (www.yale.edu/egyptology/ae.htm); Bishop Samuil and Peter Grossmann, 'Researches in the Laura of John Kolobos (Wâdî Natrûn)', in *Ägypten und Nubien in spätantiker und christlicher Zeit: Akten des 6. Internationalen Koptologenkongresses, Münster 20.–26. Juli 1996* (Wiesbaden, 1999), pp. 360-364. The main, brick altar in the old church being excavated below the walls of Deir al-Baramus presents similar features. Together with Ewa Balicka-Witakowska and Michael Gervers, we visited these sites in October 2007.

[85] Butler, *Coptic Churches*, II (see n. 15), fig. 1, p. 4; fig. 2, p. 8. On other examples, see Anne Boud'hors and Gilbert-Robert Delahaye, 'Nouvel exemple d'une pierre d'autel remployée: La stèle de Dorotheos', in *Études coptes X, Douxième journée d'études, Lyon 19-21 mai 2005*, eds. A. Boud'hors and C. Louis, *Cahiers de la Bibliothèque copte* 16 (Paris, 2008) 103-122.

[86] See the examples in the field of gospel books demonstrated by Lepage on a few occasions, whereby Middle-Eastern late-antique patterns have been in regular use in

Fig. 8: Altar at Yaḵirā Madḥanē ʿālam (Photo: Emmanuel Fritsch)

Fig. 9: Altar of St.-John-the-Short's church, Wadi n'Natrun,
showing place for *mensa* (Photo: Emmanuel Fritsch)

Fig. 10: *Mensa* of the altar of Deir Abu Hennis' village church, Upper Egypt
(Photo: Emmanuel Fritsch)

4.3. How Is a So-called Mobile Altar Supposed to Be Turned?

The fact that the morphology of altars generally includes the cavity of the *karśa ḥamar* accessed through an opening leads one to wonder how it should be turned. It is a practical concern when we describe 'mobile' altars, which often are light enough structures but have several faces (5 or 6 [4 vertical ones, top and below], let alone the inside and feet, according to the level of accuracy required). However, we could perhaps identify in the positioning of the cavity opening a reliable term of reference for describing the altar in an understandable manner. Generally, we observe the following facts:

a)   The space below Coptic altars with feet is accessible from all sides for storage. When they are built of solid material, such as bricks or marble, the opening of the cavity is always on the east side.

b)   The cavity and its opening in the Ethiopian rock-altars is on their eastern side, except in the case of Gabre'ēl Weqēn (Tembēn, Tegrāy).

c)   The altars in the churches of Lālibalā and those similar to them are generally equipped with such a cavity and opening. However, variations are found. Some altars do not show any opening, others a small one off centre a quarter distance from the side, possibly not original.[87] Chojnacki describes one carved and painted 'chest' from Lālibalā Bēta Gabre'ēl with 'small doors... cut on two sides'.[88]

d)   Indications may also be drawn from the direction the inscriptions engraved on several altars (see above) can be read in relation to the position of the niche opening.[89] At Zoz Ambā, the altar dedicated to Gabriel is read standing before the altar, opposite the side with the cavity, which positions the cavity eastwards (Fig. 2). However, the inscription which is engraved horizontally on the table of the altar of Mary is surprisingly read by a person passing from one side of the altar to the next, on the four sides, for the text is inscribed on two levels all around the mensa, reading on the outer circle which runs along the four tips of the cross: *Māryām walādita Amlāk*,

---

Ethiopia as late as the 14-15th centuries, e.g. 'Prototypes de deux Tétraévangiles du XIVe s. à cycle court de trois miniatures', *Abbay* 13 (1986-1987) 59-75.

[87] Like the one presently exposed at Gabre'ēl.

[88] It measures 'ca. 120 cm high, the box itself measuring 40 × 50 cm.' See Stanisław Chojnacki, 'Notes on a Lesser-Known Marian Iconography in 13th and 14th Century Ethiopian Painting', *Aethiopica* 5 (2002) 42-66, on p. 44.

[89] At Lālibalā Bēta Gabre'ēl wa-Rufā'ēl, it was not possible to move the altars around and examine them thoroughly.

'Mary Mother of God', and on the inner circle: *se'ali ba-'enti'a-na*, 'pray for us' (Fig. 11). If we determine where the main name, Mary, is positioned in relation to the cavity, we see that it is just above the latter and meant to be read by someone standing before the altar on the opposite side. Therefore, if we identify this place with the place where the celebrant stands at the altar, that is west of it and facing east, it appears that the opening of the cavity is east of the altar. It is the same thing as in the case of Gabriel's altar.

The smaller of the two "monoxyles" at Emmakinā Madhanē'ālam bears the words *Arbā'etu Ensesā* vertically engraved on two feet.[90] It happens that the opening of the chest is positioned opposite the inscription. It follows that the latter is written on both the west and front feet of the altar of the Four Living Creatures, where it can be read, while the cavity opens eastwards. Strangely enough, it is on the face opposite its niche that the taller Altar 2[91] presents drawings made to guide the carver

Fig. 11: Altar of Māryām with Mary's name read from the west, Zoz Ambā Giyorgis (Photo: Michael Gervers)

[90] See above the Altar 1, which measures: H 33; Width 18 × 18; box H 16; door H 9.5 × width 6 cm in frame H 8 × width 5 cm; see Fig. 5.

[91] See above the Altar 2, which measures: H 50; Width 23 × 22; box H 25; door H 9 × width 8 cm within wider frame H 14 × width 12 cm.

still there to be carved on: the altar is unfinished. Does it mean anything? Hardly, as long as it is a chance occurrence. But at Mawrē Ṭerā
Asfari Esṭifānos, again, the altars of the Paraclete, Mercurius and Stephen are engraved with the names of their 'owners' on the same side as
the opening of the cavity, just below the mensa in the first case and on
their feet in the two others. The fourth altar is similar. Remarkably
made, engraved as it is on five sides, the side with the cavity is filled
with the low relief of angel Gabriel, while the opposite side represents
Michael's image. Both are rendered in a very Byzantine manner. One
of the two other sides bears the name of Surāfēl, and the other of
Wa-Kirubēl, 'Seraphs — and Cherubs' engraved on top of the triumphal
arch of a church framing an altar, apparently with a ciborium, interestingly. On the mensa, the name *Arbā'etu Ensesā* (the 'Four Living
Creatures') has been engraved in the circular aureole which surrounds a
Crucifixion meant to be seen from Gabriel's side, the side of the cavity.[92] The Paraclete's altar differs only in that it has a beautifully carved
side opposite both its opening and its name, making it possible that this
may have been the face meant to be turned westwards, as described in
the case of other churches such as Zoz Ambā (Fig. 3, 4 and 2). Ṭerā
Asfari Esṭifānos seems to counter the evidence met hitherto. An explanation has been proposed that the cavity may have been meant to be
oriented eastwards all the same, and the names of the altars engraved in
the east and hidden on purpose.[93]

e)   How is the 15th century altar of Bēta Leḥēm Māryām (Gāyent) ori-
     ented? A beautiful cross adorns the side opposite the door of the
     karśa ḥamar, itself painted, and the angels who stretch their wings
     are three-quarters turned towards the door to the cavity, crossing
     wings on the part of the mensa which is above its entrance. Despite
     the symbolism which might ask that the priest would place the altar-
     tablet on the wings (therefore on the side of the door which would
     then be westwards), it is more likely that the angels were turned
     east, which places the door of the cavity eastwards. As a conse-
     quence, the cross both engraved and painted opposite the door of
     the cavity would be the face shown to the assembly, westwards,
     where the celebrant stands (Fig. 12). The matter is simple in the
     case of the first of the two "monoxyle" altars at Bēta Leḥēm: its

---

[92] See Gerster, *Churches in Rock* (see n. 29), pp. 141-142, plates 209-211, fig. 123.
[93] As Ugo Zanetti suggested.

Fig. 12: Altar of Bēta Leḥēm Māryām (Photo: Emmanuel Fritsch)

cavity turns east. The second case is not as obvious for the opening does not seem to be original, although probably ancient, given the patina: three sides are identical, and it is in the fourth, decorated with a floral cross that a small orifice has been arranged to access the cavity in the lower right quarter. In any case, the *karśa ḥamar* is not a necessity.

As a conclusion, we may suggest that the opening of the *karśa ḥamar* is normally turned eastwards, invisible from the west. In consequence, we propose that conventionally the faces of the altars be termed *east* (the face with the opening), *west* (its opposite), *north* and *south*. The absence of a cavity opening or its opening westwards should be regarded as exceptions and specifically noted whenever encountered.

Conclusions

At this point, we may enumerate a certain number of facts regarding the development of the Ethiopian altar.

1) Both fixed and mobile altars exist in the Coptic tradition. What was transmitted to the Ethiopian Church are notions still present in the vocabulary, although not in a rigid manner when it comes to the words and the objects represented. Due to the circumstances, the mobile altar or *tābot / ṣellāt* has prevailed in Ethiopia, not the fixed one or *meswā'*. But *meswā'* carries the essence of what an altar is and, therefore, can be applied to the *tābot* insofar as it is a true altar.

2) The *manbar* or *manbara tābot* shares in the identity of the altar but not in its own right. Besides, while the *tābot* is associated with the Ark of the Covenant, the *manbara tābot* is referred to the ark of salvation of Noah, as is shown by the cavity of the *karśa ḥamar*, lit. the 'womb of (Noah's) vessel'.

3) The large number of *tābotāt* found at Lālibalā at the time of King Lālibālā, often engraved with a text authored by him, confirms that their multiplication took place during his reign and with his involvement.

4) The invocations engraved on the altars confirm the view that the multiplication of altars had to do with the expression of devotion to such and such mystery or saint.[94]

---

[94] See Fritsch and Gervers, 'Pastophoria and Altars' (see n. 2), p. 11.

5) Characteristics of the mobile *tābot* may be observed engraved on altars of the area of Lālibalā and surroundings. As a consequence, it is possible to think that these *manābert* were in fact consecrated altars (*meswā'etāt*) which did not require the addition of any *tābotāt* to be used.

6) The absence of a complete altar table has been observed in 14th-15th century Tegrāy. From the wooden altars of Kon and examples in the Wadi n'Natrun, we see that this feature emphasizes the contrast between the sacred altar-tablet and its support. We note the differences between Māryām Dengelāt, where the table is completely missing from a central and only altar, and others where the east side appears atrophied but leaves a certain area as table. In any case, this necessarily calls for bringing in a consecrated altar-tablet if one wants to celebrate at such altars. The altar-tablet of Māryām Dengelāt was its real mensa and may, or may not, have originally been permanently set in the same way as the mensa was permanent at Saint-John Colobos' church.

7) As in the case of the development of the church architectonics which reflect Coptic developments (especially liturgical ones as the *pastophoria* or platforms, but also technological like the different forms of ceilings: flat, saddleback, barrel vaulting, cupola), here again certain morphological features are identified as originating from Coptic Egypt. Such items were then translated into Ethiopia's very different situation with a large degree of creativity. It is the case of the cavity which, sometimes adopting a strange form, become the *karśa ḥamar*; it is also the case of the high-altars themselves, or of the multiplication of altars — necessitating a *tābot* or not —, a phenomenon later simplified through the multiplication of simple altar-tablets and then the grouping of several dedications on the same tablet etc.

8) On the side of the methodology of recording, we suggest designating as 'east' the face of an altar which has its cavity, and that other cases be noted as exceptions. Descriptions should include photographs of orientation at certain angles so as to show the relation between, preferably, three faces of a certain item, which would then allow it to be described.

As a result of our study, we hope to have contributed to a better understanding of the altar in the Ethiopian context. Certain texts should be read more easily, when one has a better grasp of the notions and of the sacred objects they describe.

APPENDIX
An Overview of the Development of the Ethiopian Altar
in Connection with the History of the Churches

Prior to the presentation of each group of church-altar(s), we propose here a short overview of the general characteristics which the churches present. This will permit us to determine the line of succession in time of different types of churches. The churches may be classified into four main periods according to dating obtained from the historical context insofar as it is known and the appearance or disappearance of architectonics which often, although not always, match developments in the Coptic liturgy. The Coptic changes which have been identified mark a *terminus a quo* but do not completely determine the way things have developed in the Ethiopian area, even though the episcopacy remained in Coptic hands. In fact, phenomena triggered by Coptic developments did become authentically Ethiopian and, having developed in their own way, as we may see below, they have relatively little similarity with the original state of things.

In our context, we understand by 'architectonics' specific architectural elements built into[95] the edifices and meant for a particular, functional, purpose determined by the liturgical purpose of the building. They are meant to convey certain symbolical notions regarding the nature of that building and they facilitate the performance of the liturgical action as it was envisaged at the point in history when the church was built. Architectonics may be, for example, a cupola, a platform, a doorway, etc. While certain important features (chancel barriers, reading platforms) have already been treated and used by Claude Lepage, we have identified the *pastophoria*, the accesses to these rooms from the aisles and/ or the sanctuary, as well as their disappearance, as elements depending in great part on the development of the liturgy and contributing to a certain historical classification of these churches.[96]

Besides the liturgy, there are several factors which have an impact on the building of churches and therefore its dating (so our present viewpoint should avoid being over-functionalist): the builders themselves, influences from the court, development of techniques etc. It is not always a simple linear story.

1. The Altars up to the Early 13th Century - First Period

In the first period, the *prothesis* rite was accomplished in a *pastophorion*, whether north or south of the sanctuary occupied by only one altar. The ground-plans of the so-called Aksumite churches (4th till the end of the 7th century)

---

[95] Or reserved in the case of rock-hewn churches. Despite certain occasional re-workings, architectonics are particularly stable, hence their usefulness as witnesses of past practices.

[96] See in particular C. Lepage, 'Premières recherches sur les installations liturgiques des anciennes églises d'Éthiopie (X^e – XVe siècles)', C.N.R.S., *Travaux de la Recherche Coopérative sur Programme RCP 230: Documents pour servir à l'histoire des civilisations éthiopiennes*, fasc. 3 (Sept. 1972), pp. 77-114, 19 figures. He has sketched an analysis of the side-rooms in Lepage, *Degum* (see n. 103), p. 179.

— the oldest churches which exist only in ruins — are known and chancel barriers have been identified, but no altars.[97] *Pastophoria* existed on either side of the sanctuary, with doors opening westwards towards the aisles only. We shall proceed to our review from this starting point.

1.1. Post-Aksumite Churches (Early 8th-Early 12th Centuries)
    A number of churches still standing in and only in East-Tegrāy display significant features: chancel barrier; triumphal arch; round apse or flat east wall; central nave with high flat ceiling, then barrel-vaulted; *pastophoria* turned westwards towards the aisles, in apparent continuity with the Aksumite churches, later opening to the altar only, then to both aisle and altar; a *prothesis* niche in the south more often than the north; an eastern window and in certain cases a space behind accessed via a trench from the north or south; one west door but the two western rooms on either side of the porch have disappeared. The classification which follows depends on the characters found in the churches visited which match the features identified in the Aksumite churches.
    1.2. Gundefru Śellāsē (Wenbertā, East-Tegrāy). We place this church first, judging from the fact that the *pastophoria* doorways, which used to be filled with large doors, are turned towards the aisles. But, in apparent discontinuity with what we observe in the ruins of Aksumite churches, an additional passage connects the southern *pastophorion* with the sanctuary. However, upon close examination it is possible to discern the places where the frame of the opening used to be fixed in the rock, indicating by its dimensions that this passage was not originally arranged to be a proper doorway but, rather, a kind of window, later transformed into a doorway.[98] In contrast with the bare northern *pastophorion*, this southern *pastophorion* features a niche in its eastern wall and, in its vicinity, post-holes may be hidden under the stairs made recently in order to provide for an eastern door of the priests as demanded by the more recent

---

[97] See, e.g., 'Richerche nel luogo dell'antica Adulis (Colonia Eritrea)', ed. R. Paribeni, *Journal – Monumenti antichi* pubblicati per cura della Reale Accademia dei Lincei, vol. 18 (1907), col. 437-570, pl. XI; Francis Anfray, 'Deux villes axoumites: Adoulis et Matara', in *IV Congresso Internazionale di Studi Etiopici*, vol. I, Accademia dei Lincei 371, Problemi Attuali di Scienza e di Cultura 191 (Rome, 1974), pp. 753-760; Marilyn E. Heldman, 'Early Byzantine Sculptural Fragments from Adulis', in *Études éthiopiennes: Actes de la Xᵉ conférence internationale des études éthiopiennes*, ed. Claude Lepage (Paris, 1994), pp. 239-252.
[98] See 'Mazgaba Seelet', photograph of Gundefru 2005.024.020 (see n. 6). The large rock-church of Yohannes Matmaq at Gāzēn (north of Aṣbi) is the only one we know to display two *pastophoria* that are turned westwards and do not have any direct connection with the sanctuary. However, much re-working has taken place, let alone natural destruction of the sandstone, and the whole of the ancient chancel is disfigured. Of the ancient furnishing, one post of the chancel-barrier has survived, but no altar, whether whole or broken, has been seen so far. See Claude Lepage and Jacques Mercier, *Ancient Churches of Tigray* (Paris, 2005), pp. 90-93. Significant re-workings have taken place in Gundefru, Mikā'ēl Ambā (Wenbartā, East-Tegrāy), possibly also in the Lālibalā Bēta Marqorēwos' apsidial area.

Gondarine custom.[99] These features point to this *pastophorion* as the place where the preparation of the oblation prior to the public Eucharistic service used to be done. Significant are also the chancel barrier post-holes, the triumphal arch, the round, inscribed apse with a semi-cupola possibly ornamented with a shell motif, the central nave with a high, flat ceiling, the east window and space behind accessed via a trench from the south, the one original western door. In this ancient context, four holes appear to have received the feet of the altar in the middle of the small sanctuary at a distance of about 60 cm from the curved apse. The holes are 56 cm distant in the north-south sense, thereby indicating the length of the original altar, which was some 46 cm wide.

1.3. Māryām Barāqit (Gar'āltā, East-Tegrāy)[100] shares with Gundefru its inscribed apse with its semi-cupola, a presbyterium, its ceilings, the triumphal arch, the east window and space behind accessed via a trench from the north in this case, the one original western door, and even a 50 × 7cm flat platform connecting the outer angles of the top step of the presbyterium with the eastern side of the easternmost piers of the nave — although at Gundefru this feature continues all along the two sides of the nave, connecting all piers and the western wall. A special feature, although somewhat atrophied, connects the church with the Aksumite buildings: while the rock immediately right past the (western) entrance has not been hewn, the left side has been hollowed into a kind of small room, the opening of which is turned towards the passage created by the two blocks as in the later churches of Lālibalā and its area. The *pastophoria* doorways, however, are turned towards the altar.[101] In the centre of the sanctuary, there are no holes to receive the feet of an altar; rather, we observe under the present, recent, altar the uneven relics of a socle, which, apparently, used to be the base of the original rock-hewn altar. This feature has never been noted before. In itself, the application of rock-hewing to erecting an altar is no extraordinary thing, especially in a rock-hewn monument.[102]

1.4. The two churches of Degum Śellāsē (Gar'āltā, East-Tegrāy).[103] As already at Māryām Barāqit, the *pastophoria* open towards the sanctuary alone, although

---

[99] The circular churches generalized by the kingdom of Gondar do not have the traditional order of doorways. Instead, while the total number of doors remains three, they have kept the northern and southern doors and suppressed the western door, adding the eastern one.

[100] Described by Claude Lepage, 'L'Église rupestre de BERAKIT', *Annales d'Ethiopie* IX (1972) 147-188 (+ plates).

[101] The doors, which were sealed before, have now been walled up, which forbids any investigation.

[102] This base measures *ca.* 98 (west side) × 98 (south side) × 110 (east side) × 110 (north side) cm. The priests ascribe responsibility for the destruction of the altar to Gudit. In Egypt, the altar of the ancient church of Deir el-Moharraq (Qosqam) is monolithic.

[103] They have been described on several occasions by Claude Lepage, in particular in: Claude Lepage, 'Les monuments rupestres de Degum en Éthiopie', *Cahiers Archéologiques* XXII (1972) 167-200. Similar features are found in the neighbouring churches of Gundefru, Barāqit (see above) and Takla Hāymānot Hawzēn (an obvious case of re-naming since the saint lived in the 13th century only), as well as Gazēn, except for its large size.

the southern church has a kind of window pierced in the west wall of its otherwise poorly equipped northern *pastophorion*, thereby establishing some contact with the nave. The southern *pastophorion* of this church features post-holes below its eastern wall — likely the table of the preparation of the offerings —, and a niche in the vicinity, dug in the east end of the southern wall. The southern *pastophorion* of the northern church features post-holes below its eastern wall — again, the table of the preparation of the offerings — and a centred eastern niche which, together with its diamond-adorned ceiling, forms a room in sharp contrast with the bare northern *pastophorion*.[104] In this church, the post-holes of chancel-barriers are exposed, but cement conceals almost completely the post-holes of the chancel-barrier in the southern church.[105] In both churches, four other post-holes, almost square, have been carved out of the sanctuary rock-floor under the window of the flat east wall. They would have supported a square-like altar with a top, or mensa, measuring approx. 70 long × 60 cm wide.[106] This *dispositif* matches the details P. Grossmann provides when succinctly describing the Coptic altar: 'The Coptic Church also used movable wooden altars... The top of the altar or mensa used to be 'carried on one or more legs, which were themselves fixed in a base or into the floor' (Fig. 13).[107] The arrangement of the holes at Degum suggests that those officiating at the altar were limited to two in number (a priest and deacon), possibly assisted by other clerics standing around. Due to the confined space, the deacon could not have stood facing the priest and the assembly across the altar, as is the norm today both in the Coptic Church and in Ethiopia. Nor could there have been processions or any kind around the altar.

1.5. Zāramā Giyorgis (Wenbertā, East-Tegrāy) has a chancel, *pastophoria* with doors now opening both towards the sanctuary and the west, and a saddle-back ceiling instead of the flat ceiling found previously. Especially on account of its

---

[104] The fact that the *pastophoria* now only communicate with the sanctuary indicates that there was nothing solemn about either preparing the offerings prior to the mass or carrying them to the altar after the gospel reading during the pre-anaphora.

[105] See Georg Gerster, *Churches in Rock: Early Christian Art in Ethiopia* (London, 1970), pl. 168, between pp. 130-131. In addition, the south-east corner of the southern *pastophorion* of both northern and southern churches at Degum show holes meant for a table placed beside niches: an arrangement necessary for the preparation of the Eucharistic gifts.

[106] Lepage, *Degum* (see n. 103), p. 177 and Lepage and Mercier, *Ancient Churches of Tigray*, p. 51, have contended that a reliquary rather than an altar was meant to be installed there (see n. 98). See ground plan and picture of the northern church in Fritsch and Gervers, 'Pastophoria and Altars' (see n. 2), respectively p. 13, fig. B and p. 21, fig. 6.

[107] Peter Grossmann, 'Altar', *Coptic Encyclopedia*, in vol. I, p. 106; idem, *Christliche Architektur in Ägypten*, Handbuch der Orientalistik 1/62 (Leiden, 2002), Tafel IIa: 'Ostkirche von Abū Minā, Nebenapsis mit Altarstelle'. The same device has been used in Syria, e.g. at Dehes. See Emma Loosley, *The Architecture and Liturgy of the Bema in Fourth- to Sixth-Century Syrian Churches*, Patrimoine Syriaque 2, *Parole de l'Orient* (2003), p. 243, fig. 149.

Fig. 13: Holes to fit the altar in, Degum Śellāsē's southern church
(Photo: Emmanuel Fritsch)

late-antique Eastern Mediterranean type of ornamentation, Claude Lepage has ascribed it to the 9th century.[108] The simple, old, broken altar which survives may have something similar to the type found at Agewo (below) (Fig. 14).[109]

1.6. Agewo Qirqos (Wenbertā, East-Tegrāy).[110] The sanctuary measures 182 cm in the sense east-west and 146 cm in the north-south sense, with a 93 cm wide entrance under the triumphal arch. The doorways of the two *pastophoria* are placed at the end of the walls they share with the sanctuary, westwards. The southern *pastophorion* is narrow; it has an east window like the sanctuary and the northern *pastophorion*, as well as both a doorway to the altar and a small

---

[108] Claude Lepage, 'L'Église de Zaréma (Ethiopie) découverte en Mai 1973 et son apport à l'histoire de l'architecture éthiopienne', *Académie des Inscriptions et Belles-Lettres*, Comptes-rendus de 1973 (Paris 1974), pp. 417-454; Lepage and Mercier, *Ancient Churches of Tigray* (see n. 98), pp. 62-71.

[109] Stored in its southern *pastophorion*, the 13th century church of Gʷāhegot (Harāmāt, Tegrāy) possesses a similar altar.

[110] Also known as Agobo.

Fig. 14: Front of ancient *manbara tābot* at Giyorgis Zāramā
(Photo: Michael Gervers)

one to the south aisle.[111] The natural rock constitutes the south wall. Leaning clumsily against it is an old wooden *manbara tābot*, 100 cm high, 60 cm long, and 50 cm wide, supporting a *tābot* carefully wrapped up in a large piece of textile. The front and back sections are held together by the top mensa, and would probably collapse if the rock wall was not supporting it. The condition of its four feet, measuring 8 cm long by 6 cm wide suggests that they were long ensconced in humid holes.[112] Roughly carved, the altar is adorned with a flat, circular, decorative element at each corner. Such ornament is spontaneously attracted by the angles of the piece of furniture.[113] Given the space needed to access the sanctuary as well as the two *pastophoria*, the original altar must have been erected very close to the flat east wall of the sanctuary, as at Degum, and with the same consequences: there could be no movement around the altar, nor could the deacon stand facing the priest. Unless it came from another place, which is unlikely, the altar in the south *pastophorion* must be the original altar of the church. Where it stands at present was never meant for any type of altar and, a rarity, no other altar besides the modern one is visible in the vicinity.[114] The condition of its feet indicates that it used to be solidly secured in the ground in an appropriate place. Further, its dimensions are compatible with the proportions of the church's sanctuary.

1.7. Dabra Salām Mikā'ēl (Wenbertā, East-Tegrāy) can be ascribed to the 11th-12th century because it has kept the presbyterium guarded by a wooden chancel, the central entrance to which features the only complete, still standing, triumphal arch.[115] This arrangement agrees with the painted decoration. On either side of the sanctuary, there are two *pastophoria* with doors opening both towards the altar and, through very low doors, the aisles. While the southern one is empty, the northern one contains another, later, altar and seems to have been the *prothesis*, because its furnishing is better worked out than what there is to see in the other one and there is room for storage and the laying out of offerings. The sanctuary has an inscribed apse lined with good woodwork. The ceiling of the nave is high and flat, as in the earlier churches. The altar, placed in the middle

---

[111] The inner measurements of the doorway between the south *pastophorion* and the south aisle are 100 cm high × 38 cm wide. Because of this, as well as the flat, high ceiling above the nave, we are inclined to assign a more ancient date to this church – although it is not possible to apply rigidly this kind of argument: for example, Dabra Salām Mikā'ēl displays a flat ceiling as well as double *pastophoria* doors.

[112] Because of the nature of the floor, such holes are at present invisible, as are those where chancel post holes may once have stood.

[113] But it is all the more part of the normal description of this both earthly and heavenly piece of furniture that the expression 'the horns of the altar' is found in Ps. 117 (118):27, as Ex 27:2; Lev 4:18, and even Rev 9:13. The feature will be developed in most altars of the monumental type (see below).

[114] See a picture in Fritsch and Gervers, 'Pastophoria and Altars'(see n. 2), p. 22, fig. 7. Used for the liturgical services, a modern *manbara tābot* in iron presently occupies the south-east corner of the sanctuary.

[115] This is the triumphal arch of the chancel. The architectural triumphal arch lies between that wooden triumphal arch and the apse of the sanctuary.

of the area inscribed between the apse and the triumphal arch, below a badly damaged *Maiestas Domini* which aptly occupies the half-cupola, is a wooden, rectangular, rather large chest with its feet ensconced in the rock floor (except for the south-western foot, which seems not quite to touch the ground).[116]

1.8. Bēta Māryām, Bēta Madḥanē'ālam, Bēta Amānu'ēl at Lālibalā[117] at the turn of the 13th century, as already in the 12th century the cave-church of Yemre-hana Krestos, follow the plan developed hitherto and therefore feature the two *pastophoria* on either side of the sanctuary. However, although they maintain the space of the presbyterium, the chancel-barriers have disappeared. There are now new details which characterise the 'Zāgwē churches': a platform on either side of the nave, or only a step, or both platforms and step; west rooms, which had disappeared in the post-Aksumite churches, on either side of the western porch.[118] The altars associated with these churches are discussed below.

2. *Changes at Lālibalā - Second Period (First Part of the 13th Century)*[119]

Bēta Rufā'ēl-Gabre'ēl, Bēta Masqal, Bēta Marqorēwos, Dabra Sina, Bēta Golgotā, Bēta Denāgel, Bēta Giyorgis, Śellāsē.[120] Besides the churches men-tioned above and their architectonics, others churches of Lālibalā and the chapel

---

[116] See a picture in Fritsch and Gervers, 'Pastophoria and Altars' (see n. 2), p. 23, fig. 8. In the north aisle are two small altars. The *first* is like a box (H: 39 cm) with feet and is decorated with rough carvings (overall H: 85 × L 49 × W 39 cm). The table top has a 2cm-high frame. The lower part of the legs, to a height of 7 cm, is expanded so as easily to fit mortises in the ground (MG-2004.134:015). The *second table* is also box-like (H: 41 cm) with feet (overall H: 78 × L 47, 5 × W 41 cm), but without carving. It is where the ablutions are still done at the end of the mass. The bottom of the chest part and one of its sides have disappeared. The altar in the sanctuary is twice to three times larger than the two other altars in the north aisle, which would be compatible in size and style with the altar of Agewo Qirqos (below). The existence of these and other additional altars refers to the phenomenon of the multiplication of the altars (see below, the second period of churches).

[117] The city known today as Lalibala or Lalibela is represented as Lālibalā (it was *Warwar* until recently). The Zāg^{w}ē king is Lālibālā in the texts.

[118] Yemrehana Krestos displays a curious thing: while its outside features four 'angle towers' which would be expected to match an inner structure including two *pastophoria* in the east and two service rooms in the west, the inner structure includes the two *pasto-phoria* only. A return aisle, a typical feature of the Coptic churches, occupies the whole western area of the building. We do not treat this church, because we have not been in the position to find there the original altar, but two other altars which correspond to the fol-lowing period of the multiplication of altars (see below).

[119] Fritsch, 'Liturgical Changes' (see n. 2).

[120] Bēta Libānos is more difficult to classify. The blind western doors of its seeming *pastophoria* indicate, as at Bilbālā Qirqos, that such doors were known but, having fallen out of use, had nonetheless been kept as decorative. Our feeling is that Bēta Libānos, Bilbālā Qirqos and even Zoz Ambā belong to a time between the Bēta Māryām and the Dabra Sinā types.

inside Bēta Rufā'ēl-Gabre'ēl do not feature either the *pastophoria* or any sanctuary partition at all, and the crypt of Śellāsē even displays three rock-altars
standing side by side.[121]

The abundance of shrines is matched by an over-abundance of altars. They
are found in Lālibalā itself but also at Zoz Ambā, Ṭerā Asfari Esṭifānos, Bilbālā
Giyorgis and as far afield as Dabra Ma'ār in Gar'āltā (East-Tegrāy). They are
clearly not restricted to Lāstā. Most of these altars share a common style. The
first striking thing is that they are generally monoxyle and made of a cubic coffer standing on four (or six, even eight) feet. The proportions and quality of the
carving are often remarkable. Their frequent modest height has caused writers to
describe them as portable or mobile.[122] However, some examples, like the one
exhibited in the chapel of Bēta Masqal (Lālibalā), obviously could not be so
easily carried, due to their size and weight.[123] Therefore, the fact that they are
often small is not an essential character of theirs and their description as 'mobile
altars' should be kept for the actual occurences of that fact, not kept as a typological notion.

According to certain authors, 'the production of monoxyle altars does not
seem to have lasted beyond the 13th century'.[124] Although this is not the case,
this period of time is confirmed in Lālibalā by the texts engraved on a number
of them, in which king Lālibālā himself speaks in the first person.[125] However,
there is no other evidence yet to back the authenticity of Lālibālā's authorship,
although there is no reason to reject it either. Not all altars were made of wood,
for an apparently new phenomenon may be observed: the fashioning of monolithic altars, as observed in the crypt of Lālibalā Śellāsē, where three altars have
been hewn from the rock, which closely replicate the appearance of the altars
found in the area at the time, with both box and legs.[126]

---

[121] Having three altars side by side is the new thing. The fact that they are rock-hewn
is interesting but not crucial. The rock altar in the remote sanctuary of early 12th century
Mikā'ēl Ambā (Tegrāy) could have been made later.

[122] See the tiny altar (7,5 × 8,0 × 8,5 cm.) from the Cultural Association of Tigray,
Maqalle, donation No D3 p. 62 in J. Mercier, *L'Arche Éthiopienne: art chrétien
d'Éthiopie* (Paris, 2000-01), p. 134. Ugo Zanetti suggests that the small size of many
altars may be related to Exodus 37:1, i.e. two cubits and a half in length (114, 25 cm) ×
one cubit (45,7 cm) and a half in width, i.e. *ca.* sixty-five cm high × one cubit (45,7 cm)
and a half in height, i.e. *ca.* sixty-five cm high. Exodus 37:25 describes the altar of
incense as measuring one cubit in length × one cubit in breadth × two cubits in height.
Some altars may meet these proportions despite their great variety in size in general.

[123] Gigar Tesfaye writes about a *manbara tābot* measuring 2,30 × 2,21 m in the
church of Golgotā-Mikā'ēl. See Gigar Tesfaye, *Inscriptions* (see n. 34), p. 114. Is it a
misprint or a mistake? In the context, such a fact would demand some additional information.

[124] Claude Lepage and Jacques Mercier, 'Une église lalibelienne: Zoz Amba', *Annales
d'Éthiopie* 18 (2002) 149-154, here p. 153. The same authors have revised this statement.

[125] Texts edited in Gigar Tesfaye, *Inscriptions* (see n. 34), p.115 ff., and Strelcyn,
Mänabərt (see n. 34), on p. 138. See pictures of one *tābot* and *manāberta tābotāt* in
Monti della Corte, *Lalibala* (see n. 41), tav. 39-40.

[126] See a picture in Fritsch and Gervers, 'Pastophoria and Altars' (see n. 2), p. 26,
fig. 13. The central altar is 1,5 m high and the side altars 1,35m high. Each is roughly 70

3. The Altars up to the 15th Century - Third Period

After the fall of the Zāgwē and the emergence of King Yekunno Amlāk in 1270, churches were built with various forms which are by no means easy to sort out. Similarly, altars developed new forms. There are normally several of them in the churches, a fact systematised by King Zar'a Yā'eqob.[127]

3.1. In the Line of the Previous Altars

3.1.a. Emmakinā Madḥanē'ālam[128] lies in a large cave a relatively short distance from Lālibalā and above Gannata Māryām. This well known, but not so easily accessible, church, constructed shortly after 1270, discloses its secrets little by little. One of those is the choir platform which occupies the south-west corner of the church.[129] As for its altars, there are the two "monoxyle" ones presented above, as well as a wrought-iron altar.[130] Still used near the water point for the services of the Theophany feast (Ṭerr 10-11), this altar is usually kept standing against the west wall of the northern part of the sanctuary. The 'table' is made of a long leather thong rolled around and stretched out between the 1,3 cm thick iron bars in a criss-cross pattern. The feet are round, ensconced at their lower end through the top of wide, open conical feet. This altar is of a volume and with a table of a size compatible with the altars at Lālibalā (Fig. 15).[131] In particular, it

to 90 cm square. For a description of the chapel, see Lino Bianchi Barriviera, 'Le chiese in roccia di Lalibelà e di altri luoghi del Lasta', *Rassegna di Studi Etiopici* 18 (1962) 38-39; Michael Gervers, 'The rehabilitation of the Zaguë kings and the building of the Däbrä Sina-Golgotha-Sellassie complex in Lalibäla', *Africana Bulletin* 51 (2003) 23-49, on p. 35. There is no available description documenting the eastern side of these altars. In itself, the application of rock-hewing to erecting an altar may have been a new development in Ethiopia but not in Egypt: the altar of the ancient church of Deir el-Moharraq (Qosqam) is monolithic.

[127] Perruchon, *Les chroniques de Zar'a Ya'eqob et de Ba'eda Mâryâm rois d'Éthiopie de 1434 à 1478*(see n. 4), p. 81.

[128] Plan in Ewa Balicka-Witakowska, 'The wall-paintings in the church of [Makina] Madhane Alam near Lalibala', *Africana Bulletin* 52 (2004) 9-29, on p. 12, fig. A. Reference should also be made to Gannata Māryām, the well-known reference for this turning point, but we have no information whatsoever about its altars.

[129] This choir platform has never been mentioned so far and does not appear on any published plan. In structure, it compares with the platform of Yemrehana Krestos and measures: 200 cm long × 140 wide × 21 high on average. It may also be compared with the platform of the Lālibalā Golgotā church, also situated in the west end of the church, although in the centre.

[130] These altars and the platform in the previous note were discovered by the present author during a mission sponsored by the CFEE, May 2008. But one of the altars appears in the article by M. Gervers published in in *Wälättä Yohanna: Ethiopian Studies in Honour of Joanna Mantel-Niećko on the Occasion of the 50th Year of Her Work at the Institute of Oriental Studies, Warsaw University*, eds. Witold Witakowski and Laura Łykowska, Rocznik Orientalistyczny LIX, 1 (Warsaw, 2006), pp. 92-112, on p. 111, fig. 15.

[131] Dimensions: Height from floor to tip of crosses: 142 cm; from floor to table: 102,5 cm; from floor to first horizontal bar: 18 cm; from table to tip of crosses: 40 cm;

Fig. 15: Wrought-iron *manbara tābot* at Emmakinā Madḫanē ʿālam
(Photo: Emmanuel Fritsch)

is not covered by a canopy of any sort as many later altars will be. The golden brass flowery crosses which stand all around the eastern, northern and southern sides of the table are similar in shape as in make to examples found in the Agāmē region, or to the patterns already painted under the arches of Yemrehana-Krestos (first half of the 12th century) and to painted as well as sculptured motifs especially frequent in the surroundings of Lālibalā, such as at Bēta Māryām.[132]

3.1.b. Bēta Iyasus Gwāhegot (Harāmāt, East-Tegrāy) is a basilica with three naves and three bays hewn under a cliff in the Harāmāt by a certain Be'esē Egzi'abeḥēr, 'the Man of God', local tradition says. The decoration of false windows even in the south *pastophorion* seems remote enough from the source of inspiration. Outstanding is the ceiling, an elegant rock imitation of a saddle-roof ceiling made with real wooden beams reminiscent of Yemrehana Krestos, in particular. Its dating is uncertain, possibly sometime in the 13th century at the earliest.[133] One argument could be drawn from the answer to be given to the question: are the *pastophoria* authentic, or have they been made as sanctuaries? They have been roughly hewn, especially the northern one, but then the rock looks very hard. Furthermore, they have unconventional circular shapes, and they have no doors in the doorways connecting them with the sanctuary. In consequence, these rooms are later conceptions and have been attempts at hosting altars, which is made likely by the presence of several of these altars. In the process of the relatively recent "gondarisation"[134] of the church, door-frames have been made westwards at the doors of the *pastophoria* towards the aisles and the westernmost triumphal arch has been filled with large double doors and up to the apex of it with modern paintings in order to make sure that the 'mystery' would be preserved. A second triumphal arch rises just east of the passages between side-rooms and sanctuary — a redundancy which does not betray antiquity. The church possesses a few interesting altars besides the one presently used in the sanctuary, which is modern. It follows that one of those in the south or on the side, or even this 'Lālibalā-type' altar presently used to support the loud speaker amplifier, was in service before the present one, perhaps itself eventually replaced by another one. One expects that at one time three altars were in service at the same time and we suggest that these might have been the

from table to horizontal bar above, below the crosses: 24,5 cm. The crosses are 9 cm high. The table measures: 38,5 cm in the east-west sense, 37 in the north-south sense; in diagonal: north-east – south-west: 48 cm × north-west – south-east: 51 cm. Mid-height bars are *ca.* 33,5 cm apart.

[132] Compare, e.g., Stanislaw Chojnacki (in collaboration with Carolyn Gossage), *Ethiopian Crosses: A Cultural History and Chronology* (Milan, 2006), plates XXIII-XXVIII, nos. 47-56; LXXXVI, nos. 178, 180.

[133] Lepage and Mercier, *Ancient Churches of Tigray* (see n. 98), pp. 130-133.

[134] By this we mean the transformation of the sense of 'mystery' from the biblical notion (the mind of God about his creation is meant to be revealed by Jesus Christ and the Church, see Eph 1:3-10) to a secret sealed off not only from the non-Christians, but even from all those who are not in holy orders. This notion developed with the circular churches around Gondar from earlier dispositions triggered by the Copts and translated in the building of churches through separating the sanctuary with solid internal doors with locks and additional curtains.

three similar ones which today are one in the southern *pastophorion* (which is in the best condition especially with its angle pine-cones still on), one on the northern side of the sanctuary and one in the store for prayer-sticks and similar paraphernalia, in a recess of the rock off the southern aisle. Given their earlier construction, the second altar stored in the southern *pastophorion* — similar to the altar of Zāremā (Fig. 14) or Agewo — and the 'Lālibalā-type' one on the steps outside the sanctuary may have been there earlier, unless they were rescued from an older and abandoned church.[135]

3.1.c. Qanqānit Mikā'ēl, in the surroundings of Lālibalā, is a monolithic basilica reportedly excavated by Abuna Musē[136] under king Germā Asfarē (i.e. Newāya Māryām, 1371-1379/80), an ascription 'rare enough to attach some value to this tradition'.[137] Characteristic of it is the front colonnade in the west, associated with the northern and southern galleries of almost full walls which used to carry a rock roof above the space below in a way similar to Sārzenā Mikā'ēl's and, partly, to Ašetan Māryām's. These external galleries only go as far as the west walls of the two *pastophoria*-like rooms on either side of the sanctuary. Inside, the *pastophoria* open directly to the sanctuary.[138] The three doors of the church are of modest proportions. The sanctuary has an inscribed apse, the *maskota berhān* ('window of the light', eastern window) in the centre of the east wall and a cupola in the ceiling above the altar. The altar used to be rock-hewn, simple and without any decoration or cavity; it measured ca. 90 cm high × 60 × 60 cm.[139] It was destroyed and disposed of in around 1977 E.C. (1985 A.D.) because the rock of which it was made had decayed, to be replaced by a modern type of altar.[140] The east wall is probably not as thick as represented by Bianchi-Barriviera. There are several tombs even in the sanctuary.

---

[135] It is difficult to harmonize every detail of this church, which may lead one to think that the core of the church could belong to an older period while its *pastophoria* and certain other items may not be original but later additions. A closer examination may confirm this hypothesis or not.

[136] Abuna Musē, identified with Moses the Black according to his *Vita*, which is found at Yačerā (near Kon, Wādlā) and especially at Yadiba Māryām (Dāwent) (Claire Bosc-Tiessé, Marie-Laure Derat, Emmanuel Fritsch, Centre français des études éthiopiennes, missions 2008), is not really known from historical sources. Several churches and monasteries of the area are ascribed to him.

[137] Marie-Laure Derat about Dabra Takla Hāymānot in Dāwent, under 'Nəwayä Maryam', *Encyclopedia Aethiopica* III (see n. 17), p. 1175. See Monti della Corte, *Lalibala* (see n. 41), p. 101 ff.; plan: 102; Barriviera, *Lalibelà* (see n. 126), tav. 49, comment p. 112. Interview of the *Marigētā* of the church, in the absence of the *Qēsa gabaz* (priest administrator of a church).

[138] Such galleries are very different from those of Lālibalā Madhanē'ālam and Gannata Māryām, but it is not excluded that the original idea may have come from those churches.

[139] Rock altars have already been made in the earlier crypt of the Trinity at Lālibalā.

[140] Both the east window and the altar as well as the inscribed arch have been missed by Barriviera, *Lalibelà* (see n. 126), p. 112. Compare with the treatment of the Lālibalā Śellāsē rock altars.

3.1.d. Bēta Leḥēm Māryām (Tāč Gāyent, South Gondar) is a royal foundation, exceptional for the workmanship it displays and in that it is a constructed building exposed to all winds and yet standing. It has kept much of the structure of earlier Yemrehana Krestos with its saddle-back ceiling, three aisles, and a hitherto unstudied feature: the unusual construction of the church piers are similar in the two cases. However, Bēta Leḥēm has a transept[141] and a *qeddest* which is distinguished by its large cupola resting on the piers of the cross of the transept. The whole easternmost bay is a sanctuary without any partition in any direction except for a small step marking its limit along the full width of the building, with a cupola above the centre while lateral ceilings cover the sides like the aisles. It was built some time before the turn of the 14th to 15th century, since the church was built by Del Mogasā and her father King Dāwit I (1380-1412).[142] This church keeps three ancient altars: a comparatively large one,[143] still used today for the ablutions performed in the southern side of the sanctuary (Fig. 12), and two "monoxyles".[144] The faces of the first altar are engraved and painted. The western side, visible from the nave if the curtain opens, bears an ornate cross while the large doors of the cavity of the *karśa ḥamar* open on the eastern side. A *kirub* ('cherub') is represented on the northern side of the altar and another one on its southern side. Both angels are turned eastwards, towards the doors of the chest, the engraving of their wings joining above the mensa. The last detail is no doubt a reference to the propitiatory of the Ark of the Covenant (Ex 25:19-22; 37:8-9; Num 7:89), although the consecrated altar-tablet is placed opposite (near where the priest stands) rather than upon the carved wings — to be underneath them is naturally out of the question.[145] The angels' clothing evokes the 14th-15th century type of depiction.[146] One notices that the ends of the altar feet have not been used or worn out. Indeed, unlike in other places where they have been ensconced in stone or softer floor, in Bēta leḥēm they have rested on a stone pavement, a rare feature after the Aksumite times, otherwise found only in

[141] As the 11th-12th century Tegrean churches of Abreha wa-Aṣbeha, Weqro Qirqos and Mikā'ēl Ambā.

[142] We are preparing a note on the dating of the church, its gallery, and its circular roof.

[143] Its top surface is practically square and the chest forms a cube: 61 cm in the sense east-west × 61,5 cm in the sense north-south × 61 cm high. The total height is 110 cm.

[144] *Altar 1* measures 33 cm in the east-west sense (marked on one side by the opening of the cavity) × 33,5 cm in the north-south sense; it is engraved with the representation of a *tābot*, which identifies the piece of furniture as an altar table meant to be completed with an altar-tablet. The cavity of the *karśa ḥamar* (accidentally trapezoïdal) is 21 cm deep × 18 cm wide × 18 cm high. *Altar 2* accidentally shows a structural cavity not meant to be used: the *karśa ḥamar* is a facility, not a necessity. The top is 38 cm wide in the sense of the cross. Inventory N°: H3-V-178.

[145] As a literal understanding would demand. See Hebrews 9:4-5, 11-15, 23-28.

[146] The present altar in place shows no particular point of interest, but is painted in a naive way. It has replaced another one, even more roughly made, stored in the north-east corner of the church.

Abreha wa-Aṣbeha (11th century, East-Tegrāy) and Yemrehana Krestos (end 11th-12th century, Lasta).[147].

3.1.e. Weqro Madḥanēʿālam (South Gondar, Amhara Region) is an important landmark, for it is a hall church made under king Sayfa Arʿād (1344-1371). The threefold sanctuary is simply the easternmost bay and each of its end aisles contains one of its three rock altars. The central one is larger and has three steps, but all three are covered with a flat top and the side altars have one step. Beyond a centred eastern door, there is an unexpected additional sanctuary with one central rock-altar standing between two columns (Fig. 16).[148]

3.2. The Monumental Rock Altars

These monumental 14th century rock altars represent a striking innovation, which made its way while more traditional altars continued to be made, as we saw at Bēta leḥēm. Generally free-standing massive monoliths,[149] these new altars are sometimes over two meters high, sometimes necessitating a step. The upper part of these high-altars is hollowed out above and around the mensa and there are arched openings on all sides, or there may be only a front opening and the back between the 'canopy' and the mensa is blind, probably as a provision towards ensuring the solidity of the device, but as a result, making it impossible for the deacon standing opposite the priest and the assembly to see those he is facing. Despite their flat tops, it is not impossible to think that the monoliths may have received a wooden dome enhancing the appearance of a classic ciborium. Such is the case at Gabreʾēl Weqēn (Dabra ʿĀsā, see below), where it is not possible to decide whether the pyramidal top is rock or a wooden structure which would have been added on.[150] This is also the case with almost all posterior altars down to the present: they will have a proportionally high top part surmounted by a canopy-type *gullelāt*, of course realised in the past as nowadays using the available technology. These renditions in stone of the ciborium-style altar are common enough.[151] Despite their variations, they point to the

---

[147] As far as I know. The church of Bēta Leḥēm is also known for its 17th century sanctuary curtain, first studied by W. Staude, 'Une peinture éthiopienne datée dans une église de Beta-Léhem (région de Gaynt, province de Begemder)', *Revue d'histoire des religions* 156 (1959) 65-110, ill., p. 70.

[148] I am grateful to Habtamu Mengestie to have given me the information regarding the time-frame of the church. Roger Sauter mentions our church and provides a useful sketch of it in: 'Où en est notre connaissance des églises rupestres d'Ethiopie?', *Annales d'Ethiopie* 5 (1963) 235-293, on p. 258 N° 20; sketch p. 281.

[149] Except in the rock church of Yačerā Madḥanēʿālam (near Kon, Wādlā waradā, North-Wallo) where the rock altar is 0,87 m high, 1,97 m long, 1,50 m deep, and attached to the east wall of the sanctuary.

[150] It is difficult to read precisely the altar engraved at Dabra Ṣeyon.

[151] Lepage and Mercier, *Ancient Churches of Tigray* (see n. 98), p. 160, having said that 'the central sanctuary [of Weqro Maryam] ... contains a canopied altar cut out of the rock', state that 'such an arrangement is rare in rock-hewn churches' and that 'the only listed example [together with Weqro Maryam] is at Saint-George of May Kado'. In fact,

Fig. 16: Rock-altars at Weqro Madḫanē ʿālam (Photo: Michael Gervers)

Coptic ciborium[152] which spread throughout the Coptic area from the time of the Fatimid dynasty (972-1171) (Fig. 17).[153] The general development is, as Abu

---

one can add to Weqro Māryām and Māy Kādo the altars of Māryām Bāḥerā (the cube-shaped altar of which is no match for the side altar of Weqro Maryam, since it is an unfinished high altar, although less monumental) and Dabra Ṣeyon (where there is also a central high altar) (p. 162), Weqro Madḥanē'ālam, Abbā Yoḥanni, Gabre'ēl Weqēn, Mikā'ēl Bārkā, Walagēsā Iyasus, Yoḥannes Ma'aqudi, without forgetting 'Adi Qašo which has been erased, the more recent ones at Gundo (Gar'āltā) etc. I have not yet seen for myself the main altar of Enda Iyasus (near Guǧat). See David Buxton, *The Rock-Hewn and Other Medieval Churches of Tigré Province, Ethiopia*, Archaeologia CIII (Society of Antiquaries of London, 1971).

[152] 'Over every high altar in the churches of Egypt, and sometime also over the side altars, rises or rose a lofty canopy or baldacchino resting on four columns. The canopy, which is always of wood though sometimes upheld by stone pillars, is generally painted in rich colours within and without, and adorned with a picture of our Lord in the centre of the dome and with flying angels and emblematic figures... it may be added that the domed canopy symbolizes the highest heaven, where Christ sits enthroned in glory surrounded by angels, and the four pillars on which it is upheld typify either the four quarters of the globe, according to Germanus, or else the four evangelists, whose symbols are also sometimes painted within the canopy. The Coptic baldakyn is invariably in the form of a cupola, never having a pointed roof with gables... It seems however very possible that in some cases, where a full dome roofed the sanctuary and overshadowed the altar, a separate baldakyn on pillars was dispensed with, in later times at any rate, after the disuse of hangings. Certainly it would be quite wrong to infer that the altar-canopy was a mediaeval innovation among the Copts: for it is one of the earliest traditions of primitive church decoration'.

'Between the four columns of the canopy run four slender rods or beams, which should be painted with texts in Coptic... These beams were meant originally to hang the altar-curtains upon. For in ancient times the altar was veiled with hangings ... both the beams themselves, and the rings with which they are sometimes... still fitted, prove that even in the middle ages the practice of surrounding the altar with hangings was not disused; while the seventh or eighth century panel at Abu Sargah, in which they are figured, furnishes a good example of earlier usage. At Abu Sargah ... there remained quite room enough for the celebrant to move round the altar inside the curtains... To this day a curtain always hangs before the door of the haikal embroidered either with a red cross or with figures.' See Butler, *Coptic Churches,* II (see n. 15), pp. 28-31.

[153] Grossmann explains: 'The Coptic Church also used movable wooden altars.... Besides these simple table-altars, massive monolithic altars and altars built of stone or bricks were in use at an early date.... The form of altar in use today appears to have developed in the Fatimid period. It consists of a cube built up of quarried stone or, more rarely, of bricks, as at Dayr Sitt Dimiyanah, which in only a few cases is furnished with an upper cornice. Notable exceptions are in Cairo. The latter probably has its origin in the monolithic marble slab used earlier. A shallow rectangular depression was made in the upper surface of the block, which originally held a relic. Today, in the same place, there is a consecrated wooden board (*maqt'a'*)...'. He adds: 'ciboria of stone or wood have been found in several early Christian churches such as those in Abu Mina and Makhurah. All the older Cairo churches are furnished with altar ciboria of this kind, which confirms their use down to the present time'. See P. Grossmann, 'Altar' and 'Ciborium' respectively, in *Coptic Encyclopedia*, vol. I, pp. 106-107, 202. More sober than both Butler and Grossmann, Adeline Jeudy, 'Icônes et ciboria: relation entre les ateliers coptes de peinture d'icônes et l'iconographie du mobilier liturgique en bois', *Eastern Christian Art* 1 (2008) 67-88, on p. 67 and n. 1, writes: '... Tandis que le plus ancien ciborium conservé

Fig. 17: Ciborium of Saint-Sergius', Old Cairo (Photo: Emmanuel Fritsch)

l-Makarim already noted in his time (in A.D. 1175-76), that the altar in the central sanctuary, being the 'high altar', is adorned with a ciborium, often beautifully painted, whereas the side altars are made of a simpler cube.[154] And indeed such secondary rock-altars are found in most of the churches where high-altars have been hewn, but not at Māryām Bāḥerā or 'Adi Qašo. They can be quite large, as is the south altar of Abbā Yoḥanni — where steps were needed for the celebrant to rise to the level of the mensa. Generally they stand on a base, have a rimmed mensa, and have faces decorated with large crosses. Both high and side altars are normally equipped with a niche in their eastern side.[155]

3.2.a. Māy Kādo Giyorgis. The sanctuary is of traditional proportions and has a rock-hewn high-altar in its midst. The second sanctuary of the north aisle has a cubic rock-hewn altar with a large cross on the west face and a rimmed mensa, as in the case of certain Coptic altar tables. Here, both sanctuaries are autonomous and relate each to its own nave or aisle, respectively, the north aisle

remonte à l'époque fatimide et fait figure de cas unique (celui de l'église al-Mu'allaqa, conservé au Musée Copte), tous les autres — trois exceptions mises à part —, toujours en place dans les églises, ne sont pas antérieurs au XVIIIe siècle.'

[154] E.g. in B.T.A. Evetts, *The Churches and Monasteries of Egypt and Neighbouring Countries attributed to Abu Salih, the Armenian* (Oxford, 1895), fol. 37a.

[155] E.g. at Weqro Māryām, Māy Kādo, Dabra Ṣeyon, Enda Iyasus (near Guǧat), Abbā Yoḥanni, Gabre'ēl Weqēn, Gabre'ēl Bārkā, Walagesā Iyasus, Yoḥannes Ma'aqudi *etc.*

constituting a *parekklêsion*, at which mass was to be celebrated independently from the high altar. Otherwise the two altars would have been erected on the same horizontal line, as seen elsewhere.[156] However, the simple cubic type of altar is always second to the high-altar of the central sanctuary. It is, therefore, doubtful that the nave, for example, would have been extended eastwards at a date later than that of the rest of the church. The absence of a south wall for the north aisle's sanctuary is congruent with the time when the whole eastern bay was without any partitions and, even more, the additional altars of Seharti Enda Iyasus which have been hewn outside the sanctuary area, on either side of the *qeddest* platform. Here, there are no *pastophoria* on the sides (Fig. 18).

3.2.b. Dabra Ṣeyon is a large, multi-domed, rock-cut hall church[157] ascribed to the famous 14th century builder Abuna Abrehām (ca. 1350-1425). Characteristically, the churches ascribed to this builder have a particular decorative system, in which the walls of the church are covered with arcades and painted shallow niches.[158] The highly decorated sanctuary open space is better divided by a

Fig. 18: High rock-altar of Māy Kādo Giyorgis (Photo: Philippe Sidot)

---

[156] Having the three altars lined up is the normal arrangement in Coptic churches. See other pictures of the altars of Māy Kādo in Fritsch and Gervers, 'Pastophoria and Altars' (see n. 2), p. 19, fig. 4 and p. 20, fig. 5.

[157] Although the *qeddest* has a somewhat carved but flat ceiling.

[158] They may remind one of Selime Kalesi's basilicas (Cappadocia). See Veronica Kalas, 'The 2004 Survey of the Byzantine Settlement at Selime-Yaprakhisar in the Peristrema Valley, Cappadocia', *Dumbarton Oaks Papers* 60 (2006) 271-293.

20 cm high *qeddest* step between the west side of the two central (out of six) pillars and the north aisle side of the *qeddest*, north of the pillars.[159] Only two altars occupy the eastern bay, which is partitioned by pillars and cupolas. The centrally-positioned rock-hewn high-altar, similar to the previous 'ciborium' examples, is 214 cm high. The mensa stands at 140 cm above the floor, necessitating a stone step in order for a priest to celebrate at it. It is approximately 130 cm wide by 125 cm. There is a cavity on its east side (now closed with an iron door). In the high, flat wall behind the altar is a window with an openwork cross, above which is painted a *Maiestas Domini*, a motif normally represented in the inside of the Coptic canopy. Another rock-hewn altar stands in the southern area. There is a niche in its east side.[160]

3.2.c. Abbā Yoḥanni (in a cliff of Dabra ʿĀsā, Tambēn, Tegrāy), like Dabra Ṣeyon, is a high, multi-domed, rock-cut hall church where nothing divides the areas except the existence of three altars: a central massive rock block which has never been finished and so ended up being the support for 17th century paintings of the Crucifixion and the Descent into hell, and a northern and bigger southern one. The rimmed mensa of the south altar is quite high and used to necessitate a stone step in order for a priest to celebrate before it. There are niches in the backs of the central and southern altars, at least.

3.2.d. Gabreʾēl Weqēn (again on Dabra ʿĀsā, Tambēn, Tegrāy) also has three altars, of which two are monolithic and one constructed of stones.[161] The central, high-altar has approximately the same proportions as its counterpart at Abbā Yoḥanni, but is topped by a (original rock or added wooden structure) pyramidal canopy which makes more obvious the relation to a ciborium. The space underneath the mensa, visible from the nave, is used for storage. The north altar has a high, deeply-rimmed mensa, with a wide storage space visible below. The south-east altar, constructed off-centre, seems to have been erected later.

3.2.e. Māryām Weqro (near Nabalat, Tegrāy) has a sanctuary of traditional proportions and a rock-hewn high-altar in its midst similar to that at Māy Kādo Giyorgis. In a northern sanctuary communicating only with the sanctuary, apart from an arched window giving to the north aisle, a side rock-altar proves that the seeming *pastophorion* actually is an additional sanctuary. This feature, as also the shape of the arched window, reproduces the structure of Gannata Māryām, where at least the south room was always an additional sanctuary, which explains its murals[162] and is typical of the second part of the 13th century.

---

[159] See 'Mazgaba Seelat' (see n. 6), here pictures MG-2000.065:026-036, 2004.143:023-034, 2004.145:015-019, 2004.149:006-008. See a picture of the high altar in Fritsch and Gervers, 'Pastophoria and Altars' (see n. 2), p. 31 fig. 19.

[160] There is no altar in the northern bay of the sanctuary, nor any sign that one has been removed.

[161] For the central high-altar, see MS: MG-2004.041:002/003/004; the north-east altar: MG-2004.040:008/009; the south-east altar: MG-2004.040:023.

[162] See pictures of the altars at Māryām Weqro in Fritsch and Gervers, 'Pastophoria and Altars' (see n. 2), p. 27 fig. 14 and p. 29 fig. 17. Both a *Maiestas Domini* and a

3.2.f. Bāḥerā (first half of 15th century) has a central sanctuary occupied by a monolithic high altar. A roughly made northern room, matched on the south by a smaller room now walled because a priest has been buried there, does not contain any altar today. As is the case at Abba Yoḥanni, the central block of rock was left unfinished, without a mensa having been hewn out. Unused, its top part was to be painted with a crowned Virgin and Child in the 17th century at the initiative of a certain Walda-Māryām, and mass was celebrated at a small wooden altar.[163] Very recently, the community restored their church, built a new *qenē māḥlēt* (nave) on the west end and dug a mensa in the rock altar, now in use.[164]

4. The Altars from the 16th Century Onwards - Fourth Period

4.1. Gunda Gundē had its church re-built by 'Ezerā after the death of Nā'od (1508).[165] Its altar, placed at the centre of the easternmost bay of this late hall-basilica surrounded by a portico extended westwards, is apparently closer in style to Coptic models, with a surprisingly well made painted ciborium.[166]

4.2. The Wrought-iron Altar of Ašetan Māryām (Fig. 19). This structure in wrought-iron is definitely an altar, as its proportions and type of decoration indicate. The same proportions also show that such altars must have come in the wake of the taller type of altars witnessed in the rock of a number of churches. The four horns at the corners connect with the expected ornamentation. A craftsman in ironwork may indicate the time when the technology of welding applied to it was in use.[167] Circular churches developed according to a

Virgin and Child were painted on the east wall of Gannata Māryām's southern sanctuary in the last quarter of the 13th century. See Ewa Balicka-Witakowska, 'The Wall-Paintings in the Sanctuary of the Church of Gännätä Maryam near Lalibäla', in *Ethiopian Art: A Unique Cultural Heritage and a Modern Challenge*, eds. Walter Raunig and Prinz Asfa-Wossen Asserate (Wissenschaftliche Tagung der Gesellschaft Orbis Æthiopicus in Leipzig vom 24.-26. Juni 2005), Bibliotheca nubica et æthiopica 10 (Lublin, 2007), pp. 119-137, on pp. 134-137; Fritsch and Gervers, 'Pastophoria and Altars', pp. 37-38; p. 18 fig. 3.

[163] See Lepage and Mercier, *Ancient Churches of Tigray* (see n. 98), pp. 140-145.

[164] As a result, the painting of Mary has been destroyed and the wooden altar can nowhere be seen (January 2007).

[165] Lepage and Mercier, *Ancient Churches of Tigray* (see n. 98), p. 181.

[166] See its description in Fritsch and Gervers, 'Pastophoria and Altars' (see n. 2), on p. 32 fig. 20. This altar is likely to be the one described as 'the only antique wooden canopied altar known to this date, as yet undocumented', in Lepage and Mercier, *Ancient Churches of Tigray* (see n. 98), p. 160. 'Ciborium' is probably the apt translation of *qasta dammanā* in Getatchew Haile, 'On the House of Lasta from the History of Zena Gäbrə'el' (see n. 4), p. 11 (text) and 15 (translation). This altar has been badly damaged by fire between December 2004 and November 2006, and its canopy was almost destroyed.

[167] Claude Lepage and Jacques Mercier have discovered a significant number of similar wrought-iron structures which they have named, for the time being, 'nacelles' in French and which Lepage believes to be an altar (conversation, Paris, 20th January 2006).

Fig. 19: The Wrought-iron altar of Ašetan Māryām, near Lālibalā
(Photo: Emmanuel Fritsch)

pattern systematised by the capital city of Gondar from the 17th century onwards, even though it probably began some time in the 16th century.[168] This is the type which has prevailed in the Ethiopian religious mentality.

4.3. Guyā Abuna Takla Hāymanot (Tambēn, Tegrāy) possesses an interesting wooden altar which documents the evolution of the Ethiopian altar: a striking niche-like opening gives access to its lower hollow part (Fig. 20). The nearby Chih rock-church hosts a beautifully painted 18th century *manbara tābot* which displays the same niche-like cavity as Guyā.

5. The 20th Century - Fifth Period

To be complete, we should mention that the 20th century has seen the apparition of a first large, spacious 'cathedral', the Holy Trinity, built by Ḥāyla Sellāsē Ist. It was followed by the new cathedral of Aksum Zion (Tegrāy). Eventually, the idea took hold, and cities or pilgrimage sites like Kullubi all have their cathedral and more are under construction, the largest in size being Bolē Madhanēʿalam (Addis Ababa). All are equipped with a triple sanctuary with three altars of the baldakyn type.

Conclusion

We can attempt to articulate the following overview of the development of the altars by relying on the time-frame of the churches in which altars are found and on the relative chronology provided by the altars themselves. The altars of the period reaching King Lālibālā's reign generally are small tables, adorned with carvings, angle fittings, or practically nothing apart from the comparatively careful craftsmanship. At Lālibala, they become "monoxyle" or "monoxyle"-

We tend to ascribe to these altars a rather late date as they apparently were made after the model provided by the last altars to have appeared. The *manbara tābot* described by Alvares corresponds to this object *The Prester John of the Indies* (see notes 3 and 6), vol. II, p. 518.

[168] The oldest report known hitherto is by Manoel de Almeida about the church of Ambā Gešēn Māryām. See *Some Records of Ethiopia, 1593-1646: Being Extracts from the History of High Ethiopia or Abassia by Manoel de Almeida, together with Bahrey's History of the Galla*, eds. and trans. C.F. Beckingham and G.W.B. Huntingford, Hakluyt Society Works, ser. 2, vol. 107 (London, 1954), p. 99. Gatirā Māryām church (South Wallo, Legidā waradā) was a circular church burnt down by Grañ Muhammad, reportedly, according to the family on whose land it lies. To our knowledge, no investigations have yet been made there. The plans of circular churches include sub-types which combine a rectangular plan (not exactly basilical) with the distribution of areas in the logic of the circular churches, e.g. the church of Dāgā Esṭifānos, on Lake Ṭānā, Sayko Kidāna mehrat near Dabra Tābor (which I know of thanks to Anaïs Wion), Dabra Berhān Sellāsē at Gondar or the churches common in Tegrāy.

Fig. 20: Altar of Gụyā, Tembēn (Photo: Michael Gervers)

like, compact, with a hollow chest on top of the altar feet, both reproducing the space between the feet of ancient Coptic altars and the cavity that followed when they were made of bricks, all of which simply served for storage. The often small size of altars called for some device to raise them up to an adequate level as seen as Bilbālā Qirqos. We find numerous altars in single churches from the time of Lālibālā on, and the altars begin to be hewn out of the rock, the first identified ones being the three altars of Šellāsē (the Holy Trinity crypt) at Lālibālā. The development continues, revealing a striking development: high altars reproducing the altar-ciborium combination of the Coptic Church, often accompanied by large side altars without canopy. Some retain a more or less deep niche in their eastern side, others do not. This high altar will be reproduced systematically to the present as the dominant type of the Ethiopian altar, without totally excluding more modest forms.